LAW, ECONOMY AND SOCIETY, 1750–1914:

ESSAYS IN THE HISTORY OF ENGLISH LAW

LAW, ECONOMY AND SOCIETY, 1750–1914: ESSAYS IN THE HISTORY OF ENGLISH LAW

Edited by

G. R. Rubin

David Sugarman

PROFESSIONAL BOOKS LIMITED
1984

Published in 1984 by
Professional Books Limited,
Milton Trading Estate, Abingdon, Oxon.,
and printed in Great Britain by
Billing & Sons Ltd, Worcester

ISBN: Hardback: 0 86205 085 5
Paperback: 0 86205 098 7

CONTENTS

ACKNOWLEDGEMENTS

This anthology has been a number of years in the making, and has only been made realisable by the dedication and loyalty of our contributors, to all of whom is owed our principal debt of gratitude. A number of other individuals have also offered help and encouragement in one way or another during the preparation of the book. We, therefore, wish to express our thanks to Professor Brian Simpson, Dr. John Lovell, John Adams, and Dr. Ronnie Warrington for the kind assistance they have rendered us.

For the excellence of her typing we thank Mrs Patricia Cowley, and for the efficiency with which she compiled the index (in collaboration with David Sugarman) we are grateful to Ms Monica Trigg. We wish also to mention the co-operation of our publishers, Professional Books Ltd. In particular, we appreciate the encouragement of their editorial director, Professor John Wylie, and the assistance of Kevin Cassidy and Chris Smith at Abingdon.

For generous financial help towards the cost of publication, we record our appreciation to the Twenty-Seven Foundation, while the limited financial assistance of the University of Kent at Canterbury is also gratefully acknowledged.

G.R.R.

D.S.

CONTRIBUTORS

STUART ANDERSON is Fellow and Tutor in Jurisprudence, Hertford College, Oxford.

HARRY ARTHURS is a professor, and former dean, of Osgoode Hall Law School of York University, Toronto, Canada. He is the author of several recent articles and a forthcoming book on administrative justice and legal pluralism in nineteenth century England. His other areas of interest include the legal profession, labour law and administrative law.

P.W.J. BARTRIP is Senior Research Officer in Social History at the SSRC Centre for Socio-Legal Studies, Wolfson College, Oxford. He is the author (with S.B. Burman) of The Wounded Soldiers of Industry: Industrial Compensation Policy, 1833-1897 (Oxford University Press, 1983). He has also published a number of articles on socio-legal history and other historical topics.

MICHAEL R. CHESTERMAN is currently Commissioner, Australian Law Reform Commission, on leave from the Faculty of Law, University of New South Wales, Australia, where he holds a Chair in Law. His publications include, Charities, Trusts and Social Welfare (London: Weidenfeld, 1979) and Small Businesses (London: Sweet and Maxwell, 2nd ed., 1982). Current Research: Commissioner in Charge, Australian Law Reform Commission reference on Contempt of Court.

RAYMOND COCKS is Lecturer in Law, The University of Sussex. Relevant publications: articles and notes on Victorian barristers in Kingston Law Review and Law Quarterly Review; and a study of Victorian barristers and professional ideas in Foundations of the Modern Bar (London: Sweet and Maxwell, S.P.T.L. Series, 1983). At present he is working on aspects of Victorian jurisprudence.

BARBARA ENGLISH is a lecturer in regional and local history at the University of Hull. Her publications include John Company's Last War (1971), The Lords of Holderness (1979), and Beverley: an archaeological and architectural study (Royal Commission on Historical Monuments: co-authors K. Miller, J. Robinson and I. Hall) (1982). In 1983 she published (jointly with John Saville) Strict Settlement: a guide for historians. Her research interests cover agrarian history, both medieval and modern. She is currently working on a study of East Yorkshire landed estates.

R.B. FERGUSON is a lecturer in the Faculty of Law, Dundee University, Scotland. He has published articles in the field of legal history in the British Journal of Law and Society and the Oxford Journal of Legal Studies, and his current research interests include the regulation of financial institutions.

MICHAEL MILES is the author of " 'Eminent Practitioners': Some Aspects of West Riding Attorneyship c.1750-1800", University of Birmingham Ph.D., 1982. His articles include "The Money Market in the Early Industrial Revolution: the Evidence from West Riding Attorneys, 1750-1800", Business History (1982) and " 'A Haven of the Privileged': Recruitment into the Profession of Attorney in England, 1709-1792" (forthcoming).

WILFRID PREST is a Reader in History at the University of Adelaide, Australia. His study of The Rise of the Barristers: a Social Portrait 1590-1640 is to be published shortly. His publications include The Inns of Court under Elizabeth I and the Early Stuarts, 1590-1640 (London: Longman, 1972) and he has edited Lawyers in Early Modern Europe and America (London: Croom Helm, 1981).

EILEEN SPRING is the author of articles and reviews dealing with the history of the land laws. She is currently working on a re-assessment of the role of great landowners in the development of real property law. She teaches in the evening college of The Johns Hopkins University, Baltimore, United States of America.

GERRY R. RUBIN is holder of a law degree and a doctorate in Social History; apart from legal and historical articles, his publications include Wages and Salaries (1980) and an historical contribution to Adams (ed), Essays for Clive Schmitthoff (Professional Books, 1983). He is preparing a forthcoming study on War, Law and Labour 1915-1921. He is currently teaching law at the University of Kent at Canterbury.

DAVID SUGARMAN is Reader in Law, School of Law, Middlesex Polytechnic and Research Director, British Institute of Securities Laws. He is a graduate of the universities of Hull, Cambridge and Harvard. At Harvard he completed a historical study of the transformation of English Company Law, 1750-1930. His publications include, "Theory and Practice in Law and History" in B. Fryer et al (eds), Law, State and Society (London: Croom Helm 1981); "The Legal Boundaries of Liberty: Dicey, Liberalism and Legal Science" in Modern Law Review (1983); and Legality, Ideology and the State (London: Academic Press, 1983). He is currently completing a history of the transformation of English legal education and scholarship, c.1850-1980.

INTRODUCTION

TOWARDS A NEW HISTORY OF LAW AND MATERIAL SOCIETY IN ENGLAND, 1750-1914

by

David Sugarman and G.R. Rubin

TOWARDS A NEW HISTORY OF LAW AND MATERIAL SOCIETY

IN ENGLAND, 1750-1914

TOWARDS A NEW HISTORY OF LAW AND MATERIAL SOCIETY IN ENGLAND, 1750-1914

by

David Sugarman and G.R. Rubin *

I : INTRODUCTION

The study of legal history in Great Britain has, until very recently, been characterised by an astonishingly narrow perspective in respect both to chronology and to the sources employed. "Conventional" legal history textbooks tended to devote minimal space to developments occurring after 1688. For example, the most recent (fifth) edition of Plucknett's modestly entitled A Concise History of the Common Law[1] published in 1956, devoted, at a conservative estimate, just 75 pages out of a text of 746 pages to the period after the "Glorious Revolution". Even the author's 26 page chapter on "Legislation"[2] accorded no more than four pages to the "modern" period, during which the legislative method assuredly assumed greater historical importance than previously.

Moreover, the approach of such hefty tomes was to stress both the doctrinal development of the law and also the institutional history of the courts and of the legal profession from an essentially uncritical standpoint. This reflected, in turn, the historical material overwhelmingly relied upon, which, drawn from narrowly defined legal sources, presented an internally projected image of such institutions. Even those writers such as Holdsworth who, on occasion, embellished their works with what one might call contextual material, did so "at a fairly general level to portray the background against which the law developed".[3] The examination of specific topics in legal history still suffered from excessive narrowness of vision and composition.

More recently, there have been hopeful signs that the twin flaws of limited chronology within, and limited orientation toward, the study of legal history have begun to undergo a gradual process of rectification.[4] A distinctly modern legal history is at last being recognised, while the subject is increasingly being treated as a branch of, or as cutting across, the traditional boundaries separating modern social, intellectual, business and economic history as well as offering a significant perspective to developments in the sociology of law. It is the relationship between law and economy spanning the period circa 1750 to 1914, which we intend to explore in this chapter.

With significant exceptions, notably within the history of criminal law from the eighteenth century, this cross-fertilisation of disciplines has proceeded in a haphazard fashion. Thus, a consequence of the relative novelty of the shift towards a "new" economic and social history of law[5] is the miscellaneous quality of the published work in the area, which in turn reflects the uncertain boundaries of the subject. By plucking at random a few examples of the relevant subject matter, one might include in such a history such diverse topics as the influence of economic liberalism on contract law doctrine,[6] the legal-institutional framework within which the slave trade was conducted,[7] the development of injury compensation provisions,[8] drugs control in the nineteenth and twentieth centuries,[9] the assault on vagrancy in mid-nineteenth century Wales,[10] the regulation of street betting,[11] the legal protection of inventions,[12] or even the impact of the South African War Loan Act 1903 on the political and economic structure of South Africa.[13] In the light of such catholicity, it should be apparent that to offer a precise definition of such a history will be a hazardous exercise.

Within the span of historical studies, the arbitrary divisions which have, in the past, prevented the integration of, for example, business and labour history,[13a] have also inhibited more fruitful exploration of the kinds of themes and questions elaborated in this introductory chapter. Although much work has been done, it tends to be written in relative isolation within the confines or traditions of a particular specialism. Major pertinent literature in other disciplines or sub-areas tends to be overlooked. Outside lawyers' legal history, most attention has been afforded to the criminal law and its institutions. Private law - such as the law governing property, contracts, families and companies - has tended to receive short shrift. These reasons, and the sheer magnitude of the task, help to explain the absence of any synthetic overview of the relation between English law and economy for the period since 1700. In acknowledging the difficulties in the way of elucidating on the theme of the relation between law and economy since the Industrial Revolution, we therefore consider it more useful to offer some preliminary guidelines on the nature and scope of such examination, to attempt to pull together the disparate strands of this academic foray into uncharted, or sparsely populated, territory and, finally, to address ourselves to the tasks and possible pitfalls posed by the historical study of law and material society, rather than to impose any rigid foreclosure of the intellectual landscape. To this end, both general and specific questions might be said to arise. Like the remaining essays in this anthology, we have concentrated almost exclusively upon the private law order given its relative neglect. We have tried to provide an introductory synthesis or overview of some of the relevant literature and key issues; and also bibliographic data to assist those in a variety of specialisms who may be approaching our subject for the first time. In this way, we hope to stimulate interest in, and work towards a more avowedly inter-disciplinary economic and social history of law, society and economy. We should stress at the outset, however, that it is not our intention to offer an exhaustive summary of the work done in the area, but merely to point to the issues and subject-matter which we consider indispensable to an adequate consideration of the historical relation between English law and economy in the period 1750-1914.

II : WAS LAW IMPORTANT IN THE ECONOMY? SOME GENERAL OBSERVATIONS

A. Law As A Final Resort And The Desire For Self-Regulation

How important was law to economic development in the period 1750 to 1914? By this question is meant, in what respects did the existing legal structure facilitate economic development? As a corollary, we may ask what obstacles did the law place in the way of such advancement? If, as has often been assumed, private property rights and contract were considered essential precursors of a capitalist economy,[14] how did the legal system set out to enhance those dual legal mechanisms for such an economy? To what extent, one might ask, did there take place a shift from (crudely speaking) "status to contract"?[15] In other words, how did the role of the law and its relation to civil society and to the state change in the period after 1750? How did perceptions of the proper function of the law within industrial capitalism undergo adjustment? To what extent was there pressure to attain certainty and predictability in contractual arrangements, objectives which, it has been frequently alleged, but seldom proved, were principal concerns of both lawyers and businessmen? Which interest groups, if any, did in fact press for such ends and what opposition to this presumed development manifested itself? Lawyers, historians and sociologists have too often treated the law's "essential" role in securing certainty in commercial transactions as axiomatic.[16] The truth is, however, considerably more complex. For example, in his groundbreaking history of American law, Lawrence Friedman has concluded that American commercial law was actually,". . . too elegant (and too unknown except to lawyers) to have much effect on the actual working of the market."[17] In England the relation between the law and business practice has lacked substantial empirical analysis. There is, therefore, only relatively meagre empirical information on how much the law was actually used, why, to what effect, and by whom. The evidence that does exist suggests that the regulatory objectives of the law are often either unrealised or only imperfectly realised. In practice, for instance, the law may be mediated by relevant enforcement agencies and their officers, the economic power, wealth and influence of individuals or interest groups and through the assistance of lawyers and accountants.

In fact, it is neither clear that industry and trade wanted or needed the law, nor that the law did, or could have provided, the predictability so often asserted.

Given the devotion of business to self-regulation and given the potency of economic and financial might, why, it might be queried, should the law be necessary to such interests? Traders and entrepreneurs might, on occasions, actually have a stronger interest in a legal system characterised by confusion and complexity, which they could exploit, rather than the supposed certainty and calculability which, lawyers often argued, enterprise required of the legal order.

In addition, areas of law important to business and industry (at least in theory), such as that governing partnerships and companies were notoriously complex and ambiguous throughout the 18th and most of the 19th century, that is, throughout most of Britain's Industrial Revolution. Indeed, the historical development of the law governing business organisations is full of paradox.[18] "As late as 1919 Marshall - with an unrivalled knowledge of institutional arrangements - could write that until not very long ago the representative firm in most industries and trades was a private partnership . . . . Indeed, throughout most of the 19th century, the fundamental business unit was the individual proprietorship or partnership."[19] Yet on many central issues the law of partnership was profoundly obtuse and procedurally labyrinthine. For example, until 1890 the law of partnership was characterised by the absence of a universally accepted definition of a partnership; and, thus, a variety of sometimes contradictory tests were applied to establish the existence of a partnership. For creditors, anxious to know to whom they could look for the firm's debts, the problem was grave. The creditors' lot was compounded by the archaic rules which surrounded proceedings against a partnership, especially those concerning the correct parties to an action. Moreover, until 1916 there was no system of registration of partnerships and no requirements as to publicity. It could be extremely difficult, therefore, to know who were the partners of a particular partnership. As regards companies, the Bubble Act of 1720 had formerly made it difficult to secure the attributes of separate personality and limited liability: i.e. the vast bulk of business organisations were legally required to adopt the form of an unincorporated association, such as a partnership. Attempts to circumvent the obtuse provisions of the Bubble Act added fuel to the uncertainties which characterised this area of the law. When the liberalisation of English company law occurred, gradually over the period 1825 to 1862, limited liability and/or general incorporation were already available in New York, Ireland, Belgium, Holland, Germany and Scotland. Not only was liberalisation belated relative to England's Industrial Revolution and the laws of England's trade rivals; no enormous rush to incorporate followed the general availability of incorporation and limited liability by registration. The bulk of British trade and industry continued as previously, despite the intricacy and uncertainty surrounding the law governing unincorporated associations. Only very late in the 19th century did the corporate form supplant the partnership as the dominant form of business organisation.[20] Ironically, at the very moment when the law of partnership had at last achieved an unprecedented degree of certainty (in the codification embodied in the Partnership Act 1890) the partnership had already been eclipsed in economic import.

As an alternative hypothesis, we would ask to what extent was there a preference in some quarters of the economy for the use of non-legally binding instruments. How far, moreover, can it be taken for granted that the interests of commerce and trade were, in fact, congruous with those of the legal profession in seeking to reduce business relations to propositions of law? Any attempt to study either the efficacy or inefficacy of legal regulation of business would require to include a study of various groups' attitudes to the law, a task which must also embrace a consideration of competing conceptions of legality. For example, was there a belief that any entanglement with the law would impoverish all but the wealthy? How comprehensively did the law's delays deter legal action? Or its rules of evidence, which for long prevented the interested parties themselves giving testimony, or the stringency of the evidence required to succeed? For example, in the specific case of river pollution, the stringency required to establish nuisance might mean that if, say, the Thames was already foul, the dumping of sewage waste by the Kingston Commissioners could not constitute an actionable nuisance, for the plaintiffs could not establish the exact proportion of pollution for which the defendants were liable.[21] Moreover, large towns and large manufacturers generally did not take action against each other as all were equally engaged in river pollution. It was also asserted that even wealthy individuals disliked the cost and publicity of legal action, even when the jurisdiction of the non-jury courts of Chancery were extended, thus enabling plaintiffs to obtain more expeditious injunctive relief without requiring first to initiate a common law action for nuisance.[22] If such a reluctance to embrace legally enforceable business relations existed, was it grounded in economic reality thus depriving a substantial proportion, probably a majority of the population, from utilising the law? It is clear that such a view is too sweeping in respect to the criminal law from the mid-eighteenth century. For the personal cost of prosecutions, particularly where property was involved, was lessened following legislative provision for the expenses of prosecutors, a facility that seems to have been widely utilised.[23] In respect to the civil law, however, the issue of the disincentive to litigation is more complex. For example, did the expensive, time-consuming, private character of the civil law make it only a symbolic weapon held in terrorem by small businesses against large or vice-versa?[24] In calculating the economic cost or advantage of individual activities, to what extent did individuals and business take the perils of being sued into account? If so, what economic consequences did this have? If such a proposition of avoidance of law is correct, does this mean that because law was not widely utilised in the above sense, it therefore had little or no impact on, or relevance for, the bulk of the poor? Such an assertion would be erroneous. For we shall see shortly that the law, both instrumentally and ideologically, might directly or indirectly impinge upon every stratum in society.

It hardly requires stating that many of the rich especially, either voluntarily or by virtue of mandatory enactments, committed to legal form the arrangements they wished to make, in order to regulate aspects of their social and economic affairs. Thus the strict settlement, the turnpike trust agreement, the partnership arrangement, the indentured apprenticeship contract, the constitution of the friendly society, agreements for the sale or purchase of innumerable items, were all enclosed in legal documents. In respect to some agreements, the guidance and expertise of lawyers were called upon to assist their clients to attain given ends where institutional or practical obstacles were encountered. How to ensure the preservation of the landed estate in the event of unforeseeable contingencies affecting intended inheritors; how to provide for the permanency of an economic enterprise with fluctuating membership; how best to guarantee the right of recovery against third parties and to avoid, if possible, personal or corporate liability? For these tasks, lawyers would invent courses of action or simplify older forms; invent trusts with the assistance of the fictitious John Doe and Richard Roe;[25] adapt one mechanism of the law to a fundamentally different purpose to that for which it was originally created (for example, by applying to trade unions under the 1871 Trade Union Act, for the purpose of protecting their funds, the very doctrine, restraint of trade, with which they had formerly been beaten);[26] and no doubt advised on the degree of precision or vagueness in drafting appropriate to the objective in mind. The unclear legal status of many business enterprises in the first half of the nineteenth century would hardly have been unwelcome to those members of such organisations, deed of settlement companies, and incorporated companies lacking deeds, partnerships, joint ventures, who were all likely to be sued. In respect to appropriate drafting, the papers of both Chesterman[27] and English[28] in the present collection address themselves to the forensic qualities of the drafters of such complex arrangements and seek to establish how specific social and economic objectives were attained by means of technical legal craftsmanship. The role of the lawyer in preserving the landed interest is here depicted.

However, the use of legal formalities did not, of necessity, engulf the parties concerned in the paraphernalia of the state legal system. The use of legal formalities such as a contract or trust deed might be utilised as tools to secure a good deal of autonomy from the state legal order. This can be seen as part of a wider preference extending beyond the Stock Exchange and throughout the City, to the professions, trading and co-operative associations, trade unions and even individual contractors: namely, the desire to self-regulate one's own affairs unimpaired by the law or to utilise its coercive power only as a matter of last resort.[29] In other words, the state legal system might co-operate in its partial or complete supersession. Commerce and industry might value certainty and calculability. But often they also preferred their own adjudicators (thus, the wide use of arbitration or the demand for special "commercial" juries); and they valued the ability to formulate their own private or "home-made" legislation, as opposed to that laid down by Parliament or the courts. In short, the evidence indicates that the state legal system was utilised in a pragmatic fashion. Some of the functions or institutions of the state legal order were more valued than others. The state legal system permitted the appropriation of those facets of the state legal order deemed most useful, such as coercion and law enforcement in the final instance, whilst at the same time allowing the relevant actors considerable space for self-regulation.[30]

B. Facilitative Laws And Self-Regulation

How did the law facilitate and legitimate this desire for self-regulation? Some jurists, like most lay persons, define the law exclusively in terms of something which we either obey or disobey, as requiring persons to act in certain ways whether they wish to or not, that is, as directly coercive instrumentalities analogous to orders backed by threats. The criminal law is the paradigm of laws of this kind. However, this model of law as coercive orders obscures the variety of laws to be found in legal systems. Co-existing alongside the criminal law is another type of laws called facilitative or power-conferring laws.[31] Such laws do not impose duties or obligations. Instead, they provide individuals with facilities for realising their wishes, by conferring legal powers upon them to create, by certain specified procedures, and subject to certain conditions, structures of rights and duties within the coercive framework of the law. For example, the law conferred on individuals the power to mould their legal relations with others, by marriages, contracts, wills, companies and trusts. The law provided a skeleton for individual choice. In varying degrees, this facilitative power afforded the parties concerned the opportunity to make their own law (private law-making), and even the opportunity, on occasions, to by-pass or attenuate the state law or equitable obligations established by Parliament or the courts, that otherwise would apply.

Facilitative laws are but one instance of a wider phenomenon, namely, the role of the law in the facilitation and legitimation of a plurality of semi-autonomous realms - a role which has yet to be fully chronicled. The law simultaneously exemplified such a realm and defined and reproduced a mode of thought and practice which promoted a variety of semi-autonomous realms with powers that in some respects resembled those of the state. Here, for instance, one thinks of "the village community", the estate, the guild, the city, the church, local government and local courts, the strict settlement, corporations, the state, the Crown, the law merchant, the trust and arbitration. Thus, facilitative laws, such as the law of contract or land law, built upon as well as were imbricated within this long-standing tradition of semi-autonomous realms.[32] Facilitative laws were also dependent upon the lawyers' drafting skills in utilising, manipulating and expanding the delegations of authority permitted by state law, custom or indigenous practices. Moreover, the semi-autonomy or monopoly position that the law facilitated and legitimated was enforced by the continuous, low-key, "controlled interventionism"[33] of the state. Thus, its private law form conceals its quasi-public law, Janus-like qualities. In other words, facilitative laws straddle private <u>and</u> public law; in so doing, they illustrate the inadequacy of the traditional public/private law distinction - its insensitivity to the hybrid and ultimately coercive nature of law, public <u>and</u> private. Facilitative laws are agencies of state policy, in that they define the range of permissible conduct, albeit through the self-directing actions of private individuals. They are also instruments through which private individuals may expand or contract their autonomy and in so doing, promote, qualify or subvert official state policy.[34]

How did this relative autonomy from the mainstream of formal rules and obligations of law develop? At one end of the spectrum, it was dependent upon the lawyers' drafting skills in constructing institutional arrangements beyond, or on the fringes of, the law. Taking one step back, this in turn was stimulated both by the professions' attempts to create and control a market for their talents and also by the eagerness of potential clients to secure the advantages of the various forms of self-regulation afforded by the law.[35] The ingenious conveyancers such as Sir Orlando Bridgeman who devised the strict family settlement in order to assist the English landed classes to retain their estates in the family from generation to generation,[36] or the advice of counsel such as Serjeant Pengelly on the scope of the Bubble Act and its exceptions,[37] or of Bellenden Ker on the law of partnership,[38] created for counsel an important role in shaping the activities of the landed class and of business practice. Also vital was the often tacit support of the courts to such arrangements; and the ability of those who used them to head off litigation that might endanger such arrangements or, at least, limit them or render them uncertain. At the other end of the spectrum lay the political and economic power of the diverse interests that could secure through lawyers, the courts or Parliament, the necessary state sanction for self-regulation or other forms of assistance: the great trading companies of the sixteenth and seventeenth centuries, the great landed families, the City, the railways, manufacturers, the professions and other pressure groups.[39]

Facilitative laws illustrate the way in which the form of law itself may, through its enormous flexibility and the legal principles that sanction that flexibility, mediate or avoid the legal order. Thus, use and avoidance of the law may go hand in hand. How endemic and how costly was legitimate or illegitimate avoidance? Clearly, much research remains to be done on the role of law and lawyers in everyday commercial practice. In particular, the role of lawyers, accountants and allied professions in mediating between law and commercial practice represents an important area for future research into the use and avoidance of the law by business.

C. Freedom Of Contract

In the 19th century, the rise of freedom of contract as the pre-eminent doctrine of English private law encouraged Parliament and the courts to extend considerably the degree of legitimate autonomy afforded to the private sphere.[40] This ideology embodied the fiction that equal bargaining power must normally be assumed to exist in all commercial transactions. It has been argued that the doctrine of freedom of contract warranted the incorporation of wide exemption clauses, the growth of one-sided "standard form" contracts, and in the context of employment contracts led to drastically reduced limits being imposed on the employee's rights to sue the employer.[41] "Thus, the contractarian ideology above all expressed a market conception of legal relations . . . . Since the only measure of justice was the parties' own agreement, all pre-existing legal duties were inevitably subordinated to the contract relation . . . . The circle was complete. The law had come simply to ratify those forms of inequality that the market system produced".[42]

The ideology of freedom of contract was an important element in the liberalisation of English company law in the 19th century.[43] General incorporation by registration first became available in 1844 and limited liability was generally extended to shareholders in 1855. By 1862 the statutory regime had become extremely liberal. Robert Lowe's espousal of freedom of contract and laissez-faire was one of the major forces sustaining this liberalisation. Initially, the courts' reaction to this regime was mixed. Some attempt to construct a regulatory system can be detected. However, as in other areas of private law, the power of freedom of contract, the rise of legal formalism[44] and perhaps, on occasions, a sympathy for these agencies of economic growth, encouraged the courts frequently to adopt the mantle of legal abstentionism, rather than that of a watch-dog. Economic conditions, notably the Great Depression of c.1875-95, the rise of overseas competition and the bankruptcies that ensued encouraged the acceptance of limited liability and the use of the corporate form to control competition as well as to raise capital. The separation of ownership from control was legitimated by characterising the companies' internal relations (i.e. relations as between shareholders inter se; and shareholders and management) as primarily contractual. The evolution of the holding company and the utilisation of the corporate form by de facto partnerships or even one person was facilitated by a rigid adherence to the separate personality of the company.[45] The wave of mergers and amalgamations at the end of the 19th century could occur unimpeded by the law. Indeed, the seeming willingness of the law to permit the concentration of capital, mirrored its refusal, by and large, to use the law as means for controlling cartels and monopolies in contrast with the United States. Cartel agreements, contracts in restraint of trade, distributive agreements and intellectual property (trade marks, patents etc) enabled companies to expand the scale of their enterprises whilst conforming to the letter of the law.[46] The ideologies of legal formalism, freedom of contract and free trade constituted a kind of intellectual buffer zone which drained legal interventionism of its legitimacy. But the power of these ideologies was seemingly selective. The tendency of English law to refuse to regulate trade competition and the growing use of the corporate form by trade and industry, starkly contrasts with ". . . the courts' readiness to impose liability on trade unionists in logically similar circumstances."[47]

III : SANCTIONS, LITIGATION AND COURTS

A. Sanctions

A factor determining the use or non-use of law is the nature and effectiveness of an accompanying sanction. What type of sanction, if any, is employed, is often intimately associated with the character of the relationship between parties. Mutual economic inter-dependence will influence significantly whether any, and if so which, sanctions will be invoked. Not all employers sue their employees for breach of contract. Macaulay's well-known study of American businessmen which concluded that where the contracting parties are relatively equal and recurrently deal with each other, the law is fastidiously avoided, and that it is perceived as inimical both to that relationship and to the ability to govern one's own affairs, has received extensive comparative support.[48]

Legal enforceability, that is, lawful coercion by and through the state legal order, was probably the most important instrumental facility offered by the state legal system. "Legal enforceability lends point to adjudicative processes by supplying a motive for compliance with the decision reached. A decision whose concomitant is legal enforceability is a powerful resource for the winner confronted with the problem of extracting performance from a recalcitrant loser. The problem of the recalcitrant loser strongly suggests that few systems for the adjudication of commercial disputes could be viable without the ultimate sanction of legal enforcement. Nevertheless, legal enforceability is dispensable, albeit only in exceptional circumstances."[49] Such circumstances obtained in the mid 19th century, as Robert Ferguson's paper in the present volume demonstrates.[50] Ferguson shows that in certain circumstances, legal coercion gave way to extra-legal coercion. For example, on the Stock Exchange, ostracism was the potent force preventing the widespread repudiation of sales agreements by contractors well aware that legal sanctions for such repudiation were non-existent because the relevant bargain was legally unenforceable. Thus, commerce's need for legal coercion, directly or indirectly, cannot be assumed as axiomatic. For instance, informal collective price and output controls within a market or industry may be unenforceable in law; however, the economic sanctions cartels can impose on existing firms may be as substantial as those of the state law order. On the other hand, it is probably unlikely that parties will be unconcerned about the absence of a legal guarantee in commercial transactions unless the relevant market is characterised by an unusually high degree of self-regulation or collective cohesion. Furthermore, in the context of trade debtors and other defaulters, some plaintiffs may have regarded litigation as essential, even where this might, in itself, prove uneconomic. For ". . . unpaid bills had to be 'chased' because if it got known that their company or agency did not take defaulters to court, then nobody would pay."[51] In this way civil litigation may have a "general deterrence" function.[52]

Even where contracts were enforceable, a large body of businessmen preferred resort to arbitration to settle their contractual disagreements, to the more formal, costly and time-consuming process through the courts. Indeed, the continental tribunals of commerce were the subject of fervent enquiry.[53] As Ferguson points out, however, what was at stake was also a matter of honour as well as financial cost, though the latter may well have dictated the adoption of the former approach. By resorting to the courts, the party who did so gave notice that his or her concern was limited to the purely impersonal. The respect accorded by one gentleman-businessman to another held no place in this litigant's dealings. Such an attitude in respect to a fellow-businessman was considered by others to be undignified.

The paper by Rubin also attempts to shed light on the relation between commercial practice and litigation.[54] Whereas in Ferguson's chapter, the objective was to show how unimportant was the sanction of the law in certain specific situations when compared to the sanction of one's peers, in Rubin's paper, the role of sanction as both substance and ideology is emphasised.

"If, as Foucault suggests, we rid ourselves of 'the illusion that penalty is above all (if not exclusively) a means of reducing crime', and assume that changes in the kind and degree of punishment (and other sanctions) reveal something about the structure of the societies in which they are found, then it makes sense to give careful attention to both changes in the kind and degree of punishment (and other sanctions, both public and private law) within a specific society over time and the differences in punitive controls (and other sanctions) that exist between different societies at a fixed point in time."[55] In other words, a new history of law and economy may be able to illuminate the historical and comparative relationship between public and private law sanctions and the social organisation and economic change within and as between different nation states. This, in turn, will require that we consider state law sanctions as part of a wider, diffuse, complex of sanctions and social controls that are political, economic, ideological and social in their origins and functions.

Neither Ferguson nor Rubin dwells at length on the doctrinal development of the law, though neither contribution actually ignores this fact. Indeed, it would be foolish to assert that doctrinal development had no perceptible effect on subsequent economic behaviour, or that, alternatively, economic behaviour itself inspired no changes in the common law, for the example of Lord Mansfield's creation of the law merchant testifies otherwise.[56] What we do assert is that there is little value in adopting sweeping generalisations concerning the relationship between case law and economic development. The theme will most profitably be examined topic by topic and only once this kind of exercise has been accomplished over a sufficiently broad area, will we be in a position to point to, or to refute, the existence of a systematic pattern of development.[57]

B. Courts And Litigation

Were some courts preferred to others as a forum for dispute settlements? Mainstream English literary sources, for example, Smollett, Thackeray and Dickens are testimony enough to the low esteem in which the civil courts and the legal profession, particularly those engaged in Chancery, have been held. "No man, as things now stand", said George Spence, an authority on the Court of Chancery, in 1839 "can enter into a Chancery suit with any reasonable hope of being alive at its termination, if he has a determined adversary."[58] Thus, the relative merits of the common law as measured against those of the English civil law courts or the common law as contrasted with equity, or even local against centralised justice, were all fiercely contested.[58a] Similarly, common law versus statute law, the legislative as against administrative process, appellate as opposed to trial jurisdiction, bench as contrasted with bar, legal versus quasi-legal or non-legal personnel, "practical " law as against "academic law", state law as against indigenous norms represent a series of linkages which masked a variety of divisions and competing interests. Tensions and rivalries within the legal system perhaps, therefore, at least partly explain some change in the form and content of law over time.

Related to the issue of the role of courts in quickening the pace of economic development is the question of the extent to which legal change affected the distribution of wealth and power. For example, what were the political and economic consequences of securing legal change through the courts rather than through Parliament? Morton Horwitz has argued that in 19th century America, the impact of substantial law-making by the courts was to mystify the underlying policy choices and deny the kinds of open debate and compromises more likely to ensue from the legislative process.[59] To what extent is this thesis applicable to England; and, if it is, can we measure the costs incurred, and if so, how? Horwitz rightly warns against the casual application of the concept of laissez-faire to the common law power of judges. "Strictly speaking," he argues, "there would never be a laissez-faire regime unless judges refused to enforce all contracts and refused to compensate all injuries . . . . (Under) certain circumstances even judicial refusal to act could be motivated by developmental goals. In this sense, the contractarian ideology of 19th century judges was both instrumental (in the sense of promoting economic development) and laissez-faire (in the traditional sense of being hostile to legislative or administrative regulation). In short, when it comes to analysing the activities of private law judges deciding disputes concerning tort, contract and property, the category laissez-faire is often not useful primarily because it does not distinguish between developmental and distributional goals. It also ignores the political significance of leaving the task of government regulation primarily to judges."[60]

IV : LEGAL CONCEPTS AND INSTITUTIONS, INCENTIVES AND DISINCENTIVES

If we turn to more specific examples of the tasks confronting the legal, social, business and economic historian of the period to which the above general issues might point, we might direct our attention, first, to whether there existed legal concepts and institutions, the creations of a pre-industrial era, which were adapted to serve the purposes of a rapidly industrialising state. Thus, did the partnership form, the embodiment of the medieval commenda and societas, contribute to the thrusting entrepreneurship of the early nineteenth century? Or did more significant economic development arise through the creation of "custom built" legal forms such as the limited liability company?[61] To what extent did the creations of the lawyers of the early modern period, such as the strict settlement, the equitable trust or the equity of redemption, assist in transforming the economy into the first industrialised nation?[62]

In this section and the next we consider two examples which illustrate the complexity of the relationship between law and economy: firstly, patents and secondly, the absolute ownership of land.

A. The Illustrative Case Of Patents

By what legal instruments, if any, were the inventors of the spinning jenny and carding machine, the water frame and the mule, able to protect their inventions? What monopoly rights, if any, did Lewis Paul, Lawrence Earnshaw, Hargreaves, Arkwright, Samuel Crompton and Robert Peel enjoy in respect to their discoveries? The idea of granting a market monopoly was an old one, as the development of the guilds and boroughs exemplifies, and, until the modern period, it was intimately associated with the exercise of the royal prerogative.[63] In its efforts to declare these exercises void, Parliament challenged the Crown and indicated its preference for competition in the Statute of Monopolies of 1624. Exceptionally, section 6 permitted patent monopolies for 14 years upon "any manner of new manufacture within the realm to the true and first inventor". Parliament was concerned that England was under-developed technologically relative to France and Holland. It was the rise of industrialisation which led to a substantial increase in the number of patents. In the 1750s less than 10 patents a year were being granted; in the 1760s that number more than doubled. By the 1810s the average was 110 per annum and in the 1840s 458 per annum.[64] How important to the process of industrialisation was the protection for inventors afforded by rights of patent? "Among the famous, Boulton and Watt secured large sums from their steam engine patents, but these came partly from a special extending Act . . . (and after laborious litigation). Arkwright's main patent threatened the whole industry but proved to be too obscurely drawn to survive the attack on its validity. Crompton had to be given a parliamentary reward of £5,000 since he had virtually no commercial return from his spinning jenny. It is likely that patents provided equally sporadic encouragement for those with less celebrated improvements."[65] Henry Cort's patent of 1783, to devise a puddling and rolling process for pig-iron manufacture certainly brought him and his family little personal reward.[66]

In elucidating why this was the case, a significant factor was undoubtedly the slow, expensive and cumbersome system for obtaining and enforcing patents. Dickens satirised the obstacles the law placed in the way of inventors in Little

Dorrit.[67] As Cornish notes, "Separate patents had to be secured for England, Ireland and Scotland and a large number of officials had to give their approval."[68] Only in 1852, after Britain's technological primacy had been established, was a straightforward and relatively inexpensive patent system inaugurated.[69] Yet the advance was double-edged. The liberalisation of patent registration brought with it the increased possibility of costly and interminable litigation.

> "This might deter the genuine inventor from seeking protection, but it left the swashbuckler plenty of room to brandish dubious patents, hoping that competitors would find it simpler to treat shadow as if it were substance."[70]

Further, the courts often proved unsympathetic in their interpretation of the law when confronted with those seeking to enforce market monopolies.[71]

Did the existence of monopoly rights in inventions constitute an incentive to discovery; was it neutral in its effects or did it restrict the diffusion of new technology? Moreover, what was the relationship between inventions or discoveries and the legal form of business organisation? Charlotte Erikson, for example, has concluded that the aim of converting Ebbw Vale Steel Company from a partnership to a limited company in 1864 was to enable it to introduce fully the Bessemer process of steelmaking which the limited financial capacity of the partnership prevented.[72]

B. The Double-Edged Impact of Law On Economy

In respect to legal obstacles which might have hindered economic development, it remains, of course, an empirical question whether they did, in fact, operate to the disadvantage of a modernising economy; and if so whether their removal released scarce resources to the greater economic good of society (or of specified sections of society). Thus, discriminatory legislation, whether directed against slaves, Catholics, Non-Conformists, Jews or other groups, may well have had an inhibiting effect on the growth of the economy during the Industrial

Revolution, whilst positive discriminatory legislation, for example, the Navigation Acts or patent laws may well have worked in the other direction. Alternatively, restrictions may have channelled energies into activities which ultimately proved more productive to the economy than if the prohibitions had never existed in the first place, while protective legislation might only have had a feather-bedding, and ultimately negative, effect.

The growth of the cotton industry, for example, benefited in part from a favourable legal environment which encouraged inventions, fostered the rise of wage-labour and was free of import restrictions. By contrast, the silk industry experienced protection for the silk weavers against foreign imports, the reduction of duties on raw materials, and the fixing of wages by the justices under the Spitalfields Act 1773. As one nineteenth century writer, lamenting the fate of the silk trade, noted,

> "How unfortunate was it that the Legislature was not sufficiently enlightened on the bearing of commercial legislation. By it, both manufacturers and labourers were encouraged to make demands which were utterly irreconcilable with economic laws . . . . Witness the renewal, year after year, of the prohibition against combinations among workmen. How could the (silk) manufacturers prosper with a legislation so restrictive and meddling?"[73]

We may not agree with all the above judgments. The explicit link between legal framework and economic activity was, however, significant. An important inference to be drawn from the above discussion is that the economic impact of law is often complex and double-edged. For example, it is sometimes asserted that the usury laws impeded individual investment and economic development. However, it has also been pointed out that in practice these laws were often laxly enforced. Indeed, it has been argued that, "By setting permitted rates of interest, the law had been accommodating itself to the fact of usury ever since 1545."[74] One might add that by encouraging personal saving as the major method of raising capital between about 1750 and 1870, the usury laws indirectly encouraged the accumulation and investment of personal wealth. It is this double-edged quality of law, further exemplified by the history of the Bubble Act,[75] which is frequently overlooked in studies touching upon the operation of law in the economy.

Yet the notion of legal obstacles to economic development is not restricted solely to positive or negative statutory interventions, but also both to the absence of legal protections and to the bias of the legal system in the eighteenth century to a land-based economy. Thus, in the context of the Industrial Revolution, it is often alleged that there arose not merely new conceptions of property rights, for these arose earlier. It is also recognised that there was not simply a transformation of property rights such as patents and shares which had been developed from about the sixteenth century. What is claimed is that during the Industrial Revolution, new categories of property rights, such as bills of exchange and negotiable instruments also arose.[76] Did the law see as one of its tasks the protection of such new forms of property from depredation by others? If so, how did it set about achieving this object in the varied cases of, for example, bank clerks,[77] factors,[78] those who breached copyright,[79] poachers[80] and textile workers appropriating industrial waste?[81] Clearly, changing conceptions of property required and generated new crimes and civil wrongs. Further, how did the law seek to resolve, and with what success, conflicting property rights within, and as between, classes? Again, this calls for a more inclusive investigation than has perhaps been the case to date.

It should, indeed, be noted that the need of "authority" to secure legal fences around those instruments of the law such as patents might be said to display a continuity with a process initiated in an earlier period. However, since the law tends to mask change by retaining the same nomenclature, encouraged, perhaps, by its apparent adherence to judicial precedent, despite changes in function (the term "company" for example, applied both to the sixteenth century public institution and to the later nineteenth century private institution), it is easy to exaggerate the continuity of the law.[82] In other cases, as already noted, the existence of an unsatisfactory currency and the requirements of traders for credit, inspired a clear transformation in the law within a relatively short period of time. From outright antagonism towards negotiability, a position of full acceptance of the principle was soon established. Indeed, one might say that law might otherwise appear unimportant if it failed to give the impression either of entailing changes in concept or of creating new concepts.[83]

V : PROPERTY

A. Property And Property Relations As Symbiotic With Law

In this section we outline some of the major issues touching upon the history of property, law and economy. Inevitably, the discussion is selective rather than comprehensive.

Land was and still is a cardinal source of power and inequality. "From the earliest settlements until the Industrial Revolution the economic basis of society was agrarian. Land was wealth, livelihood, family provision, and the principal subject-matter of the law . . . . (Land) was also government and the structure of society."[84] What was the relationship between, on the one hand, property and property relations and, on the other, law and lawyers? What influences were exerted; by whom and in what directions?

" 'Property and law are born and must die together', wrote Bentham. 'Before the laws, there was no property: take away the laws, all property ceases'. The organs of the law are symbiotic with property."[85] For instance, under feudalism, the status of individuals depended in every way on their position on the land which, in turn, was defined by law and custom. The rules concerning land tenure - a system under which lord and tenant simultaneously had an estate or interest in land, though the latter had the actual occupation and use of the land held - determined political rights and duties. In the later Middle Ages, the common law helped conserve the rights of landed property against the claims of the Crown.[86]

The identification of property and production relations with law is especially intense in England given that ordinary English language uses legal terms to describe property and production relations; and that no ready-made alternative to this usage exists.[87] The two-directional, interconnection between law and property has recently been stressed in Edward Thompson's work on eighteenth century England. Thompson concludes that in the agrarian context of eighteenth century England the Marxian distinction between law as an element of superstructure, and the actualities of productive forces, is untenable. "For law", he argues, "was often a definition of actual agrarian practice . . . . How can we distinguish between the activity of farming or of quarrying and the rights to this strip of land or to that quarry? The farmer or forester in his daily occupation was moving within visible and invisible structures of law . . . . Hence, 'law' was deeply imbricated within the very basis of productive relations, which would have been inoperable without this law."[88]

The relationship between law, land and property relations is portrayed as one of reciprocal influence and reinforcement. Yet we cannot stop there, for many questions remain unanswered. "Imbrication" tells us how law, land and property relations engage with one another. But it tells us nothing about which of these constituents (if any) tends to predominate or endure in the short-run and the long-run. In other words, was the reciprocal relationship between law, land and property relations symmetrical or asymmetrical? If the relationship between law, land and property relations was functionally inter-dependent, as Thompson's use of "imbrication" seems to imply, we must ask, functional for whom and for what?

B. Capitalism And The Rise Of Absolute Private Property

Surprisingly, economic historians have tended to take for granted the relationship between law, property relations and the rise of capitalism. In effect, they have been inclined to treat that relationship as ". . . a 'given', to be held static in the background of analysis . . . ."[89] Insofar as historians and sociologists have considered the relationship between law, property and property relations, the tendency has been to focus upon a key feature of the transformation from feudalism to capitalism: the rise of absolute private property. This concern with the rise of absolute private property is not surprising: it informs the work of influential writers such as Marx, Weber and Macpherson. Even here, however, the role of law rarely receives detailed attention.[90] As we saw earlier in this introduction, there has been a marked tendency to adopt a rather simple, functionalist, state-law centred model of law and economy in the historical and sociological literature; and this is well illustrated in historical work on property and property relations. In what follows, we have tried to indicate some of the potential pitfalls of such a model.

Marx's analysis of the rise of absolute private property and the chronology he suggested has greatly influenced non-Marxist, as well as Marxist historians. Thus, a brief explication of his views still constitutes an important starting point for discussion. For Marx, the great transformation from feudalism to capitalism occurred in England in the last third of the 15th century and in the 16th century. During this period an "agricultural revolution" which forced the peasantry from the land on to a labour market, laid the foundation for the capitalist mode of production.[91] Marx argued that the "economic structure of capitalistic society has grown out of the economic structure of feudal society. The dissolution of the latter set free the elements of the former."[92] The rise of absolute private property was a fundamental constituent of the rise of capitalism; and that it did not develop until capitalist production predominated. Thus, ". . . the legal view . . . that the land-owner can do with the land what every owner of commodities can do with his commodities . . . this view . . . arises . . . in the modern world only with the development of capitalist production."[93] The history of landed property and the metamorphosis of tenurial law provides a 'mirror' in which we can observe the rise of capitalism.[94] Marx's view of feudalism stressed its dynamic character. Feudalism was not a monolithic social formation. Alongside free peasant proprietors existed a relatively small number of wage labourers from at least the latter half of the 14th century.[95] Engels reaffirmed Marx's view of a transformation in the nature of property relations and property law. Capitalist production, "by changing all things into commodities, (it) dissolved all inherited and traditional relations and replaced time hallowed custom and historical right by purchase and sale, by the 'free contract'."[96] Thus, Engels asserted that Marx had already foreseen Maine's dichotomy between 'status' and 'contract' and had located the shift from the former to the latter in the 16th century. Broadly speaking this model of transformation was endorsed by Weber though Weber's work is perhaps richer in its analysis of why capitalism supplanted feudalism in the later 16th century.[97]

Sociologists and historians, despite their diverse value-judgments, have tended to adopt this dichotomisation and the model of transition and revolution it imbibes. Indeed, it still dominates much thinking in economic history. Take, for example, Landes' attempt to explain why the first breakthrough to a modern industrial system took place in certain areas in Western Europe. "The role of private economic enterprise in the West" Landes contends, "is perhaps unique: more than any other factor, it made the modern world."[98] In terms, which echo both Marx and Weber, Landes stresses the ways in which . . . "the place of private enterprise was secure and improving with time"; and that this was reflected in . . . "the institutional arrangements that governed the getting and spending of wealth."[99] Landes takes as his example the idea and nature of property.

> "This was often hedged around in the pre-industrial period by restrictions on use and disposition and by complications of title. Land especially was caught up in a thicket of conflicting rights . . . which were a powerful obstacle to productive exploitation. Over time, however, the nations of Western Europe saw an increasing proportion of the national wealth take the form of full property - full in the sense that the various components of ownership were united in the person or persons of the possessor, who could use the object of ownership and dispose of it as he saw fit."[100]

Interconnected with the rise of absolute private property "was the growing assurance of security in one's property - an indispensable condition of productive investment and the accumulation of wealth."[101] This security, claims Landes, operated at two levels: first, as between the owners of property and the ruler; and second, as between property owners inter se. "With respect to the first, the ruler abandoned . . . the right . . . of disposition of the wealth of his subjects. This issue was joined early and its outcome was clearly linked to . . . the political as well as the economic status of the business classes. (The) ruler learned that it was easier and in the long run more profitable to expropriate with indemnification rather than to confiscate, to take by law or judicial proceeding rather than by seizure. At the same time - this is the second of our two dimensions - Europeans learned to deal with one another in matters of property on the basis of agreement rather than of force; and of contract between nominal equals rather than of personal bonds between superior and inferior."[102]

Both the traditional periodisation of the metamorphosis of property and property law and the nature of that metamorphosis have been endorsed by intellectual historians, notably C.B. Macpherson.[103] Macpherson has argued that prior to the seventeenth century, the ideas of common property and private property commonly co-existed. "It is only", he says "when we enter the modern world of the full capitalist society of the seventeenth century, that the idea of common property drops virtually out of sight . . . . (This) can be seen as a reflection of the changing facts. From the sixteenth and seventeenth centuries on, more and more of the land and resources in settled counties was becoming private property, and private property was becoming an individual right unlimited in amount, unconditional on the performance of social functions, and freely transferable, as it substantially remains to the present day."[104] Here Macpherson seems to be positing a close (but not necessarily an exact) correspondence between a major change in the concept of property (i.e. the way people saw property) as exemplified in the influential writings of Locke and Blackstone; and what was happening historically to property as an institution. As a concept and as an institution property was by the seventeenth century increasingly becoming absolute.[105]

He argues that property was conceived as a 'right' (in the sense of a claim enforceable by law, custom or the state) rather than a 'thing' until the eighteenth century. With the rise of an absolute conception of property, the distinction between property as a thing and as a right blurred. "(Limited) and not always saleable rights in things were being replaced by virtually unlimited and saleable rights to things."[106]

C. The Revisionist Challenge

Recently, the conventional chronology has been challenged. The revisionists accept the conventional view that absolute private property and the security the law afforded it were crucial to modernisation. Indeed, in some revisionist accounts, the rise of absolute private property and the central role of the law therein become the cornerstones of their explanation why capitalism first emerged in Western Europe. However, the revisionists, implicitly or explicitly, repudiate the idea that absolute property rights only began to predominate (at the earliest) from the late 15th and 16th centuries. The chronology of the transition is pushed backwards. "Possessive individualism" and its legal underpinnings were, it is asserted, alive and well in 13th century England. Let us briefly consider two such revisionist works: North and Thomas' The Rise of the Western World[107] and Macfarlane's The Origins of English Individualism.[108]

North and Thomas argue that by the end of the 13th century, freeholders had the right in law to enjoy freely and alienate their land - a right not recognised by feudal law.[109] Statutes permitting enclosure also facilitated exclusive land ownership. A major reason for these changes was the strength of central government in England (a legacy of the Norman Conquest) as compared with Continental Europe. "The centralised authority of the King's Court in England had no exact parallel on the Continent. During the thirteenth century the King's Court gradually expanded its jurisdiction relative to the seigneurial courts . . . . (The) King's Court held jurisdiction over freemen. A free man came to be defined as a man whose obligations were strictly defined . . . . These favourable developments in England were unique in the feudal world. Elsewhere, except in the Netherlands, the legal institutions still did not recognise exclusive property in land. The revival and application of Roman law on the Continent, particularly in Germany, did not afford the lessee legal protection. . . . The development of private property in land on the Continent generally lagged behind England during the thirteenth century."[110] North and Thomas are careful to note that the right freely to enjoy and alienate, being limited to freeholders, applied only to a minority of English lands. It is the precedent that they regard as "of tremendous importance."[111] They also stop short of arguing that the law recognised fee-simple ownership and, therefore, exclusive private property in its fullest, modern sense. Their conclusion is that a property right "approaching"[112] fee-simple ownership was recognised with respect to freeholders by the end of the 13th century.[113] In this way, it could be argued that their chronology does not fundamentally depart from that of Marx, Weber and conventional historiography.

Macfarlane's work, on the other hand, constitutes an explicit repudiation of the conventional periodisation. In his view, " . . . both historians and sociologists have largely misinterpreted the basic nature of English social structure between the 13th and 18th centuries . . . .[114] (If) we use the criteria suggested by Marx, Weber and most economic historians, England was as 'capitalist' in 1250 as it was in 1550 or 1750. That is to say, there was already a developed market and mobility of labour, land was treated as a commodity and full private ownership was established . . . rational accounting and the profit motive were widespread."[115]

In these revisionist studies property law is afforded unusual attention. In both works, Maitland's unearthing of individualism and proto-capitalist forms in the Middle Ages has proved inspirational. Like Maitland, Macfarlane reconstructs the lives of individuals from legal and other records, principally from two parishes: Kirby Lonsdale (Cumbria) and Earls Colne (Essex). North and Thomas' more general study places special emphasis not only on the early legal recognition of fee-simple ownership in land, but also on the ways English law from an early period (i.e. from the 14th, 15th and 16th centuries) protected privately owned goods and encouraged the protection of intangibles such as patents, thereby affording entrepreneurs, capital and inventors the institutional arrangements most conducive to modernisation.

Here, property law and other legal institutions are elevated to significant determinants of modernisation in the quest for 'why' and 'how' the industrial revolution occurred first in England.[116] The revisionist accounts, such as those of North and Thomas and Macfarlane, are stimulating and provocative contributions to the wider debate about the transition from feudalism to capitalism. Too often, historians and sociologists have adopted a static one-dimensional model of transformation or transition - from pre-capitalist to capitalist society. The revisionist contribution usefully problematises this often taken-for-granted dichotomy. In particular, Macfarlane's work re-emphasises the importance of local studies of "real" people in the generation and refinement of general theories of law, property and economy. Whether Macfarlane's findings are typical, as opposed to being peculiar to the localities investigated, will only become clear once further reconstructions of the lives of villagers have been undertaken.

A word of warning, though, about the competing explanations outlined above. The debate surrounding the chronology and changing character of property relations and property law parallels the controversy over the periodisation and content of laissez-faire and state interventionism. Both debates touch upon the general character of state and society; and both partake, in part, of "test cases" of the justice or viability of particular conceptions of property relations, state and society.[117] Thus, the politically-charged nature of both controversies.

D. Absolute Private Property Versus A Plurality of Legal Forms:

Interestingly, despite their political differences, there is a strong core of consensus shared by all the participants to the debates concerning the relationship between property, property relations and property law outlined above. They all appear to agree about the nature of the transition or transformation (captured in such phrases as "the rise of absolute private property" and "the shift from status to contract"). Indeed, for all their political differences, these studies " . . . have in common that their method posits law . . . (or 'property' or 'state') as a reified author of social change; i.e. they give legal form an active functional role in shaping the social order." They assume . . . "that law-and-society is a set of linked hierarchical structures in which legal rule induces social response (and vice-versa), instead of separate social spheres connected to one another only in the loosest and most problematic ways."[118] To accept the latter hypothesis does not necessarily entail the view that the legal order was irrelevant in economy and society. It does, however, have a number of virtues. It serves to question whether the particular regime of property, property relations and (in particular) property law that historians and sociologists have associated with the rise of modern society and the Western World in particular, was as indispensable or as absolute and pre-eminent as many seem to assume. In other words, the relation between the legal realm (state and non-state ordering) and social practice may be more discontinuous and problematic than some overly-functionalist accounts of property, property relations and property law may imply.

To illustrate this argument, let us return to some of the accounts of the metamorphosis of property, property relations and property law outlined in this section. On further investigation the much vaunted rise of absolute private property, for example, turns out to be somewhat more complex and contradictory.

One respect with which property remained qualified in practice concerns the notion that property ownership gave rise to obligations as well as rights. Whilst this idea operated with special force within the family, it also extended to the public, at least until the end of the 18th century, and probably later.[119]

Property was also qualified in practice because it was ultimately a creature of state law; and what state law protected and enforced, state law might restrict or take away.[120] For example, actions against the Crown in contract and tort for damage to the property or person of others were severely limited.[121] Whilst in theory the Crown was subject to the law, in practice this was not the case as there was no institution to enforce the law against the Crown. The courts were those of the Crown, and thus, the Crown could not be sued in its own court. The Crown could be a plaintiff but not a defendant. The Crown might, however, voluntarily abide by a decision of a court of law, and an elaborate system of petition of right was developed to facilitate this arrangement.[122] However, liability in tort, such as the employer's liability for the negligence of employees during the course of their employment fell beyond the ambit of this arrangement. This doctrine remained intact until 1947 when the Crown Proceedings Act sought to simplify and extend the law.[123] Other instances of the Crown's ability unilaterally to alter property rights include Charles II's successful struggle to control the personnel and thus the government of the borough and city corporations, notably the City of London, over which the Crown had, in 1682, slight legal control. This attack culminated in the Crown's forfeiture of the Charter of London and of other boroughs as well as bodies such as livery companies.[124] These examples illustrate that the space afforded property rights by the Crown was neither absolute nor uncontested. Indeed, once the whole range of state activity and interventionism is considered, and not just the activities of the courts alone, the notion of a pure, unequivocal private property becomes much more problematic.

A further way property rights were limited in practice was in terms of the great expense, the length of time and the sheer difficulties of enforcement which might conspire to prevent property owners fully exercising their rights. Landes and North and Thomas, for example, stress the importance of the extension of the umbrella of "property" to intangibles such as shares, copyrights and patents.

However, the average shareholder, copyrightholder and patentee did not have the financial resources, the time and the contacts to enforce their rights. The success of the Watt and Boulton partnership in protecting their patent would appear to be the exception, rather than the rule.[125] Here, again, we see historians and sociologists conflating the existence of a legal rule, right or duty with the separate questions of its operation, mediation and enforcement in practice.

But there are other reasons why property was more limited in law and practice in the 17th, 18th and 19th centuries, than the kinds of accounts outlined above recognise. What these accounts tend to de-emphasise is the continued importance of the institution of property as a "bundle of rights" i.e. a range or hierarchy of different rights vested perhaps in different people co-existing in the same piece of land or goods, which qualified the use and enjoyment of property.

The recent work of social historians testifies to the persistence, albeit in an increasingly bowdlerised form, of traditional use-rights such as the right to remove firewood and rights of pasture which in practice qualified the actualisation of absolute conceptions of property. The prohibitions upon forestalling, regrating and engrossing survived Coke's attacks and, together with customary restrictions on the price of staples (especially during periods of dearth), were sporadically resuscitated. This "moral economy" with its blend of paternalism, common property, notions of just price, and political expediency in the face of the English crowd, like use-rights and perquisites, co-existed alongside the rise of the idea of absolute property and qualified that ideal in practice well into the nineteenth century.[126]

Thus, the "restrictions on use and disposition", the "complications of title", the "thicket of conflicting rights" which Landes locates in a pre-industrial, pre-absolute propertied world, did not cease with the rise of industrialisation and general absolute private property. Indeed, all the authors so far considered ignore the notorious and persistent technicality and obscurity of English land law.[127] This survived at least until the reforms of 1925; and, thus, in turn, made all transactions in land extremely expensive in England.[128]

This qualified notion of property, reaching back to the tenures of medieval feudalism, endured in practice despite the rise of an absolute conception of property. Indeed, in the very period when Macpherson, Landes, and others detect the growing ascendency of an absolute conception of property, R.S. Neale observes that the traditionally qualified institution of property was being evolved into a vital vehicle for industrialisation.[129] Neale contends that a " . . . flexible and functional, rather than absolute and categorical (institution of property) had developed in England by the second half of the 17th century . . . ";[130] and that this grew out of the changing needs of the landed rather than the demands of middle-class traders and industrialists or because of changes in ideology. Moreover, Neale asserts that this new flexible notion of property ". . . provides the legal and a good deal of the institutional framework which alone made possible the development of industrial capitalism in Britain."[131] Because English land law recognised a wide and complex range of qualified property rights, private property rights were rarely absolute in practice. "Thus, whatever the notion in regard to property held by economic and political theorists at the turn of the 17th and 18th centuries, society and law recognised divisibility of property titles and recognised legal titles to present and future income as property, now giving legal form to the notion that property was the product of labour and capital as well as the product of land and all three together . . . . Law and society worked with a fee-simple tenure so spotted that the quantity of spots changed the quality of the beast."[132] He goes on to argue that although this flexible notion of property was originally created as a result of the needs and power of the landed, it was subsequently borrowed and exploited by the industrial sector for their own advantage - a phenomenon clearly exemplified in the gradual embourgeoisement of the trust.[133]

Thus it seems that Macpherson, Landes and others exaggerate the dominance of an absolute conception of property since the 17th century; and correspondingly tend to ignore the role played by other conceptions of property ideologically, politically and economically. Indeed, Neale rightly argues that an absolute conception of property, if put into practice, would ultimately constitute a brake upon the economic development of property and the ability to restrict the future alienation of that property. His work augments that of Macpherson by stressing the importance economically, of the traditional, flexible, qualified conception of private property in the 17th, 18th and 19th centuries. However, his thesis tends to imply that the flexible conception of property was new to the 17th century, whereas its pedigree is somewhat older. It would be more accurate perhaps to say that that conception of property became even more subtle and complex from the 17th century; and that whilst this more instrumental conception of property was no doubt originally shaped in the interests of the land relative to those of trade, it was undoubtedly assisted by the fact that legal institutions such as the trust, the settlement and the mortgage had been refined by lawyers so as better to serve the need of the 17th century landed interest. In other words, changes within the law, as well as the power of the landed, brought about a more flexible and versatile conception of property in the 17th century.

George Haskins' recent re-interpretation of the origins of the rule against perpetuities gives some support to Neale's analysis.[134] Haskins argues that prior to the Duke of Norfolk's case of 1682,[135] the case which established the rule against perpetuities, the law had not permitted unchecked perpetuities, but was a,

> ". . . rigid, already weakened system in which future interests could be found destructible or void, and present owners were often comparatively free to break their parents' wills."[136]

Thus, the ability of the great land-owner to control future ownership was hindered by a law of perpetuity that was complex, uncertain and hostile to perpetuities. The Duke of Norfolk's case resolved earlier uncertainties as to how long interests in landed property might last. Although the decision itself represented a compromise, in that it did not give conveyancers total freedom for the landed classes to control their estates, neither did it severely limit the testator's or grantor's options. It is

Haskins' thesis that the case formulated a rule of perpetuities rather than a rule against perpetuities. In other words, the case facilitated and legitimated restraints on the alienation of property after a long period when such restraints had been under attack. By clarifying the law, the case gave the landed classes the additional room to manoeuvre which they required, in order to tie up their lands with greater facility and certainty.

> "The rule meant that what had once been considered a perpetuity was no longer. In this sense, the new rule was a clear victory for the 'dead hand', not for free alienability. The rule served the fathers, not the sons and if it did not attempt to make lawful a whole panoply of perpetuities, it did at least allow most that were needed."[137]

In terms similar to those of Neale, Haskins sees the pressure for a qualified conception of property coming not from "incipient capitalists", but from the landed (including the gentry) " . . . anxious to preserve the positions of the families in a society that had recently passed through a turbulent period."[138]

The rise of "freedom of contract" facilitated and legitimated both the qualification of absolute private property and its enhancement. In other words, significant tensions arose as between the concepts of freedom of contract and absolute private property and the ostensible values they exhaled.[139]

E. The Strict Family Settlement: Accumulation And The Patriarchal Family?

Thus, the ideal of absolute ownership was qualified in practice by those very groups who, it is oft assumed, would benefit most from absolute ownership. Landowners sought legal restraints on ownership and use to ensure that property remained intact for the family over several generations. How was this qualification of property facilitated in law? There ". . . was the traditional entail by which land was held by a tenant or holder without the power to sell, mortgage, or lease, the succession to the land being predetermined usually in favour of eldest sons, one after the other. The Whig aristocrats must have felt torn by their dynastic ambitions for their descendants, and on the other hand, by their own desires to be free from the restrictions imposed upon them by the dead hand of the past. The dynastic ideology was very important . . ."[140] Now the principal medium through which the law served this ideology was the strict settlement of land, an elaborate legal device conceived by conveyancers at about the time of the Restoration. The strict settlement helped to perpetuate the great landed estates in the hands of eldest sons. It would also ". . . provide for widows, younger sons, and daughters, and, above all, maintain the property intact - or preferably augmented - in the family. These competing family rights necessarily meant that the freedom of the land 'owner' - who was often no more than a tenant for life, or tenant in tail, legally speaking - was limited. The freedom of one generation was limited by that of earlier and later generations."[141]

The strict settlement is one of the very few legal devices to which economic historians have afforded some attention. In particular, historians have scrutinised two interrelated features of the historical development of the strict settlement. First, there is an important debate concerning the role of strict settlement in the accumulation and preservation of the huge landed estates of England.[142] The essays by Chesterman, English and Spring in this anthology represent substantial contributions to this debate. Second, the strict settlement and the political controversy surrounding the reform of land in 19th and 20th century England have also interested historians.[143] The former has raised important questions about the role of property law in the preservation and accumulation of private wealth and power. The latter has served to highlight the centrality of property, and the politics of property in 19th century life. Both have illuminated the role played by lawyers in economy and society, both as the ingenious inventors of forms of private ordering and organisation designed to further certain interests and ends; and as the most powerful modern professional interest group - one which was able to play a leading role in the marginalisation of land reform, and therefore the redistribution of wealth and power in the modern period. Given the centrality of the strict settlement to three of the essays in this anthology, it is advisable to describe it.

Eileen Spring, a leading historian of the strict family settlement, offers the following succint description:

> "First, it limited the 'land-owner' to a life tenancy in his estate thus rendering him incapable of selling or mortgaging land except to the degree it might specifically allow. Second, it entailed the estate upon the land-owner's eldest son. By the entail a settlement determined that there would be but a single heir to the estate; and it did something else as well. The entail went far toward ensuring that the settlement would be renewed before it ran out. An individual settlement was of legally limited duration, usually a generation, but through the entail - in a complicated manner that need not be gone into here - this limitation was to a very considerable degree got over. It was not, to be sure, wholly got over; the rule against perpetuities was not utterly to be set aside. Settlement was a limited form of entail. Nevertheless, once an estate was settled, it tended thereafter to be bound by a chain of settlement and resettlement approaching perpetuity, son succeeding father generation after generation each limited in his power of alienation."[144]

In the words of F.M.L. Thompson, the strict settlement endowed estates with a "semi-corporate" quality.[145]

The importance of the strict settlement to landed families was advanced, in its most influential form, by Sir John Habakkuk.[146] In essence, he argued that in the sixty years after 1690, a newly improved form of strict settlement and mortgage facilitated a major shift towards oligopoly in landed power, that is, that the larger estates increased in size at the expense of the smaller ones. Other economic historians have recognised the importance of the strict settlement; and that its usage can be viewed as part of a wider movement whereby the law encouraged the elimination of the small owner-occupier of land, such as by way of Acts of enclosure and the legal forcible dispossession of the peasantry. In recent years, however, Habakkuk's stress on the importance of the strict settlement, as a mechanism for the consolidation of landed wealth, has been questioned.[147] This debate well illustrates the difficulties of assessing the importance of legal institutions to economic interests and regimes. Eileen Spring, for example, studied the history of settlement in three families from about 1780 to 1880 and concluded that their usage of the settlement varied enormously. If the families chosen were representative, the settlement was not a static institution, in which land-owners found their hands tied, as lawyers and historians have often assumed. In practice it appeared more flexible, conferring extensive power over the land to land-owners.[148] More recently she has stressed that the value of settlement to lawyers as an interest group has been neglected; whereas, their value to land-owners " . . . has possibly been exaggerated. Settlement was undoubtedly a useful aristocratic device, a kind of insurance policy . . . . But the . . . estate system . . . would not likely have crumbled without settlement . . . . The sentiment for, and the rewards of, landowning were still too great. Moreover, it is to be noted, that the estate system had survived two hundred years - between the abolition of true entails in the 15th century and the development of settlement in the 17th - without a form of entail. On the other hand . . . when settlement became a bone of class contention in the 19th century, it assumed in addition to its real usefulness a great symbolic importance."[149] Bonfield has concluded that " . . . the nexus between the strict settlement and the 'rise of great estates' is rather a weak one . . . . A combination of demographic factors such as late marriage, high mortality, and too few male children generally precluded resettlement. And without resettlement, the male heir under the existing settlement came into possession of the patrimony with a free hand."[150] Bonfield's work testifies to the importance of the demographic dimension when determining the relation between law and economy and the consequences thereof, especially in the period prior to 1780.

The papers by Chesterman, English and Spring in this anthology constitute important, though differing, assessments of the Habakkuk thesis. They also serve to extend the debate surrounding the strict settlement and economy in new directions. Whilst recognising the force of Habakkuk's critics, Michael Chesterman argues[151] that it does not follow that the strict settlement played no important role as an influential pressure against dissipation by individual family members and, therefore, the aggrandisement of landed estates. Chesterman emphasises that the law of trusts could be both sympathetic to what land-owners wanted and relatively autonomous of the needs of dominant economic interest groups. On the one hand, he points to extra-legal forces, such as the growth of commercial and industrial capital and considerations of taxation as important determinants of the law of trusts. On the other hand, he stresses the role of intra-legal factors such as the influence of legal draftsmen on the law, clients and law reform. In particular, Chesterman details for the first time the impact of a basic change in the nature of trust assets - from interests in specific land, intended to be held in specie, to a mixed fund of property (mainly personal such as shares) - on the form of modern trusts law.

Some of the problems of generalising about the nature, effect and, therefore, importance of the strict settlement have already been detailed in this introduction. Barbara English's paper[152] represents one historian's scholarly efforts to come to terms with those difficulties. As she points out, there are very few detailed investigations of individual 19th century settlements and, in that sense, generalisation is premature. English, therefore, offers a rare case history of one great land-owning family: the Sykes family, the largest land-holders in the East Riding of Yorkshire, 1792-1900. Case studies of this kind enable us to assess the extent to which the practice of settlement and resettlement followed or departed from the patterns assumed in standard legal and historical texts - as well as the operation of local land markets and the factors which most influenced land-holding families in the purchase and sale of their properties.

Habakkuk's thesis has not only influenced economic historians. In that it involves a theory of aristocratic marriage and, thus, the nature of the aristocratic family, it has focused the attention of historians of the family on the consequences of strict settlement for the character of the aristocratic family and inter-family relations. Eileen Spring's essay[153] criticises the conflicting conceptions of the aristocratic family which Habakkuk and Lawrence Stone have divined from the utilisation of the strict settlement by the aristocracy. In pointing to the ways they have misunderstood the strict settlement, Spring clarifies what the strict settlement does not tell us about aristocratic family life. What the strict settlement does tell us about aristocratic family life is the revival of traditional aristocratic ideas of inheritance, in particular, primogeniture, and thus, the cutting down of female inheritance. In this sense, the settlement was an instrument for facilitating and legitimating the patriarchal family long after some historians of the family have detected the decline of the patriarchal family. Spring's paper contributes to current debates concerning the time-span of settlements and when such settlements were made.

F. Property: Some Conclusions

The complex and contradictory relationship between the development of the concept of an absolute private property since the 17th century and a more qualified and flexible institution of property and the fractions and factions that saw one or the other as more inimical to their interests has yet to be adequately reconstructed. What is clear is that this very complexity and contradiction fostered the flexibility which enabled the common law in the 18th and 19th centuries to blur differences between realty and personalty and accept as property, intangibles such as options, shares, copyrights and patents. Yet at the same time, in the name of absolute individual property, the common and use rights of the "lower orders" were eroded.

This exercursus on property, property relations and property law illustrates a number of issues raised by the historical study of law and economy in the period 1750 to 1914. For example, the loose fit between the idea of a legal concept such as "property" or "contract" and its operation in practice; the co-existence simultaneously over relatively long periods, of competing conceptions and practices bearing the same name; the problematical relationship between legal ideas (i.e.

concepts) and practice (i.e. the law as a live institution); the manner in which a legal institution, shaped primarily with a certain economic interest in mind, could be utilised to the benefit of a different interest group, only to be turned subsequently to the advantage of yet another economic interest group (the history of the trust, for instance, is an excellent illustration of this process); the difficulty of differentiating continuity and change within law as an idea and as practised. Of course, the transformation of the concept of property must be seen in the context of the very insecurity of the landed interest under the Stuarts and their relative success in wresting greater freedom of property from the Crown, which in turn was part of the newly emerging relationship between Crown and subject.

The victory of the landed in the 17th century and their desire to consolidate their constitutional victories undoubtedly provides an important backdrop to the development of property law, and much else in the early modern period. This victory also provided the necessary foundation upon which trade and industry could expand in power, wealth and size in order to utilise and build upon itself, the legal victories of the landed class. The conflict, as well as the unity of interest, that characterised the relationship between trade and land, and its impact on law has yet to be chronicled in any depth.[154] Similarly, the effect of the agrarian revolution on land law and vice-versa has still to be systematically investigated.

What is fairly clear is that by the late 18th century, property is increasingly becoming subsumed to contract, that is, that it is taking on the qualities and functions of capital;[155] and that this function reinforced rather than negated the flexible, "instrumental", character of property as an institution. In other words, the contractualisation of property, however incomplete and schizoid, facilitated the complex holding, use or rights in property in an even more subtle form than hitherto. All this is not to deny that the so-called rise of absolute private property did not occur; but, merely, to stress that both as a concept and (especially) as a practice, property and property law operated in a more variegated and even antithetical fashion than has sometimes been recognised.

VI : THE ILLUSTRATIVE CASE OF CREDIT

A. Changing Views Of Credit, Economy And The Law

A specific, though perhaps neglected, feature of the relationship between law and economy is that between credit and the structure of the law and legal institutions.

> "Next in importance to the protection of men's lives and persons" wrote one nineteenth century pamphleteer, "is the protection of property, that property which is affected by the relation of debtor and creditor; for the proportion of national wealth that is entrusted to the hands of others in the shape of debts is, if not the largest, one of the largest sections of the whole mass."[156]

The question of credit raised issues of deep principle. Thus, there were those who, inspired by medieval ideas that any form of debt was immoral, flatly denied that bankruptcy, for example, was anything other than a crime. Others insisted that imprisonment for debt was just and condign punishment for moral failing. In the nineteenth century, by which time such medieval asceticism had been substantially diluted in the wake of widening markets, a residual legacy not absolutely opposed to credit, remained. Thus, the debate on general incorporation and limited liability for companies was influenced in part by a belief that,

> ". . . the possible inability of a limited company to meet its debts fully was regarded as immoral."[157]

Proposals to reform procedural aspects of partnership law in the 1840s, whereby it would become easier for a creditor to sue the partners without naming all of them, were, indeed, probably inspired by a concern to ensure that credit did not shift from partnerships to the joint stock company, which was at that time, as it had been in the past, identified with fraud and rash speculation.[158]

Yet moving away from such radical positions, one finds views which reflect an acknowledgement of the role of credit in the economy of the period, a recognition which determines a more qualified perception of the law's "proper" function in regulating exchange relations. Thus, as the Report of the Commissioners on Bankruptcy and Insolvency stated in 1840,

> "Credit must be, or commerce cannot be, and without it, no civilisation. All transactions have a claim to credit, from the milk score or the newspaper bill to the State loan. Therefore, the whole of such transactions, without regard to magnitude, have a claim to protection." 159

The problematic is transformed into supposedly achieving a balance between the availability of credit for both commercial and retail transactions on the one hand, and the prevention of fraud, reckless speculation and extravagance on the other. Yet the Bankruptcy Commissioners in 1840 were, surely, over-optimistic when they declared,

> "Good procedure will nearly prevent insolvency. There will be fewer losses, and creditors will then more readily act for the general good. The law is the most powerful of all teachers in showing men their social duties, and in compelling their performance. Good laws will soon extirpate those trading vultures, creditors as well as debtors, who devour men's hearts."[160]

As we have had occasion to point out already in this introductory chapter, such sentiments were frequently belied by the facts. Motives for compliance with one's obligation were often complex and multi-faceted. The existence of legal sanctions may have been one consideration. Other, socially constructed factors, were also relevant, often dictating an explicitly non-legal remedy. We, therefore, need to know which methods of settlement were more reliable to the participants, which ones were invested with a deeper sense of sanctity and reverence. In brief, did adjustments in the legal equation influence economic behaviour in respect to the availability of credit, to the likelihood of insolvency or bankruptcy occurring, or to the degree of protection to which creditors looked, or to which they felt themselves entitled?

B. Towards A More Impersonal Perception Of Law, Credit And Economy?

Yet the broader context of such debates must not be ignored. Where, for example, it was proposed to bureaucratise the procedures leading to the grant of a certificate of discharge from bankruptcy or to abolish imprisonment for debt (particularly, though not exclusively, on mesne process when legal action had just got under way), it is arguable that a more rational, impersonal perception of the law was being adopted. Coleman has suggested[161] that for the comparable period in the United States (about 1820 to 1860), the following reasons explain this new perception. First, "business in general and credit in particular became increasingly de-personalised." Thus, the corporation in the United States (though not, of course, in the United Kingdom), became the dominant form of ownership and management combined. The principal means of raising capital was through the device of stocks and bonds, with the growing banking system also clearly feeding the demand for investment. The significance of these developments for our purposes is to be found in the increasing institutionalisation of credit, extended on the basis of an impersonal evaluation of the borrower's financial standing rather than, as hitherto, on the footing of personal assessments of respectability. As Coleman, writing about the United States, alleges,

> "In short, in the orderly, systematic and de-personalised world that was emerging, the bookkeeper became the judge of the last resort for lender and borrower alike."[162]

A word of warning should be struck, however, in that until very much more information comes to light on the role and activities of attorneys and other "confidential" family advisers within local capital markets, to supplement the important researches of Anderson and Miles,[163] judgments such as the above may be premature in the context of England.

Coleman's additional points, nonetheless, possess significance. In view of the immense growth in scale and geographical dispersal of business activity, customers became mere "names on pieces of paper rather than faces and personalities", as a result of which, credit became further de-personalised. The discharge of debts thus became "normal and routine", failing which, again virtually routinely, a defaulter was likely to be sued. Bankruptcy relief became, for example, "an equitable, rational and systematic way of writing down bad debts."[164] Clearly, the stigma attached to insolvency could be written off as a sentimental throwback to a bygone age whose legal system identified "manifest criminality"[165] as one of its organising structural principles. Of course, the reality was more complex than the picture here depicted. The powerful symbolism of a public examination of the bankrupt,[166] though perhaps not rivaling the emotional atmosphere of the criminal assizes of the eighteenth century[167] is, nevertheless, one relic of the mentality of punishment by shaming, (as perhaps the Poulson affair of the 1970s reminds us). But Coleman's account of the "bookkeeper mentality" which allegedly received its "full flowering" as a result of the shift to an impersonal market place, de-personalised credit rating and a more rational-bureaucratic legal procedure did not prevail everywhere and at all times. Indeed, we have already argued that extra-judicial methods of settlement were, partly (if not wholly) on social grounds, probably preferred by businessmen - witness arbitration and tribunals of commerce - while consumer creditors such as the local grocer were more likely to write off their bad debts than to sue. There was yet room for personal assessments based on character or sympathy - at least within the world of the poor - though whether the creditors who spurned the "bookkeeper mentality" were themselves more likely to suffer eventual insolvency than those whose credit practices appeared to embody the 'status to contract' transition to a modern bureaucratised law, is a strong possibility.

Certainly, the developments noted by Coleman for the United States fail to receive full confirmation when tested against the commercial character assumed by the English county courts. While it is true that the county courts rapidly became mere debt-collecting offices (even if not every unsatisfied creditor chose to become a litigant), nonetheless, the very existence of these courts was thought, at the same time, to encourage "reckless" credit. This would be extended by determined plaintiffs, many of whom were thought to pursue questionable trading practices, but who, nevertheless, insisted that they prided themselves on their personal connections with debtors.[168] The evidence is, therefore, conflicting as to whether Coleman's model of the "bookkeeper mentality" is appropriate in the context of the working of the English county courts. Perhaps the superior courts provide more fertile ground for his analysis. Certainly, while a split between "the impersonal and barely perceived forces of system, order and rationality, and the older forces of personal responsibility and respectability"[169] undoubtedly took place, the English evidence of commercial law avoidance suggests that the scale of the shift is probably less emphatic for the United Kingdom than Coleman has suggested for the United States.

VII : THE PLURALITY OF LAW AND LEGAL INSTITUTIONS

What was or is meant by "the law" and "legal institutions" cannot be taken for granted. In fact, as we have seen, the law and legal institutions embrace a variety of discrete facets. A legal system usually possesses a range of facilities which may be analytically distinguished and which need to be differentiated if the relation between law and economy is to be advanced beyond the level of simplistic hypothesis. Here, for example, one thinks of:

(i) its procedures for establishing the facts and adjudication on the basis of those facts;

(ii) general substantive rules which guide citizens, their legal advisors and adjudicators;

(iii) appeal procedures, such as judicial review of the facts or law;

(iv) the enforcement of judgments, that is, legal coercion;

(v) its restitutive function;

(vi) its capacity to act as an insurance against financial or physical loss, for instance, by way of contract;

(vii) its provision for physical punishment signifying a "public" wrong;

(viii) its ideological and symbolic dimensions, as distinct from its instrumental concerns;

(ix) its ability to provide a degree of private ordering and organisation and, thus, a degree of autonomy from the state legal order, for example, by resort to facilitative laws, such as the laws governing companies, families, land and contracts; and

(x) its function of deterrence.

To emphasise the plurality of law and legal institutions sensitises us to their manifold dimensions thereby avoiding a monolithic usage. Moreover, attention to legal pluralism assists us to escape from a definition of law that assumes that the problems of ordering and organisation are exclusively the domain of the state. In other words, to stress legal pluralism is to recognise the complex co-existence of state law regulation (such as statute law and court decisions) and other systems of normative ordering such as custom and practice and indigenous ordering such as the family, the company, the work place, and business and social networks.[170] Sometimes these discrete but intertwined systems complement one another; on other occasions they may conflict or compete. Which tends to predominate, how and why? Robert Ferguson's essay in this volume instances the case of members of the Stock Exchange who regularly flouted the state law and, instead, applied and enforced their own "in-house" rules and sanctions.[171] The long-standing nature of the practices the law sought to prohibit; a tradition of self-regulation; the economic self-interest of Stock Exchange members; and their sense of constituting a relatively small and exclusive club governed by a code of honour, all go to explain this relative autonomy from, and supersession of, the relevant state law norms. Indeed, we have seen that the state law order actually promotes the existence of a plurality of semi-autonomous spheres such as the company, individual contractors, and so on, and therefore a margin of deviation from the state law order via, for instance, the medium of facilitative laws.

"The law" means different things to different individuals and groups. To the small trader it may be a costly and inconvenient burden, to the lawyer it may be the professional ideology of the legal profession; and to many lay persons, it may be the stereotyped "tough cop" of television fame. Similarly, the form of law, that is, its general structure, its categories, methods and procedures must be distinguished from its content, in the sense of particular case law or statutes, facilitating or prohibiting certain behaviour. The latter, in turn, must be distinguished from the ideology of the legal profession, by which is meant, for example, that law is held out to be a science which lay persons cannot properly understand (yet which is congruent with commonly held values), and that the law is both apolitical and necessary. Additionally, form, content and ideology must in turn be distinguished from the structure of the profession, for example, that High Court judges must be barristers of ten years standing and that there exists a basic separation of solicitors from the bar.[172] One reason why these distinctions between form, content, ideology and structure are important is that tensions may be generated within and between one element and another. For example, at least in the modern period, the form of law defined relevant actors for legal purposes as individuals. Recovery is, therefore, defined as recoupment by an individual for harm suffered by an individual. Similarly, collectivities such as companies, trade unions, and trusts are also conceptualised as individuals. For legal purposes, this "individuality" is an abstraction, shorn of its particular context - and its relative position and power in society. As a result, substantial differences between relevant actors are obscured and ignored.[173] Thus, the form of law (in addition to its content) may tend to define narrowly legal issues and, therefore, reinforce systematic inequalities. This is memorably conveyed in Anatole France's famous, ironic praise of "the majestic equality of the French law, which forbids both rich and poor from sleeping under the bridges of the Seine". Furthermore, the individuating, abstract form of law militates against the pursuit of class actions in the English legal system[174] and " . . . serves as an additional barrier to organisation of the under-dog to upset existing social arrangements . . . ."[175] In other words, because the legal form is inherently individualised, the expression of collective interests tends to be discouraged. Because the form of law adheres to a formal rather than a substantive conception of justice, the legal system may ratify itself merely by observing formal procedures or "precedent". Here is an instance of a wider phenomenon: namely, that the law participates " . . . in the construction of the social world, populating it with creatures of law's own devising, abstract self-determining individuals and artificial corporate persons, ascribing 'interests' to them and deciding when their sufferings are recognisable 'harms'."[176]

The relation between, first, economy, second, new forms of law associated with the rise of industrial capitalism, such as the wage labour contract, and third, the content of the law, in the sense of legal doctrine and legislation, clearly requires greater consideration by historians than hitherto. For example, John Rule has shown how the repeal of the apprenticeship clauses of the Statute of Artificers in 1814 was prefaced by a gradual whittling away of its coverage by lawyers objecting to its conflict with the common law attachment to a man's freedom of work.[177] Dobson's work on the Combination Laws in the eighteenth century is fruitful in hinting at how King's Bench sought to encourage the friendly society features of trade unions in the last decade of the century.[178] This softening of the rigours of the Combination Acts provides a suitable backcloth to the repeals of 1824-25 orchestrated by Francis Place, whose adherence to laissez-faire political economy in part inspired his campaign.[179] Finally, the doctrinal research of Napier into the transition from the pre-industrial law of master and servant to the evolution of contract of service in the nineteenth century provides an important springboard for further empirical research.[180]

Given a conceptual awareness of the distinctions between form, content, ideology and structure, there exists additionally, a need for the historical study of law and economy to give somewhat greater attention to the similarities and differences between the civil and criminal law at these levels. Especially fruitful will be those studies that examine the inter-face and inter-action between civil and criminal institutions, for example, in the context of indebtedness, bankruptcy, corporate liquidation and the regulation of trade unions. Similarly, the public law (administrative and constitutional law) interface with private law may prove especially insightful in a study of the formation of the modern State. Maitland has warned that,

> ". . . there is hardly any department of law which does not, at one time or another, become of constitutional importance . . . . If we are to learn anything about the constitution, it is necessary first and foremost that we should learn a good deal about the land law . . . . (Indeed) our whole constitutional law seems at times to be but an appendix to the law of real property . . . . (Do) not get into the way of thinking of law as consisting of a number of independent compartments . . . so that you can learn the contents of one compartment, and know nothing as to what is in the others. No, law is a body, a living body, every member of which is connected with and depends upon every other member."[181]

We would, however, stress that an historical understanding of the relations between law and economy can only be advanced where a pluralistic conception of legal phenomena is acknowledged and differentiated. Thus, one cannot conceive of law as exclusively pertaining to the decisions of Westminster Hall or to the enactments of Parliament. For if we are to secure an accurate account of the impact and usage of law in economic affairs during the later eighteenth and nineteenth centuries, the role of local courts, legal literature ("academic" and "practical"), the private law-making of lawyers, custom and practice among different and differing interest groups within the economy, the influence of or administration by quasi or non-legal personnel, the tensions between local and central regulation, indigenous versus state conceptions of legality, discretionary practices and enforcement, arbitration and other extra-legal mechanisms for dispute resolution, are just some of the other phenomena that must be considered. What links if any existed as between these different facets of ordering and organisation? Were they mutually dependent and functionally related or was their inter-action problematic?

To enrich our understanding of law, we similarly conceive of sanctions pluralistically. This includes not only the "legal", that is, those sanctions prescribed by the formal institutions of the legal system (imprisonment, damages), but also the "extra-legal", which embraces those social and customary sanctions imposed and supported by interest groups and communities. This might take the form of an informal ducking or ignominious depositing on the community's midden heap.[182] It may take the more structured form of financial penalties imposed by, for example, the "college" in King's Bench debtors' prison.[183] The impact and usage of extra-legal sanctions cannot, therefore, be divorced from a consideration of the interplay of law and economy.

VIII : EFFICIENCY, COSTS AND THE PROBLEM OF MEASUREMENT

A. Confronting The Problem From A Variety of Standpoints

Central to an examination of the historical relation between law and economy is the issue of the relative efficiency of the different legal institutions for the roles conferred upon them. Here we confront the question of the cost and measurement of the law in economy - questions which bristle with difficulty and controversy. Further, these are questions which doctrinal history cannot explicate. In tackling these questions, we can learn from the experience of a variety of realms which have attempted to confront the questions of efficiency, cost and measurement, albeit from differing perspectives. For instance, the historical debate concerning the standard of living during the Industrial Revolution exemplifies the difficulties of how one defines "efficiency" and measures "cost". As that debate testifies, social costs are notoriously more difficult to quantify than the narrowly "economic".[184]

Over the last decade Coase, Calabresi and Posner have stimulated the application of economic analysis and theory to every aspect of the legal process.[185] Landes, Posner and others have sought to demonstrate that judge-made law has evolved on the basis of an implicit economic rationale. In effect, it is argued that the common law mimics the competitive market thereby maximising efficiency and economic welfare. Posner has been attacked for a simplistic analysis of law in economy and the application of groundless normative and positive claims about "free market" economics. Clearly, it would be inappropriate to detail this controversy here.[186] Certainly, the work of writers such as Coase and Posner have undoubtedly influenced some "new" economic historians in their study of law and industrialisation.[187] However, whilst Posner's work has received most attention, a multitude of other more circumspect approaches to law and economics have been forged in recent years which might prove helpful exemplars in the development of a history of law and economy.[188]

Also pertinent is that work on the history of crime which discusses and evaluates the judicial statistics collected in the 19th century; and which has sought to incorporate quantitative evidence in order " . . . to establish how many people were prosecuted in which courts in which years with what results."[189] The use of judicial statistics and other quantitative data as indicators of past levels of crime has been the subject of a fruitful methodological debate which highlights the utility as well as the limits of such data.[190] Although much groundwork remains to be done, this debate offers valuable insights and experience of the possibilities and parameters of historical work involving the quantitative measurement of law and economy.

The questions of measurement, cost and efficiency may not, of themselves, recover the past for us, but they can usefully refine the assumptions we take for granted, make relations appear more complex and expose the problematic quality of our conceptual underpinnings. The development of techniques of demographic reconstitution are illustrative here. "Demographic reconstitution is, as both Laslett and Le Roy Ladurie have recognised from rather different points of view, largely a creature of computer technology. The sheer data-processing capacity of the computer permits historians and sociologists alike to mobilise the evidence lurking in vast accumulations of (legal) records (of births, marriages, deaths, wills, property transactions and so forth) always known to be interesting but hitherto judged unusable."[191] On the quantitative side, the new computer-based techniques have made vast masses of data accessible to interpretation. Questions of property, inheritance and kinship have undoubtedly been seen in a new light. But, as E.A. Wrigley has warned, these new data, "hold little meaning unless subject to a constant dialectical dialogue with a developing body of theory."[192] Philip Abrams, whose recent untimely death is a signal blow to the construction of a historical sociology, pointed out that even as distinguished a practitioner of the quantitative tools of demography as Peter Laslett, ". . . establishes how it was not, not how it was. Laslett's 'facts' are already categories of a certain theorisation of family history by the time they emerge from the machine room, indeed, long before the raw data are assembled for machine processing . . . . They do not, however, adequately or directly present the family to us as it 'really' was."[193] Bearing these caveats in mind, the new computer-based techniques may constitute a useful tool in the archaeology of the relation between law and economy.

The questions to be posed in an analysis of efficiency and cost are, for example, whether, in the case of those businessmen, such as traders, financiers or industrialists who were prepared to go to law, the courts satisfied their expectations as an efficient mode of recovering debts; did the existence of the facilities of the courts further encourage industrialists to expand their businesses and enter into more ambitious contracts; did it prompt financiers to broaden their horizons in lending to borrowers; did it enable traders to offer more goods on credit, in the expectation that default would quickly be remedied through the courts? Was it economically worthwhile for creditors to undertake litigation in the light of the potential returns which the courts might offer? Certainly, contemporary arguments concerning the maintenance or rejection of given sanctions and remedies offered by the legal system in general and by the courts in particular, frequently failed to rise above the level of popular belief.

Judicial attitudes in the mid and later 19th century seem to reflect a strong adherence to the principle of freedom of contract and to the desire to foster trade, industry and transportation.[194] What were the economic consequences of this judicial ideology? What was the economic impact of the rules constructed by the courts under the influence of this judicial ideology? Did their rules have the effect intended? Was a regime of fault liability really more economically efficient than one of, say, absolute liability?[195] If, in fact, one can characterise the development of 19th century law in terms of the subsidisation of trade, industry and transportation,[196] what were the economic costs and consequences of such subsidisation? What were the economic consequences of resort to one facility of the state law order, such as enforcement, relative to other facilities, such as appellate jurisdiction on points of law? And what were the relative costs of state law and extra-legal or quasi-legal facilities of enforcement and dispute settlement? Was the adversarial mode of dispute settlement - a cornerstone of the Anglo-American legal system - more or less costly and efficient than its rivals?

B. The Importance Of Civil Statistics

Rubin's paper in the present volume is suggestive of the opportunities of measuring quantitatively whether or not imprisonment for debt was a successful deterrent against default as its sponsors suggested.[197] The overall economic efficiency of the civil court system could probably also be tested by such criteria. However, in order to answer such questions, we require to know not just the practices of the different types of businessman-litigant, but also to have available meaningful civil judicial statistics which can, for example, compare the percentage of amounts sought in the courts with the amounts actually recovered and repatriated to the creditor. As yet, though many statistics are available in the Annual Returns, they have not been collected together in a convenient compendium; let alone has a thorough economic cost-benefit analysis of the civil courts in the nineteenth and early twentieth centuries been undertaken. It is symptomatic of the malaise in the historical study of law and material society that analysis of judicial statistics in this period has been virtually limited to the criminal court returns.[198] The recent publication of Professor O.R. McGregor's 1979 Hamlyn Law Lectures, entitled Social History and Law Reform has, however, drawn attention to the pioneering work of Sir John MacDonnell (1845-1921) who, from 1894 to 1919, was compiler for the Home Office of the Civil Judicial Statistics for England and Wales. MacDonnell accepted the challenge posed by the criticism of a departmental committee report on the statistics which had appeared annually since 1859. Those statistics had been prefaced by an "Introductory and Explanatory" note which, according to the Committee, was stereotyped, uninformative and unimaginative. As a consequence of this stinging rebuke, the Home Office immediately appointed MacDonnell as editor with a remit to revitalise the introductory note in order "to arrive at general conclusions". This task, MacDonnell performed with inventiveness and virtuosity. As McGregor has concluded,

> "The doing of justice requires knowledge of its own procedures. MacDonnell provided this in the tradition of the Victorian civil service which produced regularly, and commented critically, upon all the information necessary for the politically influential public to form a view about the choice of policies concerning matters within a Department's control."[199]

Modern compendia of social and economic statistics, such as that compiled by Mitchell and Deane, contain few, if any, civil judicial statistics. Perhaps figures on bankruptcies and on the proportion of gross national product devoted to legal administration have hitherto merited inclusion.[200] Why the civil historical statistics should have been so badly served while the criminal statistics have attracted considerable attention by historians must surely relate to the biases of both orthodox legal historians and of social and economic historians in choosing their research enterprises.

IX : IDEOLOGICAL DIMENSIONS OF LAW

A. Law's Legitimation Function

The ideological role of the law, especially its legitimation function, is of central importance in the historical study of law and economy. Thus, the law's role in justifying the world and existing power relations in civil society to both rulers and the ruled, thereby inducing willed obedience, cannot be neglected. Some of the major issues are the ideological role of commercial law in conceptualising business practices;[201] the relationship between legal and dominant ideology, or legal and indigenous ideologies; the diverse dimensions and functions of law as ideology; and the extent to which legal ideology is absorbed, modified or rejected by different classes or interest groups.[202] For example, what role did private law play in facilitating and legitimating absolute private conceptions of property and also the moral ethos associated with mid-Victorian, middle-class England, for instance, self-respectability, self-help, enlightened self-interest and the work-ethic? In the later nineteenth century, was imprisonment for debt a punishment visited upon those extravagant poor who supposedly failed to display the values of thrift, self-sufficiency and self-responsibility?[203]

While recognising that one function of ideology is to confer legitimacy on an institution, it nonetheless remains true that the empirical meaning of legitimacy in this context, that is, what individuals actually know or care about the legal system and how this influences, if at all, their conduct, has tended to be ignored or treated as self-evident both in the realm of history and in the sociology of law. If a gulf exists between the law in action and the (occasionally competing) values by which it claims legitimacy (for example, the values of equality, freedom of speech and expression, individuality and community), or if the law and an individual's economic self-interest are in conflict, to what extent is this perceived and if so, how?[204] Is the supposed legitimacy of the law eroded as a result? If so, with what consequences? What evidence is there to support Balbus' conclusion that what is construed as legitimacy is, in fact, mystification. Legitimacy, he argues, is unevenly trumpeted and fostered by those whose interests it avails.[205] A theoretically informed history of law and economy might be able to provide some much needed data in respect to questions of this kind. In any such work, monolithic and question-begging conceptions of "public opinion"[206] and "class interest" must give way to a recognition that individuals vary in their perceptions and experience of the legal system and of the gulf between, on the one hand, the ideals and rhetoric of the law, and, on the other hand, the reality of the law in practice. In part, this is to warn, as we shall remark later, against accepting at face-value, or generalising from, the legal profession's own pronouncements as to the centrality, purity and legitimacy of "the law"; declarations that often are little more than self-serving. On the other hand, one must avoid engaging in crude economic reductionism which views the legal professions as wholly reflective of the aims of capital or the state. Instead, there is a need to reconstruct an individual's perhaps complex and contradictory perception and experience of the legal system and of the values which that system supposedly imbibes. It would seem that there may be a tension between belief about the law and experience of the law. Law may be experienced as a coercive instrument held in terrorem or as a liberating "tool", or as something which confirms the individual's sense of helplessness and dependency. Is the law an arena wherein it was possible to advance certain political or social values?[207] For example, Brewer's account of the relationship between the Wilkites and the law is testimony to the complexity of motives and perceptions of the law revealed by the close scrutiny of actions and words.[208] The tactical use of the law as a tool in negotiation both by and with authority offers one specific perception which may not gel with more romanticised accounts of law as preserver of liberty on the one hand or as a tool of class repression on the other. Another, is the seemingly tenacious existence of behaviour inconsistent with the state law order.[209] To what extent are status, class, sex, age, family relations and geographic location important variables in mediating between perception and experience of law in history? Until we know more about the answers to the kind of questions as well as about the motives and mores grounding the use or non-use of the law in specific contexts by individuals (which may, in turn, be dictated by the nature of the wrong, and of the remedies available and the relation between the parties concerned), then the legitimacy or otherwise of the criminal and civil law will escape our understanding. Thus, at its best the history of law and economy will add to our knowledge of the lives of those touched by the law (directly or indirectly) in much the same way as the best work of historians, sociologists and anthropologists.

B. Law And Social Control

In the last decade, especially with the eruption of a sizeable body of social history, the regulation of social behaviour through the instrumentality of the law has been afforded special attention. Some of this work has been at pains to explore the law as a mode of organising beliefs and values (influenced, in part, by Gramsci's notion of "hegemony")[210] and as a means of "social control"[211] - in addition to law as a directly coercive weapon. This body of work has the virtue of transcending the tendency to treat law exclusively as a directly coercive behavioural injunction. It recognises that:

"Among other things it (the law) includes educational efforts, rewards and other incentives, symbolic deployment of legal forms, publicity (favourable or adverse), continuous supervision, public signs and signals, recognised statutes and entities, grants with strings attached, and on and on and on."[212]

Thus, in terms of its non-directly coercive facets, the law has been viewed as an instrument (together with the school system, religions, the work place, and other institutions and activities) by which certain attitudes tend to be eclipsed whilst others tend to be disseminated. It is the law's educational, disciplining, symbolic and related ideological facets which have in recent years been stressed in a number of historical and sociological studies touching on law and legal institutions. The strength and weakness of this approach are well illustrated in the recent development of a revisionist history of the prison and punishment. The history of policing and punishment has undergone a profound paradigm shift. Until recently the history of policing and punishment was written as the story of progressive reform: from physical cruelty to humanitarianism. Only rarely was the rise of the modern penitentiary, for instance, related to the political system and to economic and social changes, except loosely in terms of the evolution of the modern welfare state. A new revisionist historiography has challenged the implicit teleological bias of a history which portrayed the path of reform as simply paved with enlightenment, good intentions and uncontroverted notions of the public interest. Indeed, the revisionists have pointed to the complex nature of the motives of the reformers; and, in particular, the social control functions of the new disciplinary institutions. Changes in modes of punishment are used to illuminate the operation of power and ritual as well as the pliability of human conduct. In so doing, the very legitimacy of the reformers' reforms are questioned. The revisionists argue that the so-called progressive reforms spawned far more harmful modes of control than existed before.[213]

The new "revisionist" history of punishment, policing and crime has made a major contribution to our understanding of the relationship between law and society. It has highlighted the social control concerns of reformers, judges, jurists and administrators. It has also contributed to the recovery of popular conceptions of law and ordering. The social significance of the law, its role as a "breeder of values" and as an arena within which competing conceptions of ordering do battle has begun to be explored in ways which represent a significant advance in the field. It has also illuminated the operation of law in practice, that is, how ordinary people experienced the criminal law. By transcending the letter of the law and examining law in the context of social interaction and relations of unequal power the new history has drawn attention to the gulf that may exist between the letter and the rhetoric of the law.

Attention to the "social" as well as the "economic" aspects of history is undoubtedly long overdue. However, some work on the regulation of social behaviour through law has been inclined to treat the relation between law and social phenomena as wholly distinct from economic desiderata. While it is arguable that some social legislation or criminal law had little or no direct relation to economy (e.g. perjury, recusancy, incest), it nonetheless remains the case that economic objectives frequently underpinned such regulation explicitly or (more usually) implicitly. In view of the quantity and diversity of topics covered in this literature, one can do no more than cite examples illustrative of this point. Thus, control of the drink trade during the First World War was expressly directed to improving both workers' attendance at, and their manufacturing output of munitions from, the factories,[214] whilst the control of street gambling[215] and the prohibition on cock-fighting and bear-baiting, enacted in the mid-nineteenth century to reform manners,[216] were implicitly directed to removing workless and other individuals from the streets where they were perceived as threatening social order and into the factories and workshops where they would perform what was considered to be useful and economically beneficial toil. In this way, legislation designed ostensibly to regulate <u>social</u> behaviour might be said also to have been directed towards specific economic objectives, such as the lightening of the rates burden on the poor law unions in respect to the administration of the vagrancy and poor laws. That "social" legislation might have had an <u>indirect</u> impact on economic behaviour is not, of course, denied; and indeed it is arguable that legislation governing such diverse areas as housing, compulsory education, domestic violence, divorce and separation had more significance for their economic effects than for their "social" consequences. Thus, the alteration of the status of women in the eyes of the court, under the Married Women's Property Acts in the nineteenth century, was in respect to their economic powers as property owners or contractors and not merely a minor reflection of equalitarian philosophy.[217]

Some uses of "social control" and "hegemony" have been consciously and unconsciously premised upon an extremely functionalist model of society and a simplistic conception of ideology as "a trick" or "false consciousness". The nature and extent of ideological control has therefore been substantially overstated. Gareth Stedman Jones, in an early and important critique, pointed out that:

> It is not difficult to demonstrate that a casual usage of 'social control' metaphors leads to non-explanation and incoherence. There is no political or ideological institution which could not in some way be interpreted as an agency of social control . . . . It is as if . . . the . . . masses . . . were simply a blank page upon which each successive stage of capitalism has successfully imposed its imprint." [218]

It is also misconceived in so far as it assumes that the coercive and ideological weaponry of law and state are the cement of the social order; and that the state possesses a monopoly power to discipline and punish.[219] The potential for embourgeoisement by social control must be seen in the context of the co-existence of a plurality of orderings and organisations, state, non-state and anti-state, shaped from "below" as well as "above". This plurality of normative systems and the individuals and social groups that construct, apply and defend them, refract, mediate, obstruct or reinforce the state law order. In short, emphasis on the plurality of ordering and organisation constitutes a vital step towards breaking loose of all-embracing conceptions of social control which minimise human agency. Indeed, in the light of our earlier discussions,[220] the widespread existence and utilisation of alternative forms of normative ordering, the patchy application and enforcement of state law norms, the selective, pragmatic use of the state legal order by its clientele[221] and the significance of regional variations, the role of "ordering from above" as a fully-fledged agency of social control in 18th and 19th century England, increasingly looks double-edged and problematic.[222] Increasingly the notion of "social control" looks rather less like a solution than a short-cut both to some old intractable problems and to new modes of conceptualisation. This does not, by implication, invalidate the critique mounted of conventional histories of crime, punishment and popular recreations; nor the revisionists' quest for "connections" between social phenomena, law and the political, social and economic order.

C. The Historical Specificity Of Ideologies

Clearly, the way we conceptualise the historical specificity of ideologies is extremely important. A step towards a new way of theorising capitalist societies, and the role of law as ideology therein, has been taken in recent work on theories of ideology.[223] This work has shown the inadequacy of thinking of ideology as existing within a separate domain of ideas, or as an unreal or illusory reflection of social relations. As John Urry explains,

> ". . . there is nothing unified about 'ideology' and that much of what is located under that category is properly to be seen simply as differentiated, diverse and hetrogeneous social practices. Certain of these are linked fairly directly to capitalist social relations, others most definitely are not."[224]

In part, this work is but one instance of a wider movement: a movement which recognises the need to develop a new history and theory of capitalist society" . . . which does not presume that such societies are functionally ordered and cohesive with an effective incorporation of the subordinate social forces through a dominant ideology."[225] Real advances will require that the new theories of ideologies are tested and refined in conjunction with historical studies of real people and real communities. In particular, just as the state has no monopoly over the power of coercion, so the "ideological state apparatuses" or "economy" are not the sole institutions which produce ideological effects, though clearly they may be very important. This is merely to recognise the multiplicity and diversity of social groups and practices within capitalist societies and that some of these may exert significant ideological effects. This recognition serves as a useful counter to those concepts of ideology which lead either to an over-extension of the capital-relation or, an over-extension of the role of the state.

X : LAW, STATE AND ECONOMIC INTERESTS

A. Some Major Issues

Some of the pivotal questions in this area are: First, in respect to the state, which offered the political framework within which the legal system operated, did law possess an independent existence of its own, separate from the state or from economically dominant social groups? Was law wholly a dependent element, or was it, in a currently fashionable, though scarcely precise, phrase "relatively autonomous" of the state and economy?[226] Second, was the legal system monopolised by specific social groups in the sense both that its content was dictated by their objectives and in the sense that they alone mobilised the courts in pursuit of their aims? Third, were the courts, in moulding the shape of the law, merely functioning as the mirror-image of the economic philosophy prevailing at a particular stage of development of industrial society? Fourth, what was the relationship between law, legal change and the formation of the modern state? The political significance of the modern British state stems, in part, from the fact that the political "shell" it inhabits is that of a representative democracy. What was the relation between the law, legal thought and lawyers and the adoption and preservation of a democratic form of state?

B. Inter- And Intra-Class Conflict And The Law

The view that law, state and the "ruling class" are mutually reinforcing largely derives from much interesting work on the relation between "authority" and the operation of the criminal law and its institutions in the early modern and modern periods.[227] This research has tended, in its neglect of civil (private) law, to focus attention upon the manner in which the strongest economic and political interests and/or the state dominated weaker groups in society. In other words, it has concentrated upon inter-class "domination" and the consequences thereof for the interests of the "dominated". The study of intra-class conflicts within groups such as the working-classes, the City, the landed, mercantile and industrial interests - and the role of the law in their resolution - has correspondingly been ignored. Often there is a tendency to treat the ideology and interests of the respective groups as self-evident and homogeneous. By exploring both the criminal and the civil law and their respective institutions as fora for intra-, as well as inter-class conflict resolution, a more complete and accurate picture of the relationship between law and industrialisation, and its problematic qualities can be grasped. For example, in respect of intra-class disputes, how did Parliament and the courts balance the property rights of the landed to enjoy their land with the necessity of factory owners and railway contractors to develop their land in a manner likely to affect that enjoyment?[228] How was the issue of, for example, river pollution dealt with in the light of varying claims by private land-owners, local authorities, large factories, sewage works and river commissioners?[229] What role did the law play in mediating and legitimising disputes between, say, insurers and those requiring cover against risks; company directors and promoters as against shareholders and creditors; large firms at odds with small firms; or those Manchester industrialists who favoured free trade versus inventors who stressed that the monopoly conferred by patents was in the public interest? What were the outcomes of these conflicts: who won, how and why? What was the economic and social impact of legal dispute settlement of this kind within and as between classes?

C. The Popular Legitimacy Of The Law

The examples of intra-class disputes above could suggest that the primary fora for perhaps the bulk of intra-class dispute settlement at law lies within the province of the civil, rather than the criminal law; and that given the cost of going to law, and thus the relatively large sums involved, the main protagonists were likely to be middling to substantial property owners. However, it is too simplistic to treat the criminal law as merely that arena where, in the bulk of cases, the law was imposed upon the labouring class by an impersonal state or "the bourgeois class"; that, in short, it was simply a locus of class conflict. Peter King has argued that access to the 18th century criminal courts was not confined to the middling or upper classes, since artisans and those of similar rank were to be found among the litigants.[230] The work of David Philips suggests[231] that by the mid-nineteenth century a significant percentage of prosecutions (20% in the Black Country) were brought by unskilled workers against other members of their class. Use of the law, however, does not of itself denote a general belief in the legitimacy of the law or even of a particular law or institution. For instance, at the very same time as workers were bringing a significant proportion of prosecutions for theft, the new model police were encountering bitter (and sometimes violent) popular resistance;[232] and poaching and other new "crimes" continued to enjoy popular legitimacy.[233] This suggests a variegated, selective, pragmatic approach to the use and popular legitimacy of the criminal law by the working-classes[234] not unlike that which we seem to have found in the context of the civil law and its use by the "bourgeoisie". Thus, it is too simplistic to characterise the criminal and civil law wholly in terms of a locus of class conflict or consensus. As was indicated above, the sheer complexity of the questions surrounding the popular legitimacy of the law and attitudes thereto - as well as our lack of sufficient knowledge - is likely to make such generalisation extremely misleading.

D. The Heterogeneity Of Civil Society

In this essay, we have emphasised that law cannot be viewed as an undifferentiated unity. The different parts of the law, legal institutions and the legal professions and the manifold facilities they offer are ". . . differently integrated . . ." into the state and civil society.[235] This, amongst other things, makes it very difficult to conceive of the law as simply part of the capitalistic base or of the superstructure. Equally, the objections to the view that law is coterminous with the state or directly derived from capital seem fundamental.[236] Indeed, once the problems of ordering and organisation become viewed pluralistically - that is, once it is recognised that certain aspects of ordering and organisation are either outside the state proper, such as indigenous, customary or informal rights and practices, or connected to the state's coercive powers in complex and indirect ways, as with facilitative laws - these reductionist characterisations become untenable. The best of the recent histories of crime, for example, have revealed ". . . the tentativeness, variability and complexity of developments in the procedures and institutions . . ."[237] of 18th and 19th century justice. Changes in legal controls are seen as unplanned and highly contingent stop-gaps as much as systematic and calculated efforts to contain the conflicts of the emerging market economy. Different social groups might vary in their responses to changes in policing. Further, the alignments were rarely clear-cut and predictable. For instance, Victor Bailey's study of the policing of "outcast London" in the 1880s, especially the Trafalgar Square riots of 1886-87, brings to light the disagreements over the proper methods of control between the Chief Commissioner, the judiciary and the Home Secretary. The gradual spread of national uniformity in policing co-existed alongside differing tempos and configurations of development in specific localities.[238] This kind of work constitutes a powerful counter to those who see the whole story in terms of escalating social control.

E. The Symbolic Dimensions Of The Law

The problematic role of the state in relation to the law, especially during the period described as laissez-faire, is amply exposed when we consider the apparent contradiction of a "legal abstentionist" state authorising the enactment of such measures as the Factories Acts and the Combination Act Repeal Acts 1824-5, or, indeed, the other vast array of regulatory legislation.[239] Whence did these statutes spring? Which interests were advanced by their passing or was there simply one undifferentiated interest - the "ruling class" - which stood to gain from their enactment? While historians have agonised over whether such measures are individualist, Benthamite, collectivist or inspired by Whig or Tory sentiment and while Marxist and radical historians have sought to identify capitalist or social control, motives,[240] there remains the further critical question whether such measures had any significant impact on the economy. However, even this perspective may be too limited. Perhaps the significance of much of the legislation of that era is to be found more in their symbolic appeal, or in satisfying the political or status demands of their sponsors or supporters.[241] Thus, in the twentieth century, the Trade Disputes and Trade Union Act 1927, passed in the wake of the General Strike, can scarcely be said to have had more than a marginal influence on industrial relations following its enactment. Indeed, it is arguable that its sponsors harboured no purposive intention. Rather, the legislation might be explicable in terms of the demands made by Conservative members of Parliament, supported by a number of Cabinet ministers, for some symbol of victory over the unions in the General Strike.[242] More than that cannot be claimed for this otherwise ineffective measure of the Depression years. As The Economist remarked at the time, the introduction of the Trade Dispute Bill 1927, represented "a show of bad temper on the part of the Conservatives" that is, a symbol of victory.[243] Moreover, such an analysis is not limited to explaining how legislation comes about, but also seeks to explain why laws might remain unrepealed, despite their apparent ineffectiveness and the power of legal ritual.[244] The complex and dynamic interaction between symbolic and instrumental concerns has been described in several valuable "emergence studies" in which attention is focused upon the origins and generation of specific legislative enactments and (though less frequently) the impact of the legislation in question.[245]

F. Law, State And The Rise Of Capitalism

A leading business historian has argued that, "Historically, the most important way in which the state stimulated industrial growth in a capitalist setting was through its ability to restructure the institutions of society - i.e. through its ability to create a capitalist setting in the first instance."[246] What role did the law (including legal institutions and the legal professions) play in sustaining, constituting, legitimating, or restraining the creation of this "capitalist setting" by the state? We cannot hope to offer more than the briefest incursion into what is a vast and highly controversial area.

For Marx, "the expropriation of the agricultural producer, of the free peasant, from the soil"[247] and, thus, the rise of an absolute and exclusive private property were the basis for the emergence of capitalism. "The conditions in which the 'natural laws' of political economy could operate had to be forcibly constructed."[248] The role of the law in this process was undoubtedly multifaceted. It both confined and orchestrated the "expropriation" of free peasant and common land. The Enclosure Acts, for instance, helped to destroy independent small-holdings and created a class of landless labourers whose livelihood depended entirely on employment by landowning farmers or (later) factory owners. "Enclosure Acts are part of a wider, and centuries-long, transformation of communal and feudal into private property, within which not only who owned what but what it meant to be an owner were turned upside down. It is a far cry from feudal tenure to the *jus utendi et abutendi*, from the complicated network of personal lordship and servitude, substantial right and obligation, which enmeshed lord and serf, to the substantially rightless but formally free wage labourer voluntarily contracting with his or her chosen employer. Property did not have just to be seized, it had to be constituted."[249] The wider transformation operated at a number of levels. Socially, it encouraged ". . . the kind of progress that meant the factory bell, the workhouse, and a loss of liberty however limited"[250] a kind of progress which some social groups rejected and tried to resist.[251] Over the centuries, previously non-criminal activity became criminalised.[252] They were, variously, civil offences that became criminalised; traditional perquisites of employment (such as the coal hewer's allowance of fuel, the shipwright's right to take for firewood the chips that fell from the axe and the cooper's established claim to the draining of molasses and spilt sugar on the floor of the warehouse); and legal rights associated with common land and common rights (such as the small animals and fish found on common land), were a valuable source of food for people as well as animals; other widespread rights on the commons included pasturage for cattle and fowl, turfing and wood gathering. Legislation outlawed workers' combinations, enlarged the working day and fixed wages. The doctrine of freedom of contract was perhaps in part a response to the intrusiveness of the mercantilist state; that is, part of an attempt to bring the capricious, privileged and corrupt power of the 18th century state within greater control than previously. For some people it may have encouraged self-responsibility and a degree of individual self-determination. But alongside these desirable features, however, it underpinned a new conception of labour as a "marketable commodity". The freedom of contract doctrine also constituted a powerful intellectual and practical obstacle foreclosing state intervention on behalf of the casualties of the newly ascendent market economy. On the other hand, beginning in the 1840s, the British state also intervened to provide tighter and wider protection for workers. Does the latter indicate a shift in the character of the 19th century state, into a more neutral stance as between capital and labour; or, is it simply an instance of where sufficient political power forced major law reforms?[253]

The mid-19th century state was not simply the pliant instrument of capital nor, indeed, any other influential group. An increasing band of state administrators, officers and experts were interposed between and influenced 19th century policy-making. True, the elitist structure of the civil service and the old patronage persisted long after the Northcote-Trevelyan Report and the advent of open competition in 1870.[254] Sometimes this state expertise was undoubtedly used

". . . as an ideological weapon against working-class interests."[255] On other occasions, however, it conflicted with the interests of employers who sought to evade or neutralise the newly-emerging protections for the health and safety of labour.[256] State servants and others may act as if the state has interests of its own. In addition, although the influence of religious and humanitarian opinion has probably been exaggerated by some historians, and although their motivation was undoubtedly problematic, neither can their sway and prevalence be ignored. Residual paternalism, the need to prevent revolution and the influence of Benthamism (both its "individualistic" and "collectivistic" strands) have also been shown to have exercised influence upon and within the 19th century state. If, therefore, we cannot simply reduce the 19th century state to the needs of capital, it should not be concluded that the state was unimportant to the requirements of capitalism. As our discussion above testifies, Supple is undoubtedly correct when he warns that: ". . . before we conclude that the first Industrial Revolution owed everything to the market and nothing to government, it is worth remembering that the very characteristics of the market environment which distinguished Britain's position from that of other European countries were in large part a function of _state_ action."[257]

In fact, the evidence is clear that _laissez-faire_ and state interventionism were not polar opposites but rather, different sides of the same coin: both co-existed in 19th century England. State action and, therefore, the law were essential to the creation of _laissez-faire_ - a paradox which few historians of 19th century government have recognised.[258] Unfortunately, the historical debate as to whether there ever was an age of _laissez-faire_ has unwittingly served to narrow or exclude the kind of questions, issues and concerns that require investigation if we are to decipher the formation and changing nature of the modern state. As R.A. Lewis observed, "Historians of 19th century government growth are still in the position of the three blind men handling various parts of the elephant, and speculating from limited data and much conjecture as to the exact nature of the beast."[259] This is part of a more general process which has confined understanding of the 19th century state and society. There are several important post-war historical debates relevant to the investigation of the 19th century state and society: for instance, the debates ". . . about the 'Standard of Living'; about the nature of Class(es); about Systems and Originators of Ideas; about Voting, whether Franchise before or within Parliament; and, finally, about the 'Revolution in Government' . . . ."[260] Unfortunately, these debates ". . . have been kept almost totally separate from another."[261] One might add that the role of the law, both civil and criminal, has also been separated from these debates. Indeed, until recently there has been a tendency either to treat the role of the law as unproblematic or to ignore it completely. Corrigan's important work rightly argues that a richer understanding of state and society in 19th century England requires" . . . us to comprehend as facets of one totality"[262] the bodies of material and arguments pertaining to these debates which historians have tended to keep apart. The development of a truly inter-disciplinary history of law and economy would aid this desirable goal.

G. Central Versus Local State Law

The state in 18th and 19th century Britain was not a centralised, rational monolith. The law (civil and criminal), ". . . along with many other political and economic functions, continued in large part to be located at a local level . . . . This dichotomy (local/centre) within the state structure provides . . . (a) principal axis along which"[263] conflicts over law, state, society and economy are to be understood. "Pivotal in the local/central struggle were the local justices of the peace who were (in the 18th and 19th centuries at least) in most cases, tied very strongly to the landed gentry and the traditional pattern of social relations, and who fulfilled crucial administrative, as well as judicial, functions; in the transitional period they became the effective focus of local power and government. Justices . . . found themselves with responsibility for the bulk of the civil administration of the country - bridges, gaols, houses of correction, wages, prices, markets, enclosures, licensing, turnpikes, administration of poor relief, etc. All key functions in a developing country."[264] In the 19th century, the imperatives of local political and financial administration hindered, for instance, the creation of a national police force and prison system.[265] The political struggles around this dichotomous state structure constitute an important, though oft overlooked, factor delimiting and mediating between law, state and material society, in the modern period.

One aspect of this struggle was the tension between, on the one hand, the tradition of local and special courts and, on the other hand, a formal state system of courts. By the mid-19th century, the latter had eclipsed the former.[266] To some extent, the economic self-interest of the legal profession and its ". . . ideological opposition to the underlying values and public policies served by . . ." local and special courts account for their suppression.[267] However, in his pioneering work on the evolution of English administrative law, Harry Arthurs suggests that ". . . at the very moment when the common law courts seemed to be achieving an adjudicative monopoly, they were challenged by new manifestations of pluralism, principally commercial arbitration (which, in fact, was not new at all) and the administrative regimes which were established with increasing frequency from the 1830s onwards . . . . Whether . . . (the task) involved the resolution of commercial disputes, or the implementation of new, interventionist public policies, 'law' - in the formal sense -could not do what needed to be done."[268] In public law, as in private law, the state legal order was a last resort rather than imbricated in the day-to-day activities of public administration. "In the area of administrative law, inspectorates and government departments and commissions charged with ensuring public health, pure food, proper standards of construction and operation for railways, or safety in factories and mines and aboard emigrant ships, managed to secure increasing levels of compliance with regulatory requirements. However, although they did so within the framework of legislation and against the background of formal legal institutions, neither law nor courts contributed much to their successes: if anything the law and the courts inhibited their efforts."[269]

H. The Modern State, Public Law and Regulatory Agencies

But what of Dicey's famous remark that, "There exists in England no true droit administratif"?[270] It is now generally recognised that Dicey wholly misled lawyers and others to believe that England possessed no administrative law at all.[271] Dicey's biographer has opined that, "The most remarkable aspect of Dicey's concern with administrative law was the almost invincible ignorance he displayed about the evolution of domestic administrative jurisdiction during his own lifetime."[272] As Harry Arthurs had shown, administrative law (as opposed to judicial review) grew rapidly in the 19th century; and that it was quite well developed by 1870.[273]

Alongside the growth of public law, at both a local and central level, we find the central courts generally averse to involvement in the day-to-day administration of the 19th century state. The English judges of the latter half of the 19th century seem more afraid of intervention in the economy by the state or the overt politicisation of their position in the public's eye than of the abuse of private power.[274] Their antagonism towards administrative law, fuelled by Dicey's edict that administrative law was both un-British and inconsistent with the Rule of Law,[275] caused Parliament, from the turn of this century, deliberately to by-pass the courts so that, for example, under the new social security legislation of 1908-11, appeals to the courts were strenuously avoided. "By 1920, therefore, the judges had been removed, had removed themselves or been restrained from entering large areas of competence in the modern state."[276]

If the courts were unenthusastic about controlling the abuse of public power, how successful were the new regulators and regulatory agencies in the imposition, policing and enforcement of a plethora of minimum standards, in a variety of contexts? Indeed, there are a host of questions relating to the nature, scope and effectiveness of the new regulatory public law and its agencies (local and central) to which too little attention has been afforded. Yet clearly the historical development of modern public law may have much to tell us about business-state relations, as well as about the changing nature and scope of the modern state.

For example, to what extent did the growth of regulatory agencies preserve the "public interest" (an elastic mandate, to which all interests seek to identify themselves) as against the particular interests of those directly involved in and effected by regulation? Did a conception of the "public interest" emerge from within the process of regulation; or, was it submerged by vying interests seeking to benefit from state regulation? To what extent did regulatory functions conflict within and as between different regulatory agencies? What did business want to obtain from regulation and what did they receive in practice? How did regulatory agencies and regulators choose between and balance up the competing interests of industrial and business competitors within a particular industry or sector?; or, the interests of labour and consumers as against those of the regulated? What was the impact of industrial pressure on the shape of regulatory legislation and the policies adopted by regulatory agencies? What have been the economic effects of regulation? In the United States, during the last decade, an enormous amount of work bridging law, economics and government has largely concluded that regulation was an expensive failure.[277] In particular, economists have sought to quantify regulatory efficiency and inefficiency.[278] To date, however, much of this work has failed to combine the benefits of a micro-economic analysis with an analysis that takes on the social, political and historical dimensions of state regulation.

How did regulation and the attitudes of both regulators and those regulated change over time?: was regulation and the attitudes it engendered different as between different industries and sectors? Did regulators conceive of their roles as that of a watch-dog or as a neutral umpire, holding the balance between business and employees or consumers? In so far as administrative regulations departed from the procedural norms of the judicial process, have those regulated been treated more unfairly and prejudicially as a result? Has the machinery for making administrative regulatory decisions tended towards more political decision-making than that of the judicial process?

In answering some of these questions, we can draw, in part, on some of the excellent studies of 19th century state servants and more directly still, their reports and papers as well as several of the most famous Blue Books of the 19th century.[279] In addition, some of the areas regulated, notably, the area of safety at work, has been the subject of illuminating historical studies. It was Althorp's Act of 1833 which sought to tackle the problem of enforcement in a novel way: rather than impose higher penalties, an external inspectorate, supposedly free from local bias, was given the responsibility for law enforcement. We have here one of the first instances of a special department of the central government being created for the purpose of administering a particular Act.[280] "Of all the 19th century inventions in social organisations," wrote Sidney Webb, "Factory Legislation is the most widely diffused. The opening of the 20th century finds it . . . perhaps, more far-reaching, if not more ubiquitous, than even the public elementary school or the policeman."[281]

Yet the efficacy of the Factory Inspectorate, despite its influence as a model, in a variety of areas is questionable. Inadequate manpower and resources reduced the possible prosecutions, even assuming a willing and activist inclined inspectorate. Moreover, the magistracy were notoriously reluctant to convict. They tended to characterise regulatory offences as merely "technical" and would mitigate the statutory penalties where possible. All this is highly relevant to our understanding of the failure of the inspectorate in contemporary society. In his study of the early factory inspectorate, Carson has perceptively pin-pointed a tension which goes some way to explain the creation of an inspectorate and its relatively poor record then and now.[282] Carson argues that the emerging industrial society of the 19th century contained within itself a logic which induced regulation. For example, such regulation, ". . . was seen as having important and beneficial implications for the competitive structure of . . . industry, for the creation of a disciplined workforce, and . . . for the ideological representation of the social relations of the workplace. On the other hand, this impetus towards regulation was undercut by certain basic structural and ideological features which emerged in Victorian Britain."[283] Through an explication of this conflict Carson is able to describe the process whereby breaches of the Factory Acts began to move ". . . towards the position where, today, they are accepted as customary, are only rarely subjected to criminal prosecution and, indeed, are often not regarded as really constituting crimes at all."[284] A similar analysis might be applicable to analogous regulatory practices in the areas of consumer, creditor and shareholder protection.

XI : TOWARDS AN INTELLECTUAL HISTORY OF LAW AND ECONOMY

Here we return to the debate over the alleged autonomy or relative autonomy of law from economic determinism. What were the major intellectual currents which helped to shape modern law and which law assisted in shaping? To what extent did the intellectual structure of the law ("legal consciousness") mediate, impede or facilitate the influence of economic interests and other desiderata on lawyers and law-making?

Recently important advances have been made in attempting to relate the development of modern legal doctrine in England to economic, social and political ideas. Atiyah's important work on the relation between contract law and the rise of classical political economy is probably the most important intellectual history of English law published this century.[285] Similar, though more modest, work in related areas, much of it conducted, it must be said, by American scholars, include: Brenner's examination of nuisance law during the Industrial Revolution.[286] Danzig's examination of the leading damages case in contract, Hadley v Baxendale; [287] and the relationship between industrialisation and compensation for industrial injury (a topic on which scattered work is proceeding).[288]

Moreover, research has highlighted the rich variety of intellectual and political stimuli on 19th century legal science. For example, the influence of German legal and historical writings on legal jurists and historians - in particular Savigny, Ihering and Gierke;[289] the influence of social evolutionism and the comparativist method of Victorian anthropology and philology;[290] the appropriation and incorporation of civil law ideas by judges and jurists;[291] the influence of Roman Law on "legal science";[292] the reciprocal influence of legal scholars associated with the Law Schools of Harvard, Oxford (and to a lesser extent) Cambridge;[293] and the general and long-standing influence of the natural sciences methodology on the rhetoric and aspirations of legal scholarship, intensified by ". . . the cult of scientific knowledge so prevalent in the mid-Victorian period . . . ."[294] The links between the aspirations of university liberal law scholars such as Austin, Maine, Dicey and Bryce (who formed part of a new "intellectual aristocracy"),[295] national politics, and the fears aroused by the extension of the franchise and democracy has also begun to be explored.[296] Additionally, the political nuances of the historical debate surrounding the basis of early village communities - were they individualist or collectivist societies? - has been explicated.[297] From a very different perspective, Michel Foucault has uncovered the rise of similar social institutions designed for social control in law, medicine, education and the workplace.[298]

The period circa 1860 to 1900 is of special interest. It is in this period that the assumption of a moral basis to the legal system is challenged by Austin in England and Holmes in America.[299] Indeed, in a whole series of ways the relationship between the individual and the state was being re-examined. "The change from social contractarianism to legal positivism may not, at first, have carried much political significance. But these changing ways of thinking about the relation between the individual and the state were ultimately to be of profound importance . . . . Inevitably, the command theory (of legal positivism) carried with it implications about majority rule. If the sovereign could command, he could coerce; indeed, the whole essence of a law was that it was a command backed by a sanction. There was no longer any question about assuming that the fundamental principles of the state could not be altered without the broad consent of the landowning, or any class. Every class was now at the mercy of a Parliamentary majority."[300] This, in turn, provoked a significant debate concerning the separation (or otherwise) of law and morality. The inability to confront the consequences of this "legitimation crisis" encouraged the adoption of a new concept of social contract, that is, a new mode of reconciling law, state and the consent of the people: namely, "public opinion". "Public opinion" was the conduit pipe through which the law, state and economy achieved a degree of moral and democratic legitimacy.[301] In a period when the legitimacy of law and legal obedience was being questioned both externally, in terms of the legitimacy of Britain's imperial hegemony, especially in India and Ireland, and internally, in respect of the growing economic and political power of the working classes, this debate carried with it not inconsiderable political overtones too.[302]

The growing power and autonomy of large companies, trades unions, and an increasingly "interventionist" state helped generate an important intellectual debate concerning the nature, scope and legitimacy of this legal, political and economic "pluralism".[303] Did not the growth of corporations or quasi-corporations (i.e. of bodies autonomous or semi-autonomous of the state legal order) fundamentally challenge the traditional notion of society as composed of individuals whose collective embodiment is the state with whom (metaphorically speaking) they have individual contracts? Did it not require a new way of conceiving of the relation between individuals and state; and a new way, both sociologically and legally, of conceiving of corporate associations? For Maitland, this meant the acceptance of "the realities" of a plurality of overlapping social groups and ". . . the reversal of Maine's laissez-faire individualist version of progress from status to contracts . . . ":[304]

> "Nowadays it is difficult to get the corporation out of our heads. If we look at the doings of our law courts, we may feel inclined to revise a famous judgment and to say that while the individual is the unit of ancient, the corporation is the unit of modern law."[305]

In respect to the role of ideas in legal history, orthodox "black-letter" historians, in particular, have been prone to insist on the autonomy of the law.[306] They tend to regard the ideas and doctrines formulated by judges and legal scholars as the exclusive determinant of legal development. Is the choice simply between those accounts which are reductionist, generally assuming law, state and ideology are decisively shaped, albeit sometimes in a complex and mediated fashion, by the nature of economy; and, those accounts which are autonomist? In the United States, several recent legal histories argue for versions of the "relative autonomy" thesis in new and challenging ways.[307]

G. Edward White's history of American tort law,[308] for instance, regards ideas as a principal, but not complete, explanation of legal causation. He is critical of those who have ascribed the emergence of an independent identity for torts, and, in particular, the tort of negligence in the late nineteenth century, to industrialisation and to an accident problem of hitherto unprecedented dimensions. "The emergence of Torts as a distinct branch of law", claims White, "owed as much to changes in jurisprudential thought as to the spread of industrialisation."[309] The fact that industrialisation transformed the typical forms of tortious injury from that between individuals in a close relation to one another, to one between strangers, was undoubtedly important. But a new law of torts, characterised by broad principles, did not simply arise in response thereto. White stresses that the death of the writ system required both changes of a procedural kind and a profound restructuring of the intellectual foundations of law. Negligence provided a new conceptual basis with which to underpin the law of private wrongs. Further, this shift to broad principles was also stimulated by the intellectual preoccupations of the age. In an effort to construct order out of the increasingly fragmented world of nineteenth century society, systematisation and the articulation of broad general principles became a major object of Victorian intellectuals. Legal scholars reflected this concern also. Two of America's leading legal conceptualisers, St. John Green and Holmes, played a central role in the reconstruction of the intellectual foundations of tort law in a new, broad and unified scheme. Unlike his earlier work, the causal connections posited by White are much more complex; legal thought is no longer simply the reflection of a particular social and political milieu. Instead, the history of the intellectual form and structure of the law is treated as a discrete realm capable of analysis in its own terms, alongside more overtly "economic" interpretations of legal evolution. In part, White conceives of this approach as a counter to excessively economistic histories of law.

Other American legal historians have also been concerned with the history of legal thought, specifically with the historical specificity of legal categorising and reasoning (legal consciousness). Modern Anglo-American legal historiography has been largely devoted to explaining ". . . which, among various historical forces 'caused' a particular judicial decision."[310] Duncan Kennedy and others, however, adopt a focus wholly outside this approach to legal history. "Rather than attempting to explain the cause of particular decisions, it attempts to describe the structure of legal thought. The difference lies both in using a purely descriptive rather than explanatory approach, and in examining the structure of an entire conceptual scheme rather than the outcomes of particular decisions. The effort is not to explain why a particular side won on a given day, but to describe the conceptual apparatus by which the court justified its decisions."[311] This approach stems from the belief that a description of the nature of legal thought over time is crucial in the study of legal history, regardless of whether one sees legal thought as a dependent or independent variable. By concentrating on the legal conceptual structure it is hoped to overcome a major drawback of that approach which focuses on the forces which caused particular decisions or doctrine, especially instrumentalist approaches: namely, ". . . that of attributing so much importance to particular outcomes within the (legal) framework that the framework itself becomes invisible."[312] But what exactly is meant by a focus upon legal thought or structure? In essence, it means ". . . the activity of categorising, analysing, and explaining legal rules."[313] As Vandevelde puts is, "Legal thought is, in essence, the process of categorisation. The lawyer is taught to place phenomena into categories such as fact or law, substance or process, public or private, contract or tort, and foreseeable and unforeseeable, to name but a few. Categorising phenomena determines how they will be treated by the legal system . . . . The task of the legal historian who examines . . . legal thought is to explore the origins and structures of the categories."[314]

This approach has premised historical investigations of the concepts of form and substance in private law adjudication,[315] the conceptual structure of Blackstone's Commentaries and their influence on and relation to liberal legalism,[316] the City as a legal concept,[317] the transformation of the concepts of property, contract and tort,[318] and the structure of classical legal thought in America, 1850-1940.[319] It has the additional virtue of illuminating the ways conceptions of justice, legality, social needs and rights do not exist in a separate realm apart from law, but are constructed, in part, by the legal system itself. Moreover, it has pointed to the way the ostensible values underpinning legal concepts and structures are often contradictory. The tensions this generates may partly or wholly explain certain changes in the form and content of law over time.

Another approach utilised in some intellectual histories of modern Anglo-American law and scholarship is more directly concerned to relate law to the material world. Rather than relate legal change directly to, say, the distribution of property or the power of dominant economic interests, this work explores the striking intellectual parallels between law and other spheres such as history, politics and economics in terms of their common tasks, concerns and methods at a specific historic conjuncture.[320] J.W. Burrow, for instance, has brilliantly illuminated the common ideas and problems which help to explain why so many leading Victorian social scientists sought general laws and stages of progress; and why they tended to do so in an evolutionist and positivistic manner.[321] P.S. Atiyah has also insightfully identified parallels between legal, social and economic thought in England.[322] Two American studies further demonstrate the value of this approach to intellectual history. Thus, the revolt against legal formalism has been linked to a wider movement that embraced history, economics, philosophy and political science.[323] In an excellent study, Edward Purcell has examined the ways in which the spread of pragmatism and scientific naturalism affected developments in philosophy, the social sciences and law in the years after 1910, and traces the effect of these developments on traditional assumptions of democratic theory.[324]

These three, albeit very different, analytic frameworks have the virtue of seeking to give due weight to both the power of economic interests in influencing the content of the law and the power of legal thought and consciousness as a distinct but important influence in the evolution of the law and legal institutions, thereby transcending the either/orism implied by the reductionism versus autonomism debate. They also serve to illuminate and provide a degree of specificity to our understanding of the relative autonomy of the law. Of course, it is essential to relate legal development to its economic, social and political context. But that context also includes language systems, patriarchy, ideas and beliefs as well as (say) the economic structure of society. These are often difficult to disentangle and insofar as they can be differentiated, relate to one another in highly complex ways. This is merely to warn against a reductionist interpretation that defines "context" in such a way that an artificial confinement to purely economic desiderata thereby excludes a variety of other important social phenomena.

XII : THE LEGAL PROFESSIONS AND COURTS

It will be clear from our discussion so far that to comprehend the role of law in the growth of the economy since 1750, it will be necessary to understand the role of the legal profession in that development.[325]

Unfortunately, our knowledge of the social and economic origins and affiliations of the legal professions and the judges is still relatively slender.[326] Historians and sociologists have tended to give the legal professions and the courts less attention than other social groups or professions. As Atiyah has observed, "A great deal of biographical research is still needed . . . ; we do not know nearly enough about the judges, (the legal professions), their training, their beliefs and attitudes, in order to give a proper assessment of the influence on the detailed rules of law in any particular areas of, (say), the ideas of political economists. The tradition of the neutral, value-free judgment, based on legal doctrine rather than on any sense of justice or any particular policy, often makes it hard to detect the underlying, and perhaps unconscious influences at work."[327]

The work that does exist concerning the period since 1800, understandably perhaps, concentrates upon the relatively common elite background of bench and bar (public school, upper class etc.) and the very strong connections between Parliament and government, on the one hand, and members of the legal professions, on the other. In particular, it has been asserted that on occasions, the causal connections between the material or class self-interest of the courts and their actual decisions are extremely intense. For example, Philips has shown that from the 1830s onwards, as the social composition of the Black Country magistracy changed from predominantly landed to predominantly industrialist, so the number of prosecutions for industrial theft increased markedly. Prosecutions were commonly brought by iron and coal masters - and it was they who were now dominating the Black Country bench.[328] Bramwell's vigorous and unequivocal commitment to laissez-faire is notorious[329] (but how typical was Bramwell?). And

Halsbury's court-packing tactics so as to ensure that decisions were strongly adverse to the position of trade unions has been uncovered in the wake of Heuston's important study of the modern Lord Chancellors.[330]

Important though this data is, we would suggest that it does not, of itself, establish an invariable and direct relationship between, on the one hand, the class background of judges, legislators or winning litigants and, on the other hand, the outcome of particular cases or the enactment of specific legislation. The sometimes complex and contradictory nature of the relevant causal relations becomes apparent in the light of the historical specificity of the so-called relative autonomy of the law and legal professionalism. The characteristics usually associated with modern legal professionalism include: the supposed separation of the law from "natural" reason (and, thus, the cognisance of lay persons) - as well as its separation from "politics", "economics", and "morality"; its corresponding treatment as a neutral "science"; its "logical formal rational" form; and the asserted subjugation of society to the Rule of Law. Historically speaking, to what extent did these facets and other shared values of professionalism, mediate between and delimit, on the one hand, the economic and political needs of, say, economic dominant groups or the state - rather than simply mirror them, - and, on the other hand, the social and material self-interest of the legal professions and the judges?[331] In fact, the historical specificity of the relative autonomy of the law is only beginning to be explored by historians and sociologists.[332] Bouwsma has argued that lawyers were at the forefront of secularism throughout post-Reformation Europe in the sense of treating the claims of their craft as autonomous of and distinct from the edicts of politics, religious belief and the personal values of individual lawyers.[333] Wilfred Prest's recent study of the spiritual and material worlds of Sir Henry Finch illustrates the "segregation . . . of 'public' calling from 'private' belief", albeit a segregation which he recognises was never absolute.[334] Prest contends that this separation ". . . helps to clarify the readiness of many lawyers to accept Crown office during the 1630s, despite the distaste they must have felt for the government's ecclesiastical policies."[335] More striking still, Richard Cover has detailed the way some leading American judges felt constrained by the demands of professionalism, such as consistency, to uphold slavery despite their own personal abhorrence of black slavery.[336]

The relative workload of the courts and its impact on judicial law-making, the form and structure of legal reasoning and the presentation of judgments has only begun to be systematically explored. Friedman and Atiyah have both pointed to ". . . the growing pressure on the courts arising from the vast increases in population and commercial activity" as a possible factor in the rise of extreme legalism ("legal formalism") in the latter half of the 19th century.[337] As Friedman puts it, "Judges were rushed, and dockets were crowded; there was less time to polish and re-word opinions."[338] Further, recent histories of crime have stressed that the law may simultaneously serve as a tool of dominant economic interest groups and actually check the power of dominant groups in society vis à vis less powerful ones. A commitment to the Rule of Law limits rulers as well as the ruled.[339] Other factors seemingly reinforce the autonomy of the legal professions. For example, the fact that cases come before the courts in a relatively random fashion - the so-called "accident of litigation" - and the relatively unsystematic manner in which a minority of these are reported highlights the importance of chance and the unplanned in determining the actual content of the law.

These then are just some of the factors that appear to reinforce the autonomy of legal professionalism. Tested alongside these must be those factors which posit a strong and direct link between economic interest and power, on the one hand, and legal activity on the other. For instance, how far can lawyers not react to economic stimuli? Broadly speaking, lawyers are paid because economic agents find it profitable or necessary to do so. Did the general run of legal thinking not eventually conform to the economic forces of the age that were both shaping society and paying their fees? The fact this was or was not appreciated is not to the point. Nor would this be surprising. From their genesis as officers of the law courts at the beginning of the thirteenth century, attorneys have always been the agents of other men. The private practice of the lawyer adopts a form substantially akin to that of an ordinary commercial undertaking. A host of other factors further emphasise the closeness of the connections between economic power and wealth in practice that require empirical investigation. For example, the lack of legal aid in civil cases meant that perhaps in the past even more so than today only the economically stronger parties had the opportunity to select the best advice and advocates likely to win cases, the cases which might actually go before the courts, and thereby establish precedents which might, in turn, be reported in the law reports and thereby influence future courts and litigants, and thereby, in a real sense, determine the content of the law. The causal connections between economic power, the bringing of litigation, the use of certain counsel, the reporting of case law and thereby the construction of precedents requires our attention.[340] For instance, there may be a clear relationship between a socially and economically powerful lobby supportive of or opposed to specific laws, the amount of litigation surrounding the ambit of this law, and the range of defences and exceptions to liability under the law which are developed.

Also important are the causal connections between the economic power of a party and the ability to cause a case to be settled out of court. This may adversely affect the weaker party in a series of ways. For example, if the case had gone to court, the weaker party may have secured higher compensation - a situation that is not infrequent in a context of negligence claims against insurance companies, manufacturers and employers. It also permits the stronger party to prevent possible unfavourable precedents from being established. Credit companies and those using extensive exclusion or penalty clauses might fall into this category. Further, the power to "impose" a settlement may be used to prevent the courts considering the cases likely to establish precedents inimical to the interests of the stronger party. The stronger party will be able to use the law to wear down and even "gag" the weaker party on occasions. The successful use made by

Distillers of the law of contempt against the revelations of the Sunday Times or the unsuccessful use of "gagging writs" for defamation by Dr. William Wallersteiner are contemporary examples of this power. Moreover, since the weaker parties have not argued his case before the court, the opportunity for a precedent which might have assisted others in the position of the weaker party will have been lost. It is illusory, therefore, to ignore such considerations in assessing the efficacy of legal rights and duties. Similarly, the legal and practical problems relating to the actual enforcement of legal obligations must be considered in any historical assessment of the utility, the economic efficiency and the justice of the law and legal professionalism in the process of industrialisation. It could be suggested, therefore, that the "accident of litigation" and those cases that get reported and the establishment of precedents and, thereby the future shape of the law, appears significantly less fortuitous but is ultimately locked into the material relations within society, albeit in a manner that, on occasions, may neither be intended nor immediate in the eyes of the actors themselves.

Thus the historical specificity of the relative autonomy of the legal professions constitutes one of the most perplexing areas in a modern historical sociology of law. It is unlikely that the kind of questions enumerated above can be satisfactorily addressed at a very high level of abstraction.

Within the last decade our knowledge of the history of the English legal professions has been significantly extended. Important work has transformed our knowledge of the Inns of Court, the history of the bar, common lawyers, attorneys, solicitors, and the civilians.[341] Significant work has also been done on the history of the courts and judges.[342] In particular, the history of the House of Lords as a judicial body and the metamorphosis of the procedure of the criminal courts have been the subject of pathbreaking studies.[343] Significant work has also been done on the history of the jury and on the rise of a highly formalistic approach to legal decision-making and legal reasoning ("legal formalism").[344] What follows is a brief discussion of some of this important new literature, the relationship (if any) between the essays in Part B of this collection and that literature, and a summary of some of the major issues of a history of lawyers and the courts in the modern period.

In terms of the documentary evidence potentially available, the legal professions tend to be one of the more well-documented groups in history. Nevertheless, much of the data remains unsifted and unanalysed. In particular, we still lack a large body of local or specific case studies grounded in archival work. The quality of the data available is variable, selective and sometimes shaky. For example, the task of defining who is to be subsumed under the title of "barrister", "attorney" or "solicitor" is considerably more difficult than might be supposed. Those who formally qualified as barristers, attorneys or solicitors did not necessarily practise law; or, if they did, it was not their principal vocation. This is an acute problem in the history of the bar as a substantial proportion of those who entered the bar did not practise as barristers.

Thus, the figures that do exist for the numbers admitted and called during the nineteenth century do not reveal the number in practice. Here we are in the realm of crude (and conflicting) estimates. Contemporary estimates of the size of the professions were often vague and somewhat inconsistent. In fact, there are no accurate data on the size of the practising bar until the 1950s when the Bar Council began issuing official statistics on the subject. The data to be found in <u>The Law Lists</u> has rightly been treated with considerable caution.

Moreover, the terms "barrister", "attorney" and "solicitor" are far from unproblematic. To some extent, they were understood to mean different things by different people. These categories embraced a wide range of activities and individuals. (This was especially the case in respect of the eighteenth century attorney). Indeed, the demarcation line between these categories was not wholly clear-cut but was contested and changed over time. There is a further problem: the large number of lawyers who were not members of any professional association - a problem which in particular bedevils any historian of the attorneys. All this threatens the possibility of adopting the collective biography and other statistical techniques to the legal professions.

That significant statistical work is possible is evidenced by Duman's recent history of the English and Colonial Bars in the nineteenth century.[345] Duman suggests that the bar (rather than, say, physic) was the classic profession in nineteenth century England. Four other subsidiary themes underpin his book as a whole. Firstly, he largely discounts the importance of landed society as an influence on the bar and as a source of the bar's recruits. Instead, he insists on the increasingly middle class character, composition and clientele of the bar. Secondly, he challenges those who conflate the rise of professionalism with the Industrial Revolution. By 1835, the bar had satisfied many of the criteria usually associated with professionalisation. Thirdly, Duman argues that the Inns of Court have been overlooked by students of English society and politics. Rather than mere schools for lawyers the Inns were significant "portals of power". By the late nineteenth century, they "were one of the principal nurseries of the governing elite".[346] Fourthly, a variety of forces sought to make the Inns more democratic and improve legal education. Changes did occur. However, Duman convincingly demonstrates that these changes did not threaten the hegemony and autonomy of the Inns. The ". . . voices of conservatism prevailed and the original edifice remained with only minor alterations".[347] Duman's combination of statistical and literary evidence significantly advances our knowledge of the structure and character of the English and Colonial bars in the nineteenth century. We now know much more about the social composition, education, career patterns, wealth and income structure and political involvements of the bar than previously.

Whilst Duman's work illustrates the value of applying prosopographical and other statistical techniques to the legal profession, it also highlights their limitations. Statistical data will be misleading unless it is related to the social, political, economic and intellectual context of the institution investigated. In Duman's work the context is largely missing. The discussion of the figures often occurs in vacuo. Prosopography is notorious for its inattention to the role of ideas, principles, passions and ideologies.[348] It largely concentrates upon the vested interests of the actors concerned. Duman's work carries over the weaknesses of the Namierite perspective into the history of the bar.

What kinds of ideas might it have been pertinent to explore? As regards the period 1770-1870, Atiyah opines that laissez-faire principles may well have exercised a more tenacious hold on the mind of lawyers and judges than on any other organ of the state. "Probably, at least in the middle third of the (nineteenth) century, the majority of judges would have inclined more to Bramwell's position (i.e., a strong adherence to laissez-faire), though in the latter half of the century, opinion may have begun to moderate slightly . . . . (Once) the basic tenets of (laissez-faire) political economy had been translated into law by the judges in the form of the adoption of the principle of freedom of contract, they remained there."[349] Judicial attitudes showed little sign of movement away from adherence to laissez-faire until the present century, long after the political economists had discarded laissez-faire even to the extent that they ever espoused it.

Just why the legal profession clung so tenaciously to laissez-faire has yet to be fully explored. Some have argued that the common lawyers typified by Coke adopted ideas of economic liberalism prior to their reception throughout a wider body of the community. "What was it about the work or nature or organisation of the legal profession", asks Atiyah, "which made lawyers, or at least common lawyers, more receptive to ideas of commercial freedom?"[350] Atiyah points to the ways in which the traditions of the profession, its structure, the nature of the barristers' work, their clients as well as the political and economic context may help to explain the tenacious hold of laissez-faire over the minds of many lawyers. And that hold of laissez-faire was important; for a major part of Atiyah's history of nineteenth century contract law centres around the influence of laissez-faire ideology, especially via the doctrine of freedom of contract, on the law of contract and on the whole corpus of private law generally.

We are left to speculate upon the role of laissez-faire ideology in the history of the structure of the bar and the individuals who constituted that structure. For example, to what extent did this ideology mediate or foreclose the efforts of those members of the bar (and others) who otherwise sought reform of the bar through legislative intervention? Did it influence the attitudes of those judges who afforded the Inns considerable freedom from outside supervision? Duman stresses that whilst parliament seemed willing to impose reforms on other professions, in the view of governments and others, the Inns were untouchable. Did laissez-faire influence their attitudes towards the changing subject-matter that was coming before the courts and the rise of the regulatory state? Did all lawyers have an identical conception of laissez-faire?

Another factor seems to have shaped the ideas and values of the barrister. Several historians of the Inns of Court and their Continental counterparts, the university law school, have concluded that they were important "breeders of values" both within and without the profession. Duman's work on the nineteenth century reaffirms this thesis and adds an important political dimension to the picture.

> "In chambers and commons the novice assimilated the values and norms of the bar that each professional generation transmitted to the next. The period of studentship ensured that all barristers underwent identical rites of passage that created as far as possible a standard professional outlook and fostered occupational solidarity."[351]

In addition, members of the bar were well represented in the nineteenth century political elite. "The Inns must be ranked alongside the leading public schools and Oxbridge . . . as the principal socialising agents of the nineteenth century political establishment . . . . (The Inns) inculcated (men) with the norms of the governing classes."[352]

This recognition of the Inns as "one of the principal nurseries of the governing elite"[353] is undoubtedly important. However, many questions are left unanswered. What were the values and norms that were transmitted from generation to generation? What precisely do we mean by "a standard professional outlook" and what was its content? And what do we mean by "the norms of the governing class"? Part of the problem is that these are rather empty phrases maybe suggestive but they remain unsubstantiated assertions. Indeed, it may be queried the extent to which socialisation on the scale posited by Duman is in fact measurable. Also questionable is Duman's treatment of the bar, the ruling elite and their values as monolithic and unchanging. The bar was sufficiently heterogeneous to contain alternative conceptions of the profession and therefore differing professional ideologies. Duman's own work describes the differences within the profession on issues such as legal education, professional discipline, the efficacy of the messes as against a more centralised regulatory body, and so on. If such contradictory conceptions of the profession co-existed, they are not explored. Thus, we get no sense of the ways, if any, the profession reconciled: its concern with individual merit and social exclusiveness; the image of the barrister as "an anglicised version of the Roman iuris prudente"[354] who saw himself as part of a wider community of learning versus one which stressed the bar's autonomy and isolation, where dining was the only requirement for entry into the profession, and so on. A leading historian of the Inns of Court has acknowledged ". . . the lawyer's somewhat ambivalent moral and social position"[354a] - but Duman omits to explore the historical specificity of this ambivalence. Indeed, the notion of an unchanging ideology contradicts his own work which has sought to establish that the influx of the middle classes into the Inns gave rise to a new unified professional ideology.

In spite of these criticisms, Duman has significantly extended our knowledge of the bar. However, in order to obtain a more complete picture of the nineteenth century bar, it should be read alongside Cock's important book on the professional life of the bar.[355] Cocks describes the ideas that members of the Victorian bar had about themselves, their activities, legal education and legal science. His work is also valuable in that it conveys more sharply than Duman's work, the tensions within the bar and the importance of these tensions in explaining the transformation of the bar in the nineteenth century. Conflicts between different messes and other forms of regional divisions; the tensions between the traditional habits of the profession and the demands for organised legal education, examinations and more centralised control; and the tensions between an attachment to mere practical and technical skill and the demand for a more scientific jurisprudence are usefully explored by Cocks. In his essay in this collection, Raymond Cocks continues his work towards an intellectual history of the bar by exploring the attitudes of Victorian barristers and judges to the expansion of a new field of regulatory law - taxation. Cocks reveals the complex and contradictory attitudes of the bar and bench. He also casts new light on Dicey's involvement, as a young barrister, in revenue cases.

The work of Duman and Cocks locates the creation of the modern bar in the nineteenth century. Wilfrid Prest's essay in this collection is an important critique of the "sociological truism" that the bar, and other professions, were a Victorian creation. Prest points to the paucity of historical research on the professions before c.1800 and the Whiggish trait approach to "professionalisation" as significant factors in perpetuating the assumption that the history of the profession did not really begin until the Industrial Revolution. His data indicates that the bar took on many of the characteristics of a profession, and was so regarded, in the period before c.1800. Prest challenges the notion of a radical break in the history of the professions associated with the coming of industrial society; and, in so doing, he questions the work of several historians and sociologists of the professions, notably the influential work of Larsen.[356] Prest's essay discusses the history of the legal professions within the general context of the history and sociology of the professions. Thus, it constitutes a helpful introduction to the history and sociology of the legal professions.

One area where economic and business historians have shed important light upon the legal professions is that body of literature which investigates the role of attorneys as financial intermediaries and suppliers of credit.[357] Michael Miles' essay in this collection describes the range of work performed by country attorneys in the second half of the eighteenth century. Miles' work is significant because it is a rare example of a historian utilising an extensive collection of attorneys' working papers - day books, letter books, precedent books, ledgers, cash books, diaries, bill books, commonplace books and miscellaneous deeds - to reconstruct the changing workload and functions of attorneys. His essay describes the ways in which the eighteenth century attorney developed closer contacts with his clients than ever before. In the latter half of the eighteenth century, conveyancing already produced a third to a half of their income. The workload of the attorney expanded and reliance upon the attorney increased. This process contributed to the growing status and respectability of the eighteenth century attorney. Miles' work testifies to the significant light that lawyers' working papers can cast upon law, economy and society. More work of this kind is needed. We might do well to emulate the important collections of lawyers' papers that have recently been carefully edited in the United States.[358] These papers contain important material on commercial practice and lawyer-business networks in nineteenth century America.

Just as the history of barristers and attorneys has been transformed in recent years, so too has the history of solicitors. In the nineteenth century, land law reform evoked heated political debate because it touched upon the power and influence of the landed classes. Offer's Property and Politics, 1870-1914 includes a brilliant essay on the relations between solicitors, the land market, and legal reform.[359] Offer describes the geographical distribution of the profession and its changing workload. He also illuminates the conflicts within the profession, especially the tensions between the London dominated Law Society and the provincial "backwoodsmen". Offer provides much new and valuable information on the efforts of the profession to protect their monopoly over the conveyancing of land. The profession played a significant role in the marginalisation of the political dimensions of land reform. By the twentieth century, land law reform had become largely a technical matter, for conveyancers. Offer's work highlights the important role played by lawyers as a pressure group both within and outside parliament. It also confirms, at least in this context, Larsen's thesis that professions may significantly control the demands for their services.[360]

The work of Duman, Miles and Offer also illuminates the efforts of lawyers to improve their social status. Other concerns also seem to have been important. To what extent did elite lawyers conceive of themselves as a group with a special mediation function in society: that is, to secure social stability through the mediation of the claims of the disparate interests within society? And to what extent did they actually perform this function? Recent work has argued that lawyers influence and control through the language and symbols of the law. Lawyers translate everyday experiences into the language of the law. In so doing, it is claimed that they de-politicise and individualise issues. "In this sense law is a meta-language. Its material significance, however, derives from the fact that it is also the workaday language for certain state authorised adjudicators . . . . (Lawyers) are conceptive ideologists . . . (or "organic intellectuals") who think, and, therefore constitute the form of . . ."[361] industrial society. This emphasis upon the constitutive role of lawyers argues that the lawyers' translation function creates ideologies and/or helps construct a social consensus. Such a claim is dependent upon the assertion that legal translation, and the symbols and categories that ensue, influence the ways individuals act and understand the world. Much empirical work is required before this assertion can be verified. However, emphasis upon the constitutive role of the general practice of the lawyer has the virtue of drawing attention to the potential effectivity of the form of law and legal consciousness on lawyers and others; and how the skills of translation may partly explain the demand for the services of lawyers. In short, historians and sociologists of the professions need to give greater attention to the intellectual structure of the law[362] and the lawyers' practice of translation than hitherto, if they are to understand the demand for legal expertise and the cultural consequences of lawyering. A sensitivity to legal consciousness will also lead one to explore the tensions between the practices of lawyers and their ideals and their efforts at reconciliation.[363]

Other significant issues in the history of the professions include the failure of the codification movement;[364] the profession's attitudes to legislation vis à vis the common law; and the role of lawyers in the state, regulatory agencies and large corporations. The rise of the corporate lawyer, and the impact on the legal professions of the rise of large corporations has yet to receive adequate attention.

Also important is the role of para-legal or quasi-judicial officers in tribunals and other forms of adjudication and regulation. Peter Bartrip's essay in this collection tackles the much neglected history of County Court and superior court registrars, 1820-1875. Bartrip describes the transformation of this office, from one mainly responsible for dealing with the myriad tasks to be performed before and after judgment to a significant judicial office. In areas such as bankruptcy and divorce, registrars came to exercise important judicial duties. Why did County Court registrars become judicial figures in the period 1820-1875? Bartrip argues that the importance of these officers grew as a result of pragmatism. The success of the County Court system and the volume of the business it engendered rather than ideological or political factors ensured that the registrar's judicial role increased over time. Bartrip's work illustrates the need for historians to look beyond the judge and the central courts and explore the history of those officials in central and local courts who in practice may have exercised functions as important as those of the judge as conventionally defined.

Harry Arthurs' essay in this collection challenges the notion that the history of the English courts is the history of increasing centralisation. He points to the vital role played by local courts well into the nineteenth century. Arthurs describes the competing conceptions of legality imbibed by local and central courts and the tensions between them. He argues that this tradition of legal pluralism was not completely negated by the Courts of Westminster Hall, despite the antagonism of many lawyers to local jurisdictions. Indeed, the new administrative law and arbitration were continuing manifestations of the tradition of legal pluralism. His essay illustrates the importance of historical work on the changing business within and as between different systems of adjudication.[365] Indeed, a more inclusive approach to the study of dispute transformation and how lawyers, legal ideas and other actors affect social conflicts, such as that emerging out of recent American studies, suggests new avenues for historical research.[366]

Stuart Anderson's essay in this collection is a case study of access to the legal process: namely, to the right to remarry. It has usually been argued that until the enactment of the Matrimonial Causes Act 1857, divorce was the prerogative of the aristocracy. Anderson identifies <u>who</u> were the petitioners for legislative divorce. He argues that the upper middle class had always had access to legislative divorce. As a result, doubt is cast upon both the conventional view that attributes legal reform in part to upper middle class pressure and the importance usually attached to the 1857 Act. Anderson's essay also illuminates the causes for the changing rates of applications for statutory divorce. He argues that the common lawyer's desire to stress the superiority of courts of law, especially courts of common law, for dealing with divorce and allied matters, was an important factor in the arguments for and against legislative divorce.

The history of the civil courts, especially the lower courts, has not received extended attention by historians. Thus, the social functions performed by such courts, the ideologies which they embraced and the social composition of their personnel and of their litigants have been neglected by historians. In Part A of this collection, Gerry Rubin investigates the plight of the <u>defendants</u> in the county court system in the context of imprisonment for debt. In Part B of this collection, Rubin addresses who were the <u>plaintiffs</u> who deemed it essential to initiate county court proceedings in order to recover their debts. Here he is concerned with an important body of creditors, the tallymen, that is, peripatetic salesmen who travelled from door to door, offering goods to customers on a credit basis. Tallymen were frequently condemned and Rubin explores the attitudes of the judges in the light of this hostility. He shows that judges, if they were so disposed, could and did respond to tallymen's cases, by discriminating in favour of the debtor defendant. Proposals for the reform of the law in order to contain the litigious tallymen; the litigious activities of money-lenders and other debt collectors; and the system of consumer credit, indebtedness and the county courts are also explored in this essay. Rubin pin-points a tension between the county courts as a debt collecting agency and the desire of some county court judges to prevent county courts becoming "misery exchanges". County courts experienced a crisis of legitimacy and respectability. This crisis of legitimacy extended beyond the tallymen and other creditors to many county court judges.

XIII : HISTORIOGRAPHY OF LAW AND ECONOMY

A. Nineteenth Century Commercial Lawyers And Economy

The relationship between the legal system and credit has already been noted. In particular, it was noted that the views propounded by contemporaries lent a polemical character to the debate. However, in the spirit of scientific enquiry, a number of economists in the later nineteenth century, turned their attention to the theory underlying the distinctively legal mode of regulating credit. Thus, Sir Thomas Farrer (1819-99) noted the strong connection between "a proper law of debtor and creditor, including bankruptcy", and control of fluctuations in credit, which would, in turn, stabilise the currency and prevent "mischievous fluctuations in price."[367] The essence of the "legal" approach, in its simplicity, was to ensure, "so far as law can ensure it, that every promise to pay shall be punctually discharged." Where insolvency occurred, the nation and not only the creditors suffered, argued Farrer. For false credit, "the making of promies to pay where there are no means of performing them," was a public mischief.

> "It causes, first, an inflation and then an undue collapse, and alters prices to the injury of the honest dealer, just as the issue of bad money does."[368]

Thus, he pointed out, the recent Bankruptcy Act of 1883 (which Farrer helped to draft) was to be understood not only as a "creditors' Act or a means of punishing dishonesty, it was a remedy for unsound circulation."

Perhaps the fullest exposition of the subject was by Henry Dunning MacLeod (1821-1902) who investigated "the complete Juridical and Mathematical Theory of Credit." Publishing his work, The Theory of Credit[369] in two volumes in 1889-90, he argued that,

> "Rights of action, Credits, or Debts are now clearly shown to be the Name of a certain species of merchandise, goods and chattels, or commodities and they can be bought and sold like any other merchandise or commodities."[370]

Insistent that it was this discovery which had "most deeply affected the fortunes of the human race", he then proceeded to trace the "origin and progress of the power of selling debts". That is, he undertook a legal history, commencing with Roman law, of "Property or Rights in Contract or Obligation", intending finally to "place this branch of Mercantile Law on solid foundations", by which he sought to exhibit its empirical effects on commerce.[371]

According to the Encyclopaedia Britannica,[372] MacLeod's work on credit was his principal contribution to economics and a topic to which he was the first to give prominence. Yet as The Times noted,[373] in a brief obituary, MacLeod had been well known to students as "an authority on commercial law relating to banking, bills of exchange" and "kindred subjects". And, indeed, it is this cross-fertilisation of economic and legal ideas in the nineteenth century by writers acquainted with both disciplines, and who sought explicitly to relate economic enquiry to legal structure and institutions which we consider of importance to identify, in order both to rescue such writers from obscurity and, more significantly, to pave the way for a fuller historiography and proper understanding of the subject than hitherto, particularly in the realm of commercial law creation.

The pedigree of this genre was, of course, impressive with Adam Smith's Lectures on Jurisprudence, Bentham's Principles of Morals and Legislation and, arguably, Marx's work on the Factories Acts probably the unsurpassed products of this union.

Certainly the careers of both Farrer and MacLeod display this valuable quality of an integrated juridical and economic science. Farrer, for example, had read as a pupil in the chambers of Roundell Palmer (later Lord Selborne) and was called to the Bar in November 1844.[374] In 1848 he ceased to practise and was recruited to the Board of Trade where he drafted bills dealing with the mercantile marine. He rose through the Civil Service ranks, becoming permanent Secretary to the Board of Trade from 1865 to 1880. During this period, he exercised considerable influence on the development and character of English commercial law, especially in the fields of merchant shipping, bankruptcy and railway regulation, in much the same way that Sir Hubert Llewellyn Smith[375] and (possibly to a lesser extent) William Beveridge[376] influenced British labour legislation prior to, and during, the Great War. It has been said of Farrer that,

> ". . . so effectual was the exercise of this unseen and quiet influence that in the period between 1872 and 1886 almost all the reforms of and additions to our system of commercial law were only brought about with the concurrence of the Secretary of the Board of Trade."[377]

MacLeod similarly pursued a juridically informed career as an, occasionally unorthodox, economist. Called to the Bar in 1849, he established a moderate reputation as a mercantile lawyer.[378] In 1853, he became engaged in litigation in which he successfully challenged the claim of the Board of Trade to prohibit a joint-stock bank founded under the Act of 1845, from increasing its capital. He subsequently expounded the general conclusions indicated by the litigation in his first work, The Theory and Practice of Banking (1856), which Thomas Tooke favourably commended in his History of Prices. From 1868 to 1870, he was employed by the government to prepare a digest of the law of bills of exchange and continued subsequently to stress the intimate nexus between law and "economics", a term he popularised in preference to the then current "political economy".

Perhaps the most outstanding scholar of this genre, however, was Leone Levi (1821-88), Professor of the Principles and Practice of Commerce and Commercial Law at King's College, London, and perhaps best known for his work, The History of British Commerce, published in 1872.[379] Though called to the Bar in 1859 he had long developed an interest in the relation between commerce and the legal structure. Whilst working as a clerk in a Liverpool mercantile house, he advocated, on a wider scale than hitherto, the establishment of chambers of commerce and also the institution of permanent tribunals of commerce, presided over by a legally trained judge, with the assistance of mercantile assessors. His proposals, with the exception of that in respect to tribunals of commerce, came to fruition, with provisions in the Common Law Procedure Act 1854, embodying his recommendations for arbitration.[380]

Arguably, his magnum opus, if not necessarily his best remembered work, was Commercial Law: Its Principles and Administration; or the Mercantile Law of Great Britain Compared with the Codes and Laws of Commerce of (58 Countries) and the Institutes of Justinian, which was published between 1850 and 1852. The work was acclaimed nationally and internationally and honours and prizes were heaped upon him. One immediate consequence was a meeting of the Law Amendment Society in November 1852, to discuss practical proposals for the harmonisation of the mercantile laws of the United Kingdom. It led first to a royal commission in 1854, and eventually resulted in the Mercantile Law Amendment Acts of 1856 (19 and 20 Vict., cc.60 and 97), lasting memorials to his influence and industry.

His appointment to the chair at King's College in 1852, stimulated further endeavours in this area. His lectures formed the basis of his Manual of the Mercantile Law of Great Britain and Ireland published in 1854. In the following year, he read a paper before the Law Amendment Society on "Judicial Statistics" thereby pointing suggestively to the need for proper national compilations, particularly of civil judicial statistics. As we have seen, such a series commenced publication on an annual basis in 1859, and was fundamentally improved by Sir John MacDonnell's careful editing from 1894.

Levi's principal work on statistics was, in fact, a periodical summary of parliamentary papers entitled Annals of British Legislation, being a Classified and Analysed Summary of Public Bills, Statutes, Accounts and Papers, Reports of Committees and of Commissioners and of Session Papers, generally of the Houses of Lords and Commons, together with Accounts of Commercial Legislation, Tariffs and Facts relating to Foreign Countries. Published in 14 volumes between 1856 and 1865, it was continued in 4 volumes until 1868 under the considerably shorter title, Annals of British Legislation, being a Digest of the Parliamentary Blue Books.

The economic context of international law and the role of international arbitration received acknowledgement from Levi in such publications as Peace, the Handmaiden of Commerce, with Remarks on the Eastern Question, which originated in a lecture delivered in 1876; War and its Consequences, Economical, Commercial, Financial and Moral. With Proposals, for the Establishment of a Court of International Reference and Arbitration, published in 1881; and International Law, with Materials for a Code of International Law, which appeared one year before his death.

Thus, it was through the endeavours of authors and civil servants such as Farrer, MacDonnell, MacLeod and Levi, who attempted to forge connections between law and economy and to make accessible the statistical information necessary to mount policy initiatives, that the shape of later nineteenth century commercial law evolved as it did. If the contribution of the above writers and of, say, T.E. Cliffe-Leslie, professor of Jurisprudence and Political Economy at Queens, Belfast[381] in the second half of the nineteenth century, can be evaluated in the fashion already employed in respect to the career of Mackenzie D.

Chalmers, county court judge at Birmingham, later Home Office civil servant and commercial law codifier,[382] our understanding of the relationship between law and economy in the later nineteenth century will be richer.

B. Professional Historians of English Law

The work of the professional historians of English law is, in comparison, much better known. Some have already been cited in this chapter (or in the footnotes). Rarely, however, has their contribution to a history of law and economy in the modern period been addressed. The historiography of modern legal history has yet to be written.[383] What follows is the briefest outline, primarily concentrating upon that golden period of 1860 to 1920. Legal and historical studies in this era were especially close. Moreover, one could gather examples of legal historians whose work might have forged a more distinctively economic, social and intellectual history of law, or even a historical sociology of modern law. Yet a new legal history or historical sociology did not emerge in this period. Why was this the case? To this important, but wholly neglected question, we can here provide only the barest outline of an answer, concentrating upon internal rather than external considerations.

Although the leading English legal historians of the period 1860 to 1920 - Maine, Dicey, Maitland and Holdsworth[384] - did not write economic and social histories of law, theirs was a legal history which offered scattered and suggestive insights into the historical relation between law and material society. Indeed, in so far as their work (explicitly or implicitly) defined itself in opposition to orthodox doctrinal legal history, that is, to the study of the evolution of legal doctrine exclusively in terms of distinctively "legal" phenomena, theirs was in a sense an inherently economic, political or sociological history, though neither sociology nor political science as such. Of course their individual merits as historians varied enormously. Scorn has rightly been poured on the methods and findings of Maine and Dicey.[385] Both were ". . . deficient in a close study of the evidence and in a thorough knowledge of the literature of the subject."[386] Their differing methodologies utilised over-simplistic categorisations and crude theories of legal and social evolution. At their worst, they used ". . . the past as an ammunition dump against views with which . . . (they) disagreed . . . ."[387] However, their legacy, with its concern for the connections between law and society and between law, state formation and economic ideas and forces, was significant to contemporaries. Indeed, in the case of Dicey, it is still the focal point of a major controversy within historical scholarship. In the context of the fact-fetishism and positivism that then characterised much contemporary historical writing, the efforts of Maine and Dicey were simultaneously an instrument of a highly conservative politics[388] and a pioneering attempt to establish the relation between law, state and society as a major concern of historical and legal scholarship.

By contrast, Maitland's craftsmanship and professionalism are beyond dispute. We would emphasise Maitland's advocacy of the relevance of legal history to other sorts of history and his stress of the importance of law to economic, social and political life:

> "Think for a moment what lies concealed within the hard rind of legal history. Legal documents . . . are the best, often the only evidence that we have for the history of morality, for the history of practical religion. Take a broad subject - the condition of the great mass of Englishmen in the later Middle Ages, the condition of the villagers. That might be pictured for us . . . ; its political, social, economic, moral aspects might all be brought out (in legal documents and through legal history).[389]

Or, again,

> "It may indeed be possible for us . . . to exaggerate the importance of law; we may say . . . that it is only the skeleton of the body politic; but students of the body natural cannot afford to be scornful of bones, not even of dry bones; they must know their anatomy. Have we then any cause to speak despondently when . . . every effort after economic history is demonstrating the absolute necessity for a preliminary solution of legal problems . . . ."[390]

Maitland liked to stress what he called "the study of interactions and interdependencies".[391] We would point to three aspects of his work amongst many pertinent to the historical study of law and economy. First, his treatment of the church, and other corporate or semi-corporate bodies as semi-autonomous realms which possessed state-like characteristics, illuminated the political and constitutional dimensions of a subject-matter which political scientists and historians had tended to ignore.[392] Second, his monumental History of English Law Before the Time of Edward I in part related legal doctrine to socio-economic considerations, albeit in a highly diffused manner.[393] For instance, the law of wills and contracts is shown to have been influenced by religious ideas; the effect of a money economy is related to the manor and feudal law; and, in particular, the law of land tenure, its impact on the ways land was owned, transferred and occupied are used to extend our knowledge of state and society in feudal England. Thirdly, Maitland was a seminal force behind the movement to collect, preserve and translate the vast storehouse of neglected legal raw materials - a movement notably associated with the publications of the Selden Society.[394]

Maitland certainly had much to contribute to a new history of law and material society.[395] Yet, whilst Maitland offered occasional and suggestive ways of connecting law, society and economy, he failed to explore these connections in any systematic fashion. Perhaps to traverse the traditional province of legal history required a temperament less cautious than that of Maitland's. In addition, Maitland was part of a generation which, in effect, sought to construct and defend a historical scholarship scrupulous in its evidence and free of the influence of work, some of it variations of biological social theory, which sought to incorporate the language of universal "causes" and "laws" into history, thereby neglecting the purposive nature of human action and the contingent and complex nature of history. Their effort to avoid one-sided, mechanical and grossly simplistic historical interpretations gave rise to a tendency to eschew or distrust: general theorisation and abstraction; an explicit concern with the methodologies of history and their value-laden or political implications; "economy" and "economics" in history; and the politically-charged nature of certain historical subject-matter. Even at its best, therefore, the legal history produced in the period 1860 to 1920 tended to divorce "theory" from "history" ". . . in the interests of authenticity. This is because theory is identified as a priori mental schematism and 'history' as a quite direct (if we only listen) mediation of the real."[396]

This view of 'history' and 'theory' raises a host of problems at which we can only begin to hint. First, all research is dependent upon (frequently implicit) hypotheses and therefore theories. Second, empirical generalisations can be distinguished from laws or universals and therefore stripped of any normative force. Third, the 'facts' (a provisional conception of the real) are of themselves highly problematic and contentious. Moreover, the general analysis of facts, or the testing of hypotheses in the light of "the facts" requires that the ". . . 'facts' must already have been transformed into 'categories': into the same medium, as it were, as the 'theory'. (These facts are categories at a lower level of generality than those composing the theory)."[397] Thus, the difference between theory and history becomes one of degree rather than kind; and both are inseparable.

In short, there was a tendency to slide into empiricism. As a result, those same individuals who might have ventured beyond the confines of traditional legal history could also arguably be held to have unwittingly created and defended a historical paradigm which would inevitably frustrate rather than foster the growth of an economic and social history of law.[398] The contrast with perhaps the leading exemplar of a historical sociology of law - Max Weber - will clarify what has been said here. In contrast to Maitland, Weber was sensitive to the fact that the study of law and economy in history involved general methodological issues and hypotheses which would require conscious attention of itself; and that this was part of a more general awareness of the problem and importance of methodology in the study of society, irrespective of the discipline. Further, for Weber, economics and economic issues were part of history. Given this mode of classification, and a self-conscious sensitivity to the implications and importance of methodology, the path was open to Weber to construct a new history of law and economy. He recognised that a new legal history not only required more and better quality data, but that it also necessitated a new analytical framework, a more self-conscious methodology, and not simply the empiricist model of conventional history. In other words, in this history, unlike conventional history, questions and problems of 'theory' and 'history' were not seen as materially exclusive but as inextricably bound together.

In legal history, the divorce of 'theory' from 'history' was abetted by the then dominant tradition of jurisprudence: Austinian positivism. Indeed, it has been said that jurisprudence as it was studied in England in the late 19th and early 20th centuries meant Austin and that Austin was a religion.[399] Although Austin himself conceived of his own work as, in a sense, historically informed, Austinian jurisprudence as practised, for instance, in the writing of law textbooks and the teaching of law, was profoundly unhistorical.[400] This escaping from history in dealing with human phenomena and the need to restore the historicity of subject matter was a subject debated in the social sciences at the turn of the century. Thus, the Victorian philosopher, D.G. Ritchie, criticised Ricardian economics and Austinian jurisprudence: "In each case the attempt to work out 'pure theory' unadulterated by history has resulted in 'theory' being unintelligible and inexplicable except in the immediate surroundings of those who have enunciated it."[401] This is not to say that important and suggestive work on law and economy was not undertaken by English legal historians. However, most legal history concentrated on medieval England rather than on the modern period; and analytically speaking, it continued to operate within the traditional empiricist framework of the English historical tradition.

Concerning the study of the modern period, mention must be made of the work [402] of Sir William Holdsworth. In those volumes of his massive History of English Law devoted to the 19th and 20th centuries, Holdsworth provides much additional information which fills out and qualifies Dicey's treatment of the 19th century as a period of laissez-faire, followed by a period of increasing collectivism. But perhaps his most successful attempt at bridging the gulf between legal and economic history, is a much neglected essay he contributed to the first volume of the Economic History Review in 1927:[403]

"I have been struck" he wrote "by the fact that many of the rules of English law have an economic origin. This is true both of the enacted and the unenacted law . . . . This phenomenon is, it seems to me, a neglected aspect of the relations of economic and legal history."[404]

To illustrate ". . . the interrelation of rules of English law . . . and economic conditions" he took three specific instances: the Statute of Labourers and the labour legislation of Elizabeth's reign; the agitation against monopolies in Elizabeth's reign and James I's Statute of Monopolies; and developments in land law. After this brief but successful attempt to relate law and economy, Holdsworth concluded that . . . "the connection between law and economic history is so very close that I do not think that either the legal or the economic historian can do justice to his subject without extensive borrowings from the other's learning . . . ."[405]

Holdsworth's essay, however, failed in its objective: namely, to prompt economic historians generally to examine the relation between English law and "economic conditions". Obviously, the special skills of legal archaeology are likely to prove off-putting to historians. Perhaps Sir Frederick Pollock was right when he remarked that law is regarded by most historians ". . . as a subject so technical and difficult, not to say repulsive, that nobody but lawyers can meddle with it."[406] The problem of the peculiar nature of legal discourse is, of course, a real one. The tendency of the academic study of law to be isolated within academia (and from public life) has undoubtedly been reinforced by the fact that orthodox legal scholarship took a form which made it unlikely to be meaningful to the intellectual community. This isolation is hardly surprising given the strong traditional subservience of English legal scholarship and education to the legal professions. Thus, the vast bulk of legal scholarship has ultimately been organised around what was meaningful to the profession; law scholars usually conceived of their roles as that of "barristers without portfolio".[407] All this not only reinforced the isolation of law within academia; it also partly explains the marginalisation of legal history (especially that which sought to examine the interconnections between law and economy) within law schools.

Not all economic historians, however, took the view that only lawyers could "meddle" with the law. As we have seen, the debate surrounding the role of the strict settlement in the accumulation of landed wealth is perhaps the major instance of where economic historians and historians of the family have considerably added to our knowledge of law, economy and society. In addition, individual economic historians, including W.J. Ashley, W.L. Burn, R.M. Hartwell, R.S. Neale and Thorold Rogers[408] have attempted to connect legal and economic history from a variety of differing perspectives.

The development of a distinct business history has stimulated a limited amount of work on the role of the legal professions in trade and industry.[409] It has also encouraged historians to explore a wealth of legal and quasi-legal records generated by the law and legal processes which have previously tended to be neglected, for example, bankruptcy records and statistics, company accounts, etc.[410] Other work has highlighted the utility of English probate records as a source of information on, for instance, changes in wealth holding and the wealthy, the occupational distribution of the wealthy and their social origins.[411] This, in turn, has added to our knowledge of the character of the legal professions. The expansion of social history and, more recently, the history of gender divisions and feminist historical writing has made exciting and influential contributions to our knowledge of the linkages between law, power, authority and sexual divisions in historical causation - as has the development of historical socio-legal studies. Yet the above are representative of what is undoubtedly a relatively rare band of writers. The complaint of G.R. Elton, voiced in 1969, that,

"For the post-medieval period, the history of law, law courts and justice remains something of a Cinderella"[412]

is still a valid criticism of historical scholarship, though the remarkable growth of interest in recent years in the history of crime and criminal justice is to be warmly welcomed.[413] It is our hope that the present volume can make a modest contribution to stimulating comparable advances in the modern economic and social history and, of the historical sociology of law.

XIV : CONCLUSION

We would not pretend to have offered a full examination of the issues posed in this essay nor a complete survey of the relevant literature. We have tried, however, to show what an economic and social history of law can do as well as to indicate (although not in any exhaustive fashion) what it is or is about.

The historical study of law and economy is one way, although not the only way, of extending our knowledge of the uses and limits of the law. But it is not only "the law" that such a history may illuminate. Law is part of society and economy: it is a social, intellectual and economic as well as a legal institution. Moreover, our subject traverses the boundaries separating the disciplines of anthropology, history and sociology. Despite the differences between these nominally discrete disciplines, they confront common issues which our subject might enlighten. For instance, all three are fundamentally preoccupied with ". . . the puzzle of human agency . . . . The problem of agency is the problem of finding a way of accounting for human experience which recognises simultaneously and in equal measure that history and society are made by constant and more or less purposeful individual action and that individual action, however purposeful, is made by history and society . . . . People make their own history - but only under definite circumstances and conditions . . . . The variations on the theme are innumerable; and the failure of human sciences to work the theme to a satisfactory conclusion is inscribed on page after page of the literature of each of those sciences . . . . The estranged symbiosis of action and structure is both a commonplace of everyday life and the unbudgeable fulcrum of social analysis."[414] As our essay evidences, the historical study of law and economy has proved fertile in enhancing our understanding of the central problems of agency and structuring.

Being truly historical, our subject serves as an important counter to static, Whiggish evolutionist accounts which treat the law and economy of modern English society as an inevitable end point, simply reflecting a solid consensus of almost volksgeist proportions. "Only the successful (in the sense of those whose aspirations anticipated subsequent evolution) are remembered."[415] In contrast, some of the best social history of law has served to remind us that legal intervention or abstention did not occur in vacuo. Sometimes it involved the marginalisation, suppression, qualification or consolidation of pre-existing social and economic relations and, therefore, of specific historical alternatives. The recuperation of these alternatives must be a major task of the economic and social history of law. As Edward Thompson, in a justly celebrated passage argued, we must seek ". . . to rescue . . . "such alternatives and the individuals and groups who embodied them, ". . . from the enormous condescension of posterity . . . . After all, we are not at the end of social evolution ourselves. In some of the lost causes of the people of the Industrial Revolution we may discover insights into social evils which we have yet to cure."[416]

Unlike conventional legal history, our subject looks at law and legal institutions not just through the eyes of lawyers, but also through the eyes of individual users and non-users. Further, it is sensitive to the political dimensions of law, lawyering and law-making; and to the connection between law and objective social and economic structures. This represents a conscious attempt to transcend the confines of lawyers' legal history - without , however, jettisoning its undoubted virtues. Lawyers' legal history has tended ". . . to exhaust itself in the insular details of the legal system."[417] As a result, with several notable exceptions, it has tended to concentrate upon too little. In short, the issues our subject poses and endeavours to illuminate are formidable, long-standing and fundamental.

Despite the potential our subject holds, and its intrinsic interest and relevance to a variety of disciplines and subject areas, we have tried to indicate some of the ways in which this promise has not been consistently realised in practice. The relevant literature, whether overtly concerned with law and economy or not, has tended to regard "law", "state", "economy", "ideology" and "social classes" as undifferentiated monoliths. For example, the nature and scope of law and legal institutions is often treated in an artificially circumspect manner which must inevitably generate a misconceived view of the interconnections or otherwise between law and material society. Thus, law and legal institutions tend to be equated either with the criminal law or the civil law; as either coercive or consensual in nature; as either case law or statute law. There is also a strong tendency to give undue attention to the royal (central) courts, and correspondingly to neglect local courts, legal and quasi-legal personnel, administrative jurisdictions, tribunals, the private law-making of the legal professions and legal literature. Once these relatively discrete levels of the state legal order are recognised it becomes much more difficult to view "the law" as a coherent unity which people experience as such. In fact, one might hypothesise that the rich variety of different levels that constitute the state legal order are not yoked together in any simple, mutually dependent manner; but, instead, that their interaction and inter-penetration is problematic and indeterminate. Indeed, Weber recognised that formal rationality and justice may impede or conflict with the exercise of substantive rationality and justice. The tensions and contradiction within the state order as between its different spheres and functions and the pressures this generates towards changes in the content and form of the law, have tended to be neglected by historians, sociologists and lawyers.

It is also (and incorrectly) assumed that law, ordering, organisation, coercion and social control are the exclusive property of the state. In other words, there is a tendency to confine our subject to the legal activities of the state. In contrast, we have pointed to the importance of a pluralistic approach to law, ordering and organisation. Since coercion, social control, ordering and organisation are not the exclusive province of the state, a plural perspective requires a shift in emphasis towards all social arenas in which ordering and organisation are maintained. Thus, in addition to the state legal order, we must investigate, on the one hand, those units or systems smaller than the state legal order and their interaction (or otherwise) with the state law order. On the other hand, we must also consider the international legal order and its impact on national ordering, organisation and economy.[418]

Another common pitfall we have stressed is an inclination to assume that the linkages between law and material society can wholly be explained in simple functionalist terms: that law was essential to certain social and economic ends; and/or that law mirrored either the needs of dominant classes or a general consensus. As we have tried to indicate, the connections between law and economy may be much more complex, contradictory and double-edged than these generalisations allow. We have shown, for instance, that in at least three areas where it has often been assumed that the law reflected either the needs of an industrialising society or dominant economic interest groups - namely, the law relating to contract, land and patents - their operation and supposed importance in practice was much less clear-cut and more variegated than functionalist interpretations tend to permit. As Robert Gordon observes, "There are simply too many variables in economic growth to support a hypothesis that any . . . (particular legal regime) is socially (and economically) 'necessary' . . ." For example, ". . . it is actually very difficult to account for the emergence of negligence as a general organising principle of tort liability as if it were a technological response of the law to the 'social needs of industrialisation', for one would then have to explain, for instance, why England and the United States seem to have undertaken the systematic generalisation of the fault principle to include all tort liability at the same time (1870s and 1880s) despite England's much earlier industrialisation as well as why Germany responded to industrialisation by imposing strict liability on railroads and industrial concerns for accidents by way of exception to a pre-existing fault standard!"[419] In a similar vein, A.W.B. Simpson has argued that, "If . . . the rule in Hadley v Baxendale (1854) is, as it has been argued, peculiarly appropriate to mid-nineteenth century industrial capitalism, what was it doing in Orleans in the 1760s?"[420] Although other nation states sought to import Britain's Industrial Revolution they did not on the whole adopt the policy most associated with the British state during Britain's industrial heyday, namely, laissez-faire.[421] As Weber concluded: . . . "modern capitalism prospers equally . . . under legal systems containing rules and institutions which considerably differ from each other at least from the juridical point of view."[422] Likewise, there was no single "capitalist" form of law - whether we call it contractual, commodity form or absolute private property. It is more accurate to view these as one of several forms of capitalist law which co-existed over long periods, complementing and conflicting with one another.[423]

What of the law's latent functions or ideological dimensions? Another canon of much simple functionalist writing is the assumption that all people are more or less persuaded by the legitimacy of the law and legal institutions and of their ideological dimensions more or less all the time. Perhaps the most important variant of this view is the thesis that the law and legal institutions constitute important mechanisms of social control whose ideologies breed passivity and facilitate the embourgeoisement of the lower orders of society. However, as we have seen, legal ideologies are not static monoliths. Adherence to the legitimacy of the law may be extremely superficial for all social groups; and that traditional, semi-autonomous, indigenous norms and pragmatic considerations may influence adherence or non-adherence and the degree of adherence, as well as more immediate economic considerations and fear of the coercive might of the state.

Part of the problem has been the assumption in some work that law and state are essentially related to the relations of production. This assumption ignores the character of civil society. Law and state may not only be related (albeit in a complex manner) to relations of production but are also related to civil society. "It is within civil society that various limitations are placed on the state, that it is substantially impotent to act in various ways and that this stems from 'civil life' and the 'mutual plundering' that occurs between the various social groups . . . . It is through the interposing of civil society that we can see that similar capitalist economies do not necessarily produce similar (legal and) state forms."[424] Once we interpose civil society and the plethora of social groupings it contains; the complex of personal and impersonal relations that characterise everyday life; and the elaborate interaction between state and non-state ordering and organisation, then it becomes much more difficult to talk of the relation between law and economy in terms of a close functional fit.[425] Law, society and economy cannot, therefore, be analysed in Pavlovian terms, whereby legal norms and institutions condition social and economic behaviour or vice-versa.

Other false assumptions ground simple functionalist analyses. For example, they tend not to differentiate between discrete social actors and different levels of abstraction. Human individuals, social classes and groups, the legal professions, the courts and the state are implicitly or explicitly treated the same in respect of their links with law and the material world. However, from the standpoint of most citizens for most of the time the law, instrumentally speaking, is a last resort, a costly, time-consuming, unfamiliar and unwelcome aberration which is utilised pragmatically and often is avoided if possible. It is not that anarchy in the sense of the absence of order or uniting principle prevails (though undoubtedly a degree of anarchy exists); but that other non-state or quasi-state systems of ordering and organisation may carry greater weight and, therefore, wholly or partially supplant the formal state law order in particular situations. For most citizens at most times, the relation between the state legal order and social and economic practice is problematic and not ongoing. However, from a different perspective or at a higher level of abstraction we may be able to detect the existence of causal connections or what has been called "causally significant analogies between instances . . . ."[426] We cannot assume that all causes in history operate through intentional, conscious, individual or group behaviour. In addition, it is often necessary to embark upon an objective structural analysis at a higher level of abstraction in order to explain legal and economic change (or order). The quest for the most profitable level (or combination of levels) at which to investigate continuity and discontinuity is a major problem in historico-social research. In part, it will depend upon the questions one is asking, what one is trying to describe and the hypotheses one wants to test. In other words, both micro and macro historico-social explanations require attention.

In respect of the macro-level, we have alluded to the important role of law and state in laying the foundations of a capitalist economy through changing definitions of property and ownership, and the re-classification of common or customary rights into civil or criminal wrongs; and that the courts tended to fear state intervention in the economy or the growing power of trade unions more than the rise of "monopoly capitalism". The nature of the economic order and of the distribution of property, power and wealth therein may have crucial implications for the actual content and form (as opposed to the face-value content) of legal freedoms. Consider, for example, Max Weber's discussion of freedom of contract and coercion:

"The development of legally regulated relationships towards contractual association and of the law itself toward freedom of contract . . . is usually regarded as signifying a decrease of constraint and an increase of individual freedom . . . . The possibility of entering with others into contractual relations the content of which is entirely determined by individual agreement, and likewise the possibility of making use in accordance with one's desire of an increasingly large number of type forms rendered available by the law for purposes of association in the widest sense of the word, has, as compared with the past, been immensely extended in modern law . . . . However, the extent to which this trend has brought about an actual increase of the individual's freedom to shape the conditions of his own life or to the extent to which, on the contrary, life has become more stereotyped in spite, or, perhaps, just because of this trend, cannot be determined simply by studying the development of formal legal institutions. The great variety of permitted contractual schemata and the formal empowerment to set the content of contracts in accordance with one's desires and independently of all official form patterns, in and of itself by no means makes sure that these formal possibilities will in fact be available to all and everyone. Such availability is prevented above all by the differences in the distribution of property as guaranteed by law. The formal right of a worker to enter into any contract whatsoever with any employer whatsoever, does not in practice represent for the employment seeker even the slightest freedom in the determination of his own conditions of work, and it does not guarantee him any influence on this process. It rather means, at least primarily, that the more powerful party in the market, i.e. normally the employer, has the possibility to set the terms, to offer the job, take it or leave it; and, given the normally more pressing economic need of the worker, to impose his terms upon him . . . . A legal order which contains ever so few mandatory and prohibitory norms and ever so many 'freedoms' and 'employments' can nonetheless in its practical effects, facilitate a quantitative and qualitative increase not only in coercion in general but quite specifically of authoritarian coercion."[427]

This quote underlines the existence of causal connections between the form and content of law and the distribution of property. Sometimes linkages of this kind may be manifest; more often perhaps, they are found to be latent. Some have discerned intellectual or structural parallels between the legal sphere and other social spheres or disciplines.[428] Several of these have already been referred to in this essay. An exemplary example of this approach is Christopher Hill's work on the convergence of science, history, law and puritanism in the 17th century - their shared concerns and ideas.[429] The discovery of homologous ideas or forms in law and other spheres need not necessarily result in a variant of those histories which regard law simply as a reflection of economic needs. As Hill argues, thinkers are part of society. If ideas are to "take off" then they must be useful to some groups in society. However, ideas also have a history of their own which may refract the influence of power, politics and ideologies on ideas and vice-versa.[430]

A major problem, therefore, for the future development of our subject is the construction and testing of analytic frameworks which are sensitive to continuity <u>and</u> discontinuity, function <u>and</u> disfunction (patent and latent) within and as between law (state and non-state) and material society. Such an enterprise will require a more theoretically informed practice of historical research and scholarship than has conventionally characterised the varieties of "history".[431] The militantly positivist-empiricist methodology of orthodox legal history echoes a larger tendency within historical writing generally: namely, that the prime task of historians is conceived as the ascertainment of facts. Gareth Stedman Jones has described the premises of this method as follows:

"Historical facts were analogous to the facts of natural science: discrete, atomic and supremely indifferent to the position of the observer. What the natural scientist could reveal by the use of the test-tube, microscope and experimental method, the historian could uncover through the use of archaeology, philology and painstaking textual criticism . . . . History was a science because it was composed of 'facts'."[432]

Yet, the accumulation of facts will not, of itself, resolve the major questions raised by the historical study of law and material society. Fact-collection is of course, not a neutral or unproblematic activity. The supposed separation of "facts" from "interpretation" has been exposed as erroneous.[433] All historical work imbibes (often implicitly) value judgments and hypotheses which in turn decide what is observed. Without a conscious theory, causal connections or discontinuities either will not suggest themselves, or will suggest too many at once which seem equally necessary to explore. The fact that we feel obliged to re-assert these oft-repeated observations is testimony, in itself, to the resilience of the positivist-empiricist tradition in English historical writing. As a consequence of this tradition: "British historians have largely remained impervious to the solutions put forward by Marxism, psycho-analysis, and classical sociology. Or else they have glimpsed them through the blurred light of caricature and vulgarisation. Thus, the ingrained assumptions of British historical method have never been thoroughly shaken . . . . The result is as weird as if a Newtonian physicist were to come across Einstein, admit that relativity was probably a factor of some importance, and then attempt to carry on as before, under the impression that the occasional acknowledgement would absolve him from the necessity of further thought about it."[434]

This statement is less true of English legal, economic and social history than it was when it was written just over ten years ago. However, at least in lawyers' legal history, history and theory still tend to be invoked as wholly distinct enterprises, as polar opposites, rather than as part of the same enterprise. It is not that history needs to become more sociological but that it needs to fashion a new conceptual universe. "The truth is that British historians, with very few exceptions . . . have never aimed to construct historical totalities. Every attempt to reconstruct the structural foundations of history has been assimilated by dissolution into discrete specialisations."[435] A principal virtue of our subject, as we have conceived it, is its holistic and inter-disciplinary character. Until the tradition of positivist-empiricist history is transcended and the historical enterprise is conceived in more holistic and inter-disciplinary terms, our knowledge of the historical relation between law and economy will not advance in real insight. Balkanisation as between and within disciplines has to be overcome if relevant institutions and practices are to be understood in their entirety and connections thus far overlooked are to be perceived.

To reject outright the positivist-empiricist method and to insist upon a more inter-disciplinary and theoretically informed history of law and material society does not necessarily entail the renunciation of a continually close involvement with historical detail. Neither does it automatically involve an insensitivity to our often woeful lack of data, nor the need to rescue for posterity the wealth of pertinent historical data before it is lost for ever. Indeed, we regard the sensitivity which, say, the best lawyer's legal history has shown in these matters as also a sine qua non of the historical sociology of law and economy.

If the positivist-empiricist method is to be rejected, so too is that strand of sociological history which ransacks secondary sources in order to "theorise the facts". Such work fails to produce new evidence or take old arguments further. Further, this tradition seems ". . . unaware that many of the simplest facts about capitalist development and the emergence of . . . (new forms of law, ordering and organisation) still await research. There is an almost touching positivism in . . . (their) belief that the 'facts' can simply be read off from . . . (one secondary source or another). High theorists . . . who descend from their eyries for quick swoops over the empirical terrain are unlikely to return to their nests with anything more than the musty grain of cliche unless they are willing to settle down among the stubble to peck away with the rest of us pigeons."[436] If the history of law and economy needs better theory, theories of law and economy are best developed, we believe, through continual and close involvement with empirical sources. As Arthur Stinchcombe put it, the ". . . great theorists descend to the level of . . . detailed analogies in the course of their work. Further they become greater theorists down there among the details, for it is the details that theorists in history have to grasp if they are to be any good."[437]

No one analytical framework or viewpoint is likely to provide all the answers, let alone the perfect model. As Kenneth Burke remarked, ". . . a way of seeing is always a way of not seeing."[438] This, in turn, means being sensitive to the weaknesses as well as to the strengths of one's own perspective - to what one's theories, hypotheses and methodologies leave out or obscure as well as to what they may illuminate. Multiple approaches are, therefore, essential for the realisation of an undogmatic history of law and material society. They might enable us to re-interpret existing data and question the validity of more traditional analyses. Comparative histories of law and economy would also constitute a formidable resource for both constructive and contrastive purposes.[439]

In short, the new legal history must escape from the confines of evolutionist and functionalist histories. To argue this is merely to recognise the limits of evolutionist and functionalist histories in explaining how people think and act. Important and parallel work by sociologists, historians and anthropologists is highly suggestive of the need to re-fashion the explanatory procedures of the social sciences so as to avoid the imposition of some inner rationality upon empirical materials. We would point, for example, to the great transformation of intellectual history, deriving from the work of

Dunn, Skinner and Pocock as well as historians of science notably Kuhn.[440] Particularly relevant to the intellectual history of law is the recent work of Burrow, Collini and Winch.[441] Also important is the work of social historians such as Ginsberg, Sewell and Stedman Jones on the languages of class and popular culture and the methodological doubts cast thereby on more traditional conceptions of historical explanation.[442] A significant manifestation of the concerns expressed here is also to be found in the new feminist history and the ensuing critical dialogue with the discourse of evolutionist or functionalist histories unable to acknowledge women's specific situations and concerns.[443] Also relevant are developments within anthropology and the resultant dialogue between historians and anthropologists, notably Geertz and Sahlins.[444] The work of Corrigan and Sayer, and the work of members of the American Critical Legal Studies Movement,[444a] has argued that law is internal to everyday life and thought; that law is a constitutive language, constitutive that is, of social and economic relations. This diverse body of work is relevant because of the doubts that it casts upon those large categories that are the stock in trade of evolutionist and functionalist histories: "public opinion", "consensus", "social evolution", "social and economic needs", "interests", "labour", "class", "economy" and "social control". This body of literature is suggestive of the kinds of methodologies and concerns that the new history of law and material society might fruitfully engage with and learn from.

The broader tasks and perspectives espoused in this essay inevitably have consequences for the kind of data that is the focus of study. A compass which recognises the plurality of law (state and non-state), for example, must transcend the study of law reports and legislation and devote attention to those sources more familiar to business, economic and social historians. The resources of state papers, company records, contemporary literature, oral history, the myriad of legal, quasi-legal and extra-legal documents such as or touching upon, marriage, divorce, wills, bankruptcy, indictments and so on, the advices and private law-making housed within the offices of the legal professions or public registries and the records of village communities are just some of the more obvious sources which require attention - and which in some cases have already begun to be utilised to great effect. Clearly, this is a colossal, not to say daunting, proposition; but it cannot be shirked. Historical writing, as one commentator has recently reminded us, is undoubtedly difficult work.[445] To achieve an inter-disciplinary history of law and material society, however, is especially demanding given its avowed concern with formidable problems of theory and method. To describe the kinds of continuity, discontinuity, refraction and mediation outlined in this essay greatly complicates the task of exposition and demands the formulation of new conceptual apparatuses and, therefore, of a more sensitive language than that currently at hand. Perhaps it was with these difficulties in mind that Graham Parker wrote of "The Masochism of the Legal Historian"![446] And yet, for all the difficulties of such an enterprise, there are heartening signs that an inter-disciplinary history of law and economy is beginning to develop more vigorously than at any previous point in time. Several people have observed a sudden blooming of wild flowers.[447] We hope that this volume will encourage others to enter this important and exciting field. We also hope that this essay has cast doubt upon the dominant tradition of English legal historiography: evolutionism and functionalism. The new history of law and material society must transcend this tradition. For example, it should try to tell us more about the extent to which law was imbricated in and constitutive of social and economic relations.[448] This is not an easy task. Whilst preliminary work has been undertaken much remains to be done. Nonetheless, there are positive signs that histories which escape the confines of the dominant tradition are beginning to emerge. A new history of law and material society is in the making.

NOTES

* David Sugarman and G.R. Rubin were jointly responsible for sections I, IIA, IIIA, IV, XA and XC.

David Sugarman was responsible for sections IIB, IIC, IIIB, V, XB, XD, XF-H, XII, XIIIB and XIV; and substantially responsible for sections VII, VIIIA, IX and XI.

G.R. Rubin was responsible for sections VI and VIIIB and XIIIA; and substantially responsible for section XE.

The bibliographical material in note 4 to aid further reading was prepared by David Sugarman.

David Sugarman would like to thank Morton J. Horwitz for his inspired teaching, and Léonie Sugarman and Esther Sugarman for their support and encouragement.

1. T.F.T. Plucknett, A Concise History of the Common Law, 5th edn. (London: Butterworth 1956).
2. Ibid, Part III, Ch.4.
3. J.N. Adams, et al, "Eighteenth Century Legal Sources", Durham University Journal, (forthcoming).
4. Major general works include:- (Various authors), Select Essays in Anglo-American Legal History (Boston: Little, Brown and Co., 1907), 3 volumes; B. Abel-Smith and R. Stevens, Lawyers and the Courts: A Sociological Study of the English Legal System 1750-1965 (London: Heinemann, 1967); A.H. Manchester, Modern Legal History 1750-1950 (London: Butterworth, 1980); Sir W. Holdsworth, A History of English Law (London: Methuen Ltd/ Sweet and Maxwell) 16 volumes, esp. Vols. X-XVI; J.P. Dawson, The Oracles of the Law (Ann Arbor: University of Michigan Law School, 1968); P.S. Atiyah, The Rise and Fall of Freedom of Contract (Oxford: Clarendon Press, 1979);

R. Stevens, Law and Politics: The House of Lords as a Judicial Body, 1800-1976 (London: Weidenfeld and Nicolson, 1979); O.R. McGregor, Social History and Law Reform (London: Stevens, 1981); A.V. Dicey, Law and Public Opinion in England During the 19th Century (London: Macmillan, 1914); R.F.V. Heuston, Lives of The Lord Chancellors, 1885-1940 (London: Oxford University Press, 1964); D. Duman, The Judicial Bench in England, 1727-1825, (London: Royal Historical Society, 1982); R. Porter, English Society in the Eighteenth Century (Harmondsworth: Penguin Books, 1982) pp.113-158; E. Foss, The Judges of England 9 Vols. (London: Longman, 1848-64); J.B. Atlay, The Victorian Chancellors 2 Vols., (London: Smith, Elder, 1906); A.W.B. Simpson (ed.) Biographical Dictionary of the Common Law (London: Butterworth, 1984); J.N. Adams and G. Averley, A Bibliography of 18th Century Legal Literature (Newcastle-upon-Tyne: Avero Publications, 1982); O. Kahn-Freund, editorial introduction to K. Renner, The Institutions of Private Law and their Social Functions (London: Routledge, 1949); B. Odgers et al, A Century of Law Reform (London: Macmillan, 1901); M. Weber, Economy and Society Vol.2,"Economy and Law", (eds. G. Roth and C. Wittich) (Berkley: University of California Press, 1978) pp.641-900. J.H. Baker, An Introduction to English Legal History (London: Butterworth, 1979) and A. Harding, A Social History of English Law (Harmondsworth: Penguin Books, 1966) are useful, introductory texts.

As regards modern criminal law, its institutions and the subject of crime and disorder, the literature has grown enormously in recent years. Important work includes: L. Radzinowicz, A History of English Criminal Law (London: Stevens, 1956-1968) 4 volumes; F.C. Mather, Public Order in the Age of the Chartists (Manchester: Manchester University Press, 1959); E. Midwinter, Law and Order in Early Victorian Lancashire (University of York, 1968); D. Philips, Crime and Authority in Victorian England (London: Croom Helm, 1977); D. Hay et al (eds), Albion's Fatal Tree: Crime and Society in 18th Century England (London: Allen Lane, 1977); E.P. Thompson, Whigs and

Hunters: The Origin of the Black Act (London: Allen Lane, 1977); J.S. Cockburn (ed), *Crime in England 1550-1800* (London: Methuen, 1977); M. Ignatieff, *A Just Measure of Pain: The Penitentiary in the Industrial Revolution, 1750-1850* (London: Macmillan, 1978); J. Brewer and J. Styles (eds) *An Ungovernable People: The English and Their Law in the 17th and 18th Centuries* (London: Hutchinson, 1980); V. Gatrell *et al* (eds), *Crime and The Law: The Social History of Crime in Western Europe* (London: Europa, 1980); J. Hall, *Theft, Law and Society* (Indianapolis: Bobbs-Merrill, 1952); G. Fletcher, *Rethinking Criminal Law* (Boston: Little, Brown and Co., 1978); V. Bailey (ed), *Policing and Punishment in 19th Century Britain* (London: Croom Helm, 1981); D. Jones, *Crime, Protest, Community and Police in 19th Century Britain* (London: R.K.P. 1982); R.W. Malcolmson, *Popular Recreations in English Society 1700-1850* (Cambridge: Cambridge University Press 1973); J. Stevenson, *Popular Disturbances in England, 1700-1870* (London: Longman, 1979). R.W. Malcolmson, *Life and Labour in England, 1700-1780* (London: Hutchinson, 1981) pp.108-135; C. Steedman, *Policing the Victorian Community: The Formation of English Provincial Police Forces, 1856-80* (London: Routledge, 1984); D. Hay, "War, Dearth and Theft: The Record of the English Courts", *Past and Present*, No.95, 1982; D. Hay, "The Criminal Prosecution in England and its Historians", *Modern Law Review*, 47, 1984, pp.1-29; B.J. Davey, *Lawless and Immoral: Policing a County 1835-1857* (Leicester: Leicester University Press, 1984); L.A. Knafla (ed.), *Crime and Criminal Justice in Europe and Canada* (Calgary: Wilfrid Laurier University Press, 1981); F. Munger, "The Suppression of Popular Gatherings in England 1800-1830, *American Journal of Legal History*, 25, 1981, pp.111-140; S. McConville, *A History of English Prison Administration, Vol.I* (London: Routledge, 1981); P.B. Munsche, *Gentlemen and Poachers: the English Game Laws 1670-1831* (Cambridge: Cambridge University Press, 1981); E. Stockdale, *Law and Order in Georgian Bedfordshire* (Bedford:

Bedfordshire Historical Record Society, 1982); C. Emsley, Policing and its Context, 1750-1870 (London: Macmillan, 1983); J.H. Langbein, "The Criminal Trial before the Lawyers", University of Chicago Law Review, 45, 1978, pp.263-316 and "Shaping the 18th Century Criminal Trial: A View of the Rider Sources", University of Chicago Law Review, 50, 1983, pp.1-136; J. Styles, "Sir John Fielding and the Problem of Criminal Investigation in 18th Century England", Transactions of the Royal Historical Society, 33, 5th series, 1983, pp.127-149 and "Embezzlement, Industry and Law in England, 1550-1980" in M. Berg et al (eds), Manufacture in Town and Country Before the Factory (Cambridge: Cambridge University Press, 1984); R. McGowen, "The Image of Justice and Reform of the Criminal Law in Early 19th Century England", Buffalo Law Review, 32, 1983, pp.89-125; P. King, "Decision-Makers and Decision-Making in the English Criminal Law, 1750-1800", Historical Journal, 27, 1984, pp.25-58; M. Brogden, The Police (London: Academic Press, 1982); M.E. De Lacy, "Country Prison Administration in Lancashire, 1690-1850", Ph.D., Princeton University, 1980; M.H. Tomlinson, "Victorian Prisons", Ph.D., Bedford College, London University, 1975; J.F. Stephen, A History of the Criminal Law of England, 3 Vols. (London: 1883). For overviews of the current state of the history of crime and the criminal law see: V. Bailey, "Crime, Criminal Justice and Authority in England", Bulletin of the Society for the Study of Labour History, No. 40, Spring 1980, pp.36-40; D. Hay, "Crime and Justice in 18th and 19th Century England" in N. Morris and M. Tonry (eds), Crime and Justice, (Chicago: University of Chicago Press, 1980), Vol.2, pp.45-84; D. Sugarman, J.N.J. Palmer and G.R. Rubin, "Crime, Law and Authority in 19th Century Britain", Middlesex Polytechnic History Journal, Vol.2, 1982; J.A. Sharpe, "The History of Crime in Late Medieval and Early Modern England: A Review of the Field", Social History, Vol.7, 1982, pp.187-204; D. Philips, " 'A Just Measure of Crime, Authority, Hunters and Blue Locusts': The 'Revisionist' Social History of

Crime and the Law in Britain, 1780-1850" in S. Cohen and A. Scull (eds), Social Control and the State (Oxford: Martin Robertson, 1983) pp.50-74; M. Ignatieff, "State, Civil Society and Total Institution: A Critique of Recent Social Histories of Punishment" in D. Sugarman (ed), Legality, Ideology and the State (London: Academic Press, 1983) pp.183-212; W.R. Cornish et al, Crime and the Law in Nineteenth Century Britain (Dublin: Irish Academic Press, 1978); O. Hufton, "Crime in Pre-Industrial Europe", International Association on the History of Crime and Criminal Justice Newsletter, No.4, July 1981, pp.8-35.

On the theme of law and economy, North American historical work is particularly suggestive for future research in England. As regards Canadian work, see R.C.B. Risk: "The 19th Century Foundations of the Business Corporation in Ontario", University of Toronto Law Journal, Vol.23, 1973, pp.270-306; "The Golden Age : The Law of the Market in Ontario in the 19th Century", ibid, Vol.26, 1976, pp.307-346; "The Last Golden Age: Property and Allocation of Losses in Ontario in the 19th Century", ibid, Vol.27, 1977, pp.199-239; and "The Law and the Economy in Mid-19th Century Ontario: A Perspective", ibid, 27, 1977, pp.403-438. Also important are D.H. Flaherty, (ed) Essays in the History of Canadian Law, Vols.1 and 2 (Toronto: University of Toronto Press, 1981 and 1983).

In respect to the United States, the relevant material is enormous. Some of the most useful and pioneering texts include: J.W. Hurst, Law and the Conditions of Freedom in the 19th Century United States, (Madison: University of Wisconsin Press, 1956) and Law and Economic Growth: the Legal History of the Lumber Industry in Wisconsin, 1836-1915, (Madison: University of Wisconsin Press, 1964); L.M. Friedman, Contract Law in America: A Social and Economic Case Study, (Madison: University of Wisconsin Press, 1965) and A History of American Law, (New York: Simon & Schuster, 1973); and M.J. Horwitz, The Transformation of American Law,

1780-1860 (Cambridge: Harvard University Press, 1977).

As regards the history of the legal professions in the modern period see: R. Robson, The Attorney in 18th Century England (Cambridge: Cambridge University Press, 1959); G. Holmes, Augustan England (London: Allen and Unwin, 1982) Ch.5; M. Birks, Gentlemen of the Law, (London: Stevens, 1960); M. Larsen, The Rise of Professionalism, (Berkeley: University of California Press 1977); H. Kirk, Portrait of a Profession, (London: Oyez, 1976); C. Brooks, "Some Aspects of Attorneys in England During the Late 16th and Early 17th Centuries", D. Phil thesis, Oxford University, 1978. Abel-Smith and Stevens supra. See also the notes accompanying section XII (below).

As regards the intellectual and political history of law in the period 1750-1914 much work remains to be done. Here, as in other areas, insofar as historians have been concerned with the law, their energies have concentrated upon earlier periods. On the Middle Ages see, for instance, the important work of Walter Ullman and on the Tudor period see the work of S.T. Bindoff, S.E. Thorne and, more recently, J.H. Baker's pathbreaking essay, The Reports of Sir John Spelman (London: Selden Society Vol.94, 1978). But it is the role of law in constitutional history, especially during the turmoil of the seventeenth century and the revolution in science and thought associated with that century, that has been afforded most attention. See for example, J.W. Gough, Fundamental Law in English Constitutional History (Oxford: Clarendon Press, 1955); J.G.A. Pocock, The Ancient Constitution and the Feudal Law (Cambridge: Cambridge University Press, 1957); D.W. Hanson, From Kingdom to Commonwealth (Cambridge, Mass: Harvard University Press, 1970); C. Ogilvie, The King's Government and the Common Law, 1471-1641 (Oxford: Blackwell, 1958); H. Nenner, By Colour of Law: Legal Culture and Constitutional Politics in England 1660-1689 (Chicago: Chicago University Press, 1975); C. Hill, Intellectual Origins of the English Revolution

(Oxford: Clarendon Press, 1980); B.J. Shapiro, Probability and Certainty in 17th Century England (Princeton: Princeton University Press, 1983); and W.R. Prest, The Inns of Court under Elizabeth I and the Early Stuarts, 1590-1640 (London: Longmans, 1972). The most important intellectual history of English law for the period 1750-1914 is P.S. Atiyah, The Rise and Fall of Freedom of Contract, supra. It contains an invaluable synthesis of and reference to pertinent literature in history, philosophy and economics as well as law. Other useful building-blocks include: A.V. Dicey, supra; C. Dumont, From Mandeville to Marx (London: University of Chicago Press, 1977); A.O. Hirschman, The Passions and the Interests (Princeton: Princeton University Press, 1977); G. Jones, Social Darwinism and English Thought (Brighton: Harvester, 1980); W.E. Houghton, The Victorian Frame of Mind, 1830-1870 (New Haven: Yale University Press, 1957); T.W. Heyck, The Transformation of Intellectual Life in Victorian England (London: Croom Helm, 1982); P. Corrigan (ed), Capitalism and State Formation (London: Quartet, 1980); E. Halevy, History of the English People in the 19th Century, Vols. 5 and 6 (London: Benn, 1932); H. Perkin, The Origins of Modern English Society 1780-1880 (London: Routledge, 1969) and "Individualism versus Collectivism in 19th Century Britain", Journal of British Studies, 17, 1977, pp.105-118; H.W. Arthurs, "Rethinking Administrative Law: A Slightly Dicey Business", Osgoode Hall Law Journal, 1979, pp.1-45; R.W. Gordon, "Holmes Common Law as Legal and Social Science", Hofstra Law Review, 94, 1981, pp.903-918; C. Russell, Science and Social Change 1700-1900 (London: Macmillan, 1983); J.W. Burrow, Evolution and Society (Cambridge: Cambridge University Press, 1966); J.W. Burrow, "The Village Community and the Uses of History in Late 19th Century England", in N. McKendrick (ed), Historical Perspectives (London: Europa, 1974), pp.255-284; J.W. Burrow, A Liberal Descent (Cambridge: Cambridge University Press, 1981); R.A. Cosgrove, The Rule of Law: Albert Venn Dicey,

Victorian Jurist (London: Macmillan, 1980); C. Harvie, The Lights of Liberalism (London: Allen Lane, 1976); N. Annan, "The Intellectual Aristocracy", in J.H. Plumb (ed.), Studies in Social History (Cambridge: Cambridge University Press, 1955), pp.243-287; C. Kent, Brains and Numbers (Toronto: Toronto University Press, 1978); M. Mandelbaum, History, Man and Reason (Baltimore: Johns Hopkins University Press, 1971); E. Halevy, The Growth of Philosophical Radicalism (London: Faber, 1928); P. Abrams, The Origins of British Sociology 1834-1914 (Chicago: Chicago University Press); G. Hawthorn, Enlightenment and Despair (Cambridge: Cambridge University Press, 1976); S. Collini, Liberalism and Sociology (Cambridge, Cambridge University Press, 1979); E. Ruben, "John Austin's Political Pamphlets 1824-1859", in E. Attwool (ed.), Perspectives in Jurisprudence (Glasgow: Glasgow University Press, pp.20-41; A.W.B. Simpson, "Innovation in 19th Century Contract Law", Law Quarterly Review, Vol.91, 1975, pp.247-52 and "The Rise and Fall of the Legal Treatise", University of Chicago Law Review, Vol.48, 1981, pp.632-79; M. De Wolfe Howe (ed), Holmes-Pollock Letters (Cambridge: Harvard University Press, 1941); F.H. Lawson, The Oxford Law School 1850-1965 (Oxford: Clarendon Press, 1968); A.V. Dicey, Can English Law be Taught at the Universities? (London: Macmillan, 1883); P. Stein, Legal Evolution (Cambridge: Cambridge University Press, 1980); C.H.S. Fifoot, Judge and Jurist in the Reign of Victoria (London: Stevens, 1959); L. Goldman, "The Origins of British 'Social Science' ", Historical Journal, 26, 1983, pp.587-616; H.G. Hanbury, The Vinerian Chair and Legal Education (Oxford: Blackwell, 1958); S. Hayes, The Edwardian Frame of Mind (Princeton: Princeton University Press, 1968); G. Feaver, From Status to Contract (London: Longman, 1969); I. Hont and M. Ignatieff (eds.), Wealth and Virtue (Cambridge: Cambridge University Press, 1983); P. Anderson, "Components of the National Culture", New Left Review, No.50, 1968, pp.3-58; HaaKonssen, The Science of the Legislator (Cambridge: Cambridge University Press, 1981); J.A. Colaiaco,

James Fitzjames Stephen and the Crisis of Victorian Thought (London: Macmillan, 1983); S. Collini, D. Winch and J. Burrow, That Noble Science of Politics (Cambridge: Cambridge University Press, 1983); G. Poggi, The Development of the Modern State (London: Hutchinson, 1978); W.H. Greenleaf, The British Political Tradition, 2 Vols. (London: Methuen, 1983); S. Rothblatt, The Revolution of the Dons (Cambridge: Cambridge University Press, 1968); W.L. Morison, John Austin (London: Edward Arnold, 1971); F. Harrison, On Jurisprudence and the Conflict of Laws (Oxford: Clarendon Press, 1919); A. Engle, From Clergyman to Don (Oxford: Oxford University Press, 1983); R. Cotterrell, "English Conceptions of the Role of Theory in Legal Analysis", Modern Law Review, 46, 1983, pp.681-699; F.W. Maitland, "Why the History of English Law is not Written", and "Law at the Universities" in his Collected Papers (Cambridge: Cambridge University Press, 1911, Vol.I, pp.480-497 and Vol.3, pp.419-431 respectively; A.J. Taylor, Laissez-faire and State Intervention in 19th Century Britain (London: Macmillan, 1972) and the literature on the "revolution of government" debate cited there; L.J. Hume, Bentham and Bureaucracy (Cambridge: Cambridge University Press, 1981); D. Little, Religion, Order and Law (Oxford: Clarendon Press, 1970); D. Boorstin, The Mysterious Science of Law (Cambridge: Harvard University Press, 1942); J.W. Jones, Historical Introduction to the Theory of Law (Oxford: Clarendon Press, 1940); R. Tuck, Natural Rights Theories (Cambridge: Cambridge University Press, 1979); E.P. Thompson, "The Pecularities of the English", in his The Poverty of Theory (London: Merlin, 1978); D. Sugarman, "The Legal Boundaries of Liberty: Dicey, Liberalism and Legal Science", Modern Law Review, 46, 1983, pp.102-11.

On the questions of theory, method and historiography see R.W. Gordon, "J. Willard Hurst and the Common Law Tradition in American Legal Historiography", Law and Society Review Vol.10, 1975, pp.9-55, "Historicism in Legal Scholarship", Yale Law Journal, Vol. 90, 1981, pp. 1017-1056, (book review), Harvard Law Review, Vol. 94, 1981, pp. 903-18 and "Critical Legal Histories", Stanford Law Review 1984 (forthcoming); M.J. Horwitz, "The Conservative Tradition in the writing of American Legal History", American Journal of Legal History, Vol. 7, 1973, pp. 275-294; M.V. Tushnet, "Perspectives on the Development of American Law", Wisconsin Law Review, 1977, pp.81-109; L.M. Friedman, "Some Problems and Possibilities of American Legal History" in H.J. Bass, (ed), The State of American History, (Chicago: Quadrangle, 1970), pp. 3-21; C. Woodard, "History, Legal History and Legal Education", Virginia Law Review, Vol.53, 1967, pp. 89-121; D. Sugarman, (book review), British Journal of Law and Society, Vol.7, 1980, pp.297-310 and "Theory and Practice in Law and History: A Prologue to the Study of the Relationship between Law and Economy from a Socio-Historical Perspective", in B. Fryer et al (eds), Law, State and Society, (London: Croom Helm, 1981), pp. 70-106; H.A. Scheiber, "Regulation, Property Rights and Definition of 'The Market' ", Journal of Economic History, 1981, pp. 103-9; W. Holt, "Morton Horwitz and the Transformation of American Legal History", William and Mary Law Review 23, 1983, pp.663-723; D. Hay, "The Criminal Prosecution in England and its Historians", supra; S. Diamond, "Legal Realism and Historical Method", Michigan Law Review 77, 1979, pp.784-94; H. Hartog, "Distancing Oneself from the 18th Century" in H. Hartog (ed.) Law in the Revolution and the Revolution in the Law (New York: New York University Press, 1981); E.P. Thompson, Whigs and Hunters, supra, pp.215-269; B. Mensch, "Freedom of Contract as Ideology", Stanford Law Review, 33, 1981, pp.753-70.

5. In this essay, we have used the term, an economic and social history of law as a short hand denoting the ideal of an interdisciplinary, holistic, history of law, economy and society i.e. a history which traverses business, economic, intellectual, legal and social history, in addition to the realms of "history"

and "sociology". Alternatively, we might have used the term "historical sociology" to describe the kind of creature we had in mind: see further, P. Abrams, Historical Sociology, (Near Shepton Mallet: Open Books, 1982).

6. P.S. Atiyah, The Rise and Fall of Freedom of Contract (Oxford: Clarendon Press, 1979).

7. For example, E. Fiddes, "Lord Mansfield and the Somersett Case", Law Quarterly Review, Vol.50, 1934, pp.499-511; J. Nadelhaft, "The Somersett Case and Slavery: Myth, Reality and Repercussions", Journal of Negro History Vol.51, 1966, pp.193-208; N. Wilson "Legal Attitudes to Slavery in 18th Century Britain", Race, Vol.11, 1970, pp.463-75; F.O. Shyllon, Black Slaves in Britain (Oxford: University Press, 1974); J. Walvin, Black and White: The Negro in English Society, 1555-1914 (London: Allen Lane, 1973); W.M. Wiecek, "Lord Mansfield and the Legitimacy of Slavery in the Anglo-American World" University of Chicago Law Review, Vol.42, 1975, pp.86-146; C.P. Bauer, "Law, Slavery and Somersett's Case", New York University Ph.D., 1973.

8. For example, R.W.L. Howells, "Priestly v Fowler and the Factory Acts", Modern Law Review, Vol.26, 1963, pp.367-95; H. Smith, "The Resurgent County Court in Victorian Britain", American Journal of Legal History, Vol.13, 1969, pp.126-38; D.G. Hanes, The First British Workmen's Compensation Act 1897, (New Haven: Yale University Press, 1968).

9. V. Berridge and N.S.B. Rawson, "Opiate Use and Legislative Control: A Nineteenth Century Case Study", Social Science and Medicine - Medical Psychology and Sociology, Vol.13, 1979, pp.351-63; idem, "War Conditions and Narcotics Control: The Passing of Defence of the Realm Act Regulation 40B", Journal of Social Policy, Vol.7, 1978, pp.285-304.

10. D.J.V. Jones, "A Dead Loss to the Community: The Criminal Vagrant in Mid-Nineteenth Century Wales", Welsh Historical Review, Vol.8, 1977, pp.312-42.

11. D. Dixon, "Class Law: The Street Betting Act of 1906", International Journal

of the Sociology of Law, Vol.8, 1980, pp.101-28.

12. V.M. Batzel, "Legal Monopoly in Liberal England: The Patent Controversy in the Mid-Nineteenth Century", Business History, Vol.22, 1980, pp.189-205.

13. R.M. Kesner, "The Transvaal, the Orange River Colony and the South African Loan and War Contribution Act of 1903", Albion, Vol.10, 1978, pp.28-33.

13a. But cf. H.F. Gospel and C. Littler (eds), Managerial Strategies and Industrial Relations: An Historical and Comparative Study (London: Heinemann, 1983).

14. See, for example, K. Renner, The Institutions of Private Law and Their Social Function (London: Routledge & Kegan Paul, 1949), and the discussion in the text, infra.

15. Sir H.S. Maine, Ancient Law (London: John Murray, 1861) p.170.

16. In the realm of sociological theory, this view is especially associated with Max Weber's writings on legal rationality. In fact, on closer investigation, Weber's view of the role and importance of contract law in capitalist societies is more complex and less functionalistic than many writers assume or imply. See further, R. Cotterrell, "The Development of Capitalism and the Formalisation of Contract Law" in B. Fryer et al (eds), Law, State and Society (London: Croom Helm, 1981) pp.54-69 and D. Sugarman, "Theory and Practice in Law and History: A Prologue to the Study of the Relationship between Law and Economy from a Socio-Historical Perspective" in B. Fryer et al, ibid, pp.70-106, 81-83.

17. L.M. Friedman, A History of American Law (New York: Simon & Schuster, 1973), p.233.

18. The following account of the development of partnership and company law is drawn from D. Sugarman, Company Law and the Rise of Capitalism, (Unpublished, 1982). We are grateful to Daphne Glick for sharing her research on partnership.

Legal impediments also limited the impact the Bank of England could have on the growth of industry and the development of joint stock banking in England and Wales. Yet, the state of the law does not appear to have significantly inhibited credit facilities in Britain. As one writer puts it, in the whole context of the money market British banking legislation ". . . worked pragmatically . . . (and was) flexible enough not to impede expansion . . .": T. Kemp, Historical Patterns of Industrialization, (Harlow: Longman, 1978), p.75.

19. P.L. Payne, British Entrepreneurship in the 19th Century, (London: Macmillan, 1974), p.17. The reference to Marshall is A. Marshall, Industry and Trade, (London: Macmillan, 1923), p.314.

20. The reasons for the tenacity of unincorporated associations are complex. They include: the fact that capital needs could mostly be met without incorporation; the flexibility of the partnership; the fraudulent and speculative connotations associated with companies and limited liability; the desire for privacy (and a corresponding fear that incorporation might herald state interference) - see further, F.W. Maitland, "Trust and Corporation", in The Collected Papers of F.W. Maitland (Cambridge: Cambridge University Press, 1911), Vol.III, pp.321-60); and the desire to keep the business "in the family" (and the corresponding fear that incorporation might impede this goal. The Great Depression of 1873-96 graphically highlighted the fragile nature of unincorporated associations and precipitated a flood of incorporations so as to secure the benefits of limited liability. In this period, it was gradually apprehended that the corporate form could achieve all the attributes of unincorporated associations enumerated above with the advantage of limited liability. Thus, the growth of de facto private or close companies, a trend unintended by the original Companies Acts, but sanctioned by the courts in the celebrated case of Salomon and Co. v Salomon (1897) A.C. 22: see infra.

21. British Parliamentary Papers (BPP), 1866 (3634) XXXIII, River Commissioners

1st Report (River Thames) pp.16-17.

22. See, for example, D.M. Provine, "Balancing Pollution and Property Rights: A Comparison of the Development of English and American Nuisance Law" Anglo-American Law Review, Vol.7, 1978, pp.31-53; cf. R.C.B. Risk, "The Last Golden Age: Property and the Allocation of Losses in Ontario in the Nineteenth Century", University of Toronto Law Journal, Vol.27, 1977, pp.199-239.

23. See D. Philips, Crime and Authority in Victorian England (London: Croom Helm, 1977), Ch.4.

24. On the contemporary complaints of traders that litigation was too slow and expensive see R.B. Ferguson, "The Adjudication of Commercial Disputes and the Legal System in Modern England", British Journal of Law and Society, Vol.7, 1980, pp.141-157, esp. 142-3 and B. Abel-Smith and R. Stevens, Lawyers and the Courts: A Sociological Study of the English Legal System, 1750-1965 (London: Heinemann, 1967) pp.79-110.

    See also H. Bellenden Ker's, Report on the Law of Partnership, (B.P.P., Vol.XLIV, 399) of 1837 with its frequent references to demands for tribunals of commerce; and J. Wade, The Black Book (London: Effingham Wilson, Royal Exchange, rev. ed., 1832, reprinted 1970), ch.viii for a contemporary critique of lawyers and the courts.

25. Cf. L.L. Fuller, Legal Fictions (Stanford: Stanford University Press, 1967).

26. O. Kahn-Freund, "The Illegality of a Trade Union", Modern Law Review, Vol. 7, 1944, pp. 192-204.

27. Infra.

28. Infra.

29. For an important American study of the relation between private ordering, the state legal order (courts, administrative agencies) and government, which illustrates the quasi-public nature of the power exercised by private organizations, see J. Laurie, The Chicago Board of Trade, 1859-1905: The

Dynamics of Self-Regulation, (Urbana: University of Illinois Press, 1979).

30. See further, R.B. Ferguson, "The Adjudication of Commercial Disputes and the Legal System in Modern England", British Journal of Law and Society, Vol.7, 1980, pp.141-157 and infra. Also, D. Sugarman, Company Law and the Rise of Capitalism (Unpublished, 1982).

31. See, for example, H.L.A. Hart, The Concept of Law, (Oxford: Clarendon Press, 1961) esp. Chaps. II, III and V.

32. See, further, H.W. Arthurs, "Special Courts, Special Law: Legal Pluralism in 19th Century England" infra; G. Frug, "The City as a Legal Concept", Harvard Law Review, Vol.93, 1980, pp.1059-1154; E. Ennen, The Medieval Town (Amsterdam: North Holland Press, 1979); O. Gierke, Political Theories of the Middle Age (Cambridge: Cambridge University Press 1900); F. Gilbert (ed), The Historical Essays of Otto Hintze (New York: Oxford University Press, 1975) pp.302-356; V.G. Kiernan, "State and Nation in Western Europe", Past and Present, 31, 1963, pp.20-38; H.J. Laski, "The Early History of the Corporation in England", Harvard Law Review, 30, 1917, pp.588-603; Sir H.S. Maine, Ancient Law (London: John Murray, 1861) and Lectures on the Early History of Institutions (London: John Murray, 1874); F.W. Maitland, Township and Borough (Cambridge: Cambridge University Press, 1898), "Translators Introduction" to O. Gierke, Political Theories of the Middle Age (Cambridge: Cambridge University Press, 1900) and "The Corporation Sole", "The Crown as Corporation", "Trust and Corporation", "Moral Personality and Legal Personality", in The Collected Papers of F.W. Maitland, (Cambridge: Cambridge University Press, 1911) Vol.III, pp.210-229,Vol.II, pp.244-269, Vol.III, pp.321-360 and Vol.III, pp.304-320 respectively; G. Poggi, The Development of the Modern State: A Sociological Investigation (London: Hutchinson, 1978); F. Braudel, Afterthoughts on Material Civilization and Capitalism (Baltimore: Johns Hopkins University

Press, 1977) pp.85-99; E.P. Thompson, "The Moral Economy of the English Crowd in the 18th Century" Past and Present, 50, 1971, pp.76-109 and "18th Century Society", Social History 3, 1978, pp.133-165 esp., at 163; R.M. Unger, Law in Modern Society (New York: The Free Press, 1976) pp.66-76; M. Rheinstein (ed), Max Weber on Law in Economy and Society (Cambridge: Harvard University Press, 1954) pp.140-191; P. Vinogradoff, Villeinage in England, (London: Oxford University Press, 1892) and "Juridical Persons" in The Collected Papers of Paul Vinogradoff (Oxford: Clarendon Press, 1928) Vol.II, pp.328-340; D. Sugarman, Company Law and the Rise of Capitalism (Unpublished, 1982). See also the discussion of "Property" infra.

33. K. Polanyi, The Great Transformation: The Political and Economic Origins of Our Time (Boston: Beacon Press, 1944), p.140. See also the discussion "Law, State and Economic Interests" infra.

34. D.Sugarman, Company Law and the Rise of Capitalism, (Unpublished, 1982).

35. See further, M.S. Larsen, The Rise of Professionalism: A Sociological Analysis (Berkley: University of California Press, 1977), discussed by R. Abel, "The Rise of Professionalism", British Journal of Law and Society, Vol.6, 1979, pp.82-98.

36. See, for example, E. Spring, "The Settlement of Land in 19th Century England", American Journal of Legal History, Vol.8, 1964, pp.209-223. See also the essays by Chesterman, English and Spring infra.

37. See, for example, A.D. DuBois, The English Business Company After the Bubble Act: 1720-1800, (Cambridge: Harvard University Press, 1938) pp.3-7, 19-20, 47 n.23, 52 n. 61, 402 n. 99 and 100.

38. See, for example, B.C. Hunt, The Development of the Business Corporation in England, 1800-1867 (Cambridge: Harvard University Press, 1936), pp.46-48.

39. Cf. W.L. Guttsman, The British Political Elite (London: MacGibbon & Kee, 1963) and G. Wootton, Pressure Groups in Britain, 1720-1970, (London: Allen Lane, 1975).

40. W.J. Ashley, The Economic Organization of England (Longman: 1914); P.S. Atiyah, The Rise and Fall of Freedom of Contract (Oxford: Clarendon Press, 1979), esp. Part II; L.M. Friedman, Contract Law in America: A Social and Economic Case Study (Madison: University of Wisconsin Press, 1965), pp.15-26; J.W. Hurst, Law and the Conditions of Freedom in the 19th Century United States, (Madison: University of Wisconsin Press, 1956), pp.3-32; M.J. Horwitz, The Transformation of American Law, 1780-1860, (Cambridge: Harvard University Press, 1979) pp.160-210; G. Gilmore, The Death of Contract (Columbus: Ohio State University Press, 1974) pp.5-53; O. Kahn-Freund, "Blackstone's Neglected Child: The Contract of Employment", Law Quarterly Review, Vol.93, 1977, pp.508-528. Cf. A.W.B. Simpson, "The Horwitz Thesis and the History of Contracts", University of Chicago Law Review, Vol.46, 1979, pp.533-601.

41. See generally, M.J. Horwitz, The Transformation of American Law, 1780-1860, (Cambridge: Harvard University Press, 1979), pp.188-210; O Kahn-Freund, "Introduction" to K. Renner, The Institutions of Private Law and Their Social Functions (London: Routledge & Kegan Paul, 1949) pp.27-30; M. Rheinstein, Max Weber on Law in Economy and Society (Cambridge: Harvard University Press), pp.188-191; J.P. Dawson, "Economic Duress - An Essay in Perspective", Michigan Law Review, Vol.45, 1947, pp.253-271; M. Cain and A. Hunt, Marx and Engels on Law (London: Academic Press, 1979) pp.101-107; D. Simon, "Master and Servant", in J. Saville (ed), Democracy and the Labour Movement (London: Lawrence & Wishart, 1954) pp.160-200; R. Stevens, Law and Politics: The House of Lords as a Judicial Body 1800-1976 (London: Weidenfeld and Nicolson, 1979) pp.138-143 and 160-164; B.W. Napier, "The Contract of Service: The Concept and its Application", (Cambridge University Ph.D., 1975) Ch.2-5; W. Friedmann Law in a Changing Society (Harmondsworth: Penguin Books, 1972) pp.119-160. Cf.

J.N. Adams, "The Standardisation of Commercial Contracts, or the Contractualisation of Standard Forms", Anglo-American Law Review, Vol.7, 1978, pp.136-154 and "The Common Carrier in Legal History" (1979, forthcoming); A.W.B. Simpson, "The Horwitz Thesis and the History of Contracts", University of Chicago Law Review, Vol.46, 1979, pp.533-601.

42. Horwitz, ibid, p.210. See also A.V. Dicey, Law and Public Opinion in England During the 19th Century (London: Macmillan, 1914) pp.192-193 who argued that the new labour law of the early 19th century was premised upon ". . . the idea that the sale or purchase of labour should be as entirely a matter of free contract as the sale or purchase of boots and shoes."

43. Our discussion of the history of English company law draws upon D. Sugarman, Company Law and the Rise of Capitalism (Unpublished, 1982).

44. On the rise of legal formalism see P.S. Atiyah, supra, n.4, pp.388-397 and 660-680; R. Stevens, supra, n.4, p.77; M.J. Horwitz, supra, n.4, pp.253-266. Cf. R.B. Ferguson, "The Horwitz Thesis and Common Law Discourse in England", Oxford Journal of Legal Studies 3, 1983, 34-58.

45. See Salomon and Co. v. Salomon (1897) A.C. 22. Robert Stevens, ibid p.137, interprets Salomon as having decided that: "The company was . . . to be sacrosanct." O. Kahn-Freund referred to Salomon as a "calamitous" decision: Modern Law Review, Vol.7, 1944, pp.52-64, 54.

46. See W.R. Cornish, "Legal Control Over Cartels and Monopolization 1880-1914: A Comparison" in N. Horn and J. Jocka (eds), Law and the Formation of the Big Enterprises in the 19th and Early 20th Centuries (Gottingen: Vandenhoeck & Ruprecht, 1979), pp.277-305; L. Hannah, The Rise of the Corporate Economy (London: Methuen, 1976) pp.8-29; M. Keller, "Regulation of Large Enterprise" in A.D. Chandler Jr., and H. Daems (eds), Managerial Hierarchies: Comparative Perspectives on the Rise of the Modern Industrial Enterprise (Cambridge: Harvard University Press, 1980), pp.161-181; W. Letwin, Law and Economic Policy in America: The Evolution

of the Sherman Act, (Edinburgh: Edinburgh University Press, 1966), pp.2-99; B. Abel-Smith and R. Stevens, Lawyers and the Courts: A Sociological Study of the English Legal System 1750-1965 (London: Heinemann, 1967) pp.111-125; R. Stevens, Law and Politics: The House of Lords as a Judicial Body 1800-1976 (London: Weidenfeld and Nicolson, 1979) pp.158-164.

47. W.R. Cornish, ibid, p.297.

48. S. Macaulay, "Non-Contractual Relations in Business: A Preliminary Study", American Sociological Review, Vol.28, 1963, pp.55-66 and "Elegant Models, Empirical Pictures and the Complexities of Contract", Law and Society Review, XI, 1977, pp.507-528. See also H. Beale and T. Dugdale, "Contracts Between Businessmen: Planning and the Use of Contractual Remedies", British Journal of Law and Society, Vol.2, 1975, pp.45-60.

49. R.B. Ferguson, "The Adjudication of Commercial Disputes and the Legal System in Modern England", British Journal of Law and Society, 7, 1980, pp.141-157, 154-155.

50. Infra.

51. M. Cain, "Where Are The Disputes? A Study of a First Instance Civil Court in the U.K.", in M. Cain and K. Kalcsar (eds), The Study of Disputes, (Budapest and London: Hungarian Academy of Science and Pergamon Press, 1982), Ch.viii, p.13. We are grateful to Maureen Cain for allowing us to see her essay prior to publication.

52. See, generally, ibid.

53. See, for example, Anon., "Tribunals of Commerce", Dublin University Magazine, Vol.85, March 1875, pp.257-65; cf. H.W. Arthurs, "Commercial Disputes" (unpublished; n.d.). We are grateful to Professor Arthurs for allowing us to see his paper prior to publication.
See generally, E.S. Wolaver, "The Historical Background of Commercial Arbitration", University of Pennsylvania Law Review, 83, 1934, pp.132-146.

54. See Rubin "Law, Poverty and Imprisonment for Debt", infra.

55. S. Spitzer, "Notes Toward a Theory of Punishment and Social Control" in S. Spitzer (ed), Research in Law and Sociology, Vol.2, (Greenwood: J.A.I. Press, 1979), pp.207-229, 208. The quote is from M. Foucault, Discipline and Punish (London: Penguin Books, 1977), p.24.

56. C.H.S. Fifoot, Lord Mansfield (Oxford: Clarendon Press, 1936); E. Heward, Lord Mansfield (Chichester: Barry Rose, 1980).

57. A distinction must, however, be drawn between economic practice and economic ideas in relation to legal change. Thus, while Atiyah, supra, n.4, can demonstrate the link between economic thought and contract law in the 19th century, he holds back from stepping into the murkier waters of economic practice and thus refrains from any attempt to relate the development of economic law to what businessmen actually did.

58. Cited in Lord Bowen, "Progress in the Administration of Justice During the Victorian Period" in (Various Authors), Select Essays in Anglo-American Legal History (Boston: Little, Brown and Co., 1907), Vol.I, pp.516-557, 529. This echoes Malynes' advice to merchants that: ". . . by the common law one partner cannot proceed against another; and in Chauncerie the suits may be prolonged for the life of a man . . .": T. Malynes, Lex Mercatoria (London: Adam Islip, 1622) p.211.

58a. On the inadequacy of the common law and its courts, in commercial matters relative to the Privy Council and Chancery see J.P. Dawson, A History of Lay Judges (Cambridge: Harvard University Press, 1960), pp. 167-8 and D.E.C. Yale, "A View of the Admiral Jurisdiction", in D. Jenkins (ed), Legal History Studies 1972, (Cardiff, University of Wales Press, 1975), pp.87-109.

59. M.J. Horwitz, The Transformation of American Law, 1780-1860 (Cambridge: Harvard University Press, 1977), pp.xiv-xvi, 99-101. Cf. R. Ely, Property and Contract in Their Relation to the Distribution of Wealth, (New York: Macmillan, 1914) and R. Pessen, "Wealth in America Before 1865" in W. Rubinstein (ed), Wealth and the Wealthy in the Modern World (London:

Croom Helm, 1980), pp.165-179.

60. Ibid, p.xv. Cf. D. Sugarman, (Book Review), British Journal of Law and Society, Vol.7, 1980, pp.297-310 and W. Holt, "Morton Horwitz and the Transformation of American Legal History", William and Mary Law Review, Vol.23, 1982, pp. 663-723.

61. Cf. B.C. Hunt, The Development of the Business Corporation in England, 1800-1867, (Cambridge: Harvard University Press, 1936), pp.30-44; F.W. Maitland, "Trust and Corporation in The Collected Papers of F.W. Maitland, (Cambridge: Cambridge University Press, 1911), pp.321-360; A.D. DuBois, The English Business Company After The Bubble Act, 1720-1800, (Cambridge: Harvard University Press, 1938), pp.2-3, 44-47, 381-385; L. Hannah, The Rise of The Corporate Economy, (London: Methuen, 1976), pp.8-29; D. Sugarman, Company Law and the Rise of Capitalism (Unpublished, 1982).

62. See further the discussion of property infra, and the essays by Chesterman, English and Spring infra.

63. In the remainder of this paragraph and the next we have been especially assisted by the discussion of the history of British patents contained in W.R. Cornish, Intellectual Property, (London: Sweet & Maxwell, 1981), pp.79-84. See also H.G. Fox, Monopolies and Patents: A Study of the History and Future of the Patent Monopoly (Toronto: University of Toronto Press, 1974); E.W. Hulme,"The Early History of the English Patent System", in Various Authors, Selected Essays in Anglo-American Legal History (Boston: Little, Brown and Co., 1913), Vol.3, pp.117-147; E. Robinson, "James Watt and the Law of Patents", Technology and Culture, 1972, pp.201-249; V.M. Batzel, "Legal Monopolies in Liberal England: The Patent Controversy in the Mid-19th Century", 1980, Business History, pp. 189-205. For the common law's attack on patented monopolies see D'arcy v Allen (1602) 11 Co. Rep. 84b.

64. W.R. Cornish supra, n.63, p.81 n.17.

65. Ibid, p.81 and n. 18.

66. On inventions generally, see, for example, A.E. Musson and E. Robinson Science and Technology in the Industrial Revolution (Manchester: University Press, 1969).

67. First published in book form in June 1857.

68. W.R. Cornish supra, n.63, p.82 n. 22.

69. See The Patent Law Amendment Act 1852.

70. W.R. Cornish, supra, n.63, p.82. Further reforms were effected by the Patent Acts of 1902, 1949 and 1977.

71. See Cornish ibid, p.84. For a similar tendency in respect of the law of copyright in the 19th century see Cornish ibid, pp.295-8.

72. C. Erikson, British Industrialists: Steel and Hosiery 1850-1950, (London: Cambridge University Press, 1959), p.151.

73. L. Levi, History of British Commerce (London: John Murray, 1880), p.9.

74. A. Harding, A Social History of English Law (Harmondsworth: Penguin, 1966), p.326.

75. D. Sugarman, Company Law and the Rise of Capitalism (Unpublished, 1982).

76. See, generally, J. Milnes Holden, The History of Negotiable Instruments in English Law (London: Athlone Press, 1955).

77. Cf. J. Hall, Theft, Law and Society (New York: Bobbs, Merrill & Co., 1952).

78. R. Munday, "A Legal History of the Factor", Anglo-American Law Review, Vol.6, 1977, pp.221-62.

79. W.R. Cornish, Intellectual Property (London: Sweet and Maxwell, 1981).

80. A. Howkins, "Economic Crime and Class Law: Poaching and the Game Laws, 1840-1880", in S.B. Burman and B.E. Harrell-Bond (eds) The Imposition of Law (New York: Academic Press, 1979), Ch.15; P.B. Munsche, Gentlemen and Poachers: The English Game Laws, 1671-1831, (London: Cambridge University Press, 1981); D. Jones, Crime, Protest, Community and Police in 19th Century Britain, (London: Routledge and Kegan Paul, 1982); D. Hay, "Poaching and the Game Law on Channock Chase" in D. Hay et al (eds), supra

n.4, pp.189-254.

81. J. Styles, "Industrial Pilfering and the Law in the Eighteenth Century" (unpublished, 1979) and R. Samuel, "Industrial Crime in the 19th Century", Bulletin of the Society for the Study of Labour History, No.25, Autumn 1972, pp.7-8.

82. E.J. Hobsbawm, Industry and Empire, (Harmondsworth, Penguin Books, 1969), pp.17-19; Sir W. Holdsworth, "A Neglected Aspect of the Relations Between Economic and Legal History", Economic History Review, Vol.1 (1st series), 1927, pp.114-123.

83. Cf. D.O. Wagner "Coke and the Rise of Economic Liberalism", Economic History Review, Vol.6 (1st series), 1935-6, pp.30-44; cf. idem, "The Common Law and Free Enterprise: An Early Case of Monopoly", ibid, Vol.7, 1936-7, pp.217-20.

84. S.F.C. Milsom, Historical Foundations of the Common Law (London: Butterworths, 1981), p.99.

85. A. Offer, Property and Politics 1870-1914: Landownership, Law, Ideology and Urban Development in England (Cambridge: Cambridge University Press, 1981), p.11.

86. The Cambridge Economic History of Europe, (Cambridge: Cambridge University Press, 1952) Vol.2, pp.487-8.

87. G.A. Cohen, Karl Marx's Theory of History: A Defence (Oxford: Oxford University Press, 1978), pp.224 and 230.

88. E.P. Thompson, Whigs and Hunters (London: Allen Lane, 1975), p.261.

89. H.A. Scheiber (1981) Jr. Ec. Hist. 104.

90. See, for example, J. Saville, "Primitive Accumulation and Early Industrialisation in Britain" (eds) R. Miliband and J. Saville, The Socialist Register, (1970), Vol.4, 1969, pp.247-71, 252 and P. Sweezy et al, The Transformation From Feudalism to Capitalism (London: New Left Books, 1976).

91. Capital Vol.I, p.672 and 694.

92. Ibid. 668.

93. Capital, Vol.III, (London: Penguin Books, 1980) pp.616.

94. Grundrisse (Penguin ed. 1973) p.252.

95. K. Marx, supra n.87, pp.671 and 689.

Marx (and Weber) were also at pains to stress that changes in society "do not develop out of nothing; they develop "from within and in antithesis to the existing development of production and the intellectual relations of property: Grundrisse, ibid, p.278.

96. F. Engels, The Origin of the Family, Private Property and the State (1902 ed. Chicago), p.96.

97. Clearly, this is a rather broad generalisation. For a helpful outline of Weber's views on the rise of absolute private property see, A. MacFarlane, The Origins of English Individualism (Oxford: Blackwell, 1978), pp.44-52.

98. D.S. Landes, The Unbound Prometheus: Technological Change and Industrial Development in Western Europe from 1750 to the Present (Cambridge: Cambridge University Press, 1969), p.15.

99. Ibid.

100. Ibid, pp.15-16.

101. Ibid, p.16.

102. Ibid, pp.16-17.

103. See, for example, C.B. Macpherson, The Political Theory of Possessive Individualism (Oxford: Clarendon Press, 1962), (ed)., Property: A Controversy (New York: Pantheon, 1973), Democratic Theory: Essays in Retrieval (Oxford: Clarendon Press, 1973), (ed)., Property: Mainstream and Critical Positions (Oxford: Blackwell, 1978) and "Capitalism and the Changing Concept of Property", in E. Kamenka and R.S. Neale (eds), Feudalism, Capitalism and Beyond, (London: Edward Arnold, 1975), pp.104-125.

104. "Capitalism and the Changing Concept of Property", ibid, pp.108-109.

105. For an earlier treatment of property as a right see infra.

106. Macpherson, supra, n.104, p.111.

107. D.C. North and R.P. Thomas, The Rise of the Western World: A New Economic History (Cambridge: Cambridge University Press, 1973).

108. A. Macfarlane, The Origins of English Individualism (Oxford: Blackwell, 1978).

109. North and Thomas supra, n.107, pp.62-4. This they argue was in part influenced by the increasing economic value of land. They rightly point out that in practice, from the beginning of the manorial system, "land was never a completely 'common property' resource in the sense that economists use that phrase. Customs and precedents limited its usage to preclude overgrazing and other hazards implicit in common use", (p.19). This usefully warns against the uncritical employment of the term "common property".

110. Ibid, p.64. See also O. Kahn-Freund, "Introduction" to K. Renner, The Institutions of Private Property and their Social Functions, (London: RKP, 1949), pp. 19-24; and R.M. Hartwell, "The Industrial Revolution and Economic Growth" and "Legal Change and Legal Reform and Economic Growth Before and During the Industrial Revolution" in M. Flinn (ed), Proceedings of the 7th International History Congress (Edinburgh: Edinburgh University Press, 1978), Vol.2, pp.216-222.

111. North and Thomas, supra, n.107, p.63.

112. Ibid, p.64.

113. In this respect, they are rightly more cautious than Macfarlane vis-a-vis their recognition of a long period of transition.

114. Supra n.108, p.189.

115. Ibid. pp.195-6. Surprisingly, Macfarlane ignores the work of North and Thomas. For an excellent discussion of Macfarlane's work, see P. Abrams, Historical

Sociology (Open Books, near Shepton Mallet: 9, 182) pp.320-6. Important critiques of Macfarlane's thesis include:

P. Corrigan 1981, Sociological Review, pp.465-70 and R. Hilton "Individualism and the English Peasantry", New Left Rev, 120, 1980, pp.109-11. In particular, M. Chaytor's work concludes that perhaps the chronology and analysis espoused by Marx and conventional historiography are correct. See M. Chaytor "Household and Kinship: Ryton in the Late 16th and 17th Centuries", History Workshop Journal, 10, 1980, pp.25-60. Chaytor's critique has stimulated a considerable response, see R. Wall, letter, History Workshop Journal, 12, 1981, p.199; K. Wrightson, "Household and Kinship in 17th century England" ibid 155, and O. Harris, "Households and their Boundaries", History Workshop Journal, 13, 1982, pp.143-152.

116. See also Hartwell, supra, n.110.

117. See further J.W. Burrow's excellent, " 'The Village Community' and the Uses of History in Late 19th Century England" in N. McKendrick (ed), Historical Perspectives: Studies in English Thought and Society (London: Europa, 1974) pp.255-284 especially p.256.

118. R.W. Gordon, "Some Thoughts on Legal Form and Social Practice in American Legal Historiography" (unpublished, October 1978), pp.2 and 3. We are grateful to Robert Gordon for allowing us to quote from this manuscript.

119. See P.S. Atiyah, "The Rise and Fall of Freedom of Contract" (Oxford: Clarendon Press, 1979) pp.89-90; A. Offer supra, n.4, pp.2 and 401 et seq; E.P. Thompson, "The Grid of Inheritance: A Comment" in J. Goody et al (eds), Family and Inheritance (Cambridge: Cambridge University Press, 1976) pp.328-60.

120. See A. Offer ibid.

121. Viscount Canterbury v. Att-Gen. (1842) 1 Ph.306 and Tobin v. The Queen (1864) 16 C.B.N.S. 310.

122. See the Petitions of Rights Act 1860.

123. The above account of Crown privilege largely draws upon H.W.R. Wade, Administrative Law (Oxford: Oxford University Press, 1967) p.253 et seq.

124. See J. Levin, The Charter Controversy in the City of London 1660-1688 and its Consequences (London: Athlone Press, 1969).

125. See further our earlier discussion of the development of Patent Law infra, pp18-20.

126. P.S. Atiyah, supra, n.4, pp.61-67 and 139-193; E.P. Thompson, "The Moral Economy of the English Crowd in the 18th Century", Past and Present No. 50, pp.76-109; Thompson, supra, n.119; C. Fisher, Custom, Work and Market Capitalism, (London: Croom Helm, 1981).

127. Probably its most famous portrayal occurs in Dickens' Bleak House, first published in book form in September 1853.

128. See A. Offer, supra, n.4, Ch. 2.

129. R.S. Neale, " 'The Bourgeoisie, Historically, has Played a Most Revolutionary Part' ", in E. Kamenka and R.S. Neale (eds), Feudalism, Capitalism and Beyond (London: Edward Arnold, 1975) pp.84-103.

130. Ibid, p.95.

131. Ibid.

132. Ibid, p.99.

133. Ibid, pp.98-102.

134. G.L. Haskins, "Extending the Grasp of the Dead Head: Reflections on the Origins of the Rule Against Perpetuities", University of Pennsylvania Law Review, Vol.126, pp.19-46.

135. 3 Ch. Cas. 1, 22 Eng. Rep.931 (1682).

136. Supra, n.4, p.21

137. Ibid, p.46.

138. Ibid, p.27.

139 For examples of tension between new property rights and freedom of contract see Cornish, supra n.63, pp.297-8 and 499-500.

140. P.S. Atiyah, supra n.4, p.88.

141. Ibid. For an excellent introduction to the nature and character of the strict settlement see B. English and J. Saville, Strict Settlement: A Guide for Historians (Hull; Hull University Press, 1983).

142. See Chesterman, English and Spring infra.

143. See, for example, A. Offer supra n.4; H.J. Perkin, "Land Reform and Class Conflict in Victorian Britain" in J. Butt and I.F. Clarke (ed), The Victorians and Social Protest (Newton Abbot: David and Charles, 1973) pp. 177-217; F.M.L. Thompson, "Land and Politics in England in the 19th Century", Transactions Royal Historical Society 5th series, 1965, pp.15; D.A. Reeder, "The Politics of Urban Leaseholds in Late Victorian England", International Review Social History, Vol.6, 1961, pp.413-30.

144. E. Spring "Landowners, Lawyers and Land Law Reform in 19th Century England", American Journal of Legal History, Vol.21, 1977, pp.40-59, 41-2.

145. Cited in A. Offer, supra n.4, p.110. See also P.S. Atiyah's suggestive remarks concerning the strict settlement as the ancestor of commercial companies, P.S. Atiyah, supra n.4, pp.134-5.

146. H.J. Habakkuk, "English Landownership, 1680-1740", Economic History Review, Vol.10, 1939-40, pp. 1-29. His latest views are contained in "The Rise and Fall of English Landed Families, 1600-1800", Transactions of the Royal Historical Society, 5th series, Vols. 29 and 30 at pp. 187-207 and 123-140 respectively.

147. See Chesterman, Spring and English infra.

148. See E. Spring, "The Settlement of Land in 19th Century England", American Journal of Legal History, Vol.8, 1964, pp.209-223.

149. See E. Spring, supra n.144, p.59 n.64.

150. Economic History Review, Vol.32, 1979, pp.483-93, p.492. See also L. Bonfield, "Marriage Settlements, 1660-1740: The Adoption of the Strict Settlement in Kent and Northamptonshire", in R.B. Outhwaite, (ed), Marriage

and Society: Studies in the Social History of Marriage (London: Europa, 1980) pp.101-116.

151. M.R. Chesterman, infra.

152. B. English, infra.

153. E. Spring, infra.

154. On the unity of interest which existed between the two spheres, see, for example, D. Spring "English Landowners and 19th Century Industrialism", in J.T. Ward and R.G. Wilson (eds), Land and Industry, (Newton Abbot: David & Charles, 1971), Ch.2.

155. See P.S. Atiyah, supra n.4, pp.102-12.

156. J.H. Elliott, Credit the Life of Commerce (London: Madden & Malcolm 1845), quoted by E.J. in Westminster Review, Vol.44, 1845, pp.449-68, at p.452. According to Wellesley's Index to Victorian Periodical Literature Vol.III, p.604, 'E.J'. was the self-same Elliott, and was thus reviewing, among others, his own book.

157. P.L. Cottrell, Industrial Finance, 1830-1914, (London: Methuen, 1980) p.41.

158. See F.E. Hyde, Mr Gladstone at the Board of Trade (London: Cobden-Sanderson, 1934), Ch.8.

159. Report of Commissioners of Bankruptcy and Insolvency, BPP 1840 (274) XVI, quoted in E.J. (Elliott) op.cit, p.455.

160. Ibid, p.457.

161. P.J. Coleman, Debtors and Creditors in America: Insolvency, Imprisonment for Debt and Bankruptcy, 1607-1900 (Madison: State Historical Society of Wisconsin, 1974).

162. Ibid, pp.283-4.

163. See later in this chapter, pp.84-99.

164. Coleman, supra n.161, pp.283-5.

165. Cf. G.P. Fletcher "The Metamorphosis of Larceny", Harvard Law Review, Vol.89, 1976, pp.469-530.

166. The research of M.S. Servian at Hatfield Polytechnic into eighteenth and early nineteenth century bankruptcy law is exploring this theme in more detail. See also I.P.H. Duffy, "English Bankrupts, 1571-1861", American Journal of Legal History, Vol.24, 1980, pp.283-305.

167. D. Hay, "Property, Authority and the Criminal Law", in D. Hay et al (eds) supra, n.4.

168. For these points, see G.R. Rubin, "Packmen, Tallymen and 'Perambulating Scotchmen': Credit Drapers in Nineteenth and Early Twentieth Century England", (in preparation).

169. Coleman, supra n.161, p.286. Mike Servian's assistance in this section is gratefully acknowledged.

170. See generally: M. Brogden, "Policing and the Problem of Consent", in B. Fryer et al (eds), Law, State and Society, (London: Croom Helm, 1981), pp.202-228; P. Cohen, "Policing the Working Class City", in B. Fine et al (eds), Capitalism and the Rule of Law, (London: Hutchinson, 1979), pp.118-136; H.F. Moorhouse and C.W. Chamberlain, "Lower Class Attitudes to Property: Aspects of the Counter-Ideology", Sociology, Vol.8, 1974, pp.387-405; R. Harrison (ed), Independent Collier: The Coal Miner as Archetypal Proletarian Reconsidered, (Hassocks: Harvester, 1979); P. Joyce, Work, Society and Politics: The Culture of the Factory in Late Victorian England, (Brighton: Harvester, 1980); F.M.L. Thompson, "Social Control in Victorian Britain", Economic History Review, Vol.34, 1981, pp.189-208; J. Laurie, supra n.26; J. Mitchell, Psychoanalysis and Feminism (Harmondsworth: Penguin Books, 1975): J. Donzelot, The Policing of Families, (London: Hutchinson, 1980); Brewer and Styles (eds), supra n.4; D. Hay et al (eds), supra n.4; M. Galanter, "Justice in Many Rooms", Journal of Legal Pluralism, Vol.1, 1981, pp.1-48; J. Griffith, "Is Law Important?", New York University Law Review. Vol.54, 1979, pp.339-374; M. Ignatieff, "State, Civil Society and Total Institution: A Critique of Recent Social Histories of Punishment",

in D. Sugarman (ed), Legality, Ideology and the State (London: Academic Press, 1983); P. Fitzpatrick, "Law, Plurality and Underdevelopment",in ibid; M. Foucault, The History of Sexuality, Vol.I, (London: Allen Lane, 1979); S.F. Moore, Law as Process (London: Academic Press, 1978), Ch.2; E.P. Thompson, "The Moral Economy of the English Crowd", Past and Present, No. 50, 1971, pp.76-136 and "Rough Music! le charivari anglais", Annales, Vol.27, 1972, pp.285-312. See also the material cited supra, in n.29.

171. Ferguson, infra.

172. This approach was espoused in D. McBarnet and H.F. Moorhouse, "Business Law and Bourgeois Ideology - A Prologue to a Research Project", unpublished paper, 1977.

173. I. Balbus, The Dialectics of Legal Repression, (New York: Russell Sage Foundation, 1973) pp.12-15; A. Nekam, The Personality Conception of the Legal Entity, (Cambridge: Harvard University Press, 1938); J.T. Noonan, Jr., Persons and Masks of the Law, (New York: Farrar, Straus and Giroux, 1976); O. Kahn-Freund, Labour and the Law, (London: Stevens, 1977) pp. 1-2.

174. This point has recently been stressed in the context of U.K. race relations law. See L. Lustgarten, Legal Control of Racial Discrimination, (London: Macmillan, 1981).

175. M.V. Tushnet, "Perspectives on the Development of American Law", Wisconsin Law Review, 1977, pp.81-110, 102.

See generally, on the way recourse to law tends to diffuse reform movements: K. Klare, "Judicial Deradicalization of the Wagner Act and the Origins of Modern Legal Consciousness, 1937-41", Minnesota Law Review, Vol.62, 1978, pp.265-339; and L.M. Friedman, "Law Reform in Historical Perspective", Saint Louis University Law Journal, Vol.13, 1969, pp.351-372.

76. R.W. Gordon, "Historicism in Legal Scholarship", Yale Law Journal, Vol.90, 1981, pp.1017-1056, 1035.

177. J.B. Rule, The Experience of Labour in Eighteenth Century Industry, (London:

Croom Helm 1981), Ch.4.

178. C.R. Dobson, Masters and Journeymen, (London: Croom Helm, 1981), Ch.9.

179. On Place, see for example, J.V. Orth, "The British Trade Union Acts of 1824 and 1825", Anglo-American Law Review, Vol.5, 1976, pp.131-152; H. Pelling, A History of British Trade Unionism (Harmondsworth: Penguin, 1963), pp.29-30.

180. B.W. Napier, "The Contract of Service: The Concept and its Application", Cambridge University Ph.D., 1975, esp. pp.45-52, 65-70, 103-120. Cf. O. Kahn-Freund, "Blackstone's Neglected Child: The Contract of Employment", Law Quarterly Review, Vol.93, 1977, pp.508-528; T.S. Ashton, An English Economic History: Eighteenth Century (London: Methuen, 1954) Ch.7. For America, see J.M. Feinman, "The Development of the Employment at Will Rule", American Journal of Legal History Vol.20, 1976, pp.118-135. For the later Master and Servant Acts, see especially, Napier, ibid, pp.121-7; D. Simon "Master and Servant" in John Saville (ed), Democracy and the Labour Movement (London: Lawrence & Wishart, 1954), Ch.6; and C.J. Kauffman, "Lord Elcho, Trade Unionism and Democracy" in K.D. Brown (ed), Essays in Anti-Labour History (London: Macmillan, 1974) at pp.180-196.

181. F.W. Maitland, The Constitutional History of England, (Cambridge: Cambridge University Press, 1908), pp.538-539.

182. The treatment meted out to "outsiders" such as court bailiffs, was often of this character. Cf. R.L. Brown, "The Minters of Wapping: The History of a Debtors' Sanctuary in 18th Century East London", East London Papers, Vol.14, 1972, pp.77-86.

183. J. Innes, "The King's Bench Prison in the Later Eighteenth Century" in Brewer and Styles, supra n.4, pp.283-4.

184. The so-called "Hartwell-Hobsbawm controversy". See generally, R.M. Hartwell and E.J. Hobsbawm, "The Standard of Living During the Industrial Revolution: A Discussion", Economic History Review, Vol.16, 1963, pp.106-142.

185. R. Coase, "The Problem of Social Cost", Journal of Law and Economics, 3, 1960, pp.1-44; G. Calabresi, The Costs of Accidents (New Haven: Yale University Press, 1970); R.A. Posner, Economic Analysis of Law (Boston: Little, Brown & Co., 1977) and The Economics of Justice (Cambridge: Harvard University Press, 1981).

186. See for example, A. Leff, "Economic Analysis of Law: Some Realism About Nominalism", Virginia Law Review, Vol.60, pp.451-482; R. Cranston, "Creeping Economism: Some Thoughts About Law and Economics", British Journal of Law and Society, 4, 1977, pp.103-115; M. Polinsky, "Economic Analysis as a Potentially Defective Product", Harvard Law Review, 87, 1974, pp.1655-1681; P. Baker, "The Ideology of Economic Analyses of Law", Philosophy and Public Affairs, 5, 1975, pp.3-48; R. Dworkin, "Is Wealth a Value?", Journal of Legal Studies, 9, 1980, pp.191-226; M.J. Rizzo, "The Mirage of Efficiency", Hofstra Law Review, 8, 1980, pp.641-658; M.J. Horwitz, "Law and Economics: Science or Politics?", Hofstra Law Review, 8, 1980, pp.905-912; D. Kennedy and F. Michelman, "Are Property and Contract Efficient?", Hofstra Law Review, 8, 1980, pp.711-770.

Helpful introductions to the new law and economics include: C.G. Veljanovski, "The Economic Approach to Law: A Critical Introduction", British Journal of Law and Society, 7, 1980, pp.153-193; and P. Burrows and C.G. Veljanovski (eds), The Economic Approach to Law (London: Butterworth, 1982).

Earlier economic approaches to law can be found in the work of Bentham, J.S. Mill and Marx. In the early part of this century, several innovative economic-historical studies of law and economy appeared in the United States: see C.A. Beard, An Economic Interpretation of the Constitution of the United States (New York: Macmillan, 1924); J.R. Commons, Legal Foundations of Capitalism, (Madison: University of Wisconsin Press, 1968); and R. Ely, Property and Contract in their Relations to the Distribution of

Wealth (New York: Macmillan, 1914).

For two pioneering English essays, see D. Hughes Parry, "Economic Theories in English Case Law", Law Quarterly Review, 1931, pp.183-202 and H.W. Robinson, "Law and Economics", Modern Law Review, 11, 1939, pp.257-265.

187. See, for example, D.C. North and R.M. Hartwell, "Introduction: Law, Property Rights, Legal Institutions and the Performance of Economies" in M. Flinn (ed), Proceedings of the 7th International Economic History Congress, (Edinburgh: Edinburgh University Press, 1978), pp.211-215. This linkage is hardly surprising in view of their similar value-sympathies: cf. A.W. Coats, "The Historical Context of the 'New' Economic History", Journal of European Economic History, Vol.9, 1980, pp.185-207. D. Sugarman, supra n.16, pp.70-106, 73-74, 79-80 and n.26, briefly alludes to the influence of F.A. Hayek on certain histories of law.

188. See further, C.G. Veljanovski and Burrows and Veljanovski cited supra in n. 183.

189. D. Hay, "War, Dearth and Theft in the 18th Century: The Record of the English Courts", Past and Present, 95, 1982, pp.117-160, 117.

190. See Hay ibid, pp.117-118 n.2 which collects much of the relevant literature and his discussion thereof. See also the material in n.198 below.

In the United States, quantitative analyses have been undertaken in respect of the early American legal system. Most of this work is concerned with crime and the criminal law. See generally, M.S. Hindus and D.L. Jones, "Quantitative Methods or Quantum Meruit?", Historical Methods, Vol.12, 1980, pp.63-74.

191. P. Abrams, Historical Sociology (Near Shepton Mallet: Open Books, 1982), pp.318-319.

192. Quoted by C. Madge, "The Sociology Man", New Society, 60, 1982, No. 1014, p.147.

193. P. Abrams, supra n.191, p.321.

194. See, for example, P.S. Atiyah, supra, n.4, esp. pp.238-505; R. Stevens, supra, n.4, pp.37-181; B. Abel-Smith and R. Stevens, supra, n.4, pp.53-134; C.H.S. Fifoot, Judge and Jurist in the Reign of Victoria, (London: Stevens, 1959).

195. Cf. R. Posner, "A Theory of Negligence", Journal of Legal Studies, 1, 1972, pp.29-40.

196. Cf. G. Schwartz, "Tort Law and the Economy in 19th Century America: A Reinterpretation", Yale Law Journal, 90, 1981, pp.1717-1780.

197. See note 54.

198. Cf. L. Radzinowicz, A History of English Criminal Law, Vol.1, (London: Stevens, 1956); V.A. Gatrell and T.B. Hadden "Criminal Statistics and Their Interpretations" in E.A. Wrigley (ed), Nineteenth Century Society: Essays in the Quantitative Method for the Study of Social Data (London: Cambridge University Press, 1972); B.R. Mitchell and H.G. Jones, Second Abstract of British Historical Statistics, (London: Cambridge University Press, (1971), pp.200-10; V.A.C. Gatrell, "The Decline of Theft and Violence in Victorian and Edwardian England", in V.A. Gatrell, B. Lenman and G. Parker (eds) Crime and the Law: The Social History of Crime in Western Europe Since 1500 (London: Europa, 1981); J.M. Beattie, "The Pattern of Crime in England, 1660-1800", Past and Present, No. 62, 1974, pp.47-95; ibid, "The Criminality of Women in 18th Century England", Journal of Social History, Vol.7, 1975, J. Styles, "Criminal Records", Historical Journal Vol.20, 1977, pp.977-81; D. Hay, "War, Dearth and Theft in the 18th Century: The Record of the English Courts", Past and Present, 95, 1982, pp.117-160.

199. O.R. McGregor, Social History and Law Reform (London: Stevens, 1981), p.31.

200. B.R. Mitchell and P. Deane, Abstract of British Historical Statistics (London: Cambridge University Press, 1962), pp.246 and 396-9.

201. Cf. R.B. Ferguson, "Legal Ideology and Commercial Interests: The Social Origins of the Commercial Law Codes", British Journal of Law and Society,

Vol.4, 1977, pp.18-38.

202. But see N. Abercrombie, S. Hill and B.S. Turner, The Dominant Ideology Thesis (London: Allen & Unwin, 1980), for a recent reappraisal of this influential concept.

203. See note 54.

204. Cf. R. Abel, "From the Editor", Law and Society Review, 11, 1977.

205. I. Balbus, "Commodity Form and Legal Form: An Essay on the 'Relative Autonomy' of the Law", Law and Society Review, 11, 1977, pp.571-588.

206. Dicey's use of the term in his classic study, Lectures on the Relation Between Law and Public Opinion in the Nineteenth Century (1914), has been rightly criticised. See Orth, supra, n.179 and Richard A. Cosgrove, The Rule of Law: Albert Venn Dicey, Victorian Jurist (London: Macmillan, 1980), pp.170-194.

207. Cf. E.P. Thompson, supra, n.4, pp.258-269.

208. J. Brewer, "The Wilkites and the Law 1763-74", in Brewer and Styles, supra, n.4, pp.128-171.

209. See, for example, Brewer and Styles (eds), supra n.4; D. Hay et al (eds), supra, n.4; J. Stevenson, supra, n.4; E.P. Thompson, n.4 and "The Moral Economy of the English Crowd in the 18th Century" supra n.126. D. Jones, supra, n.4.
On the issue of the popular legitimacy, D. Hay, "Poaching and the Game Law on Cannock Chase", in Hay et al, supra, n.4, pp.189-254; P. Stearns, Lives of Labour (London: Croom Helm, 1975).

210. See A. Gramsci, Selections from Prison Notebooks (London: Lawrence and Wishart, 1971), pp.12-13, 53, 55-60, 261-264.

211. See A.P. Donajgrodski, "Introduction", in A.P. Donajgrodski (ed), Social Control in 19th Century Britain (London: Croom Helm, 1977), pp.9-26; G.S. Jones, "Class Expression versus Social Control?", History Workshop Journal, 4, 1977, pp.163-170; F.M.L. Thompson, "Social Control in Victorian Britain", Economic History Review, 34, 1981, pp.184-208; M. Ignatieff, "State, Civil

Society and Total Institution: A Critique of Recent Social Histories of Punishment", in D. Sugarman (ed), Legality, Ideology and The State (London: Academic Press, 1983).

212. R.S. Summers, "Naive Instrumentalism and the Law" in P.M.S. Hacker and J. Raz (eds), Law, Morality and Society (Oxford: Clarendon Press, 1977), pp.119-131, p.126.

213. See generally, M. Ignatieff, supra, notes 4 and 211.

The critique of "social control" in this essay might also be extended to certain uses of the notion of "labour aristocracy": for a recent overview of this cognate way of explaining the "embourgeoisement of the working-classes", see, R. Gray, The Aristocracy of Labour in 19th Century Britain, 1850-1914, (London: Macmillan, 1981).

214. D. Lloyd George War Memoirs, Vol.I (London: Ivor Nicholson and Watson Co., 1933), pp.322-44.

215. Dixon, supra, n.11.

216. R.D. Storch, "The Policeman as Domestic Missionary: Urban Discipline and Popular Culture in Northern England, 1850-1880", Journal of Social History Vol.9, 1976, pp.481-509.

217. Cf. R.J. Morris, "The Married Women's Property Act of 1870", briefly reported in Social History Newsletter, Vol.5, No.1, Spring 1980, pp.4-5.

218. G.S. Jones, supra, n.11, p.164. Jones argues that "social control" type explanations suggest that society is normally a static equilibrium which may be disturbed and then re-asserted on a new equilibrium. Thus, conflict and contradiction within society is portrayed as episodic rather than as continually present.

See also Ignatieff, supra, n.211 and F.M.L. Thompson, supra, n.211.

219. See, generally, the material in, supra, n.211.

220. See, particularly, our discussion of: "A: Was Law Important in the Economy?", supra; "B: Sanctions, Litigation and Courts", supra

and "F: The Plurality of Law and Legal Institutions", supra, and materials cited there.

221. However, the discretion to use or not to use the order may be exercised so as to secure a degree of social control. See D. Hay, "Property, Authority and the Criminal Law", in D. Hay et al, (eds), supra, n.4, pp.17-63.

222. Cf. D. Sugarman, supra, n.16, pp.84-94.

223. L. Althusser, "Ideology and Ideological State Apparatuses", in Lenin and Philosophy and Other Essays (London: New Left Books, 1977), pp.141-159; M. Foucault, Power/Knowledge (Brighton: Harvester, 1980), pp.109-133 and The History of Sexuality, supra, n.167, esp. pp.91-102; P. Hirst, On Law and Ideology (London: Macmillan, 1979); C. Sumner, Reading Ideologies (London: Academic Press, 1979); R. Williams, Marxism and Literature (Oxford: Oxford University Press, 1977), esp. pp.55-71.

224. J. Urry, The Anatomy of Capitalist Societies: The Economy, Civil Society and the State (London: Macmillan, 1981), p.57 and generally Ch.1 and 5. Cf. The material collected supra in n.170.

225. J. Urry, ibid, pp.6-7.

226. A brief analysis of the "autonomy" debate at the theoretical level is attempted by K. Foster, From Status to Contract: Legal Form and Work Relations, 1750-1850, University of Warwick School of Law Working Paper, Coventry, 1979. See, generally, J. Urry ibid, passim; B. Jessop, The Capitalist State, (London: Martin Robertson, 1982); K. Klare, supra, n. 175; E.P. Thompson, The Poverty of Theory (London: Merlin Press) pp.287-289; M. Tushnet, supra, n.175.

See also our discussion of "The Intellectual History of Law", infra pp.

227. See, for example, the following works detailed supra, n.4; D. Hay et al (eds); M. Ignatieff; D. Philips; and E.P. Thompson. For a review of this literature, see V. Bailey's overview essay, supra, n.4, pp.40-43.

On the similarities of the civil and criminal form of law in 19th century see

D. Sugarman, et al, supra, n.4.

228. Cf. R.C.B. Risk, supra, n.22.

229. D.M. Provine, supra, n.22.

230. P.J.R. King, "Decision-Makers and Decision-Making in the 18th Century Criminal Law" supra n.4.

231. D. Philips, supra, n.4.

232. R.D. Storch, "The Plague of the Blue Locusts. Police Reform and Popular Resistance in Northern England, 1840-57", International Review of Social History, Vol.20, 1975, pp.61-90.

233. See supra n.209, for examples.

234. For an instructive discussion of this phenomenon see D. Hay, "Crime and Justice in 18th and 19th Century England", in N. Morris and M. Tonry, (eds), Crime and Justice, Vol.2, (Chicago: University of Chicago Press, 1980), pp.45-84, 72-75.

235. J. Urry, supra, n.224, p.115.

236. J. Urry, ibid, pp.81-83 outlines these objections.

237. V. Bailey, "Introduction" in V. Bailey (ed), supra, n.4, p.5.

238. In V. Bailey (ed), supra, n.4.

239. For a general survey, see A.J. Taylor, Laissez-Faire and State Intervention in Nineteenth Century Britain (London: Macmillan, 1972).

240. The literature is too large and too well known to merit repetition here.

241. This is the argument advanced by Carson in his important account of the early Factories Acts. See W.G. Carson, "Symbolic and Instrumental Dimensions of Early Factory Legislation: A Case Study in the Social Origins of Criminal Law", in R.G. Hood (ed), Crime, Criminology and Public Policy (London: Heinemann, 1974). Quantitative analysis appears to support his view. See H.P. Marvel, "Factory Regulations: A Re-interpretation of Early English Experience", Journal of Law and Economics, Vol.20, 1977, pp.379-402. Other interesting historical work which has illuminated the symbolic

dimensions of the law and legal institutions include: D. Hay, supra, n. 218; J. Davis, "The London Garotting Panic of 1862": A Moral Panic and the Creation of a Criminal Class in Mid-Victorian England", in V. Gatrell et al (eds), supra, n.4, pp.190-213; and A.G. Roeber, "Authority, Law and Custom: The Rituals of Court Day in Tidewater Virginia, 1720-1750", William and Mary Quarterly, Vol.47, 1980, pp.29-52.

242. A. Anderson, "The Labour Laws and the Cabinet Legislative Committee of 1926-27". Bulletin of the Society for the Study of Labour History, No.23, Autumn 1971, pp.37-54; cf. ibid, "The Political Symbolism of the Labour Laws", in ibid, pp.13-15.

243. The Economist, May 7, 1927.

244. See Hay and Roeber, supra, n.241.

245. See Carson, supra, n.241 and Anderson, supra, n.242.

246. B. Supple, "The State and the Industrial Revolution, 1700-1914", in C.M. Cipolla (ed), The Fontana Economic History of Europe: The Industrial Revolution (Glasgow: Fontana/Collins, 1973), pp.301-357, 307.

247. K. Marx, Capital, Vol.I, (Harmondsworth: Penguin Books, 1976) p.876.

248. P. Corrigan and D. Sayer, "How the Law Rules", in B. Fryer et al (eds), supra, n.16, pp.21-53, 22.

249. P. Corrigan and D. Sayer, ibid, p.23.

250. P. Richards, "The State and Early Industrial Capitalism: The Case of the Handloom Weavers", Past and Present, No.83, 1979, pp.91-115, 113.

251. See P. Richards, ibid, and generally, E.P. Thompson, The Making of the English Working Class (Harmondsworth: Penguin Books ed., 1968).

252. For an attempted general overview which details the process of re-classification discussed here, see D. Sugarman et al, supra, n.4. See also the material on the history of crime enumerated, supra, n.4.

253. See P. Richards, supra, n.50, p.115.

254. See, generally, H. Parris, Constitutional Bureaucracy (London: Allen and

Unwin, 1969); G. Sutherland (ed), Studies in the Growth of 19th Century Government (London: Routledge and Kegan Paul, 1972); W.L. Guttsman, The British Political Elite (London: MacGibbon and Kee, 1968); G.E. Aylmer, "Bureaucracy", in P. Burke (ed), New Cambridge Modern History, Vol. XII: Companion Volume (Cambridge: Cambridge University Press, 1979), pp.164-200; S.E. Finer, Life and Times of Sir Edwin Chadwick (London: Methuen, 1952); O.R. McGregor, "Civil Servants and the Civil Service, 1850-1950", Political Quarterly, Vol.22, 1951, pp.103-120 and "Social Research and Social Policy in the 19th Century", British Journal of Sociology, Vol.8, 1957, pp.146-157; P. Richards, "The State and the Working Class, 1833-1841: MP's and the Making of Social Policy", Birmingham University Ph.D., 1975, and P. Corrigan, "State Formation and Moral Regulation in 19th Century Britain: Sociological Investigations", Durham University Ph.D., 1977.

See also P. Corrigan (ed), Capitalism, State Formation and Marxist Theory: Historical Investigations (London: Quarter, 1980).

255. P.Richards, supra, n.250, p.115.

256. See, for example, P. Richards, ibid, p.115 n.105; P.W.J. Bartrip and Fenn, infra, n.278, pp.184-185; W.G. Carson, infra, n.278, 1980.

257. B. Supple, supra, n.246, pp.314-315, our emphasis.

258. This paradox is acknowledged by P. Corrigan, supra. n. 254; B. Supple, supra, n.246, passim; K. Polanyi, supra, n.33, pp.135-150.

259. R.A. Lewis, Review, History, Vol.59, 1974, p.116, quoted in P. Corrigan, ibid, p.2.

260. P. Corrigan, ibid, p.4.

261. Ibid, p.xiv. See also P. Richards, supra, n.250, p.91-92.

262. Ibid, p.2.

263. R. Hogg, "Imprisonment and Society Under Early British Capitalism", Crime and Social Justice, No.12, 1979, pp.4-17, 7; and see generally pp.7-11.

264. R. Hogg, ibid, p.7.

265. M. Ignatieff, supra, n.4, pp.95-109; D. Philips, supra, n.4, pp.53-95 and " 'A New Engine of Power and Authority': The Institutionalization of Law-Enforcement in England, 1780-1830", in V.A.C. Gatrell, et al (eds), supra, n.4, pp.155-189.

The tensions between local and central government were also an important element in the battle over taxation in the period 1870-1914, see A. Offer, supra, n.4, Parts III, IV and V.

266. H.W. Arthurs, infra.

267. Ibid.

268. Ibid.

269. Ibid.

270. A.V. Dicey, Introduction to the Study of the Law of the Constitution (London: Macmillan, 1885), p.390.

271. See, generally, R.A. Cosgrove, The Rule of Law: Albert Venn Dicey, Victorian Jurist (London: Macmillan, 1980), pp.91-113.

272. Ibid.

273. H.W. Arthurs, infra.

274. Abel-Smith and Stevens, supra, n.4, pp.112-113; P.S. Atiyah, supra, n.4, pp.219-454; R. Stevens, supra, n.4, pp.133-184.

275. See R.A. Cosgrove, supra, n.271.

276. Abel-Smith and R. Stevens, supra, n.4, p.117.

277. T.K. McCraw, "Regulation in America: A Review Article", Business History Review, Vol.49, 1975, pp.159-183, 172.

278. T.K. McCraw, ibid, pp.171-175 discusses the relevant literature.

279. See the material cited supra in n.254. Although it relates to an earlier period, G.E. Aylmer's The State's Servants: The Civil Service in the English Republic 1640-1660 (London: Routledge and Kegan Paul, 1973) is an exemplary study, full of suggestive insights.

Also highly relevant to the questions enumerated in our text (on regulatory agencies, the public interest and private enterprise), is a wealth of American literature ably surveyed by T.K. McCraw, supra, n.73. See also K. Klare, supra, n.175, pp.270-275 and passim and J. Laurie, supra, n. 26.

Cf. C. Turpin, Government Contracts (Harmondsworth: Penguin Books, 1972); G. Ganz, Administrative Procedures (London: Sweet and Maxwell, 1974); J.A. Farmer, Tribunals and Government (London: Weidenfeld and Nicolson, 1974); H. Street, Justice in the Welfare State (London: Stevens, 1968).

280. See further, B.L. Hutchins and A. Harrison, A History of Factory Legislation (Westminster: P.S. King and Van Ltd, 1903); M.W. Thomas, The Early Factory Legislation (Leigh-on-Sea: Thames Bank, 1948); J.T. Ward, The Factory Movement, 1830-1855 (London: Macmillan, 1962) and The Factory System, 2 Vols. (Newton Abbot: David & Charles, 1970).

See also the material, infra, n.282.

281. "Preface to the New Edition", in B.L. Hutchins and A. Harrison, ibid, p.vii-viii, (1911).

282. W.G. Carson, "The Conventionalization of Early Factory Crime", International Journal of the Sociology of Law, Vol.7, pp.37-60. See also, W.G. Carson, "White-Collar Crime and the Enforcement of Factory Legislation", British Journal of Criminology, Vol.10, 1970, pp.385-400; "Early Factory Inspectors and the Viable Class Society - A Rejoinder", Vol.8, 1980, International Journal of the Sociology of Law, pp.187-192, "The Institutionalization of Ambiguity: Early British Factory Acts", in G. Geis and E. Stotland (ed), White-Collar Crime: Theory and Research (New York: Sage, 1980), pp.142-172. Cf. P.W.J. Bartrip and P.T. Fenn, "The Conventionalization of Factory Crime - A Re-assessment", International Journal of the Sociology of Law, Vol.8, 1980, pp.175-186 and P.W.J. Bartrip, "British Government Inspection", Historical Journal, Vol.25, 1982, pp.602-620.

283. W.G. Carson, "Early Factory Inspectors and the Viable Class Society - A Rejoinder", ibid, p.187.

284. W.G. Carson, 1979, supra, n.282, p.38. Cf. R. Cranston, Regulating Business: Law and Consumer Agencies (London: Macmillan, 1979).

285. Atiyah, supra, n.4. For a useful critical evaluation of Atiyah see B. Mensch, "Freedom of Contract as Ideology", Stanford Law Review, Vol.33, 1981, pp.753-770. Other commentaries include, J.H. Baker, (book review), Modern Law Review, Vol.43, 1980, pp.467-9 and A.W.B. Simpson, "Contract: The Twitching Corpse", Oxford Journal of Legal Studies, Vol.1, 1981, pp.265-77.

286. J.F. Brenner, "Nuisance Law in the Industrial Revolution in England", Journal of Legal Studies, Vol.3, 1974, pp.403-34.

287. R. Danzig, "Hadley v. Baxendale: A Study in the Industrialization of the Law", Journal of Legal Studies, Vol.4, 1975, pp.249-84.

288. L.M. Friedman and J. Ladinsky, "Social Change and the Law of Industrial Accidents", Columbia Law Review, Vol.67, 1967, pp.50-82 (in respect to the United States). See P.W.J. Bartrip and S.B. Burman The Wounded Soldiers of Industry (Oxford: University Press, 1983).

Recent interesting work on the doctrinal history of this and cognate areas of the law include: T. Ingman "The Rise and Fall of the Doctrine of Common Employment, Juridical Review, Vol.23 (N.S.), 1978, pp.106-25; idem, "A History of the Defence of Volenti Non Fit Injuria" in ibid, Vol.26, 1981, pp.1-28; H. Smith, "From Deodand to Dependency", American Journal of Legal History, Vol.II, 1967, pp.389-403; M. Pritchard, Scott v. Shepherd (1773) and the Emergence of the Tort of Negligence, (London: Selden Society, 1976). See also, G.T. Schwartz, "Tort Law and the Economy in 19th Century America", Yale Law Journal, Vol.90, 1981, pp.1717-75, 1722-27 for a succinct overview of the debate as to whether the English law of negligence shifted from strict to fault-based liability.

289. For example, on the use made by Austin of German textbooks of Institutes and Pandects to acquire a knowledge of Roman law and juristic technique,

see A.B. Schwartz, "John Austin and the German Jurisprudence of His Time", Politica, Col.I, 1934, pp.178-199 and W.L. Morison, John Austin, (London: Edward Arnold, 1982), pp.60-63. See also C.H.S. Fifoot, Judge and Jurist in the Reign of Victoria (London: Stevens, 1959) for a useful discussion of the influence of German ideas on Anglo-American jurists such as Maine, Maitland, Pollock, Story and Markby. The importance of Savigny and Ihering to Pollock was acknowledged by Pollock in his A First Book of Jurisprudence (London: Macmillan, 1929 ed.), p.vii; and their influence permeates his Principles of Contract (London: Stevens, 1876). On the influence of Ihering and Gierke on Maitland and Pollock see, for instance, F. Pollock and F.W. Maitland, The History of English Law, Vol.I (Cambridge: Cambridge University Press, 1898), Ch.1; C.H.S. Fifoot, Frederic William Maitland: A Life (Cambridge: Harvard University Press, 1971), pp.150, 188-90, 231-33 and Judge and Jurist in the Reign of Victoria, ibid, Ch.3. Also on the influence of Savigny and Ihering, see J.W. Burrow, Evolution and Society (Cambridge: Cambridge University Press, 1966), esp. at pp.142-4, 230 and A Liberal Descent: Victorian Historians and the English Past (Cambridge: Cambridge University Press, 1981), pp.97-125; P. Stein, Legal Evolution (Cambridge: Cambridge University Press, 1980), pp.51-98. The influence of German Ideas on English Legal Scholarship is also considered in E. Cambell, "German Influences on English Legal Education and Jurisprudence in the 19th Century", University of Western Australia Annual Law Review, Vol.4, 1959, pp.360-82; and P Stein, "Continental Influences on English Legal Thought, 1600-1900" in Atti Del Terzo Congresso Internazionale Della Societa Italiana Di Storica Del Diritto, La Formazione Storica Del Diritto Moderno in Europa, (Fireze: Leo S. Olschki, 1977) pp.1105-25 at 1119-25.

290. J.W. Burrow, ibid, passim; P. Stein, Legal Evolution (Cambridge: Cambridge University Press, 1980).

291. A.W.B. Simpson, "Innovation in 19th Century Contract Law", Law Quarterly

Review, Vol.91, 1975, pp.247-278 and "The Rise and Fall of the Legal Treatise", University of Chicago Law Review, Vol.48, 1981, pp.632-79.
On the earlier period, see a series of important articles by D.R. Coquillette, "Legal Ideology and Incorporation I : The English Civilian Writers 1523-1607", Boston Law Review, Vol.61, 1981, pp.1-89. "Legal Ideology and Incorporation II : Sir Thomas Ridley, Charles Mollons, and the Literary Battle for the Law Merchant, 1607-76", ibid, pp.315-71.

292. Sometimes via the work of German scholars and John Austin: see the material cited supra, n.289. The importance of Roman law in the teaching and writings of Sir Henry Maine is described in G. Feaver, From Status to Contract (London: Longmans, 1969). Maine regarded Roman law studies as an important counter to the unhistorical and insular outlook which he associated with Austinianism. The rejuvenation of Roman law studies at Oxford also owed much to James Bryce, Regius Professor of Civil Law from 1870-1893. See further, H.A.L. Fisher, James Bryce, 2 Vols (London: Macmillan, 1927), Vol.I, pp.132-134.

293. Robert Gordon's work has rightly pin-pointed the importance of this linkage: for example, (book review), Harvard Law Review, Vol.94, 1981, pp.903-18, 911. A sense of this reciprocal influence can be gauged from F.H. Lawson, The Oxford Law School 1850-1965 (Oxford: Clarendon Press, 1968), p.167; A.V. Dicey, Can English Law be Taught at the Universities? (London: Macmillan, 1883) and "The Teaching of English Law at Harvard", Contemporary Review, 76, 1899, November, pp.742-58; R.A. Cosgrove, supra, n.271, pp.54, 57, 59-60, 170-1. As these few examples testify, veneration for Harvard Law School was intense among many leading English scholars. Thus, Maitland's sad lament, when ill-health prevented him from taking up an invitation to Harvard: "You know how I regard the Harvard Law School: I feel as if I lived in the 12th century and was rejecting a 'call' to Bologna.": C.H.S. Fifoot (ed), The Letters of Frederick William Maitland (London:

Selden Society, 1965), Letter 22, p.179. See also R.A. Cosgrove, "A.V. Dicey at the Harvard Law School, 1898: A Study in the Anglo-American Legal Community", Harvard Library Bulletin, Vol.26, 1978, pp.325-35, especially the unpublished correspondence quoted on p.332. On Bryce's connections with Harvard see Fisher, supra, n.292, Vol.I, pp.135-8. Finally, O.W. Holmes Jr., who was briefly associated with Harvard Law School, exercised a profound influence on the development of the English law of Contract and Torts. See further, Fifoot, supra, n.289, pp.51-2.

294. R.A. Cosgrove, "The Reception of Analytical Jurisprudence: The Victorian Debate on the Separation of Law and Morality, 1860-1900", Durham University Journal, Vol.71, 1981, pp.47-56, 49. Cf. B. Shapiro, supra n.4.

295. N. Annan, "The Intellectual Aristocracy", in J.H. Plumb (ed), Studies in Social History (Cambridge: Cambridge University Press, 1955), pp.243-287.

296. C. Harvie, The Lights of Liberalism: University Liberals and the Challenge of Democracy, 1860-86 (London: Allen Lane, 1976); C. Kent, Brains and Numbers: Elitism, Comtism and Democracy in Mid-Victorian England (Toronto: Toronto University Press, 1978); R.A. Cosgrove, supra, n.271, passim; E. Ruben, "John Austin's Political Pamphlets 1824-1859", in E. Attwool (ed), Perspectives in Jurisprudence (Glasgow: Glasgow University Press, 1977), pp.20-41; J. Roach, "Liberalism and the Victorian Intelligentsia", Cambridge Historical Journal, Vol.13, 1957, pp.58-81; J.W. Burrow, supra, notes 117 and 289; C.J. Dewey, "Images of the Village Community: A Study of Anglo-Indian Ideology", Modern Asian Studies, Vol.6, 1972, pp.291-328.

297. J.W. Burrow, supra, n.117.

298. Mental Illness and Psychology (New York: Macmillan, 1976); Madness and Civilisation (New York: Macmillan, 1965); The Birth of the Clinic (London: Cape, 1973); Discipline and Punish (London: Allen Lane, 1977); The History of Sexuality, Vol.I (London: Allen Lane, 1979).

of Sexuality, Vol.I (London: Allen Lane, 1979).

299. J. Austin, The Province of Jurisprudence Determined, (1832), but not influential until after his death when a second edition was published in 1861 by Sarah Austin; O.W. Holmes, Jr., The Common Law (Boston: Little, Brown & Co., 1881).

On the narrowing of Austin's ideas and perspective after his death see, W.L. Morison, John Austin (London: Edward Arnold, 1982), pp.148-77.

300. Atiyah, supra, n.4, p.342.

301. See, for example, A.V. Dicey, supra, n.4.

302. See generally, R.A. Cosgrove, supra, n.294.

303. For example, see J.W. Burrow, supra, n.117, p.283; Laski, supra, n.32; Maitland supra, n.32; Gierke, supra, n.32; Vinogradoff, supra, n.32. See generally, D. Nicholls, The Pluralist State (London: Macmillan, 1975) and B. Zylstra, From Pluralism to Collectivism (Assen: Van Gorcum and Co., N.V., 1968).

304. J.W. Burrow, supra, n.117, p.283.

305. F.W. Maitland, Township and Borough (Cambridge: Cambridge University Press, 1898), p.13, cited in Burrow, ibid.

306. Cf. M.J. Horwitz, "The Conservative Tradition in the Writing of American Legal History", American Journal of Legal History, Vol.7, 1973, pp.275-294; R.W. Gordon, "J. Willard Hurst and the Common Law Tradition in American Legal Historiography", Law and Society Review, Vol.10, 1975, pp.9-55 and "Historicism in Legal Scholarship", Yale Law Journal, Vol.90, 1981, pp.1017-1056; Sugarman, supra, n.4.

307. In addition to the authors discussed in the text, see also K. Klare, supra, n.175 and M. Tushnet, "The American Law of Slavery, 1810-60", Law and Society Review, 1975, pp.119-84.

308. G.E. White, Tort Law in America (New York: Oxford University Press, 1980). Cf. R.W. Gordon, (book review), Harvard Law Review, Vol.94, 1981, pp.903-

18 and J.M. Feinman, "The Role of Ideas in Legal History", Michigan Law Review, Vol.78, 1980, pp.722-736.

309. White, ibid, p.3.

310. K.J. Vandevelde, "The New Property of the 19th Century", Buffalo Law Review, Vol.29, 1980, pp.325-367, 326.

311. Ibid.

312. D. Kennedy, "The Structure of Blackstone's Commentaries", Buffalo Law Review, Vol.28, 1979, pp.205-382, 220.

313. Ibid, p.210.

314. K.J. Vandevelde, supra, n.310, p.327.

315. D. Kennedy, "Form and Substance in Private Law Adjudication", Harvard Law Review, Vol.89, 1976, pp.1685-1778.

316. D. Kennedy, supra, n.312, passim.

317. G. Frug, "The City as a Legal Concept", Harvard Law Review, Vol.93, 1980, pp.1059-1154.

318. (Anonymous), "Tortious Interference with Contractual Relations in the 19th Century", Harvard Law Review, Vol.93, pp.1510-1539 and K.J. Vandevelde, supra, n.310, passim.

319. D. Kennedy, "Toward an Historical Understanding of Legal Consciousness", S. Spitzer (ed), Research in Law and Sociology, Vol.3 (Greenwood: JAI Press, 1980).

320. See R.W. Gordon, supra, n.308, pp.910-11; "Some Thoughts on Legal Form and Practice in American Legal Historiography", (unpublished, 1978), p.8.

321. J.W. Burrow, supra, n.289. See also P. Stein, supra, n.289.

322. P.S. Atiyah, supra, n.4. See also the discussion of Christopher Hill's work, infra, pp.

323. M. White, Social Thought in America (New York: Beacon Press, 1957).

324. E.A. Purcell, The Crisis of Democratic Theory (Lexington: University of Kentucky Press, 1973).

325. See supra pp.3-13.

326. See Stevens and Abel-Smith and Stevens, supra n.4 for pioneering studies.

327. P.S. Atiyah, supra, n.4, p.374.

328. D. Philips, supra, n.4 and "The Black Country Magistracy, 1835-60", Midland History, 1976, pp.161-90.

329. P.S. Atiyah, supra, n.4, pp.374-80, 396-7, 587.

330. R.F.V. Heuston, supra, n.4, pp.201-9. See also R. Stevens supra, n.4, pp.84-5 and 90-98; A.A. Paterson, "Judges: A Political Elite?" British Journal of Law and Society, Vol.1, 1974, pp.118-35, 120-4.

331. Cf. M.S. Larsen, The Rise of Professionalism (Berkeley: University of California Press, 1977); W.R. Prest (ed), Lawyers in Early Modern Europe and America (London: Croom Helm, 1981).

332. Cf. K. Klare, supra, n.175; P. Miller, The Life of the Mind in America (London: Victor Gollancz, 1966), pp.99-265; M. Tushnet, supra, n.175, pp.87-94.

333. W.J. Bouwsma, "Lawyers in Early Modern Culture", American Historical Review, Vol.73, 1973, pp.303-27.

334. W.R. Prest, "The Art of Law and the Law of God"; D. Pennington and K. Thomas (eds), Puritans and Revolutionaries (Oxford: Clarendon Press, 1978), pp.94-117, 116.

335. Ibid.

336. R. Cover, Justice Accused (New Haven: Yale University Press, 1978).

337. P.S. Atiyah, supra, n.4, p.390.

338. L.M. Friedman, supra, n.17, p.540.

339. E.P. Thompson, supra, n.4, pp.258-69.

340. D. McBarnet and H.F. Moorhouse, "Business Law and Business Ideology", (unpublished, 1977).

341. W.R. Prest, The Inns of Court Under Elizabeth I and the Early Stuarts, 1590-

1640 (London: Longman, 1972); R. Cocks, Foundations of the Modern Bar (London: Sweet and Maxwell, 1983); D. Duman, The English and Colonial Bars in the 19th Century (London: Croom Helm, 1983); W. Prest (ed), Lawyers in Early Modern Europe and America (London: Croom Helm, 1981); E.W. Ives, The Common Lawyers of Pre-Reformation England (Cambridge: Cambridge University Press, 1983); M. Miles, "Eminent Attorneys": Some Aspects of West Riding Attorneyship c.1750-1800, University of Birmingham Ph.D., 1982; A. Offer, Property and Politics, 1870-1914 (Cambridge: Cambridge University Press, 1981); Robson, Holmes, Brooks, Birks, Larson, supra n.4; P.H. Williams, A Gentleman's Calling - the Liverpool Attorney-at-Law (Liverpool: Incorporated Law Society of Liverpool, 1980); B.P. Levack, The Civil Lawyers in England, 1603-1641 (Oxford: Oxford University Press, 1973); G.D. Squibb, Doctors' Commons (Oxford: Oxford University Press, 1977); R. Houlbrooke, Church Courts and the People During the English Reformation 1520-1570 (Oxford: Oxford University Press, 1979); R.A. Marchant, The Church Under the Law (Cambridge: Cambridge University Press, 1969); D.E.C. Yale, "A View of the Admiral Jurisdiction", in D. Jenkins (ed), English Legal History Studies 1972 (Cardiff: Cardiff University Press, 1975).

342. B. Abel-Smith and R. Stevens, Lawyers and the Courts (London: Heinemann, 1967); J. Baker, The Reports of Sir John Spelman, 2 Vols. (London: Selden Society, 1978); Heuston, supra, n.4; Duman, supra, n.4.

343. R. Stevens, Law and Politics (London: Weidenfeld and Nicolson, 1979); J.H. Langbein, "The Criminal Trial Before the Lawyers", University of Chicago Law Review, 45, 1978, pp.263-316 and "Shaping the 18th Century Criminal Trial", University of Chicago Law Review, 50, 1983, pp.1-136.

344. Atiyah, supra n.4; Horwitz, supra, n.4; Stevens, ibid.

345. Duman, supra, n.341.

346. Ibid, p.159.

347. Ibid, p.29.

348. See L. Stone, "Prosopography", Daedalus 100, 1971, pp.46-79.

349. Atiyah, supra, n.4, p.383.

350. Ibid, p.113.

351. Duman, supra, n.341, p.78.

352. Ibid, pp.184, 194-5.

353. Ibid.

354. W. Prest, "The English Bar 1550-1700" in W. Prest (ed), supra, n.341, p.74.

354a. Prest, ibid.

355. Supra, n.341.

356. M.S. Larson, The Rise of Professionalism (Berkley: University of California Press, 1977).

357. M. Miles, "The Money Market in the Early Industrial Revolution", Business History, 1982, pp.351-74; B.L. Anderson, "The Attorney and the Early Capital Market in Lancashire" in F. Crouzet (ed), Capital Formation in the Industrial Revolution (London: Methuen, 1972); R.S. Neale, A History of Bath (London: Routledge, 1982); B.L. Anderson, "Provincial Aspects of the Financial Revolution in the 18th Century", Business History, XI, 1969, pp.57-71; B.L. Anderson, "Money and the Structure of Credit", Business History, XII, 1970, pp.41-59; B.A. Holderness, "Credit in a Rural Community, 1660-1800", Midland History, 1975, pp.55-71.

358. For example, see A. Konefsky and A. King (eds), The Papers of Daniel Webster, 3 Vols. (Hanover: University Press of New England, 1982-) and L. Wroth and H. Zoebel (eds), The Legal Papers of John Adams, 3 Vols. (Cambridge: Harvard University Press, 1965).

359. Supra, n.341.

360. Larson, supra, n.356.

361. M. Cain, "The General Practice Lawyer and the Client", International Journal of the Sociology of Law, 7, 1979, pp.331-54, 335.

362. See, for example, C. McCurdy, "Justice Field and the Jurisprudence of

Government-Business Relations", Journal of American History, 61, 1975, pp.970-999.

363. For an exemplorary study, see R.W. Gordon, "The Ideal and the Actual in the Law: Fantasies and Practices of New York City Lawyers, 1880-1910", (1983).

364. See A.H. Manchester. "Simplifying the Sources of the Law: An Essay in Law Reform", Anglo-American Law Review, 2, 1973, pp.395-413, 527-550 and R.B. Ferguson, "Legal Ideology and Commercial Interests: The Social Origins of the Commercial Codes", British Journal of Law and Society, 4, 1977, pp.18-32.

365. For suggestive American studies see L. Baum et al, "The Evolution of Litigation in the Federal Courts of Appeals 1895-1975", Law and Society Review, 16, 1981-2, pp.291-309; F.W. Laurent, The Business of a Trial Court: One Hundred Years of Cases (Madison: University of Wisconsin Press, 1959); L.M. Friedman and R.V. Percival, "A Tale of Two Courts", Law and Society Review, 1976, pp.267-301; R.A. Kagan et al, "The Business of State Supreme Courts, 1870-1970", Stanford Law Review, 30, 1977, pp.121-161; L.M. Friedman et al, "State Supreme Courts", Stanford Law Review, 1981, pp.773-818.

366. See D. Trubek, "The Construction and Deconstruction of a Disputes-Focused Approach", Law and Society Review, 15, 1981, pp.727-739; C. Felsteiner, R. Abel and A. Sarat, "The Emergence and Transformation of Disputes", ibid, pp.631-660; C. Mather and C. Yugvesson, "Language, Audience and the Transformation of Disputes", ibid, pp.775-801.

367. Sir T.H. Farrer, What Do We Pay With? Or, Gold, Credit and Prices (London: Cassell, 1889), p.56.

368. Ibid.

369. H. Dunning MacLeod, The Theory of Credit, Vols. 1 and 2 (London: Longman, Green, 1889 and 1890).

370. Ibid Vol.1, p.235.

371. Ibid, Section II, pp.235-75.

372. Thirteenth edition, Vol.17, p.262.

373. The Times, July 18, 1902.

374. D.N.B. Vol.XXII (Supplement).

375. R. Davidson, "Sir Hubert Llewellyn Smith and Labour Policy 1886-1916", Cambridge Ph.D., 1971 and various publications by R. Davidson based on his thesis.

376. J. Harris, William Beveridge: A Biography (Oxford: Clarendon Press, 1977).

377. D.N.B. op.cit, p.627.

378. D.N.B. 1901-1911.

379. D.N.B. Vol.XI for this and further biographical details.

380. Cf. L. Levi, supra, n.73.

381. For Cliffe-Leslie see Atiyah, supra, n.4, pp.612-3, 638-9 and 667-8; Perkin, supra, n.143, pp.197-200.

382. R.B. Ferguson, "Legal Ideology and Commercial Interest", British Journal of Law and Society, Vol.4, 1977, pp.18-38. See also the entry for Chalmers in A.W.B. Simpson (ed), A Dictionary of Common Law Biography (London: Butterworth, 1984). For aspects of his judicial career, see G.R. Rubin, infra. For an episode in his civil service career, see G.R. Rubin, op.cit, (in preparation).

383. See also D. Sugarman, "The Legal Boundaries of Liberty: Dicey, Liberalism and Legal Science", Modern Law Review 46, 1983, pp.102-11.

384. The group considered here has been arbitrarily limited to British-born English legal historians so as to simplify the exposition. Thus, leading figures such as Vinogradoff, Holmes and Ames, have been excluded. For reasons of space, leading figures such as Bryce, Jenks and Pollock could not be assessed here.

385. Sir H.S. Maine's work was highly influential during his lifetime. See for example, G. Feaver, From Status to Contract (London: Longmans, 1969), pp.xv-xvi, 43-6, 58, 128-33, 136, 147-7. Maitland, however, talked of Maine "with reluctance, for on the few occasions on which I sought to verify his statements of fact I came to the conclusion that he trusted much to a memory that played him tricks and rarely looked back at a book that he had once read . . .": C.H.S. Fifoot (ed), supra, n.293, Letter 279, p.222. See also Feaver, ibid, pp.54-7 and 136-43; Burrow, supra, n.289, Chs.5 and 117; and P. Stein, Legal Evolution: The Story of an Idea (Cambridge: Cambridge University Press, 1980), pp.86-114.

The criticisms of Dicey's historical method are usefully collected in R.A. Cosgrove, supra, n.271, Ch.8.

386. Sir P. Vinogradoff, "The Teaching of Sir Henry Maine", The Collected Papers of Paul Vinogradoff (Oxford: Clarendon Press, 1928), Vol.2, pp.173-89, 185. Although directed at Maine, it is equally applicable to Dicey as Cosgrove, ibid, testifies.

387. J.W. Burrow, supra, n.117.

388. See the material cited supra, notes 296 and 385.

389. "Why the History of English Law is Not Written", (inaugural lecture, 1888), The Collected Papers of F.W. Maitland, (H.A.L. Fisher, ed), Vol.I, (Cambridge: Cambridge University Press, 1911), pp.485-6.

390. "The Materials for English Legal History", ibid, Vol.II, p.3.

391. Essays on the Teaching of History, (introduction by F.W. Maitland) (Cambridge: Cambridge University Press, 1906), p.xx.

392. See, for example, the references to Maitland supra, n.32.

393. Sir F. Pollock and F.W. Maitland, The History of English Law: Before the Time of Edward I (Cambridge: Cambridge University Press, Second edition, 1898), 2 volumes. "His" because the work, as Pollock acknowledged, was very largely Maitland's. See in particular the new Chapter 1 Maitland drafted for

the second edition. This espoused a total history, an amalgam of the political, social, economic and legal.

394. Founded in 1887 "to encourage the study and advance the knowledge of the history of English Law". See further, Sir C. Carr, The Mission of the Selden Society (London: Bernard Quaritch, 1960).

395. For example, Charles Beard pointed to Maitland as the one English legal historian who had begun to explore the connections between law and economic change: C.A. Beard, An Economic Interpretation of the Constitution of the United States (New York: Macmillan, 1935 edition), p.8 and n.1.

396. R. Johnson, "Thompson, Genovese, and Socialist History", History Workshop, No.6, 1978, pp.79-100, 87, on the work of E.P. Thompson and other "culturalist" historians.

On Maitland's diffidence on the questions of theory and the politics of historiography, two examples will have to suffice. First, Maitland's empiricist tendencies are illustrated in his early but not untypical remarks that ". . . it is easier to make theories of sociology than to ascertain the facts.": Pleas of the Crown for the County of Gloucester etc. (1884), p.xxxv. Second, Burrow's fascinating explication of the ideological overtones of "The Village Community" debate in late 19th Century English history illustrates Maitland's ". . . English historian's disposition to regard historiography as historians writing about what was what in the best ways they know how": J.W. Burrow, supra, n.117, p.260. In this debate, at least, it was Vinogradoff rather than Maitland who perceived the "politically charged" nature of the competing historical arguments. See generally Burrow, ibid.

397. R. Johnson, ibid, p.89.

398. This tendency towards empiricism is applicable not only to legal history but to much of economic and social history. It is important to make clear that the problems of theory and method posed by English legal history in the period

1860-1920 are difficult to resolve; and that it is easier to articulate objections than to suggest better solutions, "especially on the vexed epistemological questions": see R. Johnson, ibid, p.87, who makes this point, in the context of social history.

399. W. Buckland, Reflections on Jurisprudence (Cambridge: Cambridge University Press, 1945), p.2. For example, Amos, Clark, Marby, Hearne, Holland and Salmond all more or less imbibed Austin's conception of jurisprudence. See, generally W.L. Morison, John Austin (London: Edward Arnold, 1982), pp.148-70.

400. Bryce, Maine, Maitland and Pollock all criticised Austin for his lack of a sense of history; and, in the case of Clark, Maitland and Pollock, the criticism extended to Austin's "superficial" knowledge of English and Roman law. See, for example, H.S. Maine, Village Communities in East and West (London: John Murray, 1871), pp.330-83 and Lectures on the Early History of Institutions (London: John Murray, 1875), pp.342-400; and C.E. Clark, Practical Jurisprudence, A Comment on Austin (Cambridge: Cambridge University Press, 1883).

401. D.G. Ritchie, Darwin and Hegel, With Other Philosophical Studies (London: 1893), p.157 and n.1, quoted in S. Collini, "Sociology and Idealism in Britain 1880-1920", Archives Europeennes de Sociologie, Vol.19, 1978, pp.3-52, 16, n.26.

402. Sir W. Holdsworth, A History of English Law, 16 volumes, (London: Methuen/Sweet and Maxwell, 1965). See, generally, H.G. Hanbury, The Vinerian Chair and Legal Education (Oxford: Blackwell, 1958), pp.186-238.

403. Sir William Holdsworth, "A Neglected Aspect of the Relations Between Economic and Legal History", Economic History Review, Vol.1, (O.S.) 1927, pp.114-23.

404. Ibid, p.114.

405. Ibid, p.123.

406. Sir F. Pollock, Jurisprudence and Legal Essays (London: Macmillan, 1961), p.185. This quote derives from a lecture published in 1882 in which Pollock argued that the linkages between the history of law and legal institutions and "politics" were closer than lay persons, lawyers and historians oft appreciated.

407. A.W.B. Simpson, "The Survival of the Common Law System" in Then and Now, 1799-1974 (London: Sweet and Maxwell, 1974), pp.51-70, 64. The full quote is revealing and provocative: "Whilst the academics have tended to behave as if their chief aim was to be really accepted as part of the system - that is as barristers without portfolio - those who have had most influence upon the law have kept a safe distance between themselves and the Inns of Court": ibid.

408. W.J. Ashley, supra, n.40; W.L. Burn, The Age of Equipoise (London: Allen and Unwin, 1964), Ch.4; R.M. Hartwell, supra, notes 110 and 187, and also The Industrial Revolution and Economic Growth (London: Methuen, 1971), pp.244-261; R.S. Neale, supra, n.129 and Bath, 1680-1850 (London: Routledge, 1981), esp. Chps.4-7; Thorold Rogers, Six Centuries of Work and Wages (1884).

409. See, for example, the citations supra, notes 338, 339 and 340.

410. For example, D. Alexander, Retailing in England During the Industrial Revolution (London: Athlone Press, 1970); S. Marriner, "English Bankruptcy Records and Statistics Before 1850", Economic History Review, Vol.33, 1980, pp.351-66; L.S. Pressnell, Country Banking in the Industrial Revolution (Oxford: Oxford University Press, 1956); H.A. Shannon, "The First Five Thousand Limited Companies and their Duration", Economic History Review, Vol.2, 1932, pp.396-424.

411. See, for example, W.D. Rubinstein, Men of Property (London: Croom Helm, 1981).

412. Cited in a book review by J.V. Orth, Tulane Law Review, Vol.54, 1980, pp.798-808, 798.

413. See the material cited supra, n.4.

414. P. Abrams, supra, n.191, pp.xiii-xiv.

415. E.P. Thompson, The Making of the English Working Class (Harmondsworth: Penguin Books, 1968), p.13.

416. Ibid. Also, P. Corrigan, supra, n.254.

417. L.M. Friedman, (book review), American Journal of Legal History, Vol.14, 1970, pp.277-279, 279.

418. J.Griffith, supra, n.170, pp.373-4.

419. R.W. Gordon, supra, n.308, p.907.

420. A.W.B. Simpson, supra, n.41, p.591.

421. B. Supple, supra, n.246, p.302.

422. M. Weber, On Law in Economy and Society (Cambridge: Harvard University Press, 1954), p.315.

423. Cf. E.B. Pashukanis, Law and Marxism (London: Ink Links, 1978), who treats the commodity form of law as the capitalist form of law. This view is inconsistent with that espoused in this essay which has emphasised the plurality of capitalist forms of law. Furthermore, Pashukanis ignores the extent to which the rise of state interventionism in the later 19th century undercut the commodity form of law. See, for example, Atiyah, supra, n.4, Part III.

424. J. Urry, supra, n.224, pp.99 and 83.

425. R. Gordon, supra, n.176, pp.1053-4.

426. A Stinchcombe, Theoretical Methods in Social History (New York: Academic Press, 1978), p.7.

427. M. Weber, supra, n.398, pp.188-91.

428. See R.W. Gordon, supra, n.118, p.8 and n.308, pp.910-11.

429. C. Hill, Intellectual Origins of the English Revolution (Oxford: Clarendon Press, 1980), pp.225-65.

430. Ibid, pp.1-3.

431. See generally, G.S. Jones, "History: The Poverty of Empiricism", Ideology in

Social Science (ed), R. Blackburn (London: Fontana/Collins, 1972), pp.96-118.

432. Ibid, pp.97-8.

433. E.H. Carr, What is History? (Harmondsworth: Penguin Books, 1964).

434. G.S. Jones, supra, n.47, pp.96-7.

435. Ibid, p.114.

436. M. Ignatieff, "Theorising the Facts", New Society, 1981, pp.237-8, 237.

437. A. Stinchcombe, supra, n.402, p.124.

438. K. Burke, Permanent Change (New York: New Republic Inc) 70 cited in Carson , supra n.283.

439. For example, T. Skocpol, States and Social Revolutions (Cambridge: Cambridge University Press, 1979).

440. J Dunn, "The Identity of the History of Ideas", History and Theory 8, 1969; Q. Skinner, "Meaning and Understanding in the History of Ideas", History and Theory 8, 1969; J.G.A. Pocock, Politics, Language and Time (London: Methuen, 1972); T.S. Kuhn, The Structure of Scientific Revolutions 2nd ed., (Chicago: University of Chicago, 1970).

441. J.W. Burrow, supra, notes 117 and 289; S. Collini, Liberalism and Sociology (Cambridge: Cambridge University Press, 1979); and D. Winch, Adam Smith's Politics (Cambridge: Cambridge University Press, 1978).

442. C. Ginzberg, "Morelli, Freud and Sherlock Holmes", History Workshop 9, 1980, pp.5-36; W. Sewell, Work and Revolution in France (Cambridge: Cambridge University Press, 1980); G.S. Jones, "Rethinking Chartism" in G.S. Jones, Languages of Class (Cambridge: Cambridge University Press, 1983), pp.90-178.

443. See, for example, B. Taylor, Eve and the New Jerusalem (London: Virago, 1983); C. MacCormick and M. Strathern (eds), Nature, Culture and Gender (London: Virago, 1983; and K. Young, C. Walkowitz and R. McCullagh, Of Marriage and the Market (London: Routledge, 1982).

444. C. Geertz, The Interpretation of Cultures (London: Routledge, 1981) and M.

Sahlins, Historical Metaphors and Mystical Realities (London: Routledge, 1982).

444a. See, for example, P. Corrigan and D. Sayer, "How the Law Rules", in B. Fryer et al (eds), Law, State and Society (London: Croom Helm, 1981) pp.21-53; P. Corrigan, "State Formation and Moral Regulation in 19th Century Britain", Ph.D., Durham University, 1977; P. Corrigan, "On Moral Regulation", Sociological Review, 1981, pp.103-29; and D. Sayer and P. Corrigan, "Late Marx" in T. Shanin (ed), Late Marx and the Russian Road (London: Routledge, 1983) pp.77-93.

The relevant work of the American Critical Legal Studies movement is voluminous. For a few examples of this important and exciting literature see: G. Frug, "The City as a Legal Concept", Harvard Law Review, 93, 1980, pp.1057-1154; R. Gordon, see supra, n.4; M. Horwitz, "The History of the Public/Private Distinction", University of Pennsylvania Law Review, 130, 1982, pp.1423-1428 and supra, n.4; D. Kairys (ed), The Politics of Law (New York: Pantheon, 1982); A. Katz, "Studies in Boundary Theory", Buffalo Law Review, 28, 1979, pp.383-435; D. Kennedy, "The Structure of Blackstone's Commentaries", Buffalo Law Review, 1979, pp.205-382; D. Kennedy, "Toward an Historical Understanding of Legal Consciousness" in S. Spitzer (ed), Research in Law and Sociology, Vol.3, (Greenwood: JAI Press); K. Klare, "Judicial Deradicalisation of the Wagner Act and the Origins of Modern Legal Consciousness 1937-1942", Minnesota Law Review, 62, 1978, pp.265-339; M. Minow, "The Properties of Family and the Family of Property", Yale Law Journal, 92, 1982, pp.376-395; J. Nockleby, "Tortious Interference with Contractual Relations in the 19th Century", Harvard Law Review, 93, 1980, pp.510-550; F. Olsen, "The Family and the Market", Harvard Law Review, 96, 1983, pp.1497-1578; M. Tushnet, "Perspectives on the Development of American Law", Wisconsin Law Review, 1977, pp.81-109; R. Unger, "The Critical Legal Studies Movement", Harvard Law Review, 96, 1982, pp.561-

675; and K. Vandevelde, "The New Property of the 19th Century", Buffalo Law Review, 29, 1980, pp.325-367. A special issue of the Stanford Law Review devoted to the Critical Legal Studies movement will be published during 1984. This issue includes an important essay by R.W. Gordon entitled "Critical Legal Histories".

We are very grateful to Michael Sonenscher for drawing our attention to the work of Ginsberg, Sewell, Geertz and Sahlins, and for impressing upon us the importance of this work in the ways described in the text.

445. S. Anderson, "The Lawyer as Historian", Modern Law Review, Vol.44, 1981, pp.227-33, 233.

446. G. Parker, "The Masochism of the Legal Historian", University of Toronto Law Journal, Vol.24, 1974, pp.279-317.

447. For example, R.W. Gordon, supra, n.176, p.1055.

448. On the imbrication of law in society and economy, see E.P. Thompson, Whigs and Hunters supra n.4 pp.215-69, "The Grid of Inheritance" in J. Goody et al (eds), Family and Inheritance (Cambridge: Cambridge University Press, 1976) pp.328-60 and "The Poverty of Theory" supra pp.288-90. See also the material collected supra n.444a.

PART A

LAW AND ECONOMY

FAMILY SETTLEMENTS ON TRUST:
LANDOWNERS AND THE RISING BOURGEOISIE *

M.R. Chesterman

Familiar summaries of the origins and development of English trusts law, such as appear at the beginning of most English texts on trusts law,[1] say little or nothing about a most important part of the story. The origins of the Lord Chancellor's equitable jurisdiction, his recognition and enforcement of uses affecting land, the enactment and effect of the Statutes of Uses and of Wills, the success of conveyancers in obviating the former Statute by means of devices such as "a use upon a use", the transformation of English property law as a whole, including many aspects of trusts, under the 1925 legislation, the emergence of implied, resulting and constructive trusts and the separate development of a law of charitable trusts - all these topics receive their due attention. What is omitted, or at best only favoured with a passing comment in the standard texts, is the long process whereby the property most commonly subjected to dispositions on trust shifted from proprietary interests in specific land, intended to be held in specie by the trustees for the general benefit of present and future beneficiaries, to a mixed collection of all forms of property (though chiefly personalty such as stocks and shares), which together constitute a floating fund of investments, in the sense that the sale of any of the assets and re-investment of the proceeds of sale is an accepted aspect of administration of the trust. While many social, economic and legal historians are thoroughly aware of these developments, their significant impact on the shape of modern trusts law remains insufficiently analysed, due chiefly to the failure of legal educators to place any real emphasis on them.

The particular context in which I propose to discuss this fundamental shift in the nature of trust assets is that of inter-generational settlements of family property within wealthy families. That such a shift did occur in this particular context can be illustrated fairly easily. In discussing the emergence of the use -the trust's forerunner - under the guidance of fourteenth and fifteenth century Lord Chancellors, legal historians concur in saying that uses were chiefly, although not wholly, employed by wealthy squires and noblemen and that land was virtually the only form of asset which they committed to uses.[2] Personal property such as an heirloom was only occasionally settled or bequeathed on trust and the value of such property was insignificant compared with the value of the land over which uses were declared - possibly approaching one-half of England by the early fifteenth century.[3] It could hardly have been otherwise in a society which was almost wholly agrarian and in which forms of intangible personal property, such as stocks, shares, patent rights and copyrights, were virtually unknown. On the other hand, in the only attempt I know of to investigate the composition of assets held in "personal trusts" in modern Britain - that of Jack Revell in The Wealth of the Nation (1967) - the estimated breakdown as at the end of 1961 is as follows:-[4]

TABLE I

Estimated balance sheet of personal trusts, 1961

Assets	£million	Percentage
Land	103	1.6
Dwellings	176	2.7
Other land and buildings	166	2.6
Cash	72	1.1
Unquoted U.K. government	10	0.2
Quoted U.K. government	846	13.1
Quoted U.K. local authority	60	0.9
Quoted U.K. debentures and preference	156	2.4
Quoted U.K. ordinary	3,810	59.1
Unquoted U.K. ordinary	108	1.7
Overseas government	66	1.0
Overseas company	312	4.8
Life policies	306	4.7
Other assets	259	4.0
Total	6,450	100.0

The very high proportion of assets in the category of personal property - particularly ordinary shares - is consistent with the hypotheses that much if not most of the surplus resources of wealthy individuals (i.e. the resources which do not relate to immediate needs) are held in the form of ordinary shares and similar forms of personalty, and that it is this surplus which, for tax and other sound reasons of expedience, they are likely to commit to an inter vivos or testamentary trust for the benefit of their spouse and/or others of their family. Lower down the financial scale, trusts affecting land are likely to be more frequent, seeing that the 1925 legislation uses the trust concept - notably the trust for sale - as a standard conveyancing device in a whole range of simple dispositions.[5] Yet even here the land often represents an investment asset rather than an item of property to be held in specie. By the same token, the increase in the proportionate value of land within "personal trusts" due to falls in the stock market and substantial rises in land prices since 1961 does not cast significant doubt on the general import of Revell's survey. To the extent that the great landed estate still exists, it is infrequently settled on trust as an asset to be enjoyed intact by present and future generations.[6] What trusts law now has to deal with, at least among wealthy families, is settlements affecting stocks, shares, debentures and other forms of transposable investment.

The reason why this process of change within family settlements forms an appropriate topic for a chapter in this book is that the period from 1750 to 1914, with which the book is concerned, was especially significant for it in two respects. First, the period marks the heyday and the decline of the last form of settlement of landed estates to achieve a dominant position within the conveyancing practice of English aristocratic families - namely the strict settlement, in which the trust concept had an important role, even though the disposition as a whole was normally not in trust form. Secondly, it was the period when, as far as can be discerned from available historical studies, substantial quantities of investments - for example, government stocks and mortgages of land - came to be included in family trusts established by industrialists, merchants and other wealthy individuals whose personal capital was not wholly or predominantly bound up in land. In the words of one of the few academic lawyers to draw attention to the overall process,[7]

> "To be sure, a hundred or more years before the time of Victoria's death trusteeship had passed, somewhat nervously, from the concept of safe conduct of a specific res into the concept of maintenance of a stated set of values. During that transition the duty of the English trustee had transformed itself from the relatively restricted obligations related to care, custody and operation of family agricultural real estate and its appurtenances to the much more intricate task of trading in commercial and financial markets and to the attempted maintenance, through the life of the trust, of a value which had been stated to exist at the time of the opening inventory."

In investigating specifically these two forms of property disposition - strict settlements of land and settlements of investments on trust - this chapter will attempt to identify the impact of background social and economic considerations - notably developments with regard to agricultural, mercantile and industrial capitalism - upon the shape of trust law from the start of the eighteenth century up to the present day.

I: Strict Settlements of Land

A. The Form of a Strict Settlement[8]

The device known as the strict settlement seems to have been invented very shortly after the Civil War. Its significance as a conveyancing mechanism derives from the fact that it successfully averted two legal pitfalls threatening any landowner who wished to tie up his landed estates over succeeding generations. These were (i) that ever since Taltarum's case (1472),[9] an entail of land could be broken (the technical term was "barred") by the current tenant in tail through the use of an ingenious procedure called a "common recovery" and (ii) that alternative fettering devices involving the creation of contingent estates of strictly limited duration coming into force one after another (e.g. a succession of life estates) were likely to fall foul of complicated and somewhat uncertain rules, whereby the later estates would be invalid ab initio (e.g. because they did not vest before the determination of prior interests created) or could be destroyed by any purported sale of the land on the part of a current holder.[10] A strict settlement could avert these traps and also confer upon the current landholder and each of his successors the form of landed interest which was most secure against fraud or double-dealing: namely, a common law freehold or leasehold estate.[11]

While strict settlements came in many shapes and sizes and manifested varying degrees of strictness, an explanation of their essential characteristics and their usefulness begins best with an outline of a typical example. On the marriage of an eldest son (ES) to a bride (B), F, the father and owner of the family estates in fee simple, made an inter vivos settlement creating the following legal estates: to himself for life, then to ES for life, then to trustees "to preserve contingent remainders" for the lifetime of ES, then to the heirs male "of the body of ES on the body of B" (i.e. an entail in the male line, known as "tail male"), then to F's younger sons successfully in tail male (this being to cover the contingency of a failure in ES's male line). In the event of a total failure of male successors, one or more female descendants could be stipulated as heiresses. Accompanying clauses, becoming more broad-ranging and permissive with the nineteenth century, regulated the important question of the current life-tenant's powers of management, covering such matters as his power to grant leases, erect buildings, fences, other improvements, or commence mining operations, without being liable to ensuing life-tenants for damages for "waste". In the absence of such clauses, life-tenants' powers to maintain and improve the estate were very limited until a series of enabling statutes came to be passed in the nineteenth century. Either in the strict settlement itself or, more commonly, in a contemporaneous marriage settlement, the land would also be charged with cash "portions" for the children of ES and B other than their heir, and with a "jointure" for B if she were to become a widow.

This example of a strict settlement is expressed to take effect on the marriage of the settlor's eldest son ES, but in this respect it may not be wholly typical. It has recently been argued[12] that strict settlements were more commonly linked to ES's coming of age. A third possibility is that the terms of the settlement were set out in F's will. By the same token, settlements did not necessarily create legal estates: instead, the legal estate could be vested in trustees, and equitable estates only be conferred on F, ES and their successors.[13]

The pattern of dispositions exemplified here wholly prevented the "barring" of the entailed estate conferred on ES's eldest son, G, until F died and G came of age; even then barring could only occur during ES's lifetime if ES consented. This is because the principle in Taltarum's case[14] only allowed barring where the holder of the entailed estate, having attained majority, was the tenant in possession or had the consent of a prior life tenant in possession. Furthermore, any attempt by ES to destroy the contingent remainder in favour of his heirs male by purporting to sell the land would be frustrated by the interposed "trust to preserve contingent remainders". In the outcome, the land was tied up at least until G turned twenty-one. By that time, however, ES would most likely be the family patriarch and as inclined as F had been to see the family lands tied up for a further period. In addition, since he would have the current income from the land and G would have only an expectancy, he could put pressure on G to resettle the land on much the same terms as before, in return for an appropriate share in the family revenue. In evidence to official inquiries in 1828 and again in 1881,[15] it was testified that individuals in G's position scarcely ever resisted this pressure. It was thus most likely that on G's marriage, the strict settlement originally created by his grandfather F would be revoked by the joint act of ES and G, and a new one would be created containing life estates for ES and G, a trust to preserve contingent remainders and an entail for G's heirs.

The particular ingredient of the strict settlement which distinguished it from other similar dispositions was the trust to preserve contingent remainders. By ensuring that the legal estate conferred upon ES's heirs could not be destroyed by any prior act of ES, it provided the finishing touches to the strict settlement, enabling it to achieve a wholly distinctive balance between fettering the family lands outright and making it excessively easy for a life-tenant to thwart the desire of his predecessors to protect the family lands from unwise dissipation by succeeding generations.

B. Extent of Use and Effects on Land Distribution

Some contemporaries believed that by the mid-nineteenth century strict settlements may have been imposed upon as much as three-quarters of English land. A modern historian's estimate of the approximate proportion is one half.[16] These observations are enough in themselves to establish one salient point: viz., that during the eighteenth and nineteenth centuries any substantial landowner, and any conveyancer consulted by him, was subject to very strong pressure, in terms of conformity with the practice adopted by members of the land-owning class and with precedents pervading both the training and the day-to-day activities of conveyancers, to adopt some variant of the strict settlement as a means of controlling the distribution of landed estates. In a word, the strict settlement was, if nothing else, fashionable. Within a social class whose status and political power depended not only on pedigree and the possession of landed estates, but also on "style" in the display and consumption of wealth,[17] adherence to fashion counted for a good deal.

This is not to say, however, that the widespread use of the strict settlement lacked any hard-nosed economic or political motivations. For a nobleman, political power, whether through membership of the House of Lords, control of the process of election to the House of Commons, court patronage, or office-holding and prestige within the local community, was dependent on continued possession of an estate of adequate size and would be enhanced by further acquisition.[18] To buy new land with spare cash, to mortgage existing holdings for this same purpose, to arrange an advantageous marriage to a wealthy heir or heiress - all these were, of course the means of acquisition of an ambitious family, but the strict settlement was, or at least appeared to be, an essential line of defence against short-sighted sales by an heir or heiress who had consumed well, and no doubt conspicuously, but not too wisely. Within the family itself, the strict settlement also represented an important patriarchial weapon against any other forms of delinquency by heirs and heiresses. G's expectation of succeeding to the family lands appeared in tangible form in his possession of a remainder in tail following the life estate of his father ES, but it was evident to him that de facto this entitlement was not immutable. It was instead open to negotiation when the time came to resettle on his majority or marriage, and at that point of time ES's control over current income gave him a very strong bargaining position. G would in practice be compelled to surrender his fee tail in exchange for a life estate on pain of losing any hope of sharing in current income so long as ES lived; in theory ES could even compel him to surrender all his interest in the land or starve in the interim. By the same token, the adoption of a clause whereby the amount of each daughter's and younger son's portion was dependent on her or his father's discretion, instead of being wholly fixed in advance, also strengthened patriarchal power.[19]

Some of the consequences of this eagerness of aristocrats following the Civil War to tie up family lands through the use of strict settlements and ancillary property dispositions have been summed up as follows: -[20]

> "In the early sixteenth century the peers refused the offer of inalienable entails included in the first draft of the Statute of Uses; in the late seventeenth, they hastened to tie up their estates in inalienable strict settlements. In the sixteenth, younger sons were often given properties outright; in the seventeenth, they were given life interests or annuities instead. In the sixteenth, men sold land to clear off debts and raise marriage portions; in the seventeenth, they conveyed property to trustees for a period of years instead, now often in their own lifetime rather than that of their heirs. In the sixteenth, they reserved a large section of their estate at their own personal disposal; often giving the

son and heir a reversionary interest only in what was left; in the seventeenth, the son and heir held the reversion of almost all the property. In the sixteenth, the father of the groom used his daughter-in-law's marriage portion on personal consumption; in the seventeenth, he was obliged to use it to buy land for settlement on the bride and groom. In the sixteenth, men raised capital from the estate by taking large fines for long leases, thus mortgaging the future; in the seventeenth, leases shortened, fines were reduced, and rents rose."

It has accordingly been argued, chiefly by Sir John Habakkuk,[21] that between the Civil War and the mid-eighteenth century there was a great deal of land acquisition by the larger landowners (many of whom had moved into this class in Tudor and Jacobean times by means of newly-acquired mercantile wealth, and who mortgaged existing holdings to facilitate new acquisitions), but that thereafter land acquisition slowed down as, with the aid of the strict settlement, the great landed families sat firm on their estates. These developments, along with increases in land tax, allegedly squeezed smaller holdings and inhibited newly-rich merchants and industrialists from acquiring landed estates. In short, the strict settlement, together with accompanying forms of marriage settlement and a recently streamlined law of mortgages (which recognised an assignment of mortgagee's interest, allowed for long-term borrowing and protected by equitable remedies the borrower whose instalment payments fell into arrears), constituted a significant legal contribution to a process of aggregation and consolidation of large landed estates between the Civil War and the mid-nineteenth century.

This account of the impact of the strict settlement was accepted as orthodox for some time after it was put forward (about 1950) and was supported to some extent by empirical study, chiefly in Bedfordshire and Northamptonshire. More recent writers, notably, Eileen Spring,[22] Clay,[23] Holderness,[24] Beckett[25] and Bonfield[26] have however challenged it on a number of points. These writers[27] argue first that a general pattern of increase in the size of large landed estates between the Civil War and the mid-eighteenth century is not discernible: indeed, in at least one further county chosen for empirical study, Cumbria, it did not occur. Secondly, they assert, with empirical evidence from Lincolnshire and Cumbria particularly, that throughout the period under discussion merchants and industrialists could buy land if they wished: there was no "squeeze" after the mid-eighteenth century due to strict settlements. It is thus misleading to talk in terms of a single-minded desire to tie up heavily mortgaged estates for the foreseeable future. Thirdly, they argue that the strict settlement did not really work along the lines claimed by Habakkuk. Not only was it fragile in the senses conceded by him - i.e., in particular, that it could be scattered to the four winds by a decision of father and heir not to resettle, or by a private Act - but it also could fail to keep the family estates in bondage if successions were not in the direct line or if the father died before the majority or marriage of the heir. As to the last of these contingencies, demographic evidence has been amassed[28] to the effect that at least until the latter half of the eighteenth century it was more likely than not that an aristocratic father would die before the marriage of his heir, though the recent assertion that more strict settlements were made on the heir's coming of age than on his marriage detracts from the significance of this conclusion.[29] Fourthly, there is clear evidence that in many cases some of an aristocratic family's land was left out of settlement, though it is of course impossible to estimate any overall proportion. Finally, Habakkuk's critics point to evidence that between the Civil War and the mid-eighteenth century - when, according to Habakkuk, large landowners were mortgaging existing holdings in order to acquire new land - mortgage interest rates were significantly higher than the rates of return to be had from leasing agricultural land. It would thus have been economic suicide to indulge extensively in a practice described by Habakkuk as a means whereby the land-owning class was "in effect raising itself by its own bootstraps."[30]

As a result of these attacks upon the Habakkuk thesis,[31] one can no longer safely regard the strict settlement as a major compelling force within a uniform process of aggregation and consolidation of large landed estates. It does not follow that it played no significant role. Beckett suggests that strict settlements and mortgages probably had a "passive role", being "utilized to realise an ever-present wish on the part of landowners to safeguard the future of their estates which had always been frustrated in the past by the lack of legal safeguards."[32] Implicit in this comment is a recognition that strict settlements remained a pervasive phenomenon: indeed the emphasis placed by Beckett et al., on the fragility of strict settlements reinforces this very point. The more it is argued that strict settlements were easily broken by positive action (such as procuring an Act of Parliament) or uncontrollable events (such as a father's early death), the more it can be asserted that the practice of settling lands must have had the character of self-imposed law; otherwise, it could scarcely have survived as an admittedly widespread practice for more than two centuries. Furthermore, even if there is inadequate evidence to support Habakkuk's assertion that the larger landed estates grew at the expense of smaller ones between the Civil War and the mid-eighteenth century and thereafter retained their dominance, it is still arguable that strict settlement assisted significantly in averting the counter-tendency, viz., the break-up of large estates through division on inheritance, sales by life tenants under financial pressure and so on. The concurrent existence of similar attempts to tie up land - sometimes called 'vinculism' - amongst aristocratic families on the Continent as well as England confirms that the settlement had at least this defensive role, given that in several of these countries (notably France) the partition of smaller holdings not subject to settlement went to considerable lengths.[33]

Accordingly, while one has to agree with the opponents of Habakkuk's thesis that as a generalised account of aspects of the land market after the Civil War it must be deemed unproven, it is possible at the same time to assert that a significant pressure towards consolidation of landed estates - or, at the least, against short-sighted dissipation by individual family members - was exerted by the widespread use of strict settlements amongst landowners from the Civil War to the late nineteenth century.

C. Strict Settlements and the Law

In the comment of Beckett quoted above,[34] the validation of strict settlements under the land law of the time is implicitly portrayed as a cause of their popularity: because the necessary 'legal safeguards' in the guise of a form of settlement sanctioned by law had become available, strict settlements became popular. By contrast, a comment of Lawrence Stone (an adherent of the Habakkuk thesis) suggests that it was the particularly strong desire of seventeenth century land-owners to tie up their lands that induced both the invention of the strict settlement form and such changes in land law as were necessary to confirm its validity. "The landed classes willed the end:" he says, "the conveyancers and the judges [my emphasis] at last provided the means."[35] With its crude Marxist overtones this comment, taken out of context, is not representative of Stone's view of the relationship between land-owners and legal development. But the clash between the two historians' "obiter dicta" provides a useful starting point for a discussion of the interrelation of the strict settlement with property law, both as it existed at the time when strict settlements became popular and in its present form.

As explained earlier, one of the achievements of the strict settlement was that it tied up common law freehold estates for a generation at least - and for longer if resettlements took place in accordance with the economic coercion upon the settlor's grandson which it envisaged - while it also countered successfully any attempt to destroy the grandson's entail by a purported sale of the son's life estate and it obviated any 'common recovery' in pursuance of the same aim. To a large measure, it achieved these aims by not attempting to do too much: that is, by not expressly purporting to render the land inalienable beyond the grandson's coming of age, it escaped any challenge to validity based on legal rules striking down more obviously dynastic settlements, such as an endless succession of life-estates. To this extent, it may be described, in conformity with the view taken by Beckett, as an ingenious and enlightened response to pre-existing rules: its inventors provided "legal safeguards" in the form of a legally inoffensive settlement which preserved the desired balance between wholesale fettering and marketability. But there were two important aspects of strict settlements which, as the law stood at the end of the Civil War, might have provoked a successful challenge to their validity and effect. The first of these was the possibility that the conveyancing device which made the strict settlement distinctive and effective, namely, the trust to preserve contingent remainders, was itself liable to destruction. The second was the more general consideration that there was no clear rule, or set of rules, to the effect that to employ common law interests to render land inalienable for the life of an existing heir and the minority of the next in line did not constitute a perpetuity. On both of these matters, the law following the invention of the strict settlement did move in a direction favourable to it: that is, the suggestion, hinted at by Stone, that the judges helped in achieving the aims desired by landowners has some force. Each of them is worthy of separate consideration.

(a) Trust to preserve contingent remainders

The effectiveness of this all-important clause within strict settlements depended, naturally enough, on its being held valid and enforceable, no matter what the life-tenant (ES) or the trustees themselves might do.

As regards ES, this meant in particular that trusts to preserve contingent remainders had themselves to be deemed vested, not contingent interests. If they had been held to be contingent interests, then, far from preserving the entailed contingent remainder in favour of the next in line, G, from any purported sale of the freehold by ES, they would themselves fail, along with G's estate, if ES purported to sell.[36] Only if they were treated as vested interests could they withstand destruction at the hands of ES. There is no doubt that the technical arguments in favour of treating them as contingent interests were strong ones:

their coming into operation clearly depended on a specific contingency which might never occur, viz., some act of ES or some other event which threatened to destroy G's remainder. Yet in 1697 the Court of Common Pleas reached a decision implying that the trustees' interest was indeed a vested one (Duncomb v. Duncomb)[37] and the House of Lords duly confirmed this in 1742 (Dormer v. Parkhurst).[38] The extent to which land-owning practice exerted pressure on the judiciary to reach this result is particularly evident in a comment of Willes C.J., delivering the opinion of the judges to the House of Lords in the latter case:[39]

> "Surely, it is a much less evil to make a construction, even contrary to the common rules of law (though I think this is not so) than to overthrow I may say 100,000 settlements; for it is a maxim in law, as well as reason, communis error facit jus."

Concurrently with these decisions, the Court of Chancery was making it clear that attempts by the trustees to upset the machinery of a strict settlement by deviating from their obligation to preserve contingent remainders would, in general, be unsuccessful. It was said in 1710 (Pye v. Gorge)[40] that for the trustees to join in a conveyance to a purchaser, defeating the remainders, would be a breach of trust. In Mansell v. Mansell (1732),[41] trustees who so acted were ordered to join with the successors of the purchasers (who had notice of the breach of trust and had not given consideration) in conveying the lands to the remainder-man in accordance with the entail originally granted to him. It was added that if the purchasers had taken for value and without notice, their rights, in accordance with normal doctrines of equity, would have prevailed over those of the remainder-man, but the trustees would have been ordered to buy equivalent land with their own money and settle them on the remainder-man. Scattered suggestions in earlier cases that trustees who broke a trust to preserve contingent remainders might not actually be punishable were thus firmly scotched. As in Dormer v. Packhurst, the court observed that enforcement of trusts to preserve contingent remainders was essential to the proper working of "all the great settlements in England."[42]

So far as modern trust law is concerned, the validation of trusts to preserve contingent remainders has not left much of a mark in terms of specific legal principle. Insofar as it conferred active duties upon trustees such as are now pervasive within trust of investments, it was forward-looking, but the same could be said of a number of other trust dispositions commonly associated with aristocratic settlements.[43] The raising of portions, for instance, was often ensured by directing trustees to sell specific lands at the time when the portion had to be paid or by empowering them to grant leases or mortgages of the settled land. Trustees might also be authorised to take possession of the settled estates when the life-tenant was threatened with insolvency and to manage these until the crisis has passed. From the point of view of the development of a modern law relating to active trusts these particular adjuncts of aristocratic land settlements may not have contributed a great deal, seeing that the principle that a trustee might have active duties was apparent, though not commonly invoked, in the very earliest days of medieval uses.[44] But they are important if one is studying changes within the dominant practices of family settlement during the rise of capitalism. They illustrate the dialectical process whereby active, managerial trusts which would relate, in due course, to funds of transposable investments became first established as a common practice within the context of earlier modes of settlement in which retention in specie of the trust property - i.e., the land - was the primary aim. Viewed in this light, trusts to preserve contingent remainders and other active trusts associated with strict settlements are a useful reminder of the law's continuity during a process of change.

(b) Perpetuities

Recent studies of perpetuities are significantly at odds with traditional accounts of judicial policy on this matter. The metaphor traditionally adopted has been one of warfare:[45] right-minded judges, carrying the banner of free alienability of land and drawing on an armoury of rules against unbarrable entails and other forms of perpetuity, battled for centuries against perverse landowners and their artful conveyancers, who persisted in erecting all manner of devious defences and fortifications in the form of ingenious conveyances and settlements. It has now been asserted more than once, however, that compromise is probably a better metaphor than warfare and, that the principal "modern" rule regarding perpetuities, stemming chiefly from the Duke of Norfolk's case (1681),[46] was viewed, even at the time of its emergence, as a rule, not against, but of perpetuities.[47] With specific regard to strict settlements, A.W.B. Simpson observes as follows:[48]

> "Modern textbooks as well as historical works tend to portray the law of real property as a body of law which has zealously protected the power of free alienation of land, and the rule against perpetuities (and associated doctrines) as an effective curb against attempts to destroy this power in landowners. It is important to realise that the strict settlement ingeniously removed the power of free alienation from a large number of the landowners of the country; it required statutory intervention to restore it to them."

This brings us back to the earlier proposition that the law relating to perpetuities responded to the invention and proliferation of strict settlements by adapting itself in their favour. The extent of this adaptation can be summed up under two heads.

In the first place, the formulation of a "modern" rule of perpetuities in the Duke of Norfolk's case (1681),[49] by shifting the emphasis onto the period within which future interest must vest, removed any possible threat to strict settlements on the ground that their general tendency de facto was to render land inalienable for an indefinite period.[50] Through concentrating on a wholly technical inquiry into remoteness of vesting, the judges cut themselves off from the issues of policy which are brought to the forefront in the above quotation from Simpson.

Secondly, the form of a strict settlement made a positive contribution to the precise terms in which the rule first adumbrated in the Duke of Norfolk's case was finally formulated. Lord Nottingham L.C. spoke in that case of vesting within the period of a life in being and a "reasonable time" thereafter. The notion that this "reasonable time" should be twenty-one years subsequently emerged by virtue of the consideration that in a strict settlement the land was rendered inalienable during the life of the tenant for like and the minority of the remainder-man in tail. This is clear from dicta in a number of decisions, notably Duke of Marlborough v. Godolphin (1759),[51] and has modern academic support.[52]

By way of elaboration of the assertion that judges simply responded to landowners' wishes, these instances of accommodation of perpetuity rules with strict settlements can be viewed as reactions to fluctuations in the land market. In the sixteenth and early seventeenth centuries, land purchases by numerous newly-rich merchants made for a highly active market[53] which would have been unduly threatened if the judges had not been quick to strike down all forms of "perpetuity": by the eighteenth century, consolidation of acquired gains by established large landowners was best served by a tolerant judicial attitude to the degree of fettering which a strict settlement provided. This interpretation is, of course, challenged by the recent articles of Spring, Clay, Holderness, Beckett and Bonfield,[54] but it is not wholly undermined. The judges at the end of the seventeenth century did have the necessary armoury, in terms of a long tradition of purported abhorrence of perpetuities, to strike down strict settlements if they had so wished, but they chose not to deploy it.

The subsequent development of the rules regarding remoteness of vesting is of major significance for the law of trusts. Recourse to the analogy with strict settlements in fixing the perpetuity period as a life in being plus the minority of the remainder-man paved the way for liberalisation of the rule to allow for any life or lives in being to be chosen (as in "royal lives" clauses) and a period of twenty-one years "in gross" (i.e. without it having to be the minority of the remainder-man). These developments had taken place by 1833.[55] The rule thus came to represent even less of an inhibition on the power of landowners to tie up their lands than the comparatively liberalised decision in the Duke of Norfolk's case[56] sought to impose, though relatively few settlements seem to have made use of the greater freedom thus conferred.[57] It would seem the traditional forms were too well entrenched by 1833, or that the economic disadvantages of tying up land for much longer than a generation at a time had become too obvious.[58]

A step of more fundamental significance was the extension of the rule regarding remoteness of vesting from its original context within land law to settlements of personalty alone or mixed personalty and realty. This step was in fact taken by 1727,[59] without apparent consideration of the fact that different policy issues are at stake. It is one thing to keep land off the market by settling it in a manner which prohibits the sale of the freehold over several generations; it is quite another to prescribe in a testamentary or inter vivos trust that a fund of transposable investments should be held for the benefit of specified beneficiaries over the same period. Both of these situations involve, in a general sense, an exercise of the power of the "dead hand" of the settlor or testator, but considerations of marketability of specific property are present in the former situation only, and considerations of fiscal policy, particularly while estate duty was in operation, have become relevant to the latter during the present century.[60] Retention of the same underlying rule to govern both situations represents a significant and not wholly satisfactory legacy from the land law surrounding the emergence and acceptance of strict settlements to the trusts law of the present day.

These short summaries of the interrelation of specific land law rules with aspects of the strict settlement show the law (which is almost wholly case-law) setting general limits to what landowners, with the aid of their legal advisers, can achieve in controlling the future disposition of their lands, but also displaying a fair degree of responsiveness to what landowners want to do. There is an interplay between law and conveyancing practice, in which the former, being itself influenced to a high degree by the conveyancers of earlier times, calls forth responses from the latter, in the form of new conveyancing devices, then responds to those devices by altering, at least incrementally, its own rules. Such alterations may then determine to a significant degree how the law will be in the future - even if the context from which the particular rule originated is substantially altered, as particularly in the case of the rule regarding remoteness of vesting.

It seems wrong, however, to view this responsiveness of the law as a simple illustration of land law's readiness to dance to landowners' tunes. A crude Marxist interpretation along these lines would lay stress on the political power exercised by eighteenth century landowners and on the land-owning status of the Lord Chancellor, the other law-lords and many of the common law judges during the period under discussion.[61] Yet if patriarchal landowners during the eighteenth century really did want to create long-term dynastic settlements of their landed estates and if they effectively controlled the course of the land law, why was any legal inhibition placed in their way? Why, for instance, when the Duke of Marlborough established a settlement of his Woodstock estates which purported to tie the hands of later generations for much longer than a strict settlement, did the Court of Chancery hold in Duke of Marlborough v. Godolphin (1759)[62] that the settlement was void for perpetuity?

The answer clearly resides in familar notions as to the relative autonomy of the law.[63] Even when, as in this case, a specific branch of the law was subject to particularly strong influence from a particularly powerful sector of the ruling classes which took a vital interest in it, other determining influences were also at work. Ideologies as to the desirability of maintaining some degree of marketability in land and specific legal principles based upon such ideologies were handed down from the Tudor-Stuart period, during which many newly-enriched traders had bought their way to landed status in a highly active land market.[64] The underlying ideological notion that the law should be certain and should adhere to precedent was taking hold even of equity (having already conquered the common law)[65] and thereby contributed to the preservation of this older doctrine despite changed attitudes on the part of landowners. A contemporary factor was the political pressure exerted by those rising non-landed classes who wished to acquire land - the merchants and industrialists whose efforts in this regard, as described by Holderness[66] and Beckett,[67] were far from unsuccessful. A proliferation of wholly unbarrable entails would have been anathema to them.

With these conflicting pressures at work, it is perhaps remarkable that strict settlements should have been widespread for as long as two hundred years, being renewed many times within individual families and operating, as already suggested, as a form of self-imposed law. The reasons must chiefly lie in the factors stressed by Habakkuk's opponents, namely, that they did not impose unbreakable chains upon the land, that they were not automatically imposed upon all lands in the hands of a great landowner and that they accordingly did leave a significant degree of leeway for land to be marketable. One must also bear in mind the contribution of the legal profession, which not only invented the relevant clauses and recommended them as the "done thing" to landowners who must often have failed to appreciate their significance, but also put up a stern resistance to nineteenth century pressures to abolish strict settlements and other forms of entail. It did so avowedly in the interests of substantial landowners (which many lawyers were), but it had its own interest in preserving the complexity of conveyancing, to which settlements and entails made a welcome contribution, against proposals for simplified methods of land transfer.[68] On this view, one can speak of a fusion of land law and conveyancing practice which pervaded, without wholly dominating, the "estate planning" of great landowners.

The overall impact of strict settlements on the economy is difficult to assess. Even allowing for the views urged by Habakkuk's critics, there seems little doubt that they facilitated, if not actually brought about, the heavy concentration of land-ownership reported in the "New Domesday Book" of 1874. Through so doing, they may have assisted in the development of agricultural capitalism, to the extent that the expansion of capital by individual tenant farmers depended necessarily on aggregation and consolidation of estates by their landlords.[69] They were, of course, often accused of inhibiting the progress of industrial capitalism, notably by nineteenth century "free traders" who argued, consistently with prevailing economic orthodoxy, that while land remained subject to fetters imposed by a conservative landed oligarchy the national economic well-being was seriously impaired.[70] Yet landowners did engage in a degree of industrial development[71] and were prepared, during the nineteenth century, to procure the enactment of a series of statutes progressively enlarging the powers of life-tenants.[72] When the most important of these, the Settled Land Act 1882, gave life-tenants a power of sale, the campaign for reform petered out, suggesting that many middle-class merchants and manufacturers who participated in it were concerned less with abolishing the now outdated relics of feudal land law than with ensuring that they might have easier access to landed estates themselves. They may, indeed, have felt concern that further moves to eliminate landowners' traditional freedom in conveyancing might encourage liberal reformers or socialists to press for nationalised or collectivised land-ownership[73] - in which concern they were joined, for different reasons already outlined, by the conveyancers themselves.

Yet the Settled Land Act 1882 was without doubt of major importance. In undermining the principal objective of a strict settlement - i.e. retention of family estates in specie in accordance with dynastic aspirations - it paved the way for the disappearance of great landed families as both a social institution and a "joint stock company" whereby large scale units of agricultural production, as well as residences and fine parklands, might be preserved.[74] More or less contemporaneously, family commercial and industrial enterprises - in which the connection between the family owners and the process of trade or production was much closer - were beginning to feel the competitive pressure exerted by firms which raised their capital through public subscription.[75] As quoted public companies increased their dominance of virtually all areas of enterprise during the twentieth century, the wealthy family became increasingly relegated to mere passive ownership of stocks and shares, as is illustrated in the ensuing discussion of settlements of investments. With the integrity of family landed estates thus ceasing to be instrumental to agricultural production in any significant way, such estates became vulnerable to high taxation (notably uniform estate duty, introduced in 1894) as well as to declining rates of return from agriculture.[76] The landed family could no longer withstand the challenge posed by the existence of newer modes of organising enterprise - rendering a family estate obsolete in this regard - along with the economic and political dominance attained by commercial and industrial interests. Within this pattern of developments, elimination of the dynastic ingredient in strict settlements through legislation such as the Settled Land Act was an essential change in the law, even though the strict settlement as a conveyancing form could still remain theoretically available to landowners. Accordingly, while strict settlements may have been merely useful, rather than essential, for the consolidation and aggregation of landed estates during the eighteenth and nineteenth centuries, their emasculation, though not total obliteration, was part and parcel of twentieth century social and economic development.[77]

II: Settlements of Investments on Trust

A. Emergence of Non-landed Wealth and the Significance of the Trust Form

Unlike strict settlements, settlements of investments on trust within wealthy families have not been closely investigated by legal, economic or social historians. Their rise to prominence has, in effect, to be inferred from evidence such as Revell's survey of "personal trusts" referred to above,[78] continued reference in trusts cases to wills and deeds settling large funds of mixed realty and personalty upon trust, and the reasonably full documentation of the decline of the strict settlement and other forms of disposition purporting to tie up land in specie. This lack of detailed discussion of the emergence of settlements of investments is, presumably, to be explained by the fact that no typical precedents as sophisticated and easily recognisable as strict settlements seem to have come into being and that, in the twentieth century at any rate, secrecy has been an almost inevitable corollary of the motivations of tax avoidance which often accompany such dispositions.[79] This is not to say that further investigation would be impossible, at least as regards the numerous testamentary trusts of investments whose provisions are filed at probate registries.

Despite the lack of detailed information, a general outline of the emergence of settlements of investments on trust can be suggested, comprising both an economic background and a set of reasons why the trust form should specifically have been adopted. An account of this background begins with the rise of a class of wealthy merchants whose early origins go back well into the Middle Ages. Significant quantities of personal wealth came to be held by them in a form other than the possession of land. The later development of an industrial bourgeoisie, particularly in the eighteenth and nineteenth centuries, gives a substantial boost to this general trend. To the extent that Habakkuk is correct in suggesting that the strict settlement contributed to a freezing of the land market in the late eighteenth century,[80] the very success of this rival form of family settlement may have encouraged the creation of settlements of investments on trust, insofar as merchants and industrialists inhibited from buying suitable landed estates would retain their wealth in non-landed form. Profit-yielding investments outside the possession of land were increasingly available to attract such wealth. In recent studies of the personal wealth of early merchants and industrialists,[81] the most prominent forms of investment, outside business assets, seem to have been government loan stock (whose availability increased greatly in the eighteenth century) and mortgages of land (which once again constitute, particularly on Habakkuk's view of things, a complement to the widespread adoption of strict settlements by wealthy landowners). Additionally, it was of course possible to participate, often as a highly speculative investor, in joint stock trading ventures or, as the Industrial Revolution progressed, in manufacturing, extractive or large-scale construction industries. Finally, it should be stressed that even where, despite Habakkuk's assertions, eighteenth and nineteenth century merchants and industrialists could break into an allegedly closed land market, they would often buy agricultural or urban land as an investment - to yield not only current income from leasing but a capital gain from resale in the future - in lieu of (or to supplement) a rural family home.[82] This approach to the acquisition of possessory rather than security interests in land was in total contrast to all that the strict settlement and other forms of entail stood for. Undoubtedly, much of the land bound up in strict settlements represented investment, insofar as it was not used for the family home, farm and pleasure grounds but was leased to tenant farmers in return for rents and lump sum premiums, but it was still never intended to be sold in the ordinary course, which marks it off from land purchased purely as an investment, i.e. with a view to annual yield and profit on a resale.

It seems unlikely that settlements of investments fell into standardised patterns comparable to that of the strict settlement of land. In the absence of detailed studies, one can conjecture that most of them are likely to have been testamentary trusts or marriage settlements, there being no fixed incentive to create other forms of inter vivos trust until the advent of high rates of income tax and estate duty in the twentieth century. Most of the former category contained life-interests for a surviving spouse with remainders for children, or possibly life interests for children (whether or not in addition to a surviving spouse) with remainders for grandchildren. Life interests often had protective trusts grafted onto them and interests in favour of children often provided for accumulations of income (with, perhaps, an accompanying power of maintenance) until the child's attaining majority or marrying beneath that age. As well as forming part of protective trust clauses, discretionary trusts were to be found from time to time, but they did not constitute a standard form until twentieth century tax considerations so dictated (i.e. in particular, between the Second World War and the advent of capital transfer tax in 1974). Accordingly, one envisages comparatively simple trust dispositions, far removed from the sophistication of strict settlements.

The principal reason why the trust, in particular, should have been the central legal concept within these family settlements of investments is simply that English law at the relevant period provided little else in the way of alternatives. In marked contrast to its attitude to land, the common law had no well-developed property concept whereby a succession of limited interests in intangible pure personalty, such as patent rights or government stock, could be created. Common law concepts conferring limited rights with regard to chattels - for example, bailments and pledges - did not extend to intangible property.[83] By the same token, corporate forms such as might now be used to hold the investments of wealthy families (were it not for close company taxation) were not sufficiently developed. Potentialities in this regard suffered a severe setback when in 1722 the Bubble Act, passed as a result of the stock market crash of 1720 known as the "South Sea Bubble" (of which more anon), held up the development of freely available limited company status for more than a century.[84]

With little available in the way of possible alternatives, the trust was the natural choice. Even in medieval times, bequests of valuable chattels such as heirlooms on successive limited interests had been created by way of uses.[85] When from the late Middle Ages onwards Chancery increasingly encroached on the jurisdiction of both common law and ecclesiastical courts in matters of testamentary personalty, it was natural that such bequests should continue to take effect by way of trust and should extend to intangible property. The Statute of Uses posed no hindrance to this because it did not apply to trusts of personalty.[86]

By the same token, the managerial function which was to become such a prominent aspect of the role of trustees of family investments had been apparent in trust dispositions from the earliest times,[87] though it had never yet been a leading feature of a predominant form of family settlement. Amongst the earliest forms of medieval use are to be found conveyances to feoffees to hold and manage the feoffor's lands while he was fighting the Saracen in a far-off country. It came to be recognised during the fifteenth century that feoffees could be empowered to mortgage, lease or sell land, that in this last case, they could confer a good title, both legal and beneficial, on the purchaser and - an important step for the future development of the law on trusts for sale - that they held the proceeds of sale subject to the uses stipulated. At the time of the Statute of Uses, trusts for sale and other kindred dispositions were still however, fairly infrequent and they too were left untouched by the Statute. Amongst the forms of land settlement which developed after the Statute, trusts conferring an active role on the trustees were, as we have seen,[88] a reasonably common feature. But such trusts were always ancillary: the trustees never became full-scale managers of the settled capital in the manner later to be encountered in settlements of investments. These ancillary trusts had, in the main, one or other of two purposes: to preserve the settled property if the life-tenant became insolvent, or to ensure that younger sons or, more significantly, female members of the family were properly provided for. In this last context, equity supplemented the common law in a significantly reformist way: that is, it recognised and enforced married women's proprietary rights at a time when common law rules regarding property still treated a husband and wife as one person, to wit the husband.[89]

To sum up so far, settlements of investments on trust brought together two separate strands of development within trusts law, relating respectively to trusts of personalty and trusts conferring active duties with regard to land. Furthermore, the potential of each of these pre-existing elements within trusts law came to be fully exploited by virtue of their link with settlements of investments. This follows from three aspects in particular of the later history of such settlements. First, the proportionate value of personal property - notably stocks and shares - settled or held within them increased substantially at the expense of realty. Secondly, the managerial function of the trustees came to dominate the whole settlement, rather than merely arising in specific and somewhat narrow circumstances such as insolvency of a life-tenant. Thirdly, settlements of investments themselves took over from strict settlements as the predominant mode of controlling accumulated private wealth within a rich family and transmitting it from one generation to the next.

By way of conclusion to this part of the discussion, it is worth noting that invested family wealth was not the only arena into which the trust made major inroads in the eighteenth century. An important essay by B.L. Anderson speaks of a "marvellous proliferation of trusts out of the context of landed property"[90] during this period, instancing the use of the trust as a substitute for incorporation by industrial and trading ventures (particularly after the Bubble Act), political, social and quasi-commercial clubs and societies (including even the Inns of Court and the London Stock Exchange) and non-conformist religious groups. Anderson suggests accordingly that "trusts of money" became as usual as "trusts of land", as this device "passed from an over-developed land law and fanned out amongst the growing commercial interest."[91] It took longer for "trusts of money" containing the investments of rich families to become as usual or as wealthy as "trusts of land" in the same context (i.e. strict settlements and the like), but ultimately this too was to happen, and the pendulum was to swing even further towards the former brand of trust.

B. Legal Developments

As stated at the beginning of this chapter, the emergence of trusts of invested wealth exerted a major influence on the development of trusts law. Numerous new questions requiring legal regulation presented themselves; in response, the eighteenth and nineteenth century courts of equity (and, to a lesser extent, the legislature) set about developing what they believed to be appropriate legal rules, often from very meagre starting points. While doubtless the basic concept of a trust and the broad outlines of modern trusts law owe their origins to the reasonably well-documented phenomenon of feudal conveyances of land to uses, the bulk of the law relating to trust administration stems from this virtually overlooked process taking place chiefly in the period under review.

Through comparing trusts of investments with strict settlements and similar dispositions of land, one may identify two general reasons why new rules of trusts law needed to be developed. First, since a trust of investments did not presuppose retention of the specific property committed to it, the question as to how far the settlor or testator should be permitted by law to prevent the beneficiaries alienating their beneficial interests, or indeed, terminating the trust as a whole, took on a new dimension. As with strict settlements and other entails, the underlying issue was still how far the "dead hand" of the settlor or testator should be able to inhibit the beneficiaries' freedom of disposition, but because the trust property was now a fund rather than a specific asset, held entirely according to rules of equity rather than under limitations created (in most cases) at common law predominantly and only subordinately in equity, this underlying issue needed to be resolved on new lines. Secondly, because the trustees of a fund of assets held for investment clearly needed to have the power (whether or not subject to the consent of beneficiaries) to sell specific assets subject to the trust from time to time and re-invest the proceeds with a view to profit, this active, managerial aspect of their role called for legal control. Guidelines had to be developed for determining, inter alia, what types of investment could legitimately be retained by a trustee, what types of investment he could legitimately buy with the proceeds of any property sold by him or with any other cash coming into the trust fund, which aspects (if any) of the process of sale or reinvestment he could properly delegate to expert agents such as valuers, estate agents, solicitors and brokers, and what overall standards of skill and care should be required of him in his handling of investments. In short, since the trust of investments was the first common-form family settlement in which active, managerial functions were performed by trustees in the ordinary course of events - i.e. not merely in emergencies such as were contemplated in trusts to preserve contingent remainders or to manage a life-tenant's affairs in the event of threatened insolvency - trusts law had to concentrate its attention, to an unprecedented degree, on the matter of legal control over the exercise of trusteeship discretions.

For reasons of space, I will not attempt to explore all the detailed ramifications of these two forms of challenge which eighteenth and nineteenth century trusts law had to face. I propose instead to dwell only on (a) selected aspects of the law's treatment of attempts by the beneficiaries of trusts of investments to assign their separate interests or terminate the trust as a whole in contravention of the settlor's or testator's wishes and (b) the development of rules specifying the range of investments available to trustees. Each of these topics is linked in significant ways to aspects of strict settlements already discussed.

(a) Assignment of beneficiaries' interests and premature termination of trusts

As explained in the first part of this chapter,[92] the questions of assignability of a life-tenant's interest under a strict settlement and destructibility of the settlement as a whole were resolved in a relatively sophisticated manner. There was nothing to stop a current life-tenant assigning his own limited interest: indeed it was expected that he might often do so by way of mortgage. What he could not do, thanks to the trust to preserve contingent remainders, was to purport to sell the fee simple in such a way as would destroy the settlement as a whole. As a matter of strict law, such premature termination did become possible if a current life-tenant and the remainder-man in tail, having come of age, agreed upon it, but for reasons already explained, the former of these individuals was likely to impose restraints upon both of them by insisting upon a resettlement. Accordingly, whatever might happen to a life-tenant's interest, it was most likely that the family lands would be preserved in specie within a series of settlements.

Because strict settlements were chiefly subject to a massive body of common law rules painfully built up over several centuries, while trusts of investments were a relatively novel concern of equity, these land law principles as to assignability and destructibility were not carried over in toto into the newer context. They formed only one of the sources upon which equity drew.

With regard to assignment of a beneficiary's interest, a series of Chancery judgments delivered in the first half of the nineteenth century extended to trusts of investments the principle of land law that prima facie the assignability of an interest once granted could not be fettered by a condition subsequent.[93] They did so on the various grounds that such a condition was repugnant to the main terms of the grant and that the legitimate expectations of creditors might otherwise be defeated. Only in one significant category of case - that of trusts for the benefit of married women - did they allow such conditions ("restraints on anticipation") to take effect, and these were explicitly limited to the period of coverture.[94] Yet, having thus conferred a significant favour upon creditors with one hand, the Chancery judges proceeded to take it away with the other. Virtually contemptoraneously, they held that a trust in favour of X for life (or a lesser period) or until he should purport to assign his interest or suffer it to be taken from him (e.g. in a bankruptcy) was valid.[95] By the mid-nineteenth century, the device of adding a discretionary trust in favour of X and his family, to take effect on termination of the prior trust, was also validated, thereby establishing the double-barrelled "protective trust".[96] This became a standard conveyancing clause, which in due course received statutory sanction in section 33 of the Trustee Act 1925. By virtue of this section, it is now sufficient to add the magic words "on protective trusts" to a trust for life or any lesser period, and a lengthy double-barrelled clause set out in the section will be incorporated into the trust instrument.[97] Conveyancers constructed this artefact, judges approved it and the legislature duly fell into line.

This equivocal approach to curbs on assignment of a single beneficiary's interest differs significantly from the straightforward approach adopted by nineteenth century Chancery judges towards premature termination. A pre-existing principle in the law of wills, originating in the practice of the ecclesiastical courts, was to the effect that an adult legatee whose interest in the legacy was vested could demand immediate payment of the capital sum of the legacy even though the testator had stipulated that income should be accumulated and the capital withheld for some specified period.[98] Despite some doubts in Lord Pawlet's case (1685)[99] as to whether such a principle should apply to trusts affecting land, this principle mushroomed in the nineteenth century[100] into a much broader doctrine of equity to the effect that all the beneficiaries (i.e. not merely a sole beneficiary, and including beneficiaries entitled in succession)[101] under any testamentary or inter vivos trust (i.e. not merely a legacy, and including, it would seem, any discretionary trust under which all the beneficiaries can be listed)[102] may bring the trust to end prematurely in spite of the trust founder's evident intentions, so long as they are of full age and sound mind. This doctrine - the so-called rule in Saunders v. Vautier (1841)[103] - is now said to be based on the beneficiaries' "equitable ownership" of the trust property[104] and is considerably wider than the starting principle that adult legatees may call for payment of their legacy despite a direction to accumulate income - which is in fact all that Saunders v. Vautier itself decided in 1841. Its emergence in such a broad form may have been made easier by judicial recognition that if a beneficial interest is prima facie freely assignable despite conditional restraints (according to the principles just outlined), assignment by the beneficiary in return for a capital sum is likely to defeat any particular aims which the trust founder had in mind in seeking to postpone the receipt of benefit.[105] It is only a short step from there to holding that the beneficiary or beneficiaries should be able to obtain the appropriate capital sum by simply calling on the trustees to transfer the trust property to them and abdicate their position as trustees.

For all this, the ease with which the rule in Saunders v. Vautier broadened from a narrow principle relating to specific legacies in favour of a sole beneficiary into a general doctrine permitting premature termination is striking, as also is the fact that neither judges nor academic writers have drawn much attention to the fact that this process of broadening was taking place. It is all the more striking for the fact that many American courts, following Claflin v. Claflin,[106] have taken the contrary view, arguing that a trust founder's intentions should not be simply swept aside by the assertion of "equitable ownership" by the beneficiaries. In the present century the rule in Saunders v. Vautier has become a particularly valuable weapon for families aspiring to minimise tax on family investments, not only because to terminate a subsisting trust under the rule may often be enough to avert a heavy charge of taxation, but also because the existence of the rule has provided both a theoretical starting point and a justification in policy terms[107] for that most generous of revenue give-aways,[108] the Variation of Trusts Act 1958.

The position as to assignability and premature termination in the case of trusts of investments thus differs in significant respects from the equivalent aspects of strict settlements. Because, as has been emphasised several times in this chapter, a trust of investments is not essentially oriented towards preservation of the specific property committed to it, there were no economic or dynastic considerations impelling either the law or the standard forms developed by conveyancers to inhibit adult beneficiaries from breaking up such a trust when they so desired.[109] Preserving the long-term integrity of family landed estates - which may have been of importance for the accumulation of agricultural capital and certainly was a matter of key importance for dynastically-minded landowners - was simply not in issue when it came to terminating a trust of investments under the rule in Saunders v. Vautier. Indeed, classical economic doctrine to the effect that entrepreneurialism and economic development depended on capital mobility may well have contributed to the emergence of this broad rule. It clearly stimulated the rapid enactment of the Thellusson Act 1800,[110] which was the first statute to set limits to income accumulation under a trust, once the eccentric Thellusson will had demonstrated that without such curbs income distribution under a trust of investments could be held up for as long as the full perpetuity period of a life or lives in being plus twenty-one years.[111] Both the Thellusson Act and, in its smaller way, the narrow ruling in Saunders v. Vautier itself exhibit a dislike of income accumulation (the former arose partly from a contemporaneous fear of the potentialities of compound interest, which Marx was later to ridicule).[112] The underlying feeling that capital should be mobile and capable of commitment to new industrial ventures which, although risky, might amass huge profits, explains both this dislike of accumulation and the broader rule developing out of Saunders v. Vautier.

This concern for mobility of capital is not, however, paramount in the judicial treatment of fetters upon the alienability of individual beneficiaries' interests under a trust of investments. If it had been, the long-established grounds on which conditions subsequent forbidding alienation were held void could easily have been invoked to invalidate forfeiture provisions making trust interests determinable on bankruptcy or attempted alienation, and thus to stifle the growth of the protective trust. The reasons why Chancery judges refused to extend the policy arguments against conditions subsequent so as to strike down such forfeiture provisions as well are not clear, because, unlike their American counterparts,[113] they did not discuss policy at all. They may have thought that forfeiture provisions represented a legitimate exercise of the settlor's or testator's jus disponendi; yet this consideration cut little ice when the question of premature termination of a whole settlement under Saunders v. Vautier had to be resolved. They may have felt that there were moral grounds for allowing a settlor or testator to protect widows, youthful children and the like from their own improvidence or inexperience in financial matters; yet there is no requirement in the law relating to protective trusts that the beneficiary should be a person for whom a "caretaker" attitude of this sort is necessary or desirable. A final possibility is that the judge saw protective trusts as a road to entrepreneurial limited liability (being a privilege not freely available to business enterprise until the Limited Liability Act 1855);[114] yet this would be misconceived because, in contrast to limited liability through incorporation, the protection of a protective trust extends to consumption debts as well as business debts and it depends upon the would-be entrepreneur/beneficiary receiving bounty in the form of a beneficial interest under a trust created by another.[115] In the outcome, a mixture of legal formalism and unarticulated considerations of policy led to judicial and (in 1925) legislative sanctioning of the protective trust, despite its apparent conflict with the notions that (a) capital should be mobile and (b) creditors for consumption debts (at least) should have recourse to the wealth from which their debtors are or have been enjoying the benefit. In the twentieth century, the second limb of the conveyancing artifice which achieved this effect - that is, the discretionary trust which arises if a bankruptcy or attempt at alienation occurs - was itself harnessed to a totally new task, that of tax avoidance on a substantial scale.[116] Throughout this whole process the law once again displayed a capacity to pursue independent lines of development while also displaying considerable responsiveness to economic and ideological forces.

(b) The range of permitted investments

It is easy to see why the emergence of trusts of investments as a common form of property disposition should have evoked a legal response in the form of a set of rules for determining the range of investments available to trustees. Since the benefit to be conferred on the beneficiaries comprised solely a money yield from investment (to which a strict settlement, which provided also a residence for the life-tenant, stood in obvious contrast), there was a paramount need to ensure that investment occurred with some degree of prudence and that the returns thereof arrived in due course into the hands of the beneficiaries. Any notion that the trustee might legitimately invest the trust property on his own behalf, receiving any profits and bearing the risk of any losses, would contravene not only the basic long-standing conception that a trustee holds property entirely for the benefit of beneficiaries, but also the specific consideration that in a trust of investments, whether comprising realty, personalty or a mixture of both, investment to produce a money return for the beneficiaries is the raison d'être.

In order to implement these seemingly self-evident principles, trusts law in the early eighteenth century went comparatively quickly through a process of emancipation from the influence of subsisting principles of law - deriving substantially from the ecclesiastical courts - as to the position of executors. The ecclesiastical courts had assimilated the role of executor of a will of personalty to that of heir to the extent that, inter alia, an executor might in certain circumstances take any undisposed residue for his own benefit. The accompanying proposition that an executor who invested any part of the estate might keep any profits for himself (provided of course that if any loss was suffered he should make it good) continued to influence the law even after equity early in the seventeenth century had firmly ruled that an executor's similarity to a trustee no longer allowed him to retain undisposed residue.[117] As late as 1718, Lord Macclesfield L.C. held in Bromfield v. Wytherley[118] that if a solvent executor or trustee invested money held by him and derived a profit, he could keep the profit because any loss would have been chargeable to him: only if he were insolvent would he be required to account for the profit to the beneficiaries, because in this event a loss would also have had to be borne by them. This decision contradicted the earlier ruling in Brown v. Litton (1711)[119] to the effect that profits received by a trustee from investment of the trust assets had to be accounted for to the beneficiary. Later decisions[120] came down on the side of Brown v. Litton, being probably impelled in that direction by the occurrence of the South Sea in 1720. This demonstrated all too clearly that a solvent trustee who was permitted to speculate with trust funds in the hope of making a profit for himself might easily be insolvent himself after a stock market crash, in which event the fact that Lord Macclesfield L.C. would declare him disentitled from retaining investment profits would be cold comfort for the beneficiaries. It has been suggested that the seminal decision in Keech v. Sandford (1726)[121], from which the modern "secret profits" doctrine is substantially derived, represents a further judicial reaction to the South Sea Bubble.[122] It is certainly in line with the emerging rule that profits from trustee investment belong to the trust, not the trustee, though the links with this rule or with the Bubble itself were not made explicit at the time.

The South Sea Bubble plays a further important role in the history of trustee investment law.[123] Even Chancery masters had indulged in the orgy of investment speculation which preceded the crash, using funds which had been paid into court. In the sober aftermath, the Chancery Court resolved to limit severely the range of investments to which funds paid into court could be committed and also - a step of major importance - to insist that without express authorisation from the settlor, testator or beneficiaries, a trustee holding cash or other property with a duty or power (express or implied) to convert it and invest the proceeds was confined to the range of investments prescribed for funds paid into court. Even if an unprescribed investment was made in good faith and seemed safe, a trustee would be liable for any loss resulting from it.[124] There thus emerged the concept of "authorised investments" to which trustees, if not otherwise authorised by the trust deed or the beneficiaries, must adhere in making trust investments if they are to avoid liability for loss.[125] They are also subject to a general duty of reasonable prudence in choosing within the range of appropriate investments.[126] A wry dictum of Lord Chancellor Hardwicke, in a case decided in 1737 involving loss suffered by the retention of the South Sea Stock in a trust fund, reflects the prevailing attitude: "[I]t is well known that during the golden dream, people were so infatuated as to look upon imaginary wealth as so much money."[127]

The concept of "authorised investment" has been a basic element in the structure of English trust investment law ever since. Even the Trustee Investments Act 1961, enacted after the depression of the 1930s and the post-war "long boom" had demonstrated how flexible an investor needed to be to make the best of changing markets, has not abandoned the notion that the law should list the categories of investment prima facie available to trustees.[128]

Having determined by the mid-eighteenth century that (a) the yields on trust investment belonged to the trust, not the trustees and (b) that such investment was prima facie to be confined to categories prescribed by law, Chancery and the legislature had also, in dealing with the emergence of trusts of investments, to prescribe the contents of this list. Throughout the period under review, the only form of investment unequivocally accepted by Chancery was government stock.

Even first mortgages of land were thought by some judges to be unsuitable,[129] and although there were dicta to the opposite effect,[130] it was left to section 32 of the Law of Property Act 1859 to confirm that mortgages of land could be a legitimate form of trustee security. In the course of the nineteenth century, other limited categories of safe investment, such as local government stock, colonial stock and shares in a number of specified statutory public utility companies, were added by statute to the authorised list. But equity investment remained unauthorised until 1961, despite ample demonstration over many years that it was, in general terms, far more profitable than the authorised investments.[131]

Some implications of this conservative view as to the proper limits for trustee investments are worthy of consideration. It would seem, paradoxically, that while the very existence of trusts of investments as an increasingly important form of disposition of family wealth was substantially attributable to the increasing economic significance of trade and industry, the capital fund contained in such trusts was being diverted by legal rules away from trade and industry.[132] By the same token, while strict settlements may have kept "new wealth" away from land and encouraged the use of mortgages by landed families (at least in Habakkuk's view), the law seemed to be inhibiting trusts into which such wealth was committed from providing the mortgage finance which landowners sought. It was instead the government which emerged as the principal party to benefit from trust investment law. Along with the litigants' funds held by Chancery - which was a very substantial investor indeed - the capital channelled towards government stock by virtue of trust investment law greatly facilitated government borrowing. According to one commentator, it "accounts, to a considerable degree, for the steadiness of British credit, in the long drawn out struggle with Revolutionary France and the Napoleonic Empire."[133] Trusts of investments, the offspring of increasingly prominent mercantile and industrial capital, thus fed into the infrastructure which supported capitalist development rather than into the process of capital formation itself. Even at the present day, despite statutes of the late nineteenth and twentieth centuries substantially extending the categories of authorised investments, this interpretation of trust investment law as a means of diverting private capital into low-yielding government securities - and thus as a form of tax upon ill-drafted trusts[134] - retains some validity.

It is not an interpretation, however, which should be pressed too far. That is to say, it should not be assumed that every pound sterling contained in trusts of investments in the eighteenth and early nineteenth centuries was held in the form of government stock. There are several reasons for this.

In the first place, trust investment law, with its categories of authorised investment, only affects the trustee who, having received ready cash from the settlor or testator or through the exercise of a power or duty to sell pre-existing trust assets, has to choose what new investments to make. It does not of itself compel a trustee to sell unauthorised investments put into the trust by the settlor or testator. Instead, a separate branch of trusts law prescribes that this need only be done where the settlor or testator so requires, or where the trust is of residuary assets under a will and no contrary intention is discernible in the will.[135]

Secondly, it is highly likely that many trustees holding investments simply did not abide by the legal rules being developed by Chancery, either through ignorance of them or because they considered them unduly restrictive. Such is the implicit view of the leading historian in this area, B.L. Anderson, who depicts eighteenth century trustees and executors as "shadowy figures" acting as "custodians of capital over a wide range of the population"[136] and draws attention to the importance of solicitors - who were often appointed as trustees or at least advised them - in local money markets. As professional brokers were scarce, solicitors provided an important link between sources of investment of funds, such as trusts of investments, and possible outlets for investment, such as mortgages sought by local landowners, share or loan finance for turnpike trusts or canal and railway construction, and the purchase of land for leasing or resale at a profit. Anderson suggests that while much of the money invested in these areas by way of solicitors as intermediaries was not held on trust, their twin roles as brokers specialising in these areas and professionals involved in trust administration probably diverted a significant quantity of trust money away from the authorised list.

Thirdly, and most significantly, the law itself left it open, as already indicated, for the terms of a will or trust deed, or for the beneficiaries themselves, to permit trustees to invest outside the authorised list. It is not known how frequently such permission was granted, but even allowing for the recent experience of the South Sea Bubble, the pressures to do so must have been reasonably strong. Even while Chancery during the eighteenth century was confirming its opposition to trust investment outside government stock, investment possibilities were widening as the Industrial Revolution gathered momentum and, as just pointed out, solicitors were consolidating their role as financial intermediaries. By the late nineteenth century, broad investment clauses were common enough to induce Chancery judges to abandon restrictive interpretation and adopt the normal and natural meaning.[137] Revell's "balance sheet" of personal trusts in 1961[138] confirms that by that time such clauses were widespread, at least in the wealthier trusts. There is no other possible explanation for the fact that, a bare six months after the Trustee Investment Act 1961 significantly widened the range of authorised investments, about 85% of the value of the trust assets surveyed by Revell was found to be represented in assets not authorised by the Trustee Act 1925. Revell himself suggests that this figure is not to be explained by a massive rush to invoke the 1961 Act, but by the prevalence of wide investment clauses in wealthy settlements.[139]

The conservatism of the eighteenth century Chancery Court in resolving, following the débâcle of the South Sea Bubble, that only government stock should be authorised unequivocally for trustees was thus the starting point for a major counter-reaction on the part of trust draftsmen. It may well be that, had the law been prepared to allow a greater element of risk in trust investment, the gap between the authorised range and the range actually adopted by trustees in pursuance of express clauses could have been narrower. Instead, Chancery's determination to confine trusteeship discretion in trust investment seems ironically to have led to the opposite result: viz., that clauses giving trustees a wide discretion became common form. Of course, other factors were at work, notably the introduction of limited liability and other forms of shareholder protection into nineteenth century company law. But the eighteenth century conception of "authorised investments", alterable only by judicial reversal of precedent or by legislation, was a major stimulus towards the development of trust precedents conferring very wide investment discretions upon trustees.

In this specific way, the law's reaction to the increasing importance of trusts of investments from the eighteenth century onwards illustrates a major theme outlined earlier, namely, that in such trusts, in marked contrast to medieval uses of land, the trustees have a substantial managerial role. This same theme is apparent in a number of other concurrent developments: for example, the rise of the discretionary trust (referred to earlier)[140] and the conferring of express or statutory discretions with regard to such matters as maintenance of minor beneficiaries, advancement of capital and other administrative questions.[141] Even the simple fact that modern investments - amongst which, as we have seen, trustees acting under wide investment clauses have considerable freedom of choice - vary greatly in terms of income yield and capital growth confers considerable (and insufficiently emphasised)[142] leeway on the trustee to favour income beneficiaries as against capital beneficiaries, or vice versa, merely through selection of specific investments. One of the chief causes of this, interestingly enough, is that, like the rules regarding perpetuities, the "fruit and trees" distinction between income and capital in trusts law (and in tax law) is imported from land law.[143] But it is the fact that a trust of investments relates to a fund, of which the specific contents may be varied within an ever-widening range of possible assets, that ultimately makes this important discretion available to trustees, with only minimal intervention on the part of the law.[144]

A final matter which should be mentioned in this catalogue of trusteeship discretions arising within trusts of investments is delegation of trustees' authority. The managerial expertise required of trustees is now seen to be so demanding that in major aspects of their work, notably investment itself, administrative duties may be and commonly are delegated to experts under section 23 of the Trustee Act 1925[145] and even discretionary decisions may be made delegable by express provision in the trust.[146] Here the managerial revolution has run its full course. The trustee, having first been a mere "stooge" or nominee (in medieval uses of land), has developed through a quasi-managerial role in special situations (strict settlements) and a fully managerial role on a day-to-day basis (most trusts of investments) into a mere supervisor of specialist management by others.[147] The analogy with company directors and even ministers of state is a fascinating one.

III: Conclusions

In the background to the various developments in trusts law and practice which this chapter endeavours to trace is, of course, the growth in commercial and industrial capital within a society still dominated politically by landed interests. The dialectical nature of this process of large-scale social change is reflected in specific aspects of the developments in private property law and practice which we have been discussing. For example, strict settlements, being a form of transaction designed to preserve a landed family's hold over its estates, tended indirectly to foster the growth of mercantile and industrial capital, both by providing investment outlets, in the form of mortgages, for the "new wealth" of merchants and industrial capitalists and by inducing reinvestment of this wealth in trade and industry to the extent that settlements kept land off the market. By the same token, essential characteristics of trusts of investments - the form of transaction most closely associated with merchants and industrialists rather than landowners - were nurtured within the settlement practices of landowners: for example, trusts to preserve contingent remainders, and trusts to rescue the estate from insolvency - an event actually encouraged by borrowing on the security of settled land[148] - conferred on trustees the brand of managerial discretion which was to become the hallmark of settlements of investments.

The legal developments being discussed also illustrate a particular facet of the notion that law enjoys a degree of autonomy from underlying economic and political changes. This notion is something of a truism, being commonly, and quite correctly, cited as a basis for arguing that the law is not simply an instrument of overt oppression of the working-classes and other disadvantaged groups on the part of those in positions of economic and political dominance.[149] Accordingly, in areas of direct conflict between labour and capital, the law may be ultimately and crudely "on the side of capital", but its form and specific content are prevented from being markedly oppressive by the very fact that there is this conflict (which the law mediates or defuses) and by the profound effects of ideologies (e.g. as to the equality of all citizens before the law, the need for certainty and stability, the requirement that law should be, and be seen to be, fair and "just", and so on). Where, as in the law relating to family settlements, fundamental opposition between oppressing and oppressed classes is not in issue, the various factors determining the autonomous character of the law require special analysis. What appears most distinctive in the material discussed in this chapter is the role of legal draftsmen. While not "calling the tune", they influenced developments significantly. They presented new patterns of disposition whose validity judges were encouraged to uphold, thereby incrementally altering the law (as in the case of trusts to preserve contingent remainders and protective trusts); they used their professional influence in appropriate cases to persuade their clients to adopt common-form clauses some of which would evade the broad thrust of judicial policy (as in the case of wide investment clauses); and they exerted a strong retarding influence on the reform of property law. Yet conveyancers are limited by the materials they have to hand, so that developments in trusts law are often explicable in terms of the manipulation of an old device for new purposes - as is illustrated classically by the harnessing of discretionary trusts, a device associated with creditor avoidance in the nineteenth century, for the purpose of tax avoidance in the twentieth century.

This representation of trusts law as something akin to a dignified game of chess between practising lawyers and judges should not be allowed to obscure the importance of pressures which, as already stressed, are exerted by social and political developments. The strict settlement ultimately faded from view not because judges and conveyancers so wished but because property and tax legislation of the late nineteenth and the twentieth centuries made it no longer viable. Such legislation owes its origin, in part at least, to the growth of commercial and industrial capital. By the same token, the emergence of the rule in Saunders v. Vautier[150] as a broad doctrine permitting premature termination of trusts of investments through "internal" attack by beneficiaries may have reflected the lack of any compelling economic or dynastic incentive to preserve the assets of such trusts in specie as well as the prevailing economic wisdom regarding mobility of capital, but it was subsequently overshadowed by the "external" attack mounted upon such trusts by the tax law of the present century. The trust of investments, being the form of family settlement which merchants and industrialists developed in rivalry to strict settlements, itself proved vulnerable to subsequent changes in the nature of capitalism. Unlike a settlement of agricultural land, its lasting integrity was wholly irrelevant to the actual process of organising capital into productive units, and as its role in financing productive enterprise became increasingly peripheral, it could more easily be subjected to fiscal attack in the interests of servicing the revenue demands of monopoly or corporate capitalism and damping down working-class political pressure for a fairer distribution of wealth. Within this wholly changed political environment, the fiscal fortunes of trusts of investments are now *defended* by judges - with, paradoxically, Saunders v. Vautier and its offshoot the Variations of Trust Act 1958 being invoked as important weapons[151] - even while internal attack under Saunders v. Vautier is permitted. If a "game of chess" is now being played, it is an undignified one between the Chancery Division and the legislature - as a law-lord recently suggested.[152] These changes constitute one of the clearest examples of the way in which trusts law doctrines and practices that stem from social and economic change within the eighteenth and early nineteenth centuries are preserved in form but transcended in function within the trusts law and practice of the present day.

In the last resort, the family trust and the law relating to it, with all their powerful moral and ideological overtones, combine to protect accumulated private wealth. What this paper has attempted to show is the extent to which, and the processes by which, they may both undergo major adaptation, when the composition of the class of private wealth-holders most dominant in society is altered in accordance with society's own political and economic development.

NOTES

* I wish to acknowledge valuable help from Ms. Anne Goodrick, formerly Research Assistant at the Faculty of Law, University of New South Wales, who tracked down numerous legal and historical articles and composed very useful summaries of their contents, and from Dr. Lloyd Bonfield, of Trinity College, Cambridge, who made helpful criticisms of my approach to strict settlements and gave me a very instructive account of his research.

1. E.g., H.G. Hanbury and R.H. Maudsley, Modern Equity, 11th ed., by R.H. Maudsley and J.E. Martin, (London: Stevens, 1981), pp.4-16, 33-4; P.H. Pettit, Equity and the Law of Trusts, 4th ed., (London: Butterworths, 1979), Ch.1.
2. E.g., J.M.W. Bean, The Decline of English Feudalism 1215-1540 (Manchester: University Press, 1968), pp.177-81; S.F.C. Milsom, Historical Foundations of the Common Law, 2nd ed. (London: Butterworths, 1981), p.207.
3. As suggested by Chief Justice Frowike, (Coke upon Littleton 272a,b), cited in P. Bordwell, "Equity and the Law of Property". Iowa Law Review, XX (1934) 8.
4. J.R.S. Revell, The Wealth of the Nation (Cambridge: University Press, 1967), p.139 (table 6.2).
5. O.L. Browder, "Recent Patterns of Testate Succession in the U.S.A. and England", Michigan Law Review, LXVII (1969), p.1351; G.W. Keeton, Modern Developments in the Law of Trusts (Belfast: Northern Ireland Law Quarterly, 1971), Ch.14.
6. Cf. O.L. Browder, op.cit., pp.1355-6.
7. M.A. Shattuck, "The Development of the Prudent Man Rule for Fiduciary Investment in the United States in the Twentieth Century", Ohio State Law Journal, XII (1951), pp.491-2.
8. See e.g. B. English, infra; H.J. Habakkuk "Marriage Settlements in the

Eighteenth Century", Transactions of the Royal Historical Society, 4th ser. XXXII (1950), pp.15-30; W. Holdsworth, History of English Law (London: Sweet and Maxwell, reprinted 1966), Vol.VII, pp.376-380, Appendix III; F. Pollock, The Land Laws (London: Macmillan, 1883), pp.105-115; A.W.B. Simpson, An Introduction to the History of the Land Law, (Oxford: University Press, 1961), pp.218-24; E. Spring, "The Settlement of Land in Nineteenth Century England", American Journal of Legal History, VIII (1964), pp.2090-23. Descriptions of the form and workings of strict settlements also appear in the sources cited in footnotes 23-26, infra.

9. (1472) Year Book 12 Edw. IV pl.25.

10. P. Bordwell, "Alienability and Perpetuities", Iowa Law Review, XXIV (1939), pp.50-66, 635-59; A.W.B. Simpson, op.cit., note 8, supra, pp.195-218.

11. The weaknesses of the holder of a purely equitable estate are outlined in H.G. Hanbury and R.H. Maudsley, op.cit., note 1, supra, pp.24-32.

12. B. English and J. Saville, "Family Settlements and the Rise of Great Estates", Economic History Review, 2nd ser. XXXIII (1980), 556-8.

13. As occurred in the settlement executed in 1847 by Tatton Sykes I, described by B. English, infra.

14. (1472) Year Book 12 Edw. IV, pl.25.

15. Report from the Select Committee on the Bill for Altering the Law Concerning Entails in Scotland (1828); Report of the Royal Commission on the Depressed Conditions of the Agricultural Interests, (1881), p.834. These sources are cited by E. Spring (op.cit., note 8, supra, p.213, note 10).

16. H.J. Habakkuk, op.cit., note 8, supra, pp.18-9; F.M.L. Thompson, English Landed Society in the Nineteenth Century, (London: Routledge and Kegan Paul, 1963), pp.66-7; A. Underhill, "Changes in the Law of Real Property", in A Century of Law Reform, (London: Macmillan, 1901), p.282.

17. See e.g. G.E. Mingay, English Landed Society in the Eighteenth Century, (London: Routledge and Kegan Paul, 1963), Ch.6.

18. See e.g. H. Perkin, The Origins of Modern English Society 1780-1880, (London: Routledge and Kegan Paul, 1969), Ch.2; F.M.L. Thompson, op.cit., note 16, supra, pp.68-70.

19. This point is further explored by E. Spring, infra; cf., L. Stone, The Family, Sex and Marriage in England 1500-1800, (London: Weidenfeld and Nicolson, 1977), pp.89, 243-4; R. Trumbach, The Rise of the Egalitarian Family, (London: Academic Press, 1978), pp.71-3.

20. L. Stone, The Crisis of the Aristocracy 1558-1641, (Oxford: University Press, 1965), p.182.

21. H.J. Habakkuk, op.cit., note 8, supra; "English Land-ownership 1680-1740", Economic History Review, 1st ser. X (1939-40), pp.2-17; "The English Land Market in the Eighteenth Century", in J.S. Bromley and E.H. Kossman (ed.), Britain and the Netherlands, (London: Chatto and Windus, 1960); G.E. Mingay, op.cit., note 17, supra, Ch.2; L. Stone, "Marriage Among the English Nobility", in R.L. Coser (ed.), The Family: Its Structure and Functions, 2nd ed., (London: Macmillan, 1974).

22. Op.cit., note 8, supra; also Spring's Chapter, infra.

23. C. Clay, "Marriage, Inheritance, and the Rise of Large Estates in England, 1660-1815", Economic History Review, 2nd ser. XXI (1968), pp.503-18.

24. B.A. Holderness, "The English Land Market in the Eighteenth Century: The Case of Lincolnshire", Economic History Review, 2nd ser. XXVII (1974), pp.557-76.

25. J.V. Beckett, "English Land-Ownership in the Later Seventeenth and Eighteenth Centuries: The Debate and the Problems", Economic History Review, 2nd ser. XXX (1977), pp.567-81.

26. L. Bonfield, "Marriage Settlements and the Rise of Great Estates: The Demographic Aspect", Economic History Review, 2nd ser. XXXII (1979), pp.483-93.

27. Other writers who also raise doubts about aspects of Habakkuk's thesis are

J.P. Cooper, "Patterns of Inheritance and Settlement by Great Landowners from the Fifteenth to the Eighteenth Centuries", in J. Goody, J. Thirsk and E.P. Thompson (ed.), Family and Inheritance: Rural Society in Western Europe 1200-1800, (Cambridge: University Press, 1976); F.M.L.Thompson, "Land-Ownership and Economic Growth in England in the Eighteenth Century", in E.L. Jones and S.J. Woolf (ed.), Agrarian Change and Economic Development, (London: Methuen, 1969).

28. L. Bonfield, op.cit., note 26, supra; T.H. Hollingsworth, "The Demography of the British Peerage", supp. to Population Studies, XVIII (1964).

29. B. English and J. Saville, op.cit., note 12, supra.

30. H.J. Habakkuk, op.cit., note 8, supra, p.28.

31. A later argument by the same historian, relating more specifically to marriage arrangements amongst the landed aristocracy, is omitted here, as it is discussed fully by E. Spring, infra. The argument is set out in "The Rise and Fall of English Landed Families, 1600-1800", Transactions of the Royal Historical Society, 5th ser. XXIX (1979), pp.187-207.

32. Op.cit., supra, note 25, p.581.

33. See P. Anderson, Lineages of the Absolutist State, (London: New Left Books, 1974), pp.56-7; J.P. Cooper, op.cit., note 27, supra; A. Goodwin, European Nobility in the Eighteenth Century, (London: A. and C. Black, 1953); V.G. Kiernan, "Private Property in History", in J. Goody, J. Thirsk and E.P. Thompson (ed.), op.cit., note 27, supra.

34. At p.134, supra.

35. L. Stone, op.cit., note 20, supra, p.183.

36. The legal reasons for this are outlined at pp.120-30, supra; see too Holdsworth, op.cit., note 8, supra, Vol.VII, pp.111-4.

37. (1697) 3 Lev. 437.

38. (1742) 3 Bro. C.C. 351.

39. (1742) 3 Atk. 135, 139.

40. (1710) 1 P. Wms. 128, 130.

41. (1732) 2 P. Wms. 678.

42. Ibid., at p.680.

43. See G.E. Mingay, op.cit., note 17, supra, pp.34, 48-9; F. Pollock, op.cit., note 8, supra, pp.111-3; L. Stone, op.cit., note 21, supra, pp.181, 185-6.

44. See pp.148-9, infra.

45. E.g., W.B. Leach, "Perpetuities in Perspective: Ending the Rule's Reign of Terror", Harvard Law Review, LXV, (1952), p.727; J.H.C. Morris and W.B. Leach, The Rule Against Perpetuities, 2nd ed. (London: Stevens, 1962), pp.3-13.

46. (1682) 3 Ch. Cas. 1.

47. G.L. Haskins, "Extending the Grasp of the Dead Hand: Reflections on the Origins of the Rule Against Perpetuities", University of Pennsylvania Law Review, CXXVI (1977), pp.19-46.

48. Op.cit., note 8, supra, p.224.

49. (1682) 3 Ch. Cas. 1.

50. Cf., accounts of the early law relating to perpetuities, in sources cited in note 10, supra.

51. (1759) 1 Eden 404.

52. P. Bordwell, "Alienability and Perpetuities VI", Iowa Law Review, XXV (1940), pp.725-7; W. Holdsworth, op.cit., note 8, supra, Vol. VII, p.232.

53. See e.g. H.J. Habakkuk, "The English Land Market in the Eighteenth Century", op.cit., note 21, supra, pp.155-6; L. Stone, op.cit., note 20, supra, pp.36-9.

54. See notes 8, 23-6, supra.

55. Cadell v. Palmer (1833) 1 Cl. & F. 372.

56. (1682) 3 Ch. Cas. 1.

57. I am indebted to Ms. Eileen Spring for this suggestion. Cf., the comment of L.M. Friedman that in Wisconsin, although the rule against perpetuities is

virtually non-existent, there is no apparent wish to create long-term trusts that would infringe such a rule: "The Dynastic Trust", Yale Law Journal, LXXIII, (1964), p.550.

58. See sources cited in note 69, *infra*.

59. *Maddox* v. *Staines* (1727) 2 P. Wms. 421.

60. J.H.C. Morris and W.B. Leach, *op.cit.*, note 45, *supra*, pp.12, 17-18.

61. See *e.g.* F.M.L. Thompson, *op.cit.*, note 16, *supra*, pp.51-9.

62. (1759) 1 Eden 404.

63. See *e.g.* I. Balbus, "Commodity Form and Legal Form: An Essay on the Relative Autonomy of the Law", in C. Reasons and R. Rich (ed.), The Sociology of Law, (Toronto: Butterworths, 1978); Pashukanis, E.B., General Theory of Law and Marxism, transl. N. Einhorn; ed. C.J. Arthur, (London: Ink Links, 1978); C. Sumner, Reading Ideologies, (London: Academic Press, 1979).

64. See sources cited in note 53, *supra*.

65. See *e.g.* W. Holdsworth, *op.cit.*, note 8, *supra*, Vol.XII, pp.222-237; G.W. Keeton, An Introduction to Equity, 3rd ed. (London: Pitman, 1952), pp.28-46.

66. *Op.cit.*, note 24, *supra*.

67. *Op.cit.*, note 25, *supra*.

68. E. Spring, *op.cit.*, note 69, *infra*, pp.56-59.

69. H. Perkin, "Land Reform and Class Conflict in Victorian Britain", in J. Butt and I.F. Clarke (ed.), The Victorians and Social Protest, (Newton Abbot: David and Charles, 1973); E. Spring, "Landowners, Lawyers and Land Law Reform in Nineteenth Century England", American Journal of Legal History, XXI (1977), pp.40-59; F.M.L. Thompson "Land and Politics in England in the Nineteenth Century", Transactions of the Royal Historical Society, 5th ser. XV (1965), pp.23-44.

70. *Cf.*, B.L. Anderson, "Law, Finance and Economic Growth in England: Some Long-term Influences", in B.M. Ratcliffe, Britain and Her World 1750-1914, (Manchester: University Press, 1975), p.101.

71. See e.g. H.J. Habakkuk, "Economic Functions of English Landowners in the Seventeenth and Eighteenth Centuries", in W.E. Minchinton (ed.), Essays in Agrarian History, Vol.I, (Newton Abbot: David and Charles, 1968); D. Spring, "The English Landed Estate in the Age of Coal and Iron, 1830-1880", Journal of Economic History, XI (1951), pp.3-19.

72. These are outlined in A. Underhill, op.cit., note 16, supra, pp.284-297. See too B. English, infra; E. Spring, op.cit., note 69, supra, pp.44-55.

73. H. Perkin, op.cit., supra, note 69, pp.206-14; F.M.L. Thompson, op.cit., note 16, supra, pp.283-5.

74. Cf., R.S. Neale, "The Bourgeoisie, Historically, Has Played a Most Revolutionary Part", in E. Kamenka and R.S. Neale (ed.), Feudalism, Capitalism and Beyond, (London: Edward Arnold, 1975), p.100.

75. See e.g. P.L. Payne, "The Emergence of the Large Scale Company in Great Britain, 1870-1914", Economic History Review, 2nd ser. XX (1967), pp.519-42.

76. Cf., C.T. Sandford, Taxing Personal Wealth, (London: Allen and Unwin, 1971), pp.64-7, 72-3.

77. Cf., F.M.L. Thompson, op.cit., note 69, supra, pp.43-4.

78. Op.cit., note 4, supra.

79. See e.g. A.B. Atkinson, Unequal Shares, rev. ed. (London: Penguin, 1974), pp.12-3; R.W. Titmuss, Income Distribution and Social Change, (London: Unwin, 1962), Ch.5.

80. See sources cited note 21, supra.

81. See e.g. R. Grassby, "English Merchant Capitalism in the Late Seventeenth Century: The Composition of Business Fortunes", Past and Present, XLVI (1970), pp.87-107; M.B. Rose, "Diversification of Investment by the Greg Family, 1800-1914", Business History, XXI (1979), pp.79-96.

82. See e.g. R.G. Wilson, "The Denisons and Milneses: Eighteenth Century Merchant Landowners" in J.T. Ward and R.G. Wilson (ed.), Land and Industry, (Newton Abbot: David and Charles, 1971); cf., B.A. Holderness, op.cit., note

24, supra, pp.359-65.

83. See P. Bordwell, "Interests in Chattels Real and Personal", Missouri Law Review, 1 (1936), pp.119-21.

84. L.C.B. Gower, Modern Company Law, 4th ed., (London: Stevens, 1980), Chs. 2, 3.

85. W. Holdsworth, op.cit., note 8, supra, Vol.III, p.548.

86. P. Bordwell, op.cit., note 83, supra, W. Holdsworth, op.cit., note 8, supra, Vol.VII, pp.477-8.

87. See generally J.M.W. Bean, op.cit., note 2, supra, pp.131-2; W.F. Fratcher, "Uses of Uses", Missouri Law Review, XXXIV (1969), pp.53, 59-60; W. Holdsworth, op.cit., note 8, supra, Vol.IV, pp.424-5; Vol.VII, pp.150-1; J.L. Lightwood, "Trusts for Sale", Cambridge Law Journal, III (1929), pp.59-74; F.W. Maitland, "The Origin of Uses", Harvard Law Review, VIII (1894), p.129; A.W.B. Simpson, op.cit., note 8, supra, pp.164-83; Note, "The Statute of Uses and Active Trusts", Michigan Law Review, XVII (1918), pp.87-90.

88. See p.138, supra.

89. See e.g. W. Holdsworth, op.cit., note 8, supra, Vol.5, pp.312-5; Vol.VI, pp.644-50; G.W. Keeton, op.cit., note 65, supra, pp.39-40. For a more general account of the trust's reformist potentialities, see A.W. Scott, "The Trust as an Instrument of Law Reform", Yale Law Journal, XXXI (1922), pp.457-68.

90. B.L. Anderson, op.cit., note 70, supra, p.103. See too F.W. Maitland, "Trust and Corporation", in H.A.L. Fisher (ed.), Collected Papers of F.W. Maitland, Vol.III, (Cambridge: University Press, 1911).

91. Op.cit., p.103.

92. See pp.143, 159, supra.

93. E.g. Brandon v. Robinson (1811) 18 Ves. 429; Graves v. Dolphin (1826) 1 Sim.66; Rockford v. Hackman (1852) 9 Hare 474, 479-80.

94. Barton v. Briscoe (1822) Jac. 603.

95. E.g. Dommett v. Bedford (1796) 3 Ves.149; Shee v. Hale (1807) 18 Ves.405;

Brandon v. Robinson, supra, at pp.433-4; Rockford v. Hackman, supra, at p.480.

96. E.g. Godden v. Crowhurst (1842) 10 Sim.642.

97. H.G. Hanbury and R.H. Maudsley, op.cit., note 1, supra, Ch.9.

98. See Lord Pawlet's case (1685) 2 Ventris 366.

99. Ibid., at p.367.

100. The key Chancery decision is Saunders v. Vautier (1841) Cr. & Ph.240: see too Barnes v. Rowley (1797) 3 Ves.305; Josselyn v. Josselyn (1837) 9 Sim.63; Curtis v. Lukin (1842) 5 Beav.147.

101. See e.g. Gosling v. Gosling (1859) Joh.265; Palairet v. Carew (1863) 32 Beav.564; Anson v. Potter (1879) 13 Ch.D. 141, 143; Re White [1901] Ch.570, 573.

102. Termination of a discretionary trust by all its beneficiaries (being of full age and sound mind) has been held effective in some decisions (e.g. Re Smith [1928] Ch.915), though academic doubts have been expressed (see e.g. J.W. Harris, "Trust, Power and Duty", Law Quarterly Review, LXXXVII (1971), pp.46-7).

103. (1841) Cr. & Ph.240.

104. J.W. Harris, Variation of Trusts, (London: Sweet and Maxwell, 1975), pp.2, 97, 103.

105. See e.g. Barnes v. Rowley (1795) 3 Ves.305; Barton v. Briscoe (1822) Jac.603.

106. 149 Mass. 19, 20 N.E. 454 (1889), discussed in L.M. Friedman, op.cit., note 57, supra, pp.586-92.

107. See J.W. Harris, op.cit., note 104, supra, pp.2-6, 97-104.

108. Ibid., pp.47-8, 85-92; G.R. Bretten, "Tax Avoidance and the Variation of Trusts Act 1958", Conveyancer, (N.S.) XXXII (1968), pp.194-203.

109. Cf., L.M. Friedman, op.cit., note 57, supra.

110. The modern equivalent is the Law of Property Act 1925, ss.164-6.

111. See Bassil v. Lister (1851), 9 Hare 177, 183; G.W. Keeton, op.cit., note 5,

supra, pp.215-75.

112. K. Marx, Capital, Vol.III (Moscow: Progress Publishers, 1959), pp.394-9.

113. E.g. Broadway Bank v. Adams 133 Mass. 170 (1882), where the public policy implications of "spendthrift trusts" (the U.S. functional equivalent of protectve trusts) are canvassed at some length. See too E. Griswold, Spendthrift Trusts, 2nd ed. (New York: Matthew Bender, 1947), Ch.10.

114. They were employed to this end in the U.S.A.: see L.M. Friedman, op.cit., note 57, supra, p.578.

115. A protective trust created by a settlor in favour of himself will not defeat his creditors if he subsequently goes bankrupt while the determinable life-interest is still operative: Re Burroughs - Fowler [1916] 2 Ch.251.

116. See e.g. J.R.S. Revell, "Settled Property and Death Duties", British Tax Review, 1961, pp.177-81; R.W. Titmuss, op.cit., note 79, supra, Ch.5. Following a sample survey, the Board of Inland Revenue estimated that the total capital settled on discretionary trusts in 1972 was of the order of £6,000 million (evidence to Select Committee on Wealth Tax, 1975, p.262, para.7).

117. W. Holdsworth, op.cit., note 8, supra, Vol.V, p.317.

118. (1718) Prec. Ch.505.

119. (1711) 1 P. Wms.140.

120. E.g. Piety v. Stace (1799), 4 Ves.620; Rocke v. Hart (1805), 11 Ves.58.

121. (1726) Sel. Cas.t.King 61.

122. G.W. Keeton, Social Change in the Law of Trusts, (Westport: Greenwood Press, 1958), p.14.

123. See generally D. Grosh, "Trustee Investment: English Law and the American Prudent Man Rule", International and Comparative Law Quarterly, XXIII (1974), pp.748-68; G.W. Keeton, "Trustee Investments and the National Investment Policy", The Accountant, April 4, 1953, pp.390-3; op.cit., note 5, supra, Ch.5; G.W. Keeton and L.A. Sheridan, The Law of Trusts, 10th ed. (London: Professional Books, 1974), pp.246-50; D.R. Marsh, Corporate

Trustees, (London: Europa, 1953), pp.218-40; D. Oosterhoff, Trustees' Powers of Investment (study prepared for Ontario Law Reform Commission, 1970).

124. E.g. Hancom v. Allen (1774) 2 Dick.498.

125. E.g. Pocock v. Reddington (1801) 5 Ves.794, 800.

126. Learoyd v. Whiteley (1887) 12 App. Cas.727.

127. Jackson v. Jackson (1737) 1 Atk.513, 514.

128. The implications of this are well brought out in the comparative study by D. Grosh, op.cit., note 123, supra.

129. See e.g. Ex parte Calthorpe (1785) 1 Cox 182; Raby v. Ridehalgh (1855) 7 De G.M. & G.104.

130. E.g. in Knight v. Earl of Plymouth (1747) Dick 120, 126; Pocock v. Reddington (1801) 5 Ves.794, 800.

131. See e.g. G.W. Keeton, op.cit., supra, note 5, pp.47-53.

132. B.L. Anderson, op.cit., note 70, supra, p.109; "Provincial Aspects of the Financial Revolution of the Eighteenth Century", Business History, XI (1969), 11-20; "The Attorney and the Early Capital Market in Lancashire", in J.R. Harris (ed.), Liverpool and Merseyside, (London: Frank Cass, 1969).

133. G.W. Keeton and L.A. Sheridan, op.cit., note 123, supra, p.247.

134. D. Grosh, op.cit., note 123, supra, p.763.

135. See e.g. H.G. Hanbury and R.H. Maudsley, op.cit., note 1, supra, pp.559-66.

136. B.L. Anderson, "Provincial Aspects . . .", op.cit., note 132, supra, p.20: see too, op.cit., note 70, supra, p.106.

137. See e.g. Re Wragg [1919] 2 Ch.58; G.W. Keeton, op.cit., note 5, supra, Ch.7.

138. See p.125, supra.

139. J.R.S. Revell, op.cit., note 4, supra, p.135.

140. See p.157, supra.

141. See generally H.G. Hanbury and R.H. Maudsley, op.cit., note 1, supra, Ch.21.

142. But see E. David, "Principal and Interest - Obsolete Concepts", Pennsylvania Bar Association Quarterly, XLIII (1972), pp.24-52; J.C. Phillips, "Some

Instances of the Trustee's Duty to Act Fairly Between Different Classes of Beneficiaries", University of Queensland Law Journal, X (1977), pp.83-101.

143. J. Flower, "A Note on Capital and Income in Trusts Law", in H.C. Edey and B.S. Yamey (ed.), Debits, Credits, Finance and Profits, (London: Sweet and Maxwell, 1974); L. Seltzer, The Nature and Tax Treatment of Capital Gains and Losses, (New York: National Bureau of Economic Research, 1951), Ch.2.

144. Though an interventionist approach was taken in the Canadian case of Re Smith (1971) 16 D.L.R. (3d) 130; (1971) 18 D.L.R. (3d) 405.

145. See generally H.G. Hanbury and R.H. Maudsley, op.cit., supra, note 1, pp.579-86.

146. For a useful illustration of the use of such delegation in a practical context, see G. Oates, "Successful Investment for Trustees", New Law Journal, CXXIII (1973), pp.935, 979.

147. Cf., G.W. Keeton, op.cit., supra, note 5, Ch.2.

148. On the relation between strict settlements and problems of liquidity experienced by life-tenants, see e.g. D. Cannadine, "Aristocratic Indebtedness in the Nineteenth Century: The Case Reopened", Economic History Review, 2nd ser. XXX (1977), pp.624-50; D. Spring, op.cit., note 71, supra, "English Land-Ownership in the Nineteenth Century: A Critical Note", Economic History Review, 2nd ser. IX (1957), pp.472-84; F.M.L. Thompson, "The End of a Great Estate", Economic History Review, 2nd ser. VIII (1955), pp.36-52.

149. See sources cited in note 63, supra.

150. (1841) Cr. & Ph.240.

151. See sources cited in note 108, supra; (also as regards Saunders v. Vautier specifically) D.B. Parker and A.R. Mellows, The Modern Law of Trusts, 4th ed., (London: Sweet and Maxwell, 1979), pp.348-50.

152. Chapman v. Chapman [1954] A.C. 429, 468, per Lord Morton of Henryton.

THE FAMILY, STRICT SETTLEMENT AND HISTORIANS

Eileen Spring

A good number of years ago, Sir John Habakkuk put forward a theory about aristocratic marriage in the eighteenth century. He was seeking to account for the growth of large estates that he believed to have then taken place, and his eye fell upon the heiress. Estates grew in part, he concluded, because eldest sons sought to marry heiresses "more systematically", than they had earlier done. This was not to be the whole of Habakkuk's thinking about women and estate growth, however; nor indeed the main part of it. Heiresses were uncommon, and the ultimate disposition of their estates was uncertain. Habakkuk extended his idea into a broad theory more significant for estate growth encompassing daughters generally. Eldest sons not only pursued heiresses but also demanded brides who, while not actual heiresses, were nevertheless increasingly well-endowed. Habakkuk deduced the substance of this theory from certain features of the strict settlement, a legal device that had been developed in the latter half of the seventeenth century to serve landowners as a form of entail. He deduced the theory from the portions, jointures, and annuities that settlement laid out for those members of the family who were not eldest sons. The strict settlement was in this way found to indicate "the increasing subordination of marriage to the increase of landed wealth."[1]

Implicitly, and indeed explicitly, Habakkuk viewed the aristocratic family as patriarchal. In recent years, however, historians have come to entertain the idea that something called the affective family came in the eighteenth century to replace the patriarchal one. Deference and authority are seen as giving way to love and mutual respect among family members. The idea stems from the work of Philippe Aries on the history of childhood. It has been expanded upon in The Family, Sex, and Marriage in England, 1500-1800 by Lawrence Stone. The strict settlement is used to support this new theory too. "The careful provision for younger sons, daughters, and widows secured the rights of all parties and thus undermined the principles of patriarchal power," Stone declares; and he specifically adds that settlement, by reducing "the arbitrary control" of the father over property, reduced "his power to enforce his will . . . over such critical issues as marriage."[2] Another recent work on the aristocratic family has much the same thing to say about settlement.[3]

These are startlingly different ideas to spring from the same legal device. In Habakkuk's theory settlement indicates that family relationships were becoming increasingly commercial; in Stone's theory settlement is a sign that the family has become tolerant and considerate. The very device that once indicated the subordination of marriage to dynastic interests has become one making for love matches! Clearly something is amiss. It is the purpose of this paper therefore to analyse the use of settlement in these two theories - and in a recent restatement by Habakkuk - in an effort to see what the strict settlement does and does not tell us about family life.

We shall find that the strict settlement is a very much misunderstood device. We shall find that it has not been properly used in either of the theories outlined. The implications of this discovery - these discoveries - are considerable for historical studies.

As historians recognise Habakkuk's misunderstanding of settlement, they will have to reassess much of the scholarly literature on the aristocratic family. Habakkuk's theory was an immensely influential one. It has come to mark aristocratic studies of the seventeenth and eighteenth centuries conspicuously. Lawrence Stone himself once used it wholeheartedly. It influences G.E. Mingay's work. It has influenced even the literature on foreign aristocracy, being traceable for example in Robert Forster's work on the French nobility. It has received recent expression in the work of Peter Roebuck on Yorkshire baronets.[4]

From Stone's misunderstanding of settlement different consequences flow, even more far-reaching ones. We shall find that settlement exhibits no lessening of patriarchal power in regard to marriage, and shall find that in property development it indicates a strengthening of patriarchal power. In other words, settlement not only fails to support the idea of the affective family but runs counter to it.

We shall proceed in this paper to look first at Habakkuk's theory; and second at his recent statement on the subject. We shall then look at Lawrence Stone's theory. Our findings will be brought together in a conclusion attempting to indicate what settlement actually did.

* * * * * * * * * * * * * *

How Habakkuk drew his theory out of the jointures, portions, and annuities in settlement may be briefly summarised. He found a fall in the ratio of jointure to portion between 1650 and 1700 that he could not account for by a change in the rate of interest or a change in the return from land. He concluded it represented a movement of the terms of marriage in favour of husbands. He went on to find that portions rose while jointures fell. Eldest sons thus seemed very clearly bent on advantage in marriage, on the one hand demanding more with their brides and on the other hand reducing their payments to those brides become widows. Habakkuk also found - what seemed to fit - that settlements discriminated against younger sons, even cutting them off with small annuities while daughters received large portions. Daughters, he reasoned, "were important as the means by which great landowners made their alliances". They had to be well provided for if they were "to make good marriages to eldest sons."[5] Younger sons, being of no dynastic account, might be slighted.

All this, of course, is to postulate much more than the existence of heiress-seeking among eldest sons. It is to postulate heiress-seeking so pervasive, so dynastically important, that the interests of all members of the family are conditioned by it - younger sons, widows, fathers, and daughters not heiresses. Habakkuk's was no simple theory that eldest sons pursued heiresses.

There are a number of things on the very surface of this theory that should have led to questioning and caution. First, the theory is based upon what are subordinate features of settlement. It little considers the main feature of settlement - the entail. Many - probably most - settlements entailed estates where there were no sons upon collateral males, postponing daughters who were heiresses-at-law to uncles, nephews, and male cousins. As settlement was clearly and directly concerned with heiresses, that is to say, it was to cut them down. This is a thing generally well-known. Jane Austen had wry sport with it in Pride and Prejudice. Mrs Bennet is "beyond the reach of reason" on the subject of entail; she never ceases "to rail bitterly against the cruelty of settling an estate away from a family of five daughters in favour of a man whom nobody cared anything about." While it is equally well-known that heiresses have at no time generally succeeded to estates as the rules for the descent of land would have it, we may assume that heiresses do better when their fathers possess power over their estates than when they do not, and thus that heiresses did better before the strict settlement than after it. Fathers in control of their estates deciding the fate of born daughters are certain overall to be more generous than fathers under the strict settlement deciding the fate of heiresses in the abstract, which was an unpleasant future possibility. It might have been wondered then how a theory emphasising the increasing importance of heiresses could be arrived at out of the strict settlement.

Second, landowners clearly demonstrated in the strict settlement a determination to preserve estates. The theory, however, has landowners endowing daughters generally in ever increasing degree. It might have been wondered whether inconsistency on such a scale was likely to have existed. Finally, it might well have been wondered whether daughters have ever, in this world dominated by males, been better endowed than sons.

That the historical profession in spite of these obvious objections was carried away by Habakkuk's theory speaks oddly for it - speaks perhaps of its hankering after novelty, or perhaps even of its own attitude to women. (How titillating to see women as objects of commerce!) To this day - thirty years later - these objections to the theory have not been mentioned, except the last of them, and that hesitantly.

There has been some criticism, but never reaching to the fundamentals of the theory. Christopher Clay came to point out that it was not always apparent at marriage who was or was not an heiress, and that heiress-seeking could be a bit of a gamble.[6] David Thomas came to show that Habakkuk had the direction of movement wrong, came to show that eldest sons had married heiresses less frequently rather than more frequently in the eighteenth century.[7] This might have been seen to indicate - what there was reason to expect - that heiresses were of less substance than they earlier had been. Eventually instead, Thomas's work was used as proof of the development of the affective family. Though he might have raised important questions, Thomas himself continued to emphasise heiress-seeking, noting that his data took no account of portions.

Habakkuk's ideas on aristocratic motives and aristocratic family principles have thus never been subjected to the analysis they deserve. There runs unchallenged through the literature on the seventeenth and eighteenth century aristocracy an extraordinary emphasis upon aristocratic daughters, upon the cost of their portions to estates, upon the difficulty of getting them married, upon their exploitation not only by eldest sons but by their own fathers. Daughters were "peculiarly expensive", says - or said -Lawrence Stone; "so hot [was] the pace" of the marriage market that their portions reached "dizzy heights."[8] More temperate in language but to the same effect is Mingay. Marriages had to be "so arranged as to bring greater wealth, land, or influence to the family"; daughters became "of more consequence to a father than his younger sons"; their portions had to be "substantial" and grew "more lavish".[9] So widespread have such ideas become that a historian of the Venetian nobility simply assumes a rise in daughters' portions continuing apparently over centuries.[10]

Let us then at last turn to analyse Habakkuk's account of the aristocratic family and its property arrangements. We shall begin with the simplest part of it, with the idea that fathers distinguished between younger sons and daughters in their settlements, favouring the latter over the former. Can this really have been so?

It may be of help in answering this question to begin with the nineteenth century and work backward, for the nineteenth century exhibits settlement full-blown, its pattern well established and widely commented on. The great nineteenth century conveyancers - Sugden, Williams, Davidson, and Key and Elphinstone - all took it for granted that younger children, male and female, were normally treated alike. The standard form of settlement they described - innumerable examples of which are known to historians from family papers - provided for younger children in the following manner: a specified sum might be raised should there be one younger child; a larger sum, though less than twice as much, should there be two younger children; a still larger sum should there be three or more younger children; all this without mentioning sex. The parents were then granted a power of apportioning the sum among their children as they should see fit. In default of such appointment the sum was to be divided equally. Thus while younger children did not necessarily receive equal portions, equality may be said to be the assumption. Insofar as inequality prevailed in practice, nineteenth century historians have found that it was the sons who did better than the daughters. Large landowners still sometimes left landed estates to younger sons.

Thus the distinguishment of daughters, if it existed earlier, was a declining practice. Let us look at the evidence that has been presented for the belief. Habakkuk has described one example of the provisioning of younger children. Daniel Finch, second Earl of Nottingham, gave a large portion to the only child of his first marriage, a daughter. To the children of his second marriage he gave annuities to the sons that when capitalised are significantly smaller than the portions of the daughters.[11] Mingay has also presented one example of a settlement - one, however, that goes to deny what he would believe.[12] Lawrence Stone has presented five examples of settlements that allow of comparison between the sexes. In two of them the sons received annuities and the daughters portions. In one of these two, the annuity if capitalised is only about half the value of the portion. In the other, however, the annuity if capitalised is about equal to the portion. In the other three examples both sons and daughters received portions, presumably equally.[13] Thus those who maintain that landowners distinguished their daughters have presented seven cases in all, only two of which clearly support their view.

Recently fuller studies of the provisioning of younger children have been undertaken. J.P. Cooper has presented forty-eight examples from the sixteenth and seventeenth centuries.[14] Randolph Trumbach has studied the settlements of thirty families in the eighteenth century.[15] Trumbach finds that eighteenth century settlements generally took the form of nineteenth century ones, and that younger sons and daughters were treated alike. Many of Cooper's examples do not allow us to compare the provision for sons and daughters either because sons received land of unstated value or because there were not children of both sexes. Of the twenty-nine examples that do permit comparison, in only four of them do we find daughters favoured over sons. In eighteen the sons did as well as or better than the daughters. Seven exhibit a mixed pattern - one sex having members above and members below the other. Cooper gives other evidence as to the preference shown for younger sons over daughters, and was led to wonder "when, if ever, it became true" that daughters were the favoured sex. Neither Cooper nor Trumbach, however, have considered the consequences of these findings, which will eventually appear here.

The evidence then would suggest that as a general rule landowners have never provided more generously for daughters than for younger sons. Under the strict settlement, they generally provided for them equally. Where they had treated sons and daughters differently, it was sons who almost always did the better. We have, to be sure, proved that water runs downhill, but the proof seems to be necessary.

The emphasis on the cost of daughters' portions that has so come to mark estate studies will not otherwise be seen to be awry. Daughters, eldest and younger together, were naturally more numerous than younger sons. In aggregate they may have been the more costly, although even that may be doubtful. Unit for unit, certainly, daughters were of no more consequence to landed estates than younger sons.

Habakkuk's main proof of his theory, however, lay not in the distinction between younger sons and daughters but in the falling ratio of jointure to portion, and to this we now turn.

It is not to be denied that the ratio fell. How and why it did so are, however, open to debate. Habakkuk held that both portions and jointures moved - the one rising and the other falling - and that both movements were the result of eldest sons seeking advantage in marriage, demanding ever more with their brides and returning ever less to their widows. It will be argued here, first, that portions did not rise, and even if they had, it would not be for the reason alleged; and, second, that there is a different and better reason for the fall of jointures.

We may begin our discussion of the movement of portions by noting that Habakkuk never presented statistical evidence for the rise he believed took place. He appealed to contemporary expressions of opinion, and pointed to demographic factors that he held must lead to a rise. These demographic factors were thus never integral to his theory, and discussing them is not strictly necessary to us here. Still a word or two about them is in order, for they have come to play a significant role in the literature on aristocracy. They are well noted as factors facilitating the increasing demands of eldest sons.

The claim is that there was an imbalance of the sexes in the aristocratic marriage market, an excess of females inevitably making the terms of marriage move against them. Several reasons for the excess are mentioned: men were killed in war; younger sons were too poor to marry; they tended to fall out of aristocratic society into the professional classes; commercial heiresses came to invade the aristocratic marriage market.[16]

There is probably little in all this. Habakkuk himself dismissed the commercial heiress. Marriages to commercial heiresses were rare. It is true that younger sons did not marry as often as their elder brothers, but most of them did marry.[17] The connected idea that younger sons drifted out of aristocratic society but that daughters had to remain locked within their class is an idea in large part deduced from the theory itself. Daughters would not be allowed to fall out of aristocratic society because dynastic significance attached to them. The thinking is circular. When Stone - who makes much of demographic movements in the marriage market - says that it was considered "indecent to marry your daughter to a mere merchant's son even though your son and heir might at a pinch marry his sister", the loading of the language is to be remarked.[18] Did not peerage daughters marry gentry sons, and did not gentry daughters in their turn marry, let us say, City aldermen, barristers, ecclesiastics, and even merchants not so mere, such as bankers? Finally, and most important, it would seem that female mortality was higher than male.[19] Women died in childbirth far more often apparently than men died in war. In the first fifteen years of marriage there was twice as great a chance of the wife's dying as of the husband doing so.[20] There would thus seem to be little reason to think that an excess of females marked the aristocratic marriage market. Indeed both Russell and Hollingsworth see a general excess of males in pre-industrial societies.[21]

Let us leave the question whether daughters' portions for demographic reasons must have risen and ask whether portions did in fact rise. Lawrence Stone has presented an estimate of the general level of portions in the early seventeenth century. He finds that the standard portion for a daughter was then roughly one year's income of the family estate, or in other words, that it was about four per cent of the family's capital.[22] No comparable figure for a later date has ever been presented. Against Stone's figure we will here venture one based on a sample - albeit small - of settlements from the nineteenth century. Sixteen out of a group of nineteen settlements provided not for a daughter but for a generation of younger children a sum twice the annual income of the estate or less.[23] From this it seems arguable that portions fell under the strict settlement. On paper they certainly fell.[24] It would be unwise to press the comparison so far, however. It seems safe though to hold that portions did not rise. (Of course they rose in money terms with the rise in prices and rents over two centuries, but it is the proportion they bear to estate income that is the appropriate measure here). Since Stone also shows that portions were rising relative to rents before the strict settlement, and K.B. McFarlane shows that the shares of younger sons increased with the increase in landowners' power over their land in the fifteenth century, it would seem that settlement put an end to an upward trend.[25]

This finding - insubstantially based though it may be - would square with legal and psychological factors as Habakkuk's theory does not. The aim of settlement being to perpetuate estates in the hands of eldest sons, its aim was to limit the cost of younger children. It limited such cost by virtue of the fact that it determined what portions were to be before children were born, before they were beings known and loved. Prior to the development of the strict settlement landowners had much power over the disposition of their property, and were freer to do what affection would prompt. Children standing before one in flesh and blood, we may be sure, are harder to cut down than children hypothetical. (That Habakkuk invoked the opposite principle of human behaviour is another thing that historians might have wondered about before taking up his theory.)[26] As settlement developed then we might expect a decrease in the size of children's portions, or at least no increase.

No matter how portions moved, however, it could not be for the reason Habakkuk alleges. Since sons and daughters were portioned more or less equally, the movement of portions is not to be explained by something operating upon daughters only - not, at least, unless one is prepared to argue that sons' portions moved merely sympathetically. Explanation of any movement of portions is to be sought in something that affected both sexes equally, in legal changes themselves or in changes in aristocratic levels of living.

It is thus clear that the upward trend of portions supposed to have been established as eldest sons demanded well-endowed brides is chimerical. No doubt some daughters received large portions. The daughter whose father possessed much personal property might well do so - a factor of general importance when personal property became substantial in the nineteenth century. No doubt such a daughter took on something of the character of an heiress and was sought as such. The idea, however, that heiress-seeking was so pervasive as to force fathers generally to portion daughters ever increasingly is mistaken. The further idea that fathers themselves were concerned with their daughters' promoting alliances for them, were themselves waging a dynastic struggle through their daughters, is also mistaken. Of course, some ambitious fathers may have so acted. It is the rule that we would establish. Fathers clearly were not generous to daughters, but by the same token they could not generally have exploited their daughters' marriages as alleged. For all their domineering ways, it would seem that English patriarchs were guiltless, at least by the eighteenth century, of one charge that has been brought against them. What settlement does indicate is that landowners desired to cut down female inheritance, and that they consistently acted to that end, reducing heiresses and putting a lid on portions.

We have thus far seen what settlement shows about younger sons and about heiresses and about daughters not heiresses. Finally then, what does it show about widows? What, in other words, is to be said about the movement of jointures? Certainly these fell, falling from 15% of portions in 1650 to 10% in 1700, as Habakkuk's figures indicate. The facts are not to be disputed in this case, and Habakkuk's claim is warranted that the fall in jointure represents a change in the terms of marriage in favour of husbands. What motivated the change is, however, open to dispute. For Habakkuk the change was part of the commercialisation of marriage. We shall find that the fall in jointure is simply coherent with the cutting down of female inheritance already described, that it tells us nothing of motives to marriage.

It is to be noted that Habakkuk deals only with what is a small part of a very great fall. When we say that jointures fell from 15% of portions to 10% we are calculating the jointure as a return on a woman's own money, or on her father's money. Legally, however, jointures were in lieu of dower; and dower was a charge upon a husband's land. It was a one-third charge for a widow's life. A 10% return on a portion - probably even a 15% one - represents overall no charge whatever on a husband's land. The apparently high "rate of interest" should not deceive us. A jointure is an annuity on one life after the falling in of another.[27] Clearly an enormous fall in the provision for widows had taken place before settlement even appeared. Settlement merely carried further an established trend.

Something of the history of widows and of landowners' attitude to them is to be gathered from the long disquisition of Justice Wilmot in the case Earl of Buckingham v. Drury (1762). In this case a plaintiff, married before the age of twenty-one, appealed to have her settlement set aside because she had been led to accept a jointure that was less than dower. Wilmot found against her. He described how landowners had evaded dower from the very development of uses. The principle long established, he declared, was that women were to accept their jointures "whether they be great or small, adequate or inadequate, whether they have been made by the agreement of themselves . . . or have been the mere spontaneous acts of the husband . . . ."[28] No relationship to land or to fortune was thus required. It is true, as historians sometimes point out, that a woman who married before a settlement was drawn could in the end choose either jointure or dower. This does not mean, however, as the implication has been, that any relationship between the two was maintained in practice. Landowners did not marry without first making a settlement. Their widows did not have the choice. The cutting down of dower was the very aim. (Dower, to be sure, was administratively more nuisance than jointure; but if increasing efficiency had been all the consideration in landowners' minds, the two things would have remained of equal value).

In the light of what has already been shown in this paper, there is no mystery to be solved here. A one-third charge on a landed estate was in landowners' eyes an unnecessarily large provision for a widow. It was never in line with the aristocratic ethos. Dower was a subject on which landowners and the common law simply differed, as they differed on the succession of females to land, or for that matter as they differed upon the total disinheritance of younger children. Accordingly, dower was virtually abolished, and widows in effect came to provide largely for their own jointures, or their fathers did.

Historians indeed have only failed to perceive how greatly landowners cut down their payments to those appropriately named relicts. Historians regularly emphasise the cost of jointures to estates. Obviously, some landowners would do less well than the average and end up with jointures that were a loss. Doubtless also there were some large jointures. Unusual things can operate in particular cases. Romantic excess is naturally sometimes to be expected; but other motives may operate as well. One dowager Duchess of Devonshire had her jointure doubled when it was learned what her Russell counterpart received.[29] More important, there developed the practice of settling a woman's portion to her own use, thus rendering the jointure a real, if overall tiny, charge upon estates. On the whole, however, historians have not appreciated the history of widows, and have exaggerated the burden of jointures to estates. Widows, it would seem, are never popular.

Having now surveyed the details of Habakkuk's theory, we may sum it up in a general way. Habakkuk claimed what we may take to be a certain truth - one hardly sensational in itself though - some heiress-seeking went on among aristocratic eldest sons. The attempt to extend this idea, to enlarge upon it through the strict settlement was, however, unfortunate. There could hardly be a less likely device to look to for the purpose. On the face of it, settlement reduced heiresses, and must have led to a decline in their importance in estate affairs. Everything about the strict settlement bespeaks the desire to preserve estates, and estates are not preserved by generosity to daughters, neither by the succession of heiresses, nor by the veritable creation of substitute heiresses in portioned daughters. Misinterpreting certain features of settlement, Habakkuk turned a device entailing estates in the male line virtually upside down, and in the process attributed to heiress-seeking extensive ramifications for aristocratic family life that it did not have.

* * * * * * * * * * * * * *

As we noted at the outset, Habakkuk has recently had something more to say on the subject of female inheritance and estate growth.[30] There are, or there seem to be, remarkable changes in his approach.

This time he barely mentions portions or the portioned daughter. He would thus seem to have turned his back on the principal part of his earlier theory, although he does not declare this to be the case. He also now uses settlement very differently than he did. Whereas he once recounted the development of settlement to prove his theory - drawing the theory out of the device - he now sets about showing that settlement was, after all, of limited effect. We are reminded that estates might be only partly settled; that they might fall out of settlement; and even be kept out of settlement. We are told that not all landowners practised settlement. The gentry particularly, we are told, came late to it. This reversal of attitude is not discussed or noted.

The emphasis has apparently narrowed to the heiress, and by implication it is now recognised that heiress-seeking and the strict settlement do not go together. Heiresses are well endowed, it seems, where settlement is not. Finally, whereas the heiress was earlier held to be uncommon, she is now noted to be "common enough".[31]

These differences would seem to make for a theory that is as much to be contrasted with the original as associated with it.

Despite these differences, despite this implied alteration of the theory, Habakkuk does still use the strict settlement to prove that marriage accounts for the growth of large estates. Settlement now simply operates automatically to limit who can marry who. It intrinsically determines that heiresses must fall to large estates. This idea had a part in the original theory, but it now assumes major importance, bearing the burden of the theory. It needs separate attention if the aristocratic family is to be properly understood.

The claim is that only large landowners could marry heiresses because only they could afford to pay the large jointures required to match the property of heiresses. "In simple terms", Habakkuk writes, "a family would need to be able to grant a jointure of £2,000 p.a. (and enjoy a total income much greater) to secure the only daughter and heiress of the owner of an estate yielding £1,000 p.a. and worth in capital terms £20,000."[32]

The arithmetic notwithstanding, this argument in the end fails. Such calculations did not even apply when the bride's fortune was in land, where a woman really did inherit an estate. As is well known in a different context the settling of landed heiresses was different from the settling of portioned daughters. A portion at common law became the immediate and absolute property of the husband, and he had to have estate sufficient to guarantee a jointure in return for it. Land at law did not pass absolutely to the husband. He gained only its use. His widow would regain her property. Settlement might be generally guided by common law principles; or it might reject them, settling the estate to the wife's own uses. In any case the widow was protected. Thus the husband owed no <u>quid pro quo</u>, and thus no landowner however small was precluded from marrying a landed heiress. The heiress did not require, nor did she receive, that lucrative jointure <u>from her husband's estate</u> that historians have imagined. Her large jointure tended to be mostly her own rents.

The calculations did normally apply to portions. However, as portions were small in relation to estate value, and as jointures were, actuarialy judged, no charge upon the husband's land - both of which things we have shown earlier - providing a jointure equal to portion was achievable within wide bounds. Where it was not to be achieved - where a portion was really large relative to the husband's estate - land might be bought and settled as above described. Eventually personalty itself came to be settlable to the wife's separate use as we have also noted, and where this was done the jointure could be determined solely with reference to the husband's estate. There is every reason to think that what would be determined upon would not be large. Thus the possibility always existed that any landowner however small could marry any woman however rich. Where there was a will to marry, be it for love or money, there was a way. Whether widely disparate matches were ever likely is another matter. What concerns us here is that settlement did nothing to prevent them.

Thus the arithmetic that allegedly stood between the small landowner and the wealthy woman did not really exist. We should only be surprised if this were not so. It would have been a perverse effect of settlement to prevent an access of good fortune. Had settlement actually stood in the way of advantageous marriages - or even dashed hope of them - it would be difficult to account for its thriving as a device for so long.

As we come to the end of our discussion of Habakkuk's theories, we should be clear what has and what has not been concluded. We have been concerned to show that those theories portray the aristocratic family, its motives and financial arrangements, incorrectly. The family scenario that Habakkuk envisions was never real. Habakkuk's theories, however, were designed to account for a growth of large estates that he held to have taken place in the eighteenth century. Settlement is inherently concerned only to preserve estates. There is no reason why it should promote estate growth. The idea that heiresses must fall to large estates because of settlement is, as we have seen, not valid. Nevertheless, settlement may account for a difference between the course of large estates and that of small. If the owners of large estates took to it earlier or if they practised it more regularly than the owners of small estates, then their estates would have been the better preserved. It has recently been shown that such a difference existed.[33] Thus settlement may have played not the spectacular role that Habakkuk assigned to it but a supporting role, accounting for the better preservation of large estates as opposed to small.

* * * * * * * * * * * * * *

Lawrence Stone, to whom we now turn, once applied Habakkuk's ideas on the family with great verve to the seventeenth century. These ideas form a large element in his Crisis of Aristocracy. As we have noted, however, he has come in The Family, Sex, and Marriage to develop a theory of his own about the meaning of strict settlement, one very different from Habakkuk's. Stone claims that settlement, by spelling out the interests of all members of the family, limited the power of the father and is therefore to be accounted an anti-patriarchal development, one of the signs of the growth of the affective family. He claims in particular that settlement gave younger children a legal right to their portions and thus that it made them independent of their parents, even putting it in their power to defy their parents.

The general idea that strict settlement is an anti-patriarchal development is surely perverse. To associate freedom of disposition with patriarchy - primogeniture and entail with its decline - will simply not do as a general rule. It is incidentally not the way that Aries, to whom the affective family is to be traced, considers these things.[34] The aim of primogeniture and entail is to preserve estates. The common threat to that end lies in younger children. The spelling out of the rights of younger children in a strict settlement is a limitation of children's rights. To note that settlement put limits upon a father's power and to claim that it is therefore anti-patriarchal is to be confused by words. Fathers were limited in the provision they might make for their younger children. They were limited in the interests of eldest sons, in the interests of patriarchy itself.

Stone confesses that "at first sight" the reaffirmation of primogeniture would seem patriarchal, and he acknowledges that settlement "preserved a highly inegalitarian distribution of family resources".[35] This is a damaging acknowledgement, but it is not all that is due. Settlement not only preserved inequity, but increased it. Stone has himself earlier declared that it did so.[36] Facts he even now cites declare the same thing. He describes an "economic crisis for younger sons" in the eighteenth century brought on by what, at the point, he only calls unspecifically "the property arrangements of the elite". Younger sons "are pushed out into the world with a small annuity [rather than as earlier being given on long lease or in perpetuity one of the ancestral estates on which to live like country gentlemen]."[37] As for daughters, Stone fails to notice that the rise in their portions that he now hails as a rise in affect took place in the seventeenth century, that is, before the strict settlement. On his own showing, settlement marks a move away from the affective family, at least if judged by the division of property.

Clearly, the most that Stone might be entitled to claim is that settlement was a mixed development for younger children, that it held some consolation for them: they were made secure of their restricted inheritances. Even this claim would be in need of scrutiny, however. Children were undoubtedly more secure under settlement, but the ways in which they were and the ways in which they were not secure are important to distinguish. Distinguishing them will tell us, leaving no room for waffling, whether settlement is an anti-patriarchal development.

In several ways younger children were secured by settlement. They were secured against intestacy on the part of their father and the consequent thoroughgoing application of the rule of primogeniture. What is much the same thing, they were secured against the earlier possibility that their father might fail to bar an old entail that left them similarly unprovided for. These are real securities: they are securities against utter disaster. One may wonder, however, whether such disasters had ever often taken place. How often had landowners died intestate disinheriting younger children? Or let old entails run that had the same result? And when these things did happen, was it owing to deliberation or to procrastination? Unless it can be shown that such things had been frequent and deliberate, settlement is not on the grounds of these securities granted younger children to be accounted an anti-patriarchal device. It is no derogation of paternal power worth the name to see to it that a father actually provides for his younger children when he has every intention of doing so.

Thus far we have seen that younger children were made secure against certain unlikely happenings that it was no derogation of paternal power to secure them against. The major question is whether younger children were in any way secured against paternal power itself. Stone claims that they were: that settlement gave them a legal right to their portions and therefore made them independent of their father. Was this true?

Possibly it was true for a while and on occasion, but it was not long nor generally true. The fact that younger children did have a legal claim to their portions at first often led to a clause being inserted in settlements requiring daughters to marry with the consent of their parents or lose their claim. Orlando Bridgeman suggests a clause to this effect.[38] Stone has noticed the disappearance of this clause, but he has then leapt to wrong conclusions. The disappearance of this clause does not mean that children became independent, nor does it prove that parents were willing "to abandon control over their children's marriages". The clause disappeared, but a more stringent replaced it that became standard. The clause concerning marriage had not been readily enforceable at law, and it had not applied to sons. It was replaced by the clause we have outlined in a different context earlier in this paper, by the clause giving parents a power of apportioning the sum for younger children in any manner they deemed fit. Trumbach finds this clause predominant by 1720.[39] All the child had under it - whether male or female - was in effect a right to be considered. He or she could, as the phrase goes, be cut off with a shilling - and could be so cut off for any reason the parents thought deserving of such a fate. Settlement here indicates no weakening of parental authority. Fathers continued to hold a warrant for younger children's good behaviour. It is true that fathers could not under settlement disinherit their eldest sons, but they had other financial powers over them.[40] Fathers may have been less likely to use their power as the eighteenth century advanced. In legal form, however, that power existed as much as ever.

We may then conclude that Stone misuses the strict settlement in his theory of the affective family. Settlement remains obstinately a patriarchal device. The spelling out of the interests of the subordinate members of the family was a limitation of those interests. Settlement did make younger children more secure of their property, but only in ways that represented no lessening of patriarchal power. In the division of property between eldest sons and younger children settlement represents a development indeed that runs counter to the theory of the affective family.

These findings are no small matter for that theory. Stone's three stages of family development are portrayed as paralleling the legal arrangements of landowners. It is in the law that Stone has attempted to find hard evidence for a theory that is otherwise impressionistic. Unfortunately, the law is largely misperceived.[41]

* * * * * * * * * * * * * *

Thus far this paper has been negative. It has been concerned with what settlement does not tell us, eminent historians to the contrary. In this section of the paper we shall consider what settlement does tell us. We shall draw together certain conclusions that have been made in passing about the positive meaning of settlement.

One thing that settlement meant has several times been touched on. It meant the cutting down of female inheritance. Heiresses-at-law became less likely to inherit estates, generally became less substantially endowed. One of the main reasons for the development of settlement must indeed have been to ensure exactly this: to make estates go more effectively in tail male - to make their descent approximate better in substance to the rules pertaining to titles, which conflict with common law rules. Under settlement, too, younger children's portions ceased to rise. This affected younger sons as well as daughters, of course, though both before and after the development of settlement some younger sons did better than their sisters. Under settlement, too, widows' rights, long in decline, reached rock bottom.

Is it because, as Jane Austen says, the pen has been in male hands that the cutting down of female inheritance, a really rather obvious development, has gone largely unnoticed by historians? What women brought to marriage, whether estates were growing through marriage, how the terms of marriage were moving and what this implied about motives to marriage, these have been the questions historians have asked. Women as marriage partners, the strict settlement as the marriage settlement, that has been the focus of historical attention. What happened to women as persons - to women as heiresses, as daughters, as widows - has been scarcely perceived, even wrongly perceived. A direct look at women and at property law and practice relative to them would seem to be in order.

The cutting down of female inheritance is, of course, part and parcel of a larger movement. This is a movement so obvious that one is surprised to find it necessary to assert it, but clearly it currently stands in need of assertion. Settlement meant a resurgence of primogeniture. It meant a tightening up of the aristocratic family structure, a tightening up after a period of relative weakness. For a century and a half after the destruction of true entails - from about 1500 to 1650 - landowners had been relatively unhampered in dealing with their land, and there are indications that this had meant what one might expect, a decrease in the proportion of estates going by the rules of primogeniture. The invention of the strict settlement marked a reassertion of traditional aristocratic ideas on inheritance, or more accurately expressed, it gave better practical effect to those ideas.

This development, however awkward to the current orthodoxy, marks a step not in the direction of the affective family but away from it. To be sure, the extent of the movement should not be exaggerated. It would have been on a limited scale because the male primogenitive ethos had marked family arrangements even when landowners were free to do as they pleased. Neither, however, is the fact of the movement to be ignored. If one looks to the inheritance of property the idea cannot be sustained that the patriarchal family declined in the eighteenth century. There are, of course, other things also to be looked at in judging of patriarchy, but there is no denying that property is fundamental.

* * * * * * * * * * * * * * *

A brief appendix needs to be added here to consider the work of Lloyd Bonfield. From a demographic analysis, Bonfield has concluded that the strict settlement could not have operated as a form of entail, that is, could not have succeeded in keeping estates perpetually in the hands of tenants for life. It frequently let into possession a landowner who being a tenant in tail was for all practical purposes an owner in fee. The power of the strict settlement to effect entail was "illusory".[42] Since entail has been taken to be the essence of the device, the implications of this finding would seem to be that the strict settlement is to be dismissed as meaningless. That is the implication that Bonfield himself seems to make.

I would not dispute - at least not in substance - the finding that settlement could not have been an effective form of entail.[43] Long ago I suggested myself that its operation as entail had been exaggerated by historians.[44] What I would point out, however, is that settlement is not rendered meaningless by its failure as entail.

Nothing in this paper depends upon it having been a form of entail. We have been looking at the strict settlement merely as a single deed, unconcerned with the possible linkage of one settlement to the next. So long as landowners settled their estates by strict settlements made before marriage they limited their future power of disposition, and it does not matter to our argument what their legal status was at the time of settling.

Of course it mattered to estates that many young men, their fathers dying before they married, succeeded to their estates as tenants in tail. If such young men were extravagant their estates were clearly open to destruction. Bonfield has shown that settlement was a weak instrument for preventing the depredations of extravagant young heirs. He finds, however, that in the eighteenth century most tenants in tail voluntarily resettled their estates when they came to marry. Most of them were thus not in possession of their estates for long. Nor are most men extravagant. It is a question for historians to consider whether, all told, a young man in possession is a greater threat to estate continuity than a father prolific or fond. Settlement could guard against the former threat only if it was an effective form of entail. Even if it was no form of entail it could by its regular presetting - its regular curtailment - of family changes guard against the latter.

Bonfield does not consider the family aspect of settlement. He recognises that the strict settlement was a limitation of a landowner's future power of disposition. He recognises that early marriage settlements were no such limitation. Early marriage settlements did not "restrict the freedom of alienation of the tenant in possession."[45] At one point he does briefly touch on the meaning of this change. He quotes a letter of Heneage Lord Finch in which Finch sets out his objections to making a strict settlement. First among the objections is that the landowner would be prevented from increasing the provision for his family. He would be unable to add "a shilling to (his wife's) jointure or to his daughters' portions". Bonfield does not pursue the matter, however, although it suggests a power in the strict settlement to alter dispositions in the family. In effect, he dismisses the matter noting "the limited restraint that a strict settlement conferred".[46] In comparison with an entail, of course, it was limited. The pertinent comparison though is with earlier settlements, and the restraint being wholly new should not be dismissed.[47] It would seem at least worth discussing.

Discussing it is what we have been doing in this paper. We have shown that the strict settlement meant the arrival of an effective estate planning device even if one limited to but one generation. That meant planning for a generation more than earlier. We have shown that the inherent tendency of such planning was to alter family dispositions in favour of eldest sons; to limit the cost of families, determining their provision at a time when the claims of estate continuity were high, and the contrary claims of younger children and heiresses were low. (Is the strict settlement to be seen as the first family planning device?) Clearly, it stabilised and preserved estates even though it was not effective as entail. For a sense of its effect one might consider some of the portions laid out by fathers of large families before the strict settlement.[48] As we have suggested, however, the arrival of the strict settlement would not have meant sudden and dramatic change. It sprang after all from a male primogenitive ethos. At the same time it powerfully reinforced that ethos, and it must be credited with having brought significant support to landed estates.

Historians have undoubtedly exaggerated the effect of settlement in the past taking it to be an effective form of entail. They would err in the opposite direction if they now dismissed it as of no consequence. Restraining early in life a landowner's power of disposition, it operated against what is arguably the major threat to the preservation of estate, division upon children and diversions out of the male line. Bonfield has discussed but one aspect of settlement.

NOTES

1. H.J. Habakkuk, "Marriage Settlements in the Eighteenth Century", Transactions of the Royal Historical Society, 4th ser. 32 (1950) (hereafter 'Habakkuk, "Marriage Settlements" ').
2. Lawrence Stone, The Family, Sex, and Marriage in England, 1500-1800 (New York, 1977), pp.244, 243. See also p.89.
3. Randolph Trumbach, The Rise of the Egalitarian Family (New York, 1978), p.71.
4. Peter Roebuck, Yorkshire Baronets, 1640-1760, (Oxford, 1980).
5. H.J. Habakkuk, "Daniel Finch, 2nd Earl of Nottingham; His House and Estate", in J.H. Plumb (ed.), Studies in Social History, (London, 1955), p.157 (hereafter 'Habakkuk, "Daniel Finch" '); and Habakkuk, "Marriage Settlements", p.24.
6. Christopher Clay, "Marriage, Inheritance, and the Rise of Large Estates in England, 1660-1815", Economic History Review, 2nd ser., 21 (1968).
7. David Thomas, "The Social Origins of Marriage Partners of the British Peerage in the Eighteenth and Nineteenth Centuries", Population Studies, 26 (1972), Table 7, p.105 (hereafter 'David Thomas, "Social Origins" ').
8. Lawrence Stone, The Crisis of the Aristocracy, (Oxford, 1965), pp.173, 638, 176.
9. G.E. Mingay, English Landed Society in the Eighteenth Century, (London, 1963), pp.32, 29, 35.
10. James C. Davis, A Venetian Family and Its Fortune, 1500-1900, (Philadelphia, 1975), p.106.
11. Habakkuk, "Daniel Finch", pp.156-7. I have assumed an annuity to be worth ten years' purchase. See Stone, Crisis of the Aristocracy, p.649, for a discussion of the value of annuities.
12. Mingay, English Landed Society, p.35.

13. Stone, Crisis of the Aristocracy, p.175.

14. J.P. Cooper, "Patterns of Inheritance and Settlement by Great Landowners from the Fifteenth to the Eighteenth Centuries", in Jack Goody, Joan Thirsk, and E.P. Thompson, (eds.), Family and Inheritance, (London, 1976).

15. Trumbach, Egalitarian Family, p.88.

16. Habakkuk, "Marriage Settlements", p.23-4.

17. David Thomas, "Social Origins", Table 2, p.101.

18. Stone, Crisis of Aristocracy, p.647-8.

19. T.H. Hollingsworth, "The Demography of the British Peerage", supplement to Population Studies, 18 (1964), pp.63-5.

20. Stone, Crisis of Aristocracy, p.590; also Family, Sex, and Marriage, p.80.

21. T.H. Hollingsworth, Historical Demography, (Ithaca, New York, 1969), p.376; J.C. Russell, British Medieval Populations, (Albuquerque, N.M., 1948), p.239.

22. Stone, Crisis of Aristocracy, p.642.

23.

Family	Estate Rental	Gross Portions
Duke of Buckingham	£50,000	£40,000
Earl of Abergavenny	30,000	60,000
Houghtons of Fryston Hall	8,000	30,000
Tylney-Long	40,000	60,000
Marquess of Hastings	18,500	40,000
Fitzwilliams of Milton	50,000	30,000
Duke of Manchester	40,000	20,000
Earl of Lucan	27,000	20,000
Grahams of Netherby	25,000	50,000
Earl of Leicester	45,000	60,000
Leghs of High Legh	10,000	12,000
Baron Petre	7,250	25,000
Blathwayts of Dyrham Park	8,700	15,000

Earl of Amherst	8,700	10,000
Elwes of Billings Hall	10,000	20,000
Duke of Portland	100,000	80,000
Baron Monson	11,000	20,000
Baron Haldon	37,500	30,000
Earl of Sandwich	13,800	11,000

24. The total sum would be raised when there were three or more younger children. Should there be only one or two such children lesser sums were specified that would be larger per child. Nevertheless, only uncommonly would a younger child receive one year's income of the estate. For a corroborating impression of the scale of portions by a nineteenth century observer see George Brodrick, English Land and English Landlords, (London, 1881), p.100. I discovered that Brodrick made an estimate of portions only after writing the text of this paper).

25. K.B. McFarland, The English Nobility in the Later Middle Ages, (Oxford, 1973), p.277; Stone, Crisis of Aristocracy, p.641.

26. Habakkuk's difficulty with the legal and psychological factors involved is quite apparent. He notes that before settlement, bequests to younger sons were "a cause of the reduction of large estates." He then claims that portions would increase with settlement. This raises the question of the purpose of the device, of course, which is said to be that of preserving estates. Then follows a psychological explanation. If he is not bound to provide portions, even a fond father might in a pinch be tempted to economise upon his younger children. This argument proves only that settlement provided some security for younger children, not that portions generally rose. Then follows a further argument - that portions set in advance for unborn children are higher than portions determined by fathers for born children because grandparents have a say in the first case.

("Marriage Settlements",pp.19-20).

27. Since a wife's portion in practice often went to her younger children, it might be objected that treating her jointure as a simple deferred annuity is not strictly correct. The landowner may end up by paying the capital to his wife and again to his children. A father, however, had the obligation to provide for his younger children. He simply often found it convenient to look upon the cash sum he had received with his wife as the basis of his provision for their younger children. For reasons inhering in family structure, it is logical to hold that portions are the business of the father no matter what fund he happens to use to pay for them, and that the wife's portion is for her own provision.

28. Sir John Eardley Wilmot, Notes of Opinions and Judgements, edited by his son (London, 1802), p.202.

29. D.M. Stuart, Dearest Bess, (London, 1955), p.182.

30. Sir John Habakkuk, "The Rise and Fall of English Landed Families, 1600-1800", Transactions of the Royal Historical Society, 5th ser. 29 (1979).

31. Ibid., p.190.

32. Ibid., p.191

33. Lloyd Bonfield, "Marriage Settlements, 1660-1740: The Adoption of the Strict Settlement in Kent and Northamptonshire", in R.B. Outhwaite (ed.), Marriage and Society: Studies in the Social History of Marriage, (London, 1981), Table 2, p.111.

    That there was a considerable difference in habits between large and small landowners is clear in the table, but the text goes on to minimise the fact. Admitting that his procedure "requires some defence", Bonfield proceeds to dismiss from consideration those small landowners who continued to practise an old minimal form of marriage settlement. In other words, he dismisses from consideration the very class whose existence is the point at issue.

    Bonfield's general thesis is that settlement had virtually no effect. For some further discussion of this claim see later here.

It may be that small gentry estates did not so regularly postpone heiresses to collateral males as large estates. Bonfield does not investigate the question. It might be significant.

34. Philippe Aries, Centuries of Childhood, (New York, 1965), pp.371, 403.

35. Stone, Family, Sex, and Marriage, p.244.

36. Stone, Crisis of Aristocracy, p.181.

37. Stone, Family, Sex, and Marriage, pp.378, 377.

38. Orlando Bridgeman, Conveyances (1690), p.331.

39. Trumbach, Egalitarian Family, p.101.

40. Despite the eldest son's great prospects, he had no current income unless he came to an arrangement with his father.

41. For a much more detailed consideration of Stone's theory of the family see my "Law and the Theory of the Affective Family", a paper delivered at the Anglo-American Conference of Historians (1982).

42. Lloyd Bonfield, "Marriage Settlements and the 'Rise of Great Estates': The Demographic Aspect", Economic History Review, 2nd ser., 32 (1979); also "Marriage Settlements, 1660-1740: The Adoption of the Strict Settlement in Kent and Northamptonshire", in R.B. Outhwaite (ed.), Marriage and Society: Studies in the Social History of Marriage, (London, 1981).

43. Bonfield does not recognise that settlements gave detailed consideration to collateral successors, though that they did so is clear in Orlando Bridgeman's classic precedent. He thus somewhat - not greatly - overstates the failure of settlement as entail. His failure to appreciate the developed form of settlement does, however, much affect his discussion of the history of settlement and his attempted reappraisal of landowners' attitudes.

44. Eileen Spring, "The Settlement of Land in Nineteenth Century England", American Journal of Legal History, 8, (1964).

45. Bonfield, "Marriage Settlements, 1660-1740", p.108.

46. _Ibid.,_ p.109.

47. The strict settlement was preceded by a half-way device, "the life-estate - entail mode." This did - in common circumstances - restrain the landowner's future power of disposition. It failed to do so in a vital respect, however. It was revocable until a son was born - even after the birth of daughters.

48. Stone, _Crisis of Aristocracy_, pp.175-6.

COMMERCIAL EXPECTATIONS AND THE GUARANTEE OF THE LAW: SALES TRANSACTIONS IN MID-NINETEENTH CENTURY ENGLAND

R.B. Ferguson

I: INTRODUCTION

The idea of "freedom of contract" has two elements.[1] First it implies that the expressed common intention of the contracting parties creates legally valid norms, albeit norms of particular rather than general application. In other words the parties may obtain legal recognition of their mutual expectations by formulating them as contract terms. Secondly "freedom of contract" connotes that at the option of the injured party breach of contract may be legally sanctioned through the mediation of the courts, i.e. that the coercive machinery of the state may be enlisted in support of the contract terms. In short "freedom of contract" means freedom to make but not freedom to break contracts. As T.H. Farrer put it (rather exaggeratedly) a century ago:

> " [The doctrine of contract] brings the whole weight of the social fabric upon the man who has bound himself by a promise. His freedom consists in being able to make or abstain from making a binding promise. But when he has made it, the State uses its whole despotic power to compel or prevent his free action."[2]

It is with the coercive aspect of freedom of contract that this essay is concerned. Its object is to assess the contribution of legal enforceability of contracts to the realisation of contractual expectations. Or more precisely, its object is to make such an assessment in relation to sales contracts in the mid-nineteenth century heyday of the market economy. Discussion is confined to commercial as opposed to consumer transactions, but sales of securities as well as sales of goods are considered. The scope of this essay is therefore limited, but the centrality of sales transactions to the operation of a market economy is clear.

The classical economic theory of contract law[3] attributes two functions to that law. First there is its reparative function: if a contractual promise is broken the law undertakes to procure compensation for the disappointed party at his behest. The law provides a "means of salvage" (Havighurst)[4] or "insurance against economic risk" (Friedmann).[5] Inseparable from this is contract law's motivational function. Weber puts it succinctly: "To the person to whom something has been promised the legal guaranty gives a higher degree of certainty that the promise will be kept."[6] The sanctions of contract law are thus seen as incentives to the performance of contractual obligations.

It may be helpful to elaborate this motivational function with reference to commercial sales in particular. The starting point is that most commercial sales do not involve immediate supply of the goods (or securities) or immediate payment of the price.[7] Rather "orders" are taken, "credit" is given - i.e. there is an exchange of promises. For this to work, however, those involved in commerce must have reasons for keeping their own promises, and solid grounds for expecting others to fulfil theirs. In Hicks' words, "Trading is trading in promises; but it is futile to trade in promises unless there is some reasonable assurance that the promises will be kept."[8] The sanctions of contract law, the theory goes, can give this assurance: the possibility that state coercion may be deployed against him can provide an affected person with one motive for taking steps to see that the expectations which he has aroused by his actions or words will not be disappointed.

But how important was the reparative and motivational function of contract law in practice? Wolfgang Friedmann, writing of "the formative era of modern industrial and capitalist society" remarks that -

> "The functioning of such an economic system depends on the guarantee of the law that enterprise or speculation, in so far as it implies contracts for labour, goods or shares, will be protected by the award of damages or specific performance."[9]

In the same vein Kessler states that with the development of a free-enterprise economy contract law "became the indispensable instrument of the enterpriser."

If, he says, reasonable expectations created by promises did not receive the protection of the law in a market society we would suffer the fate of Montesquieu's Troglodytes who perished because they did not fulfil their promises.[10] Again Hurst, in his study of Law and Economic Growth, contends: "The prime quality or function of contract law was to serve the market's need of an assured framework of dealing . . . ."[11]

The purpose of this essay is to assess the historicity of such claims. Did sales transactions "depend" on the guarantee of the law? Was its guarantee "indispensable"? Clearly to answer this question a methodological problem must be overcome. Modern studies[12] of the extent of reliance on legal guarantee have been based on interviews with businessmen, and have by and large accepted businessmen's own account of their orientation towards the legal position. Obviously if our concern is with the mid-nineteenth century such an approach cannot be used. The approach adopted here is to identify situations in which sales bargains were legally unenforceable, and to examine the consequences of that unenforceability. The way to find out how "indispensable" was the guarantee of the law is to see what happened when it was dispensed with. In the ensuing pages I focus on two statutes whose bearing on certain sorts of commercial practice was to produce legally unenforceable sales agreements. It will emerge that the relationship between legal guarantee and the realisation of commercial expectations was more variable than seems to be allowed by a statement such as Friedmann's.

II: SIR JOHN BARNARD'S ACT, LEEMAN'S ACT AND THE SALE OF SECURITIES

The Stock-jobbing Act 1733,[13] commonly called Sir John Barnard's Act, applied to sales of "public or joint stock, or other public securities" and rendered null and void both option dealings ("puts" and "calls") and speculative time bargains. Not only were these types of transaction rendered legally unenforceable, but civil and criminal penalties were stipulated for those who engaged in them. Some idea of the attitudes which prompted the enactment of this statute may be got from its title - "An Act to prevent the infamous Practice of Stock-jobbing" - and its preamble which refers to the "wicked, pernicious, and destructive practice of stock-jobbing." As Clapham remarks, in the eighteenth century the respectability of stockbrokers was "in question."[14]

In the nineteenth century the judges interpreted the Stock-jobbing Act restrictively. The milestone decisions were Wells v. Porter (1836)[15] where it was held that time bargains in foreign securities were not struck at by the Act, and Williams v. Trye (1854)[16] where it was held that dealings in shares and stock in incorporated companies were not within the Act. Thus towards the end of its span the coverage of the Act was limited to transactions in British government securities. Even at this, however, the Act applied to an important class of transactions.

Sir John Barnard's Act was consistently flouted by members of the Stock Exchange. The prohibited types of dealing were widely engaged in during both eighteenth and nineteenth centuries.[17] The Act was described as "utterly inoperative"[18] within the Exchange, a "dead letter."[19]

The same could be said of Leeman's Act.[20] Passed in 1867, it required contracts of sale involving shares in banking companies to be in writing and to designate the identifying numbers of the shares. Contracts not complying with the Act were legally null, void and criminal. The object of the Act was to prevent speculative sales of bank shares not yet in the possession of the seller. The Stock Exchange solved the problem posed by Leeman's Act by disregarding it.[21] As Morgan and Thomas say, the attitude of the Exchange was "almost contemptuous."[22] The Act was "violated with impunity every day", one dealer acknowledged.[23] Another stated that "no one would dream of talking about Leeman's Act."[24] A third could say that business was done "without reference to it at all."[25] The Chairman of the Stock Exchange Committee summed it all up very well: "We disregarded for years and years Sir John Barnard's Act, and now we are disregarding Mr. Leeman's Act . . . ."[26]

Despite the legal unenforceability, and indeed criminality, of many Stock Exchange transactions dealings on the Exchange were utterly secure. As the Royal Commission of 1878 observed, members of the Exchange were -

> ". . . bound in their dealings by rules . . . capable of affording relief and exercising restraint far more prompt and often more satisfactory than any within the reach of the courts of law."[27]

Reliance on legally unenforceable expectations was warranted by the strong internal organisation of the Exchange. A member was understood to be personally answerable for all bargains he entered into whether or not he happened to be acting for a client. A member who defaulted on his bargain was "turned out of the room."[28] The fundamental principles of the Stock Exchange were self-regulation and inviolability of bargains. The rules of the Exchange barred recourse to the courts by one member against another except with special permission from the Committee. (Such a rule is itself legally unenforceable.) At the same time, however, the Committee took it upon itself to enforce <u>all</u> bargains between members - legal or illegal - save those procured by fraud or wilful misrepresentation.

> " [Q.] Do you mean to say that it is a policy of the Stock Exchange to set at defiance an Act of Parliament which affects to restrict your dealings?
>
> [A.] We consider as the fundamental policy of the Stock Exchange, that all bargains are indefeasible in themselves.
>
> [Q.] Even if there is an Act of Parliament to prevent them?
>
> [A.] Yes, I have said so . . . ."

So answered Mr. Samuel Herman de Zoete, Chairman of the Committee of the Stock Exchange, before a Parliamentary Committee in 1875.[29] The penalty for failure to keep one's bargain was open stigmatisation as a defaulter, which brought with it expulsion from the Exchange. In de Zoete's words:

> "There is not a gentleman on the Stock Exchange who could stand on the boards one day who refused to carry out the contracts he had made, even in spite of Sir John Barnard's Act . . . he would be obliged to walk

out; he would be expelled, simply because it would be dishonourable."[30]

While the lack of legal guarantee does not seem to have led to the disappointment of expectations in affected transactions between members of the Exchange, there is some suggestion that brokers' clients sometimes took advantage of Sir John Barnard's Act to escape from a disadvantageous speculation.[31] According to one account (hostile to the Exchange) it was the risk of repudiation by clients under the Act which prompted brokers to take deposits as a safeguard.[32] Similarly it was said that Leeman's Act was "on more than one occasion . . . taken advantage of by principals [i.e. clients] to repudiate transactions entered into for them by their brokers . . . ."[33]

Sir John Barnard's Act was repealed in 1860.[34] Its repeal is not, however, evidence of a need on the part of stockbrokers for legal enforceability of contracts inter se. In 1860 the Chancellor of the Exchequer decided to impose a penny duty on transfers of stocks and shares. But the government could hardly impose a duty on criminal transactions. Legalisation was an obvious answer: "The object of the Chancellor of the Exchequer was to place a penny stamp on time bargains, and to do that it was necessary to defend the principle of time bargains."[35] Given this opportunity, the Stock Exchange appointed a subcommittee to press for the repeal of the law.[36] One can see in repeal two benefits for the Exchange: first, the stigma of criminality would be removed; and secondly, clients would no longer be able to default with legal impunity. And so it came about that the Act was removed from the statute book, "overturned by a side wind pressure upon the Chancellor, fishing for a penny on his budget."[37] (Leeman's Act was quietly repealed in 1966 under the procedure for getting rid of "obsolete, spent, unnecessary or superseded enactments.")

This analysis may be shortly summarised. The Stock Exchange was a tight-knit, well-organised commercial club. As such it had its own "code of honour" backed up by powerful sanctions.[38] That code rendered the legal enforceability of bargains between members a superfluity. It is not clear, however, that the consequences of legal unenforceability between brokers and clients were equally negligible.

III: THE STATUTE OF FRAUDS AND THE SALE OF GOODS

A. Introduction

The Statute of Frauds, passed in 1677, is of interest to us because it created a class of legally unenforceable contracts of sale. The question is what impact this had on the assuredness of commercial expectations.

The Statute specified conditions which buyers and sellers of raw materials and manufactures had to satisfy in order to secure the legal enforceability of their bargains. Section 17 was in the following terms:

> "No contract for the sale of any goods, wares and merchandises, for the price of ten pounds sterling or upwards, shall be allowed to be good, except the buyer shall accept part of the goods so sold, and actually receive the same, or give something in earnest to bind the bargain, or in part of payment, or that some note or memorandum in writing of the said bargain be made and signed by the parties to be charged by such contract, or their agents thereunto lawfully authorised."[39]

The crucial words are "No contract . . . shall be allowed to be good . . . ." In essence the Statute meant that a mere oral exchange of promises did not create a legally enforceable contract. A sale of goods bargain worth more than £10 was not legally enforceable against a defaulting buyer or seller unless it was evidenced by a written document which the defaulting party or his agent had signed. Otherwise legal enforcement of the bargain was only available if it was no longer wholly "executory" - if, in other words, the buyer had received some of the goods or the seller had received part of the price. For our purposes the important point is that a mere agreement to buy and sell could not, in the absence of a signed record of that agreement, be enforced in a court of law: that is, legal guarantee was lacking.

Where there was a signed memorandum of the bargain, we may speak of "compliance" with or "conformity" to the Statute of Frauds. Did non-compliance with the Statute, entailing the loss of legal guarantee, increase the level of insecurity in commercial dealings? In the following pages an attempt is made to answer this question. Only a tentative answer is possible, however, for there are relatively few sources of evidence. Moreover the picture that emerges is not a wholly straightforward one.

B. The Impact of the Statute of Frauds

In the North of England sales agreements rendered legally unenforceable by the Statute of Frauds were commonplace.[40] In the words of a merchant before the House of Lords Select Committee on the Mercantile Law Amendment Bill in 1856:

> "I may say that the great bulk of the business which is done throughout this country, with the exception of such as is done through brokers [as in London], and with the exception of cases where people live at some distance from one another, is by oral communication, and not by written contracts."[41]

In Manchester in particular commercial practice was "in uniform disregard of the law."[42] In 1864 Manchester Chamber of Commerce told Parliament that -

> ". . . the mode of doing business on the Manchester Exchange, where property to the value of many hundred thousand pounds daily changes hands, is entirely at variance with the Statute, orders being given and accepted without the passage of any writing whatsoever."[43]

Repudiation of these oral bargains was very rare indeed, although not unheard of.[44] Manchester Chamber of Commerce's 1856 petition claimed:

> "The enormous commercial transactions which take place in Manchester have for many years been honourably carried to completion without the employment of written contracts in such a majority of instances that your petitioners feel themselves warranted in claiming such a universality for the practice that to ask for a written contract would be generally looked upon as little short of an indignity."[45]

There are one or two indications of how it was possible to do without legal guarantee. The 1858 Select Committee on Tribunals of Commerce was informed by the Secretary of the Dublin Statistical Society of what leading merchants had told him on his visit to Manchester:

> "The merchants in Manchester said . . .'we habitually disregard the Statute of Frauds, for we carry on all our transactions in parol; we find that it does very well; our contracts are simple, and if a man violates his contract,he is read out of the market'."[46]

If a dispute did arise, then (according to a London merchant)-

> ". . . being an honorary contract, it is necessarily referred to some third party, and as it occurs in a limited community between a class of persons who know one another perfectly well . . . very small inconvenience does arise from that practice [of non-conformity to the Statute of Frauds]. Very few misunderstandings take place, and those, when they do take place, are honourably removed . . . ."[47]

Transactions unenforceable at law were not confined to Manchester. In Liverpool transactions relating to "cotton on the spot" were carried on without written contracts.[48] In the Bradford wool trade also the usage was to deal orally:

> ". . . wool is never sold scarcely by a written contract. A man goes into a woolstapler's warehouse, or meets him on change, and he makes his bargain for hundreds or thousands, and there is no evidence whatever, and not being able to establish it by viva voce evidence, or by any evidence, but your own memoranda, if you have to appeal to the law courts, of course you fail to get redress."

But "in point of custom" such a contract was just as valid as if it had been in writing.[49] As in Manchester, however, differences over unenforceable sales were unusual: "the honesty of the parties is such that they rarely want to escape from their bargains."[50]

In other contexts the impact of legal unenforceability seems to have been more appreciable. On the London Corn Exchange the usage was for the factor to give the buyer a sale note,[51] but the buyer did not sign anything:

> "The result is this, that the factor is bound, and the buyer is not. If the market goes up, the factor has to deliver; if it goes down, the buyer repudiates the bargain; and it is perfectly notorious that when there are sudden falls in the market, the buyers do repudiate the bargains to a

great extent."[52]

In general, however, London mercantile usage was in full conformity to the Statute of Frauds, so that sales were legally enforceable by both parties. In most London mercantile transactions a broker functioned as a middleman - i.e. as agent for both buyer and seller. The broker would go from one counting-house to another, learning the requirements of buyers and sellers. When in his view he had succeeded in matching a buyer and seller, he would enter in his book a contract which he might or might not sign. At the same time he would sign and send two contract notes - a bought note for the buyer, and a sold note for the seller.[53] The courts of law took the view that normally this procedure met the formal requirements of the Statute of Frauds: the judicial view being that the broker signed in his capacity as agent simultaneously for buyer and seller, so that for both parties he was an "agent lawfully authorised" within the meaning of section 17. The sales contracts made in this way were thus legally enforceable, although there was much doubt as to whether the authentic memorandum of the bargain was constituted by the entry in the broker's book (if signed) or by the contract notes.[54] Ordinarily, of course, these were identical.

Sometimes, however, the broker slipped up, with the result that there was "technical" non-compliance with the Statute. For example, take the case of Sievewright v. Archibald (1851),[55] involving a sale of iron. The broker sent to the seller a sold note, in which the object of the transaction was referred to as Dunlop's iron. To the buyer he sent a bought note, in which the goods were designated Scotch iron. Dunlop's iron was Scotch. The buyer entered the transaction as a speculation, and it was wholly immaterial to him whether it was Dunlop's or any other Scotch iron.[56] The price of iron dropped by 5 shillings a ton, so that the speculation became unprofitable for the buyer, who asked without success to be released from his bargain. In the end, he simply defaulted. The seller sued, and it was then that the variation between bought and sold notes emerged. In the Court of Queen's Bench the judges held by three to one that the discrepancy between bought and sold notes was material, that there was therefore no authentic memorandum of the contract (the broker having failed to make a signed entry in his book), and that accordingly the bargain did not comply with the Statute of Frauds and hence was legally unenforceable. The disappointed seller had to put up with his loss. Here we see the law failing to perform its reparative function just when it was needed. Another instance recorded in the law reports is Cumming v. Roebuck (1816),[57] where a buyer was moved to invoke the Statute of Frauds - with success - because the coffee in question was "at a loss in the market."

The question is how often this sort of thing happened. An indication of the frequency with which technical non-compliance with the Statute was exploited to get out of an inconvenient bargain is provided by evidence to the Select Committee on the Mercantile Law Amendment Bill, from John Hollams, a leading London commercial solicitor. Speaking from personal experience, Hollams was able to detail several cases which had occurred within the last few months where technical defects in the contract notes had defeated the reasonable expectations of one party to a sales contract. Typically the escape route provided by an accidental failure to conform to the Statute seems to have been taken by an unscrupulous entrepreneur when a deal of anticipated profitableness turned sour because of a drop in the market value of the goods:

> "There was great excitement in the sugar market about six months ago, and a very sudden rise in sugar; and that had the effect of bringing in a great many of what are called outside men, that is, speculators not ordinarily in the trade, into the market, and produced a great many questions. In several cases I found that the contracts could not be enforced. Those gentlemen who found that they had made a loss, instead of a profit, were not anxious to take the goods, and in consequence of the defects in the contracts they escaped."[58]

Hollams also mentions the case of merchants who sold a quantity of linseed cakes to arrive from New York at London. The destination of the ship was subsequently altered to Liverpool. An allowance of £130 was verbally agreed in respect of this alteration, which the sellers confirmed in writing but the buyers did not. When the cakes arrived the market price was down, and the buyers repudiated the bargain. The sellers found they could not recover what they had lost by means of a law suit, because the changed bargain was not evidenced to the stringent standard required by the Statute of Frauds. In another case the seller sold a cargo of 200 tons of raisins. He received the ordinary sold note from the brokers. But the cargo had been bought by two different houses, each buying 100 tons. When a buyer reneged the seller had to swallow his loss, because bought and sold notes did not agree as to quantity. Another case again involved a cargo of Seville oranges. The original contract was properly evidenced by writing, but the parties changed the description of the oranges. The goods shipped conformed to the changed description, but the sale could not be enforced.[59] It seems reasonable to infer, if one lawyer found it possible to list from his own recent experience so many cases in which bargains which turned out to be legally unenforceable were repudiated, that such occurrences were not particularly rare.

Among London markets the silk trade was in an exceptional position. Contracts of sale in the silk trade were indeed in writing; but they were "very loose and irregular", and hence often failed to satisfy the requirements of the Statute of Frauds. Non-compliance was not just an occasional mishap. Expectations in the silk trade remained reasonably assured, however, "in consequence of there being only one or two brokers in the trade." For these brokers, "from their great influence . . . insure the performance of the contracts."[60]

C. The Repeal of the Statute of Frauds

The matter presented in the previous section creates the impression that nowhere did the Statute of Frauds give rise to unmanageable problems for the commercial classes. In Manchester, where contractual expectations ordinarily lacked legal guarantee, wilful repudiation seems to have been a rare phenomenon.

In London, on the other hand, where it appears that the consequences of non-conformity to the Statute might be grave, the requirements of the Statute were usually satisfied. Nevertheless in 1856 a determined effort was made to secure the repeal of section 17. Does this mean that the Statute did, after all, cause intolerable problems to those engaged in trade and commerce?

To understand the attack on the existence of section 17 it is necessary to advert to one of the interests of the law reformers of the 1850s - assimilation of the commercial laws of England and Scotland.[61] The demand that the mercantile laws of Scotland and England be rendered uniform was formulated and pressed by Lord Brougham's Law Amendment Society, with the support of several Scottish and English chambers of commerce and commercial associations. Their contention was that the divergences between Scots law and the common law on mercantile matters were a harmful source of "inconvenience" and tended "to restrict and embarrass commerce, by producing uncertainty, perplexity and delay."[62] In response to the representations of the Law Amendment Society and its supporters the government of the day instructed the Mercantile Law Commission (which had been established to investigate the question of limited liability partnership) to enquire into the desirability of commercial law assimilation.[63]

Once this step had been taken it was inevitable that section 17 of the Statute of Frauds would be called into question. For no corresponding or equivalent law applied in Scotland. Assimilation on this point would therefore entail extension of the Statute to Scotland, or its repeal. The Mercantile Law Commission opted for repeal, on the ground that the Statute of Frauds (if not complied with) made it possible for a dishonest trader to escape from a firm agreement.[64] Accordingly the repeal of section 17 was provided for in the Mercantile Law Amendment Bill. The survival of section 17 thus became a public issue as a by-product of the concern with general assimilation, not as a result of overt manifestations of discontent among the commercial classes.

Nonetheless the proposal for repeal was sympathetically received in mercantile quarters outside London and Liverpool.[65] This goes to show only that even there the consequences of non-compliance with the Statute of Frauds were not entirely negligible. Legal enforceability of bargains might have enhanced further the high degree of assuredness of expectations which seems to have existed. Oddly enough, however, the mercantile interests of London put up a vigorous defence of the legal status quo. The London merchants' fear (almost certainly without foundation) was that the current usage whereby they received contract notes from their brokers would be subverted, and that they would be held bound to contracts arranged verbally by the brokers of which they had not been given adequate notice. When the Mercantile Law Amendment Bill reached the House of Commons it rapidly became clear that London commercial interests were so well represented that there was no alternative but to abandon the repeal of section 17.[66] It would survive for another 100 years.

The sale of goods section of the Statute of Frauds was ultimately repealed in 1954.[67] This step had been proposed by the Law Revision Committee in 1937.[68] It is just possible that the interwar economic depression constituted an environment in which use of the Statute of Frauds as a means of escaping one's obligations was more often than hitherto a temptation or even a necessity, and that this provided the impetus for repeal. According to one writer in 1937 it was still -

> ". . . the accepted practice on a number of Exchanges to disregard [section 17], and until post-war conditions produced a stronger spirit of sauve qui peut among businessmen, it was rare indeed that any member of these Exchanges invoked the argument of non-compliance with the section in disputes."[69]

However the repeal of section 17 was not produced by commercial pressure groups. Rather it was planned and executed by lawyers who were able to represent it as apolitical, non-contentious, technical law reform.[70] To understand why it was lawyers rather than businessmen who felt strongly about the repeal of section 17, we must remember that each group's view of the law was conditioned by its own experience of the law's practical effects. For businessmen, the disavowal of a bargain which did not comply with the Statute of Frauds was an uncommon, isolated occurrence; things usually went smoothly despite the Statute. Therefore they did not see it as a serious threat. The numerous deals which went smoothly, however, would not on the whole be referred to lawyers: in their experience, repudiation was the typical case. Encountering only an unrepresentative sample of the transactions to which the Statute formally applied, the lawyers came to regard it as the occasion for fraud and injustice. The lawyers' unfavourable perception of section 17 was thus shaped by their position in the dispute-settlement structure of English society: what they saw was mainly the "pathology" of business.

IV: CONCLUSION

Recent works on the history of contract law[71] have propounded the thesis that only in the nineteenth century did the executory contract achieve full legal recognition, and that this development is associated with the commercial and economic changes of that time. According to Atiyah, taking into account the highly volatile commercial and industrial activity "it does not seem surprising that businessmen came to demand a greater degree of legal protection for careful planning."[72] The evidence adduced in support of the proposition that the shift to the executory contract was so protracted has been critically reviewed elsewhere.[73] Here I wish to observe merely that businessmen's need for legal protection is not something that can be taken for granted; we have seen that under some circumstances businessmen could do without legal protection quite comfortably.

The aim of this study was to test the hypothesis that the guarantee of the law was indispensable to the realisation of commercial expectations founded on agreements to sell goods or securities. The case of the Stock Exchange shows how wrong it would be to postulate a blanket, across-the-board dependence on the legal enforceability of contracts. Beyond this, however, any conclusions presented can have only speculative status, given the limited extent of the evidence available.

Still, the evidence assembled here is at least consistent with the idea that the further a market departed from the model of commercial relations exemplified by the Stock Exchange the greater the risk that the absence of legal guarantee would conduce to the disappointment of commercial expectations. The case of the Stock Exchange prompts Morgan and Thomas to observe that "The less the sanction of the law in commercial dealings, the more important it is [to be able] to rely upon honour."[74] Conversely, the less the sanction of honour, the greater the need to be able to rely upon the law. But "honour" is more than a matter of character: to be effective a code of honour must be socially sustained. In Llewellyn's words:

> "Credit or reliance on a purely customary or self-interest basis presupposed for effectiveness either permanence of dealings involving long-run mutual dependence, or an ingrained traditional morality covering the point, or dealings within a face-to-face community . . . in which severe group pressure on delinquent promisors is available."

And these types of sanctions "fail increasingly as the market expands spatially and in complexity", and as the market grows more impersonal.[75] Only where markets are characterised by strong collective cohesion or are internally policed should we expect to find the lack of legal guarantee a matter of virtual indifference.[76]

ABBREVIATIONS

Sale of Corn Committee 1834	Report from the Select Committee on the Sale of Corn, P.P.1834 [517.] VII.1.
Mercantile Law Commission 1855	Second Report of the Royal Commission on Mercantile Law, P.P.1854-55 [1977.] XVIII. 653.
Mercantile Law Committee 1856	Report from the Select Committee on the Mercantile Law Amendment Bill, P.P.1856 [294.] XIV. 1.

Tribunals of Commerce Committee 1858	Report from the Select Committee on Tribunals of Commerce, P.P.1857-58 [413.] XVI. 505.
Tribunals of Commerce Committee 1871	Report from the Select Committee on Tribunals of Commerce, P.P.1871 [409.] XII. 523.
Judicature Commission 1874	Appendix to the Third Report of the Royal Commission on the Judicature P.P.1874 [C.957-I.] XXIV.13.
Foreign Loans Committee 1875	Report from the Select Committee on Loans to Foreign States, P.P.1875 [152.] XI. 1*.
Stock Exchange Commission 1878	Report of the Royal Commission on the London Stock Exchange, P.P.1878 [C.2157.] XIX. 263.

NOTES

1. See, for example, P.S. Atiyah, An Introduction to the Law of Contract, 2nd ed. (London, 1971), pp.2-10.
2. T.H. Farrer, 'Freedom of Contract', Fortnightly Review, XXIX [N.S.] (1881) 46.
3. Two recent formulations are to be found in R.B. Seidman, "Contract Law, the Free Market and State Intervention: A Jurisprudential Perspective", Journal of Economic Issues, VII (1973) pp.553-575, and S. Macaulay, "Elegant Models, Empirical Pictures, and the Complexities of Contract", Law and Society Review, XI (1977) pp.507-528.
4. H.C. Havighurst, The Nature of Private Contract (Evanston, Ill., 1961), p.82.
5. W. Friedmann, Law in a Changing Society, 2nd ed. (Harmondsworth, 1972), pp.158, 121.
6. M. Rheinstein (ed.), Max Weber on Law in Economy and Society (New York, 1954), p.98.
7. Of course, even in cash-and-carry transactions certain contingent obligations (arising, for example, from the warranty of quality) remain outstanding.
8. J. Hicks, A Theory of Economic History (Oxford, 1969), p.34.
9. Friedmann, op.cit., pp.119, 121.
10. F. Kessler, "Contracts of Adhesion - Some Thoughts About Freedom of Contract", Columbia Law Review, XLIII (1943) p.629.
11. J.W. Hurst, Law and Economic Growth: The Legal History of the Lumber Industry in Wisconsin 1836-1915 (Cambridge, Mass., 1964), p.290.
12. S. Macaulay, "Non-Contractual Relations in Business: A Preliminary study", American Sociological Review, XXVIII (1963) pp.55-66; H. Beale and T. Dugdale, "Contracts Between Businessmen: Planning and the Use of Contractual Remedies", British Journal of Law and Society II (1975) pp.45-60; D. Yates, Exclusion Clauses in Contracts (London, 1978), pp.9-22.

13. 7 Geo. 2 c.8.

14. J.H. Clapham, *An Economic History of Modern Britain: The Early Railway Age*, 2nd ed. (Cambridge, 1930), p.301.

15. 2 Bing. N.C. 722.

16. 18 Beav. 366.

17. A.P. Poley, *The History, Law, and Practice of the Stock Exchange*, 4th ed. (London, 1926), p.24; E.V. Morgan and W.A. Thomas, *The Stock Exchange: Its History and Functions*, 2nd ed. (London, 1969), pp.61-63, 147.

18. *Foreign Loans Committee* 1875, p.25.

19. *Hansard*, 3rd Series, CLVIII (1860) 1699.

20. 30 and 31 Vict. c.29.

21. See the judicial *dicta* in *Perry* v. *Barnett* (1885), 15 Q.B.D.388.

22. Morgan and Thomas, *op.cit.*, p.148.

23. *Foreign Loans Committee* 1875, p.277.

24. *Ibid*., p.238.

25. *Stock Exchange Commission* 1878, p.217.

26. *Foreign Loans Committee* 1875, p.25.

27. *Stock Exchange Commission* 1878, Report, p.5.

28. *Mercantile Law Committee* 1856, p.17.

29. *Foreign Loans Committee* 1875, p.25.

30. *Ibid*., pp.28, 25.

31. *Hansard*, 3rd Series, CLVIII (1860) 1706.

32. "The Stock Exchange", *Fraser's Magazine*, IV (1832) 721.

33. *Stock Exchange Commission* 1878, Appendix, p.356.

34. Sir John Barnard's Act Repeal Act, 23 Vict. c.28.

35. *Hansard*, 3rd Series, CLVIII (1860) 1697.

36. H. Roy, *The Stock Exchange: Strictures on . . . the proposed repeal of Sir John Barnard's Act* (London, 1860), p.30.

37. *Ibid*., p.31.

38. Cf. Morgan and Thomas, op.cit., p.148.

39. 29 Car. 2 c.3, s.17 (1677). On the origins of the Statute of Frauds, see W. Holdsworth, History of English Law, 7th ed., Vol.VI (London, 1956), pp.388-90; A.W.B. Simpson, A History of the Common Law of Contract: The Rise of the Action of Assumpsit (Oxford, 1975), pp.599-622; P.S. Atiyah, The Rise and Fall of Freedom of Contract (Oxford, 1979), pp.205-208. Section 17 of the Statute was latterly reformulated in s.4 of the Sale of Goods Act 1893.

40. Judicature Commission 1874, p.139.

41. Mercantile Law Committee 1856, p.67.

42. Ibid., p.66.

43. Quoted by A. Redford, Manchester Merchants and Foreign Trade 1850-1939 (Manchester, 1956), p.136.

44. Mercantile Law Committee 1856, p.67.

45. Manchester Chamber of Commerce, Proceedings, 21 May 1856. Cf. the remark of a Liverpool corn merchant in 1834: ". . . if you ask for a memorandum, a person would think you had a distrust of him and would be offended": Sale of Corn Committee 1834, p.74.

46. Tribunals of Commerce Committee 1858, p.73 (my emphasis).

47. Mercantile Law Committee 1856, p.10.

48. Judicature Commission 1874, p.2.

49. Tribunals of Commerce Committee 1871, p.2.

50. Ibid., p.8.

51. A. Pulling, A Practical Treatise on the Laws, Customs, Usages and Regulations of the City and Port of London, 2nd ed. (London, 1844), p.471.

52. Mercantile Law Committee 1856, p.45.

53. Ibid., pp.8-9, 14, 41; Pulling, op.cit., pp.429-30.

54. For judicial discussions of broker-mediated sales see Grant v. Fletcher (1826), 5 B. & C. 436; Goom v. Aflalo (1826), 6 B. & C. 117; Thornton v. Meux (1827), M. & M. 43; Sievewright v. Archibald (1851), 17 Q.B.103.

55. 17 Q.B. 103.

56. Mercantile Law Committee 1856, p.47.

57. Holt 172.

58. Mercantile Law Committee 1856, p.52.

59. Ibid., pp.49-53.

60. Ibid., p.18.

61. See the Law Review, XV (1851-52) 204; XVI (1852) 396; XVII (1852-53) 206; and the Law Magazine, L (1853) 318.

62. The Scotsman, 20 November 1852.

63. Mercantile Law Commission 1855. The Commission, having investigated, felt constrained to observe (p.5): "In the answers which were received there is a remarkable paucity of statements as to inconveniences actually experienced . . . ." Nevertheless, certain assimilative measures were recommended and some of these were enacted in the Mercantile Law Amendment Act 1856 and the Mercantile Law Amendment (Scotland) Act 1856.

64. Ibid., p.6.

65. Law Amendment Journal, I (1856) p.73; House of Lords Journal, LXXXVII (1856-57) pp.99, 178.

66. Hansard, 3rd Series, CXLIII (1856) 809-10.

67. Law Reform (Enforcement of Contracts) Act 1954; Decker, "The Repeal of the Statute of Frauds in England", American Business Law Journal XI (1973) pp.55-62.

68. Law Revision Committee, Sixth Interim Report (1937) Cmd. 5449, reprinted in the Canadian Bar Review, XV (1937) pp.585-619.

69. "The Law Revision Committee's Sixth Interim Report", Modern Law Review, I (1937) pp.98-99.

70. H.C. Debates, DXXIII (1954) 1574; H.L. Debates, CLXXXVII (1954) 771.

71. M. Horwitz, The Transformation of American Law 1780-1860 (Cambridge, Mass., 1977); Atiyah, op.cit., supra n.39.

72. Atiyah, op.cit., supra n.39, p.421.

73. A.W.B. Simpson, "The Horwitz Thesis and the History of Contracts", University of Chicago Law Review, XLVI (1979) pp.533-601.

74. Morgan and Thomas, op.cit., p.64.

75. K. Llewellyn, "What Price Contract? - An Essay in Perspective", Yale Law Journal, XL (1931) pp.720-21.

76. My thanks go to Charles James, Martin Albrow, Harry Calvert, Richard Lewis and David Miers for their helpful comments.

THE FAMILY SETTLEMENTS OF THE SYKES OF SLEDMERE

1792 - 1900

Barbara English

"England is governed in times of excitement by its people: in quiet times by its property."[1] This was a mid-nineteenth century view: for the writer, and for centuries before him, property meant land. Land was the principal source of wealth in pre-industrial society: it was for a long time the most important way to keep large amounts of capital. The men who held the land had economic power, and economic power was the basis of political power. Through the possession of land, successive generations of a family could move upwards through the social classes. In the nineteenth century, land was "the most permanent, transmittable and socially acceptable form of property."[2]

Because of the unique quality of land, a complex system of land law and custom existed in England, which governed how land was transferred from one man to another. Land could be freely transmitted between members of a family, as a fee simple (the nearest approximation to absolute ownership a man could have), but it was, and still is, much commoner to make transfers of large areas of land subject to settlement.

There have always been different kinds of settlement: but the commonest methods of settling land in the nineteenth century were the trust for sale and the strict settlement.[3] From the late seventeenth century the device most commonly used in England to direct the inheritance of the great landed families to the male heirs (usually the eldest sons) for successive generations was the most restricted form of family settlement known as the strict settlement. The term appears to have been first used in 1710;[4] it was not a term defined by statute, but a descriptive phrase only. Although it was often used by lawyers in the eighteenth and nineteenth centuries, the phrase "family settlement" seems to have been equally common: and a family settlement might be strict or might be more liberally constructed. One of the best known legal authorities on settlement in the nineteenth century, Joshua Williams, wrote a series of lectures on The Settlement of Real Estates published in 1879 without using the phrase strict settlement at all, although many of the lectures were concerned with family settlement of the most restricted kind. The phrases "in strict settlement" or "strictly settled" were not necessarily used in the deeds which instituted a strict family settlement.

Strict settlement combined three elements of legal doctrine: the "fee tail", estate tail or entail which came from the Middle Ages,[5] the "life interest" from the sixteenth century,[6] and a protective device, the appointment of "trustees to preserve the contingent remainders" who prevented the person with the life interest destroying the interests of possible ("contingent") successors or remainder men. This last device which made strict settlement possible was the contribution of the seventeenth century.[7] The great English landowner, standing on his terrace and looking across the parkland to his acres rolling to the horizon, was hardly ever the absolute possessor of his land: under a strict settlement he held only a life interest by which he enjoyed the occupation of the land and its rents, but he had no power to affect what would happen after his death, because the land was entailed, bound to pass to his heir, who was by custom his eldest son. If he tried to change this situation without his son's consent, the trustees would be obliged to act against him.

The life-tenant under a strict settlement suffered many disabilities. He was entitled to the income of the estate only: he could not sell land, mortgage land, or exchange it, indeed he could not even make leases beyond his own lifetime, unless these powers were written into his settlement. In default of a specific exemption, his heir could in certain circumstances sue him for "waste", for spoiling the inheritance, if he cut down trees, pulled down a cowshed, turned ploughland into pasture or pasture into ploughland.[8] In addition to these disabilities, the income of the estate was often burdened with annual sums that had to be paid to other members of the family; even if the annual charges became too great a burden, it was not possible to sell land to reduce them, unless such powers had been included in the settlement.

Settlements were not perpetual: by the nineteenth century, it was finally established that no settlement could last longer than any number of lives in being when the settlement was made, plus one additional life for 21 years. Once a settlement was imposed, the only way in which it could be broken (apart from a private Act of Parliament) was by the combination of the life-tenant and the tenant in tail acting together (or by the tenant in tail, if the life-tenant was dead). In most families, once the settlement was broken, another was imposed which lasted another generation, and which in turn could not be broken until another tenant in tail came of age.

For many centuries much English land was held by a small number of great landowners. The accumulation of land in a few hands, allegedly from the late seventeenth century onwards, was generally thought by both nineteenth century commentators and by modern historians to be the result of the type of settlement practised by the great land-owning families; however, F.M.L. Thompson has offered persuasive arguments to show that the distribution of land between estates of different sizes may not have altered greatly between 1641 and 1873, and if this view is correct, the reasons for the undoubted accumulation of land must be sought outside settlement practice.[9] "How few owned how much" was suspected but not known even approximately until the 1870s, when the government ordered a return listing all landowners and their acreages. This return, which became popularly known as the "New Domesday Book", presented the information county by county, the owners within the county being listed alphabetically. To find out how many "great landowners" there were, the county returns had to be reworked, so that one man's total acres in all counties could be ascertained. This reworking was carried out by several authors, and in particular by John Bateman, who also included corrections supplied by landowners in his later editions of The Great Landowners of

Great Britain and Ireland.[10] Bateman's analysis showed that about four-fifths of the land of Great Britain (excluding London, crown property, waste spaces, lakes, rivers and roads) was owned by less than 7,000 people. In the East Riding of Yorkshire, the area of the present study, thirty-three landed aristocrats owned just over half the rural acreage.[11]

The statistics of the 1870s succeeded in establishing in reasonably accurate detail how many landowners there were in Britain. No one, however, has ever succeeded in establishing how much land in the country was held in settlement. In the nineteenth century, informed guesses ranged from "less than a quarter" to "three-quarters and upwards."[12] As late as 1901 Sir Arthur Underhill, a lawyer of great experience (one of the select club of eminent conveyancers known as "The Forty Thieves") wrote that "nearly all the great estates, comprising perhaps the greater part of the land of England, are held in strict settlement."[13] The proportion remains unknown. Nor is it known how much of the land belonging to one family was settled, and how much was left out of settlement. Other factors which complicated the question of the total amount of land in strict settlement were the intervals that at times occurred between successive settlements, and that occasionally overriding powers (known as "general powers of appointment") were included in the settlement arrangements.

There have been few detailed investigations of individual nineteenth century settlements.[14] The main outlines of a settlement by the nineteenth century followed a set pattern, but the details of individual settlements were extraordinarily variable. The way to understanding family settlement is through the study of cases of real examples: but the generalisations of both the nineteenth and the twentieth centuries about strict settlement are founded on examples given in conveyancing textbooks, precedent books or reported cases, and have been rarely tested against the evidence from estate records.

There are a number of reasons for this. Family settlements are not always available to historians: the family may have decided not to deposit them with the rest of their archives in the local record office, because they felt they were too personal, or because the settlements were retained by the family lawyers. Their bulk and the torrent of words contained in them are daunting: the Sykes settlement of 1847 for example consisted of about 60 sheets of parchment, each about two foot square.

What is offered here is a case history of settlement in one great land-owning family. A large number of case histories should show patterns; it is hoped eventually to investigate all the large East Yorkshire estates (those that had over 10,000 acres in 1883).

The Sykes family acquired the Sledmere estates in East Yorkshire in the year 1748, through a fortunate marriage of Richard Sykes, merchant of Hull. Almost at once the merchant began to build a house at Sledmere, and to consolidate and improve the bleak land he had inherited. Later members of the family added to the acres and improved their quality, and by 1883 Sir Tatton Sykes of Sledmere owned 34,010 acres, acres which made his the largest holding in the East Riding: in the whole of England only thirty-three men held more English acres than Sir Tatton.[15]

In the last decade of the eighteenth century, Sir Christopher Sykes was tenant for life of the Sledmere estates under a settlement created by the will of his uncle Richard, who died in 1761. Christopher's son and heir Mark was tenant in tail of the settlement, and came of age in 1792: in November of that year father and son together broke the existing settlement.[16] The estates were immediately resettled: but into the new settlement was written a general power of appointment, a clause by which Christopher was allowed to alter the settlement at any time, by deed or will. The main purpose of making the settlement at all was to provide for the future of the estates in case Christopher should die unexpectedly without making proper arrangements. This settlement with a general power of appointment bound Christopher very lightly; it was in fact equivalent to ownership.[17] From

1792 to 1795 the estate was left in this unfettered state: in 1795 the power of appointment was used to settle part of the estates on the marriage of the heir, Mark, and to convey the other lands unrestrictedly to the father Christopher Sykes as a fee simple.[18]

Shortly before Christopher Sykes died in 1801 he made a long, complex and very restrictive will.[19] It was this will of 1801 which governed the Sykes estates until 1847, when another settlement was imposed, which lasted until 1900. The succession of heirs to the Sledmere estates between the late eighteenth century and 1913 is shown in the following table (which omits wives and daughters).

Table I

Succession of heirs to the Sledmere estates between the late eighteenth century and 1913

(Life tenants of Sledmere are shown in upper case letters).

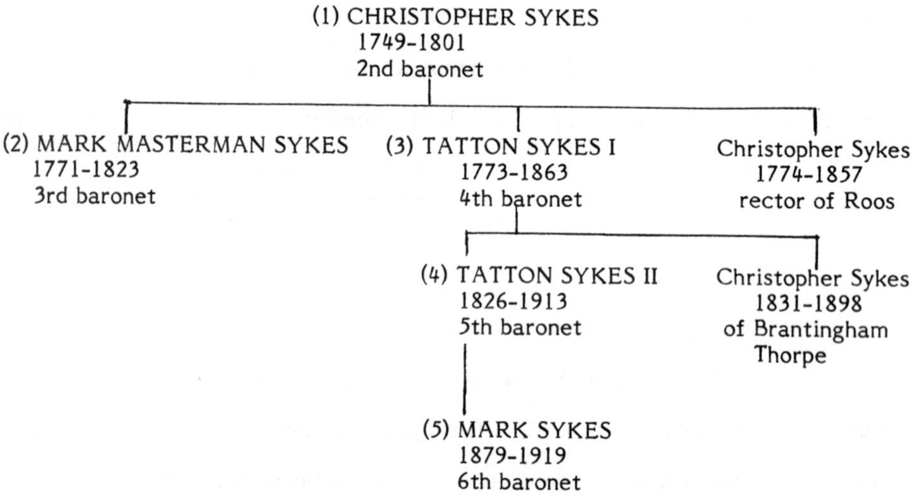

(1) & (2) broke the entail when (2) came of age in 1792 and resettled with a general power of appointment in favour of (1).
(1) settled the estates by his will in 1801 on (2) and his heirs male, then on (3) and his heirs male.
(2) died in 1823 without children and (3) inherited.
(3) & (4) broke the entail when (4) came of age in 1847 and resettled the estates on (3) for life, and then on (4) and his heirs male.
(4) & (5) broke the entail when (5) came of age in 1900 and resettled the estates on (4) for life, and then on (5) and his heirs male.

Table II

Settlement of the Sledmere estates 1792-1927

1792-1795 settled by deed of 1792 subject to a general power of appointment.

1795-1801 part strictly settled (marriage settlement 1795), part unsettled.

1801-1847 strictly settled by will of 1801.

1847-1900 strictly settled by deeds of 1847.

1900-1927 strictly settled by deeds of 1900.

Sir Christopher Sykes, in his will of 1801, devised his unsettled estates to his three sons, with a small holding of two farms to his married daughter. Only the Sledmere estates were strictly settled, on Mark, the eldest son, in tail male: if that line failed, six other potential life-tenants were named, successively and in tail male: then there was a succession of possible female life-tenants. The Holderness estates (detached from Sledmere) were settled on the second son, Tatton, and the third son, Christopher (a clergyman) was given the advowson of Roos and Hilston (places that were also in Holderness) in tail male, and was also allowed to buy the rectory and manor of Roos for £10,000, a sum which was to be paid within five years with 4% interest per annum. There is no indication how he was to find the money: Sir Christopher did not leave his third son any money, and it may have been money from his mother or his wife's dowry that purchased the Roos estate. The amount paid for Roos was to go into Sir Christopher's personal estate to discharge his debts and legacies. The two daughters were both left money: cash legacies, out of Christopher's personal estate, not charges on the lands, although the effect was the same, because the trustees of the settlement of 1801 were to take not more than £5,000 and not less than £4,000 from the "rents and profits" of the Sledmere estates each year until Christopher's debts and legacies were paid.[20.]

The settlements of Holderness and Roos under the 1801 will came into an intermediate category between strict settlement and fee simple. The estates were not strictly settled, for both the younger sons, Tatton and Christopher, were given the estates for their own lives, and then to each of their children in equal shares or in shares to be determined by their fathers. Nor were the estates given in fee simple, for there were restrictions placed on the sons concerning their powers of mortgaging for jointures or portions.

The jointure was the provision for the support of the widow of a landowner after her husband's death, given in lieu of dower, and the portion was the provision for the younger children who would not inherit the estates.[21] In nineteenth century settlement it was common to specify what size of jointures and portions could be provided. The life tenant of Sledmere under the 1801 settlement could provide not more than two jointures at any one time; not more than £80 a year per £1,000 of the wife's dowry (that is, the capital the bride brought with her as part of the marriage settlement) with a top limit of £1,500 if one jointress, and £1,500 for the first and £1,000 for the second, if two. If the second widow outlived the first, she could be promoted to £1,500 a year. There cannot, of course, be two widows of one son; the settlor was envisaging (as in fact happened) one brother succeeding the other. Mark had already married, in 1795. His power of jointuring his wife had been restricted by the settlement of 1792 to 8% of his wife's fortune, with a ceiling of £1,500 (that is, she was not likely to have a fortune of more than £20,000).

The life-tenant of Sledmere was not allowed (under the 1801 will) to raise more than £10,000 for all his younger children together (the eldest was, of course, excluded).[22] Part of the portion money could be used for the maintenance and education of the life-tenant's children, as long as it did not exceed 4% per annum of the portion: this was a standard clause in most settlements.

Leases on the Sledmere estates under the 1801 settlement were also restricted, to not more than 12 years for property in hand, and not more than 25 years for property already tenanted. There were to be no charges to tenants when they took up leases of estate farms or cottages.[23] The Sykes sons were (and this was unusual in a family settlement) liable for waste, that is, for anything they did while in possession of the estates which could be proved to injure the property their successors would one day inherit.[24]

Christopher Sykes included a special power in his will to enable the Sledmere life-tenant to spend at least £1,000 a year on Sledmere House and park, the money to come from a charge on a particular estate.[25] This was the only open-handed clause in a settlement which was in every other way very restrictive. There were no powers of mortgage except for the wives' and children's money, and such restricted powers of sale (of a few specially mentioned farms only) that within eleven years the heir under the 1801 will was obliged to obtain a private Act of Parliament to enable him to enlarge his powers of management.[26]

Christopher's heir, Mark Masterman Sykes, married twice, but had no children. When he died in 1823, the operation of the 1801 settlement ensured that the next life-tenant of the Sledmere estates was his brother Tatton, who already possessed the Holderness estates.

Tatton (called here Tatton Sykes I, to distinguish him from his son, Tatton Sykes II) married late in life, and it was 1847 before his son came of age: it was therefore 1847 before there was a tenant in tail of the 1801 settlement old enough to be able to combine with his father in breaking the settlement. Father and son together (life-tenant and tenant in tail) went through the process of disentailing, and then a new strict settlement was immediately imposed,[27] which was to last through Tatton Sykes I's death in 1863 until 1900, when Tatton Sykes II's heir in turn came of age.

The transactions that settled all the Sykes estates in the summer of 1847 were complex, and involved six deeds, dated between 22 June and 6 July.[28] There were three interrelated settlements: the strict settlement of the Sledmere estates, the strict settlement of the Holderness estates, and the money settlement on the younger children.

The deeds, in chronological order, were first the conveyance of a manor

(Ryhill in Holderness) to the younger son, Christopher;[29] then the disentailing deed; followed next day by the strict settlement of Sledmere; then the strict settlement of the Holderness estates; then the so-called money settlement on the younger children; and finally the will of Tatton Sykes I, which dealt with his personalty, such things as furniture, jewellery, his horses and so on. This last was not a negligible amount: the personal effects, apart from heirlooms which descended with the estates, were to amount to £127,406 when valued on Tatton Sykes I's death in 1863.[30]

The order of the deeds was important, for everything settled before the nomination of the tenant in tail in a strict settlement would endure, even if the entail was broken; but if, for instance, the younger children's money settlement had been set up after the designation of the tenant in tail, it could have been extinguished when the entail was next broken.[31] For this reason the power to borrow money for the younger children's money settlement, the subject of the deed of 2 July, was first set out in the deed of 30 June. The order of the trusts would in many settlements have been set out in the same deed or pair of deeds; in the Sykes settlement of 1847, separate deeds were used for the most important of the separate trusts.

The six deeds made between 22 June and 6 July were executed on a Tuesday, another Tuesday, Wednesday, Thursday, Friday and another Tuesday. No gentleman would do business on a Sunday, and it looks as if Saturday and Monday were also avoided.

In 1847 the settlor, Tatton Sykes I, divided the estates into two parts, the Sledmere estates and the Holderness estates. This pattern had been established in 1801, when the first son (Mark Masterman Sykes) had been given Sledmere and the second son (Tatton Sykes I) had been given Holderness. However, Tatton Sykes I had possessed both estates since 1823, because of his brother Mark's death without children; now he divided them once more, Sledmere to go in strict settlement to Tatton Sykes II, the elder son, and the Holderness estates to go in strict settlement to Christopher Sykes, the younger son.

The normal pattern of a strict settlement as exemplified in books of conveyancing precedents of the nineteenth century was well illustrated by the settlement of Sledmere in 1847.[32] Tatton Sykes I had himself studied law in London after his time at Brasenose, and he had also worked in banking in Hull, so it is possible that he took an active part in the drafting of the clauses of the settlement. Unfortunately, there is no correspondence in the archives about the making of the settlement, so it is not possible to estimate the respective contributions of the solicitors and the family.

In the year 1847, the law allowed the settlement to be made by a curious deed called "an indenture of settlement, made in pursuance of the act making a release as effective as a lease and release."[33] The parties named were Tatton Sykes I (the father) and his trustees, and Tatton Sykes II (the son) and his trustees. On the day of the settlement of Sledmere, 30 June 1847, the Sykes' estates were in the hands of the family solicitor, Samuel Steward (of Bell, Steward and Lloyd, Lincoln's Inn), who had been granted them by the disentailing deed of 29 June: restricted to such uses as the father and son together should by deed appoint, and in default of such appointment, the estates were to revert to the uses to which the property was settled before the disentailing deed (that is, to the 1801 settlement once more). Some such temporary cover was necessary in case one or more of the parties (the two Sykes and their solicitor) died in the night.

After giving the date of the deed and the parties, the 1847 settlement recited previous deeds showing the title to the estate and the previous charges (outstanding mortgages and jointures) which were not to be extinguished. Many lands had been bought by Tatton Sykes I during his life, and the deed next stated that he and his son had agreed that £100,000 could be taken as the 1847 value of those purchased lands (at that time unsettled), and that those lands could, therefore, be charged with £100,000 in favour of Tatton Sykes I. All the Sledmere estates (described in a schedule at the end of the settlement) were then conveyed to trustees for 1,000 years to the uses and upon the trusts described. The first provision in the settlement was usually, and in this case, a rent-charge to the son (of £1,500 as a bachelor, and £4,000 after marriage) during the joint lives of himself and his father, secured by power of distraint (all annuities in settlements were protected by some powers of distraint).[34] Subject to the heir's annuity, the estates were conveyed to the use of Tatton Sykes I for life; and after his death to Tatton Sykes II's trustees for 99 years in order to protect the jointure of Tatton Sykes I's widow, and then to the use of Tatton Sykes II for life. Should Tatton Sykes II's life-estate fail, the trustees were to preserve the contingent remainders. After Tatton Sykes II, the Sledmere estates were limited to his sons severally and successively in tail male, then to the sons of Christopher (Tatton Sykes I's younger son) severally and successively in tail male, but always according to their respective seniorities, the elder taking before the others; then to any later-born sons of Tatton Sykes II's sons, the heirs general of Christopher's sons, the heirs general of the sons of any later-born sons, then to the first and other daughters of Tatton Sykes I in succession and in tail male, to the first and other daughters in tail general and finally to the rightful heirs of the settlor. Each step involving contingent remainders was protected by trustees. Such complex remainders were normal, although some variation was possible between tail male and tail general.[35]

Remainders to daughters were protected by the "name and arms clause". Any life-tenant or husband of a life-tenant not already called Sykes was to take the name and quarter the arms of Sykes within a year of succession to the estates; and if he did not, he was to be treated as if he were dead, and the life-estate was to pass on to the next heir. This draconian clause was common in family settlements and ensured the survival of many famous names: the most celebrated perhaps being that of the Percy Dukes of Northumberland, who without the name and arms clause would have been called Smithson.[36]

After the order of succession in the 1847 settlement came the powers, that is, the recital of what the life-tenant and the trustees might do. The settlement gave the trustees of the Sledmere estates the power to borrow £100,000 (the value of the estates Tatton Sykes I had bought since 1823 which were now included in the Sledmere settlement), at a rate not exceeding 4%, and pay the money on demand to Tatton Sykes I. This was money which he was to use to provide for his younger children.

The settlement of 1847 also included a power that the trustees might charge the Sledmere estates with the purchase money of lands that Tatton Sykes I might buy after 1847 during the remainder of his life; for instance, if he bought a farm for £10,000 (and certain conditions were met), the trustees could borrow that £10,000 on the security of the estates, and return the money he had spent to Tatton Sykes I. The conditions were that the lands should be within ten miles of any part of the Sledmere estates, that Tatton Sykes I should settle the lands by deed or will to follow the Sledmere settlement, and that his heir should consent to the estates being charged for them. A similar clause in the Holderness settlements of 1847 charged those estates with the purchase money if the land bought was within five miles of the Holderness estates. In fact, Tatton Sykes I did not claim during his lifetime the money he had spent buying land, but it was credited to him and went into his personal estate for him to dispose of as he thought fit: in the event he divided the money (by his will) between his younger children.

The 1847 settlement contained powers for the life-tenants to provide jointures and portions. An additional jointure of £2,000 a year was now given to Tatton Sykes I's wife, if she survived him, added to £500 assured to her already under her marriage settlement and a further £1,500 which had been added in 1841. Her pin money (that is, pocket money during married life) was not mentioned in the 1847 deed, nor was that of any of the life-tenant's wives.

The trustees were given power to charge the estates with a once-only sum of £10,000 at 4% for Tatton Sykes II on his marriage, if that was within his father's lifetime, or in any case immediately on his father's death: Tatton Sykes II did not marry until 11 years after his father died. Tatton Sykes II, Christopher, or any later-born son if in possession of Sledmere, was in 1847 given power to raise a jointure of £4,000 a year, and the daughters, if in possession, were to be able to raise £4,000 a year for their husbands' support as widowers. No more than £6,000 a year in jointure was to be charged to the Sledmere estates. The children's portions in total were not to be more than £60,000 charged to the estates, and no one child was to have more than £20,000. There was a sliding scale for children's portions (this was usual); if there was one child, £20,000 could be raised; if two, £30,000; if three, £40,000; if four or more £50,000. All these sums were to be borrowed at not more than 4%; all were future possibilities, rather than present liabilities, and none of the sums was in fact ever raised, for Tatton Sykes II outlived his wife and only had one child, so that the estate paid neither jointure nor younger child's portion.

Powers of management were given to the life-tenants. Tatton Sykes I during his life, and all successive life-tenants or trustees in the case of minorities, were given power to make mineral leases for not more than 60 years; to make other leases for not more than 21 years; and to make improving or building leases for not more than 99 years. In addition the tenants on the estate farms and cottages were to be liable for waste;[37] but they were not to pay entry fines. The trustees on written instructions from the life-tenant could enfranchise copyholders and grant copyholders building leases. The trustees were also given a limited power to raise money by mortgage to pay for the renewal of land leases (part of the Sledmere estates was leased from the Dean and Chapter of York).

Only freehold land was settled by the ordinary deed of settlement (as was done in the 1847 Sykes' deed) and the usual clause was included that the settlor would surrender copyhold land and assign leasehold land to the uses of the settlement.

The heirlooms, family pictures, books, manuscripts, furniture, jewels and so on, were sometimes strictly settled like land. However in 1847 Tatton Sykes I merely expressed a wish that the heirlooms should follow the succession of life-tenants at Sledmere, and he did not make the condition binding. No more is heard of the 1801 clause empowering the life-tenant to spend £1,000 on Sledmere House (although in the 1900 settlement a special clause was again to be included allocating funds to the upkeep of the house).

It was customary to conclude the settlement deed with clauses about the trustees. The Sykes trustees of 1847 were all relations, not professional men. There were two sets, one acting for the settlor and one for the next life-tenant, and the trustees were chosen accordingly, older men for the first set and a younger generation for the second set. The recommended number of trustees was at least two: in fact each set of trustees of the 1847 settlement consisted of three men. They were by the settlement empowered to give receipts, to be indemnified against certain claims arising out of their position, they were reimbursed for their expenses, and they were given the power to appoint new trustees on the death, resignation or incapacity of any of their number. The trustees were not involved in the making of the settlement ; and indeed it appears from other East Yorkshire family settlements that in many cases the trustees were not asked in advance if they would agree to act, and in many cases trustees refused. The amounts of money left by Tatton Sykes I to his trustees in 1847 (£1,000 to the man who might have to act as guardian for the younger children, £100 to the other two, and nothing to the younger set of trustees) suggests that he did not expect their duties to be very onerous. They had no discretion to vary the trusts in any way, although they were allowed to advance part of the portions of the younger children. The account books and papers of the trustees of 1847 show that the work was in fact done by the London solicitors with the help of accountants and bankers.[38]

The pattern of the strict settlement of Sledmere in 1847 was followed very closely by the deed which strictly settled the Holderness lands on the younger son, Christopher. The same trustees were used, and most of the same clauses, allowing smaller jointures and portions. The settlement put Christopher's heirs before Tatton Sykes II's heirs in the succession; but as Christopher never married, the

Holderness estates at his death were once more joined to Sledmere.

Tatton Sykes I had in addition to his two sons six daughters, and he made a separate money settlement on his younger son and daughters. Money for the younger children (payable to the girls on marriage or aged 21, whichever occurred first) was to be raised by the trustees of the settlement of 1847, by a mortgage of £100,000 joined with a further £103,000 which Tatton Sykes I had in Consols. There was a clause empowering the trustees, on the written instructions of the life-tenant, to sell or exchange the lands on which the £100,000 mortgage was charged, the money raised to be used to pay off the mortgage, or to be used to buy further lands in England or Wales, to be settled to the same uses. This was a clause usually (not always) inserted in family settlements:[39] as a power, it lasted as long as the settlement. The clause was obviously of great importance, for it gave the life-tenant the ability to sell certain settled estates to remove the incumbrances of the mortgage, if they became overwhelming: of course it did not allow him to sell Sledmere itself, or any of the family lands except those which bore the mortgage, which were lands bought by the settlor Tatton Sykes I himself since his brother Mark's death. The £100,000 raised by mortgage, the £103,000 from the Consols, and most of Tatton Sykes I's personal estate, funded the money settlement on the younger children.

Each daughter under the money settlement of 1847 was to have the interest and dividends on £30,000 for her sole use during her marriage, with no power to deprive herself of the benefit. Afterwards the capital could be divided among her children as she chose. If one or more daughters died before the money was due (one did so), the others could benefit from her share, the total together with interest for each girl to be not more than £40,000. The remaining money was to be divided into 8 shares, 6 shares to be divided between the daughters and the remaining 2 shares and any surplus over the girls' maximum to be used to buy land for Christopher, the younger son. The trust was not to come into operation until the death of Tatton Sykes I, although he could anticipate the portions, and he also reserved the right to withdraw from the trust's benefits a daughter who married against his or his widow's wishes.

The settlor of 1847, although he was 75 at the time of the settlement, kept his own life-tenancy over all the estates, both Sledmere and Holderness, for another sixteen years. The two sons were mere prospective life-tenants: they would become life-tenants at their father's death and then their life-tenancies would last until their as yet unborn sons (and neither was married in 1847) came of age at 21 and broke, if they chose, the entail. Beyond that date the estate was not tied up; it was not possible to make arrangements to last beyond any number of lives in being plus 21 years.

In 1863 Tatton Sykes I died, aged 90. Since making the settlement of 1847 he had continued to buy lands to extend both the Sledmere and the Holderness estates, and as had been agreed, the purchase money for these lands was now credited to his personal estate, increasing the amount available from £100,000 (the estimated value of land bought 1823-47) to £121,316 (the value of land bought 1823-47 plus land bought 1847-63). On Tatton Sykes I's death his son Tatton Sykes II succeeded to the Sledmere estates as life-tenant, while the trustees of 1847 carried out their responsibility for raising the £121,316 for the younger children. This they did by mortgaging that part of the estate that had been bought between 1823 and 1847 to Sykes' relations[40] and in return for the capital advanced, which was invested for the younger children, the trustees paid the mortgagees each year, out of the estate income, 4% on the mortgage of £121,316. This mortgage, which lasted until well into the twentieth century, was known as the "Family Mortgage."

Tatton Sykes I's other legacies to his younger children had grown in the same way as the Family Mortgage. His money invested in Consols had risen from £103,000 in 1847 to £287,774 in 1863, and his personal effects were valued at £127,406. Altogether the father left £536,500 to his six surviving younger children.[41]

Over the years between 1863 and 1913 Tatton Sykes II paid off the original mortgagees of the Family Mortgage out of his own income, but kept the mortgage going ("on foot" was the technical word) for his own benefit. The advantage of Tatton Sykes II paying off the Family Mortgage was that the trustees no longer deducted £4,853 (4% on £121,316) from the income of the estates before it reached his pocket. In addition, by keeping the mortgage alive he had a very safe investment for his own capital, paying a higher rate than the consols he might otherwise have bought, and his investment was still his personal property, to be disposed of as he wished without regard to the settlement.[42] Similar reasoning led the trustees in 1863 to mortgage part of the Holderness estates (in order to raise the purchase money of the additional land bought between 1847 and 1863 to increase them) to Christopher Sykes, the tenant for life of the same estates;[43] this kind of complexity makes the family's financial dealings difficult to follow.

The daughters of Tatton Sykes I from 1863 onwards drew the interest of their portions under the 1847 settlement, and sometimes asked for capital sums as advances for their children. It was not until the twentieth century that they or their heirs had each received their full £40,000.[44]

In 1898 Christopher Sykes (life-tenant of the Holderness estates) died unmarried, and under the 1847 settlement his settled land reverted to his brother Tatton Sykes II as life-tenant, with Tatton's son Mark as tenant in tail. The settlement of 1847 remained unbroken until 1900, when Mark, son of Tatton Sykes II, came of age, and father and son together disentailed the estates and immediately resettled them.

The background of the 1900 settlement was the mountain of debts of Lady Jessica, the estranged wife of Tatton Sykes II. He had disclaimed her debts in 1896, but Lady Jessica continued to borrow, and some of her loans were at an interest rate of 60% per annum.[45] In 1898 there had been a court case over promissory notes signed by her: and in 1900 she owed, or disclosed, debts of

£98,000. Her son Mark, to help his mother, persuaded his father to a resettlement as soon as possible, that is, as soon as he was twenty one. The estate was disentailed and once more strictly settled, charged with a further mortgage of £110,000 raised at 3.3/8% from the Allied Assurance Company, which was used to pay Jessica's debts.[46] The mortgage of 1900 was known as the "Allied Assurance Mortgage" to distinguish it from the "Family Mortgage" of 1863. By the terms of the 1900 settlement an annuity of £2,000 per annum and powers of making jointure and portions were given to Mark, as the future life-tenant;[47] but Tatton Sykes II remained tenant for life, living at Sledmere and in command of the estates until his death in 1913.

The later history of the Sykes family settlements is outside the scope of this paper: unfortunately for the family Mark Sykes died very soon after his father, in 1919, and what is more he died intestate, leaving an encumbered estate and a number of children who were under age. The trustees therefore took over, and when Mark's eldest son, Richard (the tenant in tail of the 1900 settlement) came of age in 1927, the estates were once more disentailed and then strictly settled.

In addition to the main settlements discussed above, subsidiary settlements were made on the marriages of the Sykes men.

Mark Masterman Sykes married twice, in 1795 and 1814. His first wife, Henrietta Masterman (whose name he added to his own) brought him £11,350 in debts owed to her, and considerable estates which she held in fee simple, around Settrington, a village ten miles north west of Sledmere. A long and very complex settlement was made on the couple,[48] providing for every future contingency, and allocating a jointure of £1,360 to Henrietta. However, she died before her husband, and as Mark never had any children,[49] the settlement only added Settrington temporarily (during Mark's life) to the Sledmere estates, and then reverted to the Masterman heirs.

In 1814 Mark Masterman Sykes married again, this time his first cousin

Elizabeth Egerton (Mark's sister had already married Elizabeth's brother). By this time Mark seems to have been short of money: he had borrowed £74,000 from his bankers[50] and he was to die leaving the estates "heavily encumbered."[51] His bride of 1814 brought him £20,000 which he at once used to pay off a mortgage on land he had bought and immediately mortgaged. Mark settled £30,000 worth of insurance policies on his second wife and possible younger children, policies all taken out in 1814 with the premiums secured on his first wife's rent roll of Settrington estates. A special clause (agreed between the three Sykes brothers) assured Mark's widow an increased jointure of £3,000 a year if she survived Mark and had no son to become life-tenant of Sledmere (which in fact happened);[52] she was also given a London house until her death, which was in 1846.

Mark was succeeded in 1823 by his brother Tatton Sykes I, who had married the previous year when he was life-tenant of the Holderness estates.[53] His wife, Mary Anne Foulis, brought to the marriage £7,782 in stock and money. Tatton called this in the marriage settlement "about £7,000" and assured her a jointure based on 8% of £7,000, in addition to £500 a year out of the Holderness estates (her jointure was later increased to £1,500). In fact the jointure was never paid as Tatton outlived his wife. The marriage produced seven younger children (of which six reached their majority) to be provided for, which Tatton did very generously: in this mid-nineteenth century generation the portions to the younger children (£40,000 for each daughter and more for the younger son) far outweighed what the bride had brought to the marriage.

Tatton Sykes II made a marriage in 1874 he was to regret bitterly. At his wife's memorial service he was heard to mutter, "A remarkable woman, Jessica, a remarkable woman, but I rue the day, I rue the day I met her."[54] Under their marriage settlement, during their joint lives, Jessica Cavendish Bentinck was to have £500 for her sole use; as a widow she would have £4,000 a year, a sum which was laid down in the 1847 settlement, as were the sizes of the children's portions. In 1899 Sir Tatton and Lady Jessica separated, and he settled a further sum of

£4,500 a year on her.[55] Nevertheless, she ran up huge debts, and the family, as described above, paid most of them.

How did the marriage settlements of the Sykes family relate to the main settlements? All of them were made under the umbrella of the main settlement: all the powers of jointure and portions derived from the main settlement. The deed of 1795 strictly settled part of the Sledmere estates on the issue of one particular marriage: the other marriage settlements did not, because the succession of life-tenants was already fixed by the main settlement. The marriage settlements of 1795, 1814, 1822 and 1874 had little apparent effect on the economic history of the estates.

Table III

Capital brought to the Sykes's life-tenants of Sledmere by their brides, and the jointures proposed for their widows

Date	Capital of bride	Annual amount of jointure	Jointure as % of capital	No. of years actually paid
1770	£30,000	£690*	2.3	2
1795	£11,350 (and land)	£1,360	11.9	none
1814	£20,000	£3,000**	15.0	23
1822	£7,782	£560*	8.0	none
1874	not known	£4,000	?	none

* Later increased.

** £1,000 if the bride had a son who was life-tenant of Sledmere (which was not the case).

As can be seen in Table III, the capital the brides brought was small in comparison with the wealth of the Sykes family, as shown in their rentals (Table IV) and land purchases. Only twice in the nineteenth century did a jointure have to be paid: perhaps it was fortunate for the estates that the husbands lived so long. A curious feature is that although the jointures proposed in 1795, 1814 and 1822 should have been, according to the settlements, 8% of the brides' dowries, the rule was ignored and higher amounts were paid (with the exception of 1822, when the amount was afterwards increased threefold).

A ceiling was imposed on the power of mortgaging for the portions of younger children in all the main family settlements. In fact portions were not of great importance in the economy of the Sykes's estates in the nineteenth century. In 1801 the younger sons were given land of their own, not portions: and the two daughters were given farms and cash from Sir Christopher's personal estate.[56] In 1847 the portions charged to the estates totalled £121,316, a considerable amount, but one which the estates were well able to bear, as Tatton Sykes II paid off a large part of the portion money of his brother and sisters (the Family Mortgage) within four years of succeeding his father (he paid £42,000 in April 1867 alone)[57] and the whole sum in his lifetime. Tatton Sykes II had only one child, Mark, and so he did not have to raise portions for his own younger children.

Who made the Sykes family settlements? In most families, the main part was taken by the family lawyer. Sir Frederick Pollock wrote of the family solicitor that he was "the real possessor of the secrets of the estate, the real familiar spirit at whose bidding the magical powers of the settlement are called forth, and without whose aid, no matter of weight can be undertaken."[58] Elphinstone, in his Introduction to Conveyancing, complained that "the clients are generally so ignorant of the nature of a settlement that they are unable to see the objects which their advisers are aiming at."[59] In the Sykes family, the settlors of 1801 and of 1847 had both been trained in the law: but even so, Sir Tatton Sykes I had to ask his family solicitor in 1821 what powers he possessed. There are unfortunately no letters or diaries or even drafts for the main Sykes settlements before 1900, but something can be learned of the making of the marriage settlements of 1814 and 1822 from the very full solicitors' accounts.

In 1814, in anticipation of Sir Mark Masterman Sykes's second marriage, John Lockwood, his Beverley lawyer, went to London to advise Sir Mark on the options available. Lockwood's account recorded that he studied the former settlements (probably at Sledmere), and visited both Sir Mark and Mr. Egerton (the bride's father) in London, when the heads of the settlement were considered and directions given for it being drawn. He (or his clerk) then drew the settlement and made a fair copy. He took the settlement twice to Mr. Sanders, a conveyancing counsel of Lincoln's Inn, and to another counsel, Mr. Atherton, on behalf of Miss Egerton. The settlement, its counterpart and its memorial for registration at Beverley were then engrossed, and John Lockwood went to York to read the settlement over to Sir Mark's two brothers (who were concerned in the jointure arrangements). Both parts and the memorial were then executed by all three Sykes brothers. Lockwood charged 10 guineas for his London visit; the conveyancing counsel and his clerk were paid £11, but the bride's counsel rather less. The Beverley lawyers' bill for the whole settlement transaction was £133.10s.[60]

Events in 1821-22 were similar. Tatton Sykes I, the bridegroom, wrote to John Lockwood asking what powers he had under his father's will to make a settlement? On receiving an answer, Tatton summoned the solicitor to Sledmere House where "the instructions [were] received as to the settlement." Then followed "drawing the settlement", and making a fair copy for the bride's lawyers. Lockwood sent them the drafts with an accompanying full explanation; but some alterations were proposed by the bride's lawyers, passed on to Tatton and accepted. The settlement was then engrossed and registered.[61]

The earlier settlements were made by York or Beverley solicitors; in 1814 a London conveyancing expert was consulted by the country solicitor, not to draft the deed but to check it: a consultant's opinion. The 1801 will was witnessed by the Beverley solicitor who may have drafted it; in 1847 and 1900 the settlements were made in London, and it was a London firm that did the everyday work of the 1847 settlement with the help of accountants and bankers.[62] Neither the trustees nor the estate agents seem to have been consulted in the making of the nineteenth century settlements.

However carefully a strict settlement was drawn, some eventuality would not be foreseen, and the life-tenant was unable to alter a strict settlement: the only way he could increase the powers he had been granted was to obtain a private Act of Parliament. Private estate Acts were obtained by the Sykes family in 1776 and 1812, to modify their settlements.

By 1811 Sir Mark Masterman Sykes was in financial difficulties. He had been married for 16 years, and had no children; without an adult son, there was no way in which he could ever break the strict settlement. The 1812 Act was to enable him to sell some outlying estates which had already been mortgaged in the eighteenth century, and thus clear both the mortgages and other debts he had incurred through enclosing and draining. Any surplus money from the sales was to be paid into Chancery until it was used to buy other lands to be settled in accordance with the 1801 settlement.

Sir Mark's petition for a Bill was brought to the House of Lords in February 1811, drawn up and promoted by Robert Scott, Sir Mark's York solicitor. In the session of 1811 the Bill ran out of time; but when it was introduced again, in February 1812, it went through both houses in three months and three days, receiving the Royal Assent on 20 May.[63]

The effect of the 1812 Act on the estate was remarkable. Before 1812 there were almost no transactions involving Sir Mark Masterman Sykes in the East Riding registry of deeds (the registry which recorded all freehold land transfers in the Riding). As soon as the Act was passed, the conveyancing activity of Sykes and his trustees became much greater. Small parcels of land, cottages and farms were sold steadily from 1812, to the value of £73,500.[64]

In addition to the moderating effect on settlement of a private estate Act, life-tenants of settled land were also able to take advantage of clauses in enclosure and drainage Acts (themselves private Acts of Parliament) in order to mortgage, exchange or lease for any number of years the newly enclosed or drained land. Towards 1800 enclosure Acts came to include many standard phrases, and this tendency was reinforced by the 1801 and 1845 General Inclosure Acts. Drainage Acts followed a similar pattern.[65] Accounts of the expenses of enclosing or draining were presented to each owner or occupier, and by the Acts it was lawful for a large class of landowners under legal disabilities, including "tenants in tail or for life," with the consent of the commissioners, to charge the expenses to the lands enclosed or drained. The expenses were to be certified by the commissioners and were not to be more than £5 an acre. For example, when Sir Mark Masterman Sykes was presented with a bill, certified by the commissioners, for £3,543 for his part of the Weaverthorpe enclosure, he mortgaged the newly enclosed lands at Weaverthorpe to raise the sum demanded.[66] In a similar way private Acts for the construction of public works, canals, railways and docks, included clauses allowing life-tenants to sell land to the companies. The money paid had to be lodged in Chancery and reinvested to the uses of the settlement.[67]

The amount of land both in and out of settlement in the Sykes family is difficult to calculate in exact acreages, as they bought land almost every year and there are very few surviving rentals or surveys among the archives: every year, therefore, would need a fresh calculation. Approximate acreages and rentals of the Sledmere estates are shown in the following Table: it begins in 1823, because no figures are available for earlier years. The settlements of 1792, 1795 and 1801 name the places where land was held, but describe the tenancy by the name of the tenant and the adjoining land only, and do not give the acreage.[68]

Table IV

Sledmere estates: approximate acreage and gross rental

Date	Acreage	Gross rental[1]
1823	16,685[2]	not known
1847	25,950[3]	not known
1850	28,572[4]	£25,286[4]
1865	28,662[5]	£31,425[5]
1870	30,844[6]	£39,833[6]
1878	31,171[7]	£45,082[7]
1899	31,647[8]	£31,055[9]

1. The acreage excludes the cottages: the rental includes the cottages, but excludes woodlands, lands in hand, Sledmere Park and the home farm.
2. 1847 acreage less purchases 1823-47.
3. HCCRO/DDX/31/72 (see n.15, p.vi, post).
4. HUL/DDSY/107/4.
5. DDSY/107/6.
6. DDSY/103/7.
7. DDSY/107/8.
8. 1863 acreage plus purchases 1863-99.
9. Proposals for a mortgage in 1900, document at Crust Todd Mills & Co.

In 1801 Christopher Sykes's lands were divided between his three sons. The Sledmere estates were strictly settled: the Holderness estates and Roos were settled, but not strictly.[69] A small amount of specified land was given to the trustees of the Sledmere settlement to sell if necessary, the purchase money to be added to Christopher's personal estate. Christopher's successor, Mark, possessed very little unsettled land (principally his first wife's estates in which he had only a life interest, and also lands he bought after 1801).

Tatton Sykes I inherited his brother's settled lands by the 1801 entail, and by his brother's will made in 1819 he also inherited all Mark's unsettled land (unspecified) which was to follow the settlement of Sledmere, and the money in

Chancery which had been acquired from sales under the private estate Act of 1812.[70] The only real estate left out of settlement in 1823 was Mark Sykes's London house which he left to his widow for life and then to his in-laws.[71] From 1823 to 1847 Tatton Sykes I bought large amounts of land (9,625 acres valued at £100,000); and the vendors conveyed this land to him subject to a general power of appointment, with a proviso that if no appointment was made, the lands were to pass to his trustees: these lands were not settled until 1847. Tatton Sykes I's purchases were known as his "free lands" and represented "the greater portion"[72] of the Sledmere estates. In the 1847 settlement all the land Tatton Sykes I possessed was strictly settled except one manor, which was given to the younger son in fee simple, but settled as soon as he came of age.[73] Between 1847 and 1863 (the year of his death) Tatton Sykes I continued to buy land (another 1,480 acres) to add to the Sledmere estates, which was not settled until 1863. In 1863 all the land was again brought into strict settlement.[74]

After 1863 Tatton Sykes II went on buying lands (1,647 acres between 1863 and 1900), but these lands were not settled until 1900,[75] when they were settled subject to a general power of appointment to be exercised by Tatton Sykes II; if he did not exercise his power, those lands were to pass to Mark in strict settlement.

The outline of the area settled is clear, even if the exact acreages are not. Although almost all the land was eventually settled, it was not settled as soon as it was bought: it was not settled until the next main settlement. So there was almost always some "free land" which the life-tenant could mortgage or sell - land which he had bought since the last settlement. The limited amount of freedom this allowed depended on the estates continuing to grow. Some of the land bought was sold again: for instance, Tatton Sykes I bought the manor house and land at Barmby Moor in 1861, but it was sold again almost at once, and does not appear in the 1863 rental. It is not easy to trace lands that were bought and sold quickly, as the title deeds did not stay with the Sykes's estate records, but went to the purchaser.

In addition to the "free land", the only land that could be sold or mortgaged had to be specified in the settlements. The land in this category was a small amount in 1801 in Hull, Beverley and North Yorkshire (which was sold by Mark Masterman Sykes before 1812); and the lands which bore the Family Mortgage in 1863 (which were not sold).

As the nineteenth century advanced, the legal position of the life-tenant became less constricted. From 1833 there were numerous statutes dealing with real estate and conveyancing.[76] Many of the Acts, however, were permissive (which meant that they could be barred by the settlement); and some of the benefits to life-tenants depended upon the agreement of Chancery (which did not always return a rapid or positive answer), or the agreement of the Inclosure Commissioners. The greatest change came in 1882, when through the operation of the Settled Land Act the family capital that the land represented became the subject of the settlement, not necessarily the land itself: so it became possible, after 1882, for a life-tenant to sell his estates (though not usually the family house and park) so long as the money was kept to the uses of the settlement. There is no evidence that the Sykes family ever made use of the liberating statutes of the nineteenth century: as Dicey observed long ago, the paradox of the land law was that incessant modifications or reforms of the law left the fundamentals unchanged;[77] the framework of settlement remained unaltered throughout the century,[78] and the Sykes family's settlement of 1900 was only marginally different from that of 1801.

The economic effects of settlement on estates are usually discussed in terms of accumulation and preservation of estates; indebtedness of the life-tenant for jointures and portions; shortage of capital available to the life-tenant; and shortage of, or reluctance to invest, income. Accumulation and preservation were alleged to disorder the land market, and the indebtedness or shortage of capital and income were alleged to hinder the development of agriculture.[79]

The Sledmere estates certainly grew in the nineteenth century (see Table IV), but in this family accumulation was not primarily through marriage (see Table III). The time of greatest growth was between 1823 and 1847, when Tatton Sykes I was life-tenant; he added 9,625 acres to the Sledmere estates in those twenty-four years, an average annual increase of some 400 acres. None of this land was acquired through marriage or inheritance. The only land in the nineteenth century that might have come to the Sykes family through marriage was that of Henrietta Masterman: but as her husband had no children, the land reverted to the Masterman family. It was not settlement that caused the Sledmere acreage to grow, but settlement provided the opportunity for income to grow, and with a surplus income, the Sykes family bought lands to increase their estates.

The source of the wealth which funded the Sykes family's accumulation of land was mainly agricultural. It is not possible within the confines of this chapter to give an adequate account of their agricultural improvements; but they were famous farmers, especially Sir Christopher and Tatton Sykes I, and their work in transforming their estates is well recorded.[80] Most of their lands were on the high and windswept Wolds, around Sledmere, and it was here that their dramatic improvements in agriculture took place. The Sykes family transformed the rabbit warrens described by Arthur Young and other writers[81] and unenclosed sheepwalks, which would in the 1760s let for 1s. an acre,[82] into some of the most highly cultivated farms in the country, which by 1850 were let at an average of more than 16s. an acre.[83] From 1850 to 1880 the rents of the Sledmere estates rose steadily to an average of 27s. an acre in 1878.[84] Much of the agricultural income of the estates was used to buy further land.

Tatton Sykes I spent about £121,316 in buying 11,105 acres between 1823 and 1863; the most expensive of his purchases was £50,000 paid for four farms containing 1,800 acres which he bought in 1834.[85] All the purchase money came from his own income which was almost entirely drawn from the estate rents.

Tatton Sykes II bought much less land, 1,650 acres in 37 years, the largest purchase being 900 acres in 1866.[86]

Allied to the Sykes's agricultural income was that of the stud. It was founded in 1801 and was carried on enthusiastically into the twentieth century. How much it made is doubtful: it was at one time the largest stud in England, and yearlings at the annual Sledmere sale fetched large sums of money: about £14,000 a year in the 1890's and about £23,000 a year in the early twentieth century.[87] But the expenses of the stud were so enormous that on average there was no profit: this was accepted by a court in the 1890s.[88] The stud was not counted as part of the settled estates, but was the personal property of the life-tenant.

In the nineteenth century the Sykes family's commercial interests were few. The only industrial venture in which they were involved was a carpet mill near Driffield (the Wansford mill) which never produced a large income and was closed in 1817.[89] Christopher Sykes's partnership in the Hull bank which he had founded in 1791 was dissolved in 1801, and although Tatton Sykes I worked in the bank for some years as a young man, the premises were sold in 1811 by his brother Mark, and the family did not seem to have been interested in maintaining the connection.[90]

The family's investments were mainly in government stock. In 1847 Tatton Sykes I had £103,000 in 3% Consols, a sum which he had increased to £287,774 in 1863: but the income on even the larger sum (about £8,633) was much less than the rent receipts. Tatton Sykes II owned railway shares as well as other investments,[91] and in 1897 in the course of a law suit he proved that his investments brought him c. £12,000 a year and his net estate income was c. £20,000 a year.[92] Unfortunately, there are no account books available which might show the family's investments year by year; but it would appear that the family owned large amounts of capital, in sound but not speculative stock, and added to it constantly. The capital in stocks and shares mentioned above was the personal property of the life-tenant, not subject to settlement, so that the life-tenant could dispose of it as he wished.

Three members of the family were members of Parliament, Sir Christopher between 1784 and 1790, Sir Mark Masterman for York between 1807 and 1820, and his nephew Christopher between 1865 and 1898. But none of them held office, and their other public appointments, such as High Sheriff and J.P., were unpaid. The recorded expenses of Christopher Sykes of Brantingham Thorpe in his election for Beverley in 1865 were £3,400 and for the East Riding in 1868 were £4,169.[93] Sir Mark contested York in 1807, legendary as a very expensive election. Serving as an M.P., without office, can hardly have been a profitable venture, even though the rewards of prestige and occasional jobbery may have satisfied the family.

As a device for preserving land, the family settlement worked very well for the Sykes family: settlement with its brakes or drags on alienation of land held the Sledmere estates throughout the nineteenth century. It enabled the estates to survive the life-tenancy of Sir Mark, so that after twenty-one years of his extravagance, the estate emerged heavily encumbered but still a unit. From 1823 until the end of the century Sledmere flourished under the two Sir Tattons - nothing had to be sold off, lands were bought and settled, and the family lavishly provided for. So the family's purpose in settling the estates, which was to prevent alienation of land and to provide for the widows and younger children, was achieved.

The problem of indebtedness for jointures and portions was not a serious one: mostly the Sykes men outlived their wives, and they did not all have six daughters. Portions were only paid once, under the 1847 settlement: by the Family Mortgage of £121,316.

It cannot be said that the effect of family settlement in the Sykes family was to make them short of either capital or income. Tatton Sykes I's massive land purchases, and Tatton Sykes II's repayment of the Family Mortgage, show a continuing prosperity and ability to find capital out of income.

Every year that the net income of the estate was recorded there was a large surplus of income over expenditure;[94] and the family is said to have rebuilt farms, cottages, planted hedges, shelter belts, woods, bred sheep and horses, apparently without counting the cost. In 1900 Sir Tatton Sykes II claimed that £8,000 to £10,000 was spent on property improvements each year, about 30% of the rental.[95] Some of the family's forms of conspicuous expenditure were unusual: Tatton Sykes II estimated that he had spent £150,000 in building or rebuilding East Riding churches,[96] and both he and his father built and maintained village schools. In other expenditure on horses, hounds and houses they followed the example of their peers.

At the time of Christopher Sykes's death in 1801 the Sledmere estates went into strict settlement, a condition in which they were to remain (except for a few hours in 1847 and 1900) until 1927 and beyond. During the period discussed, there were four main settlements: one was a settlement made by will, the others were all by deed inter vivos. Three were made within a few weeks of the tenant in tail, the heir, coming of age, that is, as soon as it was possible to break the existing settlement. None of the main Sykes family's settlements of the nineteenth century were made on the marriage of the heir. The estates were held by a succession of life-tenants, and there was never a tenant in tail in possession, and never an owner of a fee simple at Sledmere. The operation of the Sykes's settlements is an example of one of the ways - it may have been the most usual way - for nineteenth century landowners to maintain their estates.

From a wider economic viewpoint, there is no doubt that the practice of strict settlement in this family restricted the scope of the local land market. For the most part the Sykes family did not want to sell; if they had wanted to, they could only sell newly bought land. There was never the slightest chance of the core of land of the Sledmere estates being sold; on the contrary, the family bought steadily to consolidate the area within ten miles of any part of the estate. The family maintained the kind of perpetual settlement, in practice if not in law, which the "free trade in land" reformers attacked unavailingly for most of the nineteenth century.

NOTES

1. M. Townsend, "Introduction" to J.L. Sandford and M. Townsend, The Great Governing Families of England 1 (1865), p.1. I am grateful to Sir Tatton Sykes of Sledmere Bt for his permission to use his family's archives for this article, Messrs Crust Todd Mills & Co., of Beverley for allowing me to work in their offices, and the archivists of Hull University and Humberside County Record Office for their help. I also wish to thank Professor John Saville of the University of Hull for commenting on earlier drafts, and for his generous help and encouragement. I have benefited greatly from discussions and correspondence with Eileen Spring, whose comments, particularly on jointures and portions, have influenced my views. The research on which this paper is based was funded by the Social Science Research Council.
2. F.M.L. Thompson, English Landed Society in the Nineteenth Century (1963), p.50.
3. See M. Chesterman, "Family Settlements on Trust: Landowners and the Rising Bourgeoisie", supra. See also for the trust for sale and the strict settlement, J.M. Lightwood, "Trusts for Sale" Cambridge Law Journal 3 (1929), pp.59-74, and E. Spring, "The Settlement of Land in Nineteenth-Century England" American Journal of Legal History 8 (1964), pp.209-23.
4. "By proof it appears a strict settlement was intended", from T. Vernon, Chancery Cases II (1728), p.659. A clear definition was given by H.J. Stephen in 1841, New Commentaries on the Laws of England I (1841), pp.306-7: "When land is settled . . . by a limitation to the parent for life, and after his death to his first and other sons in tail, and trustees are interposed to preserve the contingent remainders, this is called a strict settlement." Both these examples are cited in the Oxford English Dictionary 10 (1933), p.1120. For strict settlement generally, see B. English and J. Saville, Strict Settlement: a Guide for Historians (University of Hull Occasional Papers in Economic

and Social History No. 10; for strict settlements made on marriage, see L. Bonfield, Marriage Settlements 1601-1740 (1983).

5. By the statute De Donis Conditionalibus (1285) entails were protected by law.
6. The life interest was based on an interpretation of the Statute of Uses (1535).
7. See M. Chesterman, supra.
8. Waste is discussed by J. Williams, The Settlement of Real Estates (1879), pp.228-39.
9. An analysis of the nineteeenth century criticism of the land laws and of settlement can be found in F.M.L. Thompson, "The Economic and Social Background of the Landed Interest, 1840-1870", Oxford D. Phil., (1956). See also the same author's "The Land Market in the Nineteenth Century", Oxford Economic Papers NS 9 (1957), pp.285-308; "Land and Politics in England in the Nineteenth Century", Transactions of the Royal Historical Society 5th ser. 15 (1965), pp.23-44; "The Social Distribution of Landed Property in England since the Sixteenth Century", Economic History Review 2nd ser. XIX (1966), pp.471-86; "Landownership and Economic Growth in England in the Eighteenth Century", in E.L. Jones and S.J. Woolf eds., Agrarian Change and Economic Development (1969), pp.41-60. Adam Smith, J.S. Mill and Bentham criticised the practice of settlement (see E. Spring, "Landowners, Lawyers and Land Law Reform in Nineteenth-Century England" American Journal of Legal History 21 (1977), pp.40-59). Among the numerous nineteeenth century writers on land reform were J. Beal, Free Trade in Land (1855); J. Kay, Free Trade in Land (1879); A. Arnold, Free Land (1880), and G.C. Brodrick, English Land and English Landlords (1881). Both The Economist and The Spectator were among the periodicals which carried many articles about the necessity for land law reform; there was a vast amount of writing, including pamphlet literature, on the land question in the nineteenth century. In the twentieth century, the analysis that concentration of land was due to settlement was developed by Sir John Habakkuk: see his articles "English

Landownership 1680-1740", Economic History Review 1st ser. 10 (1939-40), pp.2-17; "Marriage Settlements in the Eighteenth Century" TRHS 4th ser. 32 (1950), pp.15-30; "England" in The European Nobility in the Eighteenth Century, ed. A. Godwin (1953), pp.1-21; "The English Land Market in the Eighteenth Century" in Britain and the Netherlands, ed. J.S. Bromley and E.H. Kossman (1960), pp.154-73; "The Rise and Fall of English Landed Families, 1600-1800" TRHS 5th ser. 29 (1979), pp.187-207. Habakkuk's views have recently been subjected to criticism from J.V. Beckett, "English Landownership in the Later Seventeenth and Eighteenth Centuries: the Debate and the Problems" Economic History Review 2nd ser. 30 (1977), pp.567-81; B.A. Holderness, "The English Land Market in the Eighteenth Century: the Case of Lincolnshire" Economic History Review 2nd ser. 27 (1974), pp.557-76; C. Clay, "Marriage, Inheritance and the Rise of Large Estates in England, 1660-1815" Economic History Review 2nd ser. 21 (1968), pp.503-18. See M. Chesterman, supra., and E. Spring, supra. See also L. Bonfield, "Marriage Settlements and the 'Rise of Great Estates': the Demographic Aspect" Economic History Review 2nd ser. XXXII (1979), pp.483-93; B. English and J. Saville, "Family Settlement and the 'Rise of Great Estates' " Economic History Review 2nd ser. XXXIII (1980), pp.556-8; L. Bonfield, "Marriage Settlements and the 'Rise of Great Estates': a Rejoinder" Economic History Review 2nd ser. XXXIII (1980), pp.559-63.

10. J. Bateman, The Great Landowners of Great Britain and Ireland (1883). The work was first published in 1877 as The Acre-Ocracy of England; then revised and expanded under the title The Great Landowners of Great Britain and Ireland in 1878 and further revised for the 1879 and 1883 editions.
11. J. Bateman, op.cit., (1883), p.511.
12. Estimates from F.M.L. Thompson, English Landed Society in the Nineteenth Century (1963), pp.66-7.
13. A. Underhill, "Changes in the Law of Real Property" in A Century of Law

Reform (1901), p.282. The nickname "The Forty Thieves" is mentioned in the same author's Change and Decay (1938), p.91.

14. E. Spring, "The Settlement of Land in Nineteenth-Century England" American Journal of Legal History 8 (1964), pp.209-23; W.A. Maguire, "The 1822 Settlement of the Donegall Estates" Irish Economic and Social History 3 (1976), pp.17-32. Works dealing incidentally with family settlement in the nineteenth century include W.A. Maguire, The Downshire Estates in Ireland, 1801-1845 (1972); R.S. Gourley, "The Social and Economic History of the Gosford Estates 1610-1876", Belfast M.Sc. (1973); T.W. Beastall, A North Country Estate: The Lumleys and Saundersons as Landowners, 1600-1900 (1975); R.A.C. Parker, Coke of Norfolk: a Financial and Agricultural Study 1707-1842 (1975); F.C. Mather, After the Canal Duke (1970). Good family histories or biographies often contain passing references to family settlement, but not detailed investigations.

15. Calculation based on Bateman, op.cit., (1883). The official return gives the same acreage to Sir Tatton Sykes II ("Return of Owners of Land 1872-3" Parliamentary Papers, 1874, LXXII). It is not clear how the figure of 34,010 acres recorded in the official return and accepted by Bateman related to the acreage of rented land shown in Table IV below. The Sykes family archives are for the most part deposited in Hull University Library (HUL) and referred to by the catalogue numbers DDSY. Documents relating to the trusts set up by Tatton Sykes I, formerly in the custody of the London solicitors Messrs. May, May and Deacon, are in the Humberside County Council Record Office (HCCRO) and referred to as DDX/31. The Beverley solicitors, Messrs. Crust Todd Mills & Co., have a further ten boxes of Sykes' papers, mainly from the nineteenth and twentieth centuries.

16. HUL/DDSY/101/13,52.

17. J. Williams, The Settlement of Real Estates (1879), p.40.

18. HUL/DDSY/108/13.

19. HUL/DDSY/110/30. Will dated 10 August; he died on 17 September 1801.

20. The debts and legacies amounted to more than £87,500: "Proceedings at Committees on Private Bills and other Matters", Session 1812, House of Lords R.O.

21. See E. Spring, supra.

22. This limit was ignored when portions were actually raised in 1863, because the portions were charged on land which had been bought between 1823 and 1847, and therefore had not been settled in 1801.

23. This was because it was legally possible for a life-tenant to demand a large entry payment and allow an artificially low rent thereafter, so acquiring more money for himself at the expense of his successor (who inherited the low rent but not the payment for entry) unless this was barred by the settlement.

24. "Waste" was spoil and destruction done by a tenant for life to the property he held for life. See above, p.210.

25. Proof that this money was spent was given to the House of Lords Committee in 1812: "Proceedings at Committees on Private Bills and other Matters", Session 1812, House of Lords R.O.

26. See p.232, post.

27. This is an over-simplification. The settlement was made in 1847 and took effect then, but some of its provisions (for instance, the younger children's money settlement) did not come into effect until the death of Tatton Sykes I in 1863.

28. The original deeds were at these locations in 1983:

    22 June 1847, conveyance of Ryhill: Crust Todd Mills & Co., Beverley;

    29 June 1847, disentailing deed: HUL/DDSY/108/26;

    30 June 1847, strict settlement of the Sledmere estates: Crust Todd Mills & Co;

    1 July 1847, strict settlement of the Holderness estates: Crust Todd Mills &

Co;

2 July 1847, money settlement: HCCRO/DDX/31/77;

6 July 1847, Tatton Sykes I's will, probate copy: HUL/DDSY/110/36.

29. There were difficulties in constructing a strict settlement around a minor, and Christopher was not of age until 1852. He was given Ryhill absolutely, and the promise of land worth £5,000 provided that when he came of age he settled both Ryhill and the Holderness estates strictly; which of course he did.

30. HCCRO/DDX/31/53. A large proportion of this was from the sale of the stud horses.

31. J. Williams, The Settlement of Real Estates (1879), p.219.

32. Standard forms of settlement are illustrated in H.W. Elphinstone, Introduction to Conveyancing (1871 and later editions) and J. Williams, The Settlement of Real Estates (1879), and in precedent books such as W.M. Bythewood and T. Jarman, Conveyancing (1827 and later editions), C. Davidson, Precedents and Forms in Conveyancing (1845 and later editions) and T. Key and H.W. Elphinstone, Precedents in Conveyancing (1878 and later editions).

33. The type of deed used in a settlement varied from time to time: see W. Holdsworth, A History of English Law 7 (1925), pp.376-80. In 1841 a simple release was substituted for the older lease and release: this was a legal contradiction, as nothing could be released which had not already been transferred in some way. In 1845 the release was generally superseded by a deed of grant, although the release form continued valid. The form used by the Sykes family in 1847 was, therefore, already old fashioned.

34. Distraint, or distress, was the right to seize property for non-payment of rent, or in this case, an annuity.

35. For the different types of fee tail, see M. Harwood, English Land Law (1975), p.13. Tail male meant succession by male descendants; tail general, any descendant.

36. G.D. Squibb, "The End of the Name and Arms Clause?" Law Quarterly Review 69 (1959), pp.219-25.

37. But unlike 1801, the life-tenants of 1847 were not themselves liable for waste.

38. HCCRO/DDX/31/49/98.

39. J. Williams, The Settlement of Real Estates (1879), pp.220-1, 250,320-37.

40. Crust Todd Mills & Co., (original mortgage deed): HCCRO/DDX/31/78-83, related papers.

41. HCCRO/DDX/31/49-53.

42. Lewin on Trusts ed. W. Banks (1928), p.738.

43. Mortgage deed at Crust Todd Mills & Co.

44. HUL/DDSY/108/30.

45. She had borrowed over £13,000 at a rate of 60% per annum from a money-lender called Jay in 1896: for the disclaimer, the case Jay brought, and other Sykes family law suits of this period, see The Times, 7, 14 December 1896 and 13-19 January 1898; also R. Adelson, Mark Sykes, Portrait of an Amateur (1975), pp.49-50, 71-4.

46. The schedule of her debts is at Crust Todd Mills & Co. The making of the 1900 settlement is described in HUL/DDSY(2)/1/2a.

47. Settlement at Crust Todd Mills & Co. Mark's annuity was to go up in stages, in 1904 and 1909.

48. HUL/DDSY/97/7.

49. The marriage settlement permitted Mark's sons by any wife to succeed to the Masterman estates: an unusual clause.

50. HUL/DDSY/98/77.

51. M.C.F. Morris, Yorkshire Reminiscences (1922), p.215. Morris knew the Sykes family very well, from about 1850. Mark Masterman Sykes was a collector (his books and pictures were sold for £34,000 in 1824); he kept a pack of hounds and ran a stud; he engaged in expensive elections such as York

in 1807; he and his wife rebuilt the entire village and manor house of Settrington; he was also a gambler, who (for instance) bet the local parson in 1802 that if he would give him 100 guineas, Sykes would give him a guinea for each day Napoleon continued to live. See also J. Fairfax-Blakeborough, Sykes of Sledmere (1929), pp.48-53; K.J. Allison, The East Riding of Yorkshire Landscape (1976), p.189.

52. HUL/DDSY/108/74: the brothers had to agree to the increase, as it exceeded the powers of jointure allowed in the 1801 settlement.

53. Marriage settlement at Crust Todd Mills & Co.

54. R. Adelson, op.cit., p.18; C.S. Sykes, The Visitors' Book (1978), p.70.

55. Abstract at Crust Todd Mills & Co.

56. See p.215, ante.

57. HCCRO/DDX/31/49.

58. F. Pollock, The Land Laws (1896), pp.119-20.

59. H.W. Elphinstone, Introduction to Conveyancing (1900), p.431.

60. HUL/DDSY/98/76.

61. HUL/DDSY/98/78.

62. HCCRO/DDX/31/49-98. The trust continued into the twentieth century.

63. House of Lords Journals XLVIII (1811, 1812), pp.97,117,581,610-11,623,699-700,722,833,844; House of Commons Journals LXVII (1811,1812), pp.282,323-4,367; HUL/DDSY/97/7-9 and 98/76. Unfortunately there are no Sykes' papers which show the cost of the private estate Act.

64. HUL/DDSY/98/77.

65. General Inclosure Acts, 41 Geo.II c.109 and 8 & 9 Vict. c.118. For drainage Acts, see E. Spring, "Landowners, Lawyers and Land Law Reform in Nineteenth-Century England" American Journal of Legal History 21 (1977), p.46.

66. HUL/DDSY/97/7-9.

67. A. Underhill, "Property" Law Quarterly Review 51 (1935), p.226.

68. For instance, "all that messuage and 2 closes of land now or lately in the

occupation of AB lying between the lands of CD to the north and the common road leading to . . ." etc.

69. See p.215, ante.

70. See p.232, ante.

71. Mark Masterman Sykes's will is HUL/DDSY/110/34.

72. Settlement deeds of 1847: see note 28, ante.

73. See p.218, ante.

74. Deed at Crust Todd Mills & Co.

75. Two deeds of 1900 at Crust Todd Mills & Co.

76. A.V. Dicey, "The Paradox of the Land Law" Law Quarterly Review 21 (1905), pp.221-32; A. Underhill, "Changes in the Law of Real Property" in A Century of Law Reform (1901), pp.280-341; idem "Property" Law Quarterly Review 51 (1935), pp.221-34.

77. A.V. Dicey, loc.cit., p.221.

78. E. Spring, "Landowners, Lawyers and Land Law Reform in Nineteenth-Century England" American Journal of Legal History 21 (1977), pp.40-59.

79. A list of some articles on accumulation and preservation is given in note 9, ante. Indebtedness of the life-tenant is discussed by D. Cannadine, "Aristocratic Indebtedness in the Nineteenth Century: the Case Re-opened" Economic History Review 2nd ser. 30 (1977), pp.624-50, who also reviews the earlier literature (writings by D. Spring and F.M.L. Thompson). See also D. Spring, "Aristocratic Indebtedness in the Nineteenth Century: a Comment" and D. Cannadine, "Aristocratic Indebtedness in the Nineteenth Century: a Restatement" Economic History Review 2nd ser. XXXIII (1980), pp.564-73. Shortage of capital and shortage of income was alleged by the nineteenth century reformers, some of whom are named in note 9 above. The case was put forcibly by J. Caird, The Landed Interest (1878), pp.79-80 and J. Kay, Free Trade in Land (1879), pp.50-2.

80. See for instance, G. Legard, "Farming of the East Riding of Yorkshire"

Journal of Royal Agricultural Society of England 1st ser. 9 (1848), pp.85-136; O. Wilkinson, *The Agricultural Revolution in the East Riding of Yorkshire* (1956); A. Harris, *The Rural Landscape of the East Riding of Yorkshire 1700-1850* (1961); K.J. Allison, *The East Riding of Yorkshire Landscape* (1976).

81. A. Young, *A Six Months Tour Through the North of England* 2 Vols (1770); W. Marshall, *The Rural Economy of Yorkshire* 2 Vols. (1788); A Harris, "The Rabbit Warrens of East Yorkshire in the Eighteenth and Nineteenth Centuries" *Yorkshire Archaeological Journal* 42 (1970), pp.429-43.

82. Legard, *loc.cit.*, pp.93,94,96,103; Young, *op.cit.*, II, p.13.

83. Legard, *loc.cit.*, p.95, calculation from the property tax returns. Similar figures can be ascertained from the Sykes's rentals, HUL/DDSY/107.

84. HUL/DDSY/107.

85. HUL/DDSY/64/24.

86. Two deeds at Crust Todd Mills & Co.

87. For the stud, see J. Fairfax-Blakeborough, *op.cit.*, *passim*: figures based on pp.235-6.

88. The *Law Times*, 9 October 1897.

89. HUL/DDSY/68; further documents in Crust Todd Mills & Co.

90. W.C.E. Hartley, *Banking in Yorkshire* (1975), pp.95-6; HCCRO, Registry of Deeds, CR/526.

91. HUL/DDSY/109/15.

92. The *Law Times*, 9 October 1897.

93. Evidence given to the Beverley Bribery Commission, p.460; Beverley Library, local history collection, Vol.C, p.8.

94. There are few account books in the Sykes's estate records. Some figures for the 1880s, based on the available records, are printed in J.T. Ward, *East Yorkshire Landed Estates in the Nineteenth Century* (1967), p.16.

95. Proposals to float a loan, a duplicated document circulated amongst insurance companies and other potential lenders. Copies at Crust Todd Mills & Co.

96. This figure is often misquoted as £1,500,000 (e.g. by M.C.F. Morris, op.cit., pp.223-6, who lists twenty churches which the Sykes family improved). "Spy" drew Tatton Sykes II in 1879 with the caption "Fifteen Churches", Vanity Fair, 23 August 1879. For Sykes's church and school building, see B. English, "On the Eve of the Great Depression: the Economy of the Sledmere Estates 1869-1878" Business History XXIV (1982), p.36.

LAW, POVERTY AND IMPRISONMENT FOR DEBT, 1869-1914

G.R. Rubin

"If there was one thing more than another which pressed hardly upon the working-classes, it was the power of committal possessed by the County Court judges."

Alexander Stavely Hill M.P. (1869)

I: INTRODUCTION

One of the hoariest legends of modern legal history is that imprisonment for debt in England was finally abolished in the later nineteenth century. Thus, it is widely believed that in the wake of the appearance of Dickens' Pickwick Papers in 1836, first, arrest on mesne (i.e., middle) process was abolished in 1838 under the Act 1 & 2 Vict., c.110.[1] Second, so the legend tell us - and dutifully repeated in the most respectable of publications[2] - arrest on final process, that is, imprisonment for debt, ceased to exist in 1869. It was supposedly swept away by the Debtors Act of that year (32 & 33 Vict., c.62), a measure unequivocally entitled "An Act for the Abolition of Imprisonment for Debt . . . ." The title, however, was a cruel and ironic deception. For instead of abolishing the civil sanction against the body, the Act proceeded to grant it a new lease of life by enacting a "saving power of committal for small debts." In effect, imprisonment for debt was being retained only in the case of those small consumer debtors whose grinding poverty prevented their meeting their everyday household bills. Compelled through penury to acquire most domestic items on credit, the "insolvent poor" remained the last hostage to a sanction supposedly done away with. Thus, the transition to a market economy, which in turn stimulated an "improved" process of consumer debt collection through the county courts, was, perhaps incongruously, accompanied by the retention of a sanction designed for the medieval age. As a result, for another one hundred years, many thousands of poor consumer debtors, but the poor alone, continued to be exposed to the intimidation of the "body warrant". Moreover, the measure proved particularly resistant to change during this period, its defenders successfully invoking moral, judicial and economic arguments (some of which were scarcely soundly based) in order to counter those predominantly humanitarian views ranged against its continued existence.

The present study is, therefore, an examination of one specific feature, imprisonment for debt, attaching to the process of consumer debt collecting through the county courts in the later nineteenth and early twentieth centuries. A number of reasons will be advanced in this paper in order to explain why it was possible for the legislature to retain imprisonment for debt whilst simultaneously enacting a measure purporting to abolish it. Such reasons, not necessarily in ascending order of significance, include that inertia characteristic of legal institutions, which habitually militates against change; together with the not unconnected hostility of legal personnel such as county court judges and registrars to any such change; the deafening silence of labour representatives preoccupied with reforming only the criminal laws and safety laws affecting trade unions and the working-class; the apparent uncritical acceptance by the working-class and poor debtors of the market ideology underpinning the sanction; the success of the judicial strategy to mystify the social phenomenon of committals by redefining imprisonment juridically as a punishment for contempt of court, rather than for failure to pay off a judgment debt; the belief that the threat of a committal was indeed an effective deterrent against default; and, finally, the conviction that the threat of imprisonment for debt, and indeed the infliction of the penalty itself, was an essential element in what was perceived by retentionists as a struggle to reform working-class habits away from extravagance and towards "sound household economy."

Whilst acknowledging the solid ideological base upon which this last-named argument, in particular, is built, it should be recognised that the retentionists possessed no monopoly of ideologically grounded theories informing policy prescriptions. For a number of abolitionists shared an image of working-class spending habits which, in fact, differed little from that of many retentionists anxious to preserve the system of committals. Both were committed to the view that the plight of the poor debtor was, basically, caused by the latter's inability to manage his own domestic arrangements successfully, rather than by the structural factors of old age, unemployment or poverty earnings. The espousal by abolitionists of repeal of the Debtors Act can principally be ascribed to two forces, the first of which was the ideology of "humanitarianism" informing the activities of many penal reform associations. The second factor was the commitment to the ideology of equality before the law. Thus, the visible contrast between the treatment afforded to bankrupts and that meted out to poor debtors stung many middle class reformers into action. In this respect, it perhaps paralleled the campaign (which included the support of those hostile to trade unionism in general) to obtain the repeal of the blatantly discriminatory Master and Servant law which prescribed criminal punishments for workers but only civil liabilities for employers.[3]

There was perhaps, therefore, more to unite the opposing forces on the issue of imprisonment for debt in the case of small debtors than there was to divide them. Both factions adhered to market principles and to the role of the courts in the debt recovery system; though they differed, of course, over the lengths to which debtors might be coerced. Both, moreover, thought that they detected similar failings in working-class mores and social economics and both desired to rectify these shortcomings, merely disagreeing over the means.

The campaign over imprisonment for debt, while casting light on the process of debt recovery through the county courts - wherein the real struggle over nineteenth century "contract" law surely took place[4] - was, therefore, conducted as a middle class diversion far removed from the structural issues surrounding the poverty which brought poor debtors to the county courts in the first place. Were the campaign of reform to have been successful, it would have offered no solution to the genuine problem, that of poverty.

II: THE LEGISLATIVE BACKGROUND

The purported abolition of imprisonment for debt in 1869 took place simultaneously with further reforms in bankruptcy law. This conjunction of objectives was not fortuitous. For the abolition of imprisonment for debt and the expansion of bankruptcy proceedings were two sides of the same coin, in that the structural principles of bankruptcy law on the one hand and of civil proceedings against the body on the other, stand in contradiction to one another. While the object of the former is to enable creditors to share equitably and to permit debtors to undergo a laundering process, offering them the opportunity of a fresh start free from debt, the object of committals was, by contrast, to substitute imprisonment for payment of the debt. The former procedure aimed to be economically rational, the latter to be punitive or obstructive to economic efficiency; an individual imprisoned for debt was not easily capable of pursuing remunerative activities and, thus, being able to pay off his debts.[5]

The nineteenth century legislative history of imprisonment for debt prior to 1869 was marked, first, by the abolition of arrest on mesne process in 1838, as we have already noted. This was followed in 1844 (by the Act 7 & 8 Vict., c.96) by the supposed cessation of arrest on final process for debts of less than £20. With the passing of the major Bankruptcy Act 1861 (24 & 25 Vict., c.134), bankruptcy status was extended to non-traders as well as to traders, thereby effecting a virtually complete encroachment by bankruptcy law on the territory previously occupied by imprisonment for debt. The Debtors Act 1869, together with the Bankruptcy Act of that year (32 & 33 Vict., c.71), put the last nail, so it was widely believed, in the coffin of the body warrant.

The assumptions informing these changes in the law were, first, that the creditor would prefer to choose the more "efficient" object of seeking the recovery of his debt, rather than choose the gratuitous and "irrational" imprisonment of his debtor as an object in itself. Second, it was assumed that the debtor's conduct was, throughout, honest, and was not tainted by misconduct, dishonesty or fraud. However, Parliament, from the 1844 Act onwards, slowly and gradually built up a reaction to the very reforms which it itself had implemented, by constantly widening the scope of behaviour on the part of debtors which would continue to render them liable to imprisonment for debt. Perhaps Parliament was indeed incapable of divesting itself of the view that there was something dishonest or fraudulent in the poor of the nation contracting debts. Whatever the explanation, the reaction, which later took a new twist with the Debtors Act 1869, commenced with a provision in the 1844 Act (which, as we saw, abolished imprisonment on final process for small debts). This measure expressly excluded cases of fraud, or misconduct by debtors amounting to fraud, from the scope of abolition. In itself, this provision was perhaps an unimpeachable safeguard. Nonetheless, it failed to placate critics, and a vigorous middle class campaign to revive imprisonment for small debts was immediately launched. As a result of the 1844 Act, it was claimed,

> "... immense sums were at once confiscated, and a state of lawless fraud and imposture destroyed many honourable traders, who had done no other wrong than to have parted in the ordinary course of commerce with various portions of their capital or of the fruits of their industry, or both, accepting a most useful, common and indispensable currency, - 'a word-of-mouth promise to pay'. This currency, which had been much debased by former Acts, was nearly destroyed by the Act of 1844, for then the real power of compelling its conversion in any more permanent form [i.e., imprisonment] was annihilated."[6]

The result of the campaign was an Act the following year (8 & 9 Vict., c.127) which accelerated the Parliamentary retreat from its bold innovation. Thus, under the 1845 Act, if the court thought that the debtor was, inter alia, guilty of fraud in contracting the debt or of having wilfully contracted it without any reasonable prospect of being able to pay, a prospect which the poor must have confronted every day, then the court could commit the debtor to prison for a period not exceeding 40 days. Moreover, by section 3 of the Act, a new dimension was added.

For the imprisonment was not to operate as the satisfaction or extinction of the debt even though this had been the previous practice in the courts of conscience and requests. The conclusion was clear. The law had become more severe towards small debtors than before.

The following year saw the enactment of the landmark measure, the County Courts Act 1846 (9 & 10 Vict., c.95). Once again, it was provided, in sections 99 to 101, that the debtor's "misconduct" in contracting without any reasonable prospect of repayment merited imprisonment for not more than 40 days.[7] A similar account could be told of the Bankruptcy Act 1861, cited earlier, which, in abolishing the Insolvent Debtors' Court and in emptying the debtors' gaols, expressly denied release from imprisonment for those whose debts did not exceed £20 or who were in custody under an order made in accordance with the County Courts Act.

The story of the progressive removal of imprisonment for debt is also, therefore, the story of the progressive tightening of the sanction against the very poor. The Debtors Act 1869, added a further dimension to this pattern and is, in fact, the legislative culmination of this development in the nineteenth century. It is hardly surprising that in 1859, one judge, Serjeant Storks, sitting at Bow County Court, declaimed in anger,

> "The Legislature had almost abolished imprisonment for debt; but they are a cowardly Legislature, a cowardly lot, and they have not done it."[8]

III: THE DEBTORS ACT 1869

The Debtors Bill which appeared in April 1869,[9] seemed at last to embody the commitment which its title, declaring the intention to abolish committals, indubitably indicated. The Times,[10] in acknowledging its assumed historical significance, noted that "few measures compete in interest and practical importance" with the proposed Act. Arrest as a coercive enforcement of debt was, it thought, now "obsolete", while the belief in a "natural and necessary connection between debt and this special penalty" was an "ancient" doctrine. It drew the conclusion, therefore, that abolition of imprisonment for debt, "once for all is only a further extension of the province of bankruptcy." It, therefore, looked forward to the rapid interment of a medieval punishment.

But law has an infinite capacity for mystification. Co-terminous with the allegedly final abolition of the traditional system of imprisonment for debt by the enactment of the 1869 Act, the government, in what amounted in substance, if not in form, to a complete about-turn, inserted in section 5 of the statute a "saving power of committal for small debts." This provided that, following a court order or judgment,

> "5 . . . any court may commit to prison for a term not exceeding six weeks or until payment of the sum due, any person who makes default in payment of any debt or instalment or any debt due from him . . .
> (2) that such jurisdiction shall only be exercised where it is proved to the satisfaction of the court that the person making default either has or has had since the date of the order or judgment, the means to pay this sum in respect of which he has made default, and has refused or neglected, or refuses or neglects, to pay the same."

Thus, deviating to a greater or lesser extent from the limited grounds upon which imprisonment for debt had been retained in the legislation since 1844, section 5 (2) of the 1869 Act was couched in terms of a contumacious refusal on the part of the debtor to transfer funds to the creditor which had been in his possession. Imprisonment was, therefore, for contumacy, not for debt as under the old system; nor for fraud or its equivalent as prescribed in parts of the legislation between 1844 and 1861 (supra). Imprisonment was, moreover, to be prescribed by the judge and not by the creditor, a step suggestive of a further breach with the pre-1869 provisions. Indeed, the judges construed imprisonment for contumacy as imprisonment for contempt of court, thus completing the image of a legal procedure finally removed from the Dickensian age when imprisonment remained the punishment for poverty.

Yet the image projected was a false one. For in substance, despite the new formulas, imprisonment continued to remain the punishment for poverty under the new Act. With the county court judge having been granted discretion to accept any manner of proof of means to pay off the debt which he considered "just" in the circumstances, thus allowing plaintiffs unprecedented licence in the presentation of what passed for evidence of means to pay; with statistics revealing that "contumacious" debtors were to be found in large numbers in some circuits, and virtually absent from others, there were grounds for belief that "contumacy" was, in fact, irrelevant. This was the view of Judge Edward Parry, one of the most outspoken critics of committals, who concluded that by 1914, over 300,000 debtors had been imprisoned under section 5 (2),

> ". . . mainly for poverty or, if you will, for improvidence - that blessed word that so insidiously describes in the poor that failure in economic asceticism, that lack of cold self-denial of luxury and extravagance, that absence of patient thrift and simplicity of life - characteristic features which are never wanting in the beautiful lives of those social classes above them that the poor must learn to look up to and to imitate."[11]

Why section 5 (2) remained on the statute book for a hundred years poses problems of explanation. There were three select committee enquiries between 1873 and 1909,[12] one critical, one favourable and one with majority and minority views divided by the chairman's casting vote. It also succeeded in resisting at least a dozen private member's bills calling for its abolition or severe limitation between 1872 and 1888. Certainly, some explanations concern verifiable issues, such as the difficulties surrounding other modes of extracting funds from the debtor. The use of executions is a case in point, where the debtor simply did not possess goods to an appropriate value which could be distrained upon. But the historian of legal institutions must also be prepared to confront less concrete phenomena. In particular, the fears, prejudices and biases of individuals, particularly, in this case, of those in favour of, but also present in some degree in the case of those hostile to, imprisonment for debt must be accommodated within such an analysis. Thus, when treating of the relationship between imprisonment for debt and working-class thrift, for example, we need to be conscious of the capacity of untested or doubtful propositions to gain and retain a hold on those who influence and determine policy. The debate over imprisonment for debt was, therefore, as much a difference over values or attitudes, as it was over matters of substance, a problematic for historical writing, but a phenomenon of significance nonetheless. It may not, therefore, be remarkable that similar, indeed identical, arguments as to the efficacy of imprisonment for debt as a deterrent to extravagance, arguments which were expounded with a conviction and, in many cases, a belief in their originality, were trotted out with astonishing regularity throughout the whole period between 1869 and 1914, despite the social and economic changes in consumption and retailing which were taking place at the time.

IV: THE RATIONALE OF THE SYSTEM

The rationale of imprisonment for debt displayed a number of characteristics. The principal claim, of course, was that it was an effective deterrent in coercing reluctant debtors to repay what they owed. This was dubbed the "screw theory" by Judge Chalmers.[13] The argument surrounding the effectiveness of imprisonment for debt in this respect was essentially a matter of statistical inference. The deterrent lobby looked at the aggregate civil judicial statistics. By pointing to the huge disparity between the number of plaints issued and the numbers actually imprisoned, the retentionists argued that this demonstrated the effectiveness of committals as a deterrent. Moreover, they argued that the amounts recovered were not significantly less than the debts adjudged owing (see Appendix, Tables A and B for these points), though returns presented to the 1909 SC suggested an important qualification, as we shall see later.[14]

However, opponents of the system considered that the annual toll of imprisoned debtors was itself testimony to the failure of committals as a deterrent, a point made more forcefully when the numbers imprisoned annually, increased around the turn of the century (see Appendix, Table B). The fact was that both views were persuasive, a matter we will explore in more detail subsequently.

In respect to the claim that it was operating in terrorem, imprisonment for debt was justified in terms of saving the working-classes from their own folly. Thus, it supposedly also revealed a pragmatic intention in the scheme of its advocates, for it was thought to act as a stimulus to sound household economy, but more especially as an inducement to the trading world to continue to offer credit to the poor. One judge went so far as to claim that he,

> ". . . could point to instances in which an unhappy home had been made into a happy one by the imprisonment which had been inflicted."[15]

The retributive theory of imprisonment for debt, by contrast, satisfied the mental urge to punish, and could particularly be located in the statutory provision which allowed a committal where the judge was satisfied that at one time since judgment, the debtor had had means to pay, even though he lacked means at the time of the committal hearing.[16] However, retributive philosophy was not prominent with respect to poor debtors, though it did dovetail with criticisms of working-class thriftlessness. Retribution, in fact, featured most often in relation to large debtors who were accused of besmirching the good name of commerce in the greatest industrialised country in the world, by their sinful conduct of incurring debts without any certainty of repayment on time.

Both deterrence and retribution were, however, dependent on the State to provide the institutional framework. We are familiar with the argument that the need for predictability and certainty in economic transactions dictates the creation of legal machinery to guarantee such arrangements. As Judge Falconer of South Wales expressed it,[17]

> "Our great towns are daily supplied with food without any official interference. Private enterprise distributes it even to the garrets of dwelling-houses, because the law governs contracts and secures their fulfilment. Want is confined to the narrowest boundaries through the enforcement of the reward [which] those who supply food and clothing to

the multitude are entitled to demand."

But the characteristic of imprisonment for debt in England was, as the Common Law Commissioners had called attention in 1832, the application of a public, criminal sanction, to a private, civil transaction. The Commissioners had recommended,[18]

> ". . . limiting the power of imprisonment itself and confining it to cases where it is warranted, on the plain and just principle of preventing the debtor from fraudulently absconding or removing his property beyond the reach of justice, or for the punishment of actual fraud, or compelling the debtor, after judgment, either to pay the debt or make a cession of the whole of his property for the benefit of the creditor. Beyond that, we believe that the practice of imprisonment for debt is neither warranted in principle nor beneficial in practice."

However, even this defence of the system exposed the legal system to criticism. By so lending itself to the deprivation of individual liberty in aid of a private dispute, the State, by maintaining imprisonment for debt, was either overreaching itself by acting "inconsistent with the genius of our Constitution and our high degree of political civilisation,"[19] or else revealing its commercial immaturity. For, as the former President of the Board of Trade, Robert Lowe, argued,[20]

> "As society advances, the power of the creditor over the debtor gradually diminishes .... As the commercial spirit advances - that is, as people lend and borrow, trust and are trusted more - the severity of the law for the fulfilment of these contracts diminishes; so that it is no exaggeration to say that the harshness or leniency of the law of debtor and creditor is an unerring guide for ascertaining the absence or presence of the true commercial spirit."

The State had no business, it was argued, in providing and maintaining prison facilities for private quarrels. In Scotland, before the total abolition of imprisonment for debt in 1880, creditors were obliged at least to provide for the maintenance of debtors in prison, albeit for bare necessities.[21] In England, on the other hand, the cost to the State and to the ratepayers of maintaining debtors in prison frequently exceeded the amount of the debt.[22]

Moreover, what interest could the State claim in enforcing payment of debts by those who did not owe the money, as most commonly happened when relatives and friends dug into their own pockets to save the debtor from imprisonment? The State had no interest in inducing a third party to pay a debt due by, for example, a relative to a creditor. The money was probably quite as useful to the State in the pocket of the third party as in that of the creditor.[23] And in contradistinction to a premise underlying the criminal law,

> "Government sits not one whit more securely on her throne, the law is not an atom more respected, nor does the framework of society receive one consolidating bond through the imprisonment of those who are caged like the beasts or criminals behind bars and bolts."[24]

V: CONTEMPT OF COURT

As stated at the outset of this paper, a major plank in the arguments of those seeking to justify the retention of committals in the "Act for the Abolition of Imprisonment for Debt", was the technical "explanation" that imprisonment was not for debt at all, but for contempt of the court order to pay the small debt outstanding. However, the explanation offered was of more than technical significance; for it was unquestionably easier, both ideologically and practically, to defend imprisonment for civil wrongs where one could stigmatise small debtors as "quasi-criminals", offending against the dignity of the court, than if the debtors were merely identified as victims of economic misfortune. Moreover, contempt of court as an offence was sufficiently distinct from the body of criminal law to enable judges to circumvent a specific self-denying ordinance against criminalisation in similar circumstances. Thus, as Cornish has recently noted,[25] the judges "persisted in requiring some further element than mere dishonesty" before labelling as criminal, both behaviour which extracted goods from another by trick, and also the conduct of those debtors who, in the words of the Small Debts Act 1845 (8 & 9 Vict., c.127), "wilfully contracted without any reasonable prospect of being able to pay."[26] By construing failure to pay under section 5 (2) of the Debtors Act as a contempt of court, the judges could imprison where, at most, "mere dishonesty" had occurred.

The fact that a literal construction of the term "imprisonment for debt" could refer only to a situation where the debt was extinguished in consideration of imprisonment, as was the case with regard to rates and maintenance[27] (as well as under the old procedure prior to 1869), made the contempt analysis intellectually attractive. Thus, in 1872, Judge W.T.S. Daniel, Q.C., speaking "not in the interest of debtors but [of] the working-class",[28] declared,

> "If he understood the meaning of the phrase 'imprisonment for debt', there was no such thing known to the law. Imprisonment for debt, to which recently objection had been made,[29] in former times was imprisonment by the creditor himself. What was called imprisonment for debt [i.e., in 1872] was in cases where debts justly incurred were honestly due from parties who were well able to pay, but who wilfully and wrongfully refused to pay. The law considered that an offence for which the party was liable to be imprisoned for a limited period."

Moreover, Judge Daniel continued,

> ".... [T]here is something quasi-criminal in disobedience... the authority of the court is set at naught, and the debtor is sent to prison because, in defiance of its authority, and having means of payment, he prefers to keep, spend, or waste the money, rather than clear off his debts like an honest man. And as he is not imprisoned because he owes money, he does not cease to owe money because he has been imprisoned."[30]

This analysis was reflected in the limited case law emanating from the superior courts, which the legislation generated. Thus, in Marris v. Ingram (1882) 13 Ch.D. 338, Jessel M.R. declared that the power of imprisonment was given, not merely as a means of enforcing payment, but as a punishment for a fraudulent or dishonest debtor, while in Mitchell v. Simpson (1890) 25 Q.B.D. 183, Lord Esher M.R. referred to the order for imprisonment in respect of "an offence against the court." Thus the stress was laid, not on the economic plight of the debtor, but on his quasi-criminal behaviour vis-à-vis the creditor and, more importantly, in relation to the court.

Indeed, the majority report of the 1909 Select Committee, which favoured the retention of imprisonment for debt, had stated that two of the three reasons why five per cent of all credit transactions came to the county courts were, first, that creditors were deceived by debtors as to their ability to pay, and second, that creditors were deceived by the statements of others concerning the debtors' position (para. 13). Yet we may note that while deception did not cease to be a civil matter, nonetheless, the mode of punishment, imprisonment, was that prescribed for those found guilty of crimes.[31] Indeed, this was especially true after the passing of the Prisons Act 1898, when the Prison Rules of the following year decreed that debtors were thenceforth to be subject to virtually the same rules as were applicable to criminals, a distinction which had always been observed up until that date. The authorities were thus prepared to countenance a criminal punishment for the benefit of a private creditor, but without extending to the debtor the protection of a criminal trial, entailing a higher standard of proof than that applicable under Part I of the Debtors Act.[32] Rights of appeal to the Home Secretary (or in subsequent years to the Court of Criminal Appeal) or to the court under the First Offenders Act were thus unavailing to debtors imprisoned alongside convicted criminals and subject to identical prison restraints.

The Daily Telegraph, however,[33] dismissed the technical reasoning in support of the contempt analysis (reasoning which, no doubt, went far to ease the consciences of many creditors and defenders of imprisonment for debt) as a "charming legal fiction." Indeed, it was a view which, to some degree, corresponded to the decision in In Re Ryley (1884-5) 15 Q.B.D. 329, that a committal was not a process for contempt of court but a method of enforcing payment of a debt; in fact, a qualified execution.

Yet even if the contempt analysis was intellectually more respectable than the analysis that imprisonment was literally for debt, the first approach was itself subject to theoretical difficulties. In particular, whereas imprisonment was normally presumed to purge a contempt of court, the Debtors Act explicitly stated that no imprisonment under section 5 (2) was to operate as a satisfaction or extinction of the debt. Logically, therefore, whatever imprisonment was for, it was not for contempt. The question had practical applications. If imprisonment were deemed to be for contempt, it would logically follow that there existed a power of recommitment of a debtor with means to pay, especially since the Act stipulated that imprisonment was not to be taken as a satisfaction of the debt. The proponents of this view pointed out that while imprisonment would purge the contempt, the purge would surely only relate to each default, any number of which could theoretically be incurred on every instalment. This was obviously an uncomfortable argument to embrace, for,

> "If compliance with such a demand could be enforced, conceive the condition of county court judgment debtors . . . . It must be difficult to believe that in such a case, a creditor is not acting vindictively."[34]

Moreover, the Law Times continued,

> ". . . it seems simply preposterous to say that a subsequent passive evasion of payment is during every day of its continuance, a new contempt, deserving renewed punishment."

Better, therefore, to manipulate the contempt theory in such a way as to argue that the punishment of imprisonment for default in payment of an instalment could apply just once. This was because,

> "By the terms of the original order, the time for the payment of the instalment is gone by, the next is becoming due, and it would be going too far to say that the whole arrangement must hang fire, and recourse continually be had to the first default for the purpose of inflicting a penalty which is really not for the failure to pay the creditor, but for contempt of court."[35]

With the adoption of this expedient, the net result was that though the instalment for which imprisonment had been imposed still remained intact, the debtor could not be imprisoned anew for default on the same instalment. It was, of course, a decidedly shaky argument, but rather than have imprisonment for debt exposed to the criticisms of the earlier system which consigned debtors to oblivion for decades in gaol, until death brought its own relief, the need for expediency and acceptability dictated the choice of a discreet management of contempt jurisdiction. Moreover, the stress on contempt sought to ensure the maintenance of the ideology of equality before the law, an object hardly attainable if the stress was placed rather on imprisonment for small debts.

The Court of Common Pleas very rapidly confirmed this interpretation in Horsnail v. Bruce (1872-3) 8 C.P. 378. This established that a debtor could only be committed once for making default in payment of a debt. However, their Lordships, in obiter dicta, also confirmed imprisonment for default on each instalment as well as for entire debts, a practice which, though already existing, soon became widespread. This, in fact, triggered off a more coercive exercise of judicial control over small debtors, with the result that many debtors would have been better off had the provision for instalment payments not been enacted. For while an order for a lump sum payment was backed by the threat of up to six weeks imprisonment, the more instalments ordered, the more spells of imprisonment up to 42 days were liable to be spent by debtors defaulting on such instalments. Indeed, on this calculation, it was undoubtedly preferable for some to be caught stealing £5 than owing it. It is hardly surprising that in his evidence to the Select Committee in 1909, Judge Henry Tindal-Atkinson (Essex) considered that Horsnail was one of the two cases which had been "a most effectual way of getting in the debts because debtors dare not disobey, as it multiplies their liability to it."[36]

VI: PROOF OF MEANS

The other decision referred to by Judge Tindal-Atkinson was the House of Lords' decision in Stonor v. Fowle (1888) 13 A.C. 20, which declared lawful the practice of making a committal order with a stay of execution so long as the debtor continued to pay the specified instalments. The result of this decision was that where a default on an instalment occurred, a creditor in possession of a committal order subject to suspension was not required to prove the debtor's means to pay at the time of the instalment default as long as proof of means had been established to the judge's satisfaction when the original committal order had been granted. The problem which remained, however, was that judges were frequently accused of committing to prison on no or on inadequate proof of means at the time of the original order, let alone at the time of a default on an instalment.

The 1873 SC had concluded that the judges were careful to enquire into the debtor's means by ascertaining the facts and adjudicating upon them "justly and equitably". The committee accepted that such matters as the debtor's wages, and the circumstances and demands of his family were "roughly proved". Nevertheless, they conceded that the debtor's liability to other creditors was "seldom, if ever, ascertained."[37]

By 1909, it was stated that,[38]

> ". . . some judges insist on legal evidence of means to pay. Others make full use of their liberty to accept evidence 'in such a manner as the Court thinks just', accepting, for example, certificates as to wages from employers, statements of bailiffs of the Court, evidence not on oath, and other hearsay evidence" (italics added).

The justification offered for the practice of hearing other than legal evidence was that the judge's discretion was principally to the advantage of the debtor. This was a most doubtful proposition. As early as 1873, The Times could point out what "evidence not on oath, and other hearsay evidence" might amount to. It declared,[39]

> "In one county unless the creditor can prove to the satisfaction of the court that the debtor is utterly without money, property or credit, the court declines to inflict a punishment, the real object of which is to enforce the payment of the debt. As this can rarely be proved, there are comparatively few imprisonments. In another county, the full powers of the Act are wielded with less stint in the interest of honesty and it must be added, long credit

and speculative trade .... For a few shillings of debt, a mere pauper, sometimes actually in receipt of parish pay is sent in charge of a policeman to a county prison thirty or forty miles off.[40] It is quite possible that the debt may be five years old, that the defaulter may be the victim of unavoidable misfortune or that he may be half an idiot. The varieties of practice arising from the various tastes and opinions of the County Court judges are such as one might expect to find in this island in the days of the Heptarchy".

Widespread criticism could be deflected by the testimonies of those judges who laid claim to a conscientious and sympathetic application of the test of debtors' means. Professional reputation and integrity were, after all, at risk. Thus, many judges giving evidence to the Select Committees, irrespective of their attitude to imprisonment for debt, proclaimed that they undertook exhaustive enquiries into the means of debtors. Judge John Russell (Manchester), an opponent of imprisonment for debt, told the 1873 Select Committee that he had published a notice detailing the kind of proof required before issuing a committal order. He would require proof on oath of someone who could speak to the debtor's means, or proof on oath of anyone who enquired at the debtor's place of employment, or the production, on oath, of books or documents showing the debtor's means. He believed that this rigorous approach limited the "vicious system" of credit and also led to a diminution in the number of plaints since 1869, despite the increase in population and in "buying and selling".[41] In demanding proof on oath, Russell's conscientiousness probably exceeded that of most judges who believed that their mode of investigation was designed to get at the truth.

Judge T.F. Falconer (South Wales), for example, explained his method in answers to a questionnaire put to him by the Committee of County Court Judges in 1874. The presence of wife, children, other debts and obligations, and the level of wages were all considered, although it was conceded that in the case of many committals, it was impossible to know if the debtor had means at the time of the judgment summons hearing. Proof of means at the time of the <u>original</u> hearing was considered sufficient.[42]

Of course, a major factor explaining why debtors' current means were unascertainable was because only a minority tended to turn up for the hearings. This ought not to have made any difference to the standard of proof acceptable, as the onus was on the creditor. But it undoubtedly allowed for a less rigorous approach to evidence when the plaintiff's testimony remained uncontroverted.[43] Non-appearance was, in fact, very common. The expense of travelling to the county court town, the prospect of losing a day's wage, perhaps other fears, fatalism or desperation, inadequacy or lack of confidence were present.[44] Such factors might have to be weighed against the allegation that debtors, according to Judge Selfe (West Kent), would pay no attention to original orders. When no appearance was entered, his Honour conceded,

> "One has to take the evidence of whoever appears on behalf of the plaintiff, and that evidence is almost necessarily of a secondary character. The plaintiff's witness is not actually in a position to say what the defendant's means are, except from information which he has obtained, and if a man tells me that he knows the debtor, that he knows he is in work, and who his employer is, and what are the average rates of wages paid in that particular employment, I consider that to be sufficient evidence of what the man's means are . . . ."[45]

Moreover, creditors were not obliged to reveal the existence of other debts which the defendant owed. This had the effect, as Joseph Collinson pointed out in an Open Letter to the Home Secretary in 1906,[46] that if a man had many debts, some of these would have to remain unpaid when the summoning creditor, by proving means, obtained a judgment. The debtor would be labelled dishonest by not paying the remainder of his debts in the event of subsequent plaints taken out against him. A premium was, therefore, put on a creditor's ability to get his claim into court first, unlike the arrangements intended to achieve equality among creditors under bankruptcy law. When a committal order was consequently issued by the first summoning creditor, it was well known that he would commonly arrest a working debtor on a Saturday afternoon after work, with his week's wages in his pocket.[47] The unfairness of this to other creditors was glaring, despite the argument that the creditor getting in first was being rewarded for his diligence.[48] As one indignant correspondent wrote,[49]

> "But whose money is this? In reality it is the money of another tradesman who has trusted the debtor with the necessaries of life during the fourteen or twenty one days, as the case may be, that he took to earn the money, and the debtor who himself had every desire to be honest towards such tradesman, is made to appear dishonest by this process of law created by the British Parliament and enforced by Her Majesty's courts of law."

Sir Richard Harington, a widely respected judge at Birmingham, pointed out that,

> ". . . [O]ne has such very unsatisfactory evidence and is obliged to transgress the rules of evidence in inquiring into the means of a debtor. I am obliged, and I think most judges are obliged, to accept hearsay evidence, ..."[50]

a modest statement when contrasted with Judge Chalmers' accusation that the atmosphere of the county court "reeks with perjury".[51]

Frequently, however, a partial obstacle to getting at the true state of affairs was the bureaucratic burden. One county court judge described the difficulty of satisfying himself that the debtor's means could be proved.[52]

> "In one large town, the judge has every morning, before the day's work begins, to deal with some thirty or forty or more judgment summonses, and on one special day in most weeks, with between one hundred and two hundred. In very many of these cases, there is direct and vigorous conflict of testimony. At great speed he has to determine as well as he can which side is telling the truth, or lying the least . . . . The best any judge can do is . . . make a shot at the right order. And all the time, in the next or some other district, one of his brethren may be, quite as conscientiously, using different means and criteria, and coming to different results."

The evidentiary difficulties attendant on ascertaining proof of means weakens the thesis that those imprisoned were contumacious, not impoverished, debtors and obliges us to take seriously the thrust of the argument of the minority report of the 1909 enquiry that most imprisoned debtors were too poor to pay. The remainder of this study will argue that various factors point in the direction of supporting this assertion.

VII: STATISTICAL VARIATIONS

Theorising about imprisonment for debt, of course, did not remain locked in the vacuum of the philosopher's world. It began to inform debate as evidence started to accumulate on the working of the system, a topic to which we now turn our attention.

We do not know how many tradesmen wrote off bad debts in order not to become entangled with the machinery of the law.[53] On the other hand, as an order of magnitude, we can fairly speak of around a million plaints a year issued through the county courts, indicating at least for the personnel of the law, a thriving and profitable trade (see Appendix, Table A). However, it was commonly observed that a lack of uniformity characterised the administration of the Debtors Act by the county court judges. Thus, the period of imprisonment varied significantly from judge to judge, usually from 10 to the 42 days maximum prescribed by the Act. Some judges created an elaborate scenario against which to fix a period of imprisonment,[54] while others employed a beautifully simple device. In Stonor v. Fowle,[55] for example, Lord Bramwell recalled,

> "A learned County Court Judge once told me that he used at first to make orders of committal for a short time, and he found that the people went to prison. He then lengthened the period and found that fewer people went to prison, and he found that the longer the period for which he committed people to prison for not paying, the shorter was the total amount of imprisonment suffered by debtors, because when they were committed for the whole six weeks, they moved heaven and earth among their friends to get the money and pay; whereas if the term was a short one, they underwent the punishment."[56]

One county court judge whose practice corresponded closely to this description, was W.T.S. Daniel, who explained,[57]

> "I have adopted a rule of 40 days imprisonment . . . . I used to make the order only for 10 days, but . . . I found 10 days imprisonment did not operate in the way in which the Act of Parliament intended it, namely, as a means of coercing a dishonest debtor, who has the means of paying, to pay; and, therefore, I tried 40 days."

It does appear, however, that Bramwell and Daniel were, in fact, at cross-purposes. While Daniel was allegedly concerned with coercing the dishonest debtor with means to pay, Bramwell's debtors, on the other hand, who "moved heaven and earth among their friends" to pay off their debts, were more likely to have been penniless, a point to which we will return.

But we may look beyond this feature and discover more significant variations in the way the Act was applied. The fact that the judges possessed discretion both as to whether to commit, and also as to the mode of proof which they thought "just", inevitably conduced to this variation in practice. The attitude to imprisonment for debt as a question of principle, on the part of the judge (indeed, arguably also on the part of creditors, many of whom found the practice distasteful), might be reflected in the statistics, as would the judge's approach to what constituted satisfactory proof of means.

Thus, a brief perusal of the returns from different circuits shows that even where the numbers of plaints issued were similar, there existed wide variations in the numbers of judgment summonses heard, the numbers of committal orders issued, and, not least importantly, the numbers of debtors imprisoned. Thus, if one looks at the Table comparing selected circuits in 1904 (Appendix, Table C), the figures reveal that in circuit 18, for example, which included Nottingham, Doncaster and Mansfield, nearly two and a quarter times as many persons were imprisoned as in the whole of London (circuits 40-44), including the City. The minority report of the 1909 Select Committee later reported that in the City of London, where consumer credit may have been less widespread, the percentage of committal orders to plaints was 1.47, and in the East Riding of Yorkshire (circuit 16) it was 38.

Similarly, if one examines some of the more revealing and dramatic tables compiled by Judge O'Connor (Durham) for the 1909 Select Committee (Appendix, Table D), one discovers that in 1906 circuits 2 and 11 (Durham and part of West Riding of Yorkshire), with a similar number of plaints, had a remarkably divergent ratio of imprisonments to plaints, as is the case when circuits 17 and 24 (Lincolnshire and Monmouthshire) are compared. Examining the numbers of judgment summonses issued by different circuits similarly compared, which may in fact be a better indicator of the judge's attitude to the principle of committals, the figures for circuit 1 (Northumberland) are in very sharp contrast to those for circuit 12 (West Riding of Yorkshire), Finally, adjoining circuits, such as circuits 2 and 15 (Durham and Yorkshire, North Riding) could pursue divergent paths, with the former reducing its annual number of committals from 309 to 19 between 1901 and 1906, and the latter increasing its numbers from 394 to 435 imprisoned debtors during the same period (Table E).

How were these anomalies explained? Indeed, how was it that certain areas of the country were infested by supposedly contumacious, indeed dishonest, debtors, while other parts, so it appeared, were not so affected? The answer was, of course, to be found in the varied manner in which the Act was administered by the judges from one circuit to another. Thus, while it is undoubtedly true that the Act itself was indefinite, nonetheless, the statistical variations surely indicated that certain judges were more punitive than others in their approach to a law which granted them discretion in dealing with defaulting debtors. Perhaps if the county court judges got together to frame rules by which they could act more uniformly, thought R.A. Cross, the Home Secretary, a remedy would be found.[58] Yet we may observe that by thus placing blame on inconsistent administration, Cross was able both to deflect criticism away from the principle of imprisonment for debt, and also away from the material basis of the "problem of administration", the issue of proof of means. For, as the Law Times, which reproduced the figures in Table C, commented,[59]

> ". . . it certainly cannot be suggested that the extraordinary difference between these figures is due to the contumaciousness of the debtors. The truth of the matter is that so far as some of our County Court districts are concerned, imprisonment for debt, pure and simple, is rife . . . ."

This perhaps could be said of Birkenhead County Court which in 1913 imprisoned more debtors than did Liverpool, or of Salford which surpassed Manchester in this respect. Indeed, five circuits out of 54 were collectively responsible for more than one third of the total number of imprisonments in that year.[60]

The proponents of imprisonment for debt also sought to use statistics to buttress their case for retention. The 1893 enquiry, for example, was favourably impressed by the figures produced by Judge Bedwell (Hull)[61] which demonstrated that once in prison, few debtors remained there to serve out their full time, but were able to secure their release in mid-sentence, either through the payment of the debt, or through the compassion of the creditor. Thus, 6.2% of prisoners remained in gaol per 100 committal warrants, on the average for five years 1887-1891, while in 1875 the figure had been 15%. The purpose of these figures was to demonstrate both the contumacious nature of imprisoned debtors who required the application of the "screw" before disgorging the funds they owed to creditors, and also the necessity to retain imprisonment.

However, critics strongly argued that if the debts were paid, they were paid not by the debtor but by third parties, such as friends or relatives, who obviously did not themselves owe the money; or alternatively, they were paid with the aid of money-lenders who themselves assumed the position of creditor. Indeed, as we have seen, no lesser an authority than Lord Bramwell, perhaps the embodiment of nineteenth century conservatism, could be cited in support of the proposition that the repayment of the debt represented a mere transference of the obligation rather than the honouring of this contractual obligation by a dishonest or contumacious debtor. Such efforts to obtain the necessary funds were surely inconsistent with an image of debtors refusing to make over to their creditors what they owed, despite their ability to pay.

Moreover, in his evidence to the 1909 enquiry, Commander Lionel Sanders, governor of Wakefield Prison, pointed out that few debtors in his experience paid after committal, but of those who did (about 10% of the total), three quarters obtained the money from friends or relatives. Of 1257 debtors of all kinds, including those committed by magistrates for defaults on bastardy, maintenance, rates and industrial school fees, 139 paid in prison while 211 were released by order of the registrar, "friends having presumably paid the money into court". Of the 139 debtors cited, it is not unreasonable to assume that friends or relatives may have handed the money to them rather than to the court.[62]

It does, therefore, appear that there was some substance to the complaint of reformers that even where money was paid over to a creditor, it did not follow that the debtor himself was in a position to pay.

As already stated, a further implication arising from Judge Bedwell's figures was that imprisonment was an effective weapon, even <u>in terrorem</u>, in the struggle to "get in" the money owed. However, figures produced by Judge O'Connor (who himself favoured retention) suggested that some circuits which seldom ordered committals could get in a larger proportion of money than other comparable circuits heavily reliant on imprisonment, as the table below shows.

TABLE I

Figures Showing Diminution in Number of Imprisonments did not Diminish the Effective Working of the Courts in the Interests of Suitors (1906)

Circuit	District	Total amount of Plaints	Amount Paid to Credit of Suitors	Debtors Imprisoned
2	Durham	£53852	£40290: over 74%	19
7	West Cheshire etc.	53969	35719: over 66%	133
12	Yorkshire, West Riding (part of)	53258	36345: over 68%	518
51	Hampshire	54539	30134: over 55%	84
58	South Devon	51028	28424: over 55%	100

(circuits with plaints £50,000 - £55,000)

Source: 1909 SC, Appendix 16B (Judge O'Connor)

Note: The numbers imprisoned in Circuit 2 fell from 309 to 19 per year between 1901 and 1906 while the national total for those years rose from 8492 to 11,986, surely a strong indication of the effect of the use of discretion in favour of the debtor (see Table B for national figures).

This potentially important finding on the amounts recovered (on which further work is proceeding) was, like so much statistical evidence, locked away in an appendix, where it failed to attract more than a cursory glance from the policy makers.

VIII: THE IMPRISONED DEBTORS

A further source shedding light on the economic position of imprisoned debtors is lists of committals compiled by county court judges and registrars. However, the usefulness of the returns made to the select committees naturally varied according to the richness of the information provided. For example, in 1873 Mr. Commissioner Kerr of the City of London Court, submitted an occupational list of defendants named in judgment summonses issued by that court in 1872 (see

Table II below). This indicated that the most numerous class of debtors were retail traders, followed by clerks, with "workpeople" well down the list. Unfortunately, no other information concerning the economic conditions of these City of London debtors, drawn predominantly, of course, from commercial rather than industrial occupations, is revealed.

TABLE II

City of London Court: Judgment Summonses for 1872
Total Number of Defendants in Each Class

Class	Defendants
Retail traders	472
Clerks	382
Wholesale traders	27
Professional classes	77
Workpeople	53
Miscellaneous	170
Total	1181

Source: 1873 SC, Appendix 4.

Similarly, lists of imprisoned debtors submitted in 1909 by Judges Hans Hamilton (Blackburn), Cyril Dodd (Hull) and William Wightman Wood (Leicester)[63] also yield insufficient information even to draw tentative conclusions. Judge Wightman Wood's list of debtors taken to gaol during the quarters ending December 1907 and March 1908 do, however, contain the judge's "remarks" on the 28 named defendants (out of 40 cases). He noted that 17 defendants paid before completing their full time in prison (though whether the money was borrowed from elsewhere or donated by friends or relatives is not known). Of those who were detained full-time, two "drank", five were in work, and the rest were either embezzlers or had suffered as a result of illness in the family or from unemployment. He also commented that a few of the full-timers were yet "honest", an admission which clearly conflicted with the alleged policy of the Act which he was charged with implementing. The most crucial flaws in the list however were the absence of sufficiently detailed information on debtors' occupations and earnings. The returns submitted by Judges

Hamilton and Dodd detailed only 10 and 8 imprisoned debtors respectively. The first-named return did, in fact, suggest a healthy earning situation for those debtors, while the remarks of Judge Dodd consistently stated that the debtor would either not pay or had not tried to pay; the archetypal contumacious debtor, in fact. Given some of the paltry amounts for which these debtors were committed (13 out of the 18 owed £2 or less, and 7 owed 15/6d or less), one would have to marvel at the determination of such debtors to face imprisonment, if contumacy were, in fact, the reason for non-payment.

Though these two returns appear on the face of it inconsistent with the general thesis put forward in this paper, they cannot, of course, be taken to invalidate the argument. For clearly, it would be impossible to argue that not one of the 217,889 debtors subject to committal warrants in 1906, or of the 12,014 debtors actually imprisoned that year, were contumacious. There must always be exceptions to the aggregate picture painted. Yet the most reliable return presented to the select committees appears to support the argument put forward in this paper that by labelling debtors as contumacious, the legislature were, in fact, seeking to disguise the fact that imprisonment was still the punishment for not being able to pay one's debts, rather than a punishment for refusing to pay when one was in a position to do so.

Thus, the 1892 returns from East Stonehouse County Court, near Plymouth (see Appendix, Table F) provide an occupational and earnings breakdown for imprisoned debtors. Ninety two defendants are listed and can be divided crudely into the following categories: gentlemen (2); professional/trader (8); skilled manual (24); semi-skilled, unskilled, widowed or unemployed (58). The earnings breakdown in Table III indicates that in the 74 cases where average earnings are given (including, in a number of cases, pension income of about £18 per annum, over half the total number of debtors, 49 in all, fell within the wage band of 15 shillings to one pound inclusive (group 1). Another 14 fell into the twenty to twenty five shillings band (group 2), 8 into the twenty five to thirty shilling band (group 3), and 3 earned above this figure (group 4). The incomes of another 11 debtors were unknown, mostly gentlemen, professionals or traders (group 5). Five others were stated to earn "considerable sums at times", but no precise figures are given (group 6), while 2 engine drivers "could easily earn 30s", but they "prefer [red] idleness" (group 7). This last example points up a difficulty with this list of debtors. For though earnings figures are provided for most cases, as we have seen, these often apply in the cases of those who were out of work at the time of arrest or in respect of whom it was not known whether they were in employment at the time. There are 24 debtors in the former category and 9 in the latter. Even in the case of the former category, it does not necessarily mean that such debtors were unemployed and seeking work, for the list of those out of work at the time of arrest also includes the gentlemen with private means, pensioners and a widow with income from trust funds. It is important, however, to emphasise that the fact of unemployment ought to reinforce the argument of this paper, that imprisonment was being meted out mainly to those unable to pay their debts, rather than to those seeking to wriggle out of paying that which they both owed and possessed.

TABLE III

East Stonehouse County Court.
Imprisoned Debtors' Approximate Earnings Band

Band	Earnings	Debtors
1	15 - 20/- inclusive	49
2	20-25/-	14
3	25-30/-	8
4	30/-	3
5	Unknown	11
6	"Considerable sums"	5
7	"Could easily earn 30/-"	2
Total:		92

Source: Extracted from Appendix, Table F.

There are, of course, abundant conceptual and analytical difficulties in attempting to substantiate arguments as to levels of poverty, income and living standards even from those tables constructed with such objects in mind. The problems are compounded when making use of tables designed for other purposes. It is apparent, therefore, that it is not feasible in the context of this paper to do more than compare crudely these income bands with tables of contemporary wage rates and earnings. Thus, the picture painted will necessarily be imprecise and impressionistic, rather than scientific and rigorous, and suggestive rather than definitive. In the light of these important qualifications, however, we can yet seek to draw instructive comparisons between average wages and the income of imprisoned (and allegedly contumacious) debtors. Thus in 1890 the rates for fitters and turners in engineering were between 32s and 39s a week depending on location; bricklayers' and labourers' rates were about 25s; adult male workers in the footwear industry in Northampton and Kettering were earning between 22s and 27s; agricultural labourers in 1892 were earning 13/10d (exclusive of payment in kind and extra payment for piecework, hay and corn harvests); while the distribution of wages for 1886 shows that 20.9% of the total employees for 38 leading industries fell into the 15s to 20s band, 35.4% in the £1 to 25s band, 23.6% in the 25s to 30s range and 11.2% in the 30s to 35s range.[64] What do these figures prove? One would have to concede that they are no more than suggestive that the imprisoned debtors in East Stonehouse (where the presence of Plymouth Naval Dockyard would tend to raise average wages in a traditionally low-earning area) were earning somewhat less than the national average, with the exception of agricultural labourers. This is an hypothesis which obviously requires more rigorous testing before one can conclude statistically that such debtors were "poor", particularly since references to "national averages" disguise the fact that regional wage variations between 1850 and 1914 were characterised both by the magnitude of these variations and also by their persistence.[65] Nonetheless, it remains incontrovertible that imprisoned debtors, in one circuit at least, were earning "low" wages, casting doubt on explanations based on the contumacy of debtors with funds.

IX: PRISON GOVERNORS

As mentioned earlier, many debtors, for one reason or another, failed to attend court hearings. Indeed, it was only at the judgment summons stage that personal service of summonses was necessary. Nonetheless, many debtors complained that their first awareness of proceedings against them was when the bailiff came to arrest them. This situation was said to arise most frequently in tallymen's cases where the tallyman had sold goods on instalments to the wife without the husband's knowledge (Rubin, infra). One consequence was that judges frequently committed to prison debtors whom they had never seen. However, one group of officials who did meet all such debtors were the prison governors into whose care the debtors were sent. The evidence of those few prison administrators who gave evidence to the enquiries is, therefore, of some importance.

Commander Sanders of Wakefield Prison, whom we have mentioned earlier, referred to 92 debtors, not all of them committed by the county courts, whom he had interviewed at length. He formed the opinion that only 10% of them could pay their debts; indeed, in some instances, they had not been given a chance, having been arrested coming from or going to work, and marched off to prison. In agreeing with the follow-up question: "Then it follows that there would be 90% who really could not pay?," he went on to explain,

> "They either get out of work, or are sick or have had bad luck. For some reason or other, they cannot pay. They cannot make up the arrears from their 25s or 30s a week if they have a wife and large family to keep."

The type of debtors who were imprisoned, according to Sanders, were "mostly working men, mechanics and labourers, not the shopkeeper class, not even the poor shopkeeper class". That there was, nevertheless, a certain amount of confusion is perhaps demonstrated by his further comment that the typical debtor prisoner was "not as a rule that of the honest working man, being degenerate rather than dishonest."[66]

Captain Carleton Haynes, governor of Brixton Prison, also gave evidence to the same enquiry. His finding was that 90% of debtors told him of their inability to pay, a statement which he thought was probably true. His view was,

> "We can only judge roughly from their letters, which they write home to their wives and friends trying to get payment of their debts. So presumably they cannot pay. I should say somewhere about 90% say they cannot pay. I have no means of proving it."[67]

Finally, in his evidence to the 1873 enquiry, Major William Fulford, governor of Stafford Prison, told the committee that the debtors he had met "are very seldom able to obtain the money", and that their families then went on parish relief. His image of such debtors diverged sharply from the model of dishonest, calculating or contumacious debtors. As he explained,

> "I have talked to those people a good deal for many years; they are not in a condition to know much about the position they are in."[68]

Though such evidence is qualitative, perhaps even impressionistic, rather than quantitative, it is submitted that the evidence is nonetheless reliable. The first two governors, moreover, had no particular axe to grind in making their points. They both opposed abolition for imprisonment for debt.

X: POVERTY AND CHARACTER

It should not be forgotten that the extent of poverty in the late nineteenth century had become well known as a result of the surveys of Booth, Seebohm Rowntree and others. In one respect, however, Rowntree's analysis could strike a sympathetic chord in the camps both of the contumacy theorists and of the poverty theorists of imprisonment for debt. Thus, an important distinction which he drew was between primary poverty where income was less than was necessary for subsistence, and secondary poverty where income was above subsistence but expenditure was extravagant. This latter category corresponded to the analysis, pursued with varying degrees of rigour, of those who detected in working-class mores the cause of imprisoned debtors' own misfortune. Basically, this view held that the working-class were thriftless and extravagant, lacking the strength of will to resist the embellishments of the tallyman or the lure of the public house.[70] Judge Daniel, for example, offered this crude characterisation,[71]

> "Those who degrade themselves into such a position as to be liable to that jurisdiction [imprisonment for debt] were not necessarily confined to the working-classes, but with reference to them, he believed it would be found that the cause which rendered it necessary for the court to interpose and exercise that jurisdiction was either intemperance, dishonesty or debauchery."

Somewhat more guarded was the comment in the Scottish Law Review[72] that,

> ". . . there are no returns discriminating between the committals where the debtors 'have had means' and where they 'have means'. Improvidence, thriftlessness, ignorance, and not deliberate intention to swindle with the ingenious artfulness of the better class debtor are responsible for most of the cases falling under the former description . . . ."[73]

For another judge, this class of debtor accounted for only one out of 5 classes, "a residue in fact", and the only group of debtors which required the threat of imprisonment to compel payment.[74]

The common strand running through these comments is, of course, the belief that the character or fecundity of debtors was at fault, and that environmental factors were not relevant. The views of "Pro Bono Publico", a correspondent to the debate on imprisonment for debt conducted in the Law Journal[75], therefore, represented, without abandoning the argument based on character, recognition that other elements should also be considered. Thus,

> "The frequent strikes, bad weather, holidays, and illnesses, etc., make an ordinary working man's lot a very unenviable one, and the most industrious

> and thrifty amongst them must have a very difficult task to keep all straight. The enormous amount spent by the improvident workmen and their wives on drink, betting, etc., make their cases almost hopeless."

Lord Derby, speaking generally,[76] ventured further that economic misery could be avoided if the want of habits of economy and forethought was corrected early enough in life, by, for example, bringing the savings banks to the people. But he appeared blissfully unaware of the tension, if not necessarily the contradiction, between this advice and his belief that,

> "You may educate a man as highly as you please; you may give him the franchise, and call upon him to exercise it as often as you think fit; you may provide the best newspapers in the world to tell him what is going on and museums and galleries without end to cultivate his taste; but no amount of political freedom, or of literary culture, or refinement will carry with them the sense of independence or of self-respect, so long as he knows that he is in somebody else's power, that he has on his shoulders a burden of debt from which he cannot shake himself loose."[77]

It was left to Clementina Black of the Women's Trade Union League to conclude that,[78]

> "The sad truth is that thrift, like cleanliness, is a virtue which can only be exercised upon a certain level of prosperity . . . you cannot save when you have barely money to keep a shelter over your head and to get a reasonable average of meals during the day."

It was this recognition of economic dependence which formed the material link between the analyses of Booth and Rowntree[79] and imprisonment for debt. On this view, imprisonment for debt was, in reality, imprisonment for poverty. Working-class thriftlessness was a comfortable scapegoat, and the occasional recitation by the judges of instances of individuals earning good wages who flaunted court orders, reinforced the stereotype.[80] Far from offering a justification for the continuance of imprisonment for debt, however, such characterisation merely sustained the class nature of this law.

XI: CLASS LAW

"[D]epend on it that so long as we have class laws, we shall have bad laws", complained the Radical political, Charles Cameron.[81] He was expressing his objection to the non-availability of bankruptcy law for small debtors, which manifestly pointed to one law for the privileged rich and another for the under-privileged poor. It is true that a concession had been made at the committee stage of the Debtors Bill to the effect that debtors owing more than £50 were to be subject to committal procedure either in the High Court or in the county courts, a development of which many legal commentators remained unaware.[82] However, cutting through the rhetoric of equality, The Times, in ringing tones, demanded,

> "What, are we entitled to ask, is the proportion of commitments of debtors owing over £50 to those of small debtors imprisoned by orders of the County Court, and how many of these small debtors have paid from time to time a proportion of their debts which would have sufficed to obtain them their discharge in bankruptcy had the amount of their obligations been greater?"[83]

For militating against substantive, as opposed to procedural, equality were a number of uncomfortable facts. First, the high fees payable in the superior courts conspired to ensure that virtually all debt cases for moderate amounts were heard in the county courts.[84] Second, the number of committals of debtors owing more than £50 rarely exceeded 3 per annum (with 350 judgment summonses)[85] as compared with an annual average of 7,246 county court debtors owing less than £50 imprisoned between 1871 and 1910.[86] Third, rich debtors could have resort to bankruptcy status to keep them out of gaol. Moreover, if the bankrupt paid out of his existing assets ten shillings in the pound, or a lesser composition acceptable to his creditors (who might be exceedingly generous if chosen specifically to cushion his obligations) he was discharged. The small debtor, on the other hand, was obliged to pay off the whole debt, mortgage his future earnings, or even his body, if proof of means had been allegedly established.[87] Finally, in order to petition for bankruptcy, a debtor had to submit a fee of £10, a prohibitive figure when the vast majority of debts sued for were for less than £20 (see Appendix, Table A).

An attempt to remedy this latter obstacle by means of administration orders, and perhaps influenced by the cheap Scottish procedure of cessio bonorum, was devised in Joseph Chamberlain's Bankruptcy Act 1883 (46 & 47 Vict., c.52), section 122. Chamberlain evidently thought that once a poor debtor had access to a cheap and modified form of bankruptcy involving the composition of all his debts and a pro rata distribution among his creditors, then no longer would any inequality exist in the law as between rich and poor.[88] But the whole basis of the argument that administration orders removed inequality was undermined by the simple fact that they relied on the threat of imprisonment for their enforcement. Indeed, in one respect, administration orders were potentially more dangerous to debtors than an ordinary unpaid judgment debt. For while proof of means had to be shown by the creditor before a committal order could be issued in the case of an ordinary debt, section 122 of the 1883 Act went further than section 5 (2) of the Debtors Act, by providing that in default of payment of instalments under the administration order, the debtor was deemed to possess means to pay unless he could prove the contrary.

One parliamentary critic, George Anderson, who was presenting his own Bill to abolish imprisonment for debt, was moved to remark that Chamberlain's scheme,

> ". . . instead of abolishing the pernicious system [of imprisonment for debt] would only give it new life. He held they [administration orders] would be found utterly illusory and unworkable in practice.[89]

As to the effectiveness of administration orders in channelling away cases which otherwise would have led to imprisonment for debt in the "conventional" manner, Judge Parry's opinion that in many county courts they remained a dead letter[90] suggests that their impact was minimal.

XII: EXECUTION AGAINST GOODS

If administration orders were unavailing to the poor debtor, then executions were unavailing to the creditor. For there was probably universal agreement even among those opposed to imprisonment for debt that executions were a generally unsuccessful means of debt recovery.[91] Statistics tended to bear this out when the numbers of executions actually carried out were contrasted with those ordered (see Appendix, Table A). Such low figures for sales could, of course, be interpreted to mean that the "screw" was operating smoothly, coercing debtors to find the necessary funds before the sales took place.[92] It is much more probable, however, that in the vast majority of cases, plans for sales were simply abandoned. For there was generally nothing left to sell after the statutory exemption of the clothes, bedding and tools of the trade, up to the value of £5, which belonged to the debtor and his family,[93] had been taken into account. Even the debtor's landlord had a prior claim under the law of distress to the debtor's furniture, allowing him to elbow aside the trade creditor.

Many judges tended to make a virtue out of necessity in criticising executions, for the opinion was expressed that,

> ". . . the most cruel and painful right that a creditor now possesses is not imprisonment for debt at all; it is execution. That is simply a cannon which the creditor takes whenever he likes to a man's door, and in so doing says, 'Pay me my bill or I will destroy your home'."[94]

Judge Bompas (Yorkshire and Lancashire) suggested to the 1909 SC[95] that goods which cost a debtor £20 to keep his wife and children in "decent comfort" would fetch perhaps not more than £5 at a forced sale, of which the expenses would be £4 or £4.10s., leaving just a few shillings for the creditor. Thus, executions were both cruel and ineffective. Another witness[96] took the view, however, that the resultant hardship which a successful execution might cause, rendered it a more effective deterrent for creditors than imprisonment. But in the light of the statistics on the use of executions, its potential could only have been applied in a very small number of cases.

It is thus difficult to resist the conclusion that the most significant explanation for the sparse use of executions against debtors' goods was the lack of items available for sale, expecially where the use of bills of sale and hire purchase became more prevalent towards the end of the century. Since goods procured by such means were not technically owned by debtors, then creditors, other than those who had provided them, could lay no claim to them in an execution. The evidence on executions is, it is submitted, consistent, therefore, with the proposition that imprisonment for debt remained essentially a sanction for poverty.

XIII: WHY NO LEGISLATION?

There remains the puzzle why no reforming legislation was passed in the period up to the First World War, nor indeed until 1970. After all, the 1873 SC supported abolition. Moreover the majority report of the 1909 SC which approved the principle of imprisonment for debt, favoured the adoption of a draft County Courts and Debtors Act Amendment Bill drawn up by Judges Selfe, Smyly and Howland Roberts. This Bill proposed the abolition of committals in the cases of money lent and of goods sold or lent on hire, unless for trade purposes, or unless the goods were "necessaries". For it was no secret that tallymen, money-lenders and, indeed, "clerks of all kinds and certain civil servants" [sic] were to be the sacrificial offerings to the critics of imprisonment for debt, thus permitting the retention of the sanction at the behest of the grocery and other "necessary" trades.[97]

Nothing, however, came of this proposal. Perhaps one of the more obvious lessons to be derived from studies of campaigns for law reform is the crucial necessity, even in the age of a powerful private members' bill constituency, to enlist government support for such programmes. On imprisonment for debt, the government will was lacking virtually throughout the whole period to 1914. Thus in 1872, in 1874-7, in 1879, and again in 1881-3, private members' bills failed to proceed despite the favourable report of the 1873 SC. In 1911, a bill sponsored by the draftsman of the 1909 SC minority report, Charles Pickersgill, failed to persuade the Inspector-General in Bankruptcy who had examined it for the Board of Trade. The latter went on to point out that even the minority report for which Pickersgill had been responsible, had agreed that abolition would remove the sole means of enforcing payment in many cases.[98] Nonetheless, that the "many cases" referred to could only have constituted a minute proportion of the total was, however, carefully hidden from view.

Perhaps the closest the government ever came to legislating in this period was in 1906-7, when the Lord Chancellor undertook to give "serious consideration" to the proposal.[99] To this end he circulated confidentially to 27 county court judges to canvass their opinions on the proposal. The results were that only 6 were in favour of total or virtually total abolition, 6 favoured partial abolition, thus excluding debts for necessaries and tort damages. Fifteen, however, were in favour of retention.[100] Once again, law reform was shelved, the reverence accorded to judicial opinions surely disposing of the possibility. The fact was that so many resources were invested in the committal system that to tamper with any of its component parts might be perceived by practitioners as threatening to upset the whole delicate machinery. Small debt collecting in the county courts did, after all, account for 90% of all county court business and provided guaranteed and continuous employment for judges, registrars and bailiffs.[101] Traders and debt collectors similarly viewed imprisonment for debt as an effective deterrent which justified its retention. It should hardly surprise us, therefore, that the majority of the judges saw the removal of imprisonment for debt as the removal of the effectiveness of the county court. As Sir Robert Collier, the Attorney-General, in introducing the Bankruptcy Bill in March 1869, had stated,[102]

"[A]lmost all the County Court judges were of the opinion that if they were deprived of this power [of committal] the efficiency of the County Court system would be destroyed."

Similarly, according to the Solicitor-General, Sir John Coleridge,[103]

"[The Government] had been informed upon sufficient authority that the County Court system, as at present constituted, could not be carried on without [imprisonment for debt]."

Such tendentious reasoning remained to haunt the campaigners for abolition and to frustrate their endeavours. Thus the 1873 SC, which in fact examined only four out of the 58 county court judges, and only two solicitors, proposed abolition in vain, in view of the admission in the report that the great majority of county court judges had been in favour of retention, a state of affairs that remained constant throughout the rest of the period. For example, in 1893 it was found that of those judges whose views had been expressed to, or reported to, the SC of that year, 23 judges were broadly in favour and 12 broadly against committals.

Moreover, registrars appear to have influenced strongly the inclination of the government to eschew legislation. At the 1909 SC there was "practical uniformity" on the part of the county court registrars against any relaxation in the law, a position identical to that reached at a conference of registrars held in 1906 where the issue had been discussed.[104] The experienced registrars examined by the 1893 SC also concurred with the views of the majority of county court judges.

Since registrars were also qualified solicitors in private practice, they attracted the criticism of want of impartiality when carrying out their duties as officers of the court. The allegation was, specifically, that the plaintiff in a debt case was potentially a client of the registrar in his capacity as family solicitor, and in such circumstances, even-handedness between creditor and debtor would be more difficult to attain. Since registrars were also paid fees on a two-tier basis according to the number of plaints issued, they had an obvious interest in the decisions of traders whether to continue using the facilities of the court. Naturally enough, a successful businessman-plaintiff would be disposed to continue a tried formula, and if, as much conventional wisdom supposed, credit and imprisonment for debt were interdependent,[105] then the majority of registrars hardly required to be instructed as to where their interests lay in the matter of committals.[106]

Apart from the overwhelming influence of the representatives of the legal process, the serried ranks of small traders and their organisations were lined up to oppose any reform proposals in the belief that abolition would threaten their capacity to conduct business. Drapers, silk mercers, accountants, ironmongers, corn factors, merchants, representatives from national and regional trade protection societies (10 regions were represented before the 1893 SC, and 6 regional and 3 national organisations appeared in 1909) all spoke to the deterrent effect of imprisonment in making debtors pay. Respectability was the image they successfully projected to the committee members; busy entrepreneurs who looked to a sympathetic legal infrastructure within which to prosper and to enhance the reputation of this nation of shopkeepers.

XIV: THE WORKING-CLASS

One possible critical source remained, however. When the setting up of the 1893 SC had been announced, the influential Draper's Record remarked[107] that the issue was possibly of some concern to the working-class. The Trades Union Congress had taken a short-lived interest in the matter after the 1873 SC, but had soon dropped it by the time of the 1874 General Election.[108] The 1893 SC did, in fact, contact three trade union representatives. These were Thomas Burt MP, who was the Northumberland miners' leader; Henry Broadhurst of the Stonemasons, who had also been an MP and Secretary of the TUC Parliamentary Committee; and also George Shipton, who had been on the Parliamentary Committee and was Secretary to the London Trades Council. Together with Charles Loch of the Charity Organisation Society, none could report any evidence of working-class dissatisfaction with the working of the Debtors Act.[109] Indeed, William Johnson, Secretary of the Warwickshire Miners Association who did give evidence to the Committee, was wholly in favour of the system.[110]

A more determined effort was made by the 1909 SC to tap union opinion. Thus, it received evidence in favour of abolition from James Seddon MP of the Shop Assistants Union, and from the somewhat puritanical George Kelley MP, Secretary of the Manchester and Salford Trades Council.[111] Together with one anonymous trade unionist and former debtor,[112] who had, in fact, never been imprisoned for debt, these three witnesses were pitched into unequal competition with about twenty tradesmen and their representatives pleading the other side. That the vote on committee was so close testified more to the strength of humanitarianism among its membership , than to the weight of the evidence which it took.

Yet would a larger representation of working-class witnesses have offered any different perspective to that presented by the trading interest? One is conscious of the absence of undiluted testimony to the system, critical or otherwise, by members of the working-class who had had experience of the grinding poverty which sent debtors to the courts. Their spokesmen, members of Parliament, powerful trade union leaders, hardly fitted the bill.[113] Evidence conveying the attitudes of the poorer classes directly affected by the Act's operation is thus extremely scarce. However, some rare letters were turned up among the Lord Chancellor's Office correspondence and may shed some light.[114] They were written by a number of individuals who had previously been imprisoned for debt in response to the announcement of the setting up of the 1893 SC. The intriguing question was whether these correspondents, victims of a system of quasi-criminal punishments for the civil wrong of being unable to pay their debts, meekly succumbed to the logic of the economically powerful. On the other hand, once freed from the threat of punishment,[115] did they grasp an opportunity to pose their own alternative interpretation to that of the dominant ideology sustaining imprisonment for debt?

The fullest letters examined tended to confirm the acceptance by these debtors of the essential correctness of imprisonment for debt. Theirs was merely a plea in mitigation to the effect that mercy from the rigours of imprisonment should be extended to those who fell victim to sickness and to old age, which in turn led to a failure to obtain work.

The first letter from one George Smith of West Kilburn in London, stated,[116]

> "As I have just been released from Holloway Prison this morning - for the crime of being 70 years old and not being able to pay the parish rates demanded of me through loss of sub-tenants not paying,[117] and being so old I cannot get work as I could when I was younger. I have just undergone one month's imprisonment making the third time during the last twelve months - I have been a tenant householder for the last 38 years in London and never been a defaulter until this last five [?] years through old age and lost eyesight - I am not so able to follow my trade of a fitter as I used to - I have never applied or had a shilling of charity in my life, but these things have no consideration in the eyes of parish Bumble or of the petty justices. All the sympathy I get is 'such people as you should not have a house. Pay or go to prison for a month' - I have done so, and would most respectfully submit to your attention many, many such and painful cases I have seen and heard of at Holloway . . . ."

He went on to instance other sad cases in like vein, including that of the "respectable" widow whose lodging-house business failed and who eventually was imprisoned for debt as a result. Her son took to pilfering from street barrows while her daughter, aged 13, went on the streets,

> ". . . in the company of a notorious woman in the neighbourhood of Hyde Park; you can guess what that means - results - the poor mother in her grave and the children God knows where. . . ."

Clearly these debtors were in a class above the "residuum",[118] or lumpen-proletariat. There was a striving for respectability, a market consciousness, thrift and individualism as long as body and soul held together during a normal working lifespan. With the onset of old age, combined with sickness and domestic tragedy, the barriers of legal charity ought to be lifted, to prohibit imprisonment for debt in these circumstances.

In one respect, George Smith's letter to Lord Herschell touched the heart of the matter. Smith was now in poverty, notwithstanding his sub-landlord status. And poverty was the cause of imprisonment for debt. It was just that his special pleading was not intended to cover the worthless, the work-shy, the casuals. As Stedman Jones has noted,[119]

> "The problem was not structural but moral. The evil to be combated was not poverty but pauperism: pauperism with its attendant vices, drunkenness, improvidence, mendicancy, bad language, filthy habits, gambling, low amusements and ignorance."

Similar sentiments were expressed in a letter from one James Beach of Hammersmith, who had taken the precaution of declaring himself bankrupt[120] with the hope of paying 2d in the £ to his creditors. But crushed by bronchitis, asthma and rheumatics at the age of 74, he could no longer carry on his trade as a joiner, while his wife's prolonged illness forced her to give up dressmaking. He fell victim to a county court committal to prison. Once again moral righteousness shone through this correspondent's plea that old age and illness should distinguish the "deserving" from the "undeserving" poor (although in contrast to the New Poor Law, the deserving poor deserved not charity, but the punishment of imprisonment).

In the case of only one correspondent was there any indication of a refusal to accept the prevailing ideology of the essential correctness of imprisonment for debt. This individual was Tom Race from Hunslet, a travelling salesman in wringers, who had apparently a lingering grievance against W.T. Greenhow[121] and Charles Cautherley,[122] respectively judge and registrar at Leeds and Wakefield County Courts. He had written a number of letters to Greenhow, eventually passed on to the Lord Chancellor's Department, in which he attacked the two court officials for having delivered a number of unfavourable judgments against him.

For example, he indignantly repudiated the judge's "right to allow your Court to be the engine for plundering poor debtors out of needless cost", and complained vigorously that,

> ". . . if a poor labourer is summoned on judgment for a 10/- debt owing to a packman, the judgment is 40 days, same as a big tradesman able to pay, owing £30."

The perceived bias in favour of richer debtors complemented Tom's conspiracy theory involving Greenhow, Cautherley,[123] the local Trade Protection Society and those employers' accountants who gave evidence for plaintiffs. Yet the manifestly intemperate, indeed hysterical, tones[124] employed in his letters strongly support Greenhow's views that, far from being a spokesman for the down-trodden, Tom was "one of those infuriated semi-madmen of whom an instance is to be found in most large County Courts", who simply refused to accept the outcome of the proceedings.

Nonetheless, when Tom unmistakably alluded to the "capture" of the County Court system by powerful, local business interests, it is plausible that Greenhow's dismissive approach reflected not just his response to a perceived threat by Tom to the enforcement of the law. It may also have been seen as his response to a challenge to the concept of law as a mechanism underpinning market exploitation. For what is most interesting, sociologically, is the apparent success of the courts in inculcating a market ideology which also embraced thrift and hard work. In this respect, Tom Race must surely be identified as a crank who could transcend the verbal game played on the judge's terms. In so doing, he appeared to be posing a somewhat modest challenge to the legitimacy of the court's official ideology. Yet in this endeavour, he was no doubt well outside the mainstream of county court debtors.[125]

XV: CONCLUSION

We ought not, then, to be surprised that debtors failed to penetrate the market ideology of which they were victims, let alone to question the efficacy of imprisonment for debt. In respect to the latter, with the trading evidence to the SCs almost wholly one way; with judicial opinion strongly in favour of retention and fully supported in this policy by the registrars; with a reluctant or even hostile government and parliament; with, as we have just seen, the apparent acceptance of the principle by many working-class spokesmen and correspondents; and with the inertia attaching to legal institutions, the legislative inaction is surely unremarkable.

In any case, retentionists might ask, on whose behalf would the risk of abolition be taken? By pointing to the numbers imprisoned relative to the number of plaints issued annually, it could be shown that less than 1% of all debtors were actually imprisoned, of whom less than a tenth stayed their full term in prison. Could one maintain a credible crusade for this paltry figure, especially where the stigmas of dishonesty, thriftlessness and gullibility were easily attached to such debtors? Moreover, did not county court judges make conscientious enquiries as to means to pay before committing for what the courts construed as contumacy (and which they further mystified as contempt) rather than for poverty? Crucially, retentionists could argue that the cure was worse than the disease, whether by suggesting that abolition would harm the interests of the working-class by, for example, encouraging profligacy, or by arguing that alternative procedures for debt recovery, such as executions, were greater evils. The value of untested propositions, such as, that abolition would result in judges going into the court room as toothless tigers, was as immense as that of the verifiable ones, for example, that executions were ineffective.

It was, moreover, highly convenient for retentionists to ignore the implications flowing from the fact that some circuits apparently suffered from a surfeit of contumacious debtors, while others appeared to be blessed by their absence. For this should, in the first place, have cast the spotlight on the exercise of the judges' discretion whether to commit. This in turn would have directed attention to the whims or fancies of different judges as to the standards of proof of means of debtors acceptable to the bench. Thus, like the alleged variations in sentencing for motoring offences today, the fate of debtors faced with committal orders - whether they were to be imprisoned or not - would turn on the fortuitous issues of geographical boundaries and judicial temperament.

For with such a wide discretion to exercise, some judges, such as Judge Chalmers, would take a less inquisitive view of the debtor's means if goods were acquired by "false pretences" (presumably short of that criminal behaviour necessary to constitute a misdemeanour under Part II of the Act) than if the debtor had "fallen into the clutches" of a money-lender. It was also claimed that a practice was followed by certain judges of enquiring into the origin of the debtor's liability, to acertain whether there were any legal grounds to set aside the contract. But as this enquiry often took place at the committal stage, rather than at the original hearing, such expedient was the object of criticism by other judges, for example, by Judge Bagshawe (Cambridge/Bedford).[126] Yet it should be noted that at the original summons stage, there was presumably no urgency, nor any reason for the judge to be "put on his guard". Nonetheless, strong feelings against certain classes of plaintiffs, such as tallymen selling to wives while husbands were at work, and money-lenders, were on occasion expressed by many judges, even by those vehemently opposed to abolition, and these classes of transaction could perhaps have been carefully scrutinised at the original summons stage - had they not been so numerous.

Yet despite the fact that certain classes of plaintiff enjoyed an unfavourable reputation as traders, we have also seen that a central strand in the justification for the retention of imprisonment for debt was the belief that those imprisoned displayed traits of character to which blame could attach. Such a view was indeed echoed in the comments of Judges Dodd and Wightman Wood, which they entered against the names of those imprisoned debtors listed in their committal books (supra).

Punishment was, therefore, appropriate. In this respect, committals were obviously designed to be an instrument of social control (that admittedly much overworked concept) regulating the behaviour of the working-class and assisting in fostering sound household economy. While Judge Daniel was celebrating the salutary qualities of imprisonment in securing a contented household, Lord Fletcher Moulton was perhaps nearer the truth with his description of the county court as a "kind of commercial police".[128]

That there could possibly exist both a different object of social control and also a different instrument for the exercise of that control was scarcely recognised. Thus, the idea was never entertained that instead of subjecting consumer debtors to a control mechanism, that is, to the artificial instrument of a threatened committal, why not subject those consumer creditors who ventured their risk capital in extending credit, to a "natural" control mechanism, the alleged discipline of the market and the invisible hand? In fact, if acted upon, and imprisonment for debt, or even the debt recovery facilities of the court system itself, were denied to consumer creditors, the new situation would probably have corresponded to that understood by most traders and businessmen who, faced with bad debts, preferred to write them off.[129] However, as we have seen, Parliament was unbended. Judicial opinions on the deterrent value of imprisonment and on the relationship between legal sanctions and consumer credit (on which subject they offered only homespun wisdoms to the exclusion of economic expertise) prevailed. And this was despite the fact that they had got it wrong in the past. First, when arrest on mesne and final process was abolished in the 1830s and 1840s, consumer credit did not disappear, despite dire warnings to the contrary.[130] Moreover, as one parliamentarian had remarked,

". . . those who had lived some time in the world must remember when a man might be hanged for stealing a shilling's worth, and plenty of learned Judges gave it as their opinion that it would be impossible to say what might happen if this penalty were taken away."[131]

Imprisonment for debt, therefore, survived for another 100 years to spite the theory that economic development proceeded in tandem with the demise of executions against the body.[132] There was surely something ironic, it was thought by some, in "lesser mercantile nations"[133] such as France, Belgium, Switzerland, Norway, Italy and Scotland, apparently displaying a mark of "civilised" development which England had rejected.[134] After the First World War,[135] the sanction lingered on until eventually buried without a whimper in 1970,[136] following the findings of the Payne Committee on the Enforcement of Judgment Debts, which had reported in the previous year.[137] The issue was disposed of in a matter of paragraphs which described many imprisoned debtors as "inadequate; incapable of managing their own affairs . . . irresponsible or feckless . . . [but] not dishonest." Prison governors similarly saw them as "physically, mentally and socially inadequate, unreceptive and unresponsive."[138] Despite the somewhat patronising tones of the Payne Committee's description, there is no reason to believe that such a judgment is not equally applicable to late nineteenth century debtors, whom Judge Parry described as "the careless, the thoughtless, the weak and the unfortunate."[139] Indeed, the spread of literacy in the twentieth century might render modern debtors more articulate and privileged by comparison. The image of the cunning debtor, dishonestly evading his obligations, an image carefully cultivated by opponents of reform, fails to shine through. Yet such a model was ideologically imperative to justify the role of a medieval barbarism within a supposedly beneficent market economy. Only those whose characters were tainted deserved such punishment. Ergo, those who were thus punished were necessarily evilly disposed, ran this argument. It was a comfortable ideology which did not, however, correspond to the facts; but its strength as a value system enabled it to survive damaging criticism. There were so many features which became the subject of social reform in the nineteenth century, such as child labour, the slave trade, or the capital punishment statutes, where some modern observers might be forgiven their amazement that such issues were matters for debate at all. That imprisonment for debt had to await the later twentieth century before abolition took place, is a stunning testimony to the combined strength, over a number of generations, of local business and legal elites who patronised most of the county courts. For the insolvent poor, it was their unfortunate fate that the majority of judges, certainly before 1914, remained both resolutely imbued with the spirit of deterrence, and also blind to the reality of poverty.[140]

TABLE A

County Court Plaints, Judgment Summonses, Executions and Debts

Quinquennial Returns 1871-1911[1]

Year	Plaints					Judgment Summonses		Executions		Debts			
	Not more than £20	£20-£50	Above £50	For Plaintiff	Non-suit or for Defendant	Issued	Heard	Issued	Sales made	Amounts sought in Plaints	Amount of debts Exclusively	Costs plus Fees	Amounts Paid In[2]
1871	904072	14431	35	504498	17446	123928	66606	181123	4435	£2662132	£1324156	£419701	N/A
1876	929159	17378	168	529455	17617	99165	51738	194635	4335	£3178202	£1471604	£506630	N/A
1881	1022340	12689	282	636753	15975	127138	74827	240709	5409	£3223973	£1601648	£561440	£1558018
1886	966948	12716	674	590816	13559	165062	97977	223877	4640	£3009838	£1523542	£546744	£1499380
1891	1019053	11685	870	632551	11786	229686	135421	228538	3854	£2975962	£1536335	£566639	£1570778
1896	1061051	12226	1010	690292	11420	301084	187519	223502	3826	£3184140	£1667692	£606881	£1695907
1901	1179886	12472	1537	772533	10312	333091	204764	268204	3961	£3479159	£1820054	£649432	£1931701[3]
1906	1265908	12578	1960	838882	9579	390729	254103	321408	3912	£3795448	£2041322	£724224	£2078760
1911	1221656	12718	2686	814319	8305	387644	242301	342219	3300	£3578060	£1959430	£710020	£2676121

Source: for 1871-91, P.P. 1892 LXV. pp.40-1; for 1896, P.P. 1898 LXXII, pp.8-9; for 1901, P.P. 1903 LXV, pp.4-5; for 1906, P.P. 1907 LXIX, pp.8-9; for 1911, P.P. 1912-13 LXIX, pp.18-19.

Notes:
(1) Figures for City of London Court are omitted
(2) Including fees
(3) 1900

TABLE B

County Courts

Warrants of Commitment and Debtors Imprisoned 1870-1906

Year	Warrants *	Debtors	Year	Warrants	Debtors
1870	26414	6605	1889	64059	6574
1871	33828	7978	1890	70725	6452
1872	33976	6910	1891	74378	5871
1873	27741	5209	1892	79211	7012
1874	23299	4203	1893	76207	6905
1875	23130	4064	1894	85045	7648
1876	23242	4239	1895	93659	8396
1877	25720	5039	1896	106699	8199
1878	28727	5687	1897	112120	7729
1879	31418	6261	1898	114376	7808
1880	37035	6883	1899	117382	7867
1881	35334	5559	1900	176959	7899
1882	40560	5407	1901	179045	8494
1883	43558	5386	1902	192331	9530
1884	42935	5222	1903	197418	10544
1885	43656	5510	1904	195013	11096
1886	44999	5502	1905	216523	11427
1887	46954	5293	1906	217889	12014
1888	55174	6447			

Source: 1909 SC, Appendix 1.

*Note: The terminology could be confusing. Warrants of Commitment and Committal Orders were the same thing and would be granted following a Judgment Summons, for which see Table A.

TABLE C

Selected County Courts Returns: 1904

1 Circuit Number	2 Circuit	3 Number of Plaints	4 Judgment Summonses	5 Warrants Issued	6 Debtors Imprisoned	7 Ratio of Col. 6/3	8 Ratio of 6/4
15	Yorkshire, N. Riding	30787	12127	8119	472	1 to 65	1 to 26
16	Yorkshire, E. Riding	38856	13847	10082	807	1 to 48	1 to 17
18	Nottinghamshire	39474	13581	9015	850	1 to 46	1 to 16
21	Birmingham	68550	8327	4004	783	1 to 88	1 to 11
25	Staffordshire, S.	39748	6188	3928	622	1 to 64	1 to 10
30	Glamorganshire	45992	11067	7748	521	1 to 88	1 to 21
40	Bow & Shoreditch	33961	2059	727	72	1 to 472	1 to 29
41	Clerkenwell	22583	1573	775	66	1 to 342	1 to 24
42	Bloomsbury & Whitechapel	32231	3032	627	41	1 to 786	1 to 74
43	Brompton & Marylebone	28750	2383	388	101	1 to 285	1 to 24
44	Westminster	22240	1922	831	69	1 to 322	1 to 28
City of London	-	42731	1304	432	30	1 to 1424	1 to 43

Source: Law Times, Vol.122, March 30, 1907, p.501 (cols. 2,7 and 8 added by author).

TABLE D

Selected County Court Returns, 1906

1 Circuit	2 District	3 Plaints under £20	4 Judgment Summonses	5 Ratio of 4 to 3	6 Debtors Imprisoned	7 Ratio of 6 to 3
1	Northumberland	18675	1535	1 to 12	43	1 to 415
2	Durham	23136	2402	1 to 9	19	1 to 1217
11	Yorkshire, West Riding (part of)	22107	10356	1 to 2	405	1 to 54
12	Yorkshire, West Riding (part of)	18467	11732	1 to 1.6	518	1 to 36
13	Sheffield	33702	11917	1 to 3	477	1 to 71
14	Leeds etc.	41653	19314	1 to 2.15	568	1 to 73
15	Yorkshire, North Riding	30193	18484	1 to 1.6	435	1 to 70
16	Yorkshire, East Riding	36632	19918	1 to 1.8	1002	1 to 36
17	Lincolnshire	25359	10233	1 to 2.5	453	1 to 56
18	Nottinghamshire	37744	20841	1 to 1.8	713	1 to 53
24	Monmouthshire	25269	4497	1 to 5.8	14	1 to 1800
48	West Kent etc.,	19925	2184	1 to 9	53	1 to 376
49	East Kent	17902	6956	1 to 2.5	164	1 to 109

Source: 1909 SC. Appendix 16D (Judge Arthur O'Connor (Durham))

TABLE E

Variations Between Two Adjoining Circuits, 1900-1906

	Circuit No. 2 (Durham)		Circuit No. 15 (Yorkshire, North Riding)	
Year	Plaints	Imprisonments	Plaints	Imprisonments
1900	30905	174 full time	22816	295 full time
1901	25587	309 altogether	26964	394 altogether
1902	29488	160 altogether	28282	546 altogether
1903	24941	59 altogether	29144	440 altogether
1904	26693	29 altogether	30517	472 altogether
1905	25271	28 altogether	30939	471 altogether
1906	23136	19 altogether	30193	435 altogether

Source: 1909 SC, Appendix 16H (Judge O'Connor)

TABLE F

East Stonehouse County Court (Devon), Imprisonments, 1892

1 No.	2 Occupation	3 Amount for which committed	4 Average earnings	5 Group	6 If in work on arrest
1	Cartman	£1.14.6	15s.	1	Yes
2	Labourer	£0.8.6	£1 plus pension	1	Yes
3	Coal Porter	£1.3.0	20-25s.	2	Yes
4	Labourer	10.0	16-18s. plus pension	2	Yes
5	Horse Cleaner	12.10	£1	1	Yes
6	Charwoman	8.0	7-8s.	1	Not known
7	Labourer	£1.4.3	18s.	1	Yes
8	Labourer	18.6	Pension of £18.5s. per annum	1	No
9	Stableman	£2.0.6	15s. plus pension of £18 p.a.	2	Yes
10	Trawler	£1.15.4	Uncertain	6	No
11	Compositor	£2.0.0	30-35s.	4	Not known
12	Mason	£1.3.0	20-25s.	2	Yes
13	Waiter	£1.16.5	25-30s.	3	Not known
14	Gentleman	£3.15.0	Private means	5	No
15	Merchant seaman	£14.1	£1 when at sea	1	Yes
16	Mason	£1.4.9	£1	1	Yes
17	Coal lumper	£1.10.0	20-25s.	2	Yes
18	Potato merchant	£4.18.4	Self-employed	5	-
19	Carpenter	17.6	25-26s.	3	Yes
20	Labourer	15.6	15-20s. including pension	1	Yes
21	Labourer	12.0	17-18s.	1	Yes
22	Gentleman	£4.10.2	Private means	5	No
23	Widow	£1.18.0	Pension of £25 p.a.	1	No
24	Millwright	£2.7.2	"Carrier in small way on arrest" - Unknown	5	Yes
25	Smith	18.0	21s	2	Yes

TABLE F

Cont.

East Stonehouse County Court (Devon), Imprisonments, 1892

1 No.	2 Occupation	3 Amount for which committed	4 Average earnings	5 Group	6 If in work on arrest
26	Billposter	£1.5.0	£1	1	Yes
27	Labourer	15.9	12s plus pension	1	Yes
28	Fish hawker	£1.14.0	10-12s	1	Not known
29	Labourer	£5.0.0	18s plus pension of £18 p.a.	2	Yes
30	Sculptor	£4.14.6	30s	3	Yes
31	Artist	£3.10.0	£3-4	4	Yes
32	Labourer	£1.13.6	15s plus £18 p.a. pension	2	Yes
33	Fisherman	£3.12.9	Uncertain	6	Not known
34	Cartman	£2.2.6	18s plus pension	2	Yes
35	Timber dealer	£12.17.10	Unknown - self-employed	5	Not known
36	Labourer	£2.16.0	18s plus pension	2	Yes
37	Commission agent	£2.0.0	Unknown	5	Not known
38	Mason	£2.2.6	£1	1	Yes
39	Lumper in docks	9.7	£1	1	Not known
40	Shoemaker	15.0	"Can easily earn 15s p.w." (widow)	1	Not known
41	Labourer	£2.3.0	Unknown	5	Yes
42	Labourer	14.6	£1	1	Yes
43	Fish hawker	£1.4.9	Unknown plus pension of £25 p.a.	5	No
44	Labourer	6.6	15s	1	Yes
45	Mason	9.6	£1	1	Yes
46	Navvy	15.0	£1	1	Yes
47	Foreman	£2.0.0	27s	3	Yes
48	Charwoman	17.0	7-8s	1	No
49	Waterman	19.0	15s	1	Yes
50	Waterman	£1.0.0	15s	1	Yes

TABLE F

Cont.

East Stonehouse County Court (Devon), Imprisonments, 1892

1 No.	2 Occupation	3 Amount for which committed	4 Average earnings	5 Group	6 If in work on arrest
51	Painter	£2.3.7	18s plus pension of £18.5s p.a.	2	Yes
52	Labourer	£2.14.5	15s plus pension of £18 p.a.	2	Yes
53	Labourer	8.3	13-15s	1	Yes
54	Mason's labourer	16.0	15-18s	1	Yes
55	Basker maker	16.0	12s	1	Yes
56	Bootmaker	17.2	17-18s	1	Yes
57	Dock labourer	14.6	Uncertain plus pension of £19 p.a.	6	No
58	Porter	£1.13.0	Uncertain plus pension of £40 p.a.	5	No
59	Carpenter	9.3	20s	1	Yes
60	Labourer	£1.8.0	16s plus pension	2	Yes
61	Painter	£1.10.0	£1	1	Yes
62	Charwoman	14.0	7-8s	1	No
63	Charwoman	6.0	7-8s	1	No
64	Charwoman	£1.2.0	Domestic servant at £12 p.a. on arrest. Previously earning as above.	1	Yes
65	Porter	£2.10.0	£1	1	Yes
66	Baker	£1.7.4	£1	1	Yes
67	Charwoman	19.0	"1s 6d a day when sober"	1	No
68	Builder	£39.9.5	Unknown: employer	5	Yes
69	General dealer	£1.5.0	£1	1	No
70	Painter	£1.1.0	21-25s	2	Yes
71	Midwife	10.0	Unknown	6	No
72	Fish dealer	£1.5.0	Unknown	6	No
73	Porter	£1.3.0	£1	1	No
74	Carpenter	£3.4.6	30s	3	Yes

TABLE F

Cont.

East Stonehouse County Court (Devon), Imprisonments, 1892

1 No.	2 Occupation	3 Amount for which committed	4 Average earnings	5 Group	6 If in work on arrest
75	Builder	£17.10.3	Unknown - self-employed	5	No
76	Engine driver	8.6	30s but "prefers loafing about"	7	No
77	Labourer	6.0	15s	1	Yes
78	Painter	12.0	20s	1	Yes
79	Butcher's assistant	10.0	18s	1	No
80	Master mariner	£11.7.8	30s	3	Yes
81	Car driver	14.0	20s	1	Yes
82	None	18.6	£40 pension p.a.	1	No
83	Painter	£2.10.4	£1	1	Yes
84	Fitter	£2.11.9	34s	4	Yes
85	Jobber	15.0	£15 pension p.a. plus odd jobs	1	No
86	Widow	£5.12.0	Unknown - trust income	5	No
87	Engine driver	15.6	30s but "prefers idleness"	7	No
88	Carpenter	£1.2.6	20s	1	Yes
89	None	9.0	£18.5s pension p.a. plus occasional labouring	1	No
90	Carpenter	£1.5.0	30s	3	Yes
91	Bootmaker	£1.12.0	16s	1	No
92	Waterman	£2.5.4	16-18s	1	Yes

Source: Extracted from 1893 SC Appendix L (Judge Edge).
Column 5 added by present author.

NOTES

1. For Dickens' relationship to imprisonment for debt, see Angus Easson, "Imprisonment for Debt in Pickwick Papers" The Dickensian, Vol.64, 1968, pp.105-12; William S. Holdsworth, Charles Dickens as a Legal Historian (New Haven, Connecticut: Yale University Press, 1928), pp.136-43.

2. See, for example, F.W. Maitland, Justice and Police (London: Macmillan, 1885), p.73; Easson, op.cit., p.109. Some writers note the exception to abolition but fail to mention that abolition of imprisonment for debt was thereby rendered nugatory. See, for example, Edward Jenks, A Short History of English Law, 3rd edn., (London: Methuen, 1924), p.356; Jay Cohen, "The History of Imprisonment for Debt and its Relation to the Development of Discharge in Bankruptcy" Journal of Legal History, Vol.3, 1982, pp.153-171, at p.164.

3. Christopher J. Kauffman, "Lord Elcho, Trade Unionism and Democracy", in K.D. Brown (ed.), Essays in Anti-Labour History (London: Macmillan, 1974); Daphne Simon, "Master and Servant", in John Saville (ed.), Democracy and the Labour Movement (London: Lawrence & Wishart, 1954).

4. Lawyers' perceptions of the "reality" of nineteenth century contract law are, of course, strongly grounded in the doctrinal analysis of the cases reported in the law reports.

5. It was not, however, uncommon for imprisoned debtors to pursue their established callings or to take up a new vocation once in prison. Cf. Holdsworth, op.cit., p.139.

6. E.J. [J.H. Elliott], "Imprisonment for Debt" Westminster Review, Vol.44, 1845, pp.449-68, at p.450. According to Wellesley's Index of Victorian Periodical Literature, Vol.III, Elliott was reviewing his own work, Credit the Life of Commerce (1845).

7. The County Courts Act also gave discretion to the judge to order the

committal of any debtor who failed merely to answer the summons. This, in fact, amounted to the reintroduction of a form of arrest on mesne process as an alternative to judgment in absentia. It was another thirteen years before this regressive step was rectified.

8. Law Times, Vol.33, October 8, 1859, p.33. A contemporary newspaper decided that his remarks merited the headline, "Extraordinary Conduct of a County Court Judge." Indeed, it went on to conclude, "Yes, there can no longer be any doubt. The Serjeant is either a monomaniac or a divinity. In neither case is he fitted to be a County Court Judge." See ibid., October 22, 1859, p.55.

9. The original Bill was amended and reissued in mid-May 1869.

10. TheTimes, April 2, 1869.

11. E.A. Parry, The Law and the Poor (London: Smith, Elder & Co., 1914), p.57. It should be noted that a greater number of debtors were imprisoned for default in payment of maintenance and affiliation, rates, taxes and industrial school debts. For example, in the twelve month period, April 1, 1911 to March 31, 1912, 15543 civil debtors were imprisoned, of whom only 6847 were County Court debtors and 2620 were rate defaulters. See Report of the Commissioners of Prisons, etc., for Year ended 31 March, 1912, Cd. 6406 (London: HMSO, 1912), appendix 2. It is not, however, proposed to deal with other than County Court debtors in this paper.

12. H.C. Select Committee on Imprisonment for Debt, P.P. 1873 (384) XV; H.L. Select Committee on the Debtors Act, P.P. 1893-4 (H.L. 156) IX; H.C. Select Committee on Debtors (Imprisonment), P.P. 1909 (239) VII (henceforth 1873 SC, 1893 SC and 1909 SC). The question was discussed more briefly in the H.C. Select Committee on the County Courts Jurisdiction (No.2) Bill, P.P. 1878 (267) XI.

13. M.D. Chalmers, "Imprisonment for Debt" Fortnightly Review, Vol.44 (N.S.), September 1888, pp.337-346. For Chalmers, see the present author's entry

in A.W.B. Simpson (ed.) Dictionary of Common Law Biography, Butterworth, 1984. See also R.B. Ferguson, "Legal Ideology and Commercial Interests: The Social Origins of the Commercial Law Codes" British Journal of Law and Society, Vol.4, 1977, pp.18-38.

14. On the disparity, see for example, Solicitors' Journal and Reporter, Vol.17, August 16, 1873, p.804.

15. W.T.S. Daniel, in Leone Levi, On the Abolition of Imprisonment for Debt (London: W. Wilfred Head, 1874), p.22.

16. However, the practice of Liverpool County Court was to commit only on proof of present means. Where this was established, Judge Collier, applying the authority of Stonor v. Fowle [1888] AC 20; 57 L.J. 387; (1886) 18 Q.B.D. 213 (H.L.), which permitted the suspension of committal orders, would request plaintiffs to suspend their execution on the ground that it was illogical to order a suspension where the means were established. See "Memorandum as to the commitment under the Debtors Act, by Judge Collier, Liverpool," 1893 SC p.189. For Stonor, see later.

17. County Courts Chronicle, Vol.24, June 1, 1874, p.405.

18. Common Law Commissioners: Fourth Report, P.P. 1831-32. (239) VVX, p.44

19. Richard Keysell, Imprisonment for Debt, Irrespective of Fraud, Shown to be Un-English, Unchristian, etc. (London: George Watson, 1860), p.5.

20. Robert Lowe, "Have we Abolished Imprisonment for Debt?" Fortnightly Review, Vol.21 (N.S.), 1877, p.312.

21. See, for example, the evidence to all three select committees of 1873, 1893 and 1909 of the remarkable Peter Morison, Solicitor, who from 1863 was secretary of the Scottish Trades Protection Society.

22. In Stafford Gaol between September 1870 and September 1871, for example, 602 persons were imprisoned for debt. The maintenance costs were £370 and the cost of conveying the prisoners to gaol was £361 4s.,

which was payable out of the consolidated fund. Yet the total debt in 100 of these cases was just £47 18s.4d. Therefore, argued the wealthy brewer, M.T. Bass, in presenting his private member's bill to abolish committals in 1872, the county might have saved 5s for each prisoner if it had paid their debts before any judgment summonses were issued, while the Chancellor of the Exchequer would have saved at least £35 and possibly £82 10s. Parish relief was also paid on top of this sum, while the deprivation of liberty would almost certainly have prevented debtors, once released, from recovering any employments they might have had prior to imprisonment. See H.C. Deb., 3rd series, Vol.211, June 19, 1872, cols. 1977-83, Cf. County Courts Chronicle, Vol.22, October 1, 1870, p.228.

23. "Appellant", "Imprisonment for Debt" Humane Review, Vol.3, 1902-3, p.113 (henceforth Appellant (1902)).

24. Keysell, op.cit., p.5.

25. W.R. Cornish, "Criminal Justice and Punishment", in W.R. Cornish et al., Crime and Law (Shannon: Irish Universities Press, 1978), p.48.

26. See Jerome E. Hall, Theft, Law and Society, 2nd edn. (New York: Bobbs, Merrill, 1952) and G.P. Fletcher, "The Metamorphosis of Larcency" Harvard Law Review, Vol.89, 1976, pp.469-530. For the Small Debts Act, see E.J. [J.H. Elliot], op.cit.

27. See generally, J.D. Unwin, The Scandal of Imprisonment for Debt (London: Simpkin, Marshall, 1935).

28. Law Times, Vol.53, May 25, 1872, p.68.

29. A reference to the private member's bill to abolish imprisonment for debt presented by M.T. Bass in 1872.

30. Judge Daniel, op.cit., note 28.

31. The 1909 committee, incidentally, failed to appreciate that if the means of the debtor were inadequate irrespective of the deception, then the requirements for committal had not been made out. Second, the

committee also failed to explain how the debtor could be held responsible for what another person had told the creditor. The 1873 SC, in fact, had earlier recommended that the provisions of Part II of the Act relating to fraudulent debtors be revised so as to extend to persons subject to judgment summons procedure. Nothing came of this suggestion, however.

32. Cf. "Resolution of the Humanitarian League to the Lord Chancellor", in Humanitarian League, Imprisonment for Debt (London: A. Bonner & Son, 1907), p.9.

33. Daily Telegraph, April 18, 1872.

34. Law Times, Vol.51, June 10, 1871, pp.97-98.

35. Ibid.

36. 1909 SC, q.1959.

37. 1873 SC, p.vi.

38. 1909 SC, p.287. From 1880 the debtor's means had to be proved by affidavit if more than four months had elapsed since the original court order.

39. The Times, May 6, 1873. The leading article was reprinted by the County Courts Chronicle, Vol.24, June 2, 1873, p.142. The Chronicle, interestingly, was no stalwart of the abolitionist cause.

40. According to one witness to the 1873 enquiry, debtors from Manchester were sent to Manchester City Gaol, while debtors from Salford, about a mile away, went to Lancaster Castle, fifty-two miles away. See 1873 SC, qq. 4889-4891 (evidence by Judge John Russell).

41. Ibid., qq. 4870-5.

42. County Courts Chronicle, Vol.25, June 1, 1874, p.405.

43. The information was more or less "conjectural" because the small debtor was usually absent through fear of losing his employment and because he had no attorney. See 1873 SC, p.vi.

44. See, for example, Supplement to Humanitarian League, October 1906, p.2

(correspondence of Judge Orr (Co. Down and North Antrim)).

45. 1893 SC, qq. 242-5.

46. The Times. August 10, 1906.

47. Appellant (1902), op.cit., p.111.

48. Law Times, Vol.55, August 9, 1873, p.268.

49. The Times, June 24, 1897 (correspondence of Walter H. Morgan).

50. 1893 SC, q.673.

51. Chalmers, op.cit., p.339. At the committee stage of the Bill, Mr. Serjeant Simon had warned that the discretion as to mode of proof granted to the judge would become open to abuse with "cooked-up affidavits" in profusion. Such latitude, it was complained, had not been conferred on the judges of any other court of law. See H.C. Deb., 3rd series, Vol.197, June 29, 1869, col. 761. The Judgment Debtors Bill 1868 had, in fact, imposed on the judge the duty of considering all the debts and liabilities of the party summoned. See Law Journal, Vol.3, April 3, 1868, p.242.

52. "A County Court Judge", "Should Imprisonment for Debt be Abolished?" Law Times, Vol.113, August 2, 1902, p.319 (henceforth Judge (1902)).

53. See later, note 129.

54. See Judge Josiah Smith (Shropshire and Herefordshire) in Law Times, Vol.61, May 20, 1876, p.52. Judge Falconer (see note 42) imprisoned between eight and ten days. A vast amount of information is contained in the three SC reports and various appendices.

55. [1888] A.C. 20, at p.29.

56. The judge was apparently Judge Motteram of Birmingham. See [Public Record Office] LC08/4, "Treasury County Court Department Circular Letters", 1887, p.57(8).

57. Solicitors' Journal and Reporter, Vol.17, October 11, 1873, p.929. See also County Courts Chronicle, Vol.23, June 1, 1872, p.283 for original statement by Judge Daniel.

58. H.C. Deb., 3rd series, Vol.218, April 14, 1874, Cols. 570-1.

59. Law Times, Vol.122, March 30, 1907, p.501.

60. "Lex", "Imprisonment for Debt", Law Magazine and Review, Vol.39, 1914, pp.155-6.

61. 1893 SC, para. 13. Bedwell was judge at first instance in the leading trade union case of Temperton v. Russell [1893] 1QB 715. See R. Brown, "The Temperton v. Russell Case (1893): The Beginning of the Legal Offensive Against the Unions" Bulletin of Economic Research, Vol.23, 1971, pp.50-66, at p.58.

62. 1909 SC, qq. 2672-7.

63. Ibid., appendices 3, 4 and 26.

64. Department of Employment and Productivity, British Labour Statistics: Historical Abstract (London: HMSO, 1971), Tables 1, 3, 6, 7 and 35.

65. E.H. Hunt, Regional Wage Variations in Britain, 1850-1914 (London: Oxford University Press, 1973), p.356. See also T.R. Gourvish, "The Standard of Living, 1890-1914" in Alan O'Day (ed.), The Edwardian Age: Conflict and Stability 1900-1914 (London: Macmillan, 1979), Ch.1. Cf. E.H. Phelps Brown The Growth of British Industrial Relations (London: Macmillan, 1959), Ch.1.

66. 1909 SC, qq. 2694-2825.

67. Ibid., qq. 2143-5.

68. 1873 SC, qq. 2003-4, 2008.

69. The accuracy of the findings may have been subject to error but there is little doubt that the population agreed with Sir Leo Chiozza Money when he wrote, "We know, thanks to the patience and accurate scientific investigations of Mr. Rowntree and Mr. Charles Booth, that there is about 30% of our population underfed on the verge of hunger." See Sir Leo Chiozza Money, Riches and Poverty (London: Methuen, 1905), p.5.

70. Where, incidentally, all transactions for immediate consumption were

required to be paid for in cash (County Courts Act 1888, s.182, 51 and 52 Vict., c.43, extending the Sale of Spirits Act 1750, s.12 (the "Tippling Act"), 24 Geo. 2, c.40). This left even less cash available for necessaries and made credit even more essential.

71. Law Times, Vol.53, May 25, 1872, p.69.

72. "Imprisonment for Debt in England" Scottish Law Review, Vol.9, February 1893, p.33.

73. The following possibly represents a combination of this view and that of Judge Daniel. It alleges, "The careless and dissipated young spendthrift is the one who marries while he is a boy, begets a family of starving babies, never has a pound put by, or a chair or a table honestly paid for. He it is who, or whose wife, borrows from money-lenders, lends his name as surety to other borrowers for a shilling or two, and runs in debt for bread and clothes with every tradesman he can get to trust him, and he it is who, when a committal order is asked against him can easily prove, that he has not, and never had, the means to pay or if he has, that he must, to keep him off the rates, be saddled with the smallest possible instalment." See "Judge" (1902), op.cit., p.319.

74. The Times, December 30, 1880, correspondence of "A County Court Judge".

75. Law Journal, Vol.28, March 4, 1893, p.161.

76. Leisure Hour, 1873, p.496.

77. Ibid., italics added.

78. Clementina Black, "Thrift for the Poor" New Review, Vol.7, 1892, p.667.

79. Names, incidentally, conspicuously absent in discussions of imprisonment for debt.

80. See, for example, the letter of Judge Greenhow (Leeds) to The Times, December 27, 1892. Writing under the pseudonym "A County Court Judge", he cited the "example" of a hypothetical miner earning 40-50 shillings a

week. See also Judge Selfe (West Kent), 1893 SC, p.203 on the case of John Beal, a hammerman at Sheerness Dockyard.

81. Charles Cameron, "The Law a Respecter of Persons" The Nineteenth Century, Vol.13, 1883, p.877. For a modern variant, see "Why some go bust and keep the Rolls" The New Standard, December 22, 1980. The opening sentence, "Is there one law for the rich and another for the poor in the bankruptcy courts?" strikes a familiar chord throughout the ages.

82. County Courts Chronicle, Vol.21, May 1, 1870, p.405. Indeed, arguably "rich" debtors were worse off than poorer ones insofar as it was believed that the opportunity to pay debts by instalment was not available in the superior courts.

83. The Times, October 2, 1873. Of course, it may be objected that "large debtors" were themselves reduced to a state of poverty. But as Jacob Viner has noted for the eighteenth century, "The poor by accident, the members of families with a tradition of at least moderate prosperity who by misfortune or misconduct had fallen into poverty, were commonly excluded from the category of 'labouring poor'." See Jacob Viner, "Man's Economic Status" in James L. Clifford (ed.) Man Versus Society in Eighteenth Century Britain (London: Cambridge University Press, 1968), p.28.

84. "Lex", "Imprisonment for Debt" Law Magazine and Review, Vol.35, 1909, p.16.

85. Solicitors' Journal, Vol.53, August 4, 1909, p.742.

86. Calculated from Report of the Committee on the Enforcement of Judgment Debts (Payne Committee), Cmnd. 3909, 1969: Table 14, "County Court Averages 1871-1964". See also Appendix, Table B.

87. Cf. 1873 SC, resolutions 9 and 10.

88. Elsie E. Gulley, Joseph Chamberlain and English Social Politics (New York: Columbia University Press, 1920), p.164.

89. Ibid.

90. E.A. Parry "The Insolvent Poor" Fortnightly Review, Vol.63 (N.S.), 1898, pp.797-804, at pp.801-2. For departmental consideration of administration orders, see for example LC02/161 and LC02/195.

91. All the SC reports commented on this failure. Though see the evidence of Adam Brown, travelling draper, to the 1873 SC, q.4228. Also letter in the Law Times, Vol.125, December 31, 1908, p.625.

92. See, for example, Judge Daniel in County Courts Chronicle, Vol.23, April 1, 1872, p.239. Another correspondent thought that the mode of issuing warrants against goods was most adopted in those districts where working men, though earning less money, were "more careful" of it than many in the ironworking and kindred districts where it was alleged that good wages were dissipated though "improvidence". See Law Journal, Vol.28, March 4, 1893, p.160.

93. County Courts Act 1888 (51 & 52 Vict., c.43) section 147.

94. The Times, January 1, 1880 (correspondence of "A County Court Judge").

95. 1909 SC, qq. 3032, 3183-8, 3212-27. In Scotland, the equivalent warrant sale has recently attracted wide criticism and one district council (Stirling) has announced its abandonment of this debt-recovery mechanism. See The Scotsman, December 22, 1980; also Scottish Law Commission, Memoranda 47-51, 1980. Judge Bompas, who had made the suggestion to the SC, had been, as Recorder of Plymouth, judge at first instance in the leading trade union case of Curran v. Treleaven [1891] 2QB. 545. See John Saville, "Trade Unions and Free Labour: The Background to the Taff Vale Decision", in A. Briggs and J. Saville (eds.), Essays in Labour History (London: Macmillan, 1960), p.342.

96. 1909 SC, qq. 5529-31 (evidence of A.O. Jennings, registrar of Brighton County Court and delegate of the Association of County Court Registrars). After 1905 the costs of abortive executions were cast on creditors, thus

further limiting their use. Cf. Judge Tindal-Atkinson, dating the shift from 1895. See ibid., qq. 2070-3.

97. Ibid., paras. 25-6. For a consideration of the tally trade and other extensive users of the facilities of the county court, see pp.321-48.

98. BT37/22/B922/11, "Memorandum on Imprisonment of Debtors (Abolition) Bill", April 27, 1911.

99. See H.C. Deb., 4th series, Vol.164, November 7, 1906, cols. 554-5; ibid., Vol.165, November 20, 1906, cols. 599-600; ibid., Vol.170, February 27, 1907, col.46.

100. LC02/211, "Lord Chancellor's Bill dealing with s.5 of the Debtors Act: Judges' Observations, 1906."

101. Cf. the remarks in Parliament: H.C. Deb., 3rd series, Vol.197, June 22, 1869, col. 424 (H.W. West); ibid., Vol.218, April 14, 1874, col. 546 (M.T. Bass).

102. H.C. Deb., 3rd series, Vol.194, March 5, 1869, col.780.

103. Ibid., Vol.197, June 29, 1869, col.763.

104. Birmingham Daily Mail, January 18, 1911.

105. For a more extended consideration of the relationship between the courts and consumer credit for the poor, see pp.341-4 and G.R. Rubin, "Packmen, Tallymen and 'Perambulating Scotchmen': Credit Drapers in Nineteenth and Early Twentieth Century England" (in preparation).

106. See, for example, Theophilus Lott, A Plea for Poor Labouring Men, etc. (Birmingham: Herald Press, 1888), pp.12-13. Lott was registrar of Shipston-on-Stour County Court.

107. Draper's Record, Vol.12, February 18, 1893, p.348.

108. Ross M. Martin, TUC: The Growth of a Pressure Group (Oxford: Clarendon Press, 1980), p.46. Some years later, one writer commented, "What must strike the observer as remarkable in connection with this subject is that although it is essentially one which affects the working classes, it has no place in the programme of the Labour Party." See C.H. Pickstone, "The

Extension of the County Court" Law Journal, Vol.42, October 26, 1907, p.645. The legislative preoccupations of the British labour movement can be gauged from, inter alia, Royden Harrison, Before the Socialists (London: Routledge & Kegan Paul, 1965); Charles Bradlaugh, Labor and Law (London: R. Forder, 1891); and F. Bealey and H. Pelling, Labour and Politics 1900-1906 (London: Macmillan, 1958). Pelling notes the passing remark of Thomas Wright, the "Journeyman Engineer", that one of the "things that sting and rankle, that perpetuate and intensify class jealousy and hatred" was the capacity of the larger debtor to file a petition in bankruptcy, while the small debtor remained exposed to imprisonment. See Henry Pelling, "Trade Unions, Workers and the Law" in Henry Pelling, Popular Politics and Society in Late Victorian Britain (London: Macmillan, 1968), p.65, quoting Thomas Wright, Our New Masters (London: Cass reprint, 1969), p.155.

109. See the correspondence in 1893 SC, p.XI.

110. Ibid., qq. 3064-3107.

111. Johnson, Seddon and Kelley were all political and industrial "moderates". Indeed Seddon eventually left the Labour Party to join the National Democratic Party in 1918, and towards the end of his life became secretary of St. Pancras Chamber of Commerce. For Johnson, see Joyce Bellamy and John Saville (eds.) Dictionary of Labour Biography, Vol.II (London: Macmillan, 1974), pp.209-11; for Seddon, ibid., pp.332-5; for Kelley, ibid., pp.211-14. Of the trade unionists mentioned previously, for Broadhurst, ibid., pp.62-8; for Burt, ibid., Vol.I (1972), pp.59-63. For Shipton, see London Trades Council 1860-1950: A History (London: Lawrence & Wishart, 1950), passim. For Loch, see C.L. Mowat, The Charity Organisation Society, 1869-1913 (London: Methuen, 1961), passim.

112. "Mr. A.A.": 1909 SC, qq. 5290-5440.

113. Cf. Zygmunt Bauman, Between Class and Elite (Manchester: Manchester University Press, 1972) on the contrasting perceptions of national trade union

leaders and the rank and file.

114. LC02/66. The views of articulate, middle class imprisoned debtors were still heard, as they had been during the Dickensian era. See, for example, "For Debt", Windsor Magazine, Vol.XV, 1902, pp.231-9.

115. Brewer and Styles have observed that the evidence of attitudes of defendants in criminal trials to the law itself must be treated with extreme care. Such defendants would tend to express only those opinions which they thought acceptable to the court trying them: John Brewer and John Styles (eds.). An Ungovernable People: The English and their Law in the Seventeenth and Eighteenth Centuries (London: Hutchinson, 1980), p.14.

116. The spelling has been corrected, and punctuation inserted where necessary.

117. Subletting was, of course, very common among late Victorian working-class householders in London. See M.S. Pember Reeves, Round About a Pound a Week (London: Bell, 1913), pp.30-8.

118. Gareth Stedman Jones, Outcast London (Harmondsworth: Peregrine, 1976), p.11.

119. Ibid.

120. Presumably under the special procedure for small bankruptcies under the Bankruptcy Act 1883 (46 & 47 Vict., c.52), s.165.

121. For a recent reference to Greenhow in the context of proposals to increase the workload of the county courts under the Employer's Liability Bill 1897, see Harry Smith, "The Resurgent County Court in Victorian Britain" American Journal of Legal History, Vol.13, 1969, p.138, note 69.

122. Cautherley was author of Costs in the County Courts (London: Wm. Clowes & Son, 1886). On the unfitness of a number of county court judges to hold office, see P.P. 1878 (267) XI, op.cit.

123. He described Cautherley ungraciously as an "empty headed thing without the intelligence to fit him for the office of a parish Beadle."

124. Among his more vivid letters was one dated February 14, 1893, which began:

"Cowardly Greenhow, you mean cowardly skunk . . . ."

125. The "verbal game" is considered in Pat Carlen, Magistrates' Justice (London: Martin Robertson, 1976). The present author is grateful to his colleague Alan Thomson for comments on this point.

126. W. Bagshawe, "Imprisonment for Debt" Law Gazette, January 13, 1893, reprinted in 1893 SC, Appendix A.

127. See, for example, The Times, December 28, 1892 (correspondence of G. Pitt-Lewis Q.C., who later edited Archbold's County Court Pleadings).

128. See Frederick Dolman, "Is the Law too Dear?" Strand Magazine, Vol.22, 1901, at p.384.

129. Cf. Judge Greenhow, under the pseudonym "A County Court Judge" in The Times, December 27, 1892: "Even under the present law, the trade creditor, the small grocer, provision dealer, baker and so forth foregoes, and for the most part foregoes cheerfully and kindly a large proportion of actual claims." Perhaps of significance was the testimony of some trade protection society members that they did not make use of the county court on the grounds that its methods were "costly, uncertain and profoundly slow": 1909 SC, q.852.

130. Parry (1914) op.cit., p.49.

131. H.C. Deb., 3rd series, Vol.197, June 22, 1869, cols.425-6 (J.W. Henley).

132. Lowe, op.cit. (supra).

133. F.K. Munton, Imprisonment for Debt (London: Spottiswoode & Co., 1890), p.1 (paper first read to annual provincial meeting of the Law Society, Nottingham, October 7-8, 1890).

134. M.D.C. [M.D. Chalmers], "Debt, Imprisonment for", in Palgrave's Dictionary of Political Economy, Vol.I (London: Macmillan, 1894), p.504.

135. Judge Artemus Jones noted that the numbers imprisoned during the war fell dramatically as a result of the need for manpower for the war effort. See Thomas Artemus Jones, "In Gaol for Debt" in Without My Wig (Liverpool: Brython Press, 1944), Ch.15.

136. Administration of Justice Act 1970. Throughout the 1930s, a number of muted voices of criticism were raised. Some criticisms were confined to imprisonment for non-payment of rates, taxes or maintenance orders, e.g. Unwin, op.cit. Others also referred to the matter dealt with in this paper, consumer debt. See, for example, "Solicitor", English Justice (London: Routledge, 1932), Ch.11. For subsequent departmental consideration, see LC02/1306 (1938) where one judge enquired whether his practice of imposing three days imprisonment was too short. He was told it was.

137. Payne Committee, op.cit.

138. Ibid., paras.980-2. Cf. O.R. McGregor, Social History and Law Reform (London: Stevens & Sons, 1981), Ch.5.

139. E.A. Parry, Ten Years Experience of the Manchester and Salford County Courts (London: Sherratt and Hughes, 1906), p.19.

140. Notwithstanding, civil imprisonment for contempt and for tax, rates and maintenance default, still blots the debt recovery landscape. Arguably these are matters of public, rather than private, law. See Geoff Wilkins, Making Them Pay (London: NACRO, 1979), Ch.5 and Boylan v. Boylan, The Times, October 3, 1980 (C.A.).

PART B

LAWYERS, COURTS AND INDUSTRIAL SOCIETY

WHY THE HISTORY OF THE PROFESSIONS IS NOT WRITTEN *

Wilfrid Prest

Certain institutional manifestations and a growing volume of published work indicate that historians are paying increased attention to the professions.[1] Of course the current surge of interest is not entirely without preparation or precedent. As long ago as 1953 Richard Pares suggested that the "enormous growth of the organised professions is perhaps the greatest change in the whole of modern history."[2] Pares was familiar with A.M. Carr-Saunders and P.A. Wilson's classic The Professions, first published in 1933. This seminal study of the historical development of professional associations remains today the standard work on the institutional history of the English professions. But it is only in the last decade that some scholars have begun to regard themselves specifically as historians of the professions, working within a distinct research field comparable to those marked out by the historian of the family or of education, the urban or the labour historian (to mention only a few of the more recently developed varieties of historical specialisation). These authors are generally more concerned than their less self-conscious predecessors to inform their work with comparative and theoretical perspectives and to relate the history of the professions to the history of society at large.

Whether the history of the professions will succeed in establishing a distinct scholarly identity remains to be seen. At present the topic labours under two major handicaps: the conceptual and semantic confusion which surround the term "profession" and the dominance of a paradigm derived from a body of sociological theory which in turn rests on inadequate historical foundations.[3] The opening section of this paper explores these problems, discussing some aspects of the relationship between historical and sociological study of the professions over the past half-century; the paper then goes on to outline an alternative approach which would shift attention to hitherto-neglected aspects of the professions in history, as well as pointing the way to a general history of the professions.

I : HISTORY AND SOCIOLOGY OF THE PROFESSIONS

There is a large body of sociological writing on the professions (if as yet no indisputably great books). Until quite recently its dominant note was a kind of functionalism which took the professions very much at their own valuation, as autonomous high-status occupations deploying esoteric but socially-important knowledge in the public interest. The proliferation of the professions was regarded as a distinguishing characteristic of modern industrial societies, the result of ever-expanding scientific knowledge combined with ever-increasing specialisation of labour.[4] This mode of interpretation was not self-evidently a-historical, since it presented both a general view of the evolution of professions over time and a good deal of data on the development of individual professions, or at least their institutional manifestations. However, the proffered overview of professional evolution was little better than theoretical history, depending far more on inference than evidence, while the use of historical examples to illustrate the general thesis could be seen as logically superfluous, however rhetorically effective. (If professions emerge and develop simply by virtue of a process of occupational differentiation, the historical details of the process - being fully determined - can hardly be of much more than antiquarian interest).[5] So, assuming that the historical "background" was well taken care of, sociologists were free to concentrate upon identifying the attributes of a true Profession, and explaining chosen combinations of characteristics in terms of their supposed harmony with objective social needs.

"Professionalisation" was said to be the process by which proto-, quasi- and would-be professions drew steadily closer to full professional status (or "professionalism") by acquiring more of the variously-denominated attributes of a profession.[6] Professionalisation (term and concept) still permeates much of what passes for the history of the professions, studies which celebrate the ascent of the so-called "new" professions, such as engineering, accountancy, surveying, teaching, nursing and librarianship, from relative impotence and obscurity towards the nirvana of full "professionalisation".[7] The Whiggish nature of this approach is obvious. Like the analogous paradigm of one-way progress, from superstitious medieval darkness to positivistic modern enlightenment, which until recently dominated the history of science, it encourages the anachronistic imposition of present-day values on the complex reality of the past, inhibiting critical scrutiny of changes in the meaning of the paradigm itself, reducing the historian's role to that of judge or quiz master, awarding the winners and ignoring the losers.[8]

While historians were discovering the functionalist "trait-analysis" approach and the allied concept of "professionalisation", sociologists were becoming increasingly conscious of their deficiencies. With the rise of radical sociological scholarship during the mid-1960s, the professions could no longer be universally accepted at their own valuation as altruistic corporations of skilled and learned men. They were rather increasingly depicted as organised conspiracies against the consumer and society at large, and their ideology of public service as a mixture of self-deception and clever public relations.[9] Such views did not sweep all before them, but forced an expansion of the hitherto narrow focus of sociological investigation. Emphasis accordingly shifted from the taxonomy of professional ideology and organisation to the strategies by which professions gain control of their markets - in particular the relationship between their market standing, the services they provide and the expertise to which they lay more or less exclusive claim. "One consequence of focussing on wider social forces is that the utility of an historical perspective becomes apparent"; or in the words of Magali Larson, who has recently published a path-breaking essay towards a systematic historical model of the rise of the professions in the West, "A first step to render modern professions sociologically intelligible is to reflect on their historical origins."[10]

These sentiments must surely be applauded. But reflection upon the historical origins of the professions is, alas, more easily advocated than achieved. The problem can be simply stated: where are sociologists to find their historical data? Since social historians typically concentrate on the bottom-most social strata, peasants and proletarians have attracted far more historical attention than professional persons. True, we do possess various studies of individual occupational groups which at some time in the past have attained the mysterious accolade of professional status. But most of the available published work is still confined to narrowly institutional or organisational themes, and hence gives little more than anecdotal or impressionistic treatment to the kinds of issues with which the new wave "power-perspective" sociologists of the professions are concerned. Thus Charles Rosenberg has recently asserted that ". . . no currently available formulation of the stages and characteristics of the professionalisation of knowledge is based on adequate historical investigation."[11]

Rosenberg is particularly concerned to stress gaps in our knowledge of the modern (i.e., post-1800) history of the professions. His remarks gain added force when it is considered that the overwhelming bulk of historical writing about the professions concentrates on the nineteenth and twentieth centuries, to the virtual neglect of earlier periods. This chronological bias is no accident, but rather reflects (as well as reinforcing) the most basic operating assumptions of the sociologists. These are summarised by Larson as follows: "professionalisation" is "part of the complex process of 'modernisation' "; the professions are "typical products of modern industrial society", and hence "the continuity of the older professions with their 'pre-industrial' past" is indeed "more apparent than real."[12]

The paucity of historical research on the professions before c.1800 must help to perpetuate the assumption that their history does not *really* begin until the nineteenth century, especially since the only extended general survey of the subject by a practising historian, W.J. Reader's influential Professional Men : The Rise of the Professional Classes in Victorian England (1966), fully endorses this sociological truism. Thus Reader asserts (p.9) that ". . . the professions as we know them are a Victorian creation, brought into being to serve the needs of an industrial society"; their pre-Victorian predecessors are correspondingly portrayed as mere dependent satellites of the ancien régime's landed ruling elite. So it is hardly surprising that the new historical dimension to the sociological study of the professions turns out, in this respect at least, little different from the older synchronic functionalist approach; both discount the history of the "pre-industrial" professions except as a backdrop to an understanding of "professionalisation" and the place of the professions in contemporary society.

Of course, it would be absurd to deny that many occupations successfully laid claim to professional status during the classical era of English industrialisation by establishing qualifying associations which gained some degree of recognition and protection from the state. It seems plain that the onward march of science and technology contributed to this process, as also the expansion of the potential market for professional services during the later eighteenth and early nineteenth centuries. Yet it does not therefore follow that these interrelated developments constituted such a decisive break in the evolution of the professions that we must regard the later eighteenth to mid-nineteenth centuries, as marking a crucial divide between "proto-professions" and modern "professions" properly so-called.

For this to be so we should need to establish that the *quantitative* proliferation of self-styled professions in the nineteenth century was accompanied by fundamental *qualitative* changes in the nature of professions. Yet the body of published historical work on the professions (however defined) before 1800 is so narrow and thin that it is hard to see how any comparison between professions before and after the supposed critical turning point could possibly be based on empirical grounds rather than a combination of conjecture and a priori reasoning. In other words, we simply do not have sufficient evidence - or rather, the evidence is not yet sufficiently explored - to determine whether or not the characteristics and functions of the professions changed drastically during, and as a result of, what it is convenient to call the Industrial Revolution. Certainly the case cannot be determined by reference to organisational matters alone, as some sociologists and historians have assumed, since (as Edward Hughes perceptively observed some time ago) ". . . most professions . . . had a long history before ever they were organised into associations." Yet it is only on organisational matters (i.e., the formal constitution of professional associations, regulations for training, certification and practice, etc.) that the available secondary literature could possibly be regarded as adequate to support the conceptual burdens now being placed upon it.[13] Here indeed is the fatal flaw which at present must disable all attempted synoptic accounts of the historical development of the professions, including Larson's elegant three-stage model of pre-industrial, competitive capitalist, and monopoly capitalist professional formations - certainly the most elaborate and fully conceived schema presented to date. A glance at Larson's bibliography and notes confirms that few of the cited secondary sources on the early modern period are of recent vintage, while most are written from an exclusively institutional standpoint which allows no more than passing treatment to the sorts of issues (particularly the class origins of both professionals and their clients) on which her general interpretation hinges. Unfortunately, even great theoretical ingenuity can hardly compensate for such a serious shortfall of data.

To summarise the argument so far: while historical interest in the professions grows apace, the definition and scope of the topic remain uncertain. Insofar as it has a theoretical basis, most recent historical writing on the professions defers to a teleological functionalism, even though the focus of sociological interest has broadened over the last decade to include a new concern with the concrete historical circumstances in which particular occupational groups succeed in winning professional status. Regrettably, the bulk of the available historical literature provides little if any systematic illumination of such matters, concentrating rather on the emergence of coherent occupational organisations ("qualifying associations") in the period after 1800. These inadequacies render attempts at formulating general theories about the historical evolution of the professions as a collective entity untenable for sheer lack of evidence. Nevertheless, both functionalist supporters and "power-perspective" critics of the professions continue to accept the sociological article of faith that the professions and professionalisation are essentially phenomena of modern industrial society, and hence that the history of the professions is marked by a fundamental discontinuity at the point of industrialisation, modernisation, or "great transformation".

II : PROFESSION : WORD AND MEANING

If the argument advanced above makes any sense, historians of the professions might benefit from temporarily abandoning the attempt to view their subject through the lens of sociological theory. This would mean giving up belief in the existence of an ideal Profession, whether benign or malignant in its social manifestations, to which individual professions conform in differing degrees at different points of time according to their ranking on the professionalisation scale. It should then become easier to look directly at particular occupational groups conventionally described, now or in the past, as professions in a narrow sense, with the aim of discovering who belonged to them and what they did, how, to whom and with what results.[14] Such an approach would regard the history of the professions as simply a branch of the history of occupations, work or the middle classes, no more and no less. It would also explicitly acknowledge the intensely subjective character of the term "profession" and its derivatives, hence cutting short debate about precisely which groups the historian of the professions is justified in taking under notice. In short, the aim would be to examine the professions as concrete historical and social entities, rather than particular manifestations of a sociological abstraction.

"Profession", word and concept, is not merely a source of intellectual confusion to academic theorists; it is also an ideology whose diverse meanings reflect the struggles of particular interest groups to appropriate the word and concept to their own purposes. Once so regarded, its history becomes a matter of pressing interest, although no historian has yet attempted to trace the changing content and connotations of the term and its derivatives since they were first introduced into the English language in the sixteenth century.

Nevertheless, it has been generally supposed that until the late eighteenth or early nineteenth century the word "profession" was simply equivalent to "job"; then a shift in linguistic usage simultaneously elevated its meaning and narrowed its application. Thus, we are informed, the word acquired a specific and rarefied connotation which it had not previously possessed, precisely as the professions established their distinctive modern identity and status, derived not from the aristocratic connections of their members but based rather on their organised command of socially-useful knowledge. Here, it would seem, is conclusive etymological evidence that the professions were indeed a creation of the Industrial Revolution.

In fact, it is nothing of the sort. Anxious to emphasise the wholly atavistic and socially-subordinate character of the pre-Victorian professions, W.J. Reader asserts (citing Johnson's Dictionary, first published in 1755), that in the eighteenth century and before " 'Profession' by itself was a word which could be used of any 'calling, vocation, known employment' ."[15] The claim is technically correct, but misleading, since the word was also used in a restricted sense as early as the mid-sixteenth century (and, conversely, is still often employed in a non-specific sense today.) The O.E.D. ascribes the first instance of the noun "profession" (derived from the Latin profiteor, profiteri: to avow or confess) used in a secular context to mean "an occupation one professes to be skilled in", to Robert Copland's The Questyonary of Cruygeons (1541): "the parts of the art of medicine cannot be separated without the damage . . . of all the medical profession." It should be noted that this "restricted" usage is distinguished in the next sub-entry from profession in a wider sense, as "any calling or occupation", the earliest recorded instance of which dates from 1576. Moreover, Johnson tightened his earlier broad definition of "profession" in the fourth revised edition of his Dictionary (1773) where the entry reads, "calling, vocation, known employment . . . *particularly used of divinity, physic and law*." Reader further claims that before the nineteenth century the term "frequently turns up in the phrase 'mechanical professions' meaning the trades of skilled workmen." This is exceedingly curious, since the phrase quoted ("mechanical profession(s)") appears in neither the O.E.D. nor any standard eighteenth-century lexicographical source; as it is cited without reference to an authority, the author has presumably made the unconscious mistake of transposing a nineteenth-century usage back in time.[16]

Harold Perkin has also recently claimed that

> ". . . the word 'profession', as now increasingly used in many languages for an especially desirable and dignified occupation with an implication of intellectual training and a largely mental expertise, is derived from a twist in Anglo-American usage in the late eighteenth and nineteenth centuries. Until then, even in English speaking countries, it still meant 'occupation' and no more, as is still normally the case with the French 'profession' and the German 'Beruf' ."[17]

Perkin goes on to shore up this point with the assertion that in Robert Campbell's careers handbook The London Tradesman (1747) no clear division was drawn between professions and other occupations, so that "pinmakers, weavers, merchants, bankers and insurance underwriters" were bracketed with clergymen, physicians and attorneys. However, Campbell's scheme does, in fact, distinguish the learned professions, both under that title and as "liberal sciences", in accordance with the plan of arrangement announced in his introductory chapter of "advice to parents": "I shall begin with the liberal sciences [i.e., the church, medicine and law] then visit the liberal arts [i.e., sculpture, painting, music and architecture] and take a view of the several mechanic trades": the latter include the building, clothing and victualling trades, as well as merchants and shipbuilders, although appropriately enough "The last trade I shall mention is the undertaker . . . ."[18]

So, contrary to received opinion, the term "profession" did have both a specific and a general sense in pre-Victorian usage. Indeed, three separate meanings can be distinguished. First, profession as job or employment tout court. Second, profession as particularly high-status or worthy job, rather than mere mechanical trade, or manual labour. This usage is exemplified in Thoman Mun's early seventeenth-century discussion of the "qualities required in a perfect merchant of foreign trade":

> ". . . many merchants here in England finding less encouragement given to their profession than in other countries, and seeing themselves not so well esteemed as their noble vocation requireth . . . do not therefore labour to attain unto the excellency of their profession . . . whereas the memory of our richest merchants is suddenly extinguished, the son being left rich, scorns the profession of his father."[19]

Third, profession in the narrowest sense of all - the three traditional learned professions, the ministry, physic and the law, as found in George Fox's journal entry for the year 1648:

> "The Lord opened to me three things, relating to those three great professions in the world, physic, divinity (so called) and law . . . and that these three, the physicians, the priests and the lawyers ruled the world out of the wisdom, out of the faith and out of the equity and law of God; the one pretending the cure of the body, the other the cure of the soul, and the third the property of the people."[20]

The word profession presumably came to be attached most specifically to those three occupations by virtue of their intimate connections with the three higher faculties of the medieval university, theology, physic and law, whose degrees were licenses both to teach and to practise or profess the discipline in question.[21]

III : PROFESSION : IDEOLOGY

So if etymology counts at all, the history of the professions, far from beginning only with the Industrial Revolution, stretches well back into the Middle

Ages. But of course the crucial question for our purposes is whether the distinctive etymological identity of "profession", as referring not just to any "calling, vocation, known employment", but specifically to one of the ancient triad of divinity, medicine and law, was merely a matter of linguistic usage, without any corresponding social reality. If the pre-nineteenth century professions were indeed no more than parasitic appendages of the landed, leisured, ruling class, we would hardly expect their members to have developed any strong sense of corporate autonomy or identity springing from the exercise of a distinctive body of knowledge and skill. Thus the sociologist Philip Elliot discerns a clear dichotomy between pre-industrial "status professionalism", when "professions were relatively unimportant in the organisation of work or community, but occupied a high niche in the system of social stratification" (by virtue of their aristocratic associations), and post-Industrial Revolution "occupational professionalism, based on specialisation of knowledge and task", where members of the professions assert "their knowledge and competence as a support for their claim to economic security and professional standing." In other words, modern professional persons are practising Benthamites in good standing, whereas their predecessors, lackeys of a decaying feudal order, merely maintained "a foothold among the ranks of gentlemen by glossing over their work responsibilities and emphasising the leisured and honourable life-style which their members could adopt."[22] Reader similarly emphasised the gentlemanly character of the "old" professions and the relative insignificance of specific knowledge or skills for their members:

> "No doubt it was desirable that a clergyman, a physician or a barrister should have the knowledge and skill appropriate to his calling . . . (but) nobody thought it necessary to make any strict enquiry into a young man's knowledge of divinity, physic and law before he took up the practice of these professions. It was, after all, assumed that a gentleman who had a liberal education could learn the rest fairly easily when the need arose."[23]

Now it cannot be denied that between the sixteenth and eighteenth centuries the English landed elite, and at least the upper ranks of the learned professions, maintained many close links, as indeed they continued to do well into the nineteenth and twentieth centuries. (Of course the landed ruling class provided a model life-style for both Victorian industrialists and professional men, as Eric Hobsbawm pointed out some time ago).[24] Indeed, the gentlemanly aura which still clings to the professions (and not only in England), has patently remained a source of high social status for their members. It is also the origin of that normative ideal of dedication to ends above and beyond the pursuit of profit which sociologists have termed the professional "service ethic", whose pervasive influence extends well beyond the traditional professions, as illustrated by the following extract from a code of occupational ethics adopted in 1884:

> "There is, perhaps, no profession, after that of the sacred ministry, in which a high-toned morality is more imperatively necessary than that of a funeral director . . . ."[25]

If that "high-toned morality" of public service before private gain still deeply embedded in the official rhetoric of most professions derived originally from the aristocratic connections and pretensions of their early forerunners, it clearly constitutes a significant element of continuity in the history of the professions. However, Magali Larson, (following Durkheim and Weber), suggests that this anti-market principle cannot be ascribed solely to a residual sense of noblesse oblige, but also derived from the Reformation doctrine of the calling or vocation, which emphasised the intrinsic ethical and moral importance of work, and hence inculcated "a sense of duty to one's calling deeper than just compliance with a set of standards."[26]

One might have thought it necessary, indeed urgent, to enquire just how far members of the pre-industrial professions managed to reconcile their supposedly aristocratic orientation with the meritocratic or even egalitarian implications of the doctrine of the calling, especially given the still-influential tradition of thought which held that "whosoever labour for their livelihood and gain have no share at all in nobility and gentry . . . ."[27] Yet these questions have yet to be examined by historians of the professions. In our present state of knowledge assertions about the attitudes and behaviour of early modern clergymen, lawyers and medical practitioners depend on an unsatisfactory amalgam of a priori reasoning, casual anecdote and impressionistic comment by contemporary observers, rather than a systematic study of the surviving evidence produced by and about these individuals.

It is obviously not possible to repair these deficiencies here. But at least sufficient evidence can be adduced to undermine the conventional picture of the pre-nineteenth century professions as so subservient to the aristocratic values of their elite patrons that they possessed no ideology of their own, and certainly no sense of self-worth based on the importance of their work. The two largest and most influential professional groups in early modern England were the clergy and the lawyers. A recent monograph by Dr. Rosemary O'Day has closely examined the training and conditions of service of the lower clergy of the Anglican church between the accession of Elizabeth I and the outbreak of the English Revolution. Dr. O'Day notes that clergymen and laity of all doctrinal persuasions shared a common concern throughout this period to improve the quality of pastoral care provided by ministers at the parish level. In this context she cites the instance of the Shropshire puritan who in the early 1580s told his bishop that he considered himself to be much more than merely the occupant of an ecclesiastical living, a parson or vicar: "I abhor these names as anti-Christian. I am pastor of this congregation." (The term pastor was popularised by Calvin's Geneva ordinances of 1541: it perfectly symbolised the characteristic Reformation emphasis upon the clergyman's duties to care for his flock by actively preaching the word of God and correcting the ungodly.) Alongside such emphasis on the clergy's vocational responsibilities we may place the parallel concern to revive the power and prestige of the clerical estate associated with Archbishop William Laud and the Arminian movement of the early seventeenth century. Taken together these suggest that the genteel somnolence of the eighteenth-century Anglican church was far from representative of "pre-industrial" normality and should rather be regarded as marking a trough between the vigorous pastoral commitment of the priesthood under Elizabeth and the early Stuarts and again in the Victorian period.[28]

While the clergy comprised the largest profession in early modern England, the lawyers were by general consent the rising men of the age. "After the coming of the Normans the nobility had the start," wrote William Harrison in his Description of England (1577), "and after them the clergy, so now all the wealth of the land doth flow unto our common lawyers."[29] The essential structural forms of the modern English legal profession were established during the century between the dissolution of the monasteries and the eve of the Civil War. Call to the bar, previously no more than a rung on the internal membership ladder of the four Inns of Court, became the basic pre-requisite for practice as a counsellor in the superior courts of the realm. The numerical expansion of the bar, the emergence of the barrister as a professional figure in his own right and changing patterns of promotion to judicial office challenged the traditional leadership of the profession by the medieval order of serjeants-at-law. An analogous change in a recognisably modern direction at the lower end of the profession was the emergence of the solicitor to join the "mechanic" attorney. Finally, the fundamental principle of strict demarcation between the profession's so-called upper and lower branches was institutionalised during this period by the promulgation of regulations designed to exclude attorneys and solicitors from membership of the four Inns of Court.[30]

These developments gain added significance for our present purpose when viewed in conjunction with a shift in ideology and rhetoric which closely accompanied them. No trace of an explicit justification of the lawyer's vocation appears among the surviving records of the medieval English legal profession. Medieval lawyers may have regarded themselves as members of a distinct occupational order and social estate; Sir John Fortescue's panegyric in praise of the laws of England, De Laudibus Legum Angliae, which was composed about 1470, describes the hierarchy of the profession and the organisation of its residential corporations, the Inns of Court and Chancery, with a good deal of pride and self-satisfaction. Yet these sentiments are expressed in a highly deferential form; thus Fortescue emphasises that students at the "academy of the laws of England" were mostly noblemen's sons, since *pauperes et vulgares* could not afford the expenses of residence, while merchants regarded such expenditure as wasteful; again, serjeants-at-law are favourably compared in dignity and learning to the holders of university doctorates, and Fortescue claims that the English serjeants constitute the richest order of advocates in the world. Yet at no point is the actual practice or vocation of the law itself asserted to be noble or ennobling. In other words, Fortescue seems to express a characteristically medieval view of the lawyer's role and social status as necessary but hardly intrinsically desirable or praiseworthy.[31]

The first positive claim for the honourable status of the lawyer, or at least certain kinds of lawyer, is found in one of the major documents of the English humanist movement, Sir Thomas Elyot's *The Boke Named the Gouernour* (1531). The son of a judge and himself a member of the Middle Temple, Elyot claimed to have acquired "no little commodity" in "that honourable study" of the common law; he was also an Oxford B.C.L. and a former protege of Thomas More. Not surprisingly, therefore, Elyot condemned the "barbarous language of the common law," which he wanted replaced with any one of English, French or Latin. Yet he also believed that intending students of the common law should first be brought up in the liberal arts and letters until they had reached the age of 21, instead of sent to the Inns of Court at 14 or 15 years of age by parents eager for monetary gain. Elyot claimed that if this course were generally adopted,

> ". . . few men in our consultations should compare with our lawyers, by this means being brought to be perfect orators, as in whom should be found the sharp wits of logicians, the grave sentences of philosophers, the elegancy of poets, the memory of civilians, the voice and gesture of them that can pronounce comedies, which is all that Tully, in the person of the most eloquent man Marcus Antonius, could require to be in an orator."

In short, Elyot maintained that the classical Roman jurisprudent, exemplified by Cicero, Quintilian, Servus Sulpitius and Tacitus - gentlemen whose learning was not confined to the law and whose involvement with the law was undertaken as a public duty, not as a direct means to wealth and power - could and should be reborn in England: "whereby at last we should have in this realm a sufficiency of worshipful lawyers and also a public weal equivalent to the Greeks and Romans."[32] While Elyot's idealised image of the good lawyer depended in part on an appeal to aristocratic virtues, particularly the disinterestedness of the gentleman of private means, its major contribution was to suggest that lawyers whose personal qualities conformed to the ideal could make highly beneficial contributions to their prince and commonwealth. As elaborated and refined in the later sixteenth and early seventeenth centuries, this concept of the good lawyer, whose prosperity was a just reward for distinguished service to country, client and calling, became the ideological correlate which justified and legitimated the rising numbers, wealth and influence of common lawyers in general and barristers in particular. Thus, in 1615 Sir John Davies, attorney general in Ireland and later very briefly Lord Chief Justice of England, maintained that his profession was

> ". . . to be preferred above all other humane professions and sciences as being most noble for the matter . . . most necessary for the common and continual use and most meritorious for the good effects it doth produce in the commonwealth. For what is the matter and subject of our profession but justice, the lady and queen of all moral virtues? And what are our professors of the law but her counsellors, her secretaries, her interpreters, her servants? And what are the professors of the law but conduit pipes deriving and conveying the streams of his justice into all the subjects of his several kingdoms?"

So, according to Davies, common lawyers both uphold the law and serve the state,

> ". . . comfort such as are grieved, counsel such as are perplexed, relieve such as are circumvented, prevent the ruin of the impotent, take the prey out of the mouth of the oppressor, protect the orphan, the widow and the stranger . . . stretch forth . . . in defence of church and true religion . . . register and keep in mind the best antiquities of our nation

. . . preserve our ancient customs and forms of government."[33]

Nor did the Roman lawyer analogy first popularised by Elyot fall into disuse. For example, in the autobiographical memoranda written for his sons in the 1630s, Sir John Lowther of Lowther asserted that

> ". . . the gravest and wisest of the Romans and of best experience were wont to come into a public place at certain times unto whom many resorted for advice in matters of importance . . . to whom I may best compare our English lawyers, men best experienced in wordly business . . . ."[34]

These examples suggest that while early modern English barristers indeed accepted and deferred to many of the values of the landed gentry and aristocracy, they were not content to rely upon mere ascribed social status, as Fortescue appears to have done in the late fifteenth century. Their spokesmen rather claimed that the inherent social importance and moral worthiness of the functions associated with the lawyer's calling ought to and did confer honour on those who followed it, so that the barrister's high status stemmed not from aristocratic associations, birth or breeding, but simply the exercise of his vocation. Of course assertions of this sort were not confined to common lawyers; similar claims were advanced on behalf of many other contemporary occupations and professions (we have already cited Thomas Mun's defence of the dignity of the merchant).[35] Does it follow that such boasts should be dismissed as mere rhetoric or cynical public-relations exercises? We might well suspect the sincerity of Francis Bacon's avowal, in his self-advertising Maxims of the Law (1597), that,

> "I hold every man a debtor to his profession, from the which as men do of course seek to receive countenance and profit, so ought they of duty to endeavour themselves . . . to be a help and ornament thereunto."[36]

Yet the frequent exhortations in barristers' wills for their sons to follow a profession and not live "idly and vainly" suggests that at least some of Bacon's colleagues did feel a strong sense of personal commitment to their calling, while rejecting the view that a gentleman should not work for his living.[37] Thus Robert

Thorpe, the son of a London vintner, who rose to the bench of the Middle Temple before his death in 1639, left his eldest son and heir only the sum of £5, "to the intent that he may apply himself to the study and practice of the law to get his living thereby . . . and not to depend upon my estate any longer for maintenance . . . ."[38]

A still more striking instance of a lawyer's close personal identification with his profession comes from the will of Edward Skipwith of South Ormsby, Lincolnshire, a bencher of Lincoln's Inn, who also served as M.P. for the borough of Grimsby in 1601, but otherwise seems to have achieved no great success at the bar, perhaps owing to the poor health which led to him being excused from his second reading in 1611. Skipwith's will (1620) includes a lengthy and somewhat garbled passage of apology for his failings in his career, which emphasises his respect for

> ". . . the most worthy and famous common law of this realm, whereof I being an unworthy member have desired to honour it in my heart, though in practice of it I have disgraced it or rather in not exercising the duties of that honourable profession as my place hath required of me, I have not rendered that public grace and ornament to it which the worthy society and fellowship of Lincoln's Inn might in regard of their favours unworthily heaped upon me though an unworthy member amongst them expect of me and now may challenge me for the same, but I desire pardon of them all, in this hope, that neither in open nor in private action of that profession, I have by no dishonest or unjust base or disgraceful means to my knowledge wronged or stained the profession."[39]

Besides such private and domestic avowals of attachment to and respect for the demands of calling, vocation, and profession may be placed the public acknowledgements of duty made in the opening speeches by readers or lecturers at Inns of Court. Explaining why he has accepted the invitation to deliver a reading or course of lectures upon a branch of statute law, despite the great expense of time and money and the hazard of reputation such a venture requires, the reader's standard assertion is that he is discharging a duty to his profession. Thus John Bankes at Gray's Inn in 1630:

"I am here called by my masters of the bench to perform a great and a weighty work; I acknowledge my many imperfections and that it is their favour not my desert, yet it is the dutie of my profession therefore I shall very willingly perform it . . . ."[40]

It would be easy to dismiss these customary tropes as empty platitude. Yet the survival of the aural learning exercise system at the Inns of Court, long after it was largely outmoded by the printed book, must be at least in some part attributed to the sense of professional obligation which they express. James Whitelock's reader's speech at the Middle Temple in 1618 exemplified this attitude, referring to

". . . the necessity of taking this place at such times as it cometh to our turns, in respect of the public. It being to preserve order and to continue the ancient forms of exercise in our profession, which exceeds all others in what profession so ever in pains, charges and magnificence."[41]

IV : CONCLUSION

I have tried to suggest that one reason for the inadequacies of most current writing about the history of the professions is the inadequacy of most current writing about the sociology of the professions, and that these two deficiencies are connected: historians have failed to supply social theorists with the data they would need to construct an adequate general theory of the professions, while sociologists have given historians a theoretical base which is both chronologically foreshortened and demonstrably incapable of reconciliation with certain familiar and readily-available data. When and if historians and sociologists have been persuaded to shed their present-minded blinkers, it will be apparent that the general history of the professions cannot be divided into a static dark age preceding the modern era of dynamic progress (or, if you disapprove of the professions, crisis and impending collapse). On the contrary, the impact of the "great transformation" on the growth of the professions (especially the expansion of effective demand for the services they provided) was not unprecedented; similar previous periods of sustained economic and demographic expansion had effects similar in kind, if not degree. About the first, which evidently occurred during the twelfth and thirteenth centuries with the rise of the universities, I am not qualified to speak;[42] the second, which in England may be dated between roughly the early sixteenth and the mid-seventeenth centuries, saw the reconstitution of the legal profession along recognisably modern lines; a partial revival in the economic fortunes and a major advance in the academic qualifications of the clergy; the appearance of a university-educated elite at the head of a nascent medical profession and the emergence of a number of new proto-or quasi-professions, including architects, schoolmasters and university dons. It is hardly surprising that during the revolutionary decades of the mid-seventeenth century, when the rights of private property were effectively secured against both monarchical absolutism and popular radicalism, professional privileges and pretensions attracted perhaps the most searching critique to which they have ever yet been subjected in the course of English history.[43] The full significance of this cluster of events for the historical development of the professions remains to be investigated. Nevertheless, it underlines the dangers of regarding the early to mid-eighteenth century as a benchmark or norm for the "pre-industrial" or "traditional" professions.

Historians of the professions, like old fashioned historians of science, are constitutionally prone to slip into a teleological frame of mind. One way to overcome the tendency to distort the past, by viewing it exclusively in terms of the present, is by attempting to listen more closely to the words of the past. For, as I have argued, the history of the professions is not just the history of professional organisations, but also the history of an idea and the words in which that idea was expressed.

Historians of the professions have a splendid opportunity to attempt "l'histoire totale" on reasonably manageable natural populations. In this enterprise the study of attitudes and perceptions towards, of, and by, professional persons can play a major part. Such a venture will probably owe as much to anthropology as sociology, and seek to follow its subject's private as well as public transactions. This is far from a call to trivialise the history of the professions, but rather to suggest that the subject has even wider bounds and possibilities than its practitioners to date would seem aware.

A synoptic history of the professions in Europe - and beyond - is well outside our present reach and likely to remain so for some time. Yet the accumulation of detailed monographic research on which it must eventually rest will meanwhile help us better to understand one of the key distinguishing characteristics of Western civilisation and society from the Middle Ages to the present day.[44]

NOTES

*The author wishes to acknowledge help and stimulus of various kinds from his former colleague Jim Kemeny and fellow participants in the seminar on the history of the professions held at the Davis Center, Princeton University, February-June 1980. None but him should, however, be held responsible for any of the views expressed below.

1. E.g., the 1978 annual conference of the Social History Society on "The Professions and Professionalisation" and the theme of the seminars held at the Shelby Cullom Davis Center for Historical Studies, Princeton University, 1979-81. Recent publications include Noel and José Parry, The Rise of the Medical Profession (London, 1976); Donald Scott, From Office to Profession : The New England Ministry 1750-1850 (Philadelphia, 1978); Rosemary O'Day, The English Clergy : the Emergence and Consolidation of a Profession 1558-1642 (Leicester, 1979); Daniel Duman, "Pathway to Professionalism: the English Bar in the Eighteenth and Nineteenth Centuries", Journal of Social History, 13 (1980), pp.615-28; Burton Bledstein, The Culture of Professionalism : the Middle Class and the Development of Higher Education in America (New York, 1976); Magali Larson, The Rise of Professionalism : A Sociological Analysis (Berkeley, 1977); Geoffrey Holmes, "The Professions and Social Change in England 1680-1730", Proceedings of the British Academy 1979 (1981), pp.313-54; Christophe Charle, "Histoire Professionnelle, Histoire Sociale" Annales E.S.C., 34 (1979), pp.787-94.
2. Richard Pares, George III and the Historians (London, 1953), pp.16-17.
3. Some discussion of these problems will be found in the unpublished Annual Reports of the Shelby Cullom Davis Center for Historical Studies for the years 1978-79 and 1979-80. See also Thomas L. Haskell, "Are Professors Professional?", Journal of Social History, 14 (1981), pp.487-93.

4. R. Lewis and Angus Maude, Professional People (London, 1952); Talcott Parsons, "The Professions and Social Structure" in Essays in Sociological Theory (Glencoe, Ill., 1954), pp.34-49; idem, "Professions", in International Encyclopaedia of the Social Sciences ed. David Sills (1968), xii, pp.536-47; William J. Goode, "Community within a community: the professions", American Sociological Review, 20 (1957), pp.194-200; Wilbert E. Moore, The Professions: roles and rules (New York, 1970).

5. I owe this point largely to an unpublished paper "Professionalisation: process without history", delivered by Terence Johnson to the Social History Society's Conference in London, 5 January 1978.

6. For an extensive discussion, see Geoffrey Millerson, The Qualifying Associations: A Study in Professionalisation (London, 1964), pp.10-13 et passim; also Howard M. Vollmer & Donald L. Mills, Professionalization (Englewood Cliffs, N.J., 1966).

7. A comprehensive list is impractical, but typical examples include Brian Abel-Smith, A History of the Profession of Nursing (London, 1960); John L. Carey, The Rise of the Accounting Profession (New York, 1969); J.M. Freedland, The Making of a Profession: A History of the Growth and Work of the Architectural Institutes in Australia (Sydney, 1971); P.H.J.H. Gosden, The Evolution of a Profession: A Study of the Contribution of Teacher's Associations to the Development of School Teaching as a Professional Occupation (Oxford, 1972); Barrington Kaye, The Development of the Architectural Profession in Britain (London, 1969); The Architect: Chapters in the History of the Profession, Spiro Kostoff (ed.) (New York, 1977); Edward Kremers and George Urdang, History of Pharmacy rev. edn. by Glenn Sonnedecker (Philadelphia, 1976); Harold Perkin, Key Profession: The History of the Association of University Teachers (London, 1969); Colin A. Russell et al., Chemists By Profession (Milton Keynes, 1977); F.M.L. Thompson, Chartered Surveyors: The Growth of a Profession (London, 1968);

Kathleen Woodroffe, From Charity to Social Work in England and the United States (London, 1962).

8. Rare exceptions include Jean Donnison, Midwives and Medical Men: A History of Interprofessional Rivalry and Women's Rights (London, 1977); Margaret Pelling and Charles Webster, "Medical Practitioners", in Health, medicine and mortality in the sixteenth century, ed. C. Webster (Cambridge, 1979).

9. The most incisive critical contribution is probably Terence J. Johnson, Professions and Power (London, 1972). But see also Eliot Freidson, Professional Dominance (Atherton, New York, 1970); Ivan Illich et al., Disabling Professions (London, 1977); Paul Boreham et al., The Professions in Australia: a critical appraisal (St. Lucia, 1976).

10. D. Klegon, "The Sociology of the Professions: An Emerging Perspective", Sociology of Work and Occupations 5 (1978), pp.271-2; Larson, Rise of Professionalism, p.9.

11. Charles Rosenberg, "Towards an Ecology of Knowledge: On Discipline, Context & History" in Alexandra Oleson and John Voss (eds.), The Organisation of Knowledge in Modern America, 1860-1920 (Baltimore, 1979), p.442.

12. Larson, Rise of Professionalism, p.xvi.

13. Edward Hughes, "The Professions in the Eighteenth Century", Durham University Journal, 44 (1952), p.47.

14. For the narrow and specific sense of "profession", see below pp.307-9.

15. Reader, Professional Men, pp.9-10.

16. Cf. Thomas Dycke and William Pardon, A New General English Dictionary (London, 1740); William Robertson, Phraesologia Generalis . . . A Full, Large and General Phrase Book (Cambridge, 1681); John Ash, The New and Complete Dictionary of the English Language (1775); John Walker A Critical Pronouncing Dictionary (London, 1791); Thomas Sheridan, A General

Dictionary of the English Language (London, 1780).

17. Harold Perkin, "Professionalism and the Game of Life", unpublished paper, Davis Center, Princeton University, Spring semester 1980, pp.2-3.

18. Ibid. Similar points are made in idem, Key Profession, 2 and "The Professions in History", Social History Society Newsletter (Spring, 1978). Cf. Robert Campbell, The London Tradesman. Being a Compendious View of All the Trades, Professions, Arts, Both Liberal and Mechanic, now practised in the Cities of London and Westminster (1747), pp.24, 88 ("I have now done with the three learned professions and shall treat no more of the Sciences, as all the rest are but auxiliaries to these . . . I now proceed to what is called the Liberal Arts . . . ").

19. Thomas Mun, England's Treasure by Forraign Trade (1664), p.36.

20. George Fox, Journal (1902), i, pp.29-30, quoted C. Hill, Change and Continuity in Seventeenth Century England (London, 1974), p.159. Cf. Sir John Stuteville's comment in 1656 that ". . . we know Divinity is the highest, as Physick the lowest of Professiones (sic)": Memoirs of the Verney Family, ed., Frances P. Verney and Margaret M. Verney (London, 1892-99), iii, p.199.

21. Cf. Hastings Rashdall, The Universities of Europe in the Middle Ages, ed. F.M. Powicke and A.B. Emden (Oxford, 1936), i, pp.19-20; Encyclopaedia Britannica (11th edn., 1910-11), s.v. Professor; P.P. Vergerius, De Ingeniis Moribus (c.1404), in W.H. Woodward, Vittorino da Feltre and other Humanist Educators (Cambridge, 1921), 108. Revised Medieval Latin Word List R.C. Latham (ed.), (London, 1965) gives "profess/io" in the sense of "admission to teach or subject taught" for the dates 1302 and 1577 (p.375).

22. Philip Elliot, The Sociology of the Professions (London, 1972), pp.14-15, 32 and ch. 2 passim.

23. Reader, Professional Men, p.11.

24. Eric Hobsbawm, Industry and Empire (1968), pp.141-2, 154-6.

25. Bledstein, Culture of Professionalism, p.34; cf., ibid., p.35 from testimony

delivered before the American Public Health Association, 1891: "Plumbing is no longer merely a trade. Its importance and value in relation to health, and its requirements regarding scientific knowledge, have elevated it to a profession." *Cf.,* Sinclair Lewis, *Babbitt* (New York, 1922), ch.13.

26. Larson *Rise of Professionalism*, pp.61-3, 220.

27. Henry Peacham, *The Complete Gentleman* (1622) ed. Virgil Heltzel (Ithaca, 1962), p.23.

28. O'Day, *English Clergy*, p.243; *cf.* W.H. Haller, *The Rise of Puritanism* (New York, 1938), chs. 1-3. *Calvin: Theological Treatises,* tr. J.K.S. Reid (Library of Christian Classics, Vol.22, London, 1954), pp.58-9.

29. William Harrison, *The Description of England*, ed. George Edelen (Ithaca, 1968), p.173.

30. *Cf.,* C.W. Brooks, "The Common Lawyers in England, c.1558-1642" in *Lawyers in Early Modern Europe and America*, ed. Wilfrid Prest, (London and New York, 1981), pp.42-46.

31. John Fortescue's *De Laudibus Legum Anglie*, ed. S.B. Chrimes (Cambridge, 1942), chs. 49-50. *Cf.* E.W. Ives, "The Reputation of the Common Lawyer in English Society", *University of Birmingham Historical Journal*, 7 (1959-60), pp.130-61.

32. Thomas Elyot, *The Boke named the Gouernour*, ed. H.H. Croft (London, 1883), ch. 14.

33. John Davies, *Le Primer Report des Cases and Matters en Ley* (Dublin, 1615), sigs. *7^{v} - *9.

34. *Lowther Family Estate Books 1617-1675* C.B. Phillips (ed.), (Surtees Society, cxci, 1979), pp.203-4.

35. Barnabe Rich, *Allarme to England* (1578); *Cf.* Thomas Trussell, *The Souldier Pleading his owne Cause* (1626); Edmund Bolton, *The Cities Advocate* (1629); Inner Temple, Petyt MS 538.151, ff.80-93, "A comparison between phisique and Lawe."

36. The Works of Francis Bacon, ed. James Spedding et.al., (London, 1857-74), vii, p.319.

37. The phrase quoted is from the will of Chief Baron Sir John Walter (d.1630), who wished his son to "undertake the profession of the law or some other honest profession to the glory of God and the good of his country and not to live idly or vainly": Public Record Office, London, PCC 93 Scroope.

38. P.R.O. PCC 47 Harvey. Cf. PCC 131 Gore; 126 Cope; 47 Rivers; 57 Scroope; 35 Dale.

39. P.R.O. PCC 19 Soame.

40. British Library, MS Hargrave 91, f.164.

41. Middle Temple, Rare Book Room, "James Whitelocke's Reading", f.3. Cf. Wilfrid Prest, The Inns of Court under Elizabeth I and the Early Stuarts 1590-1640 (London, 1972), pp.121-2.

42. But cf. John O. Ward, "Gothic Architecture, Universities and the Decline of the Humanities in Twelfth Century Europe", in Principalities, Powers and Estates: Studies in Medieval and early modern Government and Society Leighton Frappell (ed.), (Adelaide, 1979), pp.65-75; Carlo Cipolla, "The Professions - The Long View", Journal of European Economic History, 2 (1973), pp.37-51; idem, Before the Industrial Revolution (London, 1976), pp.81-4.

43. O'Day, English Clergy; Webster and Pelling, "Medical Practitioners"; Kenneth Charlton, "The Professions in Sixteenth Century England", University of Birmingham Historical Journal, 12 (1969-70), pp.20-41; Patrick Orpen, "Schoolmastering as a Profession in the Seventeenth Century: the career patterns of the grammar schoolmaster", History of Education, 6 (1977), pp.183-94; Hill, Continuity and change, ch. 7 passim.

44. This chapter was completed in August 1981. Some of its main assertions have subsequently received independent support from two important recent contributions by Geoffrey Holmes, Augustan England: Professions, State and

Society 1680-1730 (London, 1982) and Eliot Freidson, "The Theory of Professions: State of the Art", in The Sociology of the Professions, ed. Robert Dingwall and Philip Lewis (London, 1983).

THE COUNTY COURTS AND THE TALLY TRADE, 1846-1914

G.R. Rubin

"The even-handed justice which protects both debtor and creditor, it is not asserting too much to say, is seen in perfection in our County Courts. That the establishment of these courts was a boon to the public there cannot be the slightest doubt, and that in the main they have worked well is equally certain."

County Courts Chronicle (1861)

"The tallymen, the money-lenders, the flash jewellery touts, the sellers of costly Bibles in series, of gramophones and other luxuries of the mean streets, these are the knaves the State caters for . . . . To these traders the County Court is of real value."

Judge Parry (1914)

I : INTRODUCTION

Until very recently, the surge of interest in the modern social history of law was confined largely to the study of criminal law. Comparable advances in the social history of civil law and the civil courts were noticeably absent, notwithstanding the appearance of such a major work as P.S. Atiyah's The Rise and Fall of Freedom of Contract,[1] which essentially sought to explain doctrinal legal developments in the light of contemporary intellectual thought. The historical reconstruction of the civil courts since the Industrial Revolution, more especially of the lower courts, has nonetheless received only faltering attention.[2] Thus the social functions performed by such courts, the ideologies which they embraced and the social composition of their personnel and of their litigants have been neglected by economic, social and legal historians alike.

In an effort partially to rectify this omission, a study was recently made of the system of imprisonment for debt in the nineteenth and early twentieth century county courts. That research suggested[3] that the process of county court committals to prison, ostensibly reserved as a punishment for "contumacious" debtors who "deliberately" refused to pay their outstanding debts, was in fact applied against those who were simply too poor to pay off their consumer debts. Thus, in contrast with legislative policy, imprisonment for debt struck at those unable to pay rather than against those unwilling to pay. Moreover, given the immense instrumental and symbolic importance attached to imprisonment for debt by the overwhelming majority of the legal personnel of the county courts, the system of committals at the behest of private consumer creditors remained impervious, till as late as 1970, to demands for its abolition.

That research was, therefore, consciously focussed on the plight of the defendants in the county court system. The present paper, by contrast, addresses itself to the plaintiffs who considered it necessary to institute court proceedings in order to recover their debts. Many such plaintiffs were traders of various descriptions, such as grocers, coal merchants, butchers, bakers, boot dealers and even doctors. Landlords, also, were commonly listed among county court litigants. However, in respect to the numbers of summonses (or plaints) issued by different occupational groups, none of the above mentioned tradesmen could compete with the litigious activity of one particular group of traders. This numerically dominant body of creditors were the tallymen or Scotch drapers, peripatetic salesmen who travelled from door to door, offering goods to customers on a credit basis, usually of weekly or monthly instalments. Such tallymen were, perhaps, among the more colourful characters who occupied the social and economic world of the poor. Together with money-lenders and debt collectors, tallymen were "fringe" capitalists, who operated on the margins of the retailing and financial worlds. However, it was the alleged oppressively litigious activities of the tallymen, together with criticisms of their trading practices (perhaps the caricature of the South London second-hand car dealer is the modern equivalent), which tended to point up the irony of the description of the county court, since its inception in 1847, as "the poor man's court."[4]

Perhaps one way of expressing the relationship between the tally trade and the county courts in the nineteenth century is to describe it as a marriage of convenience, an uncomfortable working arrangement sustained by the respective interests of each side. For the tradesmen, the incentive was of course the opportunity to recover their debts. For the court system, the fees recoverable were justification enough, but perhaps there was the added pressure placed on the court system to demonstrate its belief in the efficacy of its own sanctions, at the pinnacle of which was the threat of imprisoning defaulting debtors. Such an analysis of the relationship between the courts and the tallyman turned on one crucial assumption. This was that the courts of law, unlike the Ritz, were in substance open to all. The logic of such an ideology of equality is that the legal-institutional facilities be available not only to "respectable" creditors, but also to those with a popular reputation for parasitism on the poor and for exploitation of customers. The courts, thus committed to equality of access, ought in principle to be powerless to register their social disapproval of specific groups of plaintiff-tradesmen by non-suiting them. However, the maintenance of a supposedly dignified legal system purporting to protect such plaintiff "knaves of the mean streets" as tallymen and money-lenders generated a crisis of legitimacy for many county court judges. Some judges might bemoan the contemptible character of their most active clients and plead inability to defend debtors from what in any case, in the view of some of those on the bench, was the folly of those debtors' own extravagance or gullibility in falling into the clutches of such "bloodsuckers." But there were other judges who sought to undermine tallymen's plaints in forensic skirmishes conducted in juridical categories, rather than in social terms of approval or disapproval. Moreover, this manoeuvre was taken notwithstanding (though it could have been because of) the restraints imposed by an ideological commitment to the rule of law, a doctrine which formally asserted that the law was no respecter of persons. The object was nonetheless social disapproval; the means employed, mystificatory.

Thus, if the analogy of a marriage of convenience between the tally trade and the courts is valid, as suggested above, it was a marriage which was frequently subjected to strain, but which never led to a divorce in the sense that the doors of the courts were closed to the tallymen. Such a step only Parliament could authorise, as it had done in respect to publicans' debts.[5] As we shall note, however, statutory provisions conferring discretion on the judges whether to grant orders to imprison debtors for default or, in the case of money-lenders, whether to enforce their debts, offered the judges a limited scope to contain "the two pests of our modern County Court,"[6] the tallymen and the money-lender.

Thus, in seeking to examine the relationship between on the one hand, the county courts, and, on the other, the activities of, primarily, the tally trade, and, secondarily, debt collectors and money-lenders, the present paper will explore both judicial and lay tactics designed to discourage those classes of unpopular tradesmen from obtaining from the county courts a legitimation of their commercial practices. In sum, therefore, the argument to be advanced is that the tally trade posed a distinct challenge to the prevailing legal order. On the one hand, the county court system, in the midst of nineteenth century capitalist expansion, was structurally incapable of disavowing its dependence on a market economy in which credit fulfilled an indispensable function for the poor. On the other hand, those suppliers of consumer goods on credit for the poor, who enjoyed an unenviable reputation for sharp practices and doubtful dealings, sought to use the facilities of the county court to press home claims, which many of the judges thought at least morally questionable. Thus, locked into debt collecting activities which they found distasteful, a number of judges, law reformers and lay critics responded to such tallymen's cases by waging a last-ditch rearguard struggle to preserve "fair" and "honest" dealings (as well as the court's own reputation for "social concern") against the overwhelming claim of bargaining "freedom." The judicial response to the systemic logic of capitalist market freedom thus illuminated the "system contradiction" to borrow Strinati's phrase,[6a] between freedom and paternalism.

II : RECOVERING DEBTS

Since the essence of the tally trade was the system of retailing on credit terms, the tallyman would naturally endeavour to sell only to those customers whom he considered would be able to maintain their payments. It frequently happened, however, that unforeseen events, such as the death of the breadwinner, unemployment, sickness or bad harvest would result in shutting off the flow of weekly or monthly payments. If accommodations could not be reached, the tally man could either write off the transaction as a bad debt or take out a summons against the debtor.

Many lawyers did, of course, lend their authority to the proposition that the very last thing a creditor should do was to go to court to try to recover a debt. Thus, Mr. Justice Willes was reputed to have said,

> "Whatever you do, never go to law; submit rather to almost any imposition, bear any oppression, rather than exhaust your spirits and your pocket in what is called a court of justice."

And indeed one author went so far as to write a book entitled How to Avoid Law.[8] Another lawyer thought fit to preface his remarks on how to recover one's debts by advising anyone who considered suing a debtor, to heed the advice Punch had some years earlier offered to those about to marry: "Don't!"[9]

However, the tally trade, if the opinions of its critics and indeed the judicial statistics are to be accepted,[10] were hardly likely to pay much attention to such advice. Thus, one legal newspaper remarked in 1868,[11]

> "We have frequently spoken with severity in condemnation of the pernicious effects of this species of trade . . . . It is at present [the tallyman's] aim to palm off a very inferior article at a price far above its value upon the poorest of our population who, attracted by the gaudy 'deception', are easily gulled by this adept at his art. They thus render themselves liable to summons and seizures, for the tallyman is an inexorable creditor" [italics added].

As Judge Parry perceived it in 1914, the result was a symbiotic relationship between fringe trading and the county courts.

> "The tallymen, the money-lenders, the flash jewellery touts, the sellers of costly Bibles in series, of gramophones and other luxuries of the mean streets, these are the knaves the State caters for."[12]

According to Alexander,[13] the hostility of the courts to the tallymen meant that the latter depended on personal rather than legal controls over their customers. It is certainly true that the activities of the tallymen attracted widespread criticism from the judges but there is little evidence that the tally trade eschewed litigation[14] (though they probably shared the common preference for extra-legal settlement). On the contrary, evidence collected for various government enquiries points to the tally trade as the most frequent user of the facilities of the county courts. Certainly, as we shall see, a number of judges devised expedients in an attempt to hold back the sea of tallymen's plaints which swamped the courts; but as noted above, the tallyman remained "an inexorable creditor" despite the obstacles put in his way by the judges.

Indeed, even prior to the establishment of the county courts in 1847, the tallymen's exploitation of the facilities of the courts of requests, and in particular, their reliance on imprisonment for debt as a sanction for non-payment, had attracted adverse criticism. McCulloch noted that the courts of requests had sought to discourage the tally trade by ordering these particular debts to be paid by extremely small instalments, at very distant intervals (italics in original).[15] Mayhew also noted that "the judges in the Court of Requests now so frequently decide against him" whenever the tallyman failed to ensure that the husband of the purchaser was cognisant with the transaction.[16] Finally, one writer, in condemning the tally trade vociferously, noted with shocked outrage that a recent statement had been issued showing that in the Westminster Court of Requests, 100 summonses had been issued in one day by a single tallyman. The amount of misery which this represented for the poor, he suggested, was truly appalling. For the tally trade was,

> ". . . a system which begins in cupidity practising on improvidence and folly, and ends for the most part in intemperance, the result of accumulating difficulties, and in ruin, the necessary consequence of summons, judgment and execution."[17]

With the establishment of the county courts themselves, following the enactment of the County Courts Act 1846, further condemnation was heaped on the tallymen. Thus, in response to Lord Chief Baron Pollock's charge to the grand jury at Bedford Assizes in 1859 where he complained that vindictive creditors caused debtors to be sentenced to repeated spells of imprisonment for the same debt, the grand jury observed,

> "We have no doubt of the truth of the statements we have heard from County Court debtors that packmen and itinerant sellers of female wearing apparel and finery are in the habit of leaving their goods in the houses of the poorer class, in the hope that, though they have declined to purchase in the first instance, they may be tempted to use or wear the articles, and thus become liable as purchasers."[18]

Shortly thereafter, the Attorney-General, Sir Robert Collier, did indeed refer the matter of committals to the Committee of County Court Judges to inquire whether the facilities afforded by the county courts for the recovery of debts did not give "undue encouragement to loan societies, to the running up of scores for beer, to the supply of goods to wives by travelling drapers, hawkers, pedlars and teamen."[19] It was perhaps significant that one of the more horrific, even if apochryphal, stories involving the death of an imprisoned debtor, a 79 year-old widow of a "respectable" licensed victualler, was occasioned by a tallyman's debt of £1.19.11d. Prior to her imprisonment, it was asserted, she had been so destitute that she could only afford to buy dry bread. On her imprisonment, therefore, her weak physical state prevented her properly masticating the more substantial prison fare which she received, and the ensuing indigestion, coupled with her infirmity, led to her death some days after her incarceration.[20] Such revelations, irrespective of their accuracy, only served to underline the alleged callousness of the tallymen in pursuit of their prey. But they also, no doubt, inspired efforts to deny the facilities of the county courts to those tallymen who resorted to sales practices which met with the judges' social, as well as their legal, disapproval. Thus, in the following two sections, we will examine the steps taken by the judges of the county courts to non-suit certain tallymen-plaintiffs. Secondly, we will consider various proposals for reforms in the law which, it was believed, would reduce the capacity of tallymen to recover their debts through the courts.

III : JUDGES AND NON-SUIT

Judges who were predisposed to adjudicating in favour of defendants sued by tallymen sought to impose rigorous conditions and to set in train searching enquiries before satisfying themselves whether a debt due to a tallyman was enforceable. Thus, Sergeant Petersdorff of Exeter County Court first observed that the tallyman's customer was frequently a married woman, and that tallymen,

> ". . . generally call at the time when the husband is supposed to be absent and that they often offer goods in the shape of dress not necessary for the station in life of the purchaser, thereby exposing the husband to a succession of judgments and executions."[21]

Second, he noted that under the existing law, the wife had no capacity to contract on her own account. In the light of these twin factors, Petersdorff therefore tended to examine closely in tally cases, whenever the husband was summoned to court, whether the goods purchased were "luxuries". If they were, then the existing state of the law, as contained in the Married Women's Property Act 1870 (33 & 34 Vict., c.93) prevented the wife from being sued, and also prevented the husband from being held liable unless he himself assumed the obligation, which he was, of course, unlikely to do. If the married woman dealt with the tallyman qua wife, and if the goods were deemed to be necessaries, the judge would look for evidence on the part of the plaintiff that the defendant husband was aware of the transaction; also whether authority had been granted by the husband and whether the circumstances of the transaction (including, no doubt, the persuasiveness of the tallyman's sales talk) justified the wife in pledging her husband's credit. Not infrequently, authority was found to be lacking, even in those cases where the tallyman's goods were held to be necessaries.[22]

A more formalised approach, apparently employed elsewhere, was suggested by Judge Hughes of Stockport County Court.

> "His Honour said he was determined to make an alteration in the mode of dealing with the "Scotchmen's" cases. The tailors in Manchester . . . would in future have to get the husband to sign a paper allowing his wife to get goods from the travelling tailors. If the tailors did that, as they did in the Midlands and elsewhere, he would allow them to collect their accounts through the County Court, but otherwise he would not allow it. The [over 50] cases brought at present by tailors, and the way they sold the goods, caused a perfect nuisance, and was a curse to the place."[23]

Other judges adopted a more robust attitude to tallymen's cases at the judgment summons stage, where, before an order of committal to prison was granted, the plaintiff was required to show that the debtor had, or had had since the date of judgment, means to pay but had refused or neglected to do so. In ascertaining the question of means to pay, the judge had discretion to accept whatever proof he considered was "just" in the circumstances. Thus, judges who disapproved of the tallyman's techniques might insist on written proof of means rather than verbal testimony of the plaintiff, thereby compelling the plaintiff to obtain documentation such as copy pay slips from the debtor's employer, if he was in work. The insistence upon rigorous, rather than hearsay, evidence by some judges no doubt diminished the enthusiasm of tallymen to proceed to committals.[24] Thus, Thomas Collins, registrar of Bury St. Edmunds County Court, told an enquiry in 1878 that his judge discouraged applications from tallymen by adopting the registrar's plan of requiring them to prove debts "a good deal more strictly than I do ordinary people." The witness concluded that whereas formerly he had had experience of a large number of tallymen's cases, he thought they were now dying out.[25] Another witness to the same committee, while agreeing that judicial restraints, together with restrictions on imprisonment, had something to do with the decline of such cases in his district (Bloomsbury), considered also that the tallymen failed to gain very much by suing their debtors. Therefore, instead of running the risk of incurring large numbers of bad debts, they became more careful about giving credit to the poor.[26]

Directly related was the determination of some county court judges to dispense, as far as possible, with the ultimate sanction of imprisonment itself. In Newcastle, for example, Judge Arthur O'Connor was able to reduce the ratio of local to national commitments from 1 in 20 in 1900, prior to his appointment, to that of 1 in 400 in 1905, after he had been on the bench for about four years. In his view, the shift in punishment policy directly led to a decline in the Scotch drapery and money-lending business in his circuit.[27]

Thus, it is clear that judges, if they were so disposed, could respond to tallymen's cases in a manner which discriminated between the latter and other, presumably more respectable, plaintiffs.[28]

IV : LAW REFORM PROPOSALS

Apart from those steps taken by judges in individual cases, a rich variety of proposals for reforming the law was offered in an attempt to contain the litigiousness of the tallymen. One widely mooted suggestion proposed by Judge Gurdon of Colchester, was to place the tallyman on the same footing as the publican and thus prevent him from recovering his debts through the courts.[29]

A further proposal was to prevent tallymen from taking out summonses in their local courts, which were then served by a foreign court on the defendant.[30] The contract usually stipulated that the price was payable at the seller's residence, notwithstanding the tallyman's practice of calling at the customer's home for payment. Therefore, the court which possessed jurisdiction to deal with the complaint was often distant from the debtor's home, frequently resulting in judgment going by default. Judge Stapylton of Durham County Court, for example, complained that,

> "I have known many instances of labouring men and mechanics, living in the county of Durham, committed for forty days for non-appearance to a summons after judgment issued out of courts from 50 to 300 miles from the county of Durham. The Judges must have acted on the ex parte evidence of the plaintiffs; and what possible evidence could they have had that the defendants (working men) had had means to travel from 50 to 300 miles, and had refused to do so?"[31]

In 1880, new regulations were framed for the judgment summons stage of the proceedings, enabling the creditor or debtor to send an affidavit to the foreign court setting forth relevant facts. This reform was presumably inadequate, since a wider alteration in the system of summonsing defendants was recommended by an enquiry into county court procedure in 1909.[32]

A somewhat polar opposite concern was the demand of plaintiffs for a more extensive power of obtaining judgment by default, such as existed in the superior courts where the defendant failed to appear. Until the case was called on for hearing, the plaintiff generally had no means of knowing whether or not it was to be defended, with the result that he was obliged to be prepared with proof of his debt. The practice was criticised as a waste of the time of the court, parties and witnesses. This led to a reform of county court procedure in 1875[33] with the institution of the default summons which enabled the plaintiff to obtain automatic judgment in the event of no appearance being put in by the defendant within the period granted for lodging appearances. However, the committee which had recommended these changes, noting the differences of opinion among its witnesses,

> ". . . as to the expediency of extending [default summonses] to the class of persons who are ordinarily the defendants in the smaller cases . . . think it will be desirable, for the protection of such persons, to make special provision as to the nature of the notice which ought to be served on the defendant so as to draw his attention specially to his liability to such judgments, and to the steps he is to take to avoid it."[34]

There clearly was some concern among the Judicature Commissioners to balance the interests of trade in "rapid debt recovery"[35] with the need to discourage what were perceived as the unacceptable practices of those traders who allegedly preyed on "the class of persons who are ordinarily the defendants in the smaller cases." The Commissioners' proposal for the above modest safeguard in such cases was, of course, wholly ineffective, as was the potentially greater restraint on abuses, whereby default summonses for amounts over £5 were only permitted by leave of the registrar. Such permission was usually granted as a "mere matter of course".[36]

One county court official, exhibiting undisguised male chauvinist tendencies, suggested that,

> ". . . if a husband finds he has unfortunately got an improvident, wasteful and drunken wife, he should be able to checkmate [his wife's] agency and protect himself, and in this way: Let there be established, in every County Court, a registry - 'Improvident Wives Registry', if you like."[37]

The husband's name would be entered on the register and any contract with his wife would be enforceable against him only if he had given oral or written authority. In one respect this was merely an extension of Sergeant Petersdorff's procedure in tally cases (supra). The suggestion was presumably influenced by the existence of the Bills of Sale Register[38] which, if efficiently maintained, would warn potential creditors whether their debtors' property could be applied as security for loans. Bills of sale were, of course, invalid in respect to hire purchase contracts which were beginning to gain wider currency.[39] However, an enquiry into bankruptcy law in 1908 had concluded that it would be inadvisable to set up a Hire Purchase Agreement Register, similarly modelled, on the grounds of cost and trouble.[40] Perhaps the county court official who volunteered the suggestion for an "improvident wives register" was writing half in jest. Had such a scheme been implemented, however, it may well have been the salvation of those tallymen who appeared before the likes of Petersdorff or Judges Parry and O'Connor.

Yet another suggestion to counter the tallyman was proposed by Judge

Gurdon, referred to earlier. Having observed that when imprisonment for debt had existed in Scotland (it was subsequently abolished in 1880), the creditor was obliged to maintain the debtor in prison, this particular judge recommended that such a system be introduced in England in the case of tallymen's debtors. Moreover, reflected the judge in 1868, the tally trade was costing the country £50,000 a year. As no case under £3 repaid the county the expenses incurred in maintaining the court system (and most of the debts sued for by tallymen scarcely ever reached that amount; indeed, many of them frequently fell in the order of four to five shillings) some charge on the tally trade was, he thought, justified.[41] At the committee stage of the Debtors Bill in 1869, one member of parliament,

> ". . . put it to the Committee as a proposition in political economy, altogether beyond dispute, that it could not be for the benefit of the community that a trade should be carried on which could not bear its own expenses, and one of these was the collection of debts. If the tallyman had to bear the expense of imprisoning his debtors, he would alter his mode of dealing if he found the expense was eating up his profits."[42]

The proposal fell on deaf ears. A few years earlier, in 1861, it had even been alleged that a tallyman who had sued 13 debtors at Sudbury County Court for a total sum of £1.3.0d was entitled to throw the legal expenses for the recovery of these debts (and not merely the expense of maintaining debtors in prison) on the State, with the result that the summonses in question cost the country - not the creditor, nor the debtors - the sum of £3.9.0d. How such an arrangement was possible was presumably because of the paltry amounts being sought. The source disclosing this additional "scandal" indeed confessed,

> "But although we have made ourselves thoroughly acquainted with every symptom of the disease, it is so complicated a disorder that it is difficult to prescribe a remedy. An alteration in the County Courts Act would at once get rid of the objectionable feature in the system of burdening the public with the expense of the actions, and it is to be hoped that this may be done."[43]

No doubt the propaganda effect of this revelation was heightened rather than diminished by the complexity of the issue of expenses. A simple explanation for the apparent anomaly would undoubtedly have lessened the impact of the criticism against the tally trade.

Two further expedients designed to strike at tallymen's cases might be mentioned. First, there were repeated calls for an amendment to the Statute of Limitations which allowed for a period of six years within which to recover debts. Lord Cairns, for example, introduced a Bill in 1881 to reduce the period to three years. As one trade journal noted,[44]

> "That some reform in this direction is required will be generally admitted since absurdly long-standing accounts do turn up every now and then in the Courts. A case of this description came on Wednesday before Mr. Bedwell, the County Court Judge, at Pontefract. His Honour commented on the fact that the accounts extended over six or seven years. In the interval since the debt was contracted, one of the defendants had been bankrupt; and in another case the wife who had ordered the work had since died. The plaintiff was non-suited, and his Honour trusted the legislature would speedily alter the law as to the Statute of Limitations from seven to three years."

It is true that there is no evidence that the case in question involved a tallyman's debt and that six to seven years may well have been considered an excessively long period during which the debt remained on the creditor's books. But one correspondent, "neither a minor tradesman nor one who carries the pack" (but who in every other respect appeared to be a Scotch draper selling clothing on instalments to 5,000 credit customers) was concerned about judicial reaction to delayed legal process.

> "It is only recently", he pointed out, "that one of the judges of our district in open court warned tradesmen . . . threatening to throw out old cases unless the creditors looked after their interests better (I suppose, as the judge thought, by putting debtors into court); but tradesmen will do this only as a last resort, and only when sheer necessity exists."[45]

Nonetheless, the more widely approved view seemed to favour a reduction in the prescriptive period. It would offer greater encouragement to demanding prompt payments, would militate against the "pernicious" system of long credit, "Which has worked so much mischief in our trade", and perhaps lend support to a reversion to cash payments.[46] It was thus seen as part of a generalised assault on credit; and as the tally trade was perceived as one of the principal factors fostering "reckless" credit, it was scarcely surprising that evidence to government enquiries into debtors' imprisonment should recommend that an amendment to the Statute of Limitations as an alternative to the abolition of committals, might be an expeditious remedy for the "canker" of the tally trade.[47]

V : MONEY-LENDERS

It is a moot point whether the unacceptable face of county court capitalism was more accurately depicted by the litigious activities of money-lenders than by those of the tallyman. Certainly, money-lenders had few defenders. Thus, according to Charles Loch of the Charity Organisation Society,

> "The working man who has contracted such a loan is considered well-nigh doomed by his mates, so great are the chances against him."[48]

The Money-lenders Inquiry of 1896-7[49] had indeed been shocked by revelations of 3,600% interest charged by money-lenders such as Isaac Gordon and the Carlton Bank Company. In the event, what came out of the report was the proposal to permit courts to go behind any transaction, as equity could do, and make an appropriate order. This would enable a court to cast aside an "agreement" which was deemed harsh and unconscionable, a recommendation embodied in the Money-lenders Act 1900 (63 & 64 Vict., c.46). While widely welcomed as a potential curb on the grosser excesses of the money-lending trade, the statute was not without notable detractors, concerned at the theoretical implications of the measure. Thus, for A.V. Dicey, the Act constituted one of the benchmarks of the age of collectivism, for which he had profound reservations. By placing restrictions on freedom of contract in money-lending transactions, he argued, the Act reversed fundamental Benthamite principles, a retrograde step undertaken by legislators who had "never taken the pains [n]or shown the ability to confute Bentham's arguments".[50] Yet it was surely convenient, however, for Dicey to ignore the welter of evidence of abuses, many of them stepping over the borderland of crime, presented to the Select Committee of 1896-7.[51] Moreover, there was evidence that even prior to the passing of the 1900 Act, some judges were prepared to take steps to discourage money-lenders' transactions being dragged through the county courts. Thus, G. Pitt-Lewis, Q.C., in a letter to The Times in 1892[52] explained how the late Sergeant Petersdorff had, in "bygone" days, "checkmated" the claims of money-lenders appearing before him in Exeter County Court, a practice followed, according to this correspondent, by "several" county court judges. More common, perhaps, was the practice of ordering repayment of the debt by many instalments of small amounts, spread over a lengthy period. Thus, in one instance, a money-lender had sued on a loan of £20 chargeable at 130% interest. As the debt was admitted, the judge at Bristol County Court was obliged to give judgment for the plaintiff. However, as he ordered the debt to be paid off in instalments at the rate of sixpence per month, it would require more than 66 years to repay the principal, let alone the interest due at judgment and thereafter. As one periodical observed,

> "The decision is a very curious one; if it were oftener repeated in flagrant cases we should hear less of such shameful transactions as still characterise the dealings of these gentry."[53]

Perhaps Commissioner Kerr of the City of London Court took note. He was once reputed to have ordered payment by instalments of a penny a month, which would take 385 years to complete.[54] Indeed, even more astonishing was the case of a 75 year-old debtor ordered by Crewe County Court to repay a debt of 70/-d at one penny a year, the first payment to commence six years after the judgment issued in

July 1893. Thus, the debt would not be liquidated for nearly one thousand years.[55] Yet even when armed with the 1900 Act,[56] some judges were unable to resist obliging money-lenders by granting judgment in severe cases. Thus, in 1906, one woman had borrowed a sovereign at the rate of 1d in the shilling per week from a female money-lender,

". . . and a'fore I knew where I was, I was two pounds in her debt."

The Bermondsey Settlement poor man's lawyer, Kingsley Wood (later Conservative Minister of Health), advised the debtor to let the money-lender sue in the county court, no doubt relying on the escape clause in the 1900 Act. The judge, however, simply ordered the borrower to pay off the debt at 2/6d a week.[57] Nor, of course, could judges prevent money-lenders from continuing to charge excessive rates of interest after the 1900 Act, so long as the matter did not come before the courts. Thus, Maud Pember Reeves, for example, reported an instance of interest at 433% being charged in 1913.[58] No doubt there were many worse cases.

VI : DEBT COLLECTORS

The network of unpopular plaintiffs who, for the judges and lawyers, embodied the most parasitical elements which invaded the county courts, also included debt collectors, or professional "duns". One reason why debts of many years standing would surface from time to time in the county courts was because of the not uncommon practice of factoring, involving the buying up of bad debts and the substitution of a new creditor for an old one. Thus, where the tallyman or money-lender was of the opinion that the expense and energy applied to recovering debts through the courts was becoming less of a paying proposition than formerly, as perhaps implied by the remarks of the registrar of Bury St. Edmunds County Court (supra), he might choose to sell his bad debts to a debt collector or to an accountant, to whom also fell the opportunity of purchasing a block of book debts from the Official Receiver.

Such debt collectors were, not unexpectedly, viewed with suspicion by "respectable" society associated with the county courts. One correspondent in The Times believed,[59] for example, that most county court committals derived from this source. Objection was taken by critics to the alleged fact that the assignee was generally harsher towards the debtor in enforcing his claim than the original creditor, particularly since the Board of Trade directed official receivers to sell a bankrupt's book debts in all cases. As we have seen, a number of such debts had almost, but not quite, expired under the Statute of Limitations 1623 (21 Jac.1., c.16) and particular grievance was felt on the part of the small debtor that he was obliged to pay 20 shillings in the £ to the trustee of a bankrupt, while the estate of the last-named paid out nothing or 2/6d to his creditors. The final damning criticism was that these book debts tended to be sold to the debt collector for a derisory sum, but that the assignee was frequently able to recover substantial amounts by threatening imprisonment.[60]

The system did have its defenders, however. In particular, The Drapers' Record[61] reminded its readers that although undoubtedly it operated harshly against the poor debtors of the bankrupt, nevertheless, in the absence of debt buying, the trustee in bankruptcy would himself require to undertake extensive litigation. Such a process, however, would fail to meet the insistence of the bankrupt's creditors on the most rapid and expeditious liquidation of his assets. Thus, the pressing interests of trade were offered as a justification for commercial practices which even the drapers' mouthpiece considered to be "one of the unpleasant consequences of modern trade"[62] and which other observers, less charitably, categorised as akin to those of the tallyman and money-lender.

The most ferocious criticism emanating from the legal profession was, however, levelled against debt collecting agents, as distinct from the purchasers of bad debts. This is scarcely surprising given that such agents were clearly perceived as a threat to the profession's market supremacy whenever they presumed to undertake court room activities which lawyers were competent to perform. As one legal correspondent, protesting vigorously against these agents, declaimed,

> "Taking them as a body they were the vilest and most worthless of men-wretched creatures, who were scouted by society, who could not obtain other employment than that of exercising their cruelty on poor unfortunate debtors by wringing from them their last penny under any circumstances of oppression, whatever might be their destitute position."[63]

They might indeed be individual agents appearing on behalf of creditors in court. Or they might be debt collecting associations or trade protection societies which might, or might not, instruct or retain attorneys to act on behalf of tradesmen-plaintiffs. It was claimed, for example, that by 1858 nine-tenths of those who appeared on behalf of clients in the county courts were debt collectors while the rest were barristers and attorneys.[64] When one agent, from the Mutual Trade Protection Society of Stalybridge, sought to appear on behalf of several plaintiffs at Upper Mill County Court in the same year, and attempted to prove admissions of debt after calling on the defendants for payment, Judge J.S. Greene complained that,

> "It was a most dangerous and improper practice, and one he could not sanction; that County Courts were never established for agents to prove in that loose manner. It was impossible an agent could know the circumstances under which a debt was contracted, and that great inducements were held out to misrepresentation thereby."[65]

One indignant solicitor, writing to The Law Times,[66] enclosed a copy of a demand sent by the Mercantile Mutual Association of Moorgate in London, to a debtor which contained the legend,

> "Messrs Henekeys, Abbott & Co., being members of this association, have placed in our hands their account against you amounting to £1.12.0d which we are requested to apply for, together with 3/6d, our charges for application and postage etc. . . ."

The usual threat of civil proceedings in the event of failure to pay was appended at the foot of the demand. What was particularly worrying this legal correspondent was, of course, the presumptuousness of an apparently unqualified organisation purporting to undertake lawyers' work. This association was,

> ". . . another of those organised invasions of our Profession. I should like to know if this is a bona fide association, or only one of the many private speculations which have assumed the title of a society?"[67]

Even where solicitors were acting on behalf of such an association, as was the case with the Southampton Trade Protection Society, indignation was not suppressed. Thus,

> "At best they are gigantic monopolies by means of which the Solicitor to the Society, who is too often the getter-up of it, brings to his own mill the harvest of an entire district by the attraction of cheapness."

Since the solicitor could not undersell directly, he attempted to do so, it was alleged, under cover in the name of a society. Thus, even if an action for maintenance could not be made out against the society, the demand for payment of charges (2/6d in the Southampton case, 3/6d in the Moorgate case) allied to threats of proceedings, might be indictable as an offence of aiding a party in litigation without just cause.[68]

As to the principal complaint, however, that is, the removal of lucrative debt recovery business from wholly independent legal practitioners, the ambiguity of the relevant statutory provision, section 91 of the County Courts Act 1846 (9 & 10 Vict., c.95), meant that the profession itself was uncertain whether non-legally qualified agents, in receipt of fees, were acting in breach of the solicitors' monopoly enshrined in the Solicitors Act 1843 (6 & 7 Vict., c.73, s.35).[69]

Of course, an alliance of the tally trade and unqualified debt collecting agents attracted the severest criticism of all. One lecturer narrated to his audience,

> ". . . a vast number of anecdotes illustrative of the rapacity of the packmen and the County Court agent . . . who had his eye only upon one thing, and that was the 2/6d in the pound he received for vampiring the unfortunate debtor for the sum due to the packman . . . . These despicable "mock attorneys", or "whippers-up", he continued, "wrote a letter in the first instance as much in the attorney style as their

> education would permit (their letters often indicating a neglect of their schooling) . . . .[70]

Attention would be drawn to overdue instalments on the tallyman's debts, and the threat of legal proceedings would prise the money from debtors who were thus compelled to sacrifice the "common necessaries of life". Only heavy fines on unqualified individuals purporting to act as county court agents would remedy this abuse. According to this lecturer, the tally trade itself should be subject to harsh restrictions (some of which have already been indicated; for example, the requirement for written authority from a husband where the wife contracted with a packman). Additionally, a judge should order instalments of no more than a shilling a month; warrants of committal should no longer be issued in tallymen's cases; purchased debts should not be recoverable through the courts "as many unprincipled persons advertised to buy these small debts up"; loss of employment might in circumstances relieve the debtor of his liability; while committals for all debts under £5 should be abolished. He concluded with the rallying cry that,

> "The working classes had now become the real parliament by virtue of the new franchise and he asked them to demand legislation on this subject to call upon the Legislature to institute a government inquiry into the system as at present carried on by packmen."[71]

Within four years, in 1873, an enquiry into the packmen's "system" was indeed mounted as part of a wider investigation into imprisonment for debt in the county courts. Moreover, similar enquiries were also carried out in 1893 and again in 1909.[72] Yet both imprisonment for debt and the tallymen's trade remained intact, basically because the argument that consumer credit should be abolished never prevailed among policy-makers, among whom must be included the majority of county judges themselves.

VII : CONSUMER CREDIT

It was true that a number of public figures identified the existence of imprisonment for debt rather than the tally trade itself as an inducement to reckless credit. Thus, one politician argued in the Commons that,

> "All political economists from Adam Smith to Mill, laid down that it was not for the interests of a State to encourage credit and he believed that if they were tomorrow to abolish imprisonment for debt, trade would be all the more flourishing . . . ."[73]

Yet others believed that the very existence of the debt recovery facilities of the county court was partly responsible for the prevalence of widespread trading "abuses". For,

> ". . . the credit given under the protection of the County Courts was given with the idea of making those courts agents for the collection of small debts. A working man's wife was induced to incur a debt for an article which perhaps she did not really want, and then the County Court obliged the husband to pay."[74]

Yet, as the 1909 Select Committee on debtors' imprisonment acknowledged,

> "Our national life is based almost entirely on a system of credit. Transactions between merchants are almost invariably conducted on the basis of credit and not of cash payments. So are transactions between wholesale and retail houses; and the retail trader must almost of necessity give credit to his customers, because a man who works for a salary or wage must, unless he has money in hand when he commences his work, obtain credit for the necessities of life until he has done sufficient work to entitle him to receive payment."[75]

The committee considered that what was crucial from the tradesman's point of view was his knowledge of, and belief in, the reliability of his customers in being able to pay off their debts. There was some evidence, it thought, that more vigorous enquiries were being undertaken in recent years into the financial standing of customers, a precaution encouraged by the trade protection societies.[76]

Yet, as we have seen, there also existed a strong belief that excessive credit was being extended to the working-class. Moreover, it was offered at a price, according to Judge Parry in 1909, which allowed the creditor a reasonable profit after having sued his debtor in court and after court fees and expenses had been met.[77] Thus, as he complained some years earlier, the "knaves" who clustered round the county courts, that is, the travelling drapers, general drapers, jewellers, money-lenders, questionable grocers, were all responsible for further immiseration of the poor. For,

> ". . . in truth, credit is given without enquiry, recklessly and equally to those in work and out of work, for necessities, luxuries, and inutilities, and given at a price which includes the profit of the credit giver, his costs of making weekly collections, the cost of his debt collector or solicitor and ultimately a considerable tribute towards the maintenance of the County Court."[78]

The trade union leader, James Seddon, M.P., president of the National Union of Shop Assistants, commented that,

> "From my own observation, credit is most demoralising, and is to a large extent responsible for much of the matrimonial unhappiness among the working-class,"[79]

a sentiment which Judge Chalmers had earlier expressed in the dictum that among the working-class, "a man marries on credit and repents on judgment summons."[80]

"Sympathetic", or "involuntary" credit, extended by doctors or tradesmen to the unemployed, to enable them to obtain the "necessaries" of life, was, for many critics of the tally trade, an unavoidable feature of economic transactions with the poor (and in respect to which, imprisonment for debt might be retained, else such credit would no longer be available; a prospect manifestly to the detriment of the working-class, according to this view). "Voluntary" or "illegitimate" credit, on the other hand, which enabled the poor to purchase jewellery, expensive watches and "all sorts of publications on the terms of payment by instalments" (among which cheap bibles apparently featured prominently), incurred the wrath of moralistic judges like Parry and Chalmers. Moreover, the widespread, if not necessarily wholly accurate view, was that the tally trade was principally responsible for fostering this "reckless", "unhealthy" or "undue" credit.[81] The majority report of the 1909 Select Committee into debtors' imprisonment indeed recommended that imprisonment be abolished in cases involving "voluntary" credit, that is, where goods other than necessaries (including "luxury" drapery) were sold on the instalment system.[82] The suggestion drew no favour with the Board of Trade, however. The Inspector-General in Bankruptcy believed that,

> "If these recommendations were adopted, I think they would lead to anomalies which could not be very well defended. There are no doubt hard cases, such as those in which tallymen induce ignorant people to purchase goods payable by instalments, but it is impossible to save people altogether from their own folly."[83]

Certainly, as we have seen, the anomalies were even more complex than is suggested here. For, in respect solely to tallymen's dealings, some believed they sold only "fripperies", while others (including, of course, the credit drapers themselves) opined that their goods were necessaries, not luxuries, and sold on realistic terms in the light of their customers' inability to pay for the goods in one instalment. Leaving aside these qualifications, what one finds in the Inspector-General's concluding observation is the supremacy of the ideology of the free market. Thus, condemnation of the debtor, not the creditor, was implicit in his remarks. The county courts were, therefore, left to resolve their crisis of legitimacy as best they could without the guidance or assistance of Parliament, for the market could not be interfered with.

VIII : CONCLUSION

The legal personnel of the county courts faced an acute dilemma in the nineteenth century in dealing with tallymen's cases. On the one hand, as an integral feature of a capitalist economy, which was dependent on the distribution and the sale of household commodities, as well as on their production, the county courts offered a vital service - perhaps not a necessary, let alone a sufficient one - to plaintiffs selling by instalment. Consumer credit was clearly the life-blood of the county courts. Moreover, despite the voices of protest levelled, as a matter of principle, against any credit for domestic purchases, a view which harked back to the late Middle Ages belief that insolvency was a mortal sin (and which was no doubt reinforced by the message of thrift of Mr. Micawber, and imbibed both by the co-operative movement and by stern judicial monetarists), there was wider approval for "legitimate" credit extended to the "worthy" poor falling on hard times, to enable them to purchase the "necessaries" of life. In respect to this "involuntary" credit, the county courts were perceived by their own personnel as guaranteeing a continuous flow of this crucial facility for the poor. Enable creditors to recover their debts, so this argument went, and these men of goodwill would ensure that the tap was never turned off. Thus, the benefits would be shared on a tripartite basis. The county court would collect its fees and justify its existence economically, socially and pragmatically; creditors would recover their debts; while debtors could again turn to credit salesmen in the future, to acquire goods which they could not hope to pay for in one instalment.

The other horn of the dilemma, however, related to the perceived domestic and moral mischief wrought by the tallymen, money-lenders, jewellery and book "touts". It was considered a social blot for which many judges felt they must share responsibility. Though sympathy was on this view often wasted on those defendants beguiled by their own vanity into extravagance on the "never-never", well might Judge Chalmers bemoan his fate as "the helpless instrument of the legalised tyranny of a small money-lender or a dishonest tallyman."[84] As Sir Henry James (later Lord James of Hereford) pointed out,

> "The County Court was not the forum for settling differences between litigants so much as it was a great debt-collecting office. It was used entirely by creditors who were traders, as against the honest portion of the community, on a reckless system of credit."[85]

Acknowledging, of course, that both Chalmers and James would not actually be helpless if sitting in judgment in a tallyman's case where the dishonesty alleged amounted to fraud or deceit or other head of criminal or civil liability, we may note that their accounts of the court system reflected the philosophy of a market economy. The courts would, therefore, adjudicate accordingly in favour of private, entrepreneurial capitalist interests. Yet the attempts of certain judges to circumscribe the tallymen's claims by according them less favourable treatment than that meted out to other, more "respectable", creditors, suggests either that the tally trade and other "fringe" traders cannot be classed as capitalist, a proposition which would be difficult to sustain, or it implies a greater degree of autonomy on the part of these courts from their economic context. The county courts - or at least some of them - were thus subject to influences not wholly dependent on the economic "substructure". They were, however, predominantly grounded in a market ideology even where judicial conceptions of liberal market economics might be ambiguous and contradictory on the extent, if at all, to which consumer transactions ought to be regulated by law. Nonetheless, one should beware overstating the significance of the maverick judges whose personal prejudices were displayed in judgments against tallymen. The county court remained, principally, a debt-collecting agency. Moreover, if it were pointed out to those judges adjudicating against tallymen that their actions were in conflict with "the rule of law", they would reply that, on the contrary, it was the rule of law with which they were concerned when they non-suited tallymen; while their exercise of discretion in respect to penalties against tallymen's debtors was itself enshrined in statute.

The choice, therefore, was stark, and it is difficult to resist the conclusion that the critical judges might have been seeking a scapegoat on whom to lay the "blame" for transforming their courts into what had vividly been called "misery exchanges". Yet as the economist, J.H. Elliot, had observed in 1845,

> "However much we may regret their 'necessity', it is better that there should be tallymen, credit and warm clothes, rather than no tallymen, no credit, rags and gin."[86]

This was a sentiment to which Judge Falconer (Merthyr) apparently gave his approval by quoting extensively from Elliot in one of his own tracts,[87] though one which the County Courts Chronicle[88] immediately repudiated in yet another condemnation of the tally trade.

There thus remained a tension which ran through the debt-collecting and decision-making processes of the county court, a crisis of legitimacy and respectability not just for the credit drapers, but for many county court judges themselves. It is probable that that tension has not as yet abated.

Certainly, for a period after the First World War, the tally trade continued to attract opprobrium. In 1929, for example, one solicitor, examining the total numbers imprisoned for debt in 1927, wrote to the Prison Commissioners that, in respect to small debtors,

> ". . . by far the greater proportion of these emanate from what is termed the 'working-classes', victims of their own petty extravagance, who have succumbed to the lure of the tallyman, the instalment system creditor and the money-lender."[89]

Of course, with specific reservations, we may say that the age of the peripatetic tallyman, hopefully knocking on doors, has long passed. Consequently the dominance of the tallyman among the lists of plaintiffs in the county courts has been replaced by that of the local authorities, gas, electricity and water companies, and, of course, by the finance houses, financing hire purchase transactions. One wonders whether such institutions are any less inexorable creditors than the tallymen ever were,[90] and whether modern county court judges display the ambivalence which clearly afflicted some of their nineteenth century predecessors. Certainly, as Ison remarked in 1975,[91]

> "A common misconception about courts is that they are engaged primarily in the task of adjudication. So far as consumer transactions are concerned, it is nearer the truth to describe the county courts as being like collection agencies, enforcing the claims of sellers and finance companies regardless of their legitimacy. Only occasionally and by way of exception is there an inquiry into the merits of the case."

We may conclude by noting that legal history has for long suffered under the blight of a Whiggish interpretation which treats of the subject as the long march of progress through the ages, and which assumes class relations as unproblematic. It is to be hoped that the above account will help to confirm the unsuitable nature of this approach.

NOTES

1. P.S. Atiyah, The Rise and Fall of Freedom of Contract (London: Oxford University Press, 1979).

2. O.R. McGregor, Social History and Law Reform (London: Stevens, 1981).

3. G.R. Rubin, supra.

4. Cf. the opinion of Robert Ellet, President of the Incorporated Law Society, cited in Frederick Dolman, "Is the Law Too Dear?" Strand Magazine, Vol.22, 1901, at p.386; and Edward A. Parry, "A Day in My Life in the County Court" Cornhill Magazine, Vol.16 (N.S.), 1904, at p.343. The phrase was used as late as 1936. See Charles Muir, Justice in a Depressed Area (London: Allen & Unwin, 1936), p.66.

5. Under the terms of the so-called "Tippling Act", 24 Geo.2, c.40, (1750).

6. G. Pitt-Lewis, quoting the opinion of Sergeant Petersdorff, judge of Exeter County Court, in The Times, December 28, 1892. On this question, see later.

6a. D. Strinati, Capitalism, the State and Industrial Relations (London: Croom Helm, 1982).

7. Cited in Alfred Emden, "Is Law for the People or for the Lawyers?" The Nineteenth Century, Vol.49, 1901, at p.859.

8. Arthur J. Williams M.P., How to Avoid Law (London: Cassell & Co., 1885).

9. See 'A Family Lawyer', "How Shall I make Him Pay?" Cassell's Family Magazine, 1891, pp.590-3. More orthodox advice is to be found in 'A Solicitor', County Court Practice Made Easy: or, Debt Collection Simplified (London: Effingham, Wilson, 1911) and Harry Impey, Debt Recovery and County Court Procedure (London: Routledge, 1909). Even trans-Atlantic advice on debt collecting through the English courts was available. See the report of the United States consul in Birmingham in Albany Law Journal, Vol.59, 1899, pp.512-4.

10. The statistics showing the predominance of tallymen among the lists of

county court plaintiffs are given in G.R. Rubin, "Packmen, Talleymen and 'Perambulating Scotchmen': Credit Drapers in Nineteenth and Early Twentieth Century England" (in preparation).

11. The Law Journal, Vol.3, September 25, 1868, p.610. Cf. County Courts Chronicle, Vol.21, June 1, 1869, p.430.

12. E.A. Parry, The Law and the Poor (London: Smith, Elder & Co., 1914), p.61.

13. David Alexander, Retailing in England During the Industrial Revolution (London: Athlone Press, 1970), p.83.

14. In litigation following the death of an insolvent tallyman, however, the Master of the Rolls (probably Lord Romilly, who was succeeded by Sir George Jessel in the same year) observed that, "It was clear what the nature of the business was - namely, the selling of clothes on credit to a number of ladies of a certain class, who require a constant supply of finery for the purpose of their calling. Many of these ladies were minors, against whom no action would lie; and in fact, it was not the policy of the tallyman to sue his customers but rather to depend on the tact of his collectors in getting instalments as often as they could, and in refusing to sell new clothes until the old ones were, at least, partly paid for." Warehousemen and Drapers' Trade Journal, Vol.2, February 22, 1873, p.104. This tallyman must have been untypical in respect to his avoidance of the courts.

15. J.R. McCulloch, A Dictionary, Practical, Theoretical and Historical, of Commerce and Commercial Navigation (London: Longman, Green & Co., 1844), p.1270.

16. Henry Mayhew, London Labour and the London Poor, Vol.1, (London: Charles Griffin & Co., 1864), p.423.

17. J.B. Kington, "The 'New' County Courts" The People's Journal, Vol.4, 1848, pp.171-2 and 194-6, at p.171.

18. The Law Times, Vol.33, April 9, 1859, p.44.

19. Ibid., June 11, 1859, pp.149-150.

20. Ibid., Vol.32, December 4, 1858, p.127. For further accounts of aged imprisoned debtors, see [Anon.] "Prisons and Poverty" Tait's Edinburgh Magazine, Vol.23, 1856, pp.242-6. Similar complaints were voiced after the turn of the century. One such case involved a debtor, John Sessions, who had died of consumption in Brixton Prison in December 1907, after having been imprisoned for a debt of one shilling. See Vanity Fair, December 28, 1907 and Joseph Collinson, "A Plea for the Honest Debtor" Humane Review, Vol.9, 1908-09, pp.97-8.

21. The Law Journal, Vol.3, December 18, 1868, p.779. The case in question was Ker v. Gregory, Mrs Gregory having purchased some items of clothing from the tallyman, Ker, who was seeking to recover a debt of £1.12.2d.

22. The law of wife's agency in the case of necessaries is discussed frequently in contemporary literature. See for example the large extract from J.W. Smith's Law of Husband and Wife, 8 Vols., (London: E. Wilson, 1872-8) in County Courts Chronicle, Vol.23, July 1, 1872, pp.310-11; also cases reported in The Drapers' Record, Vol.7, August 16, 1890, p.204; ibid., November 1, 1890, p.643; ibid., Vol.13, November 11, 1893, p.1132; the editorial on the Married Women's Property Act 1870, in Warehousemen and Drapers' Trade Journal, Vol.10, December 3, 1881, p.824, and on the 1882 and 1893 Acts, and on a Private Member's Bill in 1909, in The Drapers' Record, Vol.76, October 23, 1909, p.219.

23. The Drapers' Record, Vol.6, March 15, 1890, p.355.

24. On the general question of "means to pay", see Rubin, infra.

25. Report of H.C. Select Committee on County Courts (Jurisdiction (No.2) Bill, P.P. 1878 (267) XI, qq.3168-72.

26. Ibid., qq.2736-8.

27. LC02/211, "Lord Chancellor's Bill Dealing with s.5 of the Debtors Act: Judges' Observations, 1906."

28. Within the confines of the present work, it is not possible to offer any

definitive explanations as to why particular judges should appear to be more paternalistic than others on the county court benches in the nineteenth and early twentieth centuries. The seven or eight judges referred to in the paper, whose judicial records point to a more sympathetic posture towards the plight of the poor were not, for example, concentrated in the industrial districts. Their circuits were, indeed, widely dispersed throughout the country. Whether specific political beliefs were relevant - high Toryism, or an interventionist philosophy as contrasted to a commitment to market liberalism - requires deeper biographical research than can be attempted here. Undoubtedly, however, such prosopographical research on the county court judiciary is a matter of urgency and would enhance our understanding of many facets of social and economic development in the period such as those described here.

29. The Law Journal, Vol.3, September 25, 1868, p.610. See before, note 5.

30. Other jurisdictional difficulties not specifically related to tallymen's cases are raised in George Manley Wetherfield, County Court Reform, 5th edn., (London: privately published, 1882). Contemporary legal literature was, of course, replete with programmes for the reform of various aspects of county court procedure and jurisdiction. The literature is too vast to mention.

31. The Law Times, Vol.33, May 28, 1859, p.132.

32. Report of the Committee to the Lord Chancellor on County Court Procedure, P.P.1909 (311) LXXII, para. XXII.16.

33. County Courts Act 1875 (38 & 39 Vict., c.50), s.1.

34. Second Report of the Judicature Commission, P.P.1872 [c.631] XX, p.16.

35. Warehousemen and Drapers' Trade Journal, Vol.9, April 24, 1880, pp.260-1.

36. Ibid., Vol.10, July 30, 1881, p.528.

37. The Law Journal, Vol.28, January 21, 1893, p.46.

38. The bills of sale system itself was heavily criticised prior to the reforms of

the Bills of Sale Amendment Act 1882 (45 & 46 Vict., c.43.). Thus, in 1873, bills of sale were condemned as a device which was "frequently made use of by unscrupulous money-lenders to defraud and injure the poor, whose needy circumstances bring them within the clutches of such unprincipled men." The method was to place advertisements in the newspapers offering advances on favourable terms which "it is needless to say . . . are purely imaginary." See County Courts Chronicle, Vol.24, June 2, 1873, p.125. That the poor were the principal sufferers of the system was suggested by the return for 1880 which showed a total of 55,153 bills of sale registered for that year, of which 38,177 were for sums below £50; while 22,850 of them were for less than £20. See Warehousemen and Drapers' Trade Journal, Vol.10, August 13, 1881, p.560 and ibid., November 26, 1881, p.808. The 1882 Act abolished bills of sale for less than £30, thus affording some protection against abuse of the poor. However, creditors sought to circumvent this restriction by arranging to lend more than £30 in exchange for a bill of sale as security, and then returning to the grantor a portion of the money so that the net amount would be less than £30. See The Business Encyclopaedia and Legal Adviser, Vol.1 (London: Caxton Publishing, 1911), p.202.

39. See, for example, Warehousemen and Drapers' Trade Journal, Vol.10, June 18, 1881, p.434. For modern brief accounts, see Ralph Harris et al., Hire Purchase in a Free Society, 3rd edn., (London: Hutchinson, 1961), Ch.1, and J.J. McManus, "The Emergence and Non-Emergence of Legislation" British Journal of Law and Society, Vol.6, 1978, pp.185-201.

40. Report of Departmental Committee of Inquiry into the Bankruptcy Law, Vol.1, Cd. 4068, P.P. 1908, XXXIV, 1.

41. The Law Journal, Vol.3, September 25, 1868, p.610.

42. H.C. Debates, 3rd series, Vol.197, June 29, 1869, col.765 (J. Stapleton).

43. The Standard, n.d., cited in County Courts Chronicle, Vol.14, September 2, 1861, p.241.

44. Warehousemen and Drapers' Trade Journal, Vol.10, February 12, 1881, p.118.

45. Manchester Examiner, n.d., cited in Warehousemen and Drapers' Trade Journal, Vol.11, July 22, 1882, p.511.

46. See note 44.

47. See P.P. 1893-4 (H.L.156) IX, para.18; P.P. 1909 (239) VII, resolution viii (22), and evidence of witnesses scattered throughout the reports.

48. C.S. Loch, How to Help Causes of Distress (London: Longman, Green & Co., 1888), pp.101-2.

49. Report of H.C. Select Committee into Money-Lenders, P.P. 1897 (405) XI, and 1898 (110)X. See also T.W. Russell, "The Money-Lending Inquiry" The Nineteenth Century, Vol.44, 1898, pp.234-45, and [Anon.] "The Money-Lending Inquiry" Chambers' Journal, 6th series, Vol.1, 1898, pp.502-5; and Atiyah, op.cit., pp.711-2.

50. A.V. Dicey, Lectures on Law and Opinion in England in the Nineteenth Century (London: Macmillan, 1901), p.34.

51. S.D. Temkin, "The Influence of Public Opinion on the Development of English Law from 1880 to 1914" (M.A. thesis, Liverpool University, 1939), p.54. See also Cosgrove's recent devastating critique of Dicey's competence in this area: Richard A. Cosgrove, The Rule of Law: Albert Venn Dicey, Victorian Jurist (London: Macmillan, 1981).

52. The Times, December 28, 1892. See before, note 6.

53. The People's Lawyer, Vol.1, June 13, 1885, p.277.

54. G. Pitt-Lewis, Commissioner Kerr - An Individuality (London: T. Fisher Unwin, 1903), p.208.

55. Shoe and Leather Record, August 11, 1893, p.293.

56. On early interpretations of the "unconscionable" provisions of the Act, see L.J. Sturge, "The Construction of the Money-Lenders' Act, 1900" Law Quarterly Review, Vol.22, 1906, pp.213-221.

57. Bermondsey Settlement Magazine, Vol.12, No.2, February 1906 (copy in

Kingsley Wood Collection, University of Kent at Canterbury).

58. M.S. Pember Reeves, Round About a Pound a Week, 2nd edn., (London: Bell, 1914), p.72.

59. The Times, June 24, 1897.

60. See 1893 S.C., qq.176-7, 278 (evidence of Henry Nicol, retired Treasury Superintendent of County Courts) and q.383 (Judge William Selfe, West Kent).

61. The Drapers' Record, Vol.7, November 22, 1890, p.761.

62. Ibid.

63. County Courts Chronicle, Vol.21, April 1, 1869, p.380.

64. The Law Times, Vol.31, April 24, 1858, pp.69-70.

65. Manchester Guardian, April 19, 1858. The county courts were not, of course, encumbered by the rule of evidence in the superior courts which prevented the contractors themselves from giving evidence.

66. The Law Times, Vol.34, October 29, 1859, p.60.

67. Ibid.

68. The Law Times, Vol.32, February 5, 1859, p.231.

69. The Law Journal, Vol.7, February 16, 1872, pp.115-6.

70. County Court Chronicle, Vol.21, April 1, 1869, p.380.

71. Ibid. For muted working-class responses to county court committals, see Rubin, op.cit., p.000, ante.

72. See P.P. 1873 (384) XV; P.P. 1893-4 (H.L.156) IX; and P.P. 1909 (239) VII.

73. H.C. Debate, 3rd series, Vol.195, April 5, 1869, col.175 (P. McMahon).

74. Ibid., col.177, (W. Rathbone).

75. P.P. 1909 (239), VII, para.4.

76. Ibid., para. 13.

77. Ibid., para. 15 and q.1787.

78. Edward A. Parry, "The Insolvent Poor" Fortnightly Review, Vol.63 (N.S.) 1898, pp.797-804, at p.799.

79. P.P. 1909 (239) VII, op.cit., q.3868. For a suggested impact of the consumer

revolution on American marriages, see Elaine Tyler May, "The Pressure to Provide: Class, Consumerism and Divorce in Urban America, 1880-1920" Journal of Social History, Vol.12, 1978, pp.180-193.

80. M.D. Chalmers, "Imprisonment for Debt" Fortnightly Review, Vol.44, 1888, pp.337-46, at p.343.

81. The varied adjectival terminology relating to credit is to be found throughout the Select Committee reports of 1873, 1893 and 1909.

82. P.P. 1909 (239) VII, op.cit., para.26.

83. B.T. 37/22/B922/11, "Memorandum on Report of Select Committee on Debtors' Imprisonment, by F.A. Clarke: August 25, 1910."

84. Chalmers, op.cit., p.341.

85. H.C. Debate, 3rd series, Vol.218, April 14, 1874, Cols. 553-8. Cf. "Law is no longer merely an agency for resolving disputes: it is an active, dynamic means of social control and change." Morton J. Horwitz, The Transformation of American Law, 1780-1860 (London: Harvard University Press, 1977), pp.154-5. It is not clear that Horwitz's generalisation is apt here; for both resistance to, and acceptance of, the tally trade's practices by the courts is documented here.

86. J.H. Elliot, Credit the Life of Commerce etc., (London: Madden & Malcolm, 1845), p.97, cited in T.F. Falconer, A Husband's Liability for a Debt Contracted by his Wife (Usk: 'County Observer' Office, c.1868), p.10.

87. Ibid.

88. County Courts Chronicle, Vol.21, June 1, 1869, p.430.

89. PCOM9/61, "Memorandum upon the Law Relating to Civil Coercion, by Mr. J.A. Parker, Solicitor, Wakefield, 1929."

90. Cf. Paul Rock, Making People Pay (London: Routledge & Kegan Paul, 1973) on debt recovery means. Cf. for Canada, see T.C. Puckett, "Credit Casualties: A Study of Wage Garnishment in Ontario" University of Toronto Law Journal, Vol.28, 1978, at pp.95-7. See also Maureen Cain, "Where are

the Disputes? A Study of a First Instance Civil Court in the UK" in M. Cain and K. Kalcsar (eds.) The Study of Disputes (Budapest and London: Hungarian Academy of Science and Pergamon Press, 1982), Ch.8.

91. T.G. Ison, "Small Claims" Modern Law Review, Vol.35, 1972, pp.18-37, at p.18. See also K. Economides, "Small Claims and Procedural Justice" British Journal of Law and Society, Vol.7, 1980, pp.111-121, and, for the United States, Barbara Yngvesson and Patricia Hennessey, "Small Claims, Complex Disputes: A Review of the Small Claims Literature" Law and Society Review, Vol.9, 1975, pp.219-74.

COUNTY COURT AND SUPERIOR COURT REGISTRARS, 1820-1875: THE MAKING OF A JUDICIAL OFFICIAL

P.W.J. Bartrip

Historians in their general neglect of modern legal history have overlooked registrars. Yet today these court officials have numerous and important judicial powers. Registrars of the Family Division of the High Court, County Court and District High Court deal, for example, with practically all the ancillary work in divorce.[1] Furthermore, the registrar is also the principal figure in resolving the financial questions in a divorce. In contrast, the judge in an undefended divorce action (over 95 per cent of all cases) combines the role of rubber stamp and ritualistic symbol. Registrars are prominent not merely in matrimonial disputes; County Court and district registrars (frequently the same man occupies both positions in one locality) have a varied jurisdiction. As County Court officials they hear and determine complex contract, tort and bankruptcy cases. In short, the registrar of the later twentieth century is a central figure in the administration of civil justice whose judicial authority sometimes appears to outweigh that of his judge. Although this picture has developed in the course of this century its foundations were laid down in a period of approximately fifty years spanning the mid-nineteenth century.

In discussing registrars our first problem is one of definition; what is and was a registrar? The question is more complex than it at first might appear, for the answer depends upon the status of the court referred to and the period to which allusion is made. Victorian County Court registrars were not generally termed such until the title clerk was dropped in 1856. Since that time the duties of all types of registrar have changed fundamentally as have the qualifications required to discharge them. Registrars now have only judicial functions, whereas in the early Victorian period their tasks were clerical, administrative and domestic. But since there are differences in the work, qualifications, and powers of High Court,

County Court, and district registrars it is impossible to discuss them all under one heading. Furthermore, the duties of a High Court registrar in one division are broadly equivalent to those of masters in other divisions, though qualifications for becoming a master or registrar vary, sometimes greatly. Even amongst today's Family Division registrars there is lack of uniformity in qualifications; they may be barristers, or civil servants with no formal legal qualifications. In contrast, district and County Court registrars must be solicitors of at least seven years standing. Before the passing of the Judicature Acts of 1873 and 1875, disparities were even more pronounced. Some large towns, such as Liverpool, had more than a half dozen registrars acting in different courts and performing distinct tasks.

The anonymity of registrars forms a barrier to historical investigation. Dr. Moir, in her study of the justice of the peace, points out that the eighteenth century JP's clerk "proves an elusive figure . . . on the whole he remains anonymous."[2] The comment could apply to registrars of almost any period. It has proved possible to undertake sociological analysis of the backgrounds of judges and justices of the peace. Indeed, recent work suggests that, in the eighteenth and nineteenth centuries at least, holders of these offices were of less exalted origins than had been popularly assumed.[3] Absence of biographical data renders impossible a similar assessment of nineteenth century registrars. Thus, the main purpose of this paper is to account for the emergence of the latter as significant judicial figures in the period preceding the Judicature Acts.

I

The office of registrar is an ancient one. The thirteenth century Consistory Court of Canterbury contained an official called the notarius consistorii who has been tentatively identified as a registrar. One John Cranebourne held the post during the later fourteenth century. Registrars in the Archdeacon's Court have been traced to the mid-fifteenth century when, in August 1442, a John Penwortham was appointed.[4] However, for the most part the medieval registrars of the Ecclesiastical Courts are linked with their twentieth century counterparts by name alone. This name has become anachronistic and misleading, for today their duties do not include registering decisions.

In the first half of the nineteenth century the registrar was mainly responsible for dealing with the myriad tasks to be performed before and after judgment. This had been the basic situation for centuries. When, in 1846, the modern County Court system was established, many clerical and administrative duties were imposed upon the clerks.[5] These were consistent with those undertaken by clerks in the existing "small debts" courts and by registrars in bankruptcy since 1821.[6] The County Court clerk was also made responsible for the upkeep of the court house and offices. He had absolute power over the appointment and dismissal of servants and was obliged to make contracts, subject to Treasury regulations and the judge's sanction, for furnishing, repairing, heating, lighting and cleaning. He had to purchase the "law office books" and other stationery from the court's "general fund."[7] In short, he was responsible for the day-to-day smooth running of his court. Woodcock shows that this was precisely his role in the Ecclesiastical Courts some six centuries earlier: "If the efficiency of the courts depended on any one man, that man was the registrar."[8]

Before the establishment of the new County Court system, registrars were little in evidence in the civil courts of England and Wales. However, in 1821 an office of registrar in bankruptcy was created. The registrar, who was appointed by the Lord Chancellor, had two basic duties. First, he had to attend his office between the hours of 10.00 am and 4.00 pm for the purpose of keeping an appointment book. Second, he was obliged to attend the sittings of any commission in bankruptcy and to keep a daily journal in which were recorded the details of hearings.[9] The registrar in bankruptcy needed no legal qualifications; he performed only clerical duties and his status was low. He was, however, adequately, if not handsomely, rewarded. For every meeting of the commissioners he received ten shillings for the use of his office and one shilling for himself. In addition to such fees he received a salary of £200 per annum, an allowance for "coals and candles," living accommodation at Basinghall Street, a housekeeper (paid £50 per annum) and servants.[10]

Before 1831 ". . . all Bankruptcy proceedings were taken by suing out a commission under the great seal, directed to certain Commissioners, to take order of the bankrupt, his estate and effects and to make distribution of the bankrupt's property for the discharge of his debts."[11] There were seventy commissioners, appointed by the Lord Chancellor, divided into fourteen lists of five. The level of remuneration, which seldom exceeded £300 per annum, attracted "respectable rather than distinguished men." The commissioners had no proper premises on which to discharge their duties. Hearings took place in a Guildhall room which served as an extra kitchen on the occasion of a banquet. Within this room a number of cases might be simultaneously discussed by different groups of commissioners. The consequent disorder sometimes necessitated adjournment to the private room of a nearby coffee house.[12] After the 1831 reform, six commissioners were "to act in the prosecution of fiats" with judges forming a Court of Review.[13] This was an attempt to modernise bankruptcy proceedings, thereby making them more suitable for a rapidly industrialising economy in which efficient commercial laws and institutions were vital for continued economic growth and prosperity. However, Household Words, a not unjust critic of mid-century bankruptcy law, considered that the commissioners' duties, by this time better remunerated, were less than onerous: "The Commissioner is obliged for this salary (about £2000 per annum), to make a show of doing something."[14]

In 1831 it was also enacted that two registrars and up to eight deputies should be attached to the Bankruptcy Court.[15] Their duties were not significantly different from those imposed under the 1821 Act though, from 1832, a deputy was to attend each commissioner in order to take minutes and to draw up and have charge of proceedings under the superintendence of the chief registrar.[16] In 1842, from which time deputy registrars were known simply as registrars, clerical duties were augmented by the stipulation that registrars should keep an abstract of proceedings in the Bankruptcy Court.[17] More significantly, the 1842 Act allowed for the appointment of up to twelve "county registrars" to attend commissioners in the provinces. But the most important section of this Act, from the registrars' point of view, was that which allowed them the judicial power of acting "in the prosecution of such fiat or petition for proof of debts." By this clause they could examine parties or witnesses on oath for either purpose:

> ". . . and such officer so acting shall have and exercise all the power vested in such court for proof of debts and examination of witnesses, except the power of commitment."[18]

Thus, in 1842, the bankruptcy registrar, gained what can fairly be described as judicial authority in pre-trial issues. In 1849 the number of metropolitan bankruptcy registrars was reduced to four but the powers of these men were again increased:

> "The Registrar of the Court may, in certain cases, act for the Commissioner as his deputy, and, subject to . . . limitations . . . , exercise all his jurisdiction; and orders made by the registrar, even for the bankrupt's order of discharge, if made without opposition, have been allowed to be valid."[19]

When the County Court system, to which we must turn next, was still in its infancy, registrars in bankruptcy were significant figures. They had become such by acquiring new duties generated by efforts to modernise bankruptcy law and adapt it to changing economic circumstances. Much the same process occurred in the County Court system.

II

The year 1846 was a landmark in the history of registrars, not because it saw them acquire extra powers, but because of the vast expansion of their numbers caused by the establishment of County Courts along the lines suggested by Jeremy Bentham and Henry Brougham. County Courts were so called "because the term was a familiar one in the popular ear . . . in their jurisdiction, in their powers and in their practice, the new County Courts bear no resemblance to the Courts they have superseded."[20] They developed from the Middlesex County Court, established by statute in 1750. In fact, the name is misleading for every poor law union had a court, each served by a registrar, which formed part of a circuit under the jurisdiction of a judge.[21] They were created in an attempt to rationalise the existing profusion of small and often inefficient local "small debts" courts.[22] Their jurisdiction was in "all pleas of personal actions where the debt or damage claimed is not more than Twenty Pounds." Hence Household Words' reference to them as "establishments for low priced law."[23]

The 1840s and 1850s were years of rapid ad hoc regulation of commercial institutions and practices. The Bank Charter Act, 1844, designed to establish a safe currency, paved the way for the ascendancy of the Bank of England. The Companies Act of the same year sought to discourage irresponsible speculation. In 1856 the principle of limited liability was accepted by the Legislature in order to encourage small investors by protecting them against business collapse.[24] Several novels popularised and publicised the idea of commercial reform in this era. Dickens' Martin Chuzzlewit, written in the early 1840s showed the need for regulating the insurance business. Little Dorrit, published 1855-57, and Samuel Warren's Ten Thousand a Year, serialised in Blackwood's Magazine between 1839 and 1841, contained sub-plots underlining the need for control of unscrupulous joint-stock speculation. Writing to his daughter, Mrs Bunbury, in February 1850, Leonard Horner, the factory inspector enquired: ". . . do we not see laws passed every year to check the abuse of the application of capital, when it is productive of great moral and social evils?"[25]

The 1842 Bankruptcy Act and the 1846 County Courts legislation must be seen in the framework of this fiscal and business reform. They were designed to facilitate commercial transactions by improving "the legal and institutional framework." The new County Courts, for example, provided the small tradesman with a relatively cheap means of securing payment of debts.[26] They were, therefore, of enormous advantage to creditors. However, a critic writing in 1857, argued that County Courts impeded commerce by deterring customers from ordering goods and thereby contracting a debt for which vindictive County Court officials would demand immediate payment.[27] Indeed, it was said some years earlier that unscrupulous traders secured immediate payment of bills by lodging County Court plaints. Frightened customers then settled their bills and the trader was saved the trouble and expense of issuing reminders.[28]

For every County Court, it was enacted:

> ". . . there shall be a Clerk who shall be an Attorney of one of Her Majesty's Superior Courts of Common Law, and whom the judge shall be empowered to appoint, subject to the approval of the Lord Chancellor and, in case of inability or misbehaviour to remove, subject to the like approval."[29]

Every clerk was remunerated by fees or salary (usually, in practice, the former) supposedly up to a maximum of £600 per annum. He was expected to pay assistants from his own income.[30] In these respects the early County Court clerk was much closer to the eighteenth than the nineteenth century idea of a public official. The eighteenth century JP's clerk was also remunerated by fees regulated, from 1753, by Act of Parliament. The payment of Home Office clerks by fees ceased in the early nineteenth century.[31]

Apart from his responsibilities for the court house and offices, the clerk had four main duties:

a. To issue summons, warrants, precepts, and writs of execution.

b. To register all orders and judgments of the court (in a minute book which was admissible as evidence and could not "be contradicted by note or memorandum of the Judge").

c. To take charge of and keep account of all court fees and fines payable or paid into court, and of all monies paid into or out of court.

d. To keep an account of all court proceedings.[32]

He had a number of other tasks such as taxing costs (in certain instances) swearing in witnesses and jury (when required), taking plaints, entering and giving notice of special defences, taking recognisances for security of costs and so on.[33] The clerical nature of his duties corresponded with those undertaken by Home Office clerks during the 1830s and 1840s, for these officials had no opportunities to provide advice or record opinions on the correspondence with which they dealt. Only the chief clerk and the criminal clerk had responsibilities above the mechanical.[34]

Before long the 1846 Act was subject to a rash of amendments, the first of which became law in 1849. Apart from ending the clerk's domestic responsibilities and changing procedure for paying money to the treasurer, the 1849 Act did not much affect him.[35] Insofar as he was affected, his status was improved by making him answerable to Her Majesty's Treasury rather than the court treasurer. In 1850 another Act enhanced the clerk's status and augmented his powers. Henceforward the Lord Chancellor rather than the judge was to be responsible for dismissals. Furthermore, it was provided that where opposing parties reached agreement before an action was heard in court, they could sign a statement which the clerk (or his assistant) could record as judgment:

> ". . . and such judgment shall to all Intents and Purposes be the same, and have the same effect, and shall be enforced and enforceable in the same manner, as if it had been a judgment of the Judge of the said court."

This clause gave the clerk limited judicial power and since the jurisdiction of the County Court was raised to include disputes involving up to £50, the clerk's importance grew accordingly.[36]

In 1852 the clerk formally acquired responsibility for taxing costs between parties and between attorney and client, though any one of these could appeal to the judge against his decision. The 1852 Act increased the maximum salary payable to clerks by £100 though, as the Romilly Commission observed, not one man received £700 exclusive of fees.[37] It was also enacted that, except in special circumstances, no clerk should be appointed to more than one court. Moreover, he was obliged to reside in the district to which he was attached.[38] The reason for these regulations, which swelled the ranks of County Court clerks to 491, is not clear, though there may have been disbelief that a clerk could run offices efficiently in as many, in one instance, as twelve districts simultaneously.[39]

The Romilly Commission was established to examine the functioning of the County Court system, to consider means of cheapening it and of increasing its business. Chaired by John, second son of Sir Samuel (the renowned criminal law reformer), who was then Master of the Rolls, it made few recommendations affecting clerks. There was, however, one important proposal, namely, that all clerks should be paid by salary for, under the "fees system", "in a very large majority of instances, such an amount of remuneration is not received as is calculated to secure the services of efficient officers."[40] As Household Words observed in 1850: ". . . the Clerks' fees accumulate in each court according to the business transacted." Hence, although the remuneration of those in large courts was "comfortable", three quarters of all clerks received under £100 per annum.[41] The Romilly Commission proposed that salary levels should be determined by the annual number of plaints entered.[42] This was accepted with the Legislature imposing a minimum salary of £120. The result was that in rural areas levels of remuneration remained pitifully low because of the "one man, one court" ruling.

An example of the absurdity of the "one man, one court" ruling was given to the Judicature Commission. The registrar of the tiny Suffolk parish of Mildenhall dealt with a total of 126 plaints in the course of one year. Yet when the court was not sitting he was obliged to attend his office between the hours of 10.00 am and 4.00 pm each weekday for the purpose of entering plaints.[43] The Romilly Commission had condemned such expensive inefficiency, but in endorsing the "one man, one court" rule and failing to recommend amalgamation of court districts, the salary scale that they proposed ensured that no able man would take a rural posting. In the 1870s County Court registrars in rural districts remained low paid, underworked officials of moderate ability.[44] Such men were divided by a great gulf from their counterparts in large, important County Courts who, by the 1870s were exercising considerable judicial authority in complex bankruptcy and equity cases and being handsomely remunerated (in fees) for their trouble. Thus, having recognised the shortcomings of the "fees system" the Romilly Commission did little to circumvent them.

The 1856 County Courts Amendment Act included a number of provisions relating to clerks or registrars, as they were subsequently to be known.[45] The change of title was significant. Although the 1846 Act permitted use of the term "registrar", it was seldom employed; in fact, the word "clerk" was appropriate to the work undertaken. But, by 1856, officials of the larger County Courts had enhanced status, duties and authority. The resurrected title was in keeping with these developments.

The 1856 Act limited the registrars' responsibility for taxing costs but in all other respects continued the process of granting them extra powers. They were made eligible, on application of a plaintiff deposing that his action arose within the court's jurisdiction, to issue a summons against any defendant residing outside that jurisdiction "in like manner as any Judge of any County Court has now power to issue any such Summons." Another power, hitherto the judge's alone, was given to the registrars: "Any affidavit to be used in a County Court may be sworn before a Judge <u>or Registrar</u> of a County Court."[46] Section 63 of the Act transferred the sheriff's authority with respect to replevin bonds up to any amount.[47] Thus, it is fair to say that the County Court registrar possessed, within the limited jurisdiction of his court, a <u>quasi</u>-judicial authority which contrasted strongly with the 1846 situation. This evolution was paralleled in other sectors of the public service at this time. In the Colonial Office, for example, Sir James Stephen created an "intellectual" clerical grade responsible for a new subsection of his department.[48] As County Court jurisdiction grew, in the 1860s, the jurisdiction and authority of the registrar expanded accordingly.

Since 1847 certain County Courts had been entrusted with jurisdiction in bankruptcy to unlimited amounts.[49] In 1861 major changes in bankruptcy law and procedure were introduced. "The judge of every County Court (except of the Metropolitan County Courts) [gained] the same powers" as the Commissioners of the District Courts of Bankruptcy. Moreover, when vacancies occurred in the office of commissioner, the government was authorised "to transfer", by Order in Council, "all the Jurisdiction, Powers and Authorities . . . to the Judges of the County Courts."[50]

The 1861 Act was of the utmost significance to registrars of the larger County Courts for they inherited powers which the bankruptcy registrars had acquired over several decades. They were to discharge the duties of the registrar and the official assignee. These included taxing "all Bills of Costs, Charges, fees, and disbursements", and settling the charges of auctioneers, appraisers, valuers and accountants. But the most important section of the Act for the County Court registrar was that which gave him, along with his colleagues in the Bankruptcy Court:

> ". . . power to make Adjudication of Bankruptcy, to receive the surrender of any Bankrupt, to grant protection, to pass the last examination of any Bankrupt in cases where the Assignees and Creditors do not oppose, to hold and preside at meetings of Creditors, to audit and pass account of Assignees, and to sit in Chambers and despatch there such part of the administrative Business of the Court, and such uncontested matters as shall be defined in general orders."[51]

The Bankruptcy Court and the County Court with bankruptcy jurisdiction could direct its registrar to go anywhere within its district for the purpose of holding a meeting of creditors, receiving proof of debts:

> ". . . and generally for the prosecution of any bankruptcy or other

proceeding under the Act . . . and such Registrar so acting shall have and exercise all powers, except the power of commitment, vested in such Court for the summoning and examination of persons or witnesses and for requiring the production of books, papers, and documents."[52]

This clause, it has been observed, was similar to that of the 1849 Act[53] "except that the power given by this section seems altogether indefinite":

> ". . . this would seem to give the registrar, when acting under such direction of the Court as is mentioned in the beginning of the section, power to proceed through all the stages of prosecution of bankruptcy except commitment. By this section, taken in conjunction with the 52nd . . . the whole administrative business of the court may be executed by the registrar, and a large portion of the judicial."[54]

The registrar could also be directed by his commissioner or County Court judge to examine those imprisoned for debt. In conducting these investigations he was expected to concern himself with such wide-ranging questions as the estate, effects, debts, dealings, transactions, and places of residence and business of the prisoner in the six months preceding incarceration. His enquiries complete, the registrar had several options open to him. He could:

1. Make an order for adjudication (directing in which court it should be made having regard for the extent of debts involved and the prisoner's normal place of residence).
2. Grant the prisoner protection.
3. Order release from prison.[55]

Clearly, the 1861 Act greatly increased the powers and duties of registrars possessing a bankruptcy jurisdiction. From their point of view the Act was revolutionary. Subsequently they dealt with pre-adjudication questions in contentious business and often with <u>all</u> aspects of non-contentious business.[56] There was no statutory limitation to the sums with which they could deal. Thus, as early as the 1860s County Court registrars were undertaking critically important work in complex questions involving large sums of money. This was, of course, in marked contrast with their role in small debt litigation. The responsibilities of the provincial registrars in bankruptcy were recognised in the £1,000 per annum salaries awarded them in 1861. These put them closer to the London bankruptcy registrars, in terms of status and income, than to County Court colleagues who did no bankruptcy work.[57]

The Bankruptcy Act, 1869, did little more than ratify, as far as registrars were concerned, the changes of 1861. It clarified the extent of their powers:

> "The Chief Judge in Bankruptcy and every judge of a local court in bankruptcy may, subject and in accordance with the rules of court for the time being in force, delegate to the registrar or to any other officer of his Court such of the powers vested in him by this Act as it may be expedient for the judge to delegate to him."[58]

The Bankruptcy Rules of 1870 made the registrar the sole assistant of the bankruptcy judge. When acting in this capacity his authority was great: "Every order made by a registrar while acting under any delegated power, shall have the same force and validity, and be subject to the same appeal, as an order made by a judge."[59]

The registrar could adjourn any question for the judge's decision. Moreover, it was held that he should not hear questions of novelty and importance. But, as the Judicature Commissioners pointed out, in 1872, County Court registrars dealt with "questions of the utmost importance as to property, real or personal, whatever be their complexity or the amount involved." As Mr. Clarke, the registrar of Walsall County Court, informed the Commissioners: "I had to make an order of bankruptcy a few days ago on a question of nearly £3,000. That order was appealed against, and the decision was affirmed by Lord Justice Giffard."[60] The County Courts Chronicle reveals that in practice registrars decided cases involving large sums of money as a matter of routine.[61]

Provincial registrars' importance in the mid-nineteenth century was not transformed in the field of bankruptcy alone. In 1865 when the County Courts acquired equitable jurisdiction "in all suits by creditors, legatees, devisees, heirs at law or next of kin . . . up to £500," registrars again gained extra responsibility.

When undertaking equity work they exercised all the authority of a master in the Court of Chancery. The precise nature of their duties was defined by five County Court judges charged with framing rules and orders for regulating equity proceedings.[62] By these, a registrar was required to keep a record of each suit and proceeding, to file affidavits, and to note all documents filed;[63] he was empowered to reject any affidavit filed with him. Pending appeal he retained any money which might come into his hands; he was responsible for drawing up the final decree, in accordance with the court's judgment, for sealing it and filing it. In addition, he was obliged to tax costs. One of his most important duties, analogous to his work in bankruptcy, was "to conduct a hearing at a time and place appointed by him to hear interested parties, their counsel and attorneys, and, if required, to make enquiries or to take accounts." Finally, he was responsible for excluding decretal orders. When such an order directed an enquiry to be made, the registrar undertook that enquiry: ". . . and he shall for that purpose have all the powers and discharge all the duties of a Chief Clerk of the Master of the Rolls or a Vice Chancellor in the Court of Chancery."[64]

It is worth noting that in the 1860s a few County Courts acquired an admiralty jurisdiction.[65] These could deal with cases where the value of salvage did not exceed £1,000. Since very few registrars were involved we need not concern ourselves with the details of their duties.[66] Indeed, this is perhaps the point at which to warn against exaggerating the County Court registrars' roles in bankruptcy and equity. Important though the changes to his powers in these fields were, by no means all registrars undertook such work. About 120, approximately one-quarter of the whole, had a bankruptcy jurisdiction.[67] Even those who possessed a varied jurisdiction were far more occupied with small debt business. As Mr. Barnes, registrar of Colchester County Court, explained in 1872, "nineteen twentieths of the business of the County Court relates to small contract debts."[68]

In 1866 an Act abolishing the positions of County Court high bailiff and treasurer also regulated the mode of remunerating registrars. The object, to produce a more economical system, was familiar. As the preamble to the Act stated, ". . . it is . . . expedient to reduce the salaries of future appointed Registrars of County Courts." The minimum salary was reduced to £100 per annum.[69] Appointees to rural areas suffered; the new salary scale did not much affect officials in large courts because various Acts of the 1860s provided for payment by fees: "Many of these fees are of considerable amount and it has been stated in evidence that some of the Registrars are receiving in fees an amount equal to their fixed salaries." Expediency dictated that the registrar should take over the office of high bailiff as vacancies occurred and a twenty per cent increase in salary was offered to those prepared to accept the additional responsibility.[70]

One of the last important changes to the County Court system, before the appointment of the Judicature Commission, came in 1867 when it was enacted that in small debt cases in which the defendant failed to appear and could provide no satisfactory explanation for non-appearance;

> ". . . the Registrar may, by leave of the Judge, upon due proof of the service of the summons and of the debt being due and owing, enter up Judgment for the plaintiff and have the same power to make an order for payment by instalments, or to enter up Judgment for nonsuit, or to strike out or adjourn the cause, as the Judge of the County Court has."

When a defendant appeared and admitted a claim "the Registrar may, by leave of the Judge, settle the terms and conditions upon which it is to be paid, and enter up Judgment accordingly as a Judgment of the Court."[71] Procedure in undefended cases was outlined by the Judicature Commission:

> "The list [of summonses] is then called over by the Registrar, who gives judgment in all cases which are undefended, or where the claim is admitted. If the parties cannot agree as to the time or mode of payment, the registrar decides between them, settles the terms, fixes the instalments (if any), and makes an order accordingly."[72]

Thus, on the eve of the most comprehensive investigation of the judicature ever undertaken in Britain, County Court registrars were often exercising considerable judicial authority in a variety of jurisdictions. In practice their duties were probably more extensive and responsible than the statutes and the legal treatises indicate. Despite the fact that, formally, registrars had no contentious jurisdiction, a registrar stated, in 1872, that "many of them now help the Judges with the contentious business, and without their aid it could not often be disposed of."[73]

III

The Judicature Commissioners, reporting in 1872, were not happy with the County Court system which seemed to them a patchwork of inconsistency and, despite repeated efforts to economise, extravagance. Indeed in a mere quarter of a century several additional jurisdictions had been created; the duties of the court's officers had been either radically changed or abolished; and procedures had frequently been restructured. The outcome was not altogether satisfactory. The Commissioners found that because of the different levels of jurisdiction in the County Court (£500 in equity; £50 in contract, £10 in Common Law tort; and £150, £300, or £1,000 in Admiralty, depending on the nature of the case) justice could not be done in the "most expeditious and effective manner." A County Court judge with three jurisdictions (Common Law, Equity, and Admiralty) could not administer in one and the same suit, any of the different remedies which belonged to his three jurisdictions. This he could only do if three distinct suits were conducted under three different forms of procedure. His decision was controlled by three different courts of appeal.[74]

In bankruptcy, if there was a debt exceeding £50 and a trial was called for, it had to take place in a Superior Court. But if the debt was equitable and did not exceed £500 the County Court could determine it. Once a Superior Court declared a debtor insolvent the County Court, acting as a local Court of Bankruptcy could, as we have already observed, try questions to any amount. To remedy procedural inefficiency the Commissioners proposed "that the County Court should be annexed to and form constituent or branches of the proposed High Court of Justice." As such it should have unlimited jurisdiction in all cases.[75] Failure to implement this recommendation to this day, has meant that the unreal division between County Court and District High Court Registrars persists with the result that in some quarters the former are seen as inferior officers dispensing inferior justice in an inferior court.[76]

The Commissioners also recommended abolition of the strange rule forbidding registrars from sitting on days when the judge did not sit:

> ". . . though not necessarily present during the sitting of the Registrar, the Judge is yet compelled to remain in the neighbourhood of the Court wasting valuable time (unless there happens to be a second Court), while the Registrar is disposing of undefended cases."

Since only a "very small percentage of the plaints entered result in any real contest, or any substantial question requiring the decision of the judge," it is clear that much valuable judicial time was lost.[77]

In recommending ways of improving and cheapening the County Court system the Commissioners proposed changes which, if all implemented, would have had a very considerable effect upon the status of the registrar. They wanted to see the number of registrars cut drastically:

> "We think it right also to call attention to the expense of the very large staff of registrars and similar officers existing throughout the country, and to the waste of manpower thereby occasioned. There are forty district registrars of the Probate Court alone, maintained at an annual expense of many thousands of pounds. In Liverpool there are the following registrars - one registrar of the Admiralty Court, one registrar of the Vice Chancellor's Court, one registrar of the Court of Common Pleas of Lancaster, one registrar of the Probate Court, two registrars of the County Court, and one registrar of the Passage Court."[78]

Instead of there being a registrar in every place where the County Court was held, it was proposed that in the smaller towns on a circuit, a deputy registrar or an agent should be empowered to enter plaints and to issue summonses and subpoenas, perhaps on just one or two days per week. Moreover, circuits should be amalgamated in order to permit further reductions in the numbers of registrars and of judges also.[79]

These recommendations, inspired by the desire to retrench, were also recognition of the de facto improvement in the status of registrars in large towns and cities. The extra burden shouldered by such officers, the Commissioners felt, should be offset by substantially larger financial rewards. It was of these men that the Commissioners were thinking when they proposed that County Court registrars should assume contentious jurisdiction in small debt claims of under £5. Furthermore, the Commissioners felt that registrars, like judges, should be appointed by the Lord Chancellor and remunerated by salary alone. Various measures to improve the administrative efficiency of the County Courts were proposed. These, if implemented in harness with the Commissioners' other recommendations, would have reduced the clerical and administrative duties of registrars and augmented the judicial. In recognition of this possibility it was suggested that: ". . . there should be power of promotion from the office of the registrar to the office of the judge."[80]

The Commission's report on County Courts was potentially a revolutionary document. But most of its recommendations were ignored, either for many years or altogether. The Judicature Acts of 1873 and 1875, which restructured the Supreme Court, left the County Courts inviolate. Not until 1888 did the County Court registrar gain contentious jurisdiction in small debt cases of up to £2. Only in 1919 with the establishment of Registrars' Courts, was jurisdiction to hear disputed claims raised to the £5 proposed almost half a century earlier. Registrars have never been made eligible for promotion to the position of judge although by first becoming Recorders they have, since the Courts Act, 1971, been able circuitously to advance themselves to the rank of Circuit Judge. Only in 1924 did responsibility to make appointments pass from the judge to the Lord Chancellor. It was as late as 1967 before County Court registrars gained a divorce jurisdiction. In the post-1872 period the significant changes of the previous quarter century did not continue. In this so-called "era of stagnation", which does not directly concern us here,[81] the County Court registrars' status, duties and powers remained virtually static. The diminished pace of change in the last quarter of the nineteenth century and after, emphasises the dramatic changes in the office of County Court registrar which took place between 1846 and the 1870s.

Why did County Court registrars become judicial figures in our period? The answer is not readily revealed by the documents. Registrars were anonymous figures throughout these years and there was very little debate, either in or out of parliament, about the nature of their duties and the desirability of changing them. Neither is there evidence that registrars pressed for additional responsibilities; they were passive recipients of power who had no corporate identity. If we examine the County Court Amendment Act, 1856, which was important to registrars, we find that the three readings of the Bill in the Lords produced one short debate. In the course of this registrars were scarcely mentioned; indeed, there was no discussion of clauses dealing with the expansion of their powers. In the Commons there was no debate on the first two readings of the Bill. At the committee stage argument centred on ways of reducing expenditure on County Courts. A warning was given about over-enthusiastic retrenchment by Mr. E. Ball, Liberal Conservative M.P. for Cambridgeshire, who stated that County Court business had doubled since 1851. This provides the clue to the growth of registrars' powers and duties, for that growth did not occur as a matter of policy or as a result of pressure but of pragmatism. The success of the County Court system, and the volume of business thereby engendered, ensured that the registrar increasingly shared the judicial burden of his judge. The County Court's acquisition of additional jurisdictions, such as bankruptcy and equity, in the sixties, itself a consequence of Britain's continuing economic growth, furthered this process. Accordingly, the Judicature Commission proposed that registrars should be authorised to dispose of "the smaller class of cases" because the judge would then be able "to give his undivided attention to the more important business."[82]

As we shall see, this picture of power accumulation was mirrored by registrars in the superior courts. It is interesting to compare it with the finding of Cromwell and Steiner that reorganisation of Foreign Office personnel was also dictated by workloads: "Most of the changes which were forced on the Office in the nineteenth century arose from acute pressure of work."[83]

IV

This section examines developments affecting registrars in the superior courts. Until 1833 the office of registrar in the Court of Chancery was a valuable sinecure worth between £4,000 and £6,000 per year. The registry work was actually done by miserably paid deputies.[84] The whole fabric of the court was riddled with nepotism and sinecures at this time. In July 1832, Leonard Horner, later a factory inspector, wrote to his daughter Mary: "The Chancellor has given his brother James a sinecure in the Court of Chancery of £2,000 a year, vacant by the death of Lord Eldon's son." However, during the 1830s, the Whig administration, urged on by Henry Brougham, took action to abolish sinecures in all areas of the public service.[85] In 1832 the offices of Patentee of the Subpoena Office and Registrar of Affidavits were abolished.[86] In the following year the office of the Chancery Registrar was scrapped and replaced with a new establishment of six registrars and eight clerks. Only solicitors or those who had served five years as an articled clerk to a solicitor could be appointed.[87] The method of promotion was similar to that which obtained before the new Act - officers entered as clerks and rose by seniority. On average each registrar spent twenty years progressing through the clerking ranks. In 1855, the second registrar had been in the registry for forty-six years![88]

In 1833 there were three Chancery Courts, the Court of the Lord Chancellor, the Court of the Master of the Rolls, and the Court of the Vice Chancellor of

England. Two registrars attended each court. Acts of 1841 and 1851 altered Chancery structure and sanctioned the appointment of extra registrars and clerks bringing the number of the former to eleven. Their duties consisted of attending Court sittings for the purpose of taking minutes of orders made and entering the documentary evidence adduced in each case. Having done this they were obliged to draw up the orders, the number of which had grown phenomenally to almost 11,500 in the year 1853-4, in proper form. By the mid-nineteenth century they were involved in more mechanical clerical work. In 1875 R.H. Leach, the senior registrar, explaining that duties had changed little in the previous twenty years, stated that ". . . registrars have a great many judicial functions." He continued:

> "In drawing up these orders we have very often a point to decide quasi-judicially . . . . In every order that we draw up we have questions to decide. Various points arise, when the decision is reduced into writing which have not occurred to the parties in court, and which we determine if we can without reference back to the court."[89]

Since there was no appeal against registrars' orders it is clear that Chancery registrars were, by the mid-nineteenth century, powerful figures.[90] Pressure of work was undoubtedly the major reason for the expansion of their responsibilities.

The Common Law Procedure Act, 1854, gave the registrar in the Court of Admiralty an important quasi-judicial position in the arbitration system:

> "The practice is to refer cases which cannot be conveniently tried in Court . . . to the Registrar . . . the Registrar, from his knowledge of the law, is enabled to regulate the conduct of the case . . . . The reference proceeds like of trial of law . . . and there is an appeal at once to the Judge if the Registrar miscarries."[91]

Significant though this development was in the specialised context of maritime law, it was not until 1857 that further changes of particular pertinence to this study occurred.

In that year the Ecclesiastical Courts lost their ancient jurisdictions in probate and matrimonial causes.[92] In London a principal probate registry, employing three registrars at an annual salary of £1,500 each, was created. But the probate legislation was particularly important insofar as it implemented the idea of court branches in the provinces. In England and Wales forty-one district probate registries were opened. Existing Diocesan registrars were appointed in the provinces but where they were "unacceptable" the principal probate judge was competent to make appointments. The London positions were in the first instance made available to officers of the Prerogative Court of Canterbury. Otherwise all registrars, London or provincial, had to be (or have been) an advocate, barrister, solicitor, attorney-at-law, or proctor. All registrars and district registrars were removable by the Lord Chancellor alone. A distinction between metropolitan and provincial officials was that the latter were, in most cases, to be remunerated out of fees.[93]

The duties of probate registrars were as follows. In London, one attended practitioners, one corresponded with provincial colleagues, and the third taxed costs and attended to references from the court. District registrars, like their counterparts in London, could tax costs and administer oaths; they also had a host of administrative duties and responsibility for safeguarding fees. Where there was no contention they could grant probate of a will or letters of administration in the name of the Court of Probate. But parties resident outside the capital were not obliged to apply to the district registry for probate; in all cases the applicant could deal direct with London.[94]

V

In our period the most remarkable changes for registrars occurred in the area of divorce. We shall, therefore, look in some detail at these developments. The Matrimonial Causes Act, 1857, which introduced the possibility of divorce by civil action rather than by private Act of Parliament, did not establish district divorce registries or enact that use should be made of existing registries established under the Probate Amendment Act. Neither did it create a new central registry to administer the work of the new Court. Divorce was to remain centralised and the staff of the principal probate registry was to serve the new Divorce Court:

> "The Registrars and other Officers of the Principal Registry of the Court of Probate shall attend the sittings of the Court for Divorce and Matrimonial Proceedings thereof, and shall be directed by the Rules and Orders under this Act."[95]

Their duties in matrimonial causes, as prescribed by these rules, were complex but, for the most part, clerical and administrative. They were responsible for filing petitions, citations, answers to petitions, affidavits establishing the marriage of the parties concerned, and notice of trial. In cases tried by affidavit, the affidavits and counter affidavits had to be filed in the registry. Applications for a new trial were to be lodged with the registry. Whenever a case was to be tried by jury the Judge Ordinary (later known as the President of the Court) was required to direct questions of issue to be stated in a form of record to be settled by one of the registrars. The jury's verdict and the Court's decree had to be recorded in the Court Book by the registrar. Finally, the registrars had the quasi-judicial duty of deciding whether the cost of proving a document valid should be granted in cases where notice to admit validity was not given. If he concluded that omission to give notice saved expense he could award costs of proving documents.[96]

In the following year the Matrimonial Causes Act, 1857 was amended. By this amendment the principal probate registrars were obliged to tax costs and allowed to administer oaths. Their authority in matrimonial issues was recognised as being equal to that formerly possessed by the surrogates of the Official Principal of the Court of Arches.[97] In December 1858, when additional rules were drawn up, they again acquired extra duties and responsibilities. Their responsibility to tax costs was endorsed. They were given discretionary power to extend time limits, imposed by earlier rules, for filing various documents. They had to enter minutes of judicial orders relating to summonses in the summons book. If a summons was brought to the registry with consent to an order, signed by the party summonsed, his proctor or attorney, the registrar could, henceforth, draw up an order without having to go before the judge "provided that the order sought is in the opinion of the registrar one which the judge, under the circumstances, would make." Despite these changes it is not inaccurate to say that the divorce work of the probate registrars remained mainly administrative. Such judicial authority as they possessed, by 1859, was limited to relatively minor tangential issues. This accorded with their general responsibilities for all pre-trial questions.[98]

The amending Acts of 1859 and 1860 did not, in the short term, directly affect registrars.[99] But in December 1865, two additional duties were imposed on them by the Judge Ordinary, J.P. Wilde. One of these concerned applications for a commission or requisition to examine witnesses outside the Court's jurisdiction. These were subsequently to be made to the registrar who could approve a summons or refer the matter to the judge.[100] Of far greater import, in the historical context, were the rules giving registrars responsibility in questions of maintenance and marriage settlements.[101] In such matters, Wilde ruled, as he had power to under the 1857 Act, that a registrar "shall investigate" the averments contained in the pleadings of the parties. In the course of such investigation he:

> ". . . shall be at liberty to require the production of any documents relating to such pleadings, or to call for any affidavits, and shall report in writing to the Court the result of his investigation, and any special circumstances to be taken into consideration with reference to the prayer of the petition."[102]

This, in fact, was neither more nor less than a reproduction of similar clauses in the recent County Courts Equitable Jurisdiction Act, 1865 and the Bankruptcy Act, 1861. These recent precedents for registrars having far-reaching investigative powers in interlocutory matters, pertaining to finance, may have persuaded the Judge Ordinary to make similar extensions to the registrars' authority which would, simultaneously, materially reduce the judges' workload which, as we shall see, was overwhelming.

Notwithstanding the precedents, the 1865 ruling giving registrars some responsibility in maintenance was a significant change. There can be little doubt that it originated not so much in judicial faith in the competence of registrars, but in judicial inability to cope with the unexpectedly great burden of matrimonial petitions. From its inception the Court of Divorce and Matrimonial Causes was in chaos owing to the eccentricities of the Act of foundation. This allowed the Lord Chancellor, the Lord Chief Justice of the Court of Queen's Bench, the Lord Chief Justice of the Court of Common Pleas, the Lord Chief Baron of the Court of Exchequer, the Judge of the Probate Court, and the senior puisne judges in the Court of Queen's Bench, Common Pleas, and Exchequer to be judges in the new Court. Thus, eight of the most senior judges in the land were appointed. The Judge of the Probate Court was made Judge Ordinary and "he shall have full authority either alone or with one or more of the other Judges in all matters except for dissolving or annulling marriages." Petitions for dissolution or nullity were to be heard by at least three judges including the Judge Ordinary.[103] This stipulation initiated chaos for, as Mr. Edwin James M.P. explained in the Commons in 1859: ". . . the greatest difficulty was experienced in obtaining the attendance of the requisite number of Judges."[104]

According to Lord Brougham neither the Lord Chancellor nor any of the six designated judges of the Common Law Courts found it possible to give much of "their time and attention to the Divorce Court and the consequence was that the Court . . . got greatly into arrear." Mr. James drew attention "to the mass of causes now existing in that Court." He was referring to the 285 or so petitions pending and the 151 causes awaiting trial, "many of which had been ready for trial some twelve or eighteen months." He asked whether the Attorney-General had any intention "to bring any measure to remedy the delay[s]."[105]

One of two remedies could be applied. The Judge Ordinary could be empowered to deal with dissolutions and annulments by himself or, as Brougham desired, the "judicial force" could be increased. The latter choice was taken and, on August 13, 1859, the Divorce Court Bill empowering all puisne judges to sit in the Court in rotation, received the Royal assent. By this Act the number of competent divorce judges was raised from eight to seventeen.[106]

Before long it was realised that this change did little to improve efficiency. As Lord Lyndhurst observed in March 1860:

> ". . . much inconvenience had been experienced by the Judges, and a great suffering by the suitors. The evil did not arise from any incapacity of the learned judge who presided over the Court, but from the provisions of the Act by which the Court was constituted, and which enacted that no decree for the dissolution of any marriage could be pronounced except by a court constituted by two judges of the Common Law Courts in addition to the Judge Ordinary."[107]

The new judges had no more time to give to the Court than had their seniors. Consequently, the Lord Chancellor agreed to introduce a Bill "to allow a single judge to preside in the Divorce Court." This became law in August 1860.[108]

This Act afforded some temporary relief. But it meant that the unassisted Judge Ordinary dealt with the whole business of the Divorce Court. The incidence of petitions for nullity and dissolution, many of which posed highly complex problems, was unexpectedly high. Between 1715 and 1852, there were only 244 divorces in England and Wales.[109] In 1858, 254 petitions for dissolution or nullity were filed.[110] The Lord Chancellor believed that this high figure reflected a "backlog of grievances,"[111] and to some extent he was correct; the next four years showed consistent reductions in the number of petitions filed, though only once (in 1861) did the figure go below 200. Subsequently, the steady growth in the number of petitions confounded projections of a decrease in the business of the Divorce Court. In 1863, 262 petitions for dissolution and nullity alone were filed.

One of the most time-consuming processes for the Court was that of assessing financial settlements. Volume of business made it impossible for the Judge Ordinary to investigate the averments of husbands and wives.[112] Therefore, in 1865, as we have seen, the registrar was authorised to undertake a portion of such investigations. But his authority was limited; petitions for alimony, that is, the allowance due to the wife from the husband's estate, were still settled by oral examination before the judge in open court. Browne described the practice:

> ". . . after the time for filing an answer [to a petition] for alimony had expired, whether he [the husband] had filed one or not, the wife might proceed to examine witnesses in support of her petition; and move the court to decree her alimony, notice as required by Rule 89, 1866, being given to the other side. It followed, therefore, that in practice questions of alimony were decided as motions on motion days. And when witnesses were to be examined on a petition for alimony the practice was to hear the petition after the other motions had been disposed of. This might be done at any time after such time for filing her answer, if the husband's answer were not satisfactory to the wife; and by applying to the Court for an allotment of alimony, she was not precluded from afterwards examining witnesses in support of her petition."[113]

Such procedure was inappropriate because it was time-consuming and unlikely to facilitate balanced judgments. As Browne comments: ". . . it seems hardly possible to conceive a worse tribunal for adjusting complicated accounts."[114] Nevertheless, it continued until the mid-1870s.

In July 1875, the additional and amended Divorce Court rules gave registrars various responsibilities, hitherto borne by the judge, in relation to summonses. But the most revolutionary changes were those extending their authority in alimony. Rule 189 required that "application for an order for a further and fuller answer to a petition for alimony", hitherto made to the judge, "shall hereafter be made by summons before one of the registrars."[115] By rule 191, which overturned numbers 89 and 91:

> "All applications for an allotment of alimony pending suit, and for an allotment of permanent alimony shall hereafter be referred to one of the registrars at the principal registry, who shall investigate the averments in the petition of alimony, answer and reply, in the presence of the parties, their proctors, solicitors, or attorneys, and who, if he thinks fit, shall be at liberty to require the attendance of the husband for the purpose of being examined or cross-examined, and to take the oral evidence of witnesses, and to require the production of any document or to call for affidavits."

Except insofar as this required applications for alimony to be referred to the registrar direct, the rule, thus far, did not greatly alter the registrars' functions or authority in alimony. But the final clause gave them far-reaching powers. This stated that the registrar: ". . . shall direct such order to issue as he shall think fit."[116] He could "refer any application or any question arising out of it, to the Judge Ordinary for his decision." Moreover:

> "Any person heard on the reference as to alimony before one of the registrars, objecting to the order issued under his direction, may (subject to any order as to costs) apply to the Judge Ordinary on summons to rescind or vary the same."[117]

Notwithstanding these reservations rule 191 was of the utmost significance.

Why was the registrar given responsibility for alimony? To this vital question the contemporary professional journals and newspapers provide no answer. The Law Journal, in giving notice of the new rules in August, neither commented on them nor drew particular attention to rule 191. The Solicitors' Journal was also silent.[118] The Times saw no cause for excitement in the revised alimony procedure:

> "Several amended and additional Rules and Regulations have been issued and will take effect after this day. Under these Rules applications for leave to enter an appearance after a proceeding has been taken in default, to alter or amend pleadings, and to allot alimony pending suit which have hitherto been heard before the Judge Ordinary on motion, will for the future be disposed of by summons before the registrars, and other miscellaneous matters, including the subject of the wife's costs, are also to be dealt with by them."[119]

We may conclude, therefore, that the promulgation of rule 191 excited little attention or interest even amongst members of the legal profession. It was a classic example of (what was to become) significant change being implemented by administrative process. Be that as it may, we still have not answered our question. We have alluded to pressure of work in the Divorce Court but this does not, in itself, explain why, what seems today to have been great power, was transferred from the Judge Ordinary. We have no means of untangling the thought processes of the judge who authorised the transfer. But there can be no doubt that financial questions were felt to be less important than the sundering of a marriage. This point may be difficult to appreciate in the later twentieth century when divorce is relatively easily obtainable, socially acceptable, and contested only in about 2 per cent of all cases. In today's County Courts undefended divorce petitions are rapidly determined by the judge; far more judicial expertise and labour are brought to bear on financial questions. In the mid-nineteenth century divorce was relatively rare, difficult to obtain, and socially unacceptable.[120] That section of the Matrimonial Causes Act, 1857, which required the presence of three judges for the dissolution or annulment of marriage, testified to the awe in which the institution was held. As Edwin James M.P. put it in 1859, ". . . one judge had the power to decide on a question of life or death; but not . . . upon the simple issue of adultery or no adultery."[121] Thus, it would seem that in view of the workload in divorce and the gravity with which it was viewed (which precluded the appointment of any but the most senior judges) registrars were given responsibility for deciding questions of alimony.

Two questions arise from the 1875 Rules. First, what proportion of cases did the registrars refer to the judge? Second, what proportion of cases in which a registrar made an order was objected to and altered by the judge? These are important questions to which the Civil Judicial Statistics provide no answer. The 1875 Royal Commission on the Administrative Departments of the Courts of Justice, to which Charles Middleton, Senior Registrar of the Court of Probate gave evidence, gives no clue either.[122] A Royal Commission reporting in 1912 paid little attention to questions of alimony. The evidence of Mr. Musgrave, who had almost twenty years experience in the Probate and Divorce Registry, concerned responsibilities for the taxing of costs and for petitions in forma pauperis. The Hon. Sir Bargrave Deane, a judge in the Probate, Divorce and Admiralty Division was equally uninformative on maintenance procedure.[123]

There is, therefore, no evidence to indicate the extent to which registrars in the Principal Probate and Divorce Registry exercised a jurisdiction in alimony. However, it should be emphasised that Rule 191 did not merely permit, but "required" registrars to make the necessary investigations and orders. Furthermore, the rule was not foisted on the court by Parliament, but was drawn up by the Judge Ordinary. Thus, there is every reason to suppose that it operated in most cases. Even if the registrars' activities under the rule were not large, recognition in principle that they should assume responsibility in alimony was highly significant in terms of future practice.

VI

Also significant in terms of future practice, was the Judicature Act of 1873, which established District Registries of the Supreme Court to deal with all High Court actions, except matrimonial actions, commenced in the provinces. By this the district registrars gained responsibility for all pre-trial issues in contentious business and for giving final judgment ". . . if the plaintiff is entitled to sign final judgment or to obtain an order for an account by reason of the non-appearance of a defendant."[124] Thus, when, from 1922, divorce gradually became obtainable in the provinces, there was a long-established body of registrars capable of undertaking work previously monopolised by the London Registry.[125] Moreover, since from 1873, a qualification for being a district registrar was to be a County Court registrar it is clear, with the benefit of hindsight, that, by the beginning of the last quarter of the nineteenth century, the trend which was to lead in 1967 to County Court registrars exercising considerable authority in questions of divorce maintenance had been well and truly set in motion.

Another trend which was becoming established in our period concerned the method by which powers and authority were conferred. The early part of this paper dealt with legislation conferring additional responsibilities on registrars. By the 1860s such matters were beginning to be regulated not by Parliament but by rules of court drawn up by judges. The rule-making powers of judges in various courts were provided by Acts of Parliament in order that technical details of practice and procedure could be settled by experts. Yet, increasingly, these rules, in the case of the registrars, did more than promote court efficiency - they created significant judicial figures. We have alluded to the enormous responsibilities of today's divorce registrars; it is, perhaps, a chastening thought that these officials have gained power with only the slightest parliamentary authorisation. The same point can be made of the County Court registrars for, as a Select Committee reported in 1949, ". . . considerable powers have been conferred upon the registrar by rules." It is not surprising that the sentence should continue, ". . . but we have come to the conclusion that these powers should be extended." The justification for such extension was the normal pragmatic one: ". . . it would enable the judge to devote more of his time to substantial cases and would reduce the risk of adjournments for want of time."[126]

In recent years a considerable body of historical literature has dealt with the process of central government administrative growth. There remains much disagreement about the pattern this process followed and, indeed, whether there was a pattern. Some historians emphasise the influence of Jeremy Bentham; others, denying Bentham's impact on practical matters, argue that internal pressures or, as Macdonagh puts it, ". . . the irresistible engine of change"[127] generated the "revolution in government." Whilst it is not altogether clear whether there is inherent contradiction between these two viewpoints, it is unnecessary, here, to recapitulate a familiar debate which has been summarised elsewhere. It is interesting in the context of this controversy, however, that our examination of registrars reveals that the importance of these legal officials grew not in response to ideological or political considerations, but as a reaction to internal factors of legal administration.

NOTES

1. See W. Barrington Baker (et al), The Matrimonial Jurisdiction of Registrars (Oxford), 1977), p.iii.
2. E. Moir, The Justice of the Peace (Harmondsworth, 1969), p.92.
3. Ibid., pp.102-66; see J. Morgan, "The Judiciary of the Superior Courts 1820-1968: A Sociological Study", London University. M.Phil. thesis, (1974).
4. B.L. Woodcock, Medieval Ecclesiastical Courts in the Diocese of Canterbury (Oxford, 1952), pp.13-14, 20, 32-33.
5. Act for the More Easy Recovery of Debts and Demands in England, 1846, 9 and 10 Vict. c.95.
6. J.F. Archbold, The Law and Practice in Bankruptcy (London, 1827), p.2.
7. 9 and 10 Vict. c.95, s.55; E.W. Cox, The Law and Practice of the County Courts in England and Wales, Vol.I (London, 1848), p.112.
8. Woodcock, Medieval, p.38.
9. Bankruptcy Commissioners Act, 1821, 1 and 2 Geo. IV, c.115.
10. It has been estimated that "the average solicitor earned no more than £200 or £300 per year during the first third of the nineteenth century." See A. Harding, A Social History of English Law (Gloucester, Mass., 1973), p.351.
11. W.D. Griffith and C.A. Holmes, The Law and Practice in Bankruptcy, Vol.I (London, 1867), p.6.
12. A. Welbourne, "Bankruptcy before the Era of Victorian Reform" Cambridge Historical Journal, IV (1932) 51.
13. Court in Bankruptcy Act, 1831, 1 and 2 Will. IV c.56; see Griffith and Holmes, The Law and Practice in Bankruptcy, Vol.I, pp.6-7. In 1847 the Court of Review was abolished.
14. "Twenty Shillings in the Pound" Household Words, XVI (1852) 444-6; "Bankruptcy in Six Easy Lessons" Household Words, XVII (1858) 211; see W.L. Burn, The Age of Equipoise (New York, 1965), pp.75, 139.

15. 1 and 2 Will. IV c.56, s.9.

16. General Rules and Orders in Bankruptcy, 12 January 1832 for which see E.E. Deacon and J. de Gex, The Law and Practice of Bankruptcy, Vol. I (London, 1848), pp.181-3; see Vol. II, appendix, rule XV.

17. Bankruptcy Amendment Act, 1842, 5 and 6 Vict. c.122, ss.54, 73.

18. Ibid., ss.53, 61.

19. Griffith and Holmes, The Law and Practice in Bankruptcy, Vol. 1, p.17; Bankruptcy Amendment and Consolidation Act, 1849, 12 and 13 Vict. c.106, s.27.

20. Cox, The Law and Practice of the County Courts, Vol.1, p.1; see G.R.Y. Radcliffe and G. Cross, The English Legal System (London, 1954), Ch. XVI.

21. Sir W. Holdsworth, A History of English Law, Vol. I (London, 1956 edn.), pp.191-3.

22. See P.W.J. Bartrip, "The Career of M.D. Hill with Special Reference to his Place in Penal and Educational Reform Movements in Mid-Nineteenth Century England", University of Wales Ph.D. thesis (1975), pp.184-7.

23. 9 and 10 Vict. c.95, s.58; see "County Courts" Household Words, I (1850) 176. For a more recent criticism of the development of the County Court, see H. Smith, "The Resurgent Victorian County Court" The American Journal of Legal History, 13 (1969), pp.126-28.

24. Holdsworth, A History of English Law, Vol. XV, pp.45-61.

25. K.M. Lyell (ed.), Memoir of Leonard Horner, F.R.S., F.G.S., Consisting of Letters to his Family and from some of his Friends, Vol. II (London, 1890), p.158.

26. A. Briggs, The Age of Improvement (London, 1959), p.338; see Diana Leat, "The Rise and Role of the Poor Man's Lawyer" British Journal of Law and Society, II (1975), p.167.

27. Our County Courts: Their Practice contrasted with that of the Superior Courts; with Suggestions for the Improvement of both: By a Professional

Man cited in Burn, The Age of Equipoise, p.139. Sir L. Woodward, The Age of Reform, 1815-1870 (Oxford, 1962), p.472, argues that improved "facilities for recovering debts led to an increase in small credits, and hence to the imprisonment of small debtors." But imprisonment for debts of under £20 was abolished in 1844, and County Courts were, until 1850, only competent to deal with debts of less than £20. However, see Rubin, infra., pp.244-5.

28. Household Words, I (1850), pp.176-80.

29. 9 and 10 Vict. c.95, s.58.

30. Ibid., ss.24, 39, 40. By 1855 only fifteen registrars received payment by salary. PP 1855 XVIII, Royal Commission Appointed to Enquire into the State of the County Courts and the Course of Practice Therein, and Particularly with Respect of the Fees levied in the said Courts, First Report, p.8. (Hereafter cited as the Romilly Commission).

31. Moir, The Justice, p.91; A.P. Donajgrodski, "New roles for old: the Northcote-Trevelyan Report and the Clerks of the Home Office" in G. Sutherland (ed.), Studies in the Growth of Nineteenth Century Government (London, 1972), p.109.

32. 9 and 10 Vict. c.95, ss.27, 111; H. Broom, The Practice of the County Courts (London, 1857), pp.22-3.

33. Cox, The Law and Practice of the County Courts, Vol. I, p.97; 9 and 10 Vict. c.95, ss.70, 72, 76, 102, 104, 109, 110, 121, 126; see County Court Rules 3, 4, 18 and 46.

34. Donajgrodski, "New Roles for Old", pp.89-90.

35. Act to Amend the Act for the More Easy Recovery of Small Debts and Demands in England, and to Abolish Certain Inferior Courts of Record, 1849, 12 and 13 Vict. c.101, ss.7, 8; see 9 and 10 Vict. c.95, ss.9, 10.

36. Act to Extend the Act for the More Easy Recovery of Small Debts and Demands in England, and to Amend the Same, 1850, 13 and 14 Vict. c.61, ss.4, 9.

37. PP 1855 XVIII, Romilly Commission, First Report, p.8.

38. Ibid., pp.7-8; Act to Facilitate and Arrange Proceedings in the County Court, 1852, 15 and 16 Vict. c.54, ss.1, 14, 17. At this stage those who held appointments in more than one district were allowed to retain them. But see County Courts Amendment Act, 1856, 19 and 20 Vict. c.108, s.9.

39. PP 1855 XVIII, Romilly Commission, First Report, p.44.

40. Ibid.

41. Household Words, I (1850), 179. In 1848 incomes ranged from the £8.10s. per annum of one Welsh incumbent to the £2,731 per annum of the Westminster County Court clerk.

42. The proposed scale was:

Up to 200 plaints per annum	£60 per annum
Over 200 plaints per annum	£60 plus £5 for every additional twenty-five plaints up to 2,000 and thereafter £4 for every additional 25 plaints up to 6,000.
Over 6,000 plaints	At the Treasury's discretion.

See 19 and 20 Vict. c.108, s.82.

43. PP 1872 XX, Royal Commission on the Judicature, Evidence, qq. 2863-73. (Hereafter cited as the Judicature Commission).

44. PP 1872 XX, Judicature Commission, Second Report, pp.14-15.

45. 19 and 20 Vict. c.108, s.8.

46. Ibid., ss. 15, 34, 35, 58. My underlining.

47. Replevin was a summary process by which a man out of whose possession goods had been taken could obtain their return, until rights of ownership were determined by a court, by making a cash deposit or entering into a bond committing himself to bring an action by a certain time.

48. R.C. Snelling and T.J. Barron, "The Colonial Office and its Permanent Officials 1801-1914" in Sutherland (ed.), Studies in the Growth, p.151.

49. Act to Abolish the Court of Review in Bankruptcy and to make Alterations in the Jurisdiction of the Courts of Bankruptcy and Court for Relief of Insolvent Debtors, 1847, 10 and 11 Vict. c.102.

50. Bankruptcy and Insolvency Amendment Act, 1861, 24 and 25 Vict. c.134, ss.3, 4.

51. Ibid., ss.10, 14, 15, 52.

52. Ibid., s.58.

53. Bankruptcy Amendment and Consolidating Act, 1849, 12 and 13 Vict. c.106, s.28.

54. Griffith and Holmes, The Law and Practice in Bankruptcy, Vol. I, pp.19-20.

55. 24 and 25 Vict. c.134, s.101.

56. PP 1872 XX, Judicature Commission, Second Report, p.10.

57. 24 and 25 Vict. c.134, s.101. Schedule A laid down the following salaries for bankruptcy registrars:

Chief Registrar	£1,400 per annum
London Registrars	£1,200 per annum
County Registrars	£1,000 per annum.
Registrars in Attendance	
Upon Chief Judge	£1,200 per annum
Registrars of Meetings	£ 250 per annum.

See "Orders of the Court of Bankruptcy 12 October, 1861" in J.F. Archbold, The Practice of the New County Courts including the Practice under the New Bankruptcy Statute (London, 1861), pp.236-95.

58. 32 and 33 Vict. c.71; see J.E. Davies, The Jurisdiction and Practice of the County Courts in Equity, in Admiralty, Probate and Administration Cases (London, 1872), p.204.

59. Ibid., p.205; see Bankruptcy Rules, 1870, nos. 2, 3, 4.

60. PP 1872 XX, Judicature Commission, Second Report, 11-12, Evidence, q.2825; see 32 and 33 Vict. c.71, s.72.

61. 1853-1892, passim, consulted in the library of the Lord Chancellor's Office.

62. County Courts Equitable Jurisdiction Act, 1865, 28 and 29 Vict. c.99, ss.1, 16; see J.E. Davies, The County Courts Equitable Jurisdiction Act (London, 1865); 19 and 20 Vict. c.108, s.32.

63. General Orders in Equity, for which see Davies, The County Courts, pp.45-74, Order XX, rule 1.

64. Order VI, rule 2; order IX, rule 1; order XX, rules 3, 5, 6; order XXIII, rule 21.

65. County Courts (Admiralty Jurisdiction) Act, 1868, 31 and 32 Vict. c.81; County Courts (Admiralty Jurisdiction) Amendment Act, 1869, 32 and 33 Vict. c.51.

66. Those undertaking Admiralty work were handsomely remunerated in fees. See PP 1872 XX, Judicature Commission, Second Report, pp.10, 13-14.

67. 32 and 33 Vict. c.71.

68. PP 1872 XX, Judicature Commission, Evidence, qq.2878-9.

69. County Courts Act, 1866, 29 Vict. c.14. The new scale was:

Up to 200 plaints per annum	£100 per annum
200-6,000 plaints per annum	£4 for each additional 25.
Over 6,000 plaints per annum	By special arrangement but no salary to exceed £700 per annum.

70. PP 1872 XX, Judicature Commission, second Report, p.14; 28 and 29 Vict. c.99; 30 and 31 Vict. c.142, 32 and 33 Vict. c.71; see E. Jenks (ed.), Stephen's Commentaries on the Laws of England, Vol. III (London, 1922), p.688; 29 Vict. c.14, ss.2, 5. Existing registrars could refuse to accept the bailiff's duties. Those appointed after 1866 had to undertake them as a condition of holding office. The Lord Chancellor retained the right to appoint separate high bailiffs and the last such official did not depart until the 1950s.

71. County Courts Amendment Act, 1867, 30 and 31 Vict. c. 142, ss.16 and 17.

72. PP 1872 XX, Judicature Commission, Second Report, p.14.

73. Ibid., Evidence, q.10.

74. PP 1869 XXV, ibid., First Report, p.8.

75. PP 1872 XX, ibid., pp.11-15.

76. This point was recently made in an internal report to the Lord Chancellor to which I am not at liberty to refer.

77. PP 1872 XX, Judicature Commission, Second Report, p.14.

78. Ibid.

79. Ibid., p.19.

80. Ibid., pp.17-19.

81. The phrase is used by B. Abel-Smith and R. Stevens, Lawyers and the Courts (London, 1970), p.77.

82. 3 Hansard, CXLII (1856) cc.1-9; CXLIII (1856) cc.689-90; PP 1869 XXV, Judicature Commission, First Report, p.17.

83. V. Cromwell and Z. Steiner, "The Foreign Office before 1914: A Study in Resistance" in G. Sutherland (ed.), Studies in the Growth, p.172.

84. PP 1856 XXII, Royal Commission Appointed to Enquire into the Process, Practice and System of Pleading in the Court of Chancery, Third Report, p.208. (Hereafter cited as Chancery Commission).

85. Lyell, Memoir, Vol. I, p.271; E. Hughes, "Civil Service Reform, 1853-1855" History, XXVII (1942) 57, 60.

86. Act to Abolish Certain Sinecure Offices Connected with the Court of Chancery and to make Provision for the Lord High Chancellor on his Retirement from Office, 1832, 2 and 3 Will. IV. c.111.

87. Chancery Regulations Act, 1833, 3 and 4 Will. IV c.94. The salary scale (see Schedule) was:

1st registrar	£2,000	1st and 2nd clerks	£800
2nd and 3rd registrars	£1,800	3rd and 4th clerks	£600
4th and 5th registrars	£1,500	5th and 6th clerks	£400

6th registrar	£1,250	7th and 8th clerks	£300

88. PP 1856 XXII, Chancery Commission, Third Report, p.546; Evidence, q.1096; see 3 and 4 Will. IV s.5; 5 Vict. c.5, ss.38, 39.

89. PP 1875 XXX, Royal Commission Appointed to Enquire into the Administrative Departments of the Courts of Justice, Evidence, qq.3489, 3756.

90. Ibid., q.3603.

91. PP 1869 XXV, Judicature Commission, Firt Report, p.13.

92. Probates and Letters of Administration Act, 1857, 20 and 21 Vict. c.77; Divorce and Matrimonial Causes Act, 1857, 20 and 21 Vict. c.85.

93. 20 and 21 Vict. c.77, ss.13, 14, 18-20, 111, see Schedule A. Probate registries sometimes served an area encompassed by the county boundary, e.g., Devon, Cornwall, Wiltshire, Northumberland. Elsewhere electoral districts were followed.

94. Ibid., ss.27, 46, 48, 59, 96, 110, 111; see PP 1875 XXX, Royal Commission Appointed to Enquire into the Administrative Departments of the Courts of Justice, Evidence, qq.7696-8.

95. 20 and 21 Vict. c.85, s.14.

96. See Rules and Orders for Her Majesty's Court for Divorce and Matrimonial Causes . . . in G. Browne, A Treatise on the Principles and Practice of the Court for Divorce and Matrimonial Causes (London, 1864) Appendix II. Rules 7, 22, 24-6, 32, 34-6.

97. Divorce and Matrimonial Causes Amendment Act, 1858, 21 and 22 Vict. c.108, ss.4, 12 and 13. The Court of Arches was the oldest and leading consistory court of the Archbishop of Canterbury.

98. See Browne, A Treatise, 1st ed. for Additional Rules, 3 December, 1858, nos. 1, 3, 5 ,6, 9.

99. Matrimonial Causes Amendment Act, 1859, 22 and 23 Vict. c.61; Matrimonial Causes Amendment Act, 1860, 23 and 24 Vict. c.144.

100. See Browne, A Treatise, 4th ed. (London, 1879) Appendix II, no.132.

101. Ibid., nos. 101-2. Payments to support the wife after a decree of nullity or dissolution were called maintenance; after a decree of judicial separation or restitution of conjugal rights they were called alimony.

102. Ibid., no.101.

103. 20 and 21 Vict. c.85, ss.8-10.

104. 3 Hansard CLIV (1859) cc.555-6.

105. Ibid., cc.555-68.

106. Ibid., 559-68, 776-85; CLV 141-50, 510-18, 733-38, 992-97; 22 and 23 Vict. c.61, s.1.

107. 3 Hansard CLVII (1860) cc.815-16.

108. Ibid., 23 and 24 Vict. c.144, s.1. The Act was made perpetual by 25 and 26 Vict. c.81.

109. G. Rowntree and N.H. Carrier, "The Resort to Divorce in England and Wales, 1858-1957" Population Studies, (1958), 200.

110. Civil Judicial Statistics.

111. 3 Hansard CLV (1859) cc.141-150.

112. The number of petitions for alimony ranged from the 40 of 1858 to the 89 of 1863, the 85 of 1864, and the 86 of 1865. In these last three years an average of 26.9 per cent of all petitions included applications for alimony. Civil Judicial Statistics.

113. Browne, A Treatise, 4th ed., pp.168-9.

114. Ibid., 3rd ed., (London, 1876), p.158.

115. Ibid., Appendix nos. 86, 163, 167, 181-5. The rules issued on 14 July 1875, came into operation one week later.

116. Ibid., no.191.

117. Ibid., no.142.

118. Law Journal, X (1875), 474-5; Solicitors' Journal, XIX (1875), 761, 779-80.

119. 22 July 1875.

120. O.R. McGregor, *Divorce in England* (London, 1957), ch.3.

121. 3 *Hansard*, CLIV (1859), 555-6.

122. *PP* 1875 XXX. Middleton gave his evidence in April 1874, that is, before the promulgation of the new rules. In his evidence he spoke of the "vast number of references received from the Court on questions of alimony, and on petitions for variation of settlements." Evidence, qq.7628-987.

123. *PP* 1912-13 XVIII, Royal Commission on Divorce and Matrimonial Causes, Evidence, qq.46-218, 232, 790-1. Rule 208, July 1880, empowered registrars to consider applications to proceed *in forma pauperis*, see W. Rayden, *Practice and Law in the Divorce Division* (London, 1910), p.325.

124. Supreme Court of Judicature Act, 1873, 36 and 37 Vict. c.66, ss.60-6.

125. W. Rayden, *Practice and Law in the Divorce Division of the High Court of Justice*, 2nd ed., (London, 1926), p.1499.

126. *PP* 1948-9 XIII, Select Committee on County Court Procedure, Report, p.810.

127. O. MacDonagh, "The Nineteenth Century Revolution in Government: A Reappraisal" *Historical Journal*, I (1958), 58.

SPECIAL COURTS, SPECIAL LAW: LEGAL PLURALISM IN NINETEENTH CENTURY ENGLAND *

H.W. Arthurs

I: INTRODUCTION

By the late nineteenth century, adjudication by the ordinary courts, according to the rules of common law, was thought to be a corner-stone of English constitutionalism. Yet Holdsworth reminds us that there is a long tradition of legal pluralism in England, of adjudication by local courts, by governmental bodies and by arbitrators, according to rules which were often different from those of the common law.[1] Did this tradition of pluralism end in the nineteenth century, did it merely disappear from view, or did it rather enter the nineteenth century in the chrysalis of antique local systems and emerge in the twentieth, metamorphosed and unrecognisable, as modern administrative adjudication?

The transformation of English society which accompanied the early industrial revolution should, in one sense, have encouraged legal pluralism. As the Webbs have pointed out, the period from 1689-1832 was

> ". . . of extraordinary significance. For the first, and perhaps for the last, time in English History, the National Government abstained from intervention in local affairs . . . . Even when Parliament was appealed to for legislation, it allowed the different localities to have practically whatever constitutions and whatever powers they asked for . . . ."[2]

Conditions were obviously ripe for local experiments, and these to some extent occurred. But especially during the latter part of this period, important counter-currents developed. Shifts in population and radical changes in economic relationships undermined the social bases of older local systems, while the advent of laissez-faire destroyed the regulatory schemes of the former mercantile policies, and forestalled, at least for a time, their replacement by more suitable new instruments of state control.[3]

From about 1830 onward, however, the magnetic fields began to reverse. Local autonomy and diversity increasingly gave way to national control and uniformity. But, at the same time, laissez-faire gradually yielded to active state intervention in the economy and in social organisation. Thereafter, one would more likely be able to trace the tradition of legal pluralism through the specialised tribunals of the regulatory state than in systems of local justice.

Nor did the new pluralism entirely overtake the old. Arbitration had always attracted the loyalty of the business community. It persisted and expanded and, after mid-century, claimed a degree of autonomy and legitimacy which - if attained - would have made it an even more formidable rival to the common law. As matters transpired, arbitration continued to flourish but in a relatively subdued and domesticated form.

But it cannot be denied that from the 1830s onwards, pluralism in the English system of civil justice was under attack, and it is with this latter phenomenon that this essay is primarily concerned.

II: THE ENGLISH LEGAL SYSTEM IN THE 1830s

Despite his general acknowledgement of the historic roots of legal pluralism, Holdsworth describes the English judicial system in the early nineteenth century as very highly centralised:

> "With the exception of the petty criminal business entrusted to the justices of the peace, practically all of the judicial work of the country was done by the judges of the common law courts, the Lord Chancellor or the Master of the Rolls, and the judge of the court of Admiralty."[4]

Was the early nineteenth century, then, an unusual period insofar as the central courts enjoyed a virtual monopoly of adjudication? If so, to what extent did its atypical qualities affect the views of those concerned with English legal development throughout that century? And, if not, why did Holdsworth make such a statement, and what significance would attach to a revised view of English judicature, ascribing to other parts of the system a much larger share of "judicial work"?

In a sense, the answers to these questions depend upon a threshold decision as to what constitutes "judicial work". If this term is broadly defined to include all forms of dispute resolution, or at least of adjudication, the role of the central judiciary is to that extent diminished. If, on the other hand, the term includes only the type of work historically done by such judges, within the context of the central legal system, then they are defined into pre-eminence. But the latter definition is tautologous; only the former makes sense.

Even if "judicial work" must be broadly construed to include all forms of adjudication, it is very difficult to estimate the extent to which the central courts shared adjudicative responsibilities with other decision-makers. And it is even more difficult to assess the impact of the central courts - as exemplars and as a controlling jurisdiction -upon their behaviour. Many non-judicial adjudicators were selected privately by the parties, served ad hoc, and disappeared without any historical trace. Others staffed less transient tribunals, serving a particular social, economic or geographic constituency, but kept no records, did so only intermittently, or failed to transmit them to posterity. And yet others -including those whom Holdsworth describes as dispensing "petty criminal justice" - were part of the social fabric of all communities, exercising a jurisdiction which could only have seemed "petty" when viewed from the top down, rather than from the bottom up.

But conceding all of these difficulties of retrieving the facts and evaluating them, it seems probable that the central courts were never responsible for anything more than a minor fraction of the nation's "judicial work". Even a casual reading of the evidence illuminates the extraordinary diversity of special jurisdictions at all periods of English history, their longevity, the tenacity with which their clientele clung to them, and the unceasing disparagement they received at the hands of common lawyers. It is difficult to avoid the conclusion that Holdsworth, by no means a casual reader of evidence, had a narrow definition of law in view when he spoke of the great centralisation of the English legal system. For Holdsworth, it would seem, "law" in the nineteenth century was made by the central judiciary and parliament, not by custom or contract or the patterns of discretionary decisions by lower-level adjudicators; "law", for him, was what was produced by professional judges and lawyers rather than what was consumed by the community at large. The theoretical implications of this definition of law, and of an alternative, more pluralistic and expansive, view will be canvassed below. It is initially important, however, to appreciate that a very great number of adjudicative tribunals existed in the early nineteenth century which were neither included within, nor emanations of, the central court system.[5]

Apart altogether from arbitrators, domestic tribunals, administrative tribunals and the ubiquitous justices of the peace (with both civil and criminal powers), over 300 local courts actively exercised civil jurisdiction as late as 1830,[6] disposing of about three times as many cases as the Westminster courts,[7] virtually without scrutiny or control by the central judiciary.[8]

In a sense, the history of civil justice throughout the nineteenth century is that of an attempt to accomplish what Holdsworth described as reality - the focussing of the judicial system on its central component, the superior courts - while also seeking to enhance the convenience and efficiency of local administration and adjudication. To some extent, this attempt required rationalisation of the central courts. Integration with the common law courts was the fate of its major rivals, Equity, Admiralty and the Ecclesiastical Courts.[9] To some extent, it involved a flanking movement around rival and autonomous systems through judicial or legislative appropriation of their unique jurisdictions, doctrines, or procedures, thus enabling the central court system to compete with them more effectively.[10] To some extent, the control of the central courts was enhanced by the expansion of procedures for review and appeal.[11] And to some extent the rival systems simply atrophied with the disappearance of the communities they had served, or lingered even later, as in the case of certain feudal, borough or communal courts which have been abolished only in very recent times.[12] But today, even more than when Holdsworth wrote, the central courts are far from enjoying a monopoly.

What was at issue in the nineteenth century debate over the shape of the English judicial system was, however, not merely a matter of institutional design. Rather it was a matter of whether the common law would be the sole or pre-eminent legal regime, or merely exist as one component amongst many in a pluralistic system. Many of the special courts which eluded Holdsworth's notice did not in theory or in fact decide cases on common law principles; they administered, in effect, distinctive sub-systems of local and special law.

While this point has considerable theoretical significance, especially as it anticipates the appearance of modern administrative tribunals within the legal system, it is important at the same time not to adopt an excessively romantic view of the local and special courts. It must be conceded that by the early nineteenth century, many of them had either ceased to function,[13] or had become in effect mere local imitations of the common law courts. Indeed, as will be seen, during the protracted investigations of the British justice system in the mid-nineteenth century, it was virtually assumed that all law was, or should be, common law. Relatively little attention was paid to the substantive rules of local and special jurisdictions; concern was focussed almost exclusively on the efficiency with which they were administered. It is perhaps this focus in the work of the reforming commissions which led Dicey later in the century,[14] and Holdsworth later yet, to overlook the common law's historic rivals, and to overestimate the extent to which the "ordinary courts" and the "ordinary law of the land" monopolised adjudication.

It is neither useful, nor within the limits of this study possible, to give a comprehensive account of the rise to pre-eminence of the central royal courts of common law.[15] In general terms, however, the central legal system down to the eighteenth century was concerned with major criminal offences, disputes involving freehold property, and other civil suits concerning substantial sums of money. To be sure, the dominance of the central, over local and special, courts increased considerably over time. For example, criminal statutes and common law property rules displaced customary law in the regulation of resources such as the forests;[16] other forms of wealth (in theory, if not always in practice) came within the purview of the regular courts; and a fixed monetary limit of 40 shillings placed upon many local courts in the thirteenth century caused their jurisdiction to shrink dramatically in the face of centuries of inflation.[17] But even by the middle third of the nineteenth century, the expanding jurisdiction of the central legal system had not entirely displaced local and special justice.

Local and special court systems fell into three categories: those which administered the general law of the land (sometimes with special procedural arrangements), those with broad discretionary powers and de facto autonomy, exercised in such a way as to establish a local variant of the general law, and those which were not formally bound to apply the rules of common law, and in fact, administered a distinctive legal sub-system.[18]

A. Locally Administered Common Law Courts

The courts of the principality of Wales and the palatinates of Lancaster, Chester and Durham were not emanations of the central courts.[19] Regarded as cognate with, rather than inferior to, the central courts, each was rooted in a distinct medieval political unit and, at least initially, offered a potential breeding ground for a distinctive local legal system. However, no doubt as a result of centripetal economic and political forces, by the nineteenth century each had become largely or entirely assimilated into the national legal system. What was left was a system of specialised judicial appointments, separate tariffs of fees and costs, local procedures (sometimes simpler than those of Westminster) and whatever special local legal rules may have been preserved by legislation or custom.[20]

These large local systems enjoyed considerable support. Nonetheless, Wales and Chester were abolished in 1830, following an extensive enquiry.[21] There, a prime source of dissatisfaction appears to have been the quality of the bench; there were complaints relating to judicial tenure, competence and independence.[22] But notwithstanding these complaints, there was considerable opposition, in Wales especially, to merger with the central system of courts. In part, this reflected the persistence of local nationalism, a fact recognised by both advocates and opponents of merger.[23] In part, too, it reflected the conviction that locally based justice was cheaper and more accessible than that dispensed by the ordinary courts at Westminster or on assize.[24] This latter factor was particularly important in the case of Lancaster and Durham, which merged with the High Court only in 1971.[25] But the stress on speedy and cheap justice was a two-edged sword. Instead of persuading the central government to merely preserve this existing local jurisdiction, it helped to make the case for a new, national system of county courts.[26]

The "new" national system, ultimately established in 1846, was itself ostensibly built upon the foundations of an existing large local system of county courts, which had ancient origins as communal courts. Like the palatine courts, the county courts had been assimilated into the common law system as courts of record although they also discharged local administrative functions, especially in earlier times. But Holdsworth says of these courts that ". . . their history has been in the main a history of decline and decadence."[27] A Royal Commission investigating these (and other local) courts reported in 1833 that many of them suffered from serious weaknesses - limits of monetary and geographic jurisdiction, lack of competent staff and judges, impaired powers to issue process, compel attendance, or enforce judgment, and the cost of proceedings - and recommended their replacement.[28]

No doubt these criticisms were substantially accurate. However, the fact remains that many local courts were still extremely active in 1830, and rendered an important service annually deciding thousands of small cases relatively speedily and cheaply.[29] By contrast, almost two-thirds of the actions begun in Westminster involved sums of less than £50, and they almost certainly could not have been tried for less than several times the amount of the claim.[30] "Decline" and "decadence" thus must be treated as relative terms; neither Holdsworth's nor the Commission's strictures should be confined to the local courts; they apply to the central courts as well.

Moreover, abolition of the local common law courts was not wholly inspired by an abstract concern for more perfect justice. It is obvious that in large measure what was wanted was a more efficient mechanism for debt collection: the title of both the 1833 Report[31] and the 1846 legislation[32] make this clear, as did the text of the Report itself

> "It is a matter of sound moral as well as legal policy, that no debtor shall be exempted from the legal obligation to pay a just debt, however small . . . ."[33]

And while the earlier recommendation for the abolition of the separate Welsh courts was said to reflect -

> ". . . a very great desire on the part of the inhabitants of Wales (though not without some exceptions) for a further assimilation of the judicature of the principality to that of England . . . .",[34]

scrutiny of the evidence places this assertion in a special light. It was the "owners of property and principal inhabitants"[35] who favoured abolition of the local system, for reasons which drew the scornful criticism of popular spokesmen:

> "[N]either am I surprised [said a Welsh M.P.] that gentlemen of large fortune, many of them non-residents, connected with ironworks, and whose lawsuits must, from local and other circumstances, be conducted in England, care little about the abolition of a judicature of little utility to them, however useful to the public at large . . ."[36]

The genuine desire for reform in the administration of justice thus coincided with the desire for efficient debt collection in an expanding, modern economy. And both of these tendencies favoured a more homogeneous, national system - the reformers because local systems were in principle unscientific, the commercial interests because such systems could not be depended upon to produce favourable results.

No respectable case could ultimately be made in favour of the random and truncated jurisdiction of the old local courts, and their demise was perhaps inevitable. What was not inevitable, however, was that they should simply have been replaced with a nationwide system of common law courts based on a more rational, decentralised administration. Indeed, for a time it seemed that the new courts would be more than a localised version of the central courts. Even before the 1833 Report, legislation had been introduced (and reached second reading in the House of Commons) which created new "Local District Courts" whose judges would not only perform conventional adjudicative functions, but who would as well serve as arbitrators and "Judges of Reconcilement."[37] Although these features of the legislation disappeared in the course of the lengthy parliamentary battle to establish the new system, pressure for some such modification of common law adjudication persisted.[38] Indeed, the relatively successful experience of the courts of requests in many areas made them, as much as the county courts, a model for the new system. As will be seen, the courts of request enjoyed considerable discretion and had evolved a somewhat different style of operation from that of the common law courts.

Thus, while the County Courts Act of 1846 ultimately made no formal provision for disposition on other than common law principles, certain procedural reforms no doubt introduced a moderating influence: the adoption of a simplified system of pleadings, more liberal evidentiary rules, and a right (frequently exercised) of personal audience by the parties.[39] These reforms heightened discretion and introduced greater informality than the common law courts had previously known, although they must also have enhanced efficiency in debt collection.[40] As will be suggested next, informality and discretion are often the means by which distinctive new sub-systems of law are brought into being.

B. Local Variants of Common Law: the Role of Discretion

It can be hypothesised that in the central court system there was, in the mid-nineteenth century as now, a tendency towards predictability and uniformity of result. The theoretical commitment to precedent was not the only reason for this. The participation of advocates and judges with a common professional training, the availability of written records, treatises and reports, the hierarchical organisation of the courts to provide formal appeals, and the informal contact amongst a rather small number of judges - all of these reinforced the theoretical commitment to make decisions which were predictable and uniform throughout the legal system. And yet we know that even in the superior courts, a considerable margin of discretion must exist: the finding of facts, the application of vague standards such as "fairness" and "reasonableness", the identification of gaps in existing rules, the decision to extend them to novel situations, the choice between apparently conflicting authorities, the interpretation of statutory or common law rules, are some of the formulae through which discretion is introduced into a system which is ostensibly committed to predictability and certainty.

If discretion was in fact widely exercised in the superior courts, one would not be surprised to find that it was even more frequently encountered in local courts. All of the tasks involving the exercise of discretion were undertaken by the local courts as well, but many of the factors which constrained discretion were absent. Professionals were less often encountered (especially as advocates); written decisions were infrequent, inaccessible, and unlikely to be reported or analysed; appeals were rare or non-existent; and informal contacts amongst judges in different local courts were probably unusual.

Added to these considerations is the important fact that local justice would often be communal justice. To the extent the local court was part of the fabric of community life, it was more likely to be responsive to factors which might not impinge upon the consciousness of judges of the central system: the personality or reputation of the litigants, the state of the local economy or social climate, local custom, nuances of local speech and behaviour patterns, the judge's own continuing relationship as a member of the community; above all, a local judge may well have been less concerned to vindicate general rules of law, and more to secure what he imagined to be local social equilibrium and tranquility. This highly discretionary brand of justice might be humane or oppressive, merely idiosyncratic or perfectly attuned to local sensibilities. But it was likely to be quite different from the justice of the central system.

These speculations about the discretionary nature of local justice are offered in lieu of hard evidence that discretion in fact produced local legal regimes which differed from the general system of common law, although ostensibly a part of it. However, such evidence is not entirely lacking.

Hay's study of criminal justice in eighteenth century rural England strongly suggests that literal enforcement of the strictures of the criminal law was not the prime concern of the local magistracy. He demonstrates how the great severity of the criminal law was consciously tempered by the frequent exercise of mercy, in order to forge a flexible instrument of social control. Even when mercy was an executive, rather than a judicial, act its invocation would have come as no surprise to local justices. After all, many of them were on intimate terms with local magnates who secured pardons or other relaxations of harsh penalties, while some were themselves M.P.'s or influential political figures. Conversely, decisions to impose harsh penalties or to convict for more, rather than less, serious crimes were not taken in a political vacuum:

> "Benevolence, all patronage, was given meaning by its contingency. It was the obverse of coercion . . . . When patronage failed, force could be invoked; but when coercion inflamed men's minds, at the crucial moment mercy could calm them."[41]

In the real - as opposed to the formal - administration even of the criminal law, the local exercise of discretion played a significant role.

No doubt the activities of the justices in the expanding cities in the 1830s and 1840s differed somewhat from those of rural areas and earlier times, if only because of the changes in the political hierarchy, incipient professionalisation of the magistracy, and reform of criminal law and procedure. But it can hardly be denied that local circumstances gave local colour to an apparently neutral, national system of criminal law.[42]

On the civil side, discretion was probably even more freely exercised. The evidence to the 1833 Commission on Provincial Courts by two Commissioners of a court of requests warrants this conclusion:

"Q. Are the Commissioners guided by distinct rules of law, or according to their own notions of equity?

A. I should rather say their strict notions of equity, because we are not acquainted with strict rules of law.

Q. But occasionally you have to refer to the clerks on points of law?

A. Yes, we do.

Q. Suppose you thought the law was one way and equity another, what would be done then?

A. If it was left to our decision, I think we should give it in favour of equity . . . ."[43]

Courts of requests were generally mandated to decide cases according to "equity and good conscience", and indeed the only extended account of the actual operation of one of these courts (unfortunately from an earlier period) suggests that common sense and situation equity, rather than rules of law, did provide the norms of decision-making.[44] And discretionary departures from even basic common law institutional premises were not unknown. For example, in the busy Manchester Court of Requests[45] parties were examined directly by the judge on the inquisitorial rather than the adversarial model, and in defiance of the common law rule which then precluded the parties from testifying because they were "interested witnesses." These departures were facilitated both by the circumstances speculatively mentioned above, and by legislation which immunised them from judicial review.[46]

However, these discretion-based local systems were not destined to survive in full bloom much past the 1830s. On the criminal side, changes in the penal system diminished the occasions for the use of the prerogative of mercy and the most extreme opportunities for coercion; reform of the magistracy and (later) more extensive appellate review focussed the criminal justice system more squarely on its ostensible purposes; and legislative redrafting removed some discretion-generating ambiguities and anomalies in the law. But of course discretion did not disappear altogether.

On the civil side, a deep-rooted antipathy towards discretionary justice was expressed by the reformers:

> "The suspicion entertained . . . by Sir William Blackstone, as to the policy of erecting courts 'with methods of proceeding entirely in derogation of the Common Law, and whose large discretionary powers make a petty tyranny in a set of standing Commissioners', have not been removed by later experience."[47]

They sought to simultaneously diminish discretion and eliminate local peculiarities, while securing the advantages of a nation-wide system rather than one operating in and from Westminster. It was conceded that in litigation over small matters

> ". . . [i]f justice . . . is to be administered according to the ordinary rules of evidence, in a court regulated by certain rules of practice, the proceeding ceases to be remedial in its effect. If, on the other hand, all such restraints be dispensed with, the tribunal becomes arbitrary, and its decisions too vague and uncertain to be satisfactory."[48]

The solution proposed was that the existing local courts should be "reconstructed upon a simple and uniform model".[49] Uniformity, of course, would tend to diminish the discretionary basis of local systems, with its advantages as well as its weaknesses. But presumably simplicity would compensate for this loss by providing an efficient and accessible substitute.

The attractions of simplicity and uniformity were not restricted to court organisation. They were characteristic of proposals for scientific reform of social institutions more generally. To be sure, "scientific reform" was not a prospect which galvanised judges and lawyers into immediate and affirmative action. The new system of county courts was not established until sixteen years after it was first proposed in parliament in 1830, and even then did not at first encompass some of the more successful local and non-common law courts.[50] But when the new system finally began to operate it immediately proved itself. Conveniently located throughout the country, to some extent professionally staffed, adequately armed with powers to enforce its process, it disposed of an annual average of 433,000 cases in the first five years of its existence.[51]

It is probably fair to say that at this point the great mass of litigation moved along a spectrum from a regime of greater to a regime of lesser discretion, from the old county courts and courts of requests to the new county courts. It is only at this relatively late date that the common law can arguably be said to have secured a substantial monopoly over civil disputes. But this monopoly was challenged almost from its inception by two rival systems - private arbitration and administrative adjudication.

C. Distinctive Legal Sub-systems

Unlike County Courts, which early became involved in the local administration of common law, the courts of many manors, boroughs and other franchises established by custom, feudal grant, royal charter or parliamentary legislation were meant to administer local or specialised legal systems.

Milsom draws the distinction at any early period in the development of the feudal courts:

> "Feudal jurisdiction had started as the power to decide, not just to declare a result reached by applying <u>external</u> criteria . . . . [T]here is a great difference between a lord and his court applying rules within their own control if within anybody's and the same body applying royal rules."[52]

Nor was the distinction between external and internal legal systems confined to the feudal courts described by Milsom. Various medieval courts, for example, were entitled and expected to apply "rules within their own control". Such rules included the law merchant which was indigenous to the trading community,[53] Jewish religious law in the case of disputes among Jews or between Jews and other persons trading with them,[54] local agricultural custom,[55] and special laws governing miners and mining.[56] These "internal" legal systems did not quickly dissipate; on the contrary, they continued to flourish at least until the end of the seventeenth century,[57] to agitate Benthamite reformers in the early nineteenth century,[58] and to linger even into the twentieth.[59]

Dawson's careful description of the work of one such manor court[60] shows that both its caseload and the substantive rules it applied differed markedly from those of a common law court, as might be expected from a forum in which lawyers neither pleaded nor decided cases.[61]

Manor courts were typically concerned with minor civil and criminal-regulatory matters: use-rights in commons, personal behaviour, participation in community work such as the maintenance of watercourses, small debts and promises, and especially protection of copyhold tenure in land. Proceedings, apparently, were often not adversarial in form, and disposition was sometimes by communal decision. To the extent that a "legal" system evolved, its vehicle was the presiding officer of the court, often the steward of the manor. This official may have had some legal training, and at least often had access to one of the manuals commercially published for the guidance of those holding courts. But the basic source of "law" was not these manuals, and most certainly not the common law itself; rather it was local custom and bylaws. Indeed, the local law may well have reached results which the common law courts would not have countenanced, or which they only later adopted: enforcement of informal promises, specific performance, and a primitive form of mortgage of copyhold land.

It should not be thought that involvement in customary rather than common law was the peculiar fate of a few isolated communities. Rather the reverse was true until the industrial revolution. As Abel-Smith and Stevens remark, until the eighteenth century

> ". . . [t]he systems of law administered by the superior courts, together with the appeal courts, were the concern of a very small percentage of the population . . . . It would be wrong, however, to assume that the poor had no disputes, which today would be expected to give rise to litigation . . . . While such disputes would be of no interest to the royal judges they might well find their way into one of two types of local courts - the survivors of the communal courts such as the hundred courts, or of the feudal courts such as the manorial courts."[62]

By the nineteenth century, certainly by the 1830s, customary law was relatively less important both because of a decline in the relative (though not absolute) size of the agricultural sector, and because of the elimination through enclosure of common lands and the rights to their use.[63]

But the old customary law had by no means disappeared. Brougham's famous speech in 1828, which launched fifty years of reform in judicial administration, referred to customary tenures

> ". . . in a thousand manors, all different from the Common-law that regulates freehold estates, most of them different from each other. . . . Is it right that such varieties of custom should be allowed to have force in particular districts, contrary to the general law of the land?"[64]

Nor was customary law dispensed by manor courts alone. Custom seems to have been frequently used to regulate local economies based upon natural resources: agricultural land (as in the manor courts) but also forests and mineral deposits, especially tin.

The forest courts were organised as a separate system -"peculiar officers, peculiar courts, peculiar law", Holdsworth remarks[65] - at least from the thirteenth century. The lowest level of courts, the Swanimote, comprised the forest steward, four elected lay "Verderers" and twelve lay "Regarders". While it had power to convict and assess fines for breach of the forest laws, sentences of the Swanimote were not legally enforceable until the offender was tried by one of two Justices in Eyre, judges of the royal courts. Since trials at the Eyre were seldom held from the end of the seventeenth century, Holdsworth dates the decline and ultimate collapse of forest law from that time.[66] But Thompson's study[67] demonstrates that forest law effectively operated into the eighteenth century and perhaps beyond, its sanctions being the attachment of offenders, summary confiscation of their guns, dogs, snares, etc., and power to bind over offenders on punitive recognisances. In effect, these powers provided the forest courts with a quid pro quo which encouraged offenders to pay a small fine "in composition".

The Stannary Courts, still surviving but hardly vigorous in the 1830s, represented another significant instance of this "peculiar" customary law.[68] Rooted in the medieval franchises granted to mining communities, they appear to have survived longest in Devon and especially Cornwall. The primary function of the Stannary Courts was to decide disputes affecting mining rights according to customary rules, or enactments of the Stannary parliaments; subsequently, they also acquire a concurrent general jurisdiction over all disputes involving miners, or arising within the geographical area of the Stannaries. In the nineteenth century, however, challenges to the jurisdiction of the Stannaries, and changes in both the mining economy and the judicial organisation of the country led first to the reconstitution of these courts under special legislation,[69] and then to their ultimate abolition[70] - despite some local support for their retention.[71]

Forest law, too, is no more. It flickered briefly into local prominence between 1830 and 1860,[72] and was formally abolished only in 1971.[73] But its persistence well beyond the date when its formal sanctioning system collapsed strongly suggests that customary law may have served social interests which the common law could not serve. Thompson describes this function of forest law in terms which are equally applicable to other systems of customary law. Foresters, he says, in the eighteenth century,

". . . clung to the lowest rungs of the hierarchy of use-rights . . . .

[T]heir livelihood depended upon the survival of pre-capitalist use-rights over the land, and upon some form of social organisation (as with the old forest courts and the Verderers and Regarders) by which conflicting claims to use-rights over the same land and timber could be reconciled . . . ."[74]

And on what basis save custom could these conflicting interests be reconciled? Customary law -

". . . was often a definition of actual agrarian practice, as it had been pursued 'time out of mind'. How can we distinguish between the activity of farming or quarrying and the rights to this strip of land or that quarry? The farmer or forester in his daily occupation was moving within visible or invisible structures of law . . . ."[75]

Here, as will be suggested, lies both the strength and weakness of customary law.

D. The Relationship between Superior and Local Courts

The superior courts of common law, in theory at least, exercised supervisory jurisdiction over local, special and indeed private, tribunals. This jurisdiction in some cases rested upon specific statutory provisions, more often upon the exercise of inherent power to review through the use of prerogative writs, and occasionally upon the introduction in superior court litigation of collateral issues which had been, or might have been, decided by local courts. But scrutiny of the decisions of the superior courts in 1830 indicates that de facto if not de jure the local and special courts were largely immune from review.[76]

In a number of cases, it is true, superior courts decided collateral issues involving local custom as an evidentiary matter affecting legal or equitable claims.[77] But in only two cases was direct reliance placed upon decisions of local courts - in one case successfully,[78] in the other not.[79] In two other cases, substantive decisions of local or customary courts were directly challenged. In one case the King's Bench refused to decide a question within the jurisdiction of a domestic tribunal;[80] but in the other it overturned the decision of a customary court.[81] A pair of cases involving the judicatures of Chester[82] and Wales[83] disclosed no obvious interventionist impulse in the central courts; rather the contrary. Indeed, another group of decisions relating to forfeiture of costs for failing to resort to the appropriate lower court, based upon statutory provisions, seems to show that the central courts were content to keep their dockets clear of minor cases.[84] Spurious attempts to challenge the jurisdiction of local courts to delay or defeat execution were similarly treated with disdain.[85]

In view of the hundreds of thousands of cases tried in local or specialised tribunals the paucity of decisions relating to the interaction between the central and other court systems is surely significant. Indeed, there appears to have existed a virtual dichotomy between the two. There are, no doubt, explanations for this dichotomy: the presence of privative clauses in some cases; the relatively minor nature of claims in most local courts (although some had plenary jurisdiction); the expense of appeal or prerogative writ review, and the difficulty of securing a different decision in the higher courts; perhaps a willingness to acquiesce in the decision of local and familiar tribunals. Whichever explanation is most plausible, it does appear, however, that the central courts were not involved to any significant extent, directly or indirectly, in the supervision of local justice or in the shaping of local law.

What consequences must have resulted from this conclusion? First, it is possible that even in the absence of intervention the local courts adhered to general rules of law and normal legal procedures. But it is not likely that such adherence was universal. Not only has some direct evidence been cited to the contrary, but such a situation would be most surprising in light of the large number of local courts, their dependence on lay judges, their differing clienteles, dockets and jurisdictions, and the lack of centripetal influences such as a single code of procedure or commercial law, or a realistic possibility of appellate review. Second, since the volume of cases decided according to local law by local tribunals was so great (and that of the central system so small by comparison), it seems likely that for large parts of the population, local law was the "ordinary law", and the law of the Westminster courts was in a sense irrelevant, or at least not an ongoing juridical reality. The impact of this situation is brought home by Holmes' famous dictum, "What the judges will do in fact is what I mean by law". If "the judges" were local judges, what they would do is what was "law" for many people in the 1830s, and at least as late as 1846 when the County Courts were established.

III: THE DECLINE OF LOCAL JUSTICE

Only scant traces remain today of these local and special courts which were so important in the 1830s. A few anomalous ancient courts are still entitled to hear and determine legal proceedings,[86] while others are now limited to "the taking of presentments with respect to matters of local concern", to "management of the commons", or to purely ceremonial exercises connected with agricultural functions.[87] In light of the fact that total abolition of local inferior courts was recommended as long ago as 1833,[88] strongly reiterated in 1872,[89] and plaintively repeated as recently as 1969,[90] the wonder is that they survived at all until such a late date. Their history has been sketched here not because of mere antiquarian interest, not because of any contemporary functional significance, but rather, because it is important to appreciate their role in English socio-legal history for three reasons.

First, appreciation of the existence of rival systems helps to put in perspective the overstated claims of common lawyers to a monopoly on adjudicative business which is so sanctified by history as to virtually amount to a constitutional principle. Dawson makes this point vividly in speaking of an earlier period, but in language which has contemporary significance:

> "It has been said that the English constitution has two fundamental characteristics - 'the system of self-government and the rule of law'. If the law that 'ruled' the local courts of manor and town is identified with the common law, it did not penetrate far. Even if one reads the 'rule of law' in a larger sense as a social ordering that sets limits to power and

standards for its exercise, doubts still remain as to whether the law of the judges in the central courts contributed much to the main result . . . . It was the essence of judicial controls that they be intermittent and depend on the initiative of litigants. In the absence of stronger incentives than existed in the common law judges or in litigants, the 'rule' of the common law was a pale abstraction about which it is easy to romanticise. The question is whether the standards of the common law were transmitted through all levels of the population as meaningful guides and limits to action . . . ."[91]

Acknowledgement of the fact that the common law's hegemony was never complete will not, perhaps, provoke present-day common lawyers into an act of constitutional contrition, or even persuade them to view more modestly the claim that superior court judges enjoy a prescriptive title as ultimate custodians of our legal system. But a more accurate historical perspective may lend some legitimacy to proponents of legal pluralism, to those who believe that tribunals other than superior courts and rules other than those of the common law do not bear the mark of Cain.

And there is a second point to be made about the historical significance of customary and local courts. They should not be understood to have declined solely because of their own defects and vices.

It is no doubt true that, to an extent, local oligarchies must have been able to manipulate rules and procedures to pervert local justice, at least in any case involving a challenge to their interests. No doubt, as well, introspective local communities were themselves capable of oppression and unfairness, even when they acted through relatively democratic forms. But there are two partial answers to this point. In fact, as Dawson suggests,[92] sometimes a reasonable level of local justice was in fact achieved, and did actually constrain feudal and oligarchic power - or at least enforce the reciprocal rights and obligations existing between higher and lower orders. Moreover, if local civil justice fell below our standards, it did not necessarily suffer by comparison with contemporaneous local criminal justice, or even royal justice.[93]

The local and idiosyncratic nature of these tribunals was, no doubt, a serious and ultimately fatal weakness. Goebel's portrayal of seventeenth century courts remains generally accurate through to the nineteenth century:

> "No one who ventures into the forbidding welter of contemporary [seventeenth century] charters can fail to be appalled by the multitude and extent of franchises, the tenacity with which they were clung to, and the astounding picture of jurisdictional diversities they disclose."[94]

But so long as the boundaries of the universe were, for most people, the village or manor or hundred, so long as their economic ties were to local agriculture or even local manufacture and trade, even so long as external social and economic relationships were episodic and ordered, the multiplicity and diversity of jurisdictions and rules may have been, perhaps, less daunting than they now seem.[95]

To make an obvious point, if the users of local justice knew no other, they could hardly be troubled by what went on in other communities. The argument is not one in favour of blissful ignorance. Rather it is that so long as the system which impinged upon them functioned in a way its clients and proprietors regarded as satisfactory, neither would likely be concerned about other, remote systems - least of all what Dawson calls the "pale abstraction" of the rule of the common law. It was only when their familiar local system began to collide with other systems that the weakness of local and particular jurisdictions began to become apparent.

There was a potential for such a collision in changing patterns of local settlement, as Thompson illustrates so convincingly in relation to the forests. With the rise of the Whig gentry, with their resort to common law and lawyers, local legal systems which had evolved to regulate use-rights in a modest forest economy were swept aside.

> "During the eighteenth century one legal decision after another signalled that the lawyers had become converted to the notions of absolute property ownership, and that (wherever the least doubt could

> be found) the law abhorred the messy complexities of the coincident use-right . . . . The rights and claims of the poor, if inquired into at all, received mere perfunctory compensation . . . . Very often they were simply redefined as crimes: poaching, woodtheft, trespass."[96]

The forest law, he insists, did not perish solely because of internal decay:

> "Utilitarian bureaucrats might later see it as a toothless old relic, but in fact it was the shadowy survival of a concept both more functional and more democratic than any of their own creations. . . . Research . . . might well reveal that the old forest courts died out, not because they were impotent but because they continued to express, however feebly, the interests of the foresters. . . ."[97]

But one need not adopt such a jaundiced view of the common law and customary law. When transportation and communications improved, when a more complex and highly integrated national economy began to emerge, local legal systems became increasingly less relevant and less functional. Frankfurter reminds us: "Watt and Stephenson were much more responsible for undermining the dominantly feudal system expounded by Blackstone, than Bentham and Brougham."[98] The same can be said of the local courts which Blackstone excoriated.

The linkage between legal institutions and their social context is what was of critical importance. Thompson, we must recall, speaks of law as "a definition of actual agrarian practice"; he asks "how can we distinguish between the activity . . . and the rights?"; he describes "the farmer or forester . . . moving within visible or invisible structures of law . . .";[99] he even detects similar linkages in early forms of industrial organisation.[100] But the interweaving of social life and law, so characteristic of close-knit agricultural communities, did not easily translate into the larger, more diffuse, dynamic and diversified towns and cities which attracted an increasing proportion of the population. Simple, well-understood rules about the performance of civic tasks or the sharing of communal facilities had little meaning in the context of a society of strangers and an economy of complex and specialised services. The old system could finally survive only where the old forms of social organisation lingered.[101] In a village, for example, maintenance of watercourses might be undertaken by co-operative effort, non-participation in which would be regarded as breach of communal law. In a large town, if the task was to be performed at all, it could only be by private or public corporate undertaking. Rules and institutions designed for one situation could not easily be adapted to another.

Where such adaptation was attempted, even with considerable success, certain intrinsic institutional limitations ultimately frustrated the exercise.[102] Courts which were locally organised suffered - or were perceived to suffer - from the stigma that they were based on the political assumptions of an irrelevant _ancien régime_. In some smaller communities, no doubt, traditions of popular participation survived to confer a democratic legitimacy on the local courts. But in other cases, allegations about the inefficiency or partiality of local courts could not be addressed so long as they were controlled by local magnates rather than by an elected government. Moreover, local justice, as suggested, was plagued by the inherent weakness of a jurisdiction limited in amount and territory - a fatal defect as the amounts involved in even routine consumer and commercial transactions grew, and as trade and people flowed freely across their boundaries. Special courts, such as the Stannaries, suffered from analogous defects. Their concerns and clientele were not defined in terms which corresponded with changing social and economic realities.

And above all, it is suggested, local and special justice collided with the cherished assumptions of common lawyers about the inherent desirability of a unified, hierarchically organised, legal system. This Benthamite sentiment had emerged by the 1820s[103] and persisted throughout the next half century at least,[104] until Dicey finally consecrated it as a constitutional principle.[105] As the organising principles in the design of a new system of conventional courts, unity and hierarchy may perhaps be at least defensible, if not inevitable. But as descriptions of the past they are misleading, and as prescriptions for the future allocation of each and every task of adjudication - public and private, formal and informal, great and small - they may be fatally inadequate.

IV: THE SURVIVAL OF PLURALISM

The suppression of local and special courts in the mid-nineteenth century was in itself an event of considerable significance. It represented the victory of the central, formal legal system over its rivals. But it did not signal the end of a long tradition of pluralism. As has been suggested, at the very moment when the common law courts seemed to be achieving an adjudicative monopoly, they were challenged by new manifestations of pluralism, principally commercial arbitration (which in fact was not new at all) and the administrative regimes which were established with increasing frequency from the early 1830s onwards. It is not possible, within the confines of this essay to trace either of these developments in detail.[106] However, three important themes may be identified.

First, the procedures and substantive norms of civil and criminal law, as administered by conventional legal institutions and personnel, were not perceived by important groups of non-lawyers to be suitable for the social tasks at hand. Whether those tasks involved the resolution of commercial disputes, or the implementation of new, interventionist public policies, "law" - in the formal sense - could not do what needed to be done.

Thus, businessmen often preferred to submit their disputes to arbitration, especially in organised sectors of the economy where exchanges or trade associations or later, chambers of commerce, provided extensive systems of domestic adjudication. Here the parties could place their conflicts in the hands of knowledgeable colleagues rather than judges unfamiliar with business; here they could follow "natural" rather than legal procedures; here they could expect decisions according to trade custom rather than legal doctrine. And, in somewhat analogous fashion, in order to vindicate important regulatory policies, parliament relied primarily upon knowledgeable inspectors and commissioners rather than hostile judges or magistrates, upon informal processes of accommodation and adjudication rather than conventional prosecution or litigation, and upon special statutes, regulations, orders and circulars, rather than upon general rules of civil and criminal law.

In due course, these movements culminated in unsuccessful attempts to legitimate these alternative regimes, to confer upon them the status and powers of courts. Two examples stand out. In 1873, the Railway and Canal Commission was established as a court of record, with extensive powers to discharge its broad regulatory mandate. And in 1874, a twenty year legislative campaign by the business community to establish tribunals of commerce - arbitration tribunals with curial powers - culminated in extensive hearings on the subject by the Judicature Revision Commissioners.

But this was the high-water mark of efforts to secure formal recognition of pluralism within the legal system. The second main theme of the period was the aggressive defence of "law" by judges, lawyers and others who were outraged by the rejection of conventional legal solutions by both businessmen and administrators. To some extent their hostility towards alternative systems can be explained merely in terms of their economic self-interest, to some extent in terms of their ideological opposition to the underlying values and public policies served by these rival regimes, and to some extent in terms of their principled conviction that "law" as they knew it was a social good in and of itself. Whatever the explanation, legal periodicals of the mid-nineteenth century are replete with Dicey-like encomia to the rule of law and indignant protests against administrative and arbitral heresies.

At one level, it might seem that the efforts of the law lobby succeeded. The Railway and Canal Commission was exposed to early and intrusive judicial review, which significantly curtailed its effectiveness. The Judicature Commissioners recommended against the creation of tribunals of commerce with the rather tendentious observation that because their proponents could not all agree on their composition and powers, they should not be established. And the enactment of the Arbitration Act of 1889 completed a process begun fifty years earlier, whereby the common law courts gradually acquired the right to review arbitrators' decisions, and thus to insist that they conform to "law".

These are but examples of a more general tendency to extend and reinforce the hegemony of the formal legal system, and to deny de jure autonomy to alternative legal systems. However, this tendency was more apparent on the surface than in the deep structures of English law.

In the area of commercial disputes, for example, the rejection of tribunals of commerce did not bring businessmen to courts and to law. On the contrary. As Ferguson demonstrates, businessmen used their contractual freedom to create standard-form agreements which, in effect, codified commercial custom and provided a means of avoiding conventional legal rules. In addition, arbitration became even more widespread, and lawyers were so anxious to attract this affluent clientele that some local legal organisations actually established arbitration schemes of their own. Indeed, the creation in 1896, by judicial decree, of the Commercial Court can be seen as the court's response to the continuing competition of informal, non-"legal" adjudication.

In the area of administrative law, inspectorates and government departments and commissions charged with ensuring public health, pure food, proper standards of construction and operation for railways, or safety in factories and mines and aboard emigrant ships, managed to secure increasing levels of compliance with regulatory requirements. However, although they did so within the framework of legislation and against the background of formal legal institutions, neither law nor courts contributed much to their successes: if anything the law and the courts inhibited their efforts. Yet they were able to set standards of proper behaviour through subordinate and quasi-legislation, through orders, circulars and manuals, even through habits and routines of daily administration. And they were able to secure adherence to those standards by negotiation, bluff, compromise, exhortation and education, with only limited recourse to administrative adjudication, and very little reliance upon the courts.

It is true that participants in these informal legal systems made occasional use of law by seeking the aid of courts to enforce their orders. Moreover, they had to confront judicial review occasionally, and therefore to some extent conducted themselves so as to minimise their exposure to adverse judgments. And no doubt conventional legal values, techniques and doctrines were to some extent introduced into the other systems by their legally-trained personnel and advisers, or absorbed from the general political and social culture, which in turn was affected by "law". But to say all of these things is merely to acknowledge that formal law was one influence amongst many which helped to shape the new, special and distinctive regimes of law. Such an acknowledgement does not deny their distinctiveness, much less their very existence. Thus the third important theme in the development of English law in the nineteenth century: de facto, if not de jure, pluralism survived and indeed flourished.

V: CONCLUSION

If the persistence of legal pluralism has been described with even partial accuracy, we must confront a host of important questions. What is the significance of pluralism in terms of our understanding of nineteenth century legal history? What does it tell us, at a theoretical level, about the nature of a legal system and especially about the relationship amongst its constituent parts? And what does our historical experience imply for the future growth and development of our own legal system? These are, concededly, questions too weighty to be supported by the factual foundations which have been laid down here in a partial and speculative manner. But they deserve at least preliminary consideration.

It must first be said that the pluralist hypothesis seems strange only when we juxtapose it with traditional descriptions of the English legal system. There is, however, a growing body of literature which identifies legal pluralism not only in developing countries (of which arguably England was one in the early nineteenth century) but also in other sophisticated, modern industrial nations. Social historians, anthropologists and sociologists would find nothing startling in the proposition that formal institutions and beliefs may compete, or tacitly co-exist, with other systems which they imitate in few relevant particulars.

We gain, therefore, the not very surprising insight that the English legal system once resembled many other systems described in the literature. But when we come to consider why it took the particular shape that it did, and why we have tended to believe it was different, we open up a fruitful line of speculation. General theories relating to the emergence of powerful new economic interests, for example, might well explain the demise of local jurisdictions, and their replacement by a national system of courts which would better serve those interests. But those same theories do not explain why the new county courts should have initially been virtually lawyer-proof, why businessmen could not have their way with parliament on the issue of tribunals of commerce, or how the new regulatory regimes functioned virtually outside the framework of the formal legal system.

Without disputing the fundamental validity of any such general theories, it is necessary to pay closer attention to the role of a particular interest group, the legal profession, and to the impact of its ideology, the rule of law, upon the architecture of the legal system.

It would seem that lawyers were indeed an influential lobby. Their opposition to the old local courts was unrelenting, and their determination to control the new County Courts was outspoken. From the moment Brougham first proposed a system of Local District Courts in 1830, until the new County Courts were fully formed twenty years later, lawyers managed to win one battle after another: elements of mediation and arbitration originally proposed by Brougham were ultimately abandoned; the regime of "equity and good conscience" administered by the courts of requests was replaced by law; fees and costs in the new courts, originally fixed at low levels, were increased so that lawyers could afford to appear; and representation by "low attorneys" was ended, and the ability of parties to represent themselves diminished, leaving lawyers with a much-expanded area of work.

In a rather similar fashion, lawyers were very suspicious of arbitration and hostile to the proposed tribunals of commerce. The latter they managed to forestall, and the former to capture, by statutory and common law rules relating to review and enforcement of awards, by the development of standard legal instruments outlining the form of the submission and other aspects of arbitration procedure, and by themselves becoming arbitrators. Indeed, arbitration was used extensively by courts throughout the period as an ancillary institution, especially in regard to certain types of fact finding.

Administrative law presents a picture which is more subtle, but not dissimilar. Lawyers and their ideology did indeed manage to deny autonomy and legitimacy to the administration, particularly to independent boards and commissions. The unhelpful decisions of judges in proceedings arising out of the new regulatory regimes occasionally paralysed and demoralised them. The law officers of the crown often played a cautious and conservative role, reining in administrative initiatives, and narrowly defining the limits of administrative powers. And rule-of-law ideology quite clearly influenced parliament at critical junctures, as for example in the design of the Railway and Canal Commission, which was left vulnerable to pervasive judicial review.

Yet it must be said that if the forces of law could muster sufficient strength to win numerous battles against local supporters of the courts of requests and others, against businessmen who wished to avoid recourse to law, and against the moral entrepreneurs and professionals who conceived and implemented new schemes of regulation, they did not necessarily win all the wars. The legal profession opposed the very notion of the county courts, of arbitration, of administrative tribunals - yet all of these came into existence (albeit imperfectly formed) and performed useful "legal" work at or beyond the conventionally assumed boundaries of law.

For those who can accept a degree of indeterminacy in the very notion of law, this description poses no particular difficulties. However, the existence of indeterminacy cannot be denied. If law is simply a congeries of social facts, the presence or absence of formal legitimacy is not a matter of great significance. But if law is formal legitimacy - the "command of the sovereign", "what judges will do in fact" - pluralism becomes much more problematic. We can then define a disparate collection of activities, processes and actors that look like law only by reference to it. Decisions of administrative tribunals may be "law" if they are mandated by statute and enforced by courts. Yet decisions of domestic tribunals and similar bodies may not be "law" if they lack either characteristic. A statute is "law" because it is enacted by a competent legislature, although no one bothers about it, and it is seldom enforced in fact. Yet a custom is not law even if it moulds the conduct of important social groups or business communities and violators are exposed to significant sanctions.

There is more at stake here than terminological precision. If we accept a definition of "law" which equates it with formal legitimacy, our interpretation of historical (and contemporary) events may differ greatly from what it would be if "law" were given a more extended meaning. For example, we might be inclined to treat the decline of local and special jurisdictions in the nineteenth century as highly desirable because it contributed to the universality and systemic simplicity of law, or to deplore the growth of administrative law on the grounds that it deprived people of access to "real" law. In contemporary terms, the promotion of alternative legal systems, such as arbitration or neighbourhood courts, might look more attractive if it is viewed as but another manifestation of the pluralist tradition in law rather than as the negation of law for those strong enough to escape law's limitations or weak enough to be despoiled of its protection.

Needless to say, battles about any of these developments will ultimately not be decided by the capture of the high ground of definition. But definition is a weapon, if not an end in itself. "Law" is a value-laden term in our society, and those who can claim it as their own have secured an important advantage. At the same time, "law" is a notion which possesses when it is itself possessed, as E.P. Thompson has tried to show us. Is it not possible that self-conscious participation in "law", in its pluralist sense, was - and is - a positive virtue, contributing to stability, vitality and civility within the modest confines of everyday life?

NOTES

* This essay is based upon a paper originally presented to a Conference on the Imposition of Law at the University of Warwick in 1978, and draws upon work for a forthcoming book to be published under the title of 'Without the Law': Legal Pluralism and Administrative Law in Nineteenth Century England. I am anxious to acknowledge the hospitality of the Centre for Socio-Legal Studies, Oxford, where my research was initially pursued, the financial support of the Canada Council and the Social Sciences and Humanities Research Council of Canada, and especially the invaluable research assistance of Heather Leonoff, B.A. (Man.), LL.B. (York).

1. W.S. Holdsworth (A.L. Goodhart and H.G. Hanbury eds.), History of English Law, Vol. xiv (London: Methuen, 1964), p.182. He also records the continuing assertion by the central courts of common law of the right to control rival courts, tribunals and officials, at pp.182-3, an issue discussed infra.
2. B. Webb and S. Webb, English Local Government from the Revolution to the Municipal Corporations Act: The Parish and the County (London: Longman Green, 1906), p.vi.
3. See generally H. Perkin, The Origins of Modern English Society 1780-1880 (London: Routledge, 1976); P. Mathias, The First Industrial Nation (London: Methuen, 1969); E.P. Thompson, The Making of the English Working Class (Harmondsworth: Pelican, 1968).
4. Holdsworth, supra, note 1, Vol. i, p.188.
5. A typology of these courts was developed by R. Maugham in Outlines of the Jurisdiction of all the Courts in England and Wales (London: Spettigue, 1838). He identified the "inferior courts of common law" (the Court of Pie Poudre, the Court Baron, the Hundred Court, the County Court); the "courts of bankruptcy and insolvency" (the Court of Review, the Commissioners' Courts,

and the Court for the Relief of Insolvent Debtors); "Courts of special or local jurisdiction" (the Court of the Commissioners of Sewers, the Marshalsea and Palace Court, the Court of the Duchy of Lancaster, the County Palatine Courts, the Stannary Courts, the Courts of Cities and Boroughs, and Courts of Requests, and the Courts of the Universities); as well as numerous "ecclesiastical and maritime courts", courts "whose jurisdiction has been transferred, abolished or become obsolete", and criminal courts of "local, private or special jurisdiction". See also A.H. Manchester, A Modern Legal History of England and Wales, 1750-1950 (London: Butterworths, 1980), ch.5.

6. "Provincial Courts in England for the Recovery of Small Debts", Fourth Report of the Commissioners Appointed to Enquire into the Practice and Proceedings of the Superior Courts of Common Law (hereafter "Fourth Report") no.239 (1832), Appendix I, part V: "Return of all Process issued from Borough Courts, County Courts, Liberty Courts, Hundred Courts, Manor Courts, and Courts of Requests . . . ." It must be noted that these data related to a slightly later period than the "early nineteenth century" referred to by Holdsworth. No figures are available covering the three preceding decades. However, of the 13 largest courts (in each of which over 5,000 cases were commenced), 12 were in operation in 1800 including two courts whose jurisdiction was later statutorily revised; only one of the 13 was established as late as 1809.

7. Over 250,000 civil cases were commenced in the 47 largest local courts in 1830, distributed as follows:

1,000 - 2,000 cases	21 courts
2,000 - 5,000 cases	13 courts
5,000 - 10,000 cases	6 courts
over - 10,000 cases	7 courts.

(Source: Fourth Report, supra, note 6). By contrast, in the central courts in Westminster, barely one-third of that total, about 90,000 cases, were commenced annually, on average, at about the same time (1824-28), T. Snagge, Evolution of the County Court (London: Clowes, 1904), p.8.

8. See *infra*, "The Relationship between Superior and Local Courts".

9. These courts will not be dealt with, but see generally Holdsworth, *supra*, note 1, Vol.i, p.633 ff.

10. For example, the County Courts (established in 1846) were intended to offer the convenience of the local courts, but without many of their weaknesses; the doctrines of the law merchant were absorbed first into common law doctine, and then into legislation; and the summary procedures of arbitrators were imitated by the Commercial Court (from 1896). See *infra*.

11. For example, a limited statutory right of appeal from decisions of the County Courts was provided from the date of their establishment, County Courts Act, 1846, 9 & 10 Vict., c.95, ss.89, 90, and was later broadened, County Courts Extension Act, 1850, 13 & 14 Vict., c.61, ss.14-16. Similarly, stated case procedures were initially to be invoked by arbitrators, Common Law Procedure Act, 1854, 17 & 18 Vict., c.125, s.5, but subsequently by order of the court, Arbitration Act, 1889, 52 & 53 Vict., c.49, s.19.

12. "Local Courts of Special Jurisdiction", Report of the Royal Commission on Assizes and Quarter Sessions (hereafter "Beeching Report", 1969 Cmnd. 4153, c.X; Courts Act, Stat. 1971, c.23, ss.41-43; Administration of Justice Act, Stat. 1977, c.38, s.23, Schedule 4, part II.

13. Holdsworth, *supra*, note 1, Vol.xiv, p.188; B. Webb and S. Webb, English Local Government from the Revolution to the Municipal Corporations Act: the Manor and the Borough (London: Longmans Green, 1908), chs.1 & 2.

14. A.V. Dicey (E.C.S. Wade ed.), The Law of the Constitution (10th ed.) (London: McMillan, 1965), pp.183-93.

15. See generally Holdsworth, *supra*, note 1, Vol.i, ch.2; G.J. Thompson, "The Development of the Anglo-American Judicial System", Cornell Law Quarterly, Vol.17 (1931), pp.9-42, 203-47, 395-458.

16. E.P.Thompson, Whigs and Hunters: The Origin of the Black Act (London: Penguin, 1975).

17. J.P. Dawson, A History of Lay Judges (Cambridge: Harvard, 1960), p.180. However, the significance of the 40s. limit should not be over-emphasised for two reasons. First, 40s. was still a considerable amount of money in 1800: just over 1% of the population had a weekly income of £2.10s. per week in 1800; agricultural workers earned only about 8s.-10s, per week, unskilled industrial workers about 18s., and skilled artisans 25-40s. See Perkin, supra, note 3, p.135, Mathias, supra, note 3, p.219. Second, of the thirteen largest local courts, each disposing of over 5,000 cases per year in 1830, only five had a 40s. limit, seven had jurisdiction up to £5, and one had unlimited jurisdiction. Fourth Report, supra, note.6.

18. This categorisation deliberately ignores the various methods by which courts were originally established or their mandates renewed: custom or prescription, legislation, franchise, charter or prerogative grant. There is no consistent pattern. However, by the eighteenth century legislation was the only method by which new tribunals were created (aside from consensual bodies such as arbitration tribunals).

19. Holdsworth, supra, note 1, Vol.i, p.109; P. Archer, The Queen's Courts (Baltimore: Penguin, 1969), p.145; P.N. Walker, The Courts of Law (Devon: David and Charles, 1970), pp.153-5.

20. Anon., Rules and Orders in the Court of the County of Durham (n.p., 1775); W.D. Evans, The Practice of the Court of Common Pleas for the County Palatine of Lancaster (n.p., 1813); W.R. Ordnall, The Practice of the Court of Great Sessions on the Carmarthen Circuit (London: Butterworth, 1814).

21. First Report of the Common Law Commissioners (hereafter "First Report") 1829, (46) p.1; Act for the more effectual Administration of Justice in England and Wales, 1830, 11 Geo. IV and 1 Will. IV, c.70, s.14.

22. See e.g., H. Brougham, "State of the Courts of Common Law", 18 Hansard 127

at p.146 ff. (Feb.7, 1828); First Report, supra, note 21, p.40.

23. See e.g. evidence of Messrs Minshall and Sabine, Atty's., favouring suppression of the Welsh courts: "[A] considerable number of Ancient Britons [are opposed] because they do not like to see the ancient institutions of their country changed, and made like English ones." First Report, supra, note 21, Appendix E, p.393.

24. See e.g. evidence of D.S. Davies, Barr. and Chairman of Quarter Sessions County of Cardigan: "[J]ustice is administered cheaply and at the suitors' own doors." First Report, supra, note 21, Appendix E, p.383. The abolition of the Welsh courts in 1830 meant that all claims of over 40s. had to be sued for at Westminster, a "considerable hardship on Welsh suitors", W.B. Odgers, "Changes in Procedure and in the Law of Evidence", in A Century of Law Reform (London: Macmillan, 1901, p.231).

25. The Courts Act, Stat. 1971, c.23, s.41.

26. Holdsworth, supra, note 1, Vol.i, p.64 ff.; Snagge, supra, note 7: A.L. Cross, "Old English Local Courts and the Movement for their Reform", Michigan Law Review, Vol.30 (1931), pp.369-85.

27. Supra, note 1, Vol.i, p.65.

28. Fifth Report of the Common Law Commissioners, (hereafter "Fifth Report") 1833, (247), p.18.

29. Of the 48 local courts in which over 1,000 actions were commenced in 1830, 19 were County Courts, or were derived from other medieval jurisdictions. However, of the 13 busiest courts (5,000 or more actions) only 3 were County Courts. Most of the rest (statutorily-created, primarily in the late eighteenth century) were called "Courts of Requests". First Report, supra, note 6.

30. Snagge, supra, note 7, p.8. The apparent folly of launching an action under such circumstances may perhaps be explained in three ways. First, relatively few actions actually were tried; many no doubt resulted in out-of-court

settlements and uncontested judgments. Second, a small number of cases may have been launched in which damages were not the real or principal relief sought. And third, in many cases, no other forum except the central courts may have had jurisdiction to hear the case.

31. "Provincial Courts in England for the Recovery of Small Debts", Fifth Report, supra, note 28.

32. An Act for the more easy Recovery of Small Debts and Demands in England, 9 & 10 Vict., c.95.

33. Supra, note 28, p.11.

34. Supra, note 21, p.40.

35. Submission of the Magistrates of the County of Glamorgan, who so described themselves. First Report, supra, note 21, Appendix E, p.386. See also, e.g., submission of John Denton, Barr., id., p.460.

36. Evidence of John Jones, M.P. Barr., Chairman of Quarter Sessions, County of Carmarthen, First Report, supra, note 21, Appendix E, p.391.

37. Snagge, supra, note 7, p.10. These features had been a critical part of Brougham's strategy for law reform: "[T]he great means of shortening litigation are to be found in an enlargement of our law of arbitrament . . . " 18 Hansard 127 at 190 (Feb.7, 1828).

38. The 1833 Report itself had recommended that the new courts should have simple procedures, that actions should not be dismissed for "want of form", that lawyers should be able to recover only a limited amount in respect of costs (thus discouraging legal representation), and that the parties should be encouraged to settle their differences, supra, note 28, pp.18-30; Snagge, supra, note 7, p.22 ff.

39. Snagge, supra, note 7, p.23.

40. Snagge remarks ". . . [T]housands [of cases] were settled out of court in consequence of the intimation which the speedy despatch of business gave to debtors and wrong-doers that it was vain to resist compliance with just

demands . . .", supra, note 7, at p.14.

41. D. Hay, "Property, Authority and the Criminal Law", in D. Hay, P. Linebaugh, J.G. Rule, E.P. Thompson & C. Winslow (eds.), Albion's Fatal Tree (New York: Pantheon, 1975), p.62; Webb and Webb, supra, note 2, pp.319-64; Perkin, supra, note 3, pp.40-2.

42. See e.g. the description of the magistracy in several industrial communities in Webb and Webb, supra, note 2, pp.575-85; Perkin, supra, note 3, pp.398-9.

43. Evidence of G. Offor and J.G. Hammuck, Commissioners of the Court of Requests for Tower Hamlets, Fifth Report, supra, note 28, Appendix B, p.453. This was a local court, but hardly a typical one; in 1831, the Commissioners disposed of 22,885 cases.

44. W. Hutton, Courts of Requests (Birmingham: Pearson & Rollason, 1787). Hutton appends to his treatise an account of 99 cases decided by him as a Commissioner (judge) of the Birmingham Court of Requests over a period of fifteen years. Amongst the many examples given of reliance upon equity and conscience, rather than legal principle, is Case IV (at p.85). In that case, a neighbourhood pump broke down and was repaired on the orders of the plaintiff, one of the users; the defendant, another user, refused to pay his share of the costs. Held: the plaintiff recovered from the defendant. It is difficult to imagine how an eighteenth (or even twentieth) century court could have given the plaintiff a remedy on purely legal grounds. However, W.H.D. Winder, "The Courts of Requests", Law Quarterly Review, Vol.52 (1936), p.369 at p.375 suggests that, at a later period, courts of requests tended to follow legal rules.

45. Evidence of Sir John Cross, sometime Professional Chairman of the Manchester court: "Lawyers who have been accustomed only to the slow process of interrogation by the testimony of witnesses and the details of circumstantial evidence, can have no idea of the facility and despatch with which the truth can be ascertained by bringing the parties face to face . . . ."

Fifth Report, supra, note 28, Appendix B, p.420.

46. Each Court of Requests was established by a special, local statute. However, the statutes largely conformed to a common pattern. See e.g. London Court of Requests Act, 1800, 39 & 40 Geo.III, c.104, s.5 and Cirencester Court of Requests Act, 1792, 32 Geo.III, c.77, s.29, for typical privative clauses.

47. Fifth Report, supra, note 28, p.11.

48. Id.

49. Id., at p.12.

50. The County Courts Act, 1846, s.5, provided that existing local and specialised courts might be merged into the new system by order-in-council. See also s.14. Over a period of time, many such courts were wound up, but some exercised judicial functions (or remained theoretically free to do so) until the present time. See Courts Act, 1971, c.23, s.43; Administration of Justice Act, 1977, c.38, s.23.

51. Snagge, supra, note 7, p.14.

52. F. Pollock and F.W. Maitland, (S.F.C. Milsom, ed.) "Introduction to the second Edition", The History of English Law 2nd rev. ed. (Cambridge: University Press, 1968), Vol.1, at p.xxx, emphasis added.

53. Holdsworth, supra, note 1, Vol.xiv, pp.187-96; E.S. Wolaver, "The Historical Background of Commercial Arbitration", University of Pennsylvania Law Review, Vol.83 (1934), pp.132-146.

54. Pollock and Maitland, supra, note 52, pp.468-75.

55. Thompson, supra, note 16, p.36 ff.

56. G.R. Lewis, The Stannaries, (Cambridge: Riverside, 1908).

57. J. Goebel, "King's Law and Local Custom in Seventeenth Century New England", Columbia Law Review, Vol.31, (1931) at p.417 suggests: "So accustomed are we to focus our attention upon expansion of the 'King's law' that we have closed our eyes to the fact that at the end of the seventeenth century, local custom and local courts were still an immensely important part

of the law administration in England . . . . [T]he law of England was something greater and more multiform than that of the courts at Westminster." For developments in the eighteenth century, see Webb and Webb, supra, note 13, chs.1 and 2.

58. The Fifth Report, supra, note 28, p.17, points out that the jurisdiction of the old local courts was based on the assumption that real property, rather than commercial wealth, was the primary subject of litigation. Hence, the linkage between local courts and local law. While this suggestion is undoubtedly accurate in relation to manor courts, it is obviously inapplicable to the courts of requests which dealt only with monetary claims and had no jurisdiction to decide disputes involving title to property.

59. Beeching Report, supra, note 12.

60. Supra, note 17, ch.iv.

61. But Webb and Webb, supra, note 13, at p.17, n.4, suggest that lawyers did appear at least in some exceptional cases.

62. B. Abel-Smith and R. Stevens, Lawyers and the Courts (Cambridge: Harvard, 1967), p.12.

63. Perkin, supra, note 3, pp.125-7.

64. Supra, note 22, pp.171-2.

65. Supra, note 1, Vol.i, pp.94, 99-100.

66. Id., p.104.

67. Supra, note 16, p.36 ff.

68. Lewis, supra, note 56; Holdsworth, supra, note 1, Vol.i, p.151 ff.

69. C. Woodsworth, Joint Stock Companies (London: Saunders & Benning, 1842). The court was reorganised by the Stannaries Act, 1836, 6 & 7 Will. IV, c.106.

70. The business of the Stannary Court was transferred to the County Court by 59 & 60 Vict., c.45.

71. Second Report of the Judicature Commissioners, (hereafter "Second Report") 1872 C.631-I, XX, Vol.II, pt.II, Evidence, at n.471 ff.

72. Evidently, some final efforts to revive ancient forest rights were made in 1831. In that year a statute (1 & 2 Will. IV, c.12) authorised the appointment of a Commission to ascertain the Boundaries of the Forest of Dean, to explore the rights and privileges claimed by "the Free Miners of the Hundred of Saint Briavel's", to inquire into "the Constitution, Powers, Jurisdiction and Practice of a Court called the Mine Law Court", and to define certain interests in quarries and in the taking of timber. Further legislation was enacted as late as 1861, see C.E. Hart, The Verderers and Speech-Court of the Forest of Dean (Gloucester: Bellows, 1950), and The Free Miners (Gloucester: British Publishing, 1953).

73. The Wild Creatures and Forest Laws Act, Stat. 1971, c.47, s.1, "abrogates" forest law, although preserving any rights of common originating in it.

74. Supra, note 16, p.240.

75. Id., p.261.

76. All published decisions of the superior courts for 1830 were read. This source of information is subject to two obvious weaknesses. First, it is not clear that all cases decided by those courts in 1830 would have been reported, especially those confined to factual issues which collaterally involved issues also triable in the local or special courts. Second, the activity of the superior courts is being contrasted with that of other courts for the same year. Actual review of 1830 local court decisions would require scrutiny of superior court decisions in later years; in view of the uncertain time delays (especially where collateral review is involved) this exercise was not undertaken. However, since what is being assessed is the relative order of magnitude of original and review decisions, it is unlikely that these two weaknesses produce any serious distortion.

77. Common rights: Codling v. Johnson, (1830), 8 L.J. Rep.68 (K.B.); Doe & Sweeting v. Wellard & Griffiths, (1830), 8 L.J. Rep.79 (K.B.); Maxwell v. Martin, (1830), 8 L.J. Rep.174 (C.P.); Disputes involving tithes, access to

chapel etc.: Madison v. Nuttall, (1830), 8 L.J. Rep.27 (C.P.); Shepherd v. Bishop of Chester, (1830), 8 L.J. Rep.141 (C.P.); Lediard v. Anstie, (1830), 148 E.R. 1297 (Exch. Ch. in Eq.); Beck v. Bree, (1830), 148 E.R. 1410 (Exch. of Pleas); Denchfield v. Stong, (1830), 5 E.R. 28 (H.L.); Use of customary weights and measures: Watts v. Friend, (1830), 8 L.J. Rep. 181 (K.B.); Liability to market toll: Stamford v. Pawlett, (1830), 148 E.R. 1334 (Exch. of Pleas).

78. Bingham v. Woodgate, (1830), 8 L.J. Rep.46 (Ch.).

79. Richards v. Bassett, (1830), 8 L.J. Rep.289 (K.B.).

80. King v. Scrivener's Company, (1830), 8 L.J. Rep.199 (K.B.).

81. King v. Wilson, (1830), 8 L.J. Rep.10 (K.B.).

82. In matter of Sutton, (1830), 8 L.J. Rep.7 (K.B.).

83. Davis v. Jones, (1830), 8 L.J. Rep.88 (K.B.).

84. Wright v. Nuttall, (1830), 8 L.J. Rep.188 (K.B.); Smith v. Hurrell, (1830), 8 L.J. Rep.198 (K.B.); Copland v. Jacobs, (1830), 8 L.J. Rep.321 (K.B.); Rothery v. Munnings, (1830), 8 L.J. Rep.387 (K.B.); Harris v. Widdowson, (1830), 8 L.J. Rep.122 (C.P.); but c.f. Andres v. Phillips, (1830), 8 L.J. Rep.122 (C.P.).

85. Hall v. Taylor, (1830), 8 L.J. Rep.180 (K.B.); Furnish v. Swan, (1830), 8 L.J. Rep.224 (K.B.); Clarke v. Denton, (1830), 8 L.J. Rep.333 (K.B.); Godley v. Marsden, (1830), 8 L.J. Rep.138 (C.P.).

86. Administration of Justice Act, Stat. 1977, c.38, s.23, Schedule 4, part II.

87. Administration of Justice Act, 1977, Schedule 4, part III.

88. Fifth Report, supra, note 28, p.12.

89. Second Report, supra, note 71, pp.18-19: "We . . . recommend the abolition of all local and inferior courts of civil jurisdiction. If they did not exist no one would think of establishing them."

90. Beeching Report, supra, note 12, p.123: ". . . [I]f they were seen to meet some real and important need locally we did not wish to recommend their abolition without being sure that the system which we proposed would fulfil such need whenever it might exist . . . ."(115) But ". . . [a]s these courts are practically

moribund, we leave it to the Government to decide whether formal termination of their existence is worthwhile."

91. Supra, note 17, p.285.

92. Supra, note 17, c.v.

93. Hay, supra, note 41; Thompson, supra, note 16, pp.250-4.

94. Supra, note 57, p.417.

95. Indeed Goebel himself refrains from making such anachronistic judgments, supra, note 57, pp.420-1.

96. Supra, note 16, pp.240-1.

97. Id., pp.39-40.

98. F. Frankfurter, "Forward to a Discussion of Current Developments in Administrative Law", Yale Law Journal, Vol.47, (1938), p.515.

99. Supra, note 16, p.261.

100. Supra, note 3, c.8 & 9, esp. p.328 ff. A striking example was the "ancient constitution" of the Crowley Iron Works in the eighteenth century. This private legal code, frequently amended, and administered by a court of arbitration and other internally-established bodies, in effect governed the life of Crowley workers both as employees and as residents of the Crowley estates. "The Crowley Kingdom obtained its own laws as the laws of England gave up trying to control industrial relationships." A. Harding, A Social History of English Law (Baltimore: Penguin, 1966), p.327. See also Mathias, supra, note 3, pp.153-4.

101. But they did linger in some communities, apparently, see Administration of Justice Act, 1977, Schedule 4, part II.

102. In Manchester, an atypical case, the Court Leet of the Manor of Manchester had evolved into a virtual municipal government, until purchased by the Town Council in 1846 for £200,000. See Webb & Webb, supra, note 13, p.99 ff.

103. See e.g. Brougham, supra, note 22, at pp.171-2.

104. The possibility that special groups in the community might wish to establish

their own tribunals was apparently thought to be a sufficient reason for not permitting any such experiments. See Royal Commission on the Judicature, App. to Third Report and Mins. of Evid. relating to Tribunals of Commerce (hereafter "Third Report" 1874, c.957-I. xxiv, questions 642, 1049.

105. See e.g. the strictures of Dicey at what he understood to be the special status of public officials in France, under the droit administratif, supra, note 14, ch.xii.

106. See generally R.B. Ferguson, "The Adjudication of Commercial Disputes and the Legal System in Modern England", British Journal of Law and Society, Vol.7, p.141; H.W. Arthurs, "Jonah and the Whale: The Appearance, Disappearance and Reappearance of Administrative Law", University of Toronto Law Journal, Vol.30, p.225.

LEGISLATIVE DIVORCE - LAW FOR THE ARISTOCRACY? *

Stuart Anderson

The passing of the 1857 Matrimonial Causes Act, wrote the historian of divorce, signified nothing except that the upper-middle class henceforward had access to the previously upper class institution of divorce à vinculo matrimonii[1]. This opinion, the first precedents set by early aristocratic petitioners and the evidence of costs asserted by the Campbell Commission in 1853 has usually been enough for commentators to conclude that before 1858 divorce was indeed the prerogative of the aristocracy. The purpose of this essay is to investigate who were the petitioners for the extraordinary privilege of the right to remarry. Apart from the intrinsic interest of studying access to legal process, it is hoped to provide some background against which to see the bitter debates of the 1850s over the institution of marriage. For if, as I shall argue, the upper-middle class had always had access to legislative divorce, the 1857 Act cannot have made the qualitative difference assigned to it. Further, it will be more difficult to argue that demand for divorce from the upper-middle class, if such there was, can be explained by a real, as opposed to a perceived, exclusion theretofore. Further still, doubt may be cast upon the reliability of the Campbell Commission, on which many commentators base their views. Finally, and more tentatively, it is hoped to trace the changing rates of application for statutory divorce, and suggest reasons for its fluctuation.

Strictly speaking, English law forbade remarriage after a divorce. Ecclesiastical courts could grant divorces à mensa et thoro, but these expressly did not permit remarriage. A decree of nullity, again from the ecclesiastical courts, might sometimes serve the function of divorce and, by holding a "marriage" void, allow the "spouses" to remarry. Lack of age, lack of consent, informality, affinity or consanguinity could all have this effect; and there can be no doubt that in some cases the parties saw this as a form of divorce. There will probably have been cases of collusion to provide the court with the necessary evidence. But since these defects had to have been present at the beginning of the marriage, their usefulness to spouses who wanted to divorce - as it were - and remarry was somewhat random. As with so many other areas where the regular law disappointed, resort to the omnicompetent Parliament gave relief to those who could pay. The aristocratic precedents were set late in the seventeenth century and are well known;[2] of the 370 or more petitioners who followed them only a dozen or so have been remembered.

The early precedents established the conditions under which a private Act dissolving a marriage and enabling remarriage could be obtained. Statutory divorce was to be for adultery only, it would not be developed to duplicate other remedies, and it was to be a matter of last resort, available only after a divorce à mensa et thoro had been obtained from an ecclesiastical court.[3] Much later, when the question first arose, an additional element was required of a woman petitioner, that her husband's adultery must have been aggravated by an additional enormity like bigamy or incest. However, Parliament did not regard itself as a court of revision, merely checking that the ecclesiastical court divorce had been properly granted. The case had to be proved in its entirety before both Houses, though in time the Lords became as dominant in this as in other classes of private business like estate Acts.[4] To this end, the court documents from the proceedings for the divorce à mensa et thoro were usually, and from 1798 were required to be, forwarded to Parliament so that any discrepancies in the evidence could be investigated.[5] Since the lower court proceedings were almost entirely written, with witnesses giving evidence in writing before a court official and answering written interrogatories, the Lords, where bills were always introduced first, would know a great deal about a bill even before it came on to be heard. In Parliament evidence was given orally and was subject to cross-examination both by counsel, if they appeared, and by members of the Houses. However, the ecclesiastical court papers could not always be relied upon to disclose the whole truth,[6] for not only was cross-examination not allowed in those courts, but, more importantly, the case might not have been defended. If the defendant was willing for there to be a divorce, all manner of collusion, connivance, condonation, or ill-treatment by the plaintiff might be suppressed and, so it was argued, statutes might then be granted to undeserving petitioners. To discourage such collusion, petitioning husbands came to be required to have sued the adulterer at common law for the tort of criminal conversation - adultery with the plaintiff's wife.[7] This requirement had a further advantage for those hostile to granting divorces, that the prospect of paying heavy damages and facing public shame might induce the adulterer to defend himself in court, so that facts detrimental to the husband's petition to Parliament might become public knowledge. This requirement was not always insisted upon; it depended upon how much the Lords wished to deter statutory divorces.

This multi-stage procedure, together with the high rank of the first petitioners, has suggested an aristocratic institution designed mainly to protect the purity of the blood. This would explain the low number of petitions (Table I), for if the main object of aristocratic marriage was to provide sufficient heirs to ensure continuity of title and estate, a wife's adultery only threatened a marriage if she was still fertile but had insufficient legitimate sons. A change in the nature of marriage, it can be argued, allied with the growth of a class uncommitted to primogeniture, opened this aristocratic institution to the upper-middle class after several decades of pressure.[8] This essay suggests that if there was such a process it rested upon a misperception of men using it. When Bishop Horsley protested in 1800 that ". . . divorce bills had been applied for and obtained, not merely by the higher ranks, but even by tradesmen and mechanics",[9] he was more right than wrong.

TABLE I

Petitions for divorce[1] and their outcome.

	new petitions			subseq. pets.	statutes[4]	withdrawn or rejected	other[2]
	men		women				
	from British Isles	from India[3]					
1700-50	20			4	14	5	5
1751-60	18			1	16	2	1
1761-70	13			0	12	1	0
1771-80	35			3	33	3	2
1781-90	20			3	15	6	2
1791-1800	41	2		3[5]	40	4	2
1801-10	29	2	2	6	23	13	3
1811-20	34	1		1	27	7	1
1821-30	28	8		6	33	8	2
1831-40	30	9	3	3	34	7	3
1841-50	41[6]	12	2	5	53	8	0
1851-57	22	5[7]		2	22	5	2

Notes:

1. Petitions for separation or nullity are excluded, even if styled as divorce bills.
2. Petitions tabled but not proceeded with; dropped pending appeal to higher ecclesiastical court; prorogation.
3. This includes men petitioning in England by power of attorney from India and men using the Indian procedure under the terms of 1 G.IV cap. 101 (1820).
4. The figures for a particular decade may fail to balance, because for some Indian petitions, there was a delay between petition and the Act.
5. Includes one who first petitioned 12 years earlier.
6. Includes Joseph Cotterill who petitioned in England concerning events in Australia - unsuccessfully.
7. Excludes James Edward Dickinson who petitioned in 1857 and whose Act was passed in 1859.

Table II shows the number of petitions, both original and subsequent, from men from the British Isles, i.e., excluding men petitioning from India[10] and women, and the resulting number of statutes.

TABLE II

Decadal application and success rates for men from British Isles

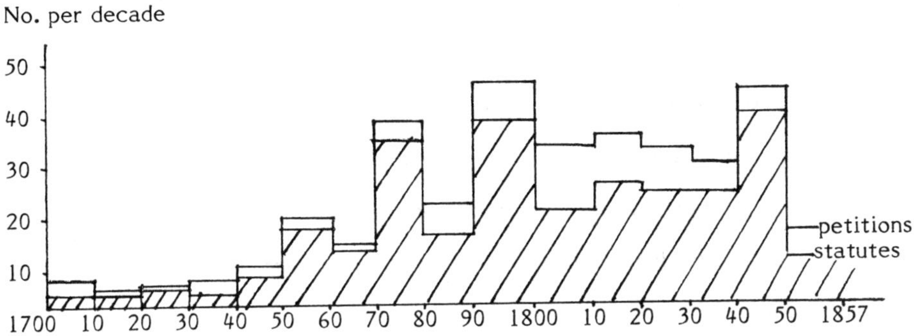

The model of social structure devised by Gregory King for fiscal purposes has been used in adapted forms by many historians and will be used here.[11] More sophisticated models dividing into segments both King's "middle" and "lower" bands may be useful for political analysis, but were not designed for questions of social stratification here being considered. King's first six "ranks, degrees, titles and qualifications" range from the great temporal peers down to the amorphous "gentlemen" and together form the landed classes. His next twelve ranks comprise the "middle orders," a wide range of wealth and status from the merchants, bankers and successful barristers who could hope to move into the upper ranks or see their children do so, down to the shopkeepers and tradesmen who were sometimes only a short step above the artisans and craftsmen of the lower orders. Changes in this model to accommodate the development of a separate group of "manufacturers," to allow for changes in the ranks of the clergy and ultimately to deal with the emergence of the modern professions may be made reasonably easily without affecting the underlying premises. The more major changes needed to the division between "middle" and "lower" do not affect us, since no petitioner for a statutory divorce came from the lower orders, though a few had belonged there at the time of their marriage.

Allocation of an individual to a precise place on the social ladder is complicated by the openness of English society, which allowed men both to rise and to fall. John Braithwaite (1777), for example, was the son of a colonel who had commanded the Africa Company's factories on the south coast of Africa; he lost the whole of his fortune to professional gamesters, started his own career as only an ensign in the East India Company, but had reached the rank of colonel by the time of his divorce; later he became commander-in-chief of the Madras army and died a baronet.[12] Further, to place petitioners by rank may be to underestimate the importance of personal qualities and style of life. Charles Francois Dumergue, for example, was a dentist, and as such he came well down King's list. But he had a coach, several servants, a fashionable address and an ambition that made him one of the royal dentists by 1785 and sole royal dentist in time to hand the position on to his nephew when he retired.[13] However, when he divorced his wife in 1779 he was just one of several fashionable dentists, and the alimony he allowed her was only £50 a year. Certainly he was middle ranking; but ambitious, able and, most interestingly, closely connected with the upper ranks, albeit in a servile capacity.

Statutory divorce was more the preserve of the upper ranks during the first half of the eighteenth century than at any later time.[14] Of the twenty petitioners between 1700 and 1750 three were English or Irish peers, four baronets, one a knight and six, probably seven, were landed gentlemen.[15] Only five belong clearly to King's middle ranks: Stephen Jermyn (1707-1711), son of a London merchant and once apprenticed in the wine trade; Ralph Box (1700), who described himself as a Citizen and grocer of London, and later as a druggist; Corbyn Morris (1746), who was just starting a career leading into the higher reaches of the customs service;

Francis Annesley (1725), son of the eminent lawyer who features in Egmont's diary, he gained his LL.D., his first parish and his divorce all in the same year after a clandestine marriage six years previously; and Thomas Cobb (1728). Cobb had been an engraver when he married Rachel Krebs, the servant daughter of a tailor. When she disappeared he "married" again, and after that "wife's" death he wanted to marry his business partner, a widow worth £500 a year according to Rachel, who had reappeared and wanted buying off. Cobb had risen from the lower ranks, and cannot be thought of as poor; but neither can he compare in status with any of the other petitioners. His success is a reminder of the openness of English institutions, especially as his conduct divided both Houses.

Annesley's was not the only clandestine marriage. The wives of Sir John Rudd (1733) and Stephen Jermyn were both alleged to be "lewd women," in the latter case the seller of oysters at a tavern door. There were two similar cases in the early 1750s and a couple a little later,[16] adding credence to Lord Hardwicke's claim that Fleet marriages and the increasing divorce rate were linked. It is noticeable, however, that Rudd was the only upper class husband of these, the rest were mainly merchants or other wealthy middle rankers. It is also noticeable that such marriages were treated differently in Parliament. In "genuine" marriages wives commonly petitioned Parliament in their defence or retained counsel to contest the bill, indeed five[17] of them defeated their husbands by one means or another. Only Mrs Jermyn of the clandestine wives contested the principle of the bill, delaying its passage by four years. Some clandestine wives argued that financial provision should be made for them, but all seem to have failed. Many regular wives also fought for provision, but they commonly succeeded - though some had to make do with property that their own families had once possessed. Finally, there are differences in clauses bastardising children of the guilty couple. For clandestine wives these commonly date from the time of separation of the spouses or even, when the marriage was very short-lived, from the date of the marriage itself. But for regular wives there is more variety, with the date of the divorce à mensa et thoro becoming more popular in the 1750s, or a date nine months after the separation. Whether these differences reflect different perceptions by Parliament or the different resources and bargaining power of the wives is difficult to say.

The pattern changes after about 1750. The rate of application quickened, a greater proportion succeeded, fewer petitions concerned clandestine marriages and the balance between the upper and middle orders shifted markedly away from the aristocracy. To demonstrate this it is necessary to identify as many as possible of the 66 petitioners between 1750 and 1780. Of the 66, there were six peers, the son of a Scottish representative peer and three baronets, two of whom were brothers-in-law.[18] The eleven other landed gentlemen[19] include several with familial links with the peerage and, at the margin perhaps, George Collier, a naval captain who later resigned his commission at not being rewarded with the baronetcy he thought he deserved. Thomas Bailey Heath Sewell should be included here; the son of the Master of the Rolls, he married the daughter of the Earl of Louth, but spent much time hiding from creditors before inheriting his father's estates five years after his divorce. John Eliot (or Elliott) should also be listed among the upper orders, for although only a physician he was patronised by Lord Melbourne, became physician to the Prince of Wales, was knighted in the year of his divorce and was made a baronet two years later. He mixed in the highest circles, as did his wife, and seems to belong there rather than as an eminent member of the middle orders. There are difficulties with Philip Cade; M.A., of Christ Church, son of the paymaster of the Band of Gentlemen Pensioners, son-in-law of the place-seeker Charles Whitworth M.P.,[20] Cade had a place in the Exchequer Office that seems to have needed his attendance, at least for part of the time. At this point we are close to the border. On the other side fall Braithwaite, already mentioned, John Weller and John Stott, commander and ex-commander in the navy, and perhaps also Thomas Edwards, captain in the 6th Foot, whose wife was the daughter of a former president of the council in Antigua; but her father had only 450 acres there, her first husband is untraceable in the standard works, and the separation agreement stipulated only £45 a year alimony.

All the petitioners classed as upper rank had been born to that station, with the exception of Eliot. Three other petitioners rose considerably in social status, but not so far as Eliot, nor did they seek their divorce coincidentally with their rise. One was Richard "Leonidas" Glover, in 1756 a voice of the London merchants but not yet a recipient of the Bubb-Doddington patronage that led to a seat in the Commons. Similarly Samuel Low, later an Irish M.P., was still an Irish barrister when he petitioned in 1753, as was the unpleasant Stephen Popham in 1774, his seat in the Irish Parliament, career in India and place in Hickey's diary still ahead of him. They must be counted as middle rank at the time of their petitions. One man's fortunes changed so suddenly that he is difficult to classify. David Moreau left his wife in 1739 after two years of marriage, went to Minorca, first as a volunteer and then as an ensign, and so effectively cut all ties with his wife and parents that they thought him dead. His wife moved in with a harness maker, and the baptismal record of their child in 1742 treats them as being husband and wife. Moreau's mother, his wife and the harness maker signed "articles of agreement" in 1749, which Moreau endorsed when he reappeared in 1750. By then, so it seems, his mother had died leaving him £10,000. His wife opposed his bill in 1754 and, by producing the articles of agreement, defeated it - perhaps with an eye on his money.

King's middle ranks, to which we now turn, begins with office holders, a category fitting for Thomas Nuthall, the elder Pitt's solicitor and confidant who had just started to accumulate the minor offices which led eventually to the lucrative post of Solicitor for the Affairs of the Treasury. Next come the merchants, ten or eleven of them, including Glover and Daniel Lascelles of the well-known West India house.[21] Five of the remainder come from London, predominantly in the wine trade or with West Indian connections, two were from Dublin and one was a wealthy Exeter merchant. None was a merchant prince, except for Lascelles, but all were comfortably off. Apart from the lawyers already mentioned there were three barristers, two of them gentlemanly and the third Westminster educated, but the son of a Derby attorney.[22] The solitary known attorney, Henry Sealy, lived in Southampton. Perhaps surprisingly, there were five clergymen. Two had advanced from academic distinction at Cambridge via college fellowships to comfortable livings in Norwich and Hertford respectively.[23] The latter, a baker's son, also taught at the local grammar school and had his death noted in the Gentleman's Magazine. St. John Haynes was a Shropshire hunting parson; Thomas Derby was a Worcestershire curate where his family had been freeholders for generations; the fifth, John Jenkins, appears not to have had a parish. Perhaps he did not need one; in his Act he agreed to forego a legacy of £10,000 left to his wife by a relative. Somewhere here in the scale comes Hugh Lewis, a Cornhill insurance broker, two men whom King would have classified as "freeholders" and three "shopkeepers" - a Bishopsgate grocer, a retired tailor and Godfrey Ambrose (Hanckwitz), well-known third generation Covent Garden chemist.[24]

By the 1760s the "men of arts and sciences" whom King ranks between the clergy and the freeholders had probably moved up a few notches. In addition to Eliot and Dumergue the dentist, there was Thomas Brooke, a fashionable London physician and son-in-law of a baronet, but a man without Eliot's claims to higher status. Charles Broomfeild had been living within the King's Bench rules before becoming a naval surgeon in India and China. He may have made money there by private trading, but when he returned to England four years after his divorce he began practice as a surgeon, so he cannot have made a fortune.[25] The sole "artist" was John Worgan,[25a] a popular and successful organist at, among other places, Vauxhall Gardens. They complete the list of the known middle ranks.[26]

Allowing for the difficulty in identifying some of the petitioners, it is still safe to say that the numbers divided about equally between the upper and middle ranks, with perhaps rather more of the latter. The merchants, clergy, lawyers and medical men formed the preponderance of the middle ranks, accounting for at least twenty five petitions. During this time also, the Acts begin to take on the standard form that becomes nearly universal by the end of the period. Some still recite the alimony and property settlement, some refer to private deeds instead, some say nothing about money - as becomes the general rule. But even when Acts are at their most secretive we know that private provision was often made, because it is sometimes announced to the Lords, and sometimes there is argument about it, even though the final Act gives no hint of the outcome. Similarly, bastardy clauses become less common, fewer than a quarter of the final Acts containing them, and most of those falling before 1765. Eventually they disappear altogether. Even the clauses that were passed need not always have caught children already born to the guilty couple, since they were still sometimes dated from nine months after the separation or divorce à mensa et thoro, even when this date fell after the passing of the Act.[27] Preambles continue to recite "fear of spurious issue" as a reason for petitioning, but this becomes a ritual form to be incanted even when there seems no likelihood of there being such a problem. More interestingly, from about 1770 petitioners also begin to recite loss of "the comforts of matrimony" as a claim on Parliament's indulgence.[28]

The increasing standardisation of the statutes is mirrored by the flavour of the examination of the witnesses in the Lords, which for the most part appears as the routine processing of relatively stereotyped claims. The same impression is gained from a reading of the court books of the London Consistory Court, one of the major ecclesiastical courts.[29] Even there serious opposition was rare, the time taken for causes was short, few claims failed. In Parliament only two wives contested liability with any tenacity, and both won.[30] A few appeared by counsel to argue over money; a few more retained counsel on a watching brief; most did not bother. One husband withdrew his bill for reasons which we cannot now tell,[31] but only two lost their bills despite lack of opposition from their wives. One was the Reverend Mr. Haynes in 1762, who appears to have been careless in concealing collusion; the other, Thomas Chism, a drysalter who petitioned in 1778, lost because his wife's father turned out to be footing the bill, presumably so that his daughter could marry the man of property named as the adulterer. They alone disturb the quiet routine of these cases during the period when the trend was generally, unmistakably, though unevenly, upwards in terms of numbers of men seeking a divorce, and equally clearly downwards in terms of their social status.

This trend did not last. The next decade saw a fall in numbers, the next a sharp rise, the following twenty years a relatively steady application rate but a reduced success rate. Internal evidence provides no explanation for the high number of petitions during the peak decades of 1770-1780 and 1790-1800. For the first of these there is little difference in social distribution compared with the previous decade, nor is there evidence (either way) of a decrease in costs. The latter decade is complicated by the war, a factor sometimes raised as an explanation. It is true that in the peak year of 1799 at least four of the twelve petitioners were serving in the forces, but there had always been some military officers among the petitioners, and the proportion for the decade as a whole did not increase. Moreover, when the proportion did increase after the turn of the century, it was against a background of a dramatic fall in the application rate. Again there is no evidence of a fall in costs; the rank of barrister engaged seems much the same as before, as does, so far as can be told, the eminence of the solicitors.

Perhaps we should instead try to explain the relative fall in application rate in the 1780s and 1800s. It is clear that during these years the success rate also fell, so perhaps this accounts for the drop. The clear fall in the success rate probably can be explained from internal evidence. During both decades debates in Parliament, especially in the Lords, showed increasing concern about the scandalously high divorce rate. The Divorce Bill of 1771 would have prevented the marriage of the guilty pair after a divorce and disinherited their children. It passed the Lords but fell by twenty votes in the Commons.[32] In 1779 the Bishop of

Landaff tried again; again the bill passed the Lords, again it lost below, this time by only nine votes.[33] Throughout the nineties Lord Auckland in Parliament and Lord Kenyon in the courts fulminated against immorality and divorce. The former tried to prevent remarriage of the guilty pair, the latter encouraged juries to award punitive damages in crim.con. cases; both had the King's support.[34] Debates in the Lords on Lord Loughborough's new Standing Orders in 1798, themselves a sign of the changing times, and in both Houses on Auckland's Adultery Prevention Bill in 1800, revealed bitter divisions of opinion.[35] Again in 1809 Auckland tried again, this time persuading the Lords that all private divorce bills must contain a clause prohibiting marriage of the guilty pair, again the Commons disagreed - though more on constitutional than matrimonial grounds.[36] Yet although these debates reached their greatest intensity during the trough decades of the 1780s and 1800s, they carried on also during the peak years of the 1770s and 1790s, so they cannot of themselves explain the dramatic differences in application and success rates.

The key lies in the Lord Chancellor. Of course, he was not as much in control of private bills as he was of judicial appeals. Often, particularly in the eighteenth century, quite large attendances are reported; several Lords, not just those of Lord Auckland's stamp, habitually spoke and voted on divorce bills.[37] But the Chancellor was usually the only lawyer present, and as such the only person who could conduct a sustained cross-examination of the witnesses. Thurlow, Loughborough and Eldon all disliked divorce and thought that it tended to collusion. But only Thurlow and Eldon habitually acted as chief inquisitor; Loughborough did not. Under Thurlow's regime Thomas Chism's failure in 1778/1779 was followed by William Gooch's in 1781, when even strenuous efforts by the Bishop of St. David's on the petitioner's behalf could not hide the collusion unearthed by the Chancellor. Another bill failed in the same year, of four cases brought in 1783 one was rejected for lack of admissible evidence and two others passed only after protracted struggle in committee.[38] A petitioner in 1784 dropped his bill and only reintroduced it in the softer climate of 1796.[39] And so it went on.

Thurlow's determined campaign against collusion is clearly reflected in the success rate, for whereas in the equivalent fourteen years before he took office all 37 petitioners eventually gained their statutes, during his chancellorship only 25 of the 32 did. Moreover, although there were thirteen petitions over the three years before he became chancellor and seven in his first year of office, the next seven years saw only thirteen altogether. This suggests a link between success rate and application rate. The same might also be true for Eldon's chancellorship. His predecessor, Loughborough, had been against divorce in general, but did not carry his opposition over into the trial of individual divorce bills. It is noticeable how lax his cross-examination was compared with either Thurlow's or Eldon's. In fact, only two petitions were rejected during his chancellorship, both after fierce opposition from the wives concerned;[40] a sign of Thurlow and Eldon's regimes was that bills failed in spite of - one is sometimes tempted to say, because of - lack of opposition from the wives. Some very weak applications passed during Loughborough's time, including one that seems to have been so doubtful that it was dropped after securing its second reading, even though its further passage through the Lords was unlikely to have been impeded.[41] One of Loughborough's laxest precedents was overturned by Eldon within four years of its happening.[42]

Although the application rates do not show an immediate increase on Loughborough's taking office, after a few years they jumped sharply, with nine, six, six and twelve in successive years, and a total of 41 over the nine years of his chancellorship. In Eldon's first year there were five petitioners, plus one from India and the first ever from a woman; in the second year there were again five, plus a man from the previous year trying again. Of these ten only four succeeded, the lowest proportion ever.[43] Eldon made full use of the new Standing Orders introduced by Loughborough in 1798 which, among other things, required petitioners to state whether they were living with their wives at the time of the adultery, and if not, why not. In Eldon's time this seemed to mean that separation for reasons other than adultery barred a divorce, just as too tardy a separation after the discovery of adultery, or too generous separation terms, were also bars. Attempts to conceal separations by not reciting them in the preamble generally meant that the bill would fail and have to be reintroduced. This was new law. It bore no relation to ecclesiastical court practice, and the only precedent for it was to be found in the attempts Lord Kenyon had made to introduce similar ideas into the crim.con. action.[44] The new rules quickly broadened into a more general examination of the state of the marriage before the adultery, particularly into the conduct of the husband to see whether he had been considerate enough to his wife to deserve the privilege of the right to remarry. In time evidence of the idyllic state of the marriage became almost ritualised, but sometimes the crim.con. trial disclosed unhappiness, or a determined wife supplied evidence of her husband's less than perfect behaviour, and then his reputation suffered as much as hers, though he usually still got his statute.

In Eldon's hands the full inquisitorial nature of the procedure quickly became apparent. Proofs of the most formal matters were required, that the wife was over 21 at the time of the marriage, for example, or that the requisite consents had been given. Separations were rigorously examined, sometimes the husband being summoned to explain himself, and the law of all aspects of collusion and condonation was expanded. Fierce cross-examination from the chair was common place, and Eldon even began to insist that certain sorts of evidence be supplied - on the state of the bed, for example, - that certain witnesses be produced, and even which acts of adultery he wanted proved. Not only were petitioners expected to have sued at common law, but they should also have pursued judgment against the defendant. Even if satisfied on all these matters Eldon might still refuse a divorce. In Miller's case (1817), for example, the fact that the wife had had four children by the adulterer was enough for Eldon to reject the application.

As with Thurlow's new broom a generation earlier, Eldon's was followed by a marked drop in the number of applications. From the heights of Loughborough's chancellorship and Eldon's first year, the figures dropped to two, two, three, two and one in the years following 1802.[45] A conjunction of an inquisitorial Chancellor and a House of Lords with a substantial body of opinion inveighing against immorality seems enough to account for both the low success rate and the low application rate. But both factors were needed. The House had been hostile to divorce in the 1770s and 1790s, but neither rate was low then. However, at neither time was there a chancellor concerned to root out collusion and deceit.

When, under Thurlow, the application rate dropped, so did the proportion of middle-ranking petitioners. The landed aristocracy was represented by the heir to the earldom of Exeter, and by the Hon. Edward Foley M.P., and Andrew Baytun M.P., who were both divorcing daughters of the Earl of Coventry. Once again some of the five landed gentlemen were related to the peerage.[46] In addition, there was John Wilmot, son of the Chief Justice of Common Pleas, F.R.S., M.P., and holder of the sinecure office of Master in Chancery, and Mathew Lewis, Deputy Secretary for War, who had extensive West Indian estates. His wife, daughter of Sewell M.R., was a favourite at court. The military present difficulties. William Arabin, supernumerary lieutenant-colonel in the Life Guards, and John Parslow, captain in the 3rd Dragoons, are clearly of upper rank. So is Henry Fortick Sheridan, for although he had been a major in only the New York Volunteers and a lieutenant in the 31st Foot, he had a New Bond Street address and moved in high circles, as did Captain James Christie, though his regiment had been disbanded after the American war. But Jonathan Twiss, who had married a naval captain's daughter, had been only a lieutenant in the marines at Bombay. And John Inglis, former naval captain himself, husband of a carpenter's daughter, had probably left the navy to become a merchant, though identification here is only tentative. These last two should probably be assigned to the middle ranks.

Certainly in the middle ranks are John Hankey, merchant and member of the wealthy banking family, John Walford junior of Bread Street Hill, though his occupation is elusive, Francis Thomas Rybot, Cheapside mercer and weaver and

William Raybould, Drury Lane ironmonger, coach-founder and painter. The group is completed by a London barrister who later acquired a landed estate, an Exeter attorney, and the architect John Nash, whose petition for a divorce from his first wife was rejected in 1787 for negligence bordering upon connivance.[47]

It is possible that this relative reduction in middle ranking applicants is related to Thurlow's campaign against collusion. Perhaps, as in Chism's case, the middle orders were more likely to try to share the costs of the process and feared detection. Perhaps the upper ranks, by earlier resort to family lawyers, more easily avoided the indulgence and consideration towards erring wives that was so readily construed as collusion or condonation. Perhaps their more frequent reliance on family servants as witnesses made them more confident of concealing such things. In the last resort the upper ranks could, and did, use their Parliamentary connections to ease the passage of a doubtful case.[48]

The departure of Thurlow marked a return to the old pattern. During the nine years of Loughborough's chancellorship and the first two of Eldon's - until his views became apparent to everyone - there were 49 men petitioning for the first time plus two men petitioning from India, Captain Christie re-petitioned after a lapse of twelve years and there was the first petition from a woman. Of the new petitioners from England and Ireland about half fall into the upper ranks. There were three peers,[49] plus John Bernard Howard, a Catholic who later became Duke of Norfolk, and the Hon. and Rev. Thomas James Twistleton, son of Lord Saye and Sele. In addition to a baronet and a knight there were ten representatives of landed families, eleven if John Buller, one of the petitioners from India, is counted.[50] The Ricketts brothers should also be included here, although they were only the sons of a bencher of Gray's Inn. William Henry Ricketts was a naval captain who had gained promotion by merit,[51] and Edward Jervis was a barrister; but both inherited West Indian estates, enabling the former to marry a daughter of the Earl of Cavan and the latter a daughter of Lord Saye and Sele. Much later Edward Jervis Ricketts succeeded his maternal grandfather as Viscount St.

Vincent. Also to be included here are Admiral Sir Hyde Parker, naval captain Shuldham Peard, the son-in-law of an admiral, and perhaps Charles Collins Campbell, an army major and district paymaster. The other military men are of middle rank: Edward Columbine, a navy commander, may have been "an officer of science and great professional knowledge",[52] but he had neither wealth nor high birth; George Hayes was a naval lieutenant of long and admirable service, but no distinction; and Edward Brown married without fortune or even marriage settlement, went to India shortly afterwards only to be invalided out as a captain. There is another adventurer who is hard to classify: James Esten, who had married actress Harriet Bennet (or Pye), gone penniless to the West Indies and returned with a reputedly huge fortune.[53]

The middle rankers again come mainly from the merchants, clergy, lawyers and doctors. The merchants included two Londoners, one of them in the West India trade, and two important local figures from Whitby and Bristol.[54] The clergy reflect the increasing links between the aristocracy and the cloth, for in addition to Twistleton two had such connections. Calverly John Bewicke was the eldest son of a landed family and had married the daughter of a baronet, and John Thoroton was patronised by the Manners family all his life. The third clergyman, William Brook Jones, may have held a college fellowship for a short time,[55] but appears to have been unbeneficed. However, three of the four lawyers were mere attorneys, from London, Manchester and Totnes,[56] with only Lancelot Shadwell, an eminent conveyancer, representing the bar. Similarly, two of the medical men were surgeons, from Tooting and Eltham; the third was a physician, but only in the service of the East India Company.[57] The solitary remaining "professional" was a Dublin banker.[58] Three master mariners petitioned, one a Liverpool slaver, the others captains of East Indiamen, all no doubt well off.[59] The remaining miscellany comprises a freeholder, a trimming maker, a well-known riding master and livery stables keeper and John Opie the artist, who, true to character, had first tried to save money by seeking annulment of his marriage.[60] The only changes from the earlier period are that London is a little less dominant in the upper-middle range, and that the junior branches of the established professions outnumber the senior. Otherwise the pattern is much like that of the 1760s and 1770s.

Once Eldon's view became known, applications dropped and the pattern seen during Thurlow's regime reasserted itself. There were 70 petitioners from 1803 to the end of 1827, plus three men petitioning from India and another woman. The upper class accounted for rather more than half. The peerage, including sons and brothers of peers, had eight petitioners, and the baronetage five, one of whom was a landless but gentlemanly naval captain.[61] Many of the gentry held military rank during the wars, usually in fashionable regiments, like Lieutenant Dunn of the 6th Dragoons and Captain Clitherow of the 3rd Foot Guards, who also held the army rank of lieutenant-colonel. Some petitioners held high rank in fashionable regiments as well as being members of old landed families, General Dyott, for example, and Lieutenant-Colonel Sir John Milley Doyle. Including these, the gentry adds a further 23 petitioners,[62] of whom six were Irish. A few naval officers should also be listed here; Sir Edward W.C.R. Owen, obviously, and Captain Foote of Bay of Naples notoriety; but not Lieutenant John Worrall who, like Hayes earlier, was professional rather than aristocratic. Similarly, one or two of the high ranking soldiers had had long military careers and seem to have lacked an upper class background. Major Thomas Weston, for example, had been in service in India before transferring to the 77th and 96th regiments, and Humphrey Dalrymple Bland had risen to Major in the 47th Foot after starting as an ensign. Two petitioners served in the army after the war; Stepney St. George had a short spell as captain in the 52nd Light Infantry, but as the son of an Irish landed family may be treated as upper ranking; Daniel Thorndike was a career soldier in the Royal Artillery and, with a long posting in Newfoundland, is perhaps more middle than upper.

The range of middle order petitioners was rather narrower than previously. The four merchants covered the usual range, there was a landed country banker and there was Andrew Jameson, the "son" who still appears on the family Irish whiskey bottles.[63] The newer professions were represented by two London attorneys and a former military surgeon about to set up in private practice.[64] The clergy continued to show links with the aristocracy. One was the son of an Irish baronet, another the son of a Somerset knight.[65] The Dean of York petitioned successfully; his father was archbishop there, having tutored two of the royal princes. The other two clerical petitioners also seem to have had important patronage: John Castleton Miller D.D., was chaplain to H.M.G. Malta for many years, and Francis Lee was patronised by Lord Paget. But apart from these traditional members of the middle orders there were few petitioners. There were two merchant marine commanders,[66] Henry Chamberlain worked for the Post Office and later had a diplomatic career culminating in a baronetcy and, at the other end of the scale, Henry Ellis was a Leadenhall butcher. Barron Grahame had been a portrait painter in India and was later a noted glass painter, but at the time of his divorce was being supported by his family. George Henry Green had recently been paymaster to a regiment of French emigrés, earning 15/- a day. Samuel Bloxham was a regimental veterinary surgeon whose wife signed merely "X" on the marriage register, and her adulterer was merely a private soldier. All points to a relatively lowly status, except that the regiment was the 1st Life Guards and that the historian of the R.A.V.C. describes Bloxham as "the classical scholar".[67] Perhaps the wider range of middle class applicants had been scared away by Eldon and by the extra costs of pursuing adulterers for damages.

Eldon's departure did not release a flood of applications. Apart from 1830, when there were seven, the rate remained much as it was; indeed, between 1831 and 1838 it was the lowest for any comparable period since Thurlow's day. Perhaps if Lyndhurst had remained Chancellor it would have been different. There were only four petitions in his first two years, but the seven in his third contained several that smacked of collusion.[68] Moreover, in 1829 Lieutenant Thorndike finally got the divorce that Eldon had twice denied him. Lyndhurst's well-known softness on divorce extended to his treatment of individual cases, and in his three chancellorships only one petitioner failed outright and only one other had to make two applications.[69] Of the eleven new petitioners between 1828 and 1831 nine were obvious members of the upper class and only one, an Ilchester attorney, clearly middle class.[70] Perhaps the middle class would have watched the turning of the tide and would have followed when it was clear that Lyndhurst was another Loughborough. But Brougham who followed him was another Eldon. It was not that he rejected many petitions - the one rejected in his first year was too unusual to count for much[71] - more his manner of proceeding. He revived Eldon's practice of cross-examining husbands about their behaviour. Both Hugh Kinnaird, a page of the backstairs in H.M. household, and Samuel Le Fevre, a Southampton customs collector, were treated brutally in this way by Brougham in 1831. He was particularly obsessed with possible collusion over the crim.con. action, frequently cross-examining the husbands' lawyers about it. One case was adjourned because Brougham would not accept hearsay evidence of the receipt of damages, the county under-sheriff had to be called. A master mariner of no great affluence was told to outlaw the adulterer in the hope of getting him to appear to defend a crim.con. action - even though he had fled to the Cape of Good Hope. Solicitors were cross-examined on the possibility of the repayment of the damages, even when there seemed to be no basis on which to suspect it. These cases[72] contrast sharply with the laxness of 1830 and with the three petitions heard in 1835/1836 after Brougham's departure, and perhaps they explain the low rate of application.

The analysis can be continued in this vein for a few more years. Brougham's departure allowed two fairly dubious petitions to get through, but Cottenham announced his arrival by rejecting two of the first four petitions that he heard.[73] That takes us to 1838, with the rate as low as it had been for sixty years. But then there is a change. There were nine petitions in 1839, with an average of four or five a year thereafter. There are indications that several of the nine could have petitioned earlier, some of them claiming that only their poverty delayed them.

Such evidence could hide less acceptable reasons,[74] but it is striking how many of these men were solidly middle class, and might therefore be expected to find the costs hard to meet. Dionysus Lardner was one; the only man to feature in the Lords as both petitioner and adulterer,[75] he was an academic and writer. Henry Coode was another, a former naval lieutenant who could now afford to petition because he had received £300 out of his trustee's bankruptcy, having previously had only his half-pay and a small leasehold investment. Joseph Deane, once a flour factor but bankrupted by fire and now a salaried salesman, Jonathan Warr, at his marriage a journeyman slater on 4/- a day, but now a master slater with his own business; it is at least credible that they were telling the truth. Even James Close, a Leeds surgeon, had the benefit of his cousin's services as solicitor, and Edward Leigh Pemberton, Whitehall solicitor and later President of the Law Society, received a discount from the Parliamentary agent as a good customer.[76] There is evidence here to suggest a new sort of petitioner, but his arrival, and the re-emerging of the middle class petitioner generally, dates rather from the early 1830s than from later in the decade when the application rate once again increased. Similarly, the increase in applications at that time came from upper and middle classes in roughly equal shares. There do not seem to be any changes in law or attitude to prompt the increasing rate of application from the middle of Cottenham's tenure onwards. It is true that Cottenham's bark turned out to be worse than his bite, and that in retrospect the two early petitions that he rejected can be seen to have little chance of success. But at about this time the character of the Lord Chancellor begins to matter less. The judicial nature of the proceedings becomes more stressed, with lay peers being discouraged from wandering in and out of the proceedings, and with more lawyer peers sitting with the Chancellor to hear the evidence. There is a slight dip in the application rate in the early 1850s, but whether this is due to Cranworth's rejection of three[77] of the first five petitions to reach him, or to hopes that a cheaper forum would soon be established, is hard to say.

Of the 124 petitioners between 1831 and 1857, 26 petitioned from India, one man recently back from Australia sought special treatment because there were no divorce courts there, and five were women.[78] The remaining 92 divide about equally between upper and middle classes. There is a solitary peer, Lord Lincoln, and three sons of baronets, who later succeeded their fathers.[79] There were 28 gentry,[80] many of them in the various editions of Burke, some related to peers, some being J.P.s, some enjoying a style of life involving frequent and extensive continental tours and yachting cruises. In addition there were seven army officers,[81] all drawn from the same strata of society. They tended to belong to fashionable regiments like the Blues, the Hussars and the Lancers, and to be captains if young, majors or lieutenant-colonels if older. At the borderline were two well-connected Royal Naval commanders,[82] John Walpole Willis, barrister, writer, son-in-law to an earl, and then in the middle of a turbulent career as a colonial judge, and Charles Lestock Boileau, a retired Indian major, son of a landed family and brother of a first baronet.

The lawyers formed the biggest middle class group, with seven solicitors and three barristers, one of whom was landed and twice mayor of St. Albans.[83] One of the other barristers practised in Leamington, and only one of the solicitors belonged to a major London firm. Three others had practices in London, two in the country and one was solicitor to a railway company. The four clergy had close ties to the upper class again.[84] There were seven men who might loosely be described as "merchants", ranging from three who traded with the East, through to Edward Ley, an oil-cooper from the New Kent Road, and Jonathan Warr the slate master.[85] As with the lawyers, the four doctors are less homogenous than earlier. There was a Leeds surgeon, and two London surgeon-apothecaries of relatively lowly status.[86] The fourth, Edward Cripps, was a young Birmingham surgeon who had married a prostitute while training in London. His horrified family, related to the Cirencester bankers and brewers, separated them as soon as they learned the truth and were paying for the divorce. There were only two other men who could be called professional, John Bernard Hartley, who succeeded his famous father as the engineer to Liverpool docks, and George Fisher, a regimental veterinary surgeon who was shortly to die in the Crimea. There were three "commercial" men, and three manufacturers, but of these only Richard Mellin from Wakefield was of the new breed - Josiah Smith made cabinets and Robert Allison pianofortes, both in London. There was a solitary official, Le Fevre, a solitary master mariner and a solitary farmer - though his mother had a life estate in the land leased to him.[88] Similar to Lardner there was Robert Montgomery Martin, once a member of the court of the East India Company, but at the time of his divorce struggling as an author and publisher. In addition to the page, the former naval lieutenant and the salaried salesman already mentioned, there was a salaried bank manager, an urban landlord, a Southwark linen draper, a Thame innkeeper and a Faversham school-master.[89] That leaves three relatively lowly petitioners: Richard Batley, who was a clerk for his father, a Pimlico job-master; William Chippendall, once a solicitor but now only a solicitor's clerk; and Edward Jones, who was a Bristol tobacconist when he petitioned in 1853 and a commercial traveller when he re-applied in 1855. He and Chippendall applied to have their cases heard in forma pauperis, but only the latter succeeded.

This range of middle class applicants is wider than earlier, even though the ratio of middle to upper class is much as it had been during the 1770s and 1790s. Many said that they found it difficult to pay for the process, and some tried to reduce costs by not suing the adulterer at common law. Similarly, several of the poorer petitioners used ecclesiastical courts other than the two big London courts, presumably to save money, though perhaps in the hope of concealing the weakness of their case from a less experienced judge. Even so, it is striking how the ratio of upper to middle class applicants remained roughly one to one during the century under consideration. The only departure from this pattern, and that only a slight one, came when the general level of applications fell. If this fall can be related to the fall in success rate, we can speculate that the relative decrease in middle class applications reflects their reluctance to run high risks when they would have to have stretched their resources to the utmost to pay for the process. Unfortunately, insufficient material survives for a reconstruction of costs for the eighteenth century and barely enough for the nineteenth. However, since the Campbell Commission was so confident in its views, and as it has been followed so frequently since, it is worth trying.

In 1853 the Campbell Commission concluded that ". . . the total cost, under the most favourable circumstances, of obtaining a divorce . . . can hardly be less than £700 or £800; and when the matter is much litigated, it would probably reach some thousands."[90] However, in reaching this total, two figures seem simply to have been invented by Campbell, those for lawyers' fees and witnesses' charges in Parliament, and those for the common law action. In the former case Campbell just ignored evidence offered by a Parliamentary agent, and where he did accept the agent's figures, on Parliamentary charges and agency fees, he treated them as minima though they were proffered as averages. Furthermore, Campbell did not investigate the circumstances in which petitioners were excused from bringing the common law action, which at the time that he wrote was in nearly a third of the cases, nor did he allow for lower costs in the ecclesiastical courts when the wife chose not to appear. Taking a more accurate view of the evidence produced to Campbell, the theoretical minimum cost should be about £280 - for a case in which the wife did not appear in the ecclesiastical court, the adulterer was not sued, and the Lords did not react by requiring more stringent proof than usual. Since there would be incidental costs in discovering that the adulterer could not, or need not, be sued, and since extra costs in Parliament would be likely, the figure could be grossed up to about £300 - which is less than half Campbell's estimate.[91] We need not, however, rest with the evidence produced to the Commission.

Usually the first step towards a divorce Act was to sue the adulterer for damages. However, some excuses for not doing so would be accepted. Table III shows how this varied with time:

TABLE III

Petitioners who had and had not sued at common law

	petitioners[1]	had sued	had not sued
1751-80	66	38	20
1781-1800	63	54	6
1801-20	65	57	1
1821-40	63	51	12
1841-57	67	44	20

Note:

1. This excludes women petitioners and men using the Indian procedure, but includes men suing in England by power of attorney from India, since for them the full English procedure applied.

Petitioners sometimes told Parliament what their taxed costs had been in the common law action, information contained in Table IV.

TABLE IV

Known taxed costs of common law action

	cases (no.)	range (£)	average (£)	median (£)
1751-1800	9	11-164	85	92
1801-1820	7	36-240	107	94
1821-40	21	31-550	185	157
1841-57	22	29-695	203	141

These taxed costs must be increased to find the actual cost to the plaintiff. Nothing is known of taxation practice, though it seems from surviving ecclesiastical court bills that about 85% was allowed on taxation there.[92] In the absence of a study of common law practice it seems reasonable to assume that 80% was allowed. Using this, an estimate of the distribution of common law costs can be attempted.

TABLE V

Estimated actual cost of common law action (% of petitioners)

	no action	£1-75	£1-100	£1-150	£1-200	£1-300	£1-500	£500+
1821-40	19	11	15	27	44	61	71	10
1841-57	31	14	19	29	37	48	57	12

So whereas between 1801 and 1840, 50% of the petitioners were spending less than £165 (extracted from Table IV and grossed up), between 1841 and 1857, 75% were paying less than £250, as the increasing cost of the action was partly offset by the decreasing proportion of petitioners who had to sue. By the end of the period nearly a third spent nothing on the action.

To estimate the cost of the divorce à mensa et thoro Campbell took evidence from ecclesiastical court officials, some of it reprinted from 1844.[93] Unfortunately, it is sometimes unclear whether actual or taxed costs are being discussed, nor do the officials clearly distinguish between "unopposed" cases and those in which the defendant did not even appear. If his wife did not appear she would incur no costs for her husband to bear; if she did appear he had to pay her taxed costs plus his own actual costs. These would be increased by her appearance since he had to provide copies of documents for her proctor and pay for his attendance at various hearings, but they would also be reduced by not having to pay for the contumacy procedure designed to force defendants to appear. On balance it is unlikely that the mere appearance of the wife significantly increased his own actual costs. Estimates of the minimum cost of an unopposed divorce ranged from £50 (Lushington 1844) to £120-£140 (Shephard 1853) in the London Consistory Court and £140-£150 in the Court of Arches. The Registrar of the Arches estimated £80 for a divorce where the defendant did not appear, and perhaps this is also what Lushington had meant. The Registrar also said that the average expense of 16 cases in the Arches between 1840 and 1843 had been £165, including the costs of both sides.

Unfortunately no bills of costs survive from the London Consistory Court for this period and only a few from the Court of Arches. Of 14 surviving final bills for suits in the Court of Arches between 1828 and 1850 in which wives were defendants,[94] half are for less than £80, three quarters are for less than £100, and the two highest by a long way are for £265 and £403. These figures were reduced to £65, £74, £201 and £210 on taxation, which is what the husbands would have to pay. While the two largest bills relate to strongly opposed suits, most of the remainder would probably be classed as unopposed. They were not, however, uncontested, and typically they involved the testing of witnesses, sometimes the taking of exceptions to the witnesses' characters and often the taking of an advocate's opinion on whether to offer a full defence. Most of the cases stretched over several terms, yet the list supplied by John Shephard, Deputy Registrar of the London Consistory Court,[95] to the Campbell Commission shows that more than half of his cases were completed within five months - two terms. Sample testing from the Assignation Books for the London Consistory Court and the Court of Arches confirms this pattern. But of the 14 bills under consideration, only two are for such a short suit, Mrs Moore's in 1838 for £16 (taxed at £12) and Mrs Lautour's in 1839 for £37 (taxed at £20), and they are the lowest of the 14. The implication may be that not all wives bothered to present bills for taxing, those in short cases did not. Perhaps then the surviving bills are untypically high. It seems safe, therefore, to conclude from these few bills, that in 75% of the cases in which the wife appeared the husband had to pay less than £75 for her costs.

Since wives never had to pay their husbands' bills, husbands did not have to present their bills for taxing, so we have no direct evidence of husbands' own costs. Surviving bills in the Court of Arches for wife-plaintiffs are of little use, since they mainly concern strongly opposed cases. Bills for suits for restitution of conjugal rights for £79 (1828) and £92 (1849) give some indication of the cost of a divorce, as the procedure and length of suit were similar, and there is a bill for £99 for a divorce in 1849 which the husband contested in the way described above.[96] Many of the bills for wife-defendants are for about £70 or £80, and assuming that the husband's bill would usually be more since he had to take the initiative in producing witnesses, we might conclude that £100 would usually cover his own costs in an "unopposed" suit. This is consistent with the opinions offered to Campbell. It is pointless to try to estimate the cost of opposed suits; Mrs Geil's defence to her husband's restitution suit plus her counter-claim for divorce in 1845 cost £1250, more modestly Mrs Kilpin's divorce in 1831 cost £424.

Shephard's list shows that about a fifth of the defendants failed to appear, and it might be supposed that this applied to cases ultimately reaching Parliament. Indeed, the list contains three such cases, and a brief look into the London Consistory Court Assignation Books quickly revealed three more.[97] However, without a full survey of the records it would be incautious to accept this figure, since the relatively greater wealth and higher status of those seeking full divorces (if that is the case) and an awareness of the probable sequel in Parliament may have led to a greater frequency of legal representation at ecclesiastical court level. It is safer to settle for 10%, and to allow, with Shephard, 20% for opposed cases. Very few petitioners after 1800 were involved in appeals to higher ecclesiastical courts,[98] so no separate allowance need be made for them. However, for those unfortunates it could be expensive. Nine bills[99] for appeals to the Court of Arches between 1830 and 1844 average £136 gross, £117 after taxation, suggesting a cost to the husband of about £250. However, Mrs Durant's bill in 1820 was for £764 (taxed at £598), while even in 1797 Lady Cadogan's bill had been £435 (taxed at £353), so averages mean even less than usually. The conclusion overall is that about 10% of the petitioners to Parliament had paid £80 to £100 for their divorce _à mensa et thoro_, a further 70% had paid £100 to £175, and that for the rest the cost could only be measured in hundreds, very occasionally in thousands.

For costs in Parliament the only evidence is that submitted to Campbell by Parliamentary Agent, John Ellicombe.[100] His list of 26 divorce bills promoted by his firm between 1837 and 1850 covers a range from £154 to £241 for Parliamentary and agency charges, with an average of £188. Ellicombe thought that a further £50-£100 should be added to cover lawyers' fees and witnesses' charges, and although Campbell simply ignored this figure and substituted £200 without saying why, there is no basis on which we can do the same. Three quarters of the petitioners in Ellicombe's list paid less than £202 in fees and charges, which can be rounded up to, say, £300 to take account of the extra items.

The elements can now be drawn together. For the common law action 75% paid less than £250; for the ecclesiastical court divorce 80% paid less than £175; in Parliament 75% paid less than £300. It would not be surprising if a particular case fell below two or even all these lines, but the safest conclusion is that nearly half the petitioners paid less than £725 for their divorce à vinculo - about the figure given by Campbell as the minimum and accepted as such ever since.

Moreover, an optimistic petitioner might hope to reduce his costs by recovering damages from the adulterer. Vindictiveness in the pursuit of penal damages may not have appealed to many - though some no doubt took grim pleasure in seeing the adulterer confined in a debtors' prison for inability to pay[101] - but many must have shared the view of John Moore who insisted to the Lords in 1805 that he intended to recover only enough damages to cover his total costs. Some observers believed that in nine cases out of ten the common law action was collusive and that any damages paid were eventually returned. Part of Eldon's sterner regime was to inquire about this, but Moore's case and numerous others in which various reasons were accepted for not executing judgment show that there was no rule that damages should actually be recovered. When, therefore, a succession of eminent solicitors and bankers told the House that damages and costs had been recovered and that there was no agreement to return them it is likely to be true. Of course, it is possible that their clients had reached secret agreements; possible even that some were encouraged by nods and winks. Reformers believed that this happened but, although there can be no proof either way, it stretches credulity too far to accept that many petitioners paid the large sums needed for a divorce and quietly handed the whole damages back. If they did return them it seems more likely that they would first have deducted their costs.[102] It seems more reasonable to believe that petitioners who said that they had recovered costs from the adulterer at least had the choice of using them to defray their costs and that some of them took it.

A large proportion (72%) of those who had sued the adulterer told the Lords whether the damages had been paid, enabling an estimate of the outcome of all such cases to be made.

TABLE VI

Damages recovered at common law (% of petitioners)

	none	£1-99	£100-499	£500 and over	(no action)
1801-20	51.5	2.5	10.3	33.5	2.0
1821-57	31.4	3.0	12.0	28.4	25.2

In all cases in which damages were recovered taxed costs were also, so only for the petitioners in the first column of Table VI was the action a net expense. The working conclusion so far has been that about three quarters of the petitioners had paid up to £250 for the common law action, but Table VI suggests that in practice, for the period 1821-1857, two thirds paid nothing at all. The total cost can now be adjusted accordingly, so that about half the petitioners can be estimated to have paid less than £475 for their divorce Act. Moreover, more than a quarter recovered enough from the common law action to pay for the entire procedure and another eighth received enough substantially to reduce their costs. In practice the action for criminal conversation was for many petitioners an effective way of shifting the cost of legally terminating the marriage on to the man deemed responsible for its breakdown. What this could mean for particular petitioners can be seen from Table VII.

TABLE VII

Estimated costs in sample cases[103] £

		common law[1]	divorce à mensa[2]	divorce à vinculo[3]	gross cost	damages rec'd	net cost
Tyrell	(1829)	350	76+(100)	(250)	776	0	776
Bayley	(1830)	?	(80)	(250)	?	100+ taxed costs	250-300
Gardiner	(1837)	231	74+(100)	190+(75)	670	285[4]	385
Carleton	(1839)	134	116+(150)	(265)	665	157[4]	500-665
Grant	(1840)	204	1300	178+(75)	1760	664[4]	1110-1760
Mitford	(1842)	61	?	183+(100)	?	1049	0
Watson	(1843)	238	(80)	(265)	583	690	0
Archbutt	(1844)	48	(80)	(265)	393	0	393
Boileau	(1845)	0	250-300	174+(75)	500-550	-	500-550
Matthyssens	(1846)	0	(150)	241+(75)	466	-	466
Martin	(1847)	0	(150)	210+(75)	435	-	435
Waldy	(1849)	0	200	(300)	500	-	500
Hoghton	(1849)	336	(175)	(350)	861	0	861
Cautley	(1850)	326	(175)	(265)	766	0	766
Hartley	(1850)	869	(150)	(400)	1419[5]	4695	0
Lincoln	(1850)	0	(200)	225+(150)	575	-	575
Tayleur	(1851)	366	(500)	(300)	1166	793	373
Berens	(1854)*	270	120-130	(350)	740-750	916	0

*Failed in the House of Commons.

Notes:

1. Taxed costs from preambles to Acts and H.L.Jo., plus 25%. Berens from H.L.P., 1854 Vol.20.

2. Sources: Tyrell, H.L.P., 1831-32 Vol.24, p.454; Gardiner and Carleton, Court of Arches records; Grant, Swabey's evidence to Campbell Commission; Boileau and Waldy, H.L.Jo., for their divorces; Berens, H.L.P., 1854 Vol.20; Bayley, Archbutt and Watson, estimates based on London Consistory Court Assignation Books; Martin, estimate based on Surrey Commissary Court Assignation Book, G.L.R.O.; remainder are estimates based on Shephard's evidence to Campbell Commission.

3. Sources: Gardiner, Grant, Mitford, Boileau, Matthyssens, Martin and Lincoln, Ellicombe's list in Campbell Report (identified from bills in H.L.R.O.) plus estimates of additional costs based on Ellicombe's evidence; remainder are estimates based on Ellicombe's evidence and House of Lords' Journals.

4. Not known whether or not recovered.

5. His solicitor estimated his costs, rather vaguely, at £2500.

Costs, therefore, were probably lower than Campbell asserted, just as the class of applicants was more varied. However, facts played but a small part in the reform debates of the 1850s. At issue was the nature of Protestantism, the power of the church, the relation between law and behaviour and, particularly, the significance of Parliament's being seen to weaken the law protecting virtue and chastity. Legislative divorce was important only insofar as it demonstrated that, contrary to the protestations of the bishops, marriage had not hitherto been indissoluble. Its cost and inconvenience were mentioned from time to time, but usually in the context of the most important minor theme of the debate, the superiority of courts of law, especially courts of common law, for dealing with such matters. But this assertion went largely unanswered. Sometimes one of Campbell's conclusions was trotted out as a factual answer to one of the Opposition's claims, but even that was rare, the Commission's main significance being seen as its share in the thorough discussion of the issue which, the Government claimed, had preceded the 1857 Bill. Indeed, it is obvious from the debates that even the main protagonists knew little about the procedure on legislative divorce and less about the petitioners. So the propaganda put forward by the Campbell Commission on behalf of the reformist common lawyers went unanswered in its details, as one would expect in debates that were, in however confused a way, persistently focussed on the major issues of principle. But, as I hope this paper has shown, the cost of a statutory divorce was less, and the range of those prepared to pay for it wider than ever one would have expected after reading the bland pages of the case put forward by the common lawyers.

NOTES

* I would like to thank Simon Roberts, Bill Cornish and Gerry Rubin for their helpful comments on an earlier draft.

1. O.R. McGregor, Divorce in England, p.19, followed, for example, by G. Rowntree and N. Carrier, "The resort to divorce in England and Wales 1858-1957" (1957-58) 11 Population Studies 118. McGregor significantly qualifies his view, without giving details, in McGregor and Finer, The History of the Obligation to Maintain, Cmnd. 5629, appendix 5, p.92.
2. See e.g., F. Clifford, A history of private bill legislation, Vol.1, ch.V.
3. Separation bills, even those purporting to be divorce bills, have been excluded from this study. Clifford, above, gives details.
4. Standing Orders of the House of Commons in 1811 providing that divorce bills should usually start in the Lords merely confirmed existing practice.
5. House of Lords Standing Order 141.
6. Compare Sir William Scott's doubts in Crewe v. Crewe (1800) 3 Hagg.Ecc.R. 123, 137, "possibly, in other places to which this case may be brought the nature of it may be more accurately disclosed."
7. House of Commons Standing Order 10 June 1773; compare House of Lords Standing Order 214, 7 July 1831, calling for the production of the court papers.
8. See e.g., J.A. Banks, Prosperity and Parenthood, p.68.
9. Parl. Hist. Vol.34, 1558.
10. Social structure among British men in India was sufficiently different for comparisons between men petitioning from there and from Britain to be worth a separate study. After 1820 most Indian cases used the new statutory procedure which allowed the evidence to be taken in India, thereby reducing the opportunities for rejection by the House of Lords.

11. King, Natural and political observations and conclusions upon the state and condition of England, 1696 (ed., George Chalmers, 1804); see W.A. Speck, Stability and Strife and H. Perkin, The Origins of Modern English Society 1780-1880 for recent adaptations.

12. For his military career see Sir J.W. Fortescue, A History of the British Army, Vol.III.

13. A. Aspinall (ed.), Correspondence of George, Prince of Wales 1770-1812 Vol.IV, 1681.

14. Note on sources. The main source of information are the divorce records themselves, the examination of witnesses printed in the House of Lords Journals and sometimes in the sessional papers. For early periods particularly these need to be supplemented by papers in the House of Lords Record Office, particularly the Main Papers and the Manuscript Minutes. Preambles to Bills and Acts often contain information on wealth not found elsewhere. Records from the ecclesiastical courts are also useful, but unfortunately the case papers for the London Consistory Court, the most popular court by far, now in the Greater London Record Office, are uncatalogued and unusable when the essay was written. My thanks are due to Mrs Kenealy of the G.L.R.O. for retrieving what she could for me. The records of the Court of Arches in Lambeth Palace Library are most useful; my thanks are due to the Librarian and staff there for their help. For social identification I have used the standard reference works, local histories, printed diaries and trade directories, too numerous to list. Military careers have been followed in the Army Lists and specialist histories; for the Navy, John Marshall, Naval Biography (1825) and W.R. O'Byrne, A naval biographical dictionary (1849) have been used. Additional sources are identified where needed. A few cases remain only tentatively identified; no doubt a systematic search of the newspapers would fill the gaps - but I lack the resources for that, and the cases are too few to affect the overall

picture.

15. Peers: Calvert (1711) (son of Lord Baltimore); Hillsborough (1734); Beaufort (1744). Barts: Yonge (1724); Rudd (1733); Morice (1737); Dinely (1739). Knight: Dillon (1700). Landed: Judge (1708-9) (Irish); Loggin (1714); Jenyns (1729); Mathew (1745) (son of Governor of Leeward Islands); Rash (1748); Copley (1748-50) and (?) Ireland (1702).

16. Benson (1752); Lascelles (1752). (See R. Pares, "A London-West Indies Merchant House 1740-69" in R. Pares and A.J.P. Taylor (eds.), Essays Presented to Sir Lewis Namier); Cooke (1759); Turner (1760).

17. Ireland (H.M.C. Manuscripts of the House of Lords, Vol.V), Calvert, Jenyns. (See A.N. Newman (ed.), Knatchbull's Diary, 28 February 1730), Hillsborough, Dinely.

18. Peers: Bolingbroke (1768); Grafton (1769); Ligonier (1772); Tyrconnel (1777); Osborne (1779); Percy (1779). Son: Weir (1757). Barts: Colleton (1772); Bunbury (1776); Blake (1778).

19. Maydwell (1754); Wymandesold (1754); Tuffnell (1757-58); Wentworth (1758); Daly (1768) (Irish); Collier (1772) (naval captain); Gordon (1773) (army captain); Horneck (1776) (captain and lieutenant); Harris (1777); Campbell (1778) (Lyon King of Arms for Scotland, see Notes and Queries (2nd series) vi, p.97).

20. Lewis Namier, The structure of politics at the accession of George the Third, p.418 et seq.

21. (?) Benson (1752); Lascelles (1752) (see note 16 above); Glover (1757); Nixon (1765); (?) Bowerbank (1773); Heatley (1772-74); Greene (1775); Williams (1776); Degen (1778); (?) Dobbin (1778); Chism (1779).

22. Henley (1754); Turner (1760) (attorney's son); Skinn (1772).

23. Greene (1773); Hazeland (1763).

24. Lewis (1772); Ennever (1753); Mathews (1766); Draper (1772); Goodflesh (1760); Hanckwitz (1772).

25. See D.G. Crawford, Roll of Indian Medical Service 1615-1930.

25a. The case papers reprinted in Trials for Adultery, or the History of Doctors Commons by A Civilian, Vol.II case 5, clearly identify Worgan as the organist. The identification in The New Grove, Dictionary of Music and Musicians (ed. Stanley Sadie), Vol.20 p.530, is erroneous (and Mrs Worgan's name wrongly given as Maclean rather than Maklecan).

26. Unidentified: Cooke (1759); Wilford (1759); Morgan (1755) and Aldcroft (1766). All appear to be middle rank.

27. E.g., Hanckwitz (1772).

28. E.g., Skinn (1772); compare L. Stone, The Family, Sex and Marriage in England 1500-1800 on "affect".

29. The Assignation Books of the London Consistory Court, in the Greater London Record Office, enable the progress of a case to be followed.

30. Moreau (1755); Edwards (1779).

31. Wilford (1759).

32. H.L.Jo. Vol.33 pp.82, 116; Parl. Hist. Vol.17, p.185.

33. Parl. Hist. Vol.20, p.592.

34. For Kenyon see G.T. Kenyon, Life of Lord Kenyon, p.364 et seq. and Anon., A sketch of the life and character of Lord Kenyon (1802); for George III see A. Aspinall (ed.), The later correspondence of George III, 2165.

35. Parl. Hist. Vol.34, p.1552; Vol.35, p.225 and see the debate on Taylor's divorce, ibid. Vol.35, 1248.

36. Hansard, Vol.14, pp.326,612.

37. The Parliamentary Register reports several debates in the 1790s and 1800s.

38. Failures: Downes (1781 and 1782); Lewis (1783); passed after a struggle: Williams (1783); Bayntun (1783).

39. Christie.

40. Esten (1798); Bartelot (1799).

41. Wilson (1798).

42. Twistleton (1798) not followed in Woodcock (1802) (or in Barker (1825)).

43. Rejected: Cope; Crewe (twice); Hoar; Woodcock. Withdrawn: Hutton; Lane. And note Williams (1801), petition only.

44. See e.g., Bartelot v. Hawker (1790) Peake 10.

45. It was against this background that the double standard was ennunciated; see Mrs Teush's case (1805-07).

46. Gooch (1781); Downes (1781-82); Newton (1782); Nisbet (1784); Fawkener (1787).

47. Errington (1787) and Williams (1783). For Nash see Sir John Summerson, The Life and Work of John Nash (1980), pp.7-12. Larking (1792) is untraced.

48. See e.g., the efforts of the Bishop of St. David's in Gooch's case, Parl. Hist. Vol.21, 1207-1222, and the reconstruction of the Cecil divorce (1791) in S.J. Watson, The Cottage Countess, ch.10.

49. Cadogan (1797); Abercorn (1799); Valentia (1799).

50. Bart: Webster (or Vassall) (1797). Knight: Hutton (1802). Landed: Stewart (1793); Martin (1793); Wakeman (1795) (later 1st Bart.); Mullins (1796) (later 2nd Baron Ventry); Biscoe (1796); Wilson (1798); (?) Bartelot (1799); Crewe (1801-02); Hoar (1802); Woodcock (1802).

51. Joseph Farington's Diary (Greig edition), Vol.III, p.73.

52. A. Aspinall (ed.), Later Correspondence of George III, 3704.

53. P.H. Highfill, K.A. Burnim and E.A. Langhans (eds.), Biographical Dictionary of Actors, Vol.V, p.104, where, however, the speculation about the reason for the failure of the divorce is groundless and wrong.

54. Moorsom (1796) (Whitby); Teast (1797) (Bristol); Boddington (1798); (?) Williams (1799).

55. A William Broke Jones is listed in Vivian H.H. Green, The Commonwealth of Lincoln College 1427-1977; cf. Foster, Alumni Oxonienses.

56. Cope (1801); Duckworth (1801) and Taylor (1800), respectively. But Taylor was also M.P. 1816-32: A. Aspinall (ed,), Correspondence of George, Prince

of Wales, 2199n.

57. Stanton (1799), Cooke (1797) and Campbell (1801) respectively. Campbell's sister, Mrs Addison, was the first woman to petition, also in 1801.

58. Woodmason (1798).

59. Farrer (1796) (E.I.C.); M'Gauley (1797); Bonham (1802) (E.I.C.).

60. Respectively, Street (1793), Bright (1796), Fozard (1797). For Opie see Joseph Farington's Diary, (K. Garlick and A. Macintyre edition), Vol.II, pp.441-2, 545; Vol.III, p.704; for the course of his nullity suit see London Consistory Court Assignation Books 1795-96 (G.L.R.O. DL/C/119,120). Lane (1802) is untraced. The remaining petitioner, by power of attorney from India, was Henry Williams, a factor with the E.I.C.

61. Peerage: Gardner (1805) (son of Baron); Boringdon (1809); Wellesley (1810); Cloncurry (1811); Rosebery (1815); Pellew (1820) (son of Viscount); Glerawly (1821); Lismore (1826). Barts: Gordon (1806); Brograve (1809); Abdy (1816); Barlow (1816); Wiseman (1824-25) (naval captain).

62. Gentry: (in addition to those named in text): Tighe (1804); Moore (1805); Simpson (1806); Campbell (1809); Powlett (1809); Guard (1810); Loveden (1811); Blachford (1812); Moore (1812); Best (1814); Garde (1814); Bailey (1817); Smith (1817); Taafe (1818-19); Miller (1821); Moore (1825); Baring (1825); Sullivan (1825); Johnston (1826).

63. Lingham (1804-05); Bazett (1809); Powles (1815); Leigh (1819); Holford (1819) (banker).

64. Gregson (1809); Taunton (1811); Allardyce (1823) (surgeon).

65. Massy (1808); Thomas (1819).

66. (?) Christie (1815); Peter (1825).

67. Sir Frederick Smith, A History of the Royal Army Veterinary Corps 1796-1919, 52. Untraced: Defries (1813); Doherty (1813) (? gentry); Dundas (1814) (probably gentry); Trelawney (1819) (ex R.N. midshipman); Temple (1820) (? gentry); Barker (1825) (middle rank). Indian: Cunliffe (1820-23);

Wilson (1823-24); Graeme (1822-25).

68. Particularly Ellenborough and Hamerton.

69. Simmons (1845-46) and Jackson (1842-43) respectively. William Hough (1841-44), an E.I.C. major in Bengal also had to petition twice.

70. Upper: Robeck; Haynes; Tyrell; Ellenborough; Hamerton; Mildmay; Muskett; Shakerley; Wallis. Attorney: Boydell. Doubtful: Lindam, formerly (as Ohle Lindam) a lieutenant in the King's German Regiment, later living at Torquay. Indian: (by power of attorney) Cazalet (judge and collector); Stock (major); Bayley (major); D'Oyley (judge etc.,). Using Indian procedure: Swetenham (collector); Keighley (captain).

71. Calcraft (1831).

72. Clayton (1832); Howell (1834) and, for example, Horlock (1834).

73. Dubious: Lambert (? collusion); Malpas (? reason for separation). Rejected: George (1836); Perry (1838).

74. Compare the readiness with which General Lautour's story that poverty had prevented his petitioning for a bill was believed by the (judicial) House of Lords, Lautour v. H.M's Proctor (1864) 10 H.L.C. 686. In fact he had petitioned in 1839 (see H.L.Jo. Vol.71), but withdrawn his petition - perhaps for the same reason that ultimately lost him his case.

75. As petitioner in 1839 and as adulterer in Major Heavisides's divorce in 1845. This probably explains the extraordinarily high damages, £8000, awarded against him, particularly as he had resisted a recriminatory plea brought by his wife on the grounds of his adultery with Mrs Heaviside. For this reason he cannot be treated as typical; cp. McGregor and Finer, op.cit. note 1, p.94.

76. He is number 5 in Ellicombe's list of divorces handled by his firm; see note 100 below.

77. Batley (1852); Bennett (1852); Jones (1853).

78. India: Wallbeoff (1830-32); Trower (1831); Blenkinsop (1833-35); Allan (1834); Moor (1834-35); Lethbridge (1837-38); Napier (1838-39); Perry

(1839-40); Larkins (1840-41); Wyatt (1841); Sewell (1842); Ashton (1842); Hough (1841-44); Cheape (1843-44); Shuldham (1845); Farquharson (1846); Jervis (1847-48); Lugard (1848); Hudson (1847-49); Cautley (1850); MacLean (1850); Wyndham (1853-55); Ewing (1854-55); Hadow (1854-55); Bellew (1855-56); Keays (1857). Australia: Cotterill (1843). Women: Turton (1831); Moffat (1832); Battersby (1840); Dawson (1848); Hall (1850). Newenham (or Wrotham)'s bill though styled a Divorce Bill was more properly called a Separation Bill; cf. Ellen Turner's Act.

79. Clayton (1832); Goring (1841); Hoghton (1849).

80. Horlock (1834); Conyers (1835); Lambert (1835); Gardiner (1837); Perry (1838); Lloyd (1839); Trafford (1840); Shawe (1841); Mitford (1842); Glegg (1842); Hawkes (1842); Kendall (1843); Watson (1843); Heaviside (1845); Curtis (1846); Heneage (1848); (?) Nicholson (1848); Waldy (1849); Hill (1849); Tayleur (1851); Webster (1851); Bennett (1852); Caton (1854); Sumner (1855); (?) Berens (1854); Talbot (1855); Smith (1857); Baring (1857).

81. Calcraft (1831); Lautour (1839); Hall (1840-41); Morgan (1843); Creagh (1846); Hawkins (1852); Rushbrooke (1853).

82. Carleton (1839); Heathcote (1851).

83. Solicitors: George (1836) (Cardigan); Pemberton (1839); Archbutt (1844); Jackson (1842-43); Clark (1846) (claimed to be solicitor to the Bristol and Exeter Railway; not in the Law Lists); James (1849) (Newnham); Davidson (1856). Barristers: Malpas (1835) (Leamington); Gape (1844) (St. Albans); Cobbe (1850).

84. Weguelin (1839); Humphreys (1846); Faussett (1849); Ashby (1850).

85. Warr (1840); Grant (1840); Todhunter (1843); Britten (1845); Matthyssens (1846); Campbell (1857); Ley (1857).

86. Close (1840), Coward (1842) and Llewellyn (1851) respectively.

87. Hodges (1836) (Lloyd's insurance broker); Mieville (1842) (partner in Kraeutler and Mieville in the City of London); Pedder (1855) (Preston banker).

88. Howell (1834) and Street (1842).

89. Cutbill (1853), Brooks (1847), Simmons (1845-46) and Stocker (1854) respectively.

90. H.C.P. 1852-53 Vol.XL, para.44.

91. The Commission is prone to exaggeration. For example, lawyers' fees are included in the computation of costs for English divorces but not for Scottish. Similarly, there are mistakes about the case law. Loveden's case (1811), which Campbell says shows the Lords rejecting a bill because the Commons insisted on inserting a clause guaranteeing the wife an income, was in fact rejected because the husband was unwilling to pay the income and asked the Lords to reject the whole bill. Similarly, Llewellyn's case (1851), does not show that the Lords had abandoned its right to call for the husband if it saw fit, only that the husband could not give evidence unless the House saw fit.

92. This is based on 77 taxed bills in the Court of Arches records, class J. Compare the taxed bills in Admiralty cases: PRO/HCA:2/36, where the procedure was similar, and the average about 80%. See also Report of the Ecclesiastical Commissioners, HCP 1831-32 Vol.xxiv at p.262.

93. Report of a Select Committee on Privy Council Appellate Jurisdiction, HLP, Vol.19, p.323.

94. Court of Arches records, class J for: Calcraft, Garlick, Birkley, Gardiner, Carleton, Moore, Grant, Lautour, Goring, May, Cutler, Knight, Parratt and Cartwright. Precise references can be found from Jane Houston, Cases in the Court of Arches 1660-1913, (Index Library, Vol.85).

95. Shephard's list wrongly says that Britten, Caton, Ashby and Tayleur did not petition Parliament and that Mrs Mathew did.

96. The cases are Currey (1828), Lakin (1849) and Smith (1849), references in Houston, op.cit., note 94.

97. Bayley (Assignation Books for 1827-30), Watson and Archbutt (Assignation Books for 1840-42).

98. To Arches: Teush (alimony) Brograve, Robeck, Hamerton, Haynes, Harris, Hamerton (again). First appeals to Delegates or Privy Council: Dunn, (Sullivan, in a nullity suit), Mellin, Grant, Curtis. Second appeals: Teush, Hamerton.

99. For Rogers, Belcher, Story, Heathcote, Trevanion, Lockwood, Frankfort, Collett and Scrivener. The appeals in Westmeath (1832) and Morse were about alimony only. References in Houston, op.cit., note 94.

100. "Costs of Divorce Acts handled by Messrs. J. Dorrington Ellicombes & Co." By referring to the printed bills in H.L.R.O. the petitioners can be identified as follows: 1 Gardiner, 2 Lethbridge, 3 Allison, 4 Coode, 5 Pemberton, 6 Battersby, 7 Grant, 8 Lloyd, 9 Trafford (probably), 10 Hall, 11 Glegg, 12 Hawkes, 13 Mieville, 14 Mitford, 15 Cheape (probably), 16 Gape, 17 Hough (probably), 18 Boileau, 19 Shuldham, 20 Curtis, 21 Matthyssens, 22 Martin, 23 Lugard (probably), 24 Hudson, 25 Cobbe, 26 Lincoln. Figures are not given for Archbutt, Sewell and Jackson, whose bills were also handled by this firm during this period.

101. In Duberley v. Gunning (1792) 4 T.R. 652, Grose J. said that new trials would not be granted solely because damages awarded might be too high, even where ". . . the damages given were tantamount to a verdict of imprisonment for life."

102. Damages might also have been used to buy an annuity for the wife, so as to fulfil the requirement that she be provided for. Lord Brougham hinted at this in Hartley's case (1850).

103. These are all the cases after about 1825, for which there is sufficient information to be worth tabulating.

VICTORIAN BARRISTERS, JUDGES AND TAXATION: A STUDY IN THE EXPANSION OF LEGAL WORK

R. Cocks

". . . in these days and in this great commercial country, the greatest and most commercial country in the world, we are bound to put a large and liberal construction upon any terms . . . in any Act of Parliament where the construction proposed to be put upon it is in favour of the trade and commerce of the country."

With these emotional words, and many others like them, Lord Chief Baron Kelly sought to justify his apparently helpful attitude towards traders in the otherwise rather solemn case of The Chartered Mercantile Bank of India, London and China v. W. Wilson (Inspector of Taxes).[1] The Bank wished to do no more to Mr. Wilson than dispute his interpretation of the Taxing Act that imposed "Inhabited House Duty." But, unfortunately for all concerned, the most important characteristic of the relevant legislation was its intense complexity. The Act exempted from liability those dwellings that were used for a "trade profession business or calling," went on in an elaborate manner to deprive any place that had someone living in it of the right to exemption, and then, in the interests of traders, exempted from liability those cases in which someone lived on the premises but did so in order to further the purposes of a trade.[2] In other words this confusing and eliptical piece of draftsmanship imposed a tax then allowed an exemption then restricted the exemption and then, by default, created an immunity.

The sheer complexity of the law was important because, at least to the outsider, it obscured the fact that Parliament had left the really important decisions to the lawyers. The range of the legislation, the extent to which it interfered with the everyday life of citizens and businesses, was entirely dependent upon the definition of a "profession" or a "business" or a "calling" or a "trade," or even of "an act done to further the purposes of a trade." In these important matters the statute provided the courts with little or no guidance and the lawyers appeared to have an almost unqualified discretion. In one or two instances suitable precedents did exist but it seems to have been felt that there was no substantial area of judge-made law that could be reinterpreted in the present context.[3] In fact in regard to revenue law in general Parliament had suddenly provided barristers with extraordinary opportunities and responsibilities. Sabine, the historian of Income Tax, has pointed out that this type of case could only come before the courts after 1874 when they were given jurisdiction in such matters by a wholly undebated section of a long and intricate piece of legislation.[4] In substance a matter that had previously been dealt with by administrators (i.e., it had not before been possible to require the officials involved - General or Special Commissioners - to state a case) was suddenly placed before these courts for analysis by the legal mind. In the past, the aggrieved tax-payer had to rely upon a (usually futile) appeal to the Treasury's good nature, but now an administrative topic had become a legal one.

In consequence the early revenue law of the 1870s provides the ideal material for an historical experiment. It should reveal as well as any other area of legal development what it was that really influenced the mid-Victorian lawyers in their creation of new law; quite simply in this area they had to cope with something which was almost wholly novel. In particular, it has the advantage of highlighting the very sensitive role of lawyers who were concerned with the appropriate role of government officials and professional men in matters relating to the creation and control of private wealth. To put it another way, it was necessary for these men to achieve an understanding as to what extent it was desirable to use the courts in response to the growth of bureaucratic activity on the part of government in the form of greatly extended tax-gathering. Could governmental functions be more closely regulated by lawyers? Conversely could lawyers be more useful than they had been in the everyday activities of complex administration; in other words could they assume a new role? In retrospect at least the importance of the lawyers' reaction to this sort of legislation in the 1870s is very clear. To use the language of the lawyers themselves it would set a precedent; it would reveal how well or badly the courts could cope with one of the new areas of concern to the state such as the imposition of strict criminal liability, factory and public health inspection, patent law etc. It would do something to reveal the possibilities for the traditional Bar and Bench in the context of a state that was gradually turning to the use of intricate and very detailed legislation as an instrument of social and economic management.

In this regard it often has been customary to see lawyers as the opponents of government and as the protectors of individuals and their property rights. In particular it has been stressed that Victorian barristers and judges had a sentiment for laissez-faire that left them hostile to both organised labour and the activities of officials who threatened the achievements of businessmen. It is not too much to say that for some historians the lawyers are little more than the agents of capital: no amount of ancient costume and heavy wigs could hide the sympathy for the modern entrepreneur who bettered himself and, in doing so, created wealth for others.[5] Indeed the determination of Lord Chief Baron Kelly to put a "large and liberal construction" upon any term in any Act where "the construction proposed is in favour of the trade and commerce in the country" would seem to confirm such views. And, in more general terms, historians who have looked in some detail at the role of law and lawyers in Victorian society can rarely resist the words of "that staunch individualist" Baron Bramwell. In a famous non-revenue case involving men who had been convicted of illegal activities during a strike by London tailors he roundly assured them that "the best men in this country . . . have been engaged in removing restraints from trade, commerce industry and labour." And he went on to stress that "everybody knows that the total aggregate happiness of mankind is increased by every man being left to the unbiased, unfettered determination of his own will and judgment as to how he will employ his industry and other means of getting on in the world."[6]

However, despite the obvious strength of feeling that lies behind such words, it is easy to show that such beliefs cannot directly explain all that happened to revenue law in the 1870s - even though Baron Bramwell himself was one of the judges involved. For example, from the very beginning of the case law it was apparent that manufacturers and mine owners were anxious to attack the tax-man's understanding of what constituted capital expenditure. These industrialists strove to argue that in computing profits for tax purposes they should be allowed to subtract the expenditure incurred in establishing their business. Thus, the owner of a coal mine would be able to subtract not only the everyday expense incurred in extracting coal but also the initial expense involved in sinking shafts into the ground.[7] Likewise the factory owner would be allowed to subtract not only the cost of running his concern but also the amount written off for depreciation of buildings and fixed plant and machinery.[8] Obviously a great deal of money was at stake and the interests of traders clearly demanded that such sums should be deducted in computing taxable profits. Indeed, they garnished their arguments with references to classical economists such as McCulloch.[9]

The judges, however, did almost nothing to help the traders in this vital matter. As with the scope of words such as "trade" and "profession" Parliament had provided the judiciary with little guidance and it was open to the Bench to interpret the law in a way that favoured the entrepreneur if it wished to do so - as elsewhere the legislation had given the judges a free hand. Yet in these years when the case-law was being established their decisions seemed to have caused so many problems for industrialists concerned with capital expenditure that it was necessary for Parliament to intervene as early as 1878. In the Customs and Inland Revenue Act of that year it gave express advantages to traders in respect of just the sort of expenditure that judges refused to regard as relevant in the computation of liability.[10] Parliament had rescued the capitalist from the judges and it is surely not too much to say that in this respect the Bench had resolutely opposed the application of laissez-faire ideas.

Of course it may be that this example, though important, was not typical, and it might also be the case that some apparently (or actually) deeper level of analysis would show that even these decisions could be reconciled with some broader commitment to laissez-faire and its associated values. For instance, an alternative analysis of the case-law in this area might lead one to place more emphasis upon the role of professional self-interest, rather than overall political ideas. And professional self-interest might, in turn, easily be associated with laissez-faire commitments. The development of the law was in the hands of a small group of men who, after years of work together, might be expected to share the same sort of outlook in defence of the same sort of interests in a non-collectivist state. After all, only about fifteen judges were involved in deciding revenue cases at this time, and the number of barristers who practised in their courts was never very large.[11] In fact the advocacy work was dominated by about twenty practitioners most of whom knew each other well, and it might be thought that these men would attempt to further the interests of lawyers in some systematic way that would be reflected in the case-law.[12] For example, they might develop a highly legalistic approach to revenue problems that would do something to ensure that lawyers rather than accountants dealt with tax. In this context "highly legalistic" means no more than that their practices would ensure that the issues came to be expressed in extremely complex ways and were identified as being the exclusive preserve of lawyers. In other words, quite apart from furthering the financial interests of Bench and Bar, they would also explore an opportunity to show the world just how indispensable the lawyers had become in this area. There would be nothing surprising in this since historians of all professions have usually explained professional change in terms of a mixture of the search for respectability and outright avarice.[13]

Unfortunately, however, this approach encounters immediate problems since it presupposes that the Bench and the Bar of the 1870s can be given a coherent identity. This is not to say that it required that all barristers and judges thought the same way about their roles; it simply involves the assertion that these lawyers had a clear idea of what it was that their profession stood for - and in fact it was just this idea that they did not have at the time in question. As far as the judiciary was concerned the story is a fairly simple one. For years there had been increasingly strident demands for the reform of the courts and much of their procedure. Newspapers such as The Times, and informed periodicals such as The Saturday Review, were unrelenting in their demand that the administration of justice should not be judged by lawyers but by the requirements of public utility.[14] And it was, of course, during these years that the very existence of the House of Lords in its judicial capacity was in doubt just because its utility was not immediately apparent to enquiring outsiders: as Robert Stevens has recently put it "utilitarian attack" had to be met with "oligarchic counter-attack."[15] Worse still, from the point of view of the less exalted judiciary, there were plans afoot to revolutionise the ancient assize system and replace it with a network of local courts that sat continuously: in other words, the old and highly centralised world of the judges was in real danger.[16] Indeed, there was a symbolic quality about the fact that Lord Chief Baron Kelly himself would be the last man to hold the title he so enjoyed.[17] The judiciary, therefore, were very much on the defensive during these years: more than at any other time in modern legal history it had to comply, willingly or otherwise, with demands for reform.

This was, if anything, even more the case with the Bar. It seems that the problems of barristers at the time of the Judicature Acts have never been explored in much detail, but what is known suggests that the profession experienced a profound crisis. Some men, particularly those who worked in the counties near London, were faced with the destruction of their practices. Old understandings such as those which regulated Circuit life were under immense stress. Indeed, one Circuit was actually to be destroyed and another to be divided in half. In some cases, notably in the Home Counties, the strain imposed upon the traditional institutions of the practising Bar - the Circuit Messes - was such as to lead men to go so far as to suggest that they may as well be abolished.[18] It was not a happy time for practitioners in the provinces.

However, there were even more problems confronting them when they came to the capital itself. The public was frequently very critical of the Inns of Court and the Bar was divided in its response to demands for reform. Some wanted these ancient bodies to continue just as they were; some supported the new system of compulsory examinations that had been forced upon the Inns in 1872 after more than a quarter of a century of acrimonious dispute; and some wished to see them entirely transformed into a sort of legal university that imposed the academic standards that were expected of lawyers in other countries.[19] Beneath these arguments there was uncertainty as to the very identity of the Inns: Lord Selborne, for example, was set upon obtaining sweeping changes and, in demanding reform, he took issue with those who claimed that the Inns were private bodies with their own property and autonomous powers. On the contrary, he claimed, they were public institutions and were, therefore, accountable to public judgment.[20] In return for his reforming efforts he encountered savage opposition to his "objectionable" course of "working from the outside, and trying by external pressure to force upon his own and the other Inns of Court fundamental changes." He was, as it were, a traitor doing the work of a hostile and ill-informed public: above all, he and other barristers who thought as he did were bringing out into the world those matters that were - in the eyes of many lawyers - best left to the Bar itself.[21]

In short, the profession of the 1870s was no better equipped than the Bench to assert its power in some forceful and novel fashion. Both were having to respond to the crude utilitarian ideas that non-lawyers held about the administration of justice, and neither could assert itself without the prospect of substantial public opposition. It would be most unlikely therefore that the development of any new era of law could be explained in terms of professional self-assertion. The profession was too disorganised and too weak to have produced such a result. It had, as it were, no very clear image of itself.

Unfortunately, however, any twentieth century reader who seeks to go beyond the debate about laissez-faire ideas and the details of professional history has also to reject the perspective put forward in modern legal text-books. These works, for obvious reasons, are primarily concerned with revenue law as it exists today rather than with the problems of its historical evolution. When one reads a modern introduction to revenue law it is sometimes rather easy to gain the impression that the lawyers of the 1870s were remarkable quarrymen hewing principles out of the unworked rock of tax law with a sense of certainty that leaves the modern barrister awe-struck. For example, the Coltness Iron and Steel case is usually quoted as the authority that laid bare the chief criteria that should be used to distinguish capital from income; and, in a way, this is undeniably true - the case is still used as a helpful authority in this regard.[22] But unfortunately such an attitude obscures many of the problems that worried the Victorian barristers who dealt with such matters; they did not see these issues with great clarity and approached them in a fashion that might seem strange to modern lawyers. For example, the judges of these years had a very different notion of the distinction between law and fact, and this inevitably coloured their reasoning in the cases before them. Indeed, the meticulous studies of Dr. Farnsworth have done much to suggest that nineteenth century revenue law as a whole has unique qualities that are easily forgotten under the burdensome weight that the vastly expanded subject has acquired during the twentieth century.[23] In a nutshell, the technical validity of an old precedent is no guide to its historical context. The fact that it can be used in a modern argument tells us nothing about the ideas of those lawyers who actually created it; it simply tells us something about modern notions of validity.

The anachronistic use of case-law is admittedly a much bigger problem than these rather casual remarks suggest, but in the present context it does have the virtue of pointing to a new approach to understanding the real origins of the cases. It suggests that instead of searching for principles that may be of use in modern analysis it is desirable to look at the way in which revenue problems really were discussed at the time the decisions were actually made: in other words, it is necessary to put at least as much emphasis upon style as upon content. The way men argued about the points involved may tell us more about the growth of the case-law than the actual conclusion that was reached at the end of a particular case. It might enable us to put on one side modern conceptions, whether they come from lawyers with their anxiety to find precedents, or from historians with their search for the influence of ideas and their emphasis upon professional self-aggrandisement.

In fact, when the case-law of the mid-1870s is looked at as a whole it becomes apparent that there were distinct themes to the arguments of counsel and judges. In particular it is immediately obvious that at times there was a strong concern with what the lawyers themselves saw as being purely legal arguments that had little or nothing to do with the economic realities of the case-law: in other words, they sought, ostensibly, to show a disregard for either pro or anti-laissez-faire thinking; they claimed to be in pursuit of neutrality. For example, counsel for the revenue usually emphasised the meaning of particular words in statutes rather than more general considerations. In one instance, Sir John Holker, the Attorney-General, went so far as to say that "the argument of the other side may be right, upon the principles required in political economy, but the very aim and object of the Income Tax Acts seem to have been to prevent the principles which a political economist would apply from applying to cases under these Acts."[24] Lord Chief Baron Kelly frequently (but, as the quotation at the start of the article indicates, not always) echoed this approach and resolutely stuck to what he saw as being non-economic criteria. The court, he thought, should follow "the plain and natural meaning of the words" in the statute; it should adhere to the usage adopted by the great English writers during the past two or three centuries. When the Act was clear the court should follow its obvious meaning regardless of the need to do justice and fairness to commercial and manufacturing interests. It had to be recognised that tax law itself was not always what it ought to be - the tax-payer might be able to produce "the most reasonable mode that could be determined" for the computation of profits in most cases, "but it really would not be according to law."[25]

Other judges and barristers were prepared to take a somewhat broader view whilst sticking to the same sort of "non-economic" approach. For example, they were at times anxious to construe the meaning of a statutory word or phrase by considering its use in a past taxing Act. Some such as Thesiger and Brett JJ. sought to follow this sort of analysis whilst still being determined to avoid a dogmatic attachment to any one particular meaning of the words before them.[26] Bramwell B. himself emphasised that the judges should analyse legislation carefully and critically; he pointed out that although the courts were not concerned with the hardship that a particular interpretation might cause a litigant they should also bear in mind that it was unlikely that the Act was intended to cause such hardship rather than to be reasonable and just.[27]

This rather technical approach with its emphasis upon the law itself, rather than the commercial realities involved in taxation, received further support when the judges went in search of legal principles. Even in these early years the judges made confident references to "the general principles of the Income Tax Acts" but unfortunately it is not always easy to discover exactly what the principles that they had in mind actually were. In fact, at times they became almost obscure, as when they went beyond the legislation itself and considered "Income Tax Acts and the principles of the Law" and it is very difficult indeed to see where these ideas, independent of statute law, came from. For example, the remarkable Kelly L.C.B. sometimes referred to the latter type of principle, usually in the course of regretting that it had been overruled by statute. There were, he claimed "great principles of the law," "principles of great weight as affecting the Law of England and I may almost say as affecting the international law of the world;" for instance, "the great principle of the Law of England in relation to taxation is that taxation shall only be imposed upon persons or things actually within this country." In this respect our modern statute law was "an infringement upon one of the principles on which taxation is levied by the laws of any country."[28]

The Scottish judges were also interested in principles and appear to have applied them with much more confidence. For example, Lord Deas asserted that "in administering an Act of this kind" - he was dealing with an Act that imposed a general tax and not a tax on a particular group or class - "the great principle comes in that there is to be equality of liability among all the parties for whose benefit it is laid on."[29] In another case Lord Ardmillan remarked that "we have been told that a taxing statute must be construed liberally and favourably to the subject"; and he went on to add that "in one sense this is true and the remark is well-founded, but on the other hand, equality and impartial justice in the incidence of taxation are of greater moment, and the statutes should be construed so as to promote that equality and that impartiality of justice."[30] It is not suggested that the use of these principles was (or was not) typical of Scottish lawyers faced with revenue problems. For present purposes what matters is that they were contributing to the development of a general British approach to tax problems since it is noticeable that English judges were very interested in the Scottish case-law at this time.[31]

In England, however, the usual approach of those judges who wished to use legal arguments, and who found it difficult to rely on the statutes by themselves, was to look for other areas of the law that were in some way analogous to the case in hand. In one instance the court considered (in effect) the right of a company to set against its profits any annual reduction in the value of mines that were having coal taken out of them. In response to this Herschell Q.C. looked beyond the common law and asked "Would not the Court of Chancery interfere if the company were going to pay a dividend when, though it had made a sum of money, it had exhausted an amount of coal more than representing that sum of money?"[32] In a similar fashion there was a preparedness on the part of some judges to look to what they thought of as being "reasonable." Pollock B. in particular was happy to stress this consideration, and Kelly L.C.B. - cheerfully contradicting what he said on other occasions - was happy to assert that "We must really look at these cases with the eye of common sense."[33] However, it is apparent that when the lawyers spoke in terms such as these they were anxious to consider arguments that were not based solely on the problems of statutory interpretation and old principles.

In other words, they tried also, even from the very start, to introduce what they saw as being economic criteria to their analysis of the revenue problems that confronted them. In some instances, and in direct contradiction to the emphasis placed on legal criteria by men such as Holker, they regarded economic ideas and trading experience as being relevant. For example, this approach produced one of Kelly's most condescending remarks when he said that "I have the greatest respect for the decisions of the Court of Session in Scotland, even upon commercial questions."[34] In short, Scottish law was relevant because in some way it reflected, or was part of, economic success. Clearly it was not a very long step from this to Kelly's outright enthusiasm for trade, and he was supported in voicing such sentiments by Baron Cleasby who, in construing a statute and the phrase "the purpose of trade" said that "it is desirable to encourage trade, and it is a matter of importance to give it that encouragement."[35] The interest in laissez-faire is very obvious, but it can now be seen as just one of a number of sometimes mutually opposing criteria that barristers and the judges were happy to use in the course of argument. The important and consistent theme is the preparedness to use a variety of 'tests'. Indeed, in the case above, for all his formidable remarks about trade, Cleasby - balancing this matter with other considerations - found against the trader.

The variety of approaches used by the judges is further illustrated by the fact that they were sometimes anxious to go beyond economic matters in general and relate the problem in front of them to specific commercial practices - without regard to whether or not they favoured laissez-faire. In one Scottish case the Lord President said ". . . I am quite clear that the making of a new pit in a trade of this kind is in every sense of the term just an expenditure of capital . . . it must be placed to capital account in any properly kept books applicable to such a concern."[36] In an English case Baron Huddlestone was influenced by the fact that the expenditure in question "would be treated for all purposes of bookkeeping and for all usual purposes as capital."[37] In the same vein when considering the word "profit", Kelly L.C.B. was very happy to talk about what he saw as being economic realities at considerable length.[38] Baron Pollock was content to place reliance upon the opinions of informed outsiders as when he had to consider the significance of "depreciation" in a company's balance sheet, and he was assisted by the ideas of a company director, Mr. Chadwick M.P., "who thoroughly understands the matter."[39] Nevertheless, the same judge was shrewdly aware of the fact that this approach could make for many problems; it was easy for difficulties to grow "from a sort of misapprehension which often unfortunately arises, not only in matters of law, but still more perhaps, in matters of commercial accounts, by the nomenclature which is used."[40]

However, most of the lawyers were unconcerned with the detailed problems of nomenclature. When it became clear that varied economic ideas as well as more conventional legal arguments could be used in the course of debate, judges and counsel obviously enjoyed discussion about such matters in an everyday and amateur fashion. The Attorney General, Herschell, once argued that "in any ordinary case of trading you must see in estimating the profits how much less the stock was at the end than at the beginning of the year," and Pollock B. responded by saying (in effect) that in the case of land they were not dealing with stock but rather with something like the soil in a market garden. If, the judge continued, you overworked a market garden, the declining value of the soil was hardly a deductible expense. Herschell Q.C. immediately responded by saying that when (as in his case) someone mined coal, the coal left forever - but the market garden could be made profitable once again.[41]

In fact, as subsequent case-law has made clear, these simple analogies contained a great number of complicated implications for revenue law. They raised matters relevant to the definition of stock in trade; they pointed to the difficult distinction between deductible income expenditure and non-deductible capital "losses"; they involved the vague idea that land itself must usually be regarded as a form of capital rather than income. Above all they pointed to the pervasive belief that the lawyer is capable of solving intricate commercial problems by using ideas culled from his experience of everyday life.

Indeed, at times this apparently simple, apparently common sense, approach could become somewhat involved; and this was particularly so when strong social or moral issues were bound up in economic problems. For instance, in one case Kelly L.C.B. and Hawkins J. were faced with an important decision in regard to pubs.[42] In substance they had to consider the nature of payments made in order to ensure that certain pubs sold the beer of the brewery that was being taxed; in other words, they had to consider the sums of money that were used to turn pubs into 'tied' houses. The appellant brewery claimed that "for the purpose of arriving at the just balance of the profits and gains of their trade, it is necessary each year to make an allowance in respect of a portion of the amount which was paid by them to acquire the leaseholds, and without which they would not have been able to make any profits . . . and that such an allowance represents only the portion of their capital exhausted during the year in earning the said profits."[43] In other words, to use the language of Grantham Q.C. who represented the appellants, a proportion of the initial expense should be set against each year's gross profits. But Kelly L.C.B. was not impressed by these propositions. As he saw it, payments for tied houses were a form of advertising (the idea that they involved an "anti-free trade" monopoly does not seem even to have occurred to him) and he went on to ask Grantham Q.C. if the act of giving dinners to prospective clients could be deductible.[44] The latter fell back on some things that Kelly L.C.B. himself had said in a previous case: "the tax-payer", he had then stated, "has the right to take into consideration before the amount of profit can be said to be ascertained all that he has expended of every description in order to enable him to acquire the right to dispose of it, and thus to obtain the sum in respect of which he is to be assessed."[45] In other words, Grantham Q.C. - who was perhaps rather less than a legal and fiscal luminary - saw the problem solely in terms of traditional ideas about property.

The judges set about solving the problem by looking to the meaning of the word "production"; only the costs and expenses of actual "production" were to be deducted. Hence raw material, wages, even the rent of a brewery might be deducted in assessing the appellant's liability, but the payments in respect of the pubs did not come into this category. They were seen as being of a character and description quite unconnected with the production of the article. Hawkins J. admitted that it was difficult to know where exactly the line should be drawn: for example, what about the costs of transport between the brewery and the customer? In other words, "common sense," and analogies from everyday life, were not of great assistance in "drawing the line" and it is difficult to see this as other than a social judgment about the proper scope of 'true' trading. In brief, social, and even moral, tests were just as useful as economic ones.

In many cases the issues were a great deal more complex than this and they necessarily involved a jumbled mixture of all the criteria used by the lawyers. This became particularly apparent when the judges considered whether or not the "profits" made by Municipal Corporations were taxable. It was clear that even if a Corporation made money out of a water-works it was hardly a conventional trading concern. At the same time, however, it was equally plain that it was carrying on some sort of economic activity. It was an unsettling area in which the judges were concerned about the very fact that government (even local government) was involved in such a matter, particularly if it made a profit out of its work. At times, as elsewhere, the judges took what they saw as being the purely legal approach and spoke of the meaning of words: income from such things as a water rate was to be contrasted with income from other local "taxes"; the former was more like a due or toll and the latter was more like a public payment that could not be related to profit making.[47] At times legal ideas were borrowed from other areas of the law: local authorities might be associated with the ideal of trusteeship; in the words of Lord Deas "the Corporation is the mere trustee, hand and instrument of the ratepayer. There is no room, therefore, for saying that the Corporation can make a profit."[48] And at times they might try to use all possible approaches as in another Scottish case where the Lord President balanced economic and legal considerations when he observed that "it seems to me that the Corporation of the City of Glasgow is, by virtue of this statute, empowered to enter into a speculation as traders in gas. No doubt it may have been for the benefit of the community . . . but they have all the character and attributes of a trading company."[49]

Plainly, as the judges themselves sensed, these problems indicate that there comes a stage where it is very difficult to draw clear lines between legal and economic or social analysis. Much of the explicit and implicit reasoning in the cases takes a form similar to the following line of reasoning: What activity did the tax-payer engage in? He mined coal. What is a mine like? It is like a market garden because something of value is taken out of the ground. What is the ground like? It is something that can depreciate in value but it is permanent. What are permanent things like? They are capital - they are not temporary income. Therefore, we may conclude, the declining value of a coal-mine is a capital and not an income matter.

Of course there are all sorts of ways in which such an approach to legal problems might have been justified. It was possible for the lawyers to emphasise that it frequently reflected the virtues of common sense; it seemed to link the law to some of the realities behind the cases; it had a certain air of reasonableness about it. But when it is broken down into its constituent elements the results appear chaotic and it is increasingly difficult to discover anything like the borderline between legal and economic ideas. It is surely an economic judgment to say that mining is (or is not) like market-gardening; and it is surely a legal judgment to say that such matters should be discussed in tax cases or, on a different tack, to say that the court will give a word a certain meaning. And the results are likely to be most confusing when the analogies are based upon traditional legal terms reflecting very different types of economic activity. For instance, it is difficult to obtain a clear picture of the issues involved when the tax liability of a mining enterprise is judged in the light of a comparison between mining and the Court of Chancery's ideas about a company's duties to its shareholders. Similarly, there are obvious problems when the notion of trusteeship is associated with the trading activities of a Municipal Corporation.

However, beneath all the confusion there is one consistent commitment. The lawyers never despaired of being able to cope with the problems before them - indeed they rather enjoyed themselves. They never expressed doubts as to their own suitability in being the ultimate tribunal in the matters that came to court and, curiously, the chief reason for this confidence seems to have been based on their obvious sense of continuity with the legal past. To the outsider the rapidly expanding volume of revenue case-law looked like a radically new phenomenon and in a sense, as we have seen, it really was the important novelty it appeared to be in that lawyers were dealing with very important matters that, by and large, had not previously been left to them. But for the lawyers there was nothing revolutionary about the event: the subject matter of their work had changed but they were fully capable of dealing with the innovation: they simply debated the issues partly in terms of the words used in the statutes, partly in terms of established legal concepts, partly in everyday economic terms, and above all in the light of what they took to be common sense. There was no need for sharp distinctions between the economic and legal elements in the arguments; they could both be integrated so easily into acceptable discussion. The case-law was really the scene of a triumph for a traditional ad hoc "common law" approach to litigation, and the great volumes of legislation coming from Parliament could do nothing to change this state of affairs. Revenue law had been accommodated with the traditional pattern of debate between barristers and judges. One might almost say that a form of linguistic imperialism had taken place: the lawyers had "carved out" a new area of public debate for themselves.

However, the matter cannot be left to rest at this point. For one thing it suggests a reassessment of the way the Victorian lawyers are so frequently described. If a brief survey of how one very small area of case-law developed reveals inadequacies in conventional interpretations much greater surveys might indicate that the wrong questions have been asked about the making of Victorian case-law in general. It is not just that it is impossible to label the revenue lawyers as either "laissez-faire men" or "collectivist men"; it is rather that such labels are of necessity wholly inappropriate in that they guide attention away from what it was that really concerned these men - which was, of course, the desire to sustain a tradition of analysis that was not attached to any particular ideas beyond the implicit assumption that it was sensible for lawyers to make these important decisions. In this part of the law at least, what mattered was the preservation of a court room tradition in which a great variety of criteria could be used in the course of argument without any taint of unorthodoxy. To put it loosely, lawyers were concerned with a way of doing things, not with specific ideas.

By the same token these matters invite a reassessment of the Bar and Judiciary in their historical context. It is not just that it is impossible to regard them as being uniformly strong throughout the Victorian era. It is also necessary to emphasise the importance of individual advocates and judges who were hardly likely to accept the constraints of some single principle or idea. The importance of Lord Chief Baron Kelly in these early years of tax law is beyond dispute - yet he had behind him the strangest of careers at the Bar in which he combined an enormous practice with professional ostracism. He was known to be corrupt - even those parts of the legal press that defended him admitted this - and on one occasion he was actually flung out of his Circuit Mess.[50] His appointment to the Bench was regarded as being more than somewhat dubious, and in his later years as

Chief Baron, his behaviour was at times sufficiently odd for even the respectful Holdsworth to comment on it as being strange.[51] A man such as this could hardly be categorised with any ease.

The same could be said, not only of many of the other judges, but also of the advocates who appeared before them. Holker, for example, had behind him a career that was also in many respects a professional oddity: he was one of the first advocates to build up a local practice (in Liverpool) not based exclusively upon Circuit work who then, having established his reputation, went on to achieve further fame in London.[52] Farrer Herschell also had a distinguished and unusual career behind him.[53] Benjamin, the authority on "Sale of Goods", appeared in tax cases and, as is well known, he had a strange past involving distinguished legal work in Louisiana, the offer of a position in the Supreme Court of the United States, and a leading political role in the Confederate states.[54] Giffard - Sir Hardinge Giffard - is even better known as a man who already had vast political and professional experience behind him and who, in his capacity as Lord Chancellor Halsbury, was to have so much influence in the legal world of the late nineteenth century.

The point of these remarks is, of course, that they hint at the enormous breadth of experience behind those who were involved in the early revenue cases. It would be easy to amplify both their lives, and the lives of others, with a view to showing that it was in the highest degree unlikely that such men could have agreed upon anything other than what they saw as being the standards of general debate in broad common sense terms. The modern lawyer may not regard them all as being very endearing personalities but the commanding power of their characters was beyond dispute.

In respect of one of the barristers, in particular, the analysis should be carried a little further. A.V. Dicey found it much more difficult to take for granted the idea that widely informed men of affairs, who happened to have a love of public speaking, should be entrusted with the interpretation of legislation in such an important area. Although his own practice was not particularly distinguished - he had been called to the Bar in 1863 and he had done more in the years since then to impress the world of scholarship than the world of clients - he nevertheless was briefed in revenue cases from an early date.[55] In particular, he was given the task of assisting the tax authorities with the more technical aspects of the law.

For some years before he did this work, he had been very concerned about the profession and its proper role in British society. As early as 1867 he had defended the Bar from the accusation that it was some form of "Trade Union" and, although his defence did not even satisfy all the lawyers, it revealed an anxiety on Dicey's part to find some publicly acceptable justification for the Bar's existence.[56] In regard to the revenue cases of the 1870s, this could only have given him cause to think. It must have been obvious to him that here was a matter of vital importance to the citizen and his property which until recently had been dealt with by government officials rather than lawyers. The need to justify the increasing use of lawyers was clear and it does not seem fanciful to claim that Dicey's experience in this area reinforced his subsequent interest in the "rule of law" and does something to explain his shrill and hostile attitude to "administrative" powers. In other words, he may well have sensed that much was at stake for the lawyers.

At the same time, his possible concern presents an apparent paradox. Dicey's name was inseparably linked after the publication of Law and Opinion in England with devotion to the laissez-faire rather than the collectivist elements in Benthamite thought.[57] In other words, unlike the Dicey of the 1870s who argued in general terms with other revenue lawyers and avoided any commitment to particular ideas, the Dicey of later years had become the classic example of those who see nineteenth century law as the model for individualistic values. In part the paradox is resolved by pointing out that Dicey himself saw the period of collectivism as beginning in the 1870s - for him it was a time of confusion when many ideas might be entertained.[58] But in part, also, the paradox is explained away by assuming that Dicey foresaw a very clear challenge to the traditions of the

Bench and Bar arising out of the fact that they were going to be called upon to interpret and apply immensely complicated statutes that sought to regulate vast areas of social and economic activity. The temptation to see the lawyers as useful means to an administrative end rather than as capable independent men maintaining a tradition of civilized public debate was likely to become stronger and stronger. And one of the defences that could be raised with a view to preventing this from ever happening was, of course, to praise the individual in the way that Dicey did, and to interpret the law of the nineteenth century in such a fashion as to show that the judges and the Bar should be identified with the cause of those who opposed collectivism. Specific values were to be injected into a debate that had previously avoided them. Legal history, as interpreted by Dicey, would serve the purpose of revealing the dangers that lay ahead and at the same time it would highlight a crucial role for lawyers in modern conditions. Lawyers had a role in the society of the future but it had to be as the agents of an individual's rights - it had, as it were, to have a specific content. Far from seeking to defend the old Bar, Dicey sought to revolutionise its functions and replace impartial debate with a radical commitment to individualistic values.

Whatever the explanations for Dicey's responses to revenue law, the legacy of the ad hoc way in which the lawyers approached these problems is still of great importance and is immediately apparent in the quality of modern tax law. The comparative lack of principles in this area has made informal understandings between what may loosely be described as the revenue authorities, accountants and lawyers, of particular importance. For example, commercial practice may (or may not) have the force of law but its influence is undeniable - and, in general, tax is a branch of law that cannot properly be understood apart from the conventions of its practitioners. Indeed, Megarry V.C. has cautioned those who apply dogmatic methods of interpretation: in his own words, judicial common sense is needed and "the adjective 'judicial' may be useful as indicating that the kind of common sense needed is one that is not at large, but is guarded and tutored by the authorities."[59]

Unfortunately, it is arguable that this very reasonable reaction has in itself produced massive problems for the modern citizen. Just because the interpretation of revenue statutes is a craft with its own, almost intuitive qualities, the drafting of revenue legislation is a nightmare. The possible responses of civil servants, accountants, tax advisers, solicitors, barristers and judges are so numerous that, with a view to eliminating uncertainty, the draftsman has to produce very detailed legislation indeed. And the result of course is the all but overwhelming weight and complexity of modern tax statutes. The strange legacy of the mid-Victorian determination to deal with revenue cases in what was seen as being a "common sense" manner is the creation of a body of law that is frequently far beyond the grasp of the most intelligent and "common sense" citizen.

CONCLUSION

Plainly, the very early revenue cases cannot be explained in terms of a devotion to a particular economic creed or a programme of sustained professional self-assertion. The common theme to the case-law, and the explanation for its qualities, lies in an attachment on the part of the lawyers involved to a tradition of debate within which a great variety of arguments were permissible. At one time a judge might support a proposition that would further the interests of laissez-faire; at another time he would do the opposite. One barrister would argue that economic considerations were irrelevant; another would make them the corner-stone of his argument. And so on.

As a result it seems reasonable to suggest three things. Firstly, it appears that Dicey in particular reacted to this challenge presented to the lawyers by the modern state in a singularly radical fashion. He was not (as is commonly suggested) the stout defender of every legal tradition; he was instead an innovator who sought to preserve the old powers of the legal profession by new means. As he seems to have seen it, barristers were faced with difficulties that made it increasingly desirable to identify the Bar with a particular set of values rather than with standards of debate that allowed for the use of a great variety of ideas. He sensed, perhaps, a need to replace mid-Victorian "openness" with a particular dogma: for him, the modern Bar had to be seen as the defender of "individualistic" laissez-faire ideas, and the mid-Victorian tradition of apparent "neutrality" had to be put to one side.

Secondly, if these cases are any guide, it also follows that the legal profession of these years cannot be seen as some homogeneous entity pursuing a consistent policy of support for one set of ideals rather than another: admittedly, it resolutely adhered to the ideal of open argument but, beyond this, it could not be identified with any particular school of thought. Perhaps, however, we should not be too surprised at this: other recent investigations have stressed the importance of tensions within the professions and the complexity of their response to nineteenth century problems.[60]

Thirdly, and most significantly, these facts suggest further research into Victorian legal ideas along the lines suggested in recent years by those who have been looking at non-legal subjects. For example, Christopher Harvie's analysis of mid-Victorian academic life suggests in a particularly forceful manner that not much of value is going to be revealed by looking for the "manipulative skills of an elite": modern theories of "elite rule" are hardly applicable to the realities of these decades in Britain.[61] Instead, an increasing interest in intellectual history has produced a situation in which "the role of ideology in nineteenth century British politics is now seen as more important and more complex than a mere rationalisation by groups of their situation and ambitions . . . it influences the groups who profess it, not simply as a programme but as a factor within their own constitution which affects their perception of 'social reality'."[62]

In this context Christopher Harvie had done a great deal to chart the ideology of university liberalism, and there is no reason why the same sort of approach cannot be used with Victorian barristers and judges in general. In fact, just because many barristers were also academics, Harvie's study itself makes suggestions as to the possible links between legal thought, the professional problems of the Bar, and a much broader crisis in the public life of the nation.[63]

It is in this area in particular that the present study may be helpful. By itself it provides a simple interpretation of what it was that the mid-Victorian barristers and judges were doing with tax law and, in concluding that what counted for them was an open tradition of debate, and not particular ideas, it accepts much of what they said at face value. Obviously, it has to be conceded at once that it would be very naive to suggest that a tradition of debate provides the final explanation for the case-law that has been analysed. Phenomena such as the appearance of neutrality, the cultivation of very complex chains of argument, and the accommodation of novel economic problems within the confines of traditional legal discussion suggest further and much deeper investigations into the problems of Victorian lawyers.

However, the present approach does claim to have two virtues. It highlights the shortcomings of conventional investigations into the law, with their emphasis on the public beliefs of individuals or the self-interest of the profession: these instruments are too blunt when it comes to understanding the intricate details of the early tax cases. And, more positively, the approach favoured by this article suggests an alternative method of analysis in which primary attention is given to the style of argument. This leads attention away from the biographical details of individual judges and barristers (did "X" believe in laissez-faire?, etc.,) and reveals a variety of beliefs which are not easily explained in terms of immediate professional self-interest. It points instead to professional ideas, conventions, understandings etc., that had, as it were, a momentum of their own. As Harvie puts it, we cannot confine ourselves to "a mere rationalisation by groups of their situation and ambitions": beliefs as to what was appropriate legal conduct were themselves an important part of professional life, and did much to determine the pace and quality of legal change. As yet we know almost nothing about these professional understandings, and further research may show that they explain more than some aspects of the case-law: for example, in looking at later years it also may be possible to show that Dicey's shrill concern with the rule of law and the proper function of lawyers in modern society was itself, in part, the product of a crisis in late Victorian professional conventions.[64]

NOTES

I am grateful to Professor Cornish for his comments upon a first draft of this essay.

1. 1 Tax Cases (hereafter cited as T.C.) 179 at p.185. For the purposes of modern tax law the case is obsolete; but this does not, of course, deprive it of real significance in the early development of ideas about how tax cases in general should be approached. In fact, Kelly's remarks were not sufficient to help the trader involved in this case: and it will be seen in the article that follows that there was nothing very surprising in such an outcome.
2. The most important provisions may be found at 14 and 15 Victoria, c.36, ss.2 and 32 and 33 Victoria, c.14, s.11 (exemption where relevant premises were used for the purposes of a trade only).
3. This was not a simple matter. Lawyers did (and still do) refer to tax legislation passed before 1874. And there were precedents for assessed taxes- although these were apparently very brief and uninformative; see V. Grout and B.E.V. Sabine, "The First Hundred Years of Tax Cases" British Tax Review, 1976, Part I (Grout) p.75 and Part II, (Sabine) 239 at p.239. The judiciary rarely responded to the use of an old case by counsel (see for example the present case involving the Chartered Mercantile Bank, 1 T.C. 179 at p.180 - no response seems to have been forthcoming from counsel's use of such a precedent). Some judges did plunder non-revenue cases for what they saw as being suitable analogies, but, if only because of the vast range of cases - the entirety of all case-law - this practice did nothing to restrict the scope of the lawyers' discretion. They certainly did not feel obliged to follow even those decisions concerned with the same words (e.g., trade) in other parts of case-law (e.g., bankruptcy).
4. Customs and Inland Revenue Act 1874, 37 and 38 Victoria, c.16. At the same

time income tax was a very small burden upon the individual - there was even a real possibility of its extinction and the provision was wholly undebated: in fact, the only discussion about the Act consisted of a question and answer concerning the specific gravity of beer - see Grout and Sabine, supra, p.239. It was an odd beginning for a vast body of case-law that cannot now be contained in one hundred volumes: in so far as a complex system of tax regulations is characteristic of modern government this is a "classic" example of England stumbling into the modern "administrative" state. Cf., P.S. Atiyah, The Rise and Fall of Freedom of Contract, Clarendon Press, Oxford, 1979, p.236. For Sabine's works on the history of income tax see his A History of Income Tax, Allen and Unwin, 1960 and A Short History of Taxation, Butterworth 1980.

5. Atiyah, supra, has recently emphasised that as far as descriptions of British society in general are concerned the "laissez-faire" men are a dying breed: "almost every modern historian who has written of the question has come to the same conclusion - the idea of an age of laissez-faire is a myth . . ." (p.234); the chief exception is E.J. Hosbawm, Industry and Empire, p.230 (see Atiyah p.234, fn. 39). But in the present context the laissez-faire school of thought has to be taken very seriously since if the lawyers (who might have had their own distinct ideas anyway) did have such commitments they were very likely to appear in tax cases where the freedom of the individual trader, man of commerce etc., was clearly threatened. There is also the fact that A.V. Dicey, the chief inventor of the laissez-faire perspective on nineteenth century law, was himself a revenue lawyer; the significance of this is considered below.

6. W.L. Burn, in The Age of Equipoise, George Allen & Unwin, 1964, was unable to resist these words at pp.68-9: cf., pp.102-3 and 303. But, as Atiyah himself points out (supra, p.234, fn. 42), Burn was not dogmatic in his use of these quotations (cf., Burn, supra, pp.132-3).

7. See Coltness Iron Foundry v. Black, 1 T.C. 287 and L.R. 6 App. Case. 315; expense of pit sinking held not deductible - see also in Re Addie and Sons 1 T.C. 1. These cases destroyed the chance of any wavering in favour of the tax-payer that arose in Knowles v. McAdam 1 T.C. 161 and L.R. 3 Ex.D. 23.

8. Forder v. Andrew Handyside Ltd 1 T.C. 65. The judges (Kelly L.C.B., Pollock and Huddlestone BB.) argued that in this instance the statute gave them very little discretion; in fact it would have been possible for them to get around it - the Commissioners, from whom the Crown appealed, had found for the tax-payer.

9. See for e.g., Lord Blackburn in Coltness Iron Co. v. Black 1 T.C. 287 at p.315. The reference embellished the argument; it was not conclusive - indeed it was circumvented.

10. Customs and Inland Revenue Act, 1878 51 Vict., c.8, s.12. Cf., J.R. Edwards "Tax Treatment of Capital Expenditure and the Measurement of Accountancy Profit" British Tax Review, 1976, p.36: the "doctrinal" concerns of the judges frequently conflicted with the ideas of the Commissioners, some of whom were entrepreneurs. This is stressed in 1955, Cmd. 9474, 308-28, at 309, and see also, more generally, the Richardson Committee on Turnover Taxation, 1964, Cmnd. 2300, Ch.6. Some parts of the Act were debated at quite extraordinary length, but there seems to have been no discussion about the present provision: presumably this was because the only people who suffered from it were the Government and they, obviously, had decided to concede the point.

11. In the early years, the judges included Kelly C.B., Bramwell, Cleasby, Pollock, Huddlestone and Amphlett BB: after the reforms of the mid-1870s, there was also James, Brett, Colton, Thesiger, Baggallay LJJ. and Hawkins J. On rare occasions there were also, of course, the judges in the House of Lords.

12. These included men such as (to use their contemporary titles) A.V. Dicey, Sir John Holker, Farrer Herschell Q.C., Saunderson, Benjamin, A.L. Smith,

Meadows White Q.C., Sir Hardinge Giffard, Solicitor-General, Gorst Q.C., Bush Cooper, Waugh, Grantham Q.C., and Graham.

13. For example, R. Robson, The Eighteenth Century Attorney, Cambridge, Ch.10 (emphasis upon respectability): H. Kirk, Portrait of a Profession, Oyez, 1976 (refreshingly honest about avarice). Admittedly these categories do not do full justice to the much broader analysis of M. Larsen, The Rise of Professionalism, 1977, University of California, and some very recent work.

14. For examples, not long before the tax cases, see Saturday Review, Vol.34, 7 December, 1872, pp.716-7, and - more moderately, but insistently - The Times, 21 December 1872, p.9.

15. Robert Stevens, Law and Politics, The House of Lords as a Judicial Body, 1800-1976, Weidenfeld and Nicolson, 1979, p.47 (utilitarian attack) and p.57 (oligarchic counter-attack).

16. This was not discussed by non-lawyers as much as the reform of the courts themselves, but the threat was apparent in the first of the reports on the legal system: see 1 Judicature Commission: First Report of the Commissioners, No. 4130, (1869), at, e.g., p.16.

17. The three separate common-law divisions were merged in 1880: Radcliffe and Cross, The English Legal System, 6th ed. (by Hand and Bentley), Butterworth, p.291.

18. For all of these points, see R.C.J. Cock's, "The Bar at Assizes: Barristers on Three Nineteenth Century Circuits", Kingston Law Review, Vol.6, Spring 1976, p.36 and "Dignity and Emoluments: Blofeld's Life as a Victorian Barrister", Kingston Law Review, Vol.8, Spring 1978, p.37.

19. See, generally, W.C. Richardson, A History of the Inns of Court, Baton Rouge, Claitors, 1975, Ch.10. I do not however accept some of Richardson's ideas about the Inns of Court, and I am attempting to assess the modern role of these institutions elsewhere in a study of the nineteenth century Bar as a whole: also, not all of the present examples are used by Richardson. Abel-

Smith and Stevens refer to the Inns at some length in their Lawyers and the Courts, Heinemann, 1967 and 1970; see in particular pp.71-76.

20. See, for example, his ideas in the Parliamentary debate at Hansard, 3rd Series, (H. of C.) Vol.CCIX, 1 March 1872, Col.122 et seq. Cf., Abel-Smith and Stevens, supra, at p.73.

21. See "The English Bar and the Inns of Court" Quarterly Review, Vol.138, January 1875, pp.138-176. According to the Wellesley Index to Victorian Periodicals 1824-1900, E.W. Houghton ed., Toronto and R.K.P., 1966, Vol.1, the author was Henry Warwick Cole Q.C. (see analysis of Quarterly Review for January 1875). In retrospect, this article reads most oddly; it is almost fanatical. For Victorians, however, it expressed ideas that had to be taken seriously: cf., E.B.V. Christian, A Short History of Solicitors, Reeves and Turner, London, 1896, pp.213 and 216. (For further information on Cole see F. Boase, Modern English Biography, Frank Cass, London, 1965 ed., Vol.1, p.672).

22. See, e.g., Tiley, Revenue Law, 2nd, ed., Butterworths, 1978, p.374. I am indebted to the author's references to the history of Capital Allowances; see reports etc., mentioned in fn. 10, supra.

23. See, generally, A. Farnsworth, Income Tax Case Law: Judicial Interpretation of the Income Tax Acts, Stevens, 1947.

24. Knowles v. McAdam 1 T.C. 161 at p.164.

25. Imperial Fire Insurance Co. v. William Wilson 1 T.C. 71 at p.73.

26. For Brett, see Jones v. Cwmmorthin Slate Co. 1 T.C. 267 at pp.270-1. For Thesiger, see Yewens v. Noakes 1 T.C. 260 at pp.264-6 . . . "Now definitions are proverbially dangerous . . . ."

27. See Weavers Hall . . . 1 T.C. 15 at p.19. There was always a limit to what Bramwell was prepared to do for entrepreneurs: see, e.g., Jones v. Cwmmorthin Slate Co. 1 T.C. 267 at pp.269-70.

28. Calcutta Jute Mills Co. Ltd. v. H. Nicholson and Cesena Sulphur Co. Ltd.

1 T.C. 83 at pp.92, 101 and 102. For "the principle of the law", see, e.g., Imperial Fire Insurance Co. v. William Wilson 1 T.C. 71 at p.73.

29. In Re Young 1 T.C. 57 at p.61.

30. In Re Edinburgh Life Assurance 1 T.C. 5 at p.10. Cf., re general principles, Coltness Iron Co. v. Black 1 T.C. 287 at p.307.

31. See Kelly C.B. in Chartered Mercantile Bank of India, London and China v. Wilson 1 T.C. 179 at p.187: quoted below, see n.34.

32. Knowles v. McAdam 1 T.C. 161 at p.165.

33. Octavius Jepson v. Frederick Gribble 1 T.C. 78 at p.80.

34. Chartered Mercantile Bank of India, London and China v. Wilson 1 T.C. 179 at p.187.

35. W.G. Keen v. Peyton Dashwood 1 T.C. 130 at p.133. Cf., Weavers Hall 1 T.C. 15 at p.19.

36. In Re Robert Addie and Sons 1 T.C. 1 at p.3.

37. Forder v. Handyside 1 T.C. 65 at p.70.

38. See, e.g., Watney v. Musgrave 1 T.C. 272 at pp.275-278.

39. Knowles v. McAdam 1 T.C. 161 at p.175. Cf., Sabine, supra, p.107 when he refers to Chadwick M.P. - presumably the same man, (note also pp.102-3, 179, 132).

40. Ibid. at p.175.

41. Ibid. at pp.163-4.

42. Watney & Co. v. Musgrave 1 T.C. 272.

43. Ibid. p.273.

44. Ibid. p.274.

45. Ibid. p.275.

46. Ibid. pp.278-9.

47. See, e.g., the arguments in In Re Glasgow Corporation Waterworks 1 T.C. 28.

48. Ibid. at p.50.

49. In Re Glasgow Commissioners 1 T.C. 122 at p.127.

50. For his activities in Circuit, see R.C.J. Cock's, "The Bar at Assizes", supra. For the capacity to tolerate some of his dubious activities, see Law Times, Vol.5, 5 July 1845, p.294.

51. Sir William Holdsworth, A History of English Law, Methuen, (1965 ed.,) Vol.XV, p.483: even in earlier days, "he was not an admirable character" ibid., p.484.

52. Dicey was, to some extent, his protégé and knew all about his achievements in the North: see, e.g., Bryce MSS., Bodleian Library, Oxford, letters to Bryce 21 December 1867 (Vol.2 fol. 3); ? 1879 (Vol.3 fol. 25); 16 July 1889 (Vol.2 fol. 115).

53. For his rather unconventional family background and education, see R.F.V. Heuston Lives of the Lord Chancellors, Clarendon, 1964, pp.85-113, particularly at p.85.

54. Holdsworth, supra, pp.303-4: Benjamin had "a more unique and remarkable career than any other English lawyer."

55. Bryce MSS., supra; and numerous tax cases - e.g., Knowles v. McAdam 1 T.C. 161. R.S. Rait, Memorials of Albert Venn Dicey, Macmillan, 1925, Chs.4 and 6, and pp.108-9, 140.

56. "Legal Etiquette", Fortnightly Review, Vol.2 N.S. August 1867 p.169. For legal doubts, see Law Journal, Vol.2, August 16, 1867, p.371 and, more generally, Raymond Cock's, Law Quarterly Review, Vol.94, at p.509. Rait, supra, emphasises Dicey's early and enduring concern with public opinion: see pp.1-2. A different interpretation of Dicey's vision of the legal profession emerges from R.A. Cosgrove's biography The Rule of Law: Albert Venn Dicey, Victorian Jurist, Macmillan 1980. It is an intricate problem on which further work on the Victorian Bar is proceeding.

57. Law and Public Opinion in England, Macmillan, London, 1905. It is notorious that Dicey suppressed the collectivist elements in Benthamite thought. H. Parris considers the legacy in general in Constitutional Bureaucracy, George

Allen & Unwin, 1969, pp.258-66.

58. Law and Public Opinion, supra, Lectures 7 and 8, pp.210-301, particularly at p.257.

59. Pitt v. Castle Hill Warehousing Co. Ltd. 49 T.C. 638 at p.645. The case is also reported at [1974] 1 W.L.R. 1624; [1974] 3 All E.R. 146; [1974] S.Y.C. 420; 118 S.J. 864.

60. E.g., D. Podmore, British Journal of Law and Society, Vol.7, No.1, Summer 1980, pp.1-21, and M.S. Larson, The Rise of Professionalism, University of California Press, 1977.

61. C. Harvie, The Lights of Liberalism, Allen Lane, 1976, Ch.1, particularly at p.14. N.b. C. Harvie, "Concept of Elites" and "Intellectuals and Society" in British Elites 1750-1870, Open University, 1974.

62. Ibid. p.16. Significantly, just before this quote, Harvie refers to John Vincent, The Formation of the British Liberal Party, 1857-1868, 2nd ed., Harvester, 1976: this contains a very interesting study of the Victorian lawyers in Parliament; see pp.39-47 and 23, 127.

63. See, e.g., pp.162-9.

64. Since this article was finished I have written a book on barristers which considers some of the issues discussed above: see Foundations of the Modern Bar, Sweet and Maxwell, S.P.T.L. series, 1983. For a stimulating - if rather more orthodox - study of late Victorian revenue law see Robert Stevens', Law and Politics, supra,-pp.170-76: this concentrates on cases decided after those looked at in the present study. Since this article was finished I have written a book on barristers which considers some of the issues discussed above: see Foundations of the Modern Bar, Sweet and Maxwell, S.P.T.L. series, 1983.

"EMINENT PRACTITIONERS" : THE NEW VISAGE OF COUNTRY ATTORNEYS c.1750-1800

M. Miles

This paper describes the range of duties performed by country attorneys in the second half of the eighteenth century; and what this meant for a region like the West Riding of Yorkshire which was just about to experience its first industrial revolution. The study concentrates upon the activities of the provincial practitioner since it was in the country towns and villages that the extent of the changes to be discussed below had been most acute; and as a result of which the country attorney was metamorphosed from being little more than a conductor of lawsuits into a dispenser of a much greater variety of non-litigious services in addition to, and sometimes at the expense of his ostensible reason for existence - summed up in the misleading and rather anachronistic title: Attorney at Law.

A comparison with seventeenth-century practice is more difficult in the total absence of working papers before 1660. In the sole study of this earlier period, Brooks has shown the provincial attorney as principally an agent in litigation, but occasionally taking on the role of town clerk, manorial steward or clerk of the peace.[1] In 1796 a pamphleteer defined his role: ". . . the very meaning of the word attorney, the principal law agent, denotes factor, doer, substitute, or actor for another person, in a matter where that person cannot act for himself; hence the dignity of the office."[2] From his genesis as an officer of the law courts at the beginning of the thirteenth century, the attorney had always been the agent of other men. But as this study will show, the original role was already by 1750 widened far beyond the definition just quoted.

The West Riding was chosen for this study because of its extensive collections of attorneys' working papers. The area contains some of the richest in the whole country and consists of: Day Books, Letter Books, Precedent Books, Ledgers, Cash Books, Diaries, Bill Books, Commonplace Books and miscellaneous deeds. The material was of such a quality as to allow for a detailed investigation of the business dealings of attorneys over a large number of years. It was, therefore, possible to isolate any changes in practice and procedure which might have occurred. John Howarth of Ripponden, near Halifax (1721-1804), and John Eagle of Bradford (1723-1787), have left behind the largest collections of papers and so form the principal source for this study. Three smaller deposits relating to attorneys who practised in Halifax, Birstall and Leeds have been used to check the reliability of the information derived from the other two collections. All of the data collected have been set against a background of evidence gleaned from a wealth of pamphlet material depicting the state of the profession in the eighteenth century.

Tables 1 and 2 contain a business analysis of the two attorneys' practices in terms of relative profitability. These tables have been reconstructed by recording every business entry in the Ledgers and Day Books of the two men between the specified dates. In John Eagle's case, his first and last ten years in business for which accounts survive have been chosen. With John Howarth, it is the central ten years of his career which have been selected for scrutiny. By subtracting the disbursements made in conducting a piece of business (which are recorded separately) from the overall charge in the bill, it was possible to calculate the yearly profits accruing to the attorneys. Each micro-transaction of business has been placed under one of eleven major categories. Most of the categories are self-explanatory; but two need clarification. The one entitled "potential litigation" relates to business in which the attorney attended to settle disputes and advise clients without the development of a lawsuit. The serving of Notices to Quit and the making of Distresses for rent arrears on tenants (if they did not develop into ejectment suits) have been included under this heading. The miscellaneous category relates primarily to those types of agency work which did not fit under any of the major headings. Any parliamentary business (whether electioneering or the soliciting of private bills in London) has been included under this category.

What must be pointed out is that the calculations of profits are notional, being based on that which the attorneys would have received each year if they had been paid immediately after presenting their bills. However, in reality things were not so straightforward. Credit was given on most types of litigation work which meant that many bills were not paid for one or more years. Nor do the tables include salaries paid for acting as land stewards, agents or rent receivers. Having been qualified in these ways, the tables can still tell us much about the relative popularity and profitability of the wide range of departments in a country attorney's office.

TABLE 1. JOHN EAGLE'S ESTIMATED BUSINESS PROFITS 1748-80

Year	Convey-ancing	Common Law	Chancery	Exchequer	Ecclesiastical Courts	Sessions & Assizes Prosecutions	Potential Litigation	Bankruptcy Commissions	Navigation Business	Parish	Misc.	Total
	£	£	£	£	£	£	£	£	£	£	£	£
1748	61	36	11	-	1	1	1	-	-	12	-	123
1749	95	74	16	1	3	4	1	-	-	7	-	201
1750	106	34	16	-	1	1	3	-	-	5	-	166
1751	76	50	6	-	3	-	5	-	-	4	-	144
1752	111	41	1	-	3	1	4	-	-	5	-	166
1753	105	45	5	1	-	3	1	-	-	2	-	162
1754	87	24	15	-	-	4	6	6	-	12	-	154
1755	148	47	5	-	11	3	3	11	-	12	1	241
1756	111	42	16	1	-	24	2	1	-	9	-	206
1757	136	46	17	1	2	-	4	2	-	16	-	224
1758	148	29	5	2	-	1	3	1	-	1	-	190
1768	94	49	63	-	-	3	10	-	6	4	1	230
1769	124	66	34	-	2	4	6	1	25	12	12	286
1770	114	26	9	-	1	4	8	-	110	9	1	282
1771	71	46	22	-	1	-	5	-	82	5	-	232
1772	110	29	10	-	1	7	6	-	81	14	2	260
1773	65	21	1	-	1	18	4	-	98	9	3	220
1774	91	36	2	-	1	1	2	-	93	6	1	233
1775	114	34	2	-	-	2	11	-	85	1	1	250
1776	127	11	2	-	-	7	3	11	93	1	-	255
1777	66	24	1	-	-	6	2	-	82	1	-	182
1778	86	45	-	-	-	-	3	-	81	6	3	224
1779	83	24	-	-	1	19	2	-	104	2	10	245
1780	107	28	67	-	1	3	3	-	80	1	3	293
Total	2436	907	326	6	33	116	98	33	1020	156	38	5169

SOURCE: L.C.A., DB250, LEDGERS 1-4

TABLE 2. JOHN HOWARTH'S ESTIMATED BUSINESS PROFITS 1768-80

Year	Convey-ancing	Common Law	Chancery	Exchequer	Ecclesiastical Courts	Sessions & Assizes Prosecutions	Potential Litigation	Bankruptcy Commissions	Navigation Business	Parish	Misc.	Total
	£	£	£	£	£	£	£	£	£	£	£	£
1768	142	33	25	-	-	11	-	5	-	31	-	247
1769	161	46	16	-	1	3	-	6	7	27	3	270
1770	137	32	4	1	2	34	68	5	1	18	-	302
1771	129	39	10	-	1	28	111	11	-	38	1	368
1772	160	56	5	-	-	46	114	14	4	29	1	429
1773	178	38	10	-	1	39	122	10	20	27	1	446
*1774	158	40	19	1	1	14	117	23	30	38	1	442
1777	138	20	6	-	-	25	129	17	-	32	154	521
1778	175	37	22	-	1	56	151	12	25	23	1	503
1779	195	47	9	6	1	38	144	22	-	23	1	486
1780	214	48	14	-	-	26	131	15	4	9	1	462
Total	1787	436	140	8	8	320	1087	140	91	295	164	4476

* Accounts Incomplete

SOURCE: C.A.D., HAS 9-13

II

The major area of change in the preserves of the country attorneys' practice occurred in their acquisition of a large share of conveyancing work. In contrast to later, narrower definitions of conveyancing, the word was used in eighteenth-century attorneys' papers to cover a greater variety of business, and as one writer has pointed out it stood for "not only instruments required on the transfer or mortgage of property, but all that is done in the Conveyancing Room."[3] A partnership agreement drawn up between two Leeds attorneys in 1792 had described conveyancing as ". . . the Drawing and Ingrossing any Wills Writings Conveyances and other Assurances"[4]; and a guide to the professions published in 1747 had provided an even fuller definition of conveyancing as:

> ". . . the drawing of Deeds, Mortgages and Conveyances of Estates. This is the most profitable Branch of the Law; for to that of Drawing Deeds they commonly add the Trade of a Money-Scrivener; that is, they are employed to find out Estates to purchase, or have Money to lay out for some, and borrow for others, and receive Fees from Borrower and Lender; and of course are employed to draw the Securities."[5]

Exactly when the attorneys first obtained their firm hold on the conveyancing branch is not know since there was no Act of Parliament recognising them as conveyancers before the nineteenth century. The take-over bid was slow and piecemeal; but nonetheless real and can be chronicled roughly from the 1670s when, in an edition of the Practique Part of the Law[6] - at that time the Bible and step-by-step guide to practice in the law for attorneys old and young - conveyancing is conspicuous by its absence; through 1724 when Bohun's Practising Attorney and Lawyers Office[7] dealt with conveyancing as one of the four main divisions of the attorneys' business; to the middle of the eighteenth century when the London Tradesman could confidently assert that conveyancers are usually bred as attorneys.[8]

Before this period the conveyancing business had been (in theory at least), the exclusive duty of the bar. Those clients who needed to have "writings" drawn were expected to approach counsel direct. However, it seems probable that in country areas at least, Tudor and early Stuart attorneys did prepare very simple conveyances such as money bonds, promissory notes and the less complicated wills and indentures. The crucial changes came after the Restoration when the attorneys came to be employed to draw even the most intricate deeds and to tighten their hold on the local capital market.[9]

This acquisition of lucrative conveyancing work meant a revival of financial prospects for the aspiring attorney. This must be the major factor in accounting for the rapid growth in size of the profession between 1660 and 1730 - a phenomenon that caused much alarm to contemporaries with demands for regulation and reform.[10] Calculations of numbers for the seventeenth century are bound to be unreliable owing to the lack of accurate roll keeping at Westminster and due to the large numbers who practised without ever gaining formal recognition.[11] All figures, therefore, must be accepted as underestimates. What evidence we do possess suggests an increase from around 1773 officially enrolled attorneys in 1672,[12] to 4000 in 1731[13] and taken at their face value these figures imply a doubling of the number of attorneys per head of the population.[14] Much of this growth was in the provinces. Attorneys had settled themselves in most of the important country towns by 1730. Counsel were too few in numbers to cope with the increase in conveyancing. Moreover, as we shall see below, the new attorneys were prepared to live out each working year in their own localities and found ample business there to forego the trips to London to attend their clients' case hearings in the central courts.

Judging from the silence of the records, these encroachments by country attorneys on what had previously been the preserves of the bar, passed without a murmur. The evidence from the West Riding suggests that relations between the two classes of Practitioner continued to stay harmonious. This may have been because counsel were still consulted on the very difficult settlements, transfers of property and trusts. Their fees were so adequate on these occasions that they could live very comfortably by merely giving "opinions". The lowest charge of provincial barristers for perusing, settling or advising clients (and they rarely took very long about it) was one guinea.[15] Not surprisingly, the loss of the drawing and ingrossing side of conveyancing, although lucrative enough in itself, could pass without much pain.

Each of the several attorneys whose papers were examined showed a high degree of similarity in both the quantity and range of the conveyancing work which passed through their hands. Table 3 therefore, although showing detail from only one practice, can be taken as being representative of the average firm during the second half of the eighteenth century. The table divides the clientele into four main categories and aims to demonstrate both the extent of the attorneys' conveyancing expertise and the requirements of the different social groups who consulted them on such business. As can be seen, it was the gentry and prosperous 'middling people' who provided the largest demand for conveyancing services. The attorneys were kept very busy by these groups, almost on a daily basis: buying or selling land and drawing the necessary agreements; arranging transfers and assignments of property; procuring money on personal or landed security; settling and winding-up estates or businesses; arranging marriage settlements; drawing wills and handling trusts.

The 'lower middling element' in the population also required conveyancing services, but not in such great quantity or frequency as the upper strata. They still borrowed money on mortgage and bond, bought and sold property, went into and dissolved co-partnerships, made wills and appointed trustees; but in all cases the size of such transactions, agreements and provisions was much smaller. Category four consisted entirely of servants of one kind or another who consulted the attorney only once each on such matters as advice on a small legacy which was due to them or on a purchase of property; and which suggests a higher income than their occupation would normally confer. There were no representatives of the

TABLE 3. JOHN HOWARTH'S CONVEYANCING CLIENTELE 1768-80: ATTRIBUTED OCCUPATIONS

'GENTRY': 55 Clients

CONVEYANCING WORK: wills and trusts; mortgages; establishing titles; buying and selling property; money-scrivening; deeds of appointment, exchange and partition; partnership agreements; marriage settlements; releases; winding-up and settling of estates; leases to tenants; subscription papers; assignments of property or mortgages; bonds; fines.

'UPPER MIDDLE SORT': 201 Clients

CONVEYANCING WORK: searching for titles; leases to tenants; mortgages; marriage settlements; wills and trusts; buying and selling of property; money-scrivening; partnership agreements; settlements of estates; settling partnership accounts; releases; deeds of feoffment; bonds; transfers of property and mortgages; petitions to enclose land; deeds of appointment; fines; indentures of apprenticeship.

'LOWER MIDDLE SORT': 61 Clients

CONVEYANCING WORK: leases from landlords; money-scrivening; mortgages; wills; deeds of partition; assignments of leases; examining titles; partnership agreements; releases; indentures of apprenticeship; bonds; fines; sales of houses and cottages; transfers of mortgages.

'POORER SORT': 9 Clients

CONVEYANCING WORK: legacy payments; executory advice; memoranda of cottage purchases; copies of wills.

Source: C.A.D., Howarth Papers, HAS 9-14; Miscellaneous Working Papers.

labouring poor in any of the attorneys' accounts considered.

Two of the conveyancing functions of attorneys stand out clearly from amongst the rest. The first concerns their role in the local capital market. The position of the West Riding attorneys as financial intermediaries between prospective borrowers and lenders of money has recently been dealt with elsewhere and need not be dwelt upon here.[16] The second function was their position in the property sales market. The attorneys were evidently the estate agents and mediators between sellers and purchasers of property. They saw to all the preliminaries of a sale: assessing the value of the property and searching to see if there were any conveyances, mortgages, judgments or other incumbrances affecting the title, and drawing and inserting the advertisement in the local newspaper. Their advice might also be sought on what they thought the property would bring on the open market. It could be that the property was incumbered in some way and therefore a sale would not be the best procedure:

> ". . . if you think of selling, I think it will be best to advertise a publick sale & try what can be got for ye Est but tho ye Est as you say may be improveable yet these joint affairs seldom sell well unless where those who have ye o^{r}. part are of ability to purchase ye whole."

If the attorney did advise a sale he would be employed to draw up the conditions and attend to sell the property himself at the appointed time, either by auction (for which method he usually possessed a licence) or by private contract; as well as to draw the purchase agreement. In addition, the attorney might be asked to purchase property on behalf of a client. This could involve keeping a close eye on the local land market for the type of property which his particular client had in mind, or just receiving instructions to bid for them at some imminent sale.

III

Another area in which the country attorney had come to be important by the early eighteenth century was in the affairs of his local parish. This usually brought him business at the local Quarter Sessions. However, unless he acted as a Justice clerk, the average attorney was unlikely to get involved in the handling of criminal cases;[18] and so most of this work was of a regulative and obligation enforcement kind. Although attorneys held no official positions in the running of the parish, they did occupy a number of "unofficial roles". For example, they were highly important as intermediaries between the Overseers of the Poor and the local Justice. The J.P.s had no direct responsibility for poor law administration as most of this had been delegated to the Overseers. When an Overseer was experiencing difficulty in fulfilling his office, he often approached an attorney first for advice and not the Justice. It might be that the Overseer's accounts had been objected to and he sought the attorney's help to draw them out and assist him to get them allowed before the Justice.[19] The most frequent problem, however, arose from the operation of the Settlement Laws; and in particular, the disputes between townships and parishes as to who was liable to maintain a certain pauper and his family. Such disputes commonly went to Quarter Sessions and formed the mainstay of the attorney's work there. When a pauper had been removed from one township to another, the receiving township might appeal against the order at the Sessions. The attorney was retained in order to prove the place of the pauper's settlement by searching for a record of birth or apprenticeship and examining witnesses.[20]

In addition to disputes between appellant and respondent townships, the attorney could also be involved in appeals against the filiation of bastard children, or prosecutions for neglect of statute duty on the local turnpike roads. Here the attorney was employed to enter into recognizances for appearance at the Sessions and to prefer, respite or discharge indictments. Non-contentious business included: motions for leave to obtain treasury grants in order to repair bridges; deciding whether property was assessable to the poor and other parochial rates; attending town meetings and entering up accounts; or drawing assignments of poor apprentices. Whatever the truth of Thompson's accusation that the gentry J.P.s were withdrawing "increasingly from face-to-face relations with the people in village or town",[21] the evidence from the West Riding would at least support the contention that in much of the routine business of parish administration, the Justices were quite prepared to allow the attorneys to advise and officiate in the problems of that administration without recourse to themselves. A more likely explanation, however, for the attorney's increased involvement with parish business can be found in the nature of things - the increased complexity of eighteenth-century society. The sheer increase in volume of Justice work (and in particular, the non-Sessions business such as enclosure movements, turnpikes and the land tax), compelled the J.P.s to look to the large numbers of attorneys in local society who had the necessary degree of social standing and legal acumen, on whose shoulders they were willing to see some part of the burden of parish administration fall.

The volume of parish business which came an attorney's way was greatly augmented when he acted as a Justice's clerk.[22] Such positions carried no official salary, but the clerk was amply compensated for this by his share of the fees taken on summonses, writs, warrants, orders, informations, convictions, commitments, licences, bonds and certificates; as well as for giving advice on various matters. These fees could add a substantial bonus to an attorney's income. John Howarth of Ripponden secured the position of clerk to Joshua Horton of Howroyd in Barkisland after the latter had received his Dedimus to act as a Justice in December 1769.[23] Howarth's yearly emoluments from this source ranged from £68 in 1770 to as much as £151 in 1778.[24] When such fees are added to the increased profits which accompanied the parish work at Quarter Sessions and Assizes, one would think that such positions must have been greatly coveted.

When an attorney was chosen as a Justice's clerk it is clear that he was expected to undertake much business that was, strictly speaking, the duty of the J.P. This situation arose from the fact that it was the clerk who was often the first person to be consulted on a whole host of complaints and problems: poaching, embezzlement of yarn, false reeling, short weights and measures, bastardy, theft, forcible entry through turnpike bars, refusal to do statute duty on roads, non-payment of poor rates, arrears of wages, burglary, trespass, hauling vessels or working on the Sabbath, tippling and so on. He was expected to offer advice to complainants and issue summonses.[25] The clerk might also at this stage examine some witnesses.[26] This combination of the roles of adviser and examiner in the first instance, meant that the clerk was in effect sifting the reliability of accusations and controlling what went before the Justice. The clerk was usually present at the hearings of cases at the house of the Justice; and afterwards he was responsible for such duties as drawing and issuing any convictions or commitments to the House of Correction. A clerkship with a local Justice also increased the attorney's share in profitable Sessions and Assizes prosecutions. Some of these cases were concerned with criminal matters. Howarth's Day Books reveal him advising both plaintiffs and defendants in prosecutions for theft, coining and malicious damage; as well as conducting proceedings on their behalf.[27] His yearly profits from conducting these prosecutions rose from an average of £6 in 1768 and 1769 to as much as £34 between 1770 and 1780.[28]

IV

Virtually every West Riding attorney enjoyed the salary and profits of at least one clerkship or stewardship during the course of his career.[29] These offices could take several forms: clerk to a navigation, turnpike or public utility scheme; clerk to an enclosure commission; land steward or agent (which may or may not carry the added pecuniary benefit of holding the manorial court); Clerk or Deputy Clerk of the Peace; County Court Clerk; Town Clerk; Coroner; Justice's clerk and insurance agent. Some attorneys held multiple offices, either all at the same time or over the course of a career.[30] Most types of office seem to have been acquired by a mixture of reputation and patronage.[31] A regular and wealthy client who sat on the board of trustees to such a body or company, or who was on close terms with someone who did, could be a powerful ally when canvassing for a place and well worth propitiating.

A position as steward or agent to an influential family could be equally as beneficial. John Howarth - as the successor of his old master, Charles Radcliffe of Elland - early gained the favour of the Horton family. In the early 1750s he acted as steward and trusted family attorney to Dame Susanna Horton, and such was his intimacy with the family that on her death he organised and attended the funeral.[32] He continued to appease other members of the Horton family such as, Sir Watts Horton of Chadderton, and the inheritor of the Howroyd estates, Joshua Horton. During the 1760s he acted as Joshua's confidential agent: advising him on property purchases, mortgages, government securities and tenancy disputes - all of which helped gain for him the position of Justice's clerk. Yet Horton must have taken into consideration Howarth's reputation as a practitioner of some distinction in conducting parish and Sessions business; as well as his unusual role as adviser on felonies and misdemeanours. For instance, a full two years before his appointment as an acting Justice, Horton approached Howarth for advice on what to do about some night hunters he had discovered poaching on his lands.[33]

A similar combination of skill and fortuitous contacts was behind John Eagle's acquisition of the position of law clerk to the Leeds and Liverpool Canal Company in 1770. Eagle had already been concerned as attorney for the company since 1768, although that position carried no salary. It was doubtless his ex-partner Abraham Balme who, as a wealthy Bradford businessman and one of the major instigators and largest shareholders in the enterprise, nominated him for the post. Positions of this nature carried a good deal of responsibility, and as with the Justice's clerk, the person was generally the first to be consulted on a variety of business. John Eagle's papers tell us much about the duties of a law clerk to an embryónic navigation company. In a letter to his London agent he described the extent of his duties:

> ". . . besides being concerned as Atty for ye Compy I am by office their Law Clerk with a salary of £80 per ann. & as such do all ye conveyancing Business prepare all or most of ye contracts for ye Lands

> give Notices & attend ye Meetings when ye Com^{rs} & jurys are called, when ye Land owners cannot be agreed with or when they are incapacitated to sell & c. I also frequently attend ye Commee meetings & do any o^{r}. Business that may be wanted, but as to ye Law Suits I am employed in by ye Company for, If I was to undertake them for my sallary, I shd have very little for myself, Besides this I keep ye Book contain^{g} an acct of ye Transfers . . . .[34]

In addition to the £80 a year salary, Eagle enjoyed a monopoly of the litigation work. Exactly how much profit he made on these lawsuits is unclear since his records do not mention the fees and expenses; and they were probably entered separately in some Cash Book which has not survived. What the papers do tell us about the lawsuits is that they caused him a great deal of headache. The growth of huge trustee-based concerns like navigation and turnpike companies was throwing up new questions and problems for which the subject matter of the law - heavily based as it was on precedent - was sometimes inadequate to cope. Many of the Leeds to Liverpool Canal disputes arose about the taking and valuing of the lands belonging to those through whose property the canal had been, or was to be, cut. For instance, in early 1771, a group of landowners refused to allow the commissioners to value their lands and, contrary to the express directions of the Act, proceeded to value their property themselves. Eagle was at a loss about how to act, he being "never concerned in any proceedings of this nature", and so contacted his agent in London for advice.[35] However, such was the lack of precedents for disputes of this nature, that both London attorneys and counsel were sometimes unsure what to advise. Consequently, we find Eagle directing his agents to enquire out the Duke of Bridgewater's solicitor and agent to see how he had proceeded in matters of this kind and to procure a copy of the Duke's Navigation Act.[36]

Other problems arose when a landowner did give his consent for a jury to value his lands, but then disputed the result of that valuation. If a lawsuit developed on these lines the attorney had to contend not only with a type of case for which he possessed no precedents; but also with the general hostility of much of the local populace towards canals and turnpikes; all of which made the collection of evidence in support of his employers extremely difficult. The case of *Rookes Esq.,* v. *Proprietors of the Leeds to Liverpool Company* helps to illustrate the point.[37] In this suit, a landowner named Rookes disputed the fact of whether the jury had included the woodland in their valuation of his lands to be taken for the canal. Originally the jury had sworn on oath that they did value all his lands. However, Rookes and some other landowners, along with their attorney, induced the jury members to join in an affidavit swearing that the evidence given previously on oath after the valuation was all a mistake. By proving that the original verdict was false, Rookes was entitled to bring an action of Trover against the company to make him satisfaction for the wood. Eagle was outraged at the degree of injustice involved, but he was sure how easily it had been accomplished. He had this to say of the jury:

> ". . . if they had been seperated immed^{y} after giv^{g} the verdict & asked whe^{r} they had valued ye Wood or not & not one of ym known what answer his Fellow Jurymen had given all or ye greatest part of y^{m} wod have declared with^{t} Hezitation yt they had valued both ye Wood & Soil but ye Sense of ye greatest part of ye Country people being ag^{t} undertakin^{gs} of this nature this prejudice on their minds generally opperates more strongly upon ym than ye Duty or obligat^{n} they are bound to by their oath."[38]

V

The last of the major changes in the range of functions performed by the country attorney concerns the giving of advice and the reorganisation of the attorney-barrister relationship. What the eighteenth century saw was a much greater range of advisory services provided by the provincial attorney and an increase in the frequency of administering that advice. As with conveyancing, the dispensing of advice was not originally the business of the attorney, but was confined to counsel.[39] The client was expected to consult his chosen counsellor in person and to pay him for his opinion without the intercession of an attorney. Nevertheless, it seems likely that this clear-cut division between attorneys and counsellors in their advisory roles was more strictly adhered to in conveyancing matters than in litigation; since in a situation where the attorney was the first person to be resorted to in a lawsuit he was in a very strong position to offer advice. We know that the Tudor and early Stuart attorneys possessed a sound enough knowledge of procedural law to enable them to advise their clients; although the nature of that advice does not appear to have been very substantial. The main advisory function of those attorneys was to inform the client whether a particular grievance could be made to lie as an action at law on the basis of what the client could tell them about the nature of the case. It would then be the attorneys' duty to fit the grievance into one of the several categories of case.[40]

By the late seventeenth century many more attorneys were apparently beginning to advise their clients all the way through a lawsuit. Roger North could lament this gaining of ground at the expense of the long robe; but he was clear about the way it had come about:

> "The truth is, the gentlemen of the law, having left the mechanic part of their practice, that is to speak with the client at first instance to state his business and to advise the action, and not griping for fees at first, but making their conversation easy to the suitor, hath been the cause that the attorneys carry all from them; for the first undertaker in business doth all, and he must go through in the cause; he is instructed, and can instruct others; he is resorted to on all occasions."[41]

The real issue is whether or not the attorney was advising clients entirely on his own, or if he still consulted counsel when the need arose. In reality a situation developed in which the client dealt exclusively with his attorney, who still sought advice from and instructed counsel when necessary. Retainers were placed and opinions taken by way of the attorney. Indeed, the contacting of counsel in this way engineered a shift in the wielding or patronage away from a client-counsellor towards an attorney-counsellor relationship. The country barrister became directly dependent upon the attorney for much of his work and the client was often willing to leave to him the choice of counsel. In the West Riding, for example, the attorney could choose from amongst a small number of local counsellors whom he could consult with and retain.[42] An attorney, might, however, choose to take the opinion of a London counsellor who, due to the greater range of choice, must have been even more dependent upon the patronage of the attorney. The reputations of the most eminent London lawyers fanned-out over the rest of the country vis-à-vis the London agent-country attorney system. The country practitioner retained and took advice from London Counsel on the basis of his agent's recommendations. Since the majority of London attorneys in profitable practice conducted agency business on behalf of their country colleagues, we may conclude that their relationship was of mutual advantage. There can be no doubt that the London attorneys were the senior partners because of the large patronage at their disposal.

Nevertheless, as a result of the growth of a system in which the attorneys were the first to be resorted to on most legal problems, it was natural that the latter group should come to share more prominently in the giving of advice. The attorneys, as the first to be consulted, could control what went before counsel: advising on all that they thought themselves qualified and reserving only the very difficult matters for a second opinion. A glance at the working papers of eighteenth-century country attorneys would give the impression that they were running what was, to all intents and purposes, a citizens' advice bureau in which they alone were the oracle. Their advisory duties were extremely wide-ranging. The Day Books of John Howarth reveal some 579 instances of advice-giving between the years 1768 and 1780. The papers of John Eagle record him advising clients only 181 times between the years 1748 to 1758, and 1768 to 1780. With this attorney, however, only his Ledgers have survived, and as these do not provide such a precise record of business activity as the Day Books, they probably underestimate his advisory role. A further 276 problems, initially taken to Howarth and Eagle, were later referred to counsel. It is by studying the difference between what the attorneys were advising on themselves and what they passed over to counsel, that we get one of our clearest insights into the extent of their business expertise.

A precise categorisation of the advice administered by the two attorneys shows that 40 per cent of it related to conveyancing, 15 per cent was on parish and Sessions business, and 18 per cent each related to litigation and "potential" litigation respectively. A further 9 per cent of advice was on Justice business, for which John Howarth alone was responsible. As can be seen, it was on conveyancing matters that they felt most confident to advise. One of the most frequent calls for assistance came from executors and trustees who needed guidance in dealing with the affairs of the testator: could somebody apply a portion of his childrens' legacies towards their maintenance before they came of age?; could an executor undertake the receipt of the rents from the real estate of a testator?; was it possible to claim a cottage as heir at law of a late brother?[43] The attorney might also be called in to advise on business partnerships: could a partner in a dyers' company leave and begin business elsewhere, or did the clauses in the articles of co-partnership compel him to stay?; what were the financial prospects for those who wished to continue in a brewing business on the death of the principal partner?[44] Other of the more usual questions concerned the problem of cutting-off entails;[45] whether it was right for the tenants of a mortgaged estate to "attorn" to the mortgagee without the consent of the mortgagor;[46] and about the proper evidence to be given on a commission of bankruptcy.[47] These are just some of the more complex questions on which both attorneys were commonly expatiating to their clients or pronouncing judgment. Only the most perplexing problems were referred to counsel and even here the skill of the attorneys was such that it was more a case of having their own opinions confirmed or corrected, than of being totally devoid of ideas on the proper mode of proceeding.

The other major area of advice (parish affairs and Quarter Sessions business) has been mostly dealt with already. Both attorneys dispensed advice on such issues as: pauper settlements, disputes about statute duty, the mode of passing accounts as late Surveyor of the Highways, whether militiamen were liable to be "lotted" to a certain township, or what was necessary to be done when a mother affiliated a bastard child on two different persons, and so on. Virtually none of these and other like questions were ever referred to counsel.

What the attorneys were able confidently to advise by themselves and what was referred to counsel reflects both the frontiers of their legal knowledge and the relative degree of importance which they placed on the different departments of their work. A discussion of the relative attractions of different types of business will take place below; but for an understanding of how the attorneys came to acquire their legal knowledge and hence dispense advice, it is necessary to say something at this stage. As in the earlier period, the usual method of amassing knowledge of the practical side of the law was by compiling Precedent Books. These came to be filled with examples of all the most common forms of work. As conveyancing became the single most important area of business for the country attorneys, so their Precedent Books came to be filled with the forms and precepts of such work. What soon becomes evident is that most of their knowledge of the law was obtained in a very haphazard fashion based on the principle of slowly compiling Precedent Books from first-hand experience of handling the business. The average country attorney was unlikely to possess any great depth of learning in the law to form a background to his own compilations of cases; although he might make his precedents more full by supplementing them with extracts from up-to-date law books or manuals which he possessed.[48] Basically, the more precedents an attorney could amass on a given topic - he may even have inherited the books of his late father or master to whose business he had succeeded - the more qualified he was to judge and advise personally on that topic.

As litigation declined from its position of pre-eminence in the country attorneys' zone of activity, so it began to figure less in their Precedent Books. The knowledge of Eagle and Howarth in litigious matters was such that unless the proceedings were relatively straightforward they quickly became confused and unsure on how best to act. Their main advisory function in litigation was still to advise the client in the first instance on whether a grievance could be maintained as an action at law. Even here, however, counsel's opinion was frequently sought. They possessed enough knowledge of procedural law to enable them to know roughly what was necessary to be done in a suit. This information could be gleaned from the standard practitioners' manuals. What they lacked was expert knowledge on the repetitious and tautologous minutiae of practice and the prolixity of pleadings which were starting to befog central court litigation.[49] Opinions were taken along well-trodden lines: what pleas to make and what evidence to collect in support of a claim.

However, this decrease in central court expertise on the part of the country practitioners was compensated for by the rise of the London agency system. The London attorneys continued to depend on litigation for a large proportion of their income; and being in frequent attendance on the hearing of cases in the courts at Westminster, meant that they stood in need of a greater depth of learning in procedural law than their country counterparts. They were, therefore, often able to advise the country practitioners on points of practice. Moreover, the improved postal services of the second half of the century ensured that the opinions of eminent City counsellors and special pleaders could be taken and speedily dispatched when the agent was unable to solve the problem:

> ". . . from the facility with which cases are sent and opinions returned from the Metropolis, the Practiser in the Country stands in but little need of more deep-founded knowledge of his profession . . . it is only necessary to add the expence of postage to his bill, and he will be able to obtain for his client every advantage which fees can command in this profession, from great abilities united with great experience . . . a kind of Law factor has succeeded . . . and the London Agent has superceeded all necessity of an intricate knowledge of the Law among the Country practisers; and has left them but little skill, and less profit."[50]

VI

Having outlined the more important changes in the preserves of the country attorney's practice, it is now time to show the effect of those changes on the traditional function of the attorney - litigation. Conveyancing was by far the most profitable single source of business for the country attorney. Just how profitable can be seen from Tables 1 and 2. In John Eagle's table conveyancing accounts for 47 per cent of his overall profits between the specified years; whereas all types of litigation work combined: common law (superior and inferior courts), Chancery, Exchequer, ecclesiastical courts, Quarter Sessions, Assizes prosecutions and potential litigation - amounted to just 29 per cent. In John Howarth's case the corresponding figures are 40 per cent conveyancing and 23 per cent litigation. The marked similarity between the two sets of figures should be evident. Both Eagle and Howarth therefore obtained the bulk of their overall profits from sources other than litigation, the figures being 71 and 77 per cent respectively. Smaller collections of attorneys' papers relating to practitioners in other parts of the Riding reveal that conveyancing work entailed the entering up of many more precedents than any other type of business.[51]

As the country attorneys began to centre their practices on this lucrative base it is possible to discern a pronounced shift in their interests away from litigation. The first indication of this change can be seen in the relatively rapid break up of the attorney's profession from a single body of men with only a vague division between country and City practitioners; and its consequent realignment into an established system of permanently-resident country attorneys and regularly retained London agents who conducted central court business on their behalf. The picture of the provincial attorney and his clerk treading the roads to London personally to attend the hearings of his clients' causes at Westminster during each of the four legal terms, rapidly became a subject for reminiscence.[52]

The practice wherein country attorneys employed London agents appears to have been commenced in the early years of the eighteenth century, and had become widespread by mid-century. One author in 1792 echoed the earlier sentiments of Campbell when he remarked that ". . . country business in the law is, in general, much decreased, or else conducted by agents in the Inns of Court."[53] It was the imposition of an annual duty on all practising attorneys in 1785 which finally made the distinction absolute, since after that date no country attorney could practise in the superior courts without having a permanent London address and by paying a higher annual duty.[54]

At the same time that conveyancing was proving an attractive proposition for the country attorney, complaints were raised that the profits and emoluments for conducting lawsuits were fast diminishing in value. The basic attorney's fee for conducting a lawsuit for one term (excluding of course the fees for attendances, advice and the drawing of instruments) was still only 3s.4d. in the late eighteenth century.[55] The attorney was by no means silent about this fact:

> ". . . no Man earns a sordid Livlihood so hardily; for his Fees are the same now, they were some hundred Years ago when a penny would purchase near as much of Life's Necessaries as Sixpence will now."[56]

Another attorney was equally displeased:

> "And what-ever Men may think of our great Gains, I am most confident there's no such thing as saving any great Estate out of 'em, for he that lives purely upon his Practice as Attorney or Sollicitor, and in 20 or 30 years, with great Business and great Husbandry, saves 4 or 5000L. I think does a very remarkable thing."[56]

This writer went on to acknowledge the more rewarding areas of business which had thankfully come the attorneys' way:

> "I confess there are many other gainful Businesses fall in a Practiser's Way, as Conveyancing, Court-Keeping, the Opportunity of picking good Bargains out of the many Estates he sees sent to Market, & c. by which some gain great Wealth; but these are foreign to my Subject, and arise not by Fees as an Attorney or Sollicitor."[58]

Moreover, the biggest proportion of an attorney's bill for a lawsuit was money for which he was personally out of pocket in conducting that suit. This could sometimes be as much as two-thirds of the whole bill; a factor usually overlooked when a client complained about the excessive size of his bill.[59] When due allowance had been made for fees and expenses of London agents, monies disbursed to clerks in court and other officers, counsel, parchment, stamp duty and many incidental expenses, the attorney was by no means over-compensated for his trouble.[60] Nor can we support the argument that the attorney, because of the London agent taking much of the business of litigation out of his hands, had little to do for his money. He was still responsible for such duties as: examining witnesses, attending to look into the nature of disputes, issuing writs, serving declarations, and writing long instructive letters on the state of cases to his agents; as well as the divers tedious attendances which accompanied litigation. The fees in the inferior courts were equally dismal. In the generality of such courts the attorney's regulated fee for conducting a suit was either 1s. 6d. or 2s. 6d; although there was rarely more than one motion or step of procedure necessary.[61]

Chancery suits could be profitable, especially when a practitioner managed to secure the work of attending on the commissions which heard evidence locally. But even here, the perplexing nature of many of the cases and the work that accompanied them: settling complicated accounts,[62] searching for and proving titles, collecting evidence; which when added to the longevity of many suits with the attendant inconvenience to the attorney of being very large sums out of pocket - all made them far less of an attraction.

John Eagle experienced the acute difficulties of long Chancery suits at first-hand during the 1760s and 1770s; and his letters help us to understand the nature of the burden which many attorneys must have laboured under. The major problems were twofold. Firstly, Chancery suits were very expensive if they dragged on for more than one or two terms. The attorney (or solicitor as he needed to be) was obliged to pay his agent at the end of each term all that the latter had disbursed in the conducting of the proceedings in London. To facilitate this payment the country practitioner needed to remit regular bills of exchange to cover this expenditure. Without such payment, regularly remitted, the London agent refused to be employed. These payments were usually very large.[63] However, at the same time as being compelled to pay his agents as he went along with the cause, the attorney was not normally expected to present his own bill to his client until all was over. Consequently, as Chancery suits notoriously stretched on for a number of terms - and not infrequently years, owing to the great difficulty commonly experienced in forming equitable decisions - the attorney could be considerably out of pocket before a cause reached settlement. In April 1769, for example, Eagle was already owed above £120 by a Yorkshire merchant for business done in one Chancery suit alone.[64] He bewailed the mentality of his clients on numerous occasions: ". . . they never like to pay for Law, if they can avoid it . . . ."[65]

The second problem facing the attorney was also of a pecuniary nature. When large sums were laid out on credit (in lawsuits), there was a loss of interest which might have been accruing to the attorney if he had lent that sum out on personal or landed security. In the above mentioned Chancery suit, which lasted from 1759 until 1772, Eagle received only £20 to sustain him during the whole period.[66] No wonder that after this experience he meddled very little with Chancery business for the rest of his career; and that which was undertaken was speedily concluded. He summed up his discontent in a letter to his client:

> "In looking over the Bill which has been taxed & considering ye large Sum I am out of Pocket in this Cause, & on comparing the Profitts with the Loss I sustain in the Int. of my Money. I am clear that for some years past, if I am paid no more than common fees, I shall have nothing for my Trouble, but be more a looser than gainer by ye Cause. My agent complains of being heartily tired of ye Cause, but I have far greater Reason to complain, for after he & ye Clerk in Court he employs are paid there is small Profitts remain for me, & as I pay my agent as I go along, & am all ye Money out of Pocket, you must be sensible that ye Loss I have sometime sustained in Interest takes away

anything I get . . . ."[67]

In contrast to litigation, other types of business brought a quicker, and generally more profitable, return. Virtually all of an attorney's bill for conveyancing business (excluding parchment, stamps, travelling expenses and other minor costs) was clear gain. This factor, when added to the above disadvantages of litigation, was an added incentive to concentrate energies on the other sides of the practice.

A further indication of the attorney's decreasing preoccupation with litigious matters can be seen in his behaviour towards those clients who were involved in disputes. When a dispute arose between two or more parties the attorney attempted to settle it out of court, ostensibly to save expense to his clients, but probably also to save himself a time-consuming and relatively unprofitable piece of work which stole his time and energy away from more lucrative business. The attorneys in this study were certainly active in steering their clients away from litigation when this was humanly possible. When a client approached the attorney with a complaint against his neighbour (whether for debt, trespass, abuse, assault and so on), the attorney would either write or attend on the offending party and endeavour to get an amicable settlement without suit. The defendant was prevailed upon to make satisfaction for damages by making a monetary recompense or an apology, depending on the nature of the offence. Sometimes a dispute reached the stage where both parties had retained the services of an attorney; but where the conciliatory skills of each practitioner were enough to achieve a satisfactory accommodation. Alternatively, both of the disputants might agree to refer the matters in contention to anything from one to three indifferent persons who would agree to act as arbitrators.[68] Such men would listen to the evidence of both sides, as prepared and presented by their attorneys, and then proceed to make an award between them. If the arbitrators could not agree matters, the next step was for them to refer the dispute to an umpire on whom they could all agree.

Over the whole period 1748 to 1758 and 1768 to 1780, John Eagle's accounts reveal a yearly average of 25 disputes which were settled in this way by private compromise. By way of contrast, the yearly average of disputes which did enter the law courts was: superior courts 20, inferior courts eight. Over the whole time he handled only 31 Chancery or Exchequer suits and only nine in the ecclesiastical courts.[69] So roughly one in two of all disputes were settled out of court. The records of the other attorneys' firms, although not permitting such precise calculations, show that private compromise by an indifferent third party was frequently a preferred alternative to litigation. Moreover, once a lawsuit had been commenced, the attorney lost no time in attempting to accommodate matters at every possible opportunity. The actual commencement of an action was usually enough to bring about an agreement. Between the above mentioned dates, no less than 73 per cent of all superior court actions handled by Eagle (509) were over before the expiration of one legal term. Only a mere 16 per cent went through to advanced stages to last in excess of two terms.[70] Settlement was again either by the defendant making his reparations voluntarily in response to the entreaties of the attorney, or by abiding by the decisions of referees.

Before proceeding with the discussion, it is necessary to say something about the types of person who acted as arbitrators. The most frequently appointed arbitrator was the attorney himself. Apart from attending as above to settle amicably matters in contention between his own clients (which was not the same as sitting on a reference), an attorney could be called in by other practitioners to arbitrate in a dispute between their own clients. Here it was necessary for the employing party to appoint a time and place, usually at some inn or tavern, for the reference to take place; and ensure that everything was ready for the chosen attorney or attorneys to make the award. John Howarth acted as arbitrator or umpire in this way at least once a year between 1768 and 1780.

The attorneys, however, were not the only people to be nominated as arbitrators. The small number of local counsel were also a popular choice, and they made their awards either alone or in co-operation with attorneys.[71] Nor was legal expertise always a necessary prerequisite. Respectability and a reasonable degree of intelligence were often the only qualifications required. Esquires and gentlemen formed another group who accepted such roles, possibly in an attempt to cultivate an image of paternal responsibility in the community. Other candidates included merchants, clothiers and yeomen. An interesting factor that does emerge when investigating the social origins of arbitrators is that the appointments were sometimes expected to be made along the lines of social class. As a result we find gentlemen mediating between gentlemen, shalloon and kersey makers presiding over other clothiers or merchants, and yeomen arbitrating between yeomen. If these "mores" were not followed, there might be friction. For instance, in 1749 John Eagle was concerned in an action for trespass in which his client, a Manningham gentleman, was defending the claims of his own tenant against another person of the same yeoman status. When proposals of reference were offered, the plaintiff insisted that no gentleman should act as arbitrator, whereon the defendant refused to consider the offer and the case was settled in court.[72]

All this does not, of course, imply that the attorneys were totally unconcerned about litigation and were prepared to turn such business away. On the contrary, business was business, however small the return, and those clients who were adamant about going to law would receive every assistance. The comments of John Eagle at two different points in time, one written to his London agent, the other to one of his regular clients, are probably indicative of the attitudes of many country attorneys towards litigation:

> "I know you get little by suing out a Writ no more do I. but one Thing with ano^r makes up . . . .[73] . . . you must be satisfyed it is my Business to push on ye Law where my Client is able to pay & I am sure you are but it is always my Disposition to get Differences accommodated with as little charges in Law as may be . . . ."[74]

This change in direction away from litigation on the part of country attorneys is very important if we are to understand the attitudes of the population at large towards the law. Given a situation in which the attorneys were the first persons to be consulted for advice in the legal process (as well as the first to set the wheels of the civil law machine in motion when an action was commenced), then surely the nature of that advice is highly significant in determining the propensity of people in going to law. This seems a fairly obvious point to be making, but it is one which has been hitherto overlooked by historians. The attorneys, by the nature of their advisory role, must have had a certain amount of personal control in determining the volume of disputes which entered the law courts. Having outlined a situation where attorneys were much less preoccupied with taking disputes into the courts and - failing that - with seeing causes through to advanced stages; then we should perhaps expect to see a relative decrease in the volume of litigation in all courts in relation to earlier periods in history.

It is precisely this trend which has been commented on by historians, who inform us that it was the Tudor period which was the most litigious time in English history. One recent historian has explained the Tudor fashion for Central Court litigation in terms of: a rapid rise in the number and availability of attorneys; the surprisingly low cost of lawsuits in the superior courts; and that credit was given on such suits by the attorneys. As a result of all these factors the law was within the reach of many more people than was once thought possible.[75] Yet the eighteenth century had all the same prerequisites for a great age of litigation. The rapid upsurge in the size of the attorney ranks has already been shown. Nor does the evidence from the West Riding suggest that anything had changed since the Tudor period in the relative cost of Superior Court lawsuits. Taking the evidence of John Eagle's bills, it appears that a suit in the King's Bench or Common Pleas averaged from as low as £3. 9s.10d in 1751, to as much as £19.16s.9d in 1778.[76] These averages, however, conceal great discrepancies. Altogether, between the years 1748-1758 and 1768-1780, Eagle conducted some 509 superior court actions which mostly cost from between three and seven pounds. If we deduct the high cost of the handful of suits which reached trial at <u>nisi prius</u> from the majority which were over within two terms, the average cost of a suit falls below three pounds.[77] Moreover, many of these suits were conducted on credit. It has already been remarked upon that clients were in no hurry to pay their bills for Chancery suits; this was equally the case with common law actions. Very few bills were paid in under six months and many were not settled for over a year or more.

When we consider the social status of superior court litigants in Table 4, it can be seen that although the 'gentry' and 'upper middling strata' dominate the list, there is a fairly strong contingent from the 'lesser middling' and 'poorer sections' of society. Taking the bottom section of the list (below dealers and shopkeepers), we find a total of 39 people whose occupations would have conferred only a moderate life-style. Five of the litigants were even near the bottom of the social hierarchy[78] and one was a pauper. Yet as with the sixteenth century, a scrutiny of the social status of litigants will show that the law was largely out of reach of the very poor sections of society. None of the attorneys here considered handled more than one pauper cause during the course of their entire careers.[79]

Might not the golden age of Tudor litigation be due to a hidden factor- a much greater disregard on the part of the attorneys for counselling their clients away from actions at law? This is not to say that all Tudor attorneys were actively engaged in stirring up trouble amongst their clients in order to secure the work of settling it in court. What is being suggested is that those attorneys who commonly dissuaded their clients away from lawsuits were doing themselves a pecuniary disservice since they depended upon such work for most of their income. If this was so then they would possibly have been more concerned about lengthening the size of their yearly suit-roll and seeing causes go through in the courts as far as possible. It is reasonable to argue that the eighteenth century was just as "potentially litigious" as the Tudor period in having those two major essentials in making people flock to law: an abundance of attorneys and reasonably cheap legal costs, providing a case was quickly concluded. What may have prevented this state of affairs developing into an imbroglio of litigants was a significant change in the nature of the advice administered by country attorneys, as a direct result of their increased concern with more profitable non-contentious business.

TABLE 4. CLIENTS OF JOHN HOWARTH INVOLVED IN CENTRAL COURT LITIGATION 1768-1780 : ATTRIBUTED OCCUPATIONS

Esquires	4	25	Gentry
Gentlemen	21		
Merchants	10	80	Upper Middle Sort
Clothiers	21		
Yeomen	18		
Dealers, Shopkeepers and Manufacturers	31		
Innkeepers	9	33	Lower Middle Sort
Weavers	6		
Craftsmen	18		
Servants and Carriers	5	6	Poorer Sort
Paupers	1		
Widows	12	12	Unknown
	Total	156	

Sources: C.A.D., Howarth Papers, Miscellaneous Working Papers.

NOTE: Gentlemen includes landed proprietors, professional men, and all merchants, woolstaplers and clothiers who used the title.

Clothiers: shalloon makers, stuffmakers, white kersey makers, broad clothiers.

Yeomen: principally farmers, but some clothiers, dealers, chapmen and traders.

Dealers: Shopkeepers and Manufacturers: woollen and worsted drapers, linen drapers, mercers, corn factors, maltsters, dyers, combe and card makers, druggists, etc.

Craftsmen: includes butchers, masons, glaziers, cordwainers, painters, carpenters, blacksmiths, whitesmiths, etc.

Finally, having argued a case for a decrease in the quantity of litigation handled by provincial attorneys, it is time to say something about the content of the suits which they did undertake. The greatest proportion of superior court actions handled by the West Riding attorneys involved debts of one kind or another. In John Eagle's papers 80 per cent of all central court actions in which the type of dispute is recorded, are of this kind. These debts had usually been incurred in business transactions: money due for goods sold or ordered; on bills of exchange returned for non-acceptance; outstanding partnership debts; or by lending money on personal and landed security. They reflect the mercantile and commercial society of the West Riding during the second half of the eighteenth century. What can be classed as the more personal forms of action, such as trespass, assault, trover, replevin, case or ejectment, accounted for only 20 per cent of the suits, with the latter category topping the list with 12 per cent. The inferior court actions (190) showed a similar bias towards trade with 76 per cent of all suits being for debt.[80] Very few of the actions would seem to have been the result of feuding or vindictiveness on the part of the local population.

VII

It was during the period 1660-1750 that the true family attorneys were born. This was largely as a result of their acquisition of the conveyancing business. The creation of a situation in which attorneys were consulted not only on lawsuits, but on wills, trusts, marriage settlements, the buying and selling of land, as well as on the procuring or lending of money, ensured that such men could never be the mere givers and receivers of instructions. Conveyancing work (and especially that undertaken for the more prosperous local inhabitants) meant regular attendances on clients and receiving information on their personal affairs. The attorneys had the chance of becoming the confidential and trusted advisers with whom, as with the local physician, it was perfectly natural to dine and be on first name terms.

Such positions with the more illustrious families, could confer extra benefits in the way of agency work, manorial stewardships or even a match of marriage.[81] If anything contributed more to the growth in respectability and status of the eighteenth-century attorneys it was this infiltrating of themselves into the confidence of the wealthiest persons in the neighbourhood to whose discerning eyes they were exposed.[82]

In the earlier period, the contact between attorneys and their clients (mostly for litigious purposes) was likely to have been much more casual and infrequent. A client did not commence a lawsuit every week; but he might well lend or borrow a few pounds, make a tenancy agreement, alter a will or seek advice on a host of other like matters. Very casual business encounters with attorneys, especially those which proved unsatisfactory, might leave a distrustful or even jaundiced view of the profession as a whole. Attorneys in established practice secured most of their work on the basis of the recommendations of their existing clients. The eighteenth-century attorneys, the nature of whose work entailed a closer contact with their clients than ever before, were therefore in a much stronger position to prove their worth and propitiate those clients.

It has been argued in this study that the prime mover in initiating the changes in the functions of country attorneys was the great influx of entrants into the profession after the Restoration. The new attorneys responded quickly to the changes in economic conditions which had made conveyancing and related business a more attractive proposition. The result was a relegation of their traditional vocation: litigation. Yet this major change, which witnessed the rise of the permanently-resident country attorneys who were able to concentrate their energies within their own locality, and extend their range of functions, had occurred by 1750 -before the onset of sustained industrial growth. The 1760s and 1770s did bring new types of business for attorneys as a direct consequence of nascent industrialisation. This primarily took the form of clerkships to navigation and turnpike companies or enclosure committees. The work which these positions brought was new and time-consuming and included much business in unprecedented areas of trusteeship and contract. In most cases the work involved the handling of larger sums of money than ever before and principles which were more difficult to apply.

But we must not overestimate the impact of industrialisation on the world of the country attorneys before 1800. The biggest proportion of their business continued to reflect the very localised, albeit commercially active, region in which they lived. With a few conspicuous exceptions, both of the attorneys in this study were conducting similar business in 1780 to that undertaken thirty years earlier on setting-up in practice. For instance, if we take the evidence of the contents of lawsuits, there was no real change over the whole period: actions for debt were by far the most common, and, as a study of the central courts has shown, they had been a century earlier.[83]

It is perhaps best to see the period 1750-1800 as an age of transition for the country attorneys. The next major catalyst of change must have come after 1800 with the rise of the great manufacturers in the north, the creation of joint-stock companies, and later of course, with the birth of the railways - all of which helped to bring about the commercial solicitor of the nineteenth century.

NOTES

I would like to thank Maurice Beresford, David Allen, Stuart Anderson and David Sugarman for their useful comments on an earlier draft of this paper. Where appropriate, original spellings have been retained in all quotations.

1. C.W. Brooks, "Some aspects of attorneys in England during the late sixteenth and early seventeenth centuries" (unpublished Ph.D. thesis, Oxford, 1979), pp.6, 191.
2. A. Grant, The Progress and Practice of a Modern Attorney, Exhibiting the Conduct of Thousands Towards Millions (London, 1796), p.15.
3. E.B.V. Christian, Solicitors: an Outline of their History (London, 1925), p.129.
4. L(eeds) C(ity) A(rchives), Bolland Papers, DB69, Bolland and Atkinson's Partnership Agreement.
5. R. Campbell, The London Tradesman, being a compendious view of all the trades, professions, arts, both liberal and mechanic, now practised in the cities of London and Westminster. Calculated for the information of parents, and instruction of youth in their choice of business (London, 1747), pp.79-80 (hereafter London Tradesman).
6. The Practique Part of the Law, shewing the Office of a Compleat Attorney (London, 1676).
7. W. Bohun, Practising Attorney or Lawyer's Office containing the business of an attorney in all its branches (London, 1724).
8. London Tradesman, op.cit., p.79.
9. The second half of the seventeenth century witnessed a conveyancing boom in the field of real estate. Lawyers were kept busy with the intricate and prolonged problems of land sales and recoveries after the Civil War and the Restoration. At the same time, the perfection of the practice of entailing estates; and the immense benefits this practice conferred on landowners who

could now have mortgages with equity of redemption, ensured a flood of business for the lawyers. In both areas of business the attorneys gained a generous share, and consolidated their position as financial intermediaries. B.L. Anderson, "The attorney and the early capital market in Lancashire" in F. Crouzet (ed.), Capital Formation in the Industrial Revolution (London, 1972), pp.226-7.

10. All the major attempts at a systematic regulation of the profession after the Restoration had mentioned a reduction in the excessive numbers of attorneys as their principal objective. A committee was appointed in February 1672 to consider the inconvenience arising from the multitudes of attorneys and to prepare a bill for their regulation. The judges gave evidence before the committee and returns of numbers of practitioners were produced; but the committee never reported. In January 1697, a select committee sat to consider how to prevent the great expense and length of suits; and one of the three heads agreed to be considered for a Bill was that the number of attorneys in every County be reduced. Leave was given to bring in this Bill in March 1701, but it failed to get beyond a second reading. These and other earlier efforts at reform culminated in the Strickland Committee and the great Regulating Act of 1729. For the interesting evidence of these committees see Historical Manuscripts Commission, Vol.8, Ninth Report Part II, (House of Lords) (1884) pp.20-21; ibid., House of Lords Papers, New Series III (1697-1699) (1905), pp.70-88; H. of C. Journals, XXI (1727-1732), pp.236-7.

11. We cannot hope to arrive at any precise calculations of the size of the fringe element amongst the attorneys, either before or after 1730. That large numbers of men were practising with little or no previous training, the records leave us in no doubt. An interesting fact which does emerge from reading the evidence is the great numbers of bankrupt merchants, dealers and tradesmen who evidently set themselves up as attorneys or solicitors. Attorneyship was being used as a safety net for hard times in business which

could be conveniently folded up when their principal vocation again proved financially viable. For examples of this practice before the Regulating Act, see H. of C. Journals, XXI (1727-1732), 236-7; Dim Sasson, Law-Visions, or, Pills for Posterity, (with) Plain Truth by way of a dialogue between Truman and Skinall, two Attorneys, and Season, a Bencher (1736), p.8; F North, The Compleat Solicitor Entring Clerk and Attorney, 2nd ed., (London, 1683), p.13; that such practices were continuing unchecked during the second half of the century, see Observations on the Use and Abuse of the Practice of the Law, interspersed with Remarks on the Character and Conduct of Persons of a Description more numerous than respectable, who encourage litigious Disputes to the great Inconvenience of Mankind in general and the Disgrace of the better part of the Profession of the Law, and illustrated with several professional anecdotes. By a Friend to the Profession (1786), pp.32-33, 36; Joseph Day, An Address to the Attorneys at Law and Solicitors practising in Great Britain upon the proceedings of the London Law Club relative to the Bill . . . for incorporating and better regulating the practitioners, etc., (1796), p.27.

12. H.M.C., Ninth Report, op.cit., p.20.

13. This is probably a gross underestimate. Professor G.S. Holmes has opined that the total number of official practitioners must have reached 3000 by the eve of 1688. I am grateful to the author for having allowed me to see, prior to publication, the chapter on attorneys from his book on the professions. See G.S. Holmes, Augustan England: Professions and Society, Allen & Unwin, 1983.

14. The most recent estimates suggest 4.98 million people for England and Wales in 1672 and 5.2 million in 1731. E.A. Wrigley and R.S. Schofield, The Population History of England 1541-1871: a Reconstruction (Cambridge, 1981), tables 7.8, 7.15.

15. London counsel fees for perusing and giving an opinion on a single case were usually between one and three guineas, depending on reputation and experience.

A letter from John Eagle to Allen and Atkinson, his London agents, illustrates the policy when feeing counsel: ". . . as he is a young Councel I sho^{d} think 2 Gua^{s} wo^{d} be sufficient with the present Case & Papers but if you think it will not be sufficient then Give him 3 Guineas." L.C.A., Eagle Papers, DB250, Letter Book, 20 November 1768 (no pagination).

16. M. Miles, "The Money Market in the Early Industrial Revolution: the Evidence from West Riding Attorneys c.1750-1800" Business History, Vol.23, July 1981, pp.351-74.

17. L.C.A., Eagle Papers, DB250, Letter Book, 25 July 1772.

18. After 1695, defendants who were charged with felonies were all allowed to be represented by a lawyer. The work of attorneys, however, was still largely confined to matters of civil law. J.H. Baker, "The Criminal Courts and Procedure at Common Law 1555-1800" in J.S. Cockburn (ed.), Crime in England, 1550-1800 (London, 1977), pp.37-38. The West Riding attorneys, however, were responsible for drawing agreements amongst the local inhabitants to bear an equal expense in the prosecution of felons. Thomas Sayer of Halifax was the solicitor to an association for prosecuting persons for buying embezzled wool or yarn. C(alderdale A(rchives) D(epartment), Howarth Papers, HAS 8, fo.57. The services of attorneys on the side of the prosecution were also in demand in times of crisis. For instance, during the campaign against the Yorkshire coiners, Eagle did business for an association of local gentlemen who were concerned with suppressing their activities. He was responsible for such duties as taking descriptions of coiners and circulating advertisements for their apprehension; and drawing the commitments of those taken by the vigilance of the association. L.C.A, Eagle Papers, DB250, Letter Book, 16 November 1772; Ledger 1768-77, fos.138-9. Moreover, the brilliant career of Robert Parker of Halifax - the only comet amongst the Yorkshire attorneys - included the position as the Crown's prosecuting solicitor against the coiners from 1768 to 1783: C.D. Webster, "Robert

Parker, Attorney Part I" Transactions of the Halifax Antiquarian Society, (1966), pp.65-66.

19. C.A.D., Howarth Papers, HAS 14, Day Book, fo.68.

20. A typical example of a settlement dispute occurs in L.C.A., Eagle Papers, DB250, Ledger 1747-59, fo.373. Fielding once said that ". . . in cases of settlement of paupers an appeal was almost certain if an attorney lived in the parish, but if a Justice of the Peace lived there, it was almost certain to succeed." Quoted in E.B.V. Christian, A Short History of Solicitors (London, 1896), p.125.

21. E.P. Thompson, "Patrician Society, Plebeian Culture" Journal of Social History, VII (1974), p.389.

22. To what extent the West Riding attorneys monopolised the position of J.P.s' clerks is difficult to assess. Only one other Justice's clerk has come to light during my cursory researches. John Waugh, the Rothwell attorney, was acting as Justice's clerk to Edward Leedes of Royds Hall in 1780. The origins of J.P.s' clerks have proved awkward to trace in other parts of the country. E. Moir, The Justice of the Peace (Harmondsworth, 1969), p.92. It is hoped that a comparison of the lists of West Riding Justices' clerks and attorneys, compiled by John Styles and myself respectively, will shed more light on the backgrounds of such men.

23. It was through John Howarth and his London agents that Horton (then on the Commission of the Peace) procured his Dedimus. C.A.D., Howarth Papers, HAS 10, Day Book 1769-71, fo.120.

24. C.A.D., Howarth Papers, HAS 16, 19, Cash Books.

25. As a Justice's clerk, Howarth advised defendants as well as prosecutors. For instance, in 1770, Samuel Whitely of Norland came to Howarth for advice when he had been summoned before Justices Lamplugh and Wickham on the pretence that he had clandestinely assisted James King to remove his goods and so prevent the landlord from distraining for his rent. C.A.D., Howarth

Papers, HAS 10, Day Book, fo.137.

26. For example, in January 1778, he attended to examine Thomas Knowles who had been apprehended at Ripponden on suspicion of stealing a piece of cotton out of the bleaching yard of Mr. Bentley of Bury. Again, in August of that same year, he examined six witnesses in a case of felony. C.A.D., Howarth Papers, HAS 13, Day Book, fos.103, 173.

27. In January 1770, Luke Dewhirst of Turvin was arrested for diminishing the coin, whereupon his wife consulted Howarth for advice. C.A.D., Howarth Papers, HAS 10, Day Book, fo.131.

28. C.A.D., Howarth Papers, HAS 9-14, Day Books.

29. Some of these offices, such as Clerkships of the Peace, land stewardships, and Town Clerkships, were long-established and had always been open to attorneys. During the eighteenth century, however, the public offices became more numerous and varied and came to be regarded as the preserve of lawyers. After 1760, the range of offices was extended further with the first stage of increased industrial activity. It was at this time that positions as clerks to navigation and turnpike companies became available.

30. For instance, Lucas Nicholson of Leeds in 1798 held the offices of Town Clerk and agent for the Royal Exchange Insurance; whereas James Hebdin of that town was clerk to the Trustees of the Selby to Leeds and Leeds to Elland Turnpikes, the Leeds to Liverpool Canal Company, and the Committee appointed for preventing frauds in the woollen and worsted manufactures. Leeds Intelligencer, 30 April 1798, 31 August 1773, 14 March 1780, 24 November 1794.

31. It was Robert Parker's connections with the wealthy Prescot family, as well as his reputation in London as an eminent attorney, that led to his acquisition of the lucrative stewardship of the Honour of Pontefract in 1775. C.A.D., Parker Papers, RP/3, 409.

32. C.A.D., Howarth Papers, HAS 1, Day Book, fo.18.

33. C.A.D., Howarth Papers, HAS 9, Day Book, fo.141.

34. L.C.A., Eagle Papers, DB250, Letter Book, 5 November 1774.

35. Ibid., 29 March 1771.

36. Ibid., 30 August, 1774.

37. L.C.A., Eagle Papers, DB250, Ledger 1768-77, fos.26-31.

38. L.C.A., Eagle Papers, DB250, Letter Book, 1 June 1773.

39. E.B.V. Christian, A Short History . . . op.cit., pp.91-93.

40. C.W. Brooks, thesis op.cit., p.176.

41. Augustus Jessopp (ed.), The Lives of the Right Hon. Francis North, Baron Guildford; The Hon. Sir Dudley North; And The Hon. And Rev. Dr. John North. By The Hon. Roger North, Together With The Autobiography of the Author, Vol.3 (London, 1890), p.139.

42. At various times during their careers, both Eagle and Howarth were dependent upon the local services of Lawyer John Stanhope of Horsforth, Recorder Wilson, elder and younger, of Leeds, Serjeant Aspinal and Mr. Fearnley of Oakwell Hall near Birstall.

43. C.A.D., Howarth Papers, HAS 9, fo.171; HAS 11, fo.161; HAS 12, fo.31; HAS 14, fo.58.

44. C.A.D., Howarth Papers, HAS 13, fo.18; L.C.A., Eagle Papers, DB250, Ledger 1759-71, fo.407.

45. C.A.D., Howarth Papers, HAS 13, fo.50.

46. Ibid., fo.98.

47. Ibid., fo.306.

48. John Eagle's law library included such works as: Blackstone's Commentaries; Horn's Executor Devises, Trusts and Remainders; Burrow's Reports; Lilly's Conveyancer; Green's Law of Bankruptcy; Atkin's Reports; Greenwood on Courts; Hobart's Reports; Coke's Institutes; Jacob's Law Dictionary; The Attorney's Practice in the Court of King's Bench.

49. The Attorney's Practice in the Court of Common Pleas and The Attorney's

Practice in the Court of King's Bench by R. Richardson were first published in 1739. These became the standard manuals for practising attorneys. It is interesting that both books deal with pleading as well as practice. But whatever skills in pleading the attorneys had once possessed, by this time they had lost them to a new class of special pleaders. In the preface to the second edition of The Common Pleas, the author points out that: ". . . he can never be an able attorney who is not tolerably well skilled in special pleading. Formerly all attorneys drew their own pleadings, and never had occasion for any assistance . . . . This kind of learning, which is too much neglected, led them into the very reasons of the practice, and into a knowledge of the Common Law, which none but a special pleader can be said to be thoroughly master of: an attorney, without being acquainted with special pleading, can have no other than a confused knowledge of such particular instances of practice only as have passed through his own hands, and upon the least variation is as much at a loss as if he never knew anything of the matter; . . . for which reasons the loss of this branch of learning amongst the generality of the profession is greatly to be lamented . . . ."

50. The London Tradesman . . . op.cit., pp.30-31.

51. For example, in the six volumes of precedents compiled by James Carr of Birstall, some 54 per cent out of a total of 859 precedents of the period 1735-1800, relate to conveyancing. L.C.A., Carr Manuscripts, CA 1-6.

52. One grudging writer in 1736 could confidently assert that the change in the geographical distribution of the profession was in the compass of the last eighty to one hundred years: "Formerly you us'd to trudge up to London with your green Bags, some of you a Foot, and scarce two or three were to be found in a Country: God knows since, how the Number is increas'd." Read Hodshon, The Honest Man's Companion: or, the Family Safeguard. Illustrated with Copper Plates, and done at the Request of Several Gentlemen and Others, occasion'd by an Attorney's defying any Person to paint him or his

Brotherhood in their proper Colours, or to propose any method to regulate them or their Practice. As also Remarks upon Roman Catholick Lawyers practising as Chamber-Counsel and Conveyancers, etc. (Newcastle upon Tyne, 1736), p.9.

53. T. Ruggles, The Barrister: or, strictures on the education proper for the Bar (London, 1792), p.31.

54. 25 Geo.III, c.80. For a discussion of this Act and other taxation measures on the profession, see Robert Robson, The Attorney in Eighteenth-Century England (Cambridge, 1959), pp.13-17.

55. The fee list of the King's Bench attorneys, as taken from The Practique Part of the Law, is reproduced in E.B.V. Christian, A Short History . . . op.cit., pp.98-99.

56. Some Advice To The Gentlemen Members of the late instituted Society of Attorneys From one of their Members, with some general Hints, humbly offered to the Public for regulating and improving the Profession of an Attorney (Dublin, 1753), p.16.

57. Proposals Humbly Offered to the Parliament for remedying the great charge and delay of Suits of Law and in Equity (London, 1707), p.18.

58. Ibid.

59. A humorous hit at the excessive size of attorneys' bills occurs in John Arbuthnot's Law is a Bottomless Pit (1712), pp.24-25. For a more caustic attack the reader is referred to An Essay in Praise of Knavery (London, 1723), p.10-12.

60. Charles Ilsley, A Brief Inquiry concerning the origins, progress, and impolicy of taxing attorneys; including remarks ascribed to a suggestion from the late Right Honourable Lloyd, Lord Kenyon (London, 1804), pp.20-21.

61. Considerations on the Attorney Tax, and proposals for altering and equalising the same, so as to render it easy in operation, and just in principle (London, 1786), pp.7-8.

62. One writer, when listing the qualifications of an attorney, mentioned that he should be "well versed in . . . Mathematicks, and especially in Geometry, as several Questions do frequently arise about the Means and Bounds of Lands, in which a knowledge of Surveying might be materially useful; he should be a perfect Master of Figures and Book-keeping, as most of the suits in the Court of Equity are upon Matters of Account . . . ." Some Advice To the Gentlemen (as n.56 above), pp.19-20.

63. In late 1790, John Howarth dispatched bills to the value of £1053.13s.3d. to his London agents Messrs. J. & A. Allen of Furnival's Inn, which was for law business done in Hilary Vacation, Easter, and Trinity Terms of that year. Again in 1791, he remitted a further £1019.17s.10½d. for agency work. C.A.D., Howarth Papers, HAS 22, Ledger, fo.199.

64. L.C.A., Eagle Papers, DB250, Letter Book, 17 April 1769.

65. Ibid.

66. The total cost of this Chancery suit was £252.0s.9d. L.C.A., Eagle Papers, DB250, Ledger 1768-77, fo.211.

67. L.C.A., Eagle Papers, DB250, Letter Book, 22 January 1772.

68. The following are typical examples of the procedure in a dispute. In July 1768, John Ward of York gave John Eagle instructions to attend on a Mr. Lund to procure payment for a survey which Ward had made on his property. He gave orders for an action to be commenced against him only if he refused to pay the debt or submit the affair to arbitration. In 1753, Solomon Thwaite of Elland ordered John Howarth to sue out a writ against Henry Wormald, his neighbour; whereupon Howarth journeyed to Elland to acquaint the defendant with this and to prevail with both disputants to refer the matter to arbitration. L.C.A., Eagle Papers, DB250, Ledger 1768-77, fo.227; C.A.D., Howarth Papers, HAS 1, Day Book, fo.68.

69. L.C.A., Eagle Papers, DB250, Ledgers 1-4.

70. Ibid.

71. In one letter Eagle told another practitioner that he was willing to refer a dispute "either to Councel or Gentlemen to determine"; by which latter designation he presumably meant attorneys. Attorneys and counsellors were certainly active together on arbitrations. For instance John Howarth and Serjeant Aspinal were called in by Mr. Lancashire, a Rochdale attorney, to preside over a reference together in October 1779. L.C.A., Eagle Papers, DB250, Letter Book, 30 August 1769; C.A.D., Howarth Papers, HAS 13, Day Book, fo.301.

72. L.C.A., Eagle Papers, DB250, Ledger 1747-59, fo.16.

73. L.C.A., Eagle Papers, DB250, Letter Book, 24 August 1773.

74. Ibid., 23 January 1772.

75. C.W. Brooks, thesis, op.cit., pp.35-39, 40-42, 44, 58.

76. L.C.A., Eagle Papers, DB250, Ledgers 1-4.

77. In the period 1560-1640, a superior court action cost between £6 and £8. C.W. Brooks, thesis, cit., p.39.

78. The servants who sued, usually did so at their masters' expense.

79. In theory, very poor people were entitled to try for a remedy at law, there was some slender provision for their representation. A statute of the reign of Henry VII had stipulated that poor persons could pursue their claims in the law courts free of all fees to attorneys and counsel by petitioning the Chancellor to sue in forma pauperis. Since the statute failed to specify just what precisely constituted a definition of pauperism, it became a rule of court to limit the remedy to all those who could prove themselves not worth five pounds (exclusive of wearing apparel). But, as more than one contemporary writer pointed out, this rather vague remedy was all but self-defeating in its object. In the first place, very few attorneys were prepared to take on such business - unless it was a young practitioner who took the work because he could get no other, or, an older one who bestowed his services as charity - and without an attorney, a pauper was unable to introduce his petition, and so

carry his claim into action. A second and more crushing barrier arose from the fact that to obtain an order from the Judge to be admitted to sue in such a manner, cost at least one-sixth of what the pauper had sworn he was not worth in the world. For discussions of pauper causes see Observations on the Use and Abuse of the Practice . . . op.cit., pp.48-50; Dim Sasson, The Law and Lawyers Laid Open in Twelve Visions. To which is Added Plain Truth in Three Dialogues, Between Truman, Skinall, Dryboots, Three Attorneys, and Season, a Bencher (London, 1737), pp.190-1.

80. L.C.A., Eagle Papers, DB250, Ledgers 1-4.

81. Amongst those West Riding attorneys who married into the families of their rich clients was John Howarth. He married Mary, the daughter of John Royds of Soyland, and sister of the wealthy Royds Brothers, merchants of Halifax, in 1753. Similarly, both John Eagle and Abraham Balme married into the family of their prosperous clients, the Hodgsons of Fairweather Green near Bradford. C.D. Webster, "Halifax Attorneys (Second Part)" Transactions of the Halifax Antiquarian Society, (1969), p.121; L.C.A., Eagle Papers, DB250, Miscellaneous Deeds, Hodgson and Eagle's Pedigree.

82. Professor G.S. Holmes has pointed out how the attorneys ". . . by the beginning of the eighteenth century could claim a very substantial top layer of able, honest and socially acceptable practitioners, now fully assimilated into the ranks of the town gentry, if not of the country gentry." See Holmes, supra, n.13.

83. C.W. Brooks, thesis, op.cit., pp.266-67.

<u>INDEX</u>

INDEX